Strategic Paper P9

MANAGEMENT ACCOUNTING – FINANCIAL STRATEGY

For exams in 2007

Practice & Revision Kit

In this January 2007 new edition

- We discuss the **best strategies** for revising and taking your CIMA exams

- We show you how to be well prepared for the **2007 exams**

- We give you **lots of great guidance** on tackling questions

- We include **genuine student answers** with BPP commentary

- We show you how you can **build your own exams**

- We provide you with **three** mock exams including the **November 2006 exam**

BPP's **i-Pass** product also supports this paper.

LEARNING MEDIA

First edition 2005
Third edition January 2007

ISBN 9780 7517 4199 5 (previous ISBN 0 7517 2525 0)

British Library Cataloguing-in-Publication Data
A catalogue record for this book
is available from the British Library

Published by

BPP Learning Media Ltd
BPP House, Aldine Place
London W12 8AA

www.bpp.com/learningmedia

Printed in Great Britain by
Page Bros
Mile Cross Lane
Norwich
WR6 6SA

Your learning materials, published by BPP Learning
Media Ltd, are printed on paper sourced from
sustainable, managed forests.

We are grateful to the Chartered Institute of Management
Accountants for permission to reproduce past
examination questions. The answers to past examination
questions have been prepared by BPP Learning Media
Ltd, unless where otherwise stated.

Contents

	Page

Finding questions

Question index 4
Topic index 7

Using your BPP Practice and Revision Kit 9

Passing CIMA exams

Revising and taking CIMA exams 13
How to revise 14
How NOT to revise 15
How to PASS your exams 16
How to FAIL your exams 17
Using your BPP products 18

Passing P9

Revising P9 21
Passing the P9 exam 22
Recent exams 25
What the examiner means 28
Useful websites 29

Planning your question practice

BPP's question plan 33
Build your own exams 39

Questions and answers

Questions 43
Answers 149

Exam practice

Mock exam 1
- Questions 411
- Plan of attack 423
- Answers 425

Mock exam 2
- Questions 445
- Plan of attack 455
- Answers 457

Mock exam 3 (November 2006)
- Questions 473
- Plan of attack 487
- Answers 489

Mathematical tables 509

Review form & free prize draw

Question index

The headings in this checklist/index indicate the main topics of questions, but questions often cover several different topics.

Questions set under the old syllabuses *Management Accounting – Financial Strategy (FLFS)* are included because their style and/or content are similar to those that appear in the Paper P9 exam.

		Marks	Time allocation Mins	Page number Question	Page number Answer

Part A: Formulation of financial strategy

Relevant costs and short-term decisions

		Marks	Mins	Question	Answer
1	Goals	25	45	43	149
2	Educational Institution (FLFS, 5/03)	25	45	43	151
3	Objectives (Pilot paper)	25	45	44	154
4	JS	25	45	44	157
5	PQD	25	45	46	159
6	HG (11/05)	25	45	47	162
7	CBA	25	45	48	165
8	Question with analysis: Emcos (FLFS, 11/02 amended)	25	45	49	168
9	KOL	25	45	55	172
10	RJ (11/05)	25	45	56	175
11	RG	25	45	58	178
12	AB and YZ (FLFS, 11/04)	25	45	59	180
13	DRY	25	45	59	184
14	TED	25	45	60	186

Part B: Financial management

		Marks	Mins	Question	Answer
15	PJH (FLFS, 11/02)	25	45	61	189
16	RUMP	25	45	62	191
17	XTA (5/05)	25	45	63	194
18	EFG (5/06)	25	45	64	197
19	AIR	25	45	65	199
20	DDD	25	45	66	202
21	BAC	25	45	67	206
22	XYZ	25	45	68	208
23	TFC	25	45	69	211
24	Question with helping hand: RZ (Pilot paper)	25	45	70	213
25	FLG (5/05)	25	45	71	217
26	GREBE	25	45	72	219
27	UR (FLFS, 11/03)	25	45	73	221
28	MNO (5/06)	25	45	74	224
29	LE International	25	45	75	226

BPP
LEARNING MEDIA

	Marks	Time allocation Mins	Page number Question	Answer
30 WZ (11/05)	25	45	75	229
31 IML	25	45	76	231
32 CAP	25	45	77	234
33 DEA	25	45	78	238
34 AB (FLFS, 5/02)	25	45	79	241
35 MAN	25	45	80	243
36 KM	25	45	80	247
37 HH (FLFS, 11/02)	25	45	81	250

Part C: Business valuations and acquisitions

	Marks	Time allocation Mins	Page number Question	Answer
38 CD (FLFS, 5/03)	25	45	82	252
39 Synergy	25	45	83	255
40 Question with student answer: MC	25	45	84	258
41 PP	25	45	85	265
42 PR (FLFS, 5/02)	25	45	87	269
43 BA (FLFS, 11/02)	25	45	87	272
44 PDQ (FLFS, 11/03)	25	45	88	274
45 PCO (Pilot paper)	25	45	89	277
46 BiOs (Pilot paper)	25	45	91	281
47 BST (FLFS, 11/04)	25	45	92	284
48 FS (11/05)	25	45	93	287

Part D: Advanced investment appraisal

	Marks	Time allocation Mins	Page number Question	Answer
49 VEN	25	45	95	289
50 Canada	25	45	96	292
51 IT (FLFS, 11/01)	25	45	97	294
52 GH (FLFS, 5/01)	25	45	97	297
53 Question with student answer: QE	25	45	98	300
54 KH (FLFS, 11/01)	25	45	99	305
55 DAC	25	45	100	308
56 CTC (5/05)	25	45	101	311
57 XZ (FLFS, 5/01)	25	45	102	313
58 Question with helping hand: REM (FLFS, 11/02)	25	45	103	315
59 GHI (5/06)	25	45	104	318
60 RS (5/06)	25	45	105	319

		Time allocation	Page number	
	Marks	Mins	Question	Answer

Scenario questions

	Marks	Mins	Question	Answer
61 Casarina	50	90	106	321
62 Question with analysis: Spearhead	50	90	108	327
63 Premoco	50	90	115	332
64 Garden World	50	90	117	339
65 Almond Arts	50	90	119	343
66 Eros (FLFS, 5/01)	50	90	122	351
67 Margate (FLFS, 11/01)	50	90	124	355
68 KL (FLFS, 5/02)	50	90	127	361
69 Dobbs (FLFS, 5/03)	50	90	129	367
70 C&C Airlines (FLFS, 11/03)	50	90	131	372
71 RGB (FLFS, 11/04)	50	90	133	377
72 JHC (Pilot paper)	50	90	136	383
73 Groots (5/05)	50	90	138	391
74 Gas (11/05)	50	90	141	398
75 PM (5/06)	50	90	143	403

Mock exam 1

Questions 76 to 80

Mock exam 2

Questions 81 to 85

Mock exam 3 (November 2006)

Questions 86 to 90

Planning your question practice

Our guidance from page 33 shows you how to organise your question practice, either by attempting questions from each syllabus area or by **building your own exams** – tackling questions as a series of practice exams.

Topic index

Listed below are the key Paper P9 syllabus topics and the numbers of the questions in this Kit covering those topics.

If you need to concentrate your practice and revision on certain topics or if you want to attempt all available questions that refer to a particular subject (be they preparation or exam-standard questions), you will find this index useful.

Syllabus topic	Question numbers
Accounting rate of return	51, 71
Acquisitions and mergers	39, 41–43, 45–48, 53, 63, 66, 67, 69, 73, 75
Adjusted discount rate	57
Adjusted present value	57, 59
Business plans	8
Capital asset pricing model	29–32, 45, 48, 58, 70, 71
Capital rationing	53, 57, 60
Capital structure decision	17–20, 26, 30, 33, 34, 61
Certainty equivalents	51, 62, 64, 70
Corporate governance	14
Cost benefit analysis	4
Cost of debt	18, 20, 22, 23, 25
Convertible debt	17, 18
Cost of equity	11, 14, 34, 62, 63
Current and emerging issues	14
Debt issue	16, 18, 20, 21, 24, 70
Distribution of earnings	11, 12, 13
Dividends	11–13, 38
Dividend valuation model	11, 39, 45, 63, 67
Economic factors	64, 65
Equity issue	16, 20, 64
Euro finance	17
Exchange rates	62
Financial control	3, 13, 36
Financial management	1, 3, 5, 8, 13, 24, 34, 36, 38, 55, 61, 65, 66
Financial modelling	7–10, 17, 26, 61, 65
Financial performance	2, 5, 9, 61
Financial statements	61, 64
Flotation	5, 40, 66
Forecasts	7–10, 26, 61, 65
Foreign investment	50, 52, 62, 74
Funding	1, 7, 8, 15, 18, 20, 23, 24, 29, 34, 38, 39, 50, 55, 61, 68, 69
Gearing	17, 18, 19, 30
Inflation rates	52, 65, 70
Information technology	49
Intangible assets	40
Internal rate of return	49, 51
Investment appraisal	34, 49–59, 62, 64, 69, 70, 71, 74
Leasing	21–25

Syllabus topic	Question numbers
Management buyouts	19, 44
Modified internal rate of return	49, 72
Net present value	34, 49–60, 64, 68–74
Objectives	1–3, 5, 6, 15, 62, 65, 68, 71, 72, 75
Offer for sale	16
Payback	51
Performance measures	2, 5, 10
Placing	16, 17
Post acquisition strategy	41, 57
Post completion audit	8, 58, 73
Preference shares	29
Product development	50
Profitability	9
Profitability index	53, 57, 60
Public offer	16
Ratio analysis	3, 5, 8, 10, 45, 61, 65
Real options	68, 72
Regulatory authorities	4
Relevant costs	4, 49, 56
Rights issue	15–17, 19, 61, 64
Risk and risk management	5, 29, 54, 55, 62, 64, 68, 70, 71, 74
Settlement methods	19, 39, 41–43, 63, 67
Share price	11, 40, 64, 67, 74, 75
Share repurchase	11, 12
Shareholders	11, 41
Stakeholders	1
Structure	20, 23, 26, 35, 38
Synergy	39
Treasury function	3, 36, 37
Valuation of organisations	38-40, 42–48, 63, 65, 66, 74, 75
Venture capital	46, 49, 66
Weighted average cost of capital	19, 21, 22, 29, 30, 32–35, 51, 55
Working capital management	7, 9, 27, 28

Using your BPP Practice and Revision Kit

Tackling revision and the exam

You can significantly improve your chances of passing by tackling revision and the exam in the right ways. Our advice is based on recent feedback from CIMA examiners.

- We look at the dos and don'ts of revising for, and taking, CIMA exams

- We focus on Paper P9; we discuss revising the syllabus, what to do (and what not to do) in the exam, how to approach different types of question and ways of obtaining easy marks

Selecting questions

We provide signposts to help you plan your revision.

- A full **question index**

- A **topic index** listing all the questions that cover key topics, so that you can locate the questions that provide practice on these topics, and see the different ways in which they might be examined

- A **BPP question plan** highlighting the most important questions and explaining why you should attempt them

- **Build your own exams**, showing you how you can practise questions in a series of exams

Making the most of question practice

At BPP we realise that you need more than just questions and model answers to get the most from your question practice.

- Our **Top tips** provide essential advice on tackling questions, presenting answers and the key points that answers need to include

- We show you how you can pick up **Easy marks** on questions, as we know that picking up all readily available marks often can make the difference between passing and failing

- We summarise **Examiner's comments** to show you how students who sat the exam coped with the questions

- We refer to the **BPP 2006 Study Text** for detailed coverage of the topics covered in each question

- A number of questions include **Analysis** and **Helping hands** attached to show you how to approach them if you are struggling

- We include **annotated student answers** to some questions to highlight how these questions can be tackled and ways answers can be improved.

Attempting mock exams

There are three mock exams that provide practice at coping with the pressures of the exam day. We strongly recommend that you attempt them under exam conditions. **Mock exams 1 and 2** reflect the question styles and syllabus coverage of the exam; **Mock exam 3** is the actual November 2006 exam. To help you get the most out of doing these exams, we not only provide help with each answer, but also guidance on how you should have approached the whole exam.

Passing CIMA exams

Revising and taking CIMA exams

To maximise your chances of passing your CIMA exams, you must make best use of your time, both before the exam during your revision, and when you are actually doing the exam.

- Making the most of your revision time can make a big, big difference to how well-prepared you are for the exam

- Time management is a core skill in the exam hall; all the work you've done can be wasted if you don't make the most of the three hours you have to attempt the exam

In this section we simply show you what to do and what not to do during your revision, and how to increase and decrease your prospects of passing your exams when you take them. Our advice is grounded in feedback we've had from CIMA examiners. You may be surprised to know that much examiner advice is the same whatever the exam, and the reasons why many students fail don't vary much between subjects and exam levels. So if you follow the advice we give you over the next few pages, you will **significantly** enhance your chances of passing **all** your CIMA exams.

How to revise

☑ Plan your revision

At the start of your revision period, you should draw up a **timetable** to plan how long you will spend on each subject and how you will revise each area. You need to consider the total time you have available and also the time that will be required to revise for other exams you're taking.

☑ Practise Practise Practise

The **more exam-standard questions** you do, the **more likely you are to pass** the exam. Practising full questions will mean that you'll get used to the time pressure of the exam. When the time is up, you should note where you've got to and then try to complete the question, giving yourself practice everything that the question tests.

☑ Revise enough

Make sure that your revision covers the breadth of the syllabus, as in most papers most topics could be examined in a compulsory question. However it is true that some topics are **key** – they often appear in compulsory questions or are a particular interest of the examiner – and you need to spend sufficient time revising these. Make sure you know the basics – the fundamental calculations, proformas and report layouts.

☑ Deal with your difficulties

Difficult areas are topics you find dull and pointless, or subjects that you found problematic when you were studying them. You mustn't become negative about these topics; instead you should build up your knowledge by reading the **Passcards** and using the **Quick quiz** questions in the Study Text to test yourself. When practising questions in the Kit, go back to the Text if you're struggling.

☑ Learn from your mistakes

Having completed a question you must try to look at your answer critically. Always read the **Top tips** guidance in the answers; it's there to help you. Look at **Easy marks** to see how you could have quickly gained credit on the questions that you've done. As you go through the Kit, it's worth noting any traps you've fallen into, and key points in the **Top tips** or **Examiner's comments** sections, and referring to these notes in the days before the exam. Aim to learn at least one new point from each question you attempt, a technical point perhaps or a point on style or approach.

☑ Read the examiners' guidance

We refer throughout this Kit to **Examiner's comments**; these are available on CIMA's website. As well as highlighting weaknesses, examiners' reports often provide clues to future questions, as many examiners will quickly test again areas where problems have arisen. CIMA's website also contains articles that are relevant to this paper, which you should read.

☑ Complete all three mock exams

You should attempt the **Mock exams** at the end of the Kit under **strict exam conditions** to gain experience of selecting questions, managing your time and producing answers.

How NOT to revise

☒ Revise selectively

Examiners are well aware that some students try to forecast the contents of exams, and only revise those areas that they think will be examined. Examiners try to prevent this by doing the unexpected, for example setting the same topic in successive sittings or setting topics in compulsory questions that have previously only been examined in optional questions.

☒ Spend all the revision period reading

You cannot pass the exam just by learning the contents of Passcards, Course Notes or Study Texts. You have to develop your **application skills** by practising questions.

☒ Audit the answers

This means reading the answers and guidance without having attempted the questions. Auditing the answers gives you **false reassurance** that you would have tackled the questions in the best way and made the points that our answers do. The feedback we give in our answers will mean more to you if you've attempted the questions and thought through the issues.

☒ Practise some types of question, but not others

Although you may find the numerical parts of certain papers challenging, you shouldn't just practise calculations. These papers will also contain written elements, and you therefore need to spend time practising written question parts as well.

☒ Get bogged down

Don't spend a lot of time worrying about all the minute detail of certain topic areas, and leave yourself insufficient time to cover the rest of the syllabus. Remember that a key skill in the exam is the ability to **concentrate on what's important** and this applies to your revision as well.

☒ Overdo studying

Studying for too long without interruption will mean your studying becomes less effective. A five minute break each hour will help. You should also make sure that you are leading a **healthy lifestyle** (proper meals, good sleep and some times when you're not studying).

How to PASS your exams

☑ Prepare for the day

Make sure you set at least one alarm (or get an alarm call), and allow plenty of time to get to the exam hall. You should have your route planned in advance and should listen on the radio for potential travel problems. You should check the night before to see that you have pens, pencils, erasers, watch, calculator with spare batteries, also exam documentation and evidence of identity.

☑ Select the right questions

You should select the optional questions you feel you can answer **best**, basing your selection on the topics covered, the requirements of the question, how easy it will be to apply the requirements and the availability of easy marks.

☑ Plan your three hours

You need to make sure that you will be answering the correct number of questions, and that you spend the right length of time on each question – this will be determined by the number of marks available. Each mark carries with it a **time allocation** of **1.8 minutes**. A 25 mark question therefore should be selected, completed and checked in 45 minutes. With some papers, it's better to do certain types of question first or last.

☑ Read the questions carefully

To score well, you must follow the requirements of the question, understanding what aspects of the subject area are being covered, and the tasks you will have to carry out. The requirements will also determine what information and examples you should provide. Reading the question scenarios carefully will help you decide what **issues** to discuss, what **techniques** to use, **information** and **examples** to include and how to **organise** your answer.

☑ Plan your answers

Five minutes of planning plus twenty-five minutes of writing is certain to earn you more marks than thirty minutes of writing. Consider when you're planning how your answer should be **structured**, what the **format** should be and **how long** each part should take.

Confirm before you start writing that your plan makes **sense**, covers **all relevant points** and does not include **irrelevant material.**

☑ Show evidence of judgement

Remember that examiners aren't just looking for a display of knowledge; they want to see how well you can **apply** the knowledge you have. Evidence of application and judgement will include writing answers that only contain **relevant** material, using the material in scenarios to **support** what you say, **criticising** the **limitations** and **assumptions** of the techniques you've used and making **reasonable recommendations** that follow from your discussion.

☑ Stay until the end of the exam

Use any spare time to **check and recheck** your script. This includes checking you have filled out the candidate details correctly, you have labelled question parts and workings clearly, you have used headers and underlining effectively and spelling, grammar and arithmetic are correct.

How to FAIL your exams

☒ Don't do enough questions

If you don't attempt sufficient questions on the paper, you are making it harder for yourself to pass the questions that you do attempt. If for example you don't do a 20 mark question, then you will have to score 50 marks out of 80 marks on the rest of the paper, and therefore have to obtain 63% of the marks on the questions you do attempt. Failing to attempt all of the paper is symptomatic of poor time management or poor question selection.

☒ Include irrelevant material

Markers are given detailed mark guides and will not give credit for irrelevant content. Therefore you should **NOT** braindump into your answer all you know about a broad subject area; the markers will only give credit for what is **relevant**, and you will also be showing that you lack the ability to **judge what's important.** Similarly forcing irrelevant theory into every answer won't gain you marks, nor will providing uncalled for features such as situation analyses, executive summaries and background information.

☒ Fail to use the details in the scenario

General answers or reproductions of old answers that don't refer to what is in the scenario in **this** question won't score enough marks to pass.

☒ Copy out the scenario details

Examiners see **selective** use of the right information as a key skill. If you copy out chunks of the scenario that aren't relevant to the question, or don't use the information to support your own judgements, you won't achieve good marks.

☒ Don't do what the question asks

Failing to provide all the examiner asks for will limit the marks you score. You will also decrease your chances by not providing an answer with enough **depth** – producing a single line bullet point list when the examiner asks for a discussion.

☒ Present your work poorly

Markers will only be able to give you credit if they can read your writing. There are also plenty of other things as well that will make it more difficult for markers to reward you. Examples include:

- Not using black or blue ink
- Not showing clearly which question you're attempting
- Scattering question parts from the same question throughout your answer booklet
- Not showing clearly workings or the results of your calculations

Paragraphs that are too long or which lack headers also won't help markers and hence won't help you.

Using your BPP products

This Kit gives you the question practice and guidance you need in the exam. Our other products can also help you pass:

- **Learning to Learn Accountancy** gives further valuable advice on revision

- **Passcards** provide you with clear topic summaries and exam tips

- **Success CDs** help you revise on the move

- **i-Pass CDs** offer tests of knowledge against the clock

- **Learn Online** is an e-learning resource delivered via the Internet, offering comprehensive tutor support and featuring areas such as study, practice, email service, revision and useful resources

You can purchase these products by visiting www.bpp.com/mybpp.

Visit our website www.bpp.com/cima/learnonline to sample aspects of Learn Online free of charge.

Passing P9

Revising P9

This is a time pressured exam that combines calculations with discussion. It is very important that you do not concentrate completely on the calculations at the expense of fully understanding the strategic issues involved.

Topics to revise

You need to be comfortable with **all areas of the syllabus** as questions, particularly compulsory Question 1, will often span a number of syllabus areas.

Formulation of financial strategy

- How financial objectives of different types of organisation are identified and attained

- The links between investment, financing and dividend decisions

- The constraints on formulating financial strategy

- The techniques of ratio analysis and forecasting. The emphasis in this exam is always on discussion of techniques you employ and using your calculations to support your analysis

- Recommending alternative financial strategies - probably the most important learning outcome in this paper

Financial management

- The determination of long-term capital structure in the form of debt finance, equity finance and leasing
- How securities markets work
- The roles of the finance and treasury functions
- Essential techniques such as calculating the cost of capital and using the capital asset pricing model

Business valuations and acquisitions

- Methods of calculating the valuations of organisations of different types. The most important use of these techniques is in a merger or acquisition situation and this area is frequently examined

Investment decisions and project control

- Issues connected with investment appraisal
- Complex calculations and techniques need to be practised

Question practice

Question practice under timed conditions is essential, so that you can get used to the pressures of answering exam questions in **limited time** and practise not only the key techniques but allocating your time between different requirements in each question. Our list of recommended questions includes 50 mark Section A and 25 mark Section B questions; it's particularly important to do a number of Section A questions in full to see how the numerical and written elements balance in longer questions.

Passing the P9 exam

Avoiding weaknesses

Although there have only been three sittings of P9, the examiners have already identified weaknesses that occur in many students' answers at every sitting. You will enhance your chances significantly if you ensure you avoid these mistakes:

- Failure to read the question

- Failure to pick up scenario details e.g. size of company, listed or unlisted, attitude to risk, dividend policy

- Muddling up scenario details from different questions

- Time management – spending excessive time on strong areas

- Poor English, structure and presentation

- The discursive question is often answered poorly, suggesting for many students that it's the question of last resort

- Poor knowledge of basic concepts and calculations (earnings per share, cost of debt)

- Calculations producing unrealistic results, and no comments being made on these

- Unable to distinguish coupon rate and cost of debt

- Believing retained earnings are cash

- Poor knowledge of tax and capital allowance calculations

- Lack of application of knowledge to scenario

Using the reading time

We recommend that you spend the first part of the reading time choosing the Section B questions you will do, on the basis of your knowledge of syllabus areas tested and whether you can fulfil all the question requirements. We suggest that you should note on the paper any ideas that come to you about these questions.

However don't spend the reading time going through and analysing the Section B question requirements in detail; leave that until the three hours writing time. Normally Section B requirements are more step-by-step than Section A requirements and so require less planning and thinking time. Instead you should be looking to spend as much of the reading time as possible looking at the Section A scenario, highlighting and annotating the key points on the question paper.

Choosing which questions to answer first

Spending most of your reading time on the Section A scenario will mean that you can get underway with planning and writing your answer to the Section A question as soon as the three hours start. It will give you more actual writing time during the one and a half hours you should allocate to it and it's writing time that you'll need.

During the second half of the exam, you can put Section A aside and concentrate on the two Section B questions you've chosen.

However our recommendations are not inflexible. If you really think the Section A question looks a lot harder than the Section B questions you've chosen, then do those first, but **DON'T run over time on them.** You must leave yourself an hour and a half to tackle the Section A question. When you come back to it, having had initial thoughts during the reading time, you should be able to generate more ideas and find the question is not as bad as it looks.

Tackling questions

You'll improve your chances by following a step-by-step approach to Section A scenarios along the following lines.

Step 1   **Read the requirement**

You need to identify the knowledge areas being tested and what information will therefore be significant.

Step 2   **Identify the action verbs**

These convey the level of skill you need to exhibit. See the list on page 28.

Step 3   **Identify what each part of the question requires**

When planning, you will need to make sure that you aren't reproducing the same material in more than one part of the question.

Step 4   **Check the mark allocation to each part**

This shows you the depth anticipated and helps allocate time.

Step 5   **Read the scenario through quickly, highlighting key data**

- Size of the organisation
- Factors influencing the decisions (business strategies, financial resources, constraints)
- Changes in circumstances that are about to take place

Step 6   **Read the scenario carefully**

Put points under headings related to requirements (e.g. by marginal notes). Consider the techniques you'll need to use.

Step 7   **Consider the consequences of the points you've identified**

Remember that in the answer you will often have to provide recommendations based on the information you've been given. Consider the limitations of any analysis you undertake or other factors that may impact upon your recommendations.

Step 8   **Write a plan**

You may be able to do this on the question paper as often there will be at least one blank page in the question booklet. However any plan you make should be reproduced in the answer booklet when writing time begins.

Step 9   **Write the answer**

Make every effort to present your answer clearly.

Numerical questions

You are likely to see calculation questions covering:

- Forecasts
- Performance evaluation
- Methods of valuation
- Cost of capital
- CAPM
- Net present value, probably with an international dimension
- Purchasing power parity

Given the examiner's comments about poor calculations, we suggest you revise the basic techniques and formats for these, and also their limitations that you may have to discuss. Even if you do make a mistake on the numbers, you will gain credit for the correct approach.

Discussion questions

As well as the limitations of your calculations, you should expect to discuss their results in the context of the organisation's wider situation and strategy. As well as discussing financing, be prepared also to bring relevant knowledge from other strategic level papers such as the risks affecting investment or how well proposals support the organisation's optimum business strategy. Another important area is implementation of strategy (for example what should happen after an acquisition, how an investment project should be controlled).

Remember that strategies you recommend must be suitable and feasible for the organisation, and acceptable to shareholders, managers and perhaps other stakeholders as well.

One important aspect of time allocation is not to spend excessive time on the calculations at the expense of the discussion parts. You need to be strict with yourself as you won't at this level see a question that purely consists of calculations.

Remember that the marking schemes for discussion questions will be fairly general, and you will gain credit for all relevant points. Good discussion focused on the question scenario, with evaluation of pros and cons supported by examples, will score well.

Gaining the easy marks

Unsurprisingly perhaps for a strategic level paper, it is not possible to say where there will definitely be easy marks. However when you're using techniques such as company valuation methods, you will generally be expected to comment on your calculations, so knowledge of the limitations of each technique will earn you marks.

There may be some discussion parts, such as 1 (b) (iv) in the May 2005 exam on the benefits and limitations of post-completion audits, which are straightforward provided you revise those areas.

If you get a large investment appraisal with lots of different items, there will be easy marks for slotting the simpler figures into your proforma straightaway, before you concentrate on the figures that need a lot of adjustment such as cost of capital.

In the end the easiest marks may be gained (or avoided being lost) through following certain basic techniques:

- Setting out calculations and proformas clearly

- Clearly labelling the points you make in discussions so that the marker can identify them all rather than getting lost in the detail

- Providing answers in the form requested, particularly using report format if asked for and giving recommendations if required.

Recent exams

Format of the paper

		Number of marks
Section A:	A compulsory scenario-based question with up to 4 parts	50
Section B:	2 out of 4 questions, 25 marks each	50
		100

Time allowed: 3 hours

The examiner has stated that in all questions marks will be available for structure and presentation, and marks will be allocated for correct structure and approach.

For calculations, the marks allocated are 'the maximum marks assuming the calculations are all correct. Marks are available for recognition of correct approach and understanding.'

For discussion questions, 'where the marking scheme says 'up to 3 marks for each valid point', 0.5 marks are awarded for a bullet point, 1 mark for some attempt at a correct and valid discussion, rising to 3 marks for good discussion of the point using appropriate illustrative examples.'

The examiner has given the following further guidance:

- The numerical content of the paper may be up to 50%, and may require calculations that are not specified in questions.

- The paper will usually include one question that contains no specific requirements for calculations.

- No new topic will be included in a compulsory question until it has featured in an optional question.

- All topics will be covered over three diets.

- Question weightings will be within 10% of the stated weightings for each syllabus section in each exam.

November 2006

Section A

1   Investment appraisal; forecast balance sheets; investment evaluation; roles and responsibilities of treasury and finance departments

Section B

2   Business valuation with intellectual capital

3   Venture capital valuation and as a source of finance

4   Investment appraisal, NPV, IRR and MIRR

5   Objectives; dividend, investment and financing policies

This paper is Mock Exam 3 in this Kit.

May 2006

Section A		*Questions in this Kit*
1	Post-merger values; attainment of objectives; post-merger value enhancing strategies	75

Section B		
2	Working capital requirements; financing policies; advantages and disadvantages of aggressive policy; treasury department structure	28
3	Debt finance, calculations of conversion value and yield to maturity; creditworthiness of an investment	18
4	APV; functions of project committee	59
5	NPV and profitability index; capital rationing in publicly owned entities.	60

Examiner's comments. The performance on this paper was extremely disappointing with many candidates appearing to have done little preparation. Candidates still demonstrate poor knowledge of even basic calculations and their grasp of basic concepts is limited. Poor presentation and structure of solutions is a further weakness.

November 2005

Section A		*Questions in this Kit*
1	Investment; risk issue; share prices; rights issues	74

Section B		
2	Corporate objectives and financing	6
3	Cost of capital; bid price; consideration	48
4	Financial data calculations; sources of finance	30
5	Forecast statements; company objectives	10

Examiner's comments. Performance was again disappointing with many candidates lacking knowledge of even quite basic financial calculations. For example:

- TERP calculations
- Calculating forward exchange rates from interest rates
- Distinguishing between profit and cash
- Using a tabular format for investment appraisal calculations
- De-gearing and re-gearing a beta value

Candidates must also **apply** knowledge to a given case scenario.

May 2005

Section A   *Questions in this Kit*

1   Acquisition consideration, financing acquisition; value-enhancing acquired
     company; post-completion audits.   73

Section B

2   Financing new subsidiary; forecast balance sheet; gearing   17

3   Forecast balance sheet and income statement; cash flow analysis; financial
     management decisions   ME2

4   Cost of debt; lease or buy decision   25

5   Net present value; project control, real options   56

Examiner's comments. Performance was generally poor, with several basic failings:

- Failure to lay out computations, particularly investment appraisals well
- Failure to use market price information when assessing a takeover bid
- Inability to calculate forward exchange rates
- Inability to calculate breakeven
- Suggesting that a bonus issue resulted in an injection of cash
- Suggested retained earnings are cash (better to say retained cash surpluses)

Pilot paper

Section A   *Questions in this Kit*

1   Net present value of acquisition; MIRR ; contribution of new investment to
     objectives; real options   72

Section B

2   Sources of finance for an investment; overseas finance   24

3   Stock market ratios; cost of equity; share price; offer price; offer consideration;
     business implications   45

4   Inter-relation of investment, financing and dividend policies; treasury and
     financial control departments   3

5   Company valuation; venture capital or stock market funding   46

What the examiner means

The table below has been prepared by CIMA to help you interpret exam questions.

Learning objective	Verbs used	Definition	Examples in the Kit
1 Knowledge What you are expected to know	• List • State • Define	• Make a list of • Express, fully or clearly, the details of/facts of • Give the exact meaning of	
2 Comprehension What you are expected to understand	• Describe • Distinguish • Explain • Identify • Illustrate	• Communicate the key features of • Highlight the differences between • Make clear or intelligible/state the meaning of • Recognise, establish or select after consideration • Use an example to describe or explain something	3 46 73
3 Application How you are expected to apply your knowledge	• Apply • Calculate/compute • Demonstrate • Prepare • Reconcile • Solve • Tabulate	• To put to practical use • To ascertain or reckon mathematically • To prove the certainty or to exhibit by practical means • To make or get ready for use • To make or prove consistent/compatible • Find an answer to • Arrange in a table	 72 7
4 Analysis How you are expected to analyse the detail of what you have learned	• Analyse • Categorise • Compare and contrast • Construct • Discuss • Interpret • Produce	• Examine in detail the structure of • Place into a defined class or division • Show the similarities and/or differences between • To build up or complete • To examine in detail by argument • To translate into intelligible or familiar terms • To create or bring into existence	68 51 24 40
5 Evaluation How you are expected to use your learning to evaluate, make decisions or recommendations	• Advise • Evaluate • Recommend	• To counsel, inform or notify • To appraise or assess the value of • To advise on a course of action	45 17 25

Useful websites

The websites below provide additional sources of information of relevance to your studies for *Management Accounting – Decision Management.*

- BPP   www.bpp.com

   For details of other BPP material for your CIMA studies

- CIMA   www.cimaglobal.com

   The official CIMA website

- *Financial Times*   www.ft.com

- *The Economist*   www.economist.com

- *Wall Street Journal*   www.wsj.com

Planning your question practice

BPP LEARNING MEDIA

Planning your question practice

We have already stressed that question practice should be right at the centre of your revision. Whilst you will spend some time looking at your notes and the Paper P9 Passcards, you should spend the majority of your revision time practising questions.

We recommend two ways in which you can practise questions.

- Use **BPP's question plan** to work systematically through the syllabus and attempt key and other questions on a section-by-section basis

- **Build your own exams** – attempt the questions as a series of practice exams

These ways are suggestions and simply following them is no guarantee of success. You or your college may prefer an alternative but equally valid approach.

BPP's question plan

The plan below requires you to devote a **minimum of 45 hours** to revision of Paper P9. Any time you can spend over and above this should only increase your chances of success.

Step 1   **Review your notes** and the chapter summaries in the Paper P9 **Passcards** for each section of the syllabus.

Step 2   **Answer the key questions** for that section. These questions have boxes round the question number in the table below and you should answer them in full. Even if you are short of time you must attempt these questions if you want to pass the exam. You should complete your answers without referring to our solutions.

Step 3   **Attempt the other questions** in that section. For some questions we have suggested that you prepare **answer plans or do the calculations** rather than full solutions. Planning an answer means that you should spend about 40% of the time allowance for the questions brainstorming the question and drawing up a list of points to be included in the answer.

Step 4   **Attempt Mock exams 1, 2 and 3** under strict exam conditions.

Syllabus section	2007 Passcards chapters	Questions in this Kit	Comments	Done ☑
Objectives and constraints	1, 2	1	Worth doing an answer plan to get you thinking about objectives.	☐
		2	Answer in full.	☐
			This question introduces a number of issues that are important for organisations, their overall objectives and performance measures, not just financial ones.	
		3	Prepare a plan for this question.	☐
		4	Answer in full.	☐
			This question will give you practice on different areas of the syllabus, covering the regulatory environment that many businesses face, and also relevant costs and benefits.	
		5	Answer in full.	☐
			This question tests your ability to measure financial performance and status against objectives.	
		6	Answer in full.	☐
			This question gives you practice at applying your discussion to a specific organisation, an essential skill in this exam.	
Performance analysis and forecasting	3	9	Do the calculations in (a) and brief notes of the relevant points for (b).	☐
		10	Answer in full.	☐
			This November 2005 question tests the preparation of forecasts thoroughly and also requires you to analyse the performance of the company.	
		61	Answer in full.	☐
			This question tests your ability to prepare forecasts and discuss sources of finance, which are both areas stressed by the examiners.	
		65	Answer in full.	☐
			This question is a good example of the sort of longer question you might be asked in this area.	
Financial strategies	4	12	Answer in full.	☐
			This question is a good one on dividend policy, requiring you to examine the interaction between dividend policy and share price, and also covers share repurchase.	
		14	Answer in full.	☐
			This question demonstrates the sorts of issues you need to consider when discussing the impact of recent developments in accounting on financial strategy.	
Equity capital	5	16	Attempt the calculations in (a) as they are useful practice, and plan your answer to the report in (c).	☐

Syllabus section	2007 Passcards chapters	Questions in this Kit	Comments	Done ☑
Debt finance	6	17	Answer in full. This May 2005 question indicates the breadth a sources of finance question may have, covering different methods, gearing and effect on financial statements.	☐
Leasing	8	24	Answer in full.	☐
		25	Answer in full. These leasing questions, from the Pilot paper and May 2005 exam, are good examples of what you might be asked about leasing and its relations with other sources of finance.	☐
Securities' market and the capital structure decision	7, 10	15	Answer in full. This question is a good link between the financing decision and wider objectives and valuation issues.	☐
		18	Answer in full. This May 2006 question provides practice at debt finance calculations and some common sense analysis.	☐
		19	Answer in full. This question illustrates how methods of finance can affect the attainments of wider business objectives.	☐
		20	Answer in full. This question provides practice in calculating the cost of debt, which is a common weak area in exams. It also involves consideration of a number of financing options.	☐
		26	Answer in full. Another good illustration of how financing can affect a company's accounts.	☐
		27	Answer in full. This question shows how Paper P9 brings in strategic aspects of a topic first encountered at a lower level (here management of working capital).	☐
		28	Answer parts (a) and (b) in full. This May 2006 question is a good test of working capital calculations and discussion.	☐
The cost of capital	9	29	Answer in full. A good WACC calculation, with discussion parts that require some thought.	☐
		30	Answer in full. The calculations in part (a) are a useful test of how to maximise marks in as short a time as possible. Part (b) provides good practice at discussion of choice of finance.	☐

Syllabus section	2007 Passcards chapters	Questions in this Kit	Comments	Done ✓
		33	Answer in full. Another good calculation, and discussion requiring thought on the reasons for choosing a cost of capital.	☐
Portfolios and CAPM	11, 12	32	Answer in full. Good practice at using CAPM and considering the issues involved in using it.	☐
		34	Carry out the calculations in (a) and prepare an outline for the rest of the answer.	☐
The finance and treasury functions	13, 14	36	Answer in full. This question covers most of the main areas relating to the finance and treasury functions.	☐
Business valuations and acquisitions	15, 16	38	Answer in full. This question ranges quite broadly over the syllabus, and it raises a couple of issues connected with valuation.	☐
		39	Carry out the calculations in (a), and summarise briefly the advantages and disadvantages of each method as you may need to discuss these in your exam.	☐
		42	Answer in full. This question is a good test of your ability to consider practical merger issues (terms, consideration) from the viewpoint of the acquiring company.	☐
		43	Answer in full. And this question provides an equally good test of acquisitions from the viewpoint of the shareholders in the acquired company.	☐
		44	Answer in full. This question gives a slightly different perspective by looking at valuation from the venture capitalists' viewpoint.	☐
		45	Answer in full. A very good merger and acquisition from the pilot paper.	☐
		46	Answer in full. A good valuation question from the pilot paper that also brings in venture capital.	☐
		48	Answer in full. This November 2005 question gives you practice at using betas to calculate cost of capital which is then used to value the business.	☐
		63	Answer in full. A wide-ranging question, covering valuation and various merger issues.	☐

Syllabus section	2007 Passcards chapters	Questions in this Kit	Comments	Done ✓
		66	Answer in full.	☐
			This question is a good illustration of the breadth of issues that compulsory questions can cover including valuation methods, financing and risk management.	
		73	Answer in full.	☐
			The compulsory question from the May 2005 exam.	
		75	Answer in full.	☐
			The compulsory question from May 2006.	
Investment decisions and project control	17–20	49	Answer in full.	☐
			A good introduction to this section, covering mainstream calculations as well as MIRR and also IT investment which has been emphasised as important.	
		51	Jot down a plan for this question as it is useful revision of a number of issues relating to investment appraisal. Include in your plan notes on how the answer would relate to each of the companies.	☐
		53	Answer in full.	☐
			A question testing both your ability to appraise investments in a capital rationing situation and to discuss wider strategic issues.	
		54	Do the net present value calculation and plan your answer to the rest of the question.	☐
		55	Answer in full.	☐
			A question testing not just your investment appraisal skills, but also requiring discussion of the use of WACC and risks of foreign investment.	
		57	Answer in full.	☐
			(a) examines your ability to apply the adjusted present value method, while (b) is a good illustration of various issues that arise when capital is scarce.	
		58	Answer in full.	☐
			A test of your ability to manipulate beta factors to come up with a cost of capital used in an investment appraisal.	
		59	Answer in full.	☐
			This question from May 2006 covers calculation of K_e double taxation relief and APV.	
		60	Answer in full.	☐
			Another question from May 2006 which tests capital rationing techniques.	

Syllabus section	2007 Passcards chapters	Questions in this Kit	Comments	Done ☑
		62	Answer in full. A good question requiring a lot of thought about how contracts are evaluated, and bringing in purchasing power parity.	☐
		69	Answer in full An investment question which brings in a number of important issues in discussion part (b).	☐
		72	Answer in full. The compulsory question on the pilot paper.	☐
		74	Answer in full. The compulsory question from November 2005.	☐

BPP LEARNING MEDIA

Build your own exams

Having revised your notes and the BPP Passcards, you can attempt the questions in the Kit as a series of practice exams. You can organise the questions in the following ways:

- Either you can attempt complete old papers; recent papers are listed below.

	P9			
	Pilot paper	May'05	Nov'05	May'06
Section A				
1	72	73	74	75
Section B				
2	24	17	6	28
3	45	ME2	48	18
4	3	25	30	59
5	46	56	10	60

- Or you can make up practice exams, either yourself or using the mock exams that we have listed below.

	Practice exams								
	1	2	3	4	5	6	7	8	9
Section A									
1	63	64	65	66	67	68	69	70	71
Section B									
2	2	4	5	6	7	8	9	11	12
3	15	16	19	20	21	22	23	26	27
4	38	39	40	41	42	43	44	47	37
5	49	50	51	52	53	54	55	57	58

- Whichever practice exams you use, you must attempt **Mock exams 1, 2 and 3** at the end of your revision.

Questions

FORMULATION OF FINANCIAL STRATEGY

Questions 1 to 14 cover formulation of financial strategy, the subject of Part A of the BPP Study Text for Paper P9.

1 Goals

45 mins

(a) Assume you are Finance Director of a large multinational company, listed on a number of international stock markets. The company is reviewing its corporate plan. At present, the company focuses on maximising shareholder wealth as its major goal. The Managing Director thinks this single goal is inappropriate and asks his co-directors for their views on giving greater emphasis to the following:

   (i) Cash flow generation

   (ii) Profitability as measured by profits after tax and return on investment

   (iii) Risk-adjusted returns to shareholders

   (iv) Performance improvement in a number of areas such as concern for the environment, employees' remuneration and quality of working conditions and customer satisfaction

Required

Provide the Managing Director with a report for presentation at the next board meeting which:

   (i) Discusses the argument that maximisation of shareholder wealth should be the only true objective of a company, and

   (ii) Discusses the advantages and disadvantages of the MD's suggestions about alternative goals

(15 marks)

(b) The company is already considering improving the methods of remuneration for its senior employees. As a member of the executive board, you are asked to give your opinions on the following suggestions:

   (i) A high basic salary with usual 'perks' such as company car, pension scheme etc but no performance-related bonuses

   (ii) A lower basic salary with usual 'perks' plus a bonus related to their division's profit before tax

   (iii) A lower basic salary with usual 'perks' plus a share option scheme which allows senior employees to buy a given number of shares in the company at a fixed price at the end of each financial year

Required

Discuss the arguments for and against *each* of the *three* options from the point of view of both the company and its employees. Detailed comments on the taxation implications are *not* required.   **(10 marks)**

(Total = 25 marks)

2 Educational institution (FLFS, 5/03)

45 mins

You are a newly-appointed Finance Manager of an Educational Institution that is mainly government-funded, having moved from a similar post in a service company in the private sector. The objective, or mission statement, of this Institution is shown in its publicity material as:

'To achieve recognised standards of excellence in the provision of teaching and research.'

The only financial performance measure evaluated by the government is that the Institution has to remain within cash limits. The cash allocation each year is determined by a range of non-financial measures such as the number of research publications the Institution's staff have achieved and official ratings for teaching quality.

However, almost 20% of total cash generated by the Institution is now from the provision of courses and seminars to private sector companies, using either its own or its customers' facilities. These customers are largely unconcerned about research ratings and teaching quality as they relate more to academic awards such as degrees.

The Head of the Institution aims to increase the percentage of income coming from the private sector to 50% over the next five years. She has asked you to advise on how the management team can evaluate progress towards achieving this aim as well as meeting the objective set by government for the activities it funds.

Required

(a)   Discuss the main issues that an Institution such as this has to consider when setting objectives.

Advise on

- Whether a financial objective, or objectives, could or should be determined; and
- Whether such objective(s) should be made public.   **(9 marks)**

The following is a list of financial and non-financial performance measures that were in use in your *previous company:*

FINANCIAL	NON-FINANCIAL
Value added	Competitive position
Profitability	Customer satisfaction
Return on investment	Market share

Required

(b)   Choose *two of each* type of measure, explain their purpose and advise on how they could be used by the Educational Institution over the next five years to assess how it is meeting the Head of the Institution's aims.

(16 marks)

Note: A report format is NOT required in answering this question.   **(Total = 25 marks)**

3 Objectives (Pilot Paper)   45 mins

When determining the financial objectives of a company, it is necessary to take three types of policy decision into account: investment policy, financing policy and dividend policy.

Required

(a)   Discuss the nature of these three types of decision, commenting on how they are inter-related and how they might affect the value of the firm (that is the present value of projected cash flows).   **(12 marks)**

(b)   Describe the different functions of the treasury and financial control departments of an organisation and comment on the relative contributions of these two departments to policy determination and the setting and achievement of financial objectives.   **(13 marks)**

(Total = 25 marks)

4 JS   45 mins

The JS Company was established in Ruritania a few years ago to participate in the telecommunications industry in that country. It has developed a subsidiary that sells mobile phones mainly via telephone sales, with 150 sales representatives communicating with customers exclusively on the telephone.

Within the JS Company, sales representatives require information such as:

- Stocks of telephones

- Popular brands of telephones, to try and offer acceptable telephones to each type of customer (such as young, middle-aged or business users)

- Special offers and promotions

- Details of which offers and promotions are effective for different categories of customer

Sales representatives tailor their sales advice according to the different customer types. Sales representatives are paid a commission on all telephones sold. The range of computer systems currently available to provide information to the sales representatives is relatively old and generally inefficient to use. The company is implementing a groupware system to enable employees to share more knowledge more efficiently within the organisation. The new system is being implemented on the recommendation of an external consultant. Sales representatives have had very little input into the overall system design.

The consultant produced the following Cost Benefit Analysis summary (CBA) to help justify the implementation of the new system:

	Ruritanian £
Costs Hardware, to include new PCs for each sales representative	(150,000)
Software	(50,000)
Implementation, including data conversion	(75,000)
Lost sales as staff receive on-the-job training	(5,000)
Total costs	(280,000)

Benefits Increase in sales estimated at £100,000 in year one, rising at 10% per annum for each of the following four years to total £610,510.

Net benefit of new system £330,510

Required

(a)   Evaluate the CBA, explaining any deficiencies and justifying any amendments you may wish to make.

(14 marks)

The government of Ruritania has established a regulatory body to oversee the telecommunications industry in that country. The body was set up to protect consumers and ensure that monopoly or near monopoly suppliers did not abuse their position for financial gain.

Required

(b)   (i)   Explain the factors that might cause a regulator to intervene in the management of a regulated industry.

(ii)   Describe the activities a regulator might perform to enhance competition in a regulated industry.

(iii)   Explain why it might be necessary to retain a regulatory body even when competition enters an industry.

(11 marks)

(Total = 25 marks)

5 PQD

45 mins

(a) PQD is an unquoted company aiming for a stock exchange listing. Its directors have commissioned a firm of consultants to conduct a wide-ranging review of the company's public image and market position. Although this is not predominantly a financial review, the consultants need to examine the company's financial performance. The company has the following summary information for the last five years.

	Year 1 £m	Year 2 £m	Year 3 £m	Year 4 £m	Year 5 £m
Revenues	51.2	58.3	63.9	75.2	78.2
Cost of sales	20.5	22.2	24.3	30.1	30.5
Salaries and wages	15.4	16.8	17.2	15.8	15.2
Other costs	6.1	7.9	9.9	16.3	17.9
Profit from operations	9.2	11.4	12.5	13.0	14.6
Interest	1.5	1.6	1.3	0.3	0.2
Tax	2.5	3.2	3.7	4.2	4.8
Profit after interest and tax	5.2	6.6	7.5	8.5	9.6
Dividends payable	2.1	2.6	3.0	3.4	4.8
Average receivables	10.5	11.7	13.3	14.8	15.2
Average payables	3.8	4.2	5.1	6.7	6.9
Average total assets	41.2	45.2	46.7	63.3	67.1
Shareholders' funds	26.2	30.2	34.7	59.8	64.6
Long-term debt	15.0	15.0	12.0	3.5	2.5
Number of shares in issue (millions)	6.0	6.0	6.0	8.0	8.0
P/E ratio:					
Company	8.0	8.5	9.0	9.2	9.5
Industry	8.5	9.0	9.1	9.0	9.1
Number of employees	1,720	1,750	1,820	1,720	1,690

Notes

1   Each P/E ratio is the average for the year.

2   The increased equity in year 4 was the result of a 1-for-3 rights issue at 1,000p per share which took place at the beginning of the year. Some of the money raised was used to reduce debt.

For the past five years, PQD has stated its objectives as: 'To maximise shareholder wealth whilst recognising the responsibility of the company to its other stakeholders'.

As one of the consultants working on this assignment, you have been asked to assess whether the company has achieved its objectives in the five-year period under review and to discuss the key factors which have determined your assessment.

Required

(i)   Discuss whether the company has met its objectives, based solely on the information available.

(12 marks)

(ii)   Explain what other financial information you would need in order to provide your client with a more accurate assessment.   **(8 marks)**

(b)   Describe the role of the financial managers if PQD decides to seek a flotation.   **(5 marks)**

(Total = 25 marks)

6 HG (11/05)

45 mins

HG is a privately-owned toy manufacturer based in a country in the European Union, but which is not in the European Common Currency Area (ECCA). It trades internationally both as a supplier and a customer. Although HG is privately owned, it has revenue and assets equivalent in amount to some public listed companies. It has a large number of shareholders, but has no intention of seeking a listing at the present time. In fact, the major shareholders have often expressed a wish to buy out some of the smaller investors.

The entity has a long history of sound, if unspectacular, profitability. The directors and shareholders are reasonably happy with this situation and are averse to adopting strategies that they think might involve a substantial increase in risk, for example, acquisition or setting up manufacturing capability overseas, as some of HG's European competitors have done. As a consequence, HG accepts its growth rate will be relatively low, compared with some of its competitors.

The entity is financed 70% equity and 30% debt (based on book values). The debt is a mixture of secured and unsecured bonds carrying interest rates of between 7% and 8·5% and repayable in 5 to 10 years' time. Inflation in HG's country is near zero and interest rates are low and possibly falling. The Company Treasurer is investigating the opportunities for, and consequences of, refinancing.

HG's main financial objective is simply to increase dividends each year. It has one non-financial objective, which is to treat all stakeholders in the organisation with 'fairness and equality'. The Board has decided to review these objectives. The new Finance Director believes maximisation of shareholder wealth should be the sole objective, but the other directors do not agree and think a range of objectives should be considered, for example profits after tax and return on investment and performance improvement across a number of operational areas.

Required

(a)   Evaluate the appropriateness of HG's current objectives and the Finance Director's suggestion, and discuss the issues that the HG Board should consider when determining the new corporate objectives. Conclude with a recommendation. **(15 marks)**

(b)   Discuss the factors that the treasury department should consider when determining financing, or re-financing strategies in the context of the economic environment described in the scenario and explain how these might impact on the determination of corporate objectives.

(10 marks)

(Total = 25 marks)

7 CBA

45 mins

CBA is a manufacturing company in the furniture trade. Its sales have risen sharply over the past six months as a result of an improvement in the economy and a strong housing market. The company is now showing signs of 'overtrading' and the financial manager, Ms Smith, is concerned about its liquidity. The company is one month from its year end. Estimated figures for the full 12 months of the current year and forecasts for next year, on present cash management policies, are shown below.

	Next year £'000	Current year £'000
Income statement		
Revenues	5,200	4,200
Less		
Cost of sales (Note 1)	3,224	2,520
Operating expenses	650	500
Operating profit	1,326	1,180
Interest paid	54	48
Profit before tax	1,272	1,132
Tax payable	305	283
Profit after tax	967	849
Dividends declared	387	339
Current assets and liabilities as at the end of the year		
Inventory/work-in-progress	625	350
Receivables	750	520
Cash	0	25
Trade payables	464	320
Other payables (tax and dividends)	692	622
Overdraft	11	0
Net current assets/(liabilities)	208	(47)

Note 1:		
Cost of sales includes depreciation of	225	175

Ms Smith is considering methods of improving the cash position. A number of actions are being discussed.

Debtors

Offer a 2% discount to customers who pay within 10 days of despatch of invoices. It is estimated 50% of customers will take advantage of the new discount scheme. The other 50% will continue to take the current average credit period.

Trade payables and inventory

Reduce the number of suppliers currently being used and negotiate better terms with those that remain by introducing a 'just in time' policy. The aim will be to reduce the end-of-year forecast cost of sales (excluding depreciation) by 5% and inventory/WIP levels by 10%. However, the number of days credit taken by the company will have to fall to 30 days to help persuade suppliers to improve their prices.

Other information

- All trade is on credit. *Official* terms of sale at present require payment within 30 days. Interest is not charged on late payments.

- All purchases are made on credit.

- Operating expenses will be £650,000 with the existing or proposed policies.

- Interest payments would be £45,000 if the new policies are implemented.

- Capital expenditure of £550,000 is planned for next year.

Required

(a)   Explain the main uses of overdraft facilities as part of a company's working capital management policy.

(5 marks)

(b)   Prepare a cash flow forecast for next year, assuming:

(i)   The company does not change its policies
(ii)   The company's proposals for managing customers, suppliers and inventory are implemented

In both cases, assume a full twelve-month period, that is the changes will be effective from day 1 of next year.   **(14 marks)**

(c)   As Assistant to Ms Smith, write a short report to her discussing the proposed actions. Include comments on the factors, financial and non-financial, that the company should take into account before implementing the new policies.   **(6 marks)**

(Total = 25 marks)

8 Emcos (FLFS, 11/02 amended)   45 mins

Company background and objectives

Emcos designs and develops emission control systems for motor vehicles. The company is based in the United Kingdom. When it was listed in 20X0 it forecast trading losses for the first three full years of listing (20X1 – 20X3) but then substantial profits from 20X4 onwards.

Emcos patents its designs and receives its income in the form of royalty payments from manufacturing companies in the UK, Spain, Norway and Japan to which it licenses its designs. The company's main objective is to become the market leader in its field, as measured by turnover and industry quality standards, by 20X6. To achieve these goals, it spent large sums of capital in the five years up to 20X2. This investment has yet to yield results in terms of positive cash flow.

Forecast financial statements for 20X2

Financial results are available for the first 10 months of the current year (20X2). The accounts departments has produced the following full-year forecasts based on these first 10 months' results.

FORECAST PROFIT AND LOSS ACCOUNT FOR THE YEAR TO 31 DECEMBER 20X2

	£'000
Turnover	261
Development expenses	5,315
Administration/other expenses (Note 1)	2,615
Operating loss	(7,669)
Interest receivable	140
Loss before taxation	(7,529)
Taxation	0
Loss after taxation	(7,529)

Note 1: Including £1.2 million depreciation.

FORECAST BALANCE SHEET AT DECEMBER 20X2

	£'000	£'000
Non-current assets (net book value)		
Patents and copyright		751
Tangible assets		7,850
Investments		58
		8,659
Current assets		
Inventory and work-in-progress	98	
Marketable securities (Note 1)	2,150	
Cash and bank	200	
	2,448	
Less amounts falling due within one year		
Trade payables	(1,450)	
Net current assets		998
Total assets less current liabilities		9,657
		£'000
Financing		
Called-up share capital (ordinary shares of £0.10)		9,985
Share premium account		37,522
Profit and loss account		(37,850)
Equity shareholders' funds		9,657

Notes

1   Marketable securities are short-term, interest-bearing investments.
2   Today's share price (19 November 20X2) is 85 pence.

Forecast receipts for the year to 31 December 20X3

The company's UK licensees pay royalties in £ sterling; those overseas pay in their domestic currency. Forecast receipts for the next 12 months are as follows. Assume for simplicity that all receipts are received at the end of the year.

Licensee number	Country	Receipts expected Amount '000s	Currency	Forecast rates at 31.12.20X3	Forecast interest rates % per annum
1	UK	260	£ sterling	n/a	4.50
2	Spain	425	Euro	1.664	3.50*
3	Norway	1,365	Kroner	13.502	3.75
4	Japan	25,000	Yen	174.310	0.25

* Assume this is the rate applicable throughout the countries within the common currency area.

Other forecast financial information for 20X3

- Development expenses are expected to fall to £4.5 million.

- Administration/other expenses will rise by 10%.

- Interest receivable will be £140,000.

- Capital purchases planned during the year will be:

  –   Patents   £320,000
  –   Tangible assets   £250,000

- Depreciation on tangible assets will be charged at 20% on net book value. Patents are not depreciated at present. Investments are in shares in unlisted companies and their value is not expected to change.

- Inventory and work-in-progress will increase to £285,000 by the end of the year.

- The value of trade payables will decrease by 10%.

Other relevant information

- The company has to date agreed with the bank to maintain a minimum cash balance at bank of £200,000. Sales of marketable securities will be used to help maintain this balance.

- Ignore any interest payable on overdrawn bank balances.

Required

(a)   Assume you are the senior management accountant with Emcos and that today is 19 November 20X2. Using the forecast accounts for 20X2 as a base, you have been asked to construct:

  (i)   A forecast profit and loss account for the year to 31 December 20X3
  (ii)   A forecast balance sheet at 31 December 20X3
  (iii)   A cash flow forecast, in £ sterling, for the year to 31 December 20X3   **(17 marks)**

(b)   On the basis of your forecast financial statements, you have some concerns about the financial strategy of the business. Write a report to the company's directors that discusses and recommends a financing strategy for a business such as Emcos plc that has a requirement for substantial amounts of cash to continue to develop intellectual property whilst maintaining investor confidence.   **(8 marks)**

(Total = 25 marks)

8 Question with analysis: Emcos (FLFS, 11/02 amended)

45 mins

Company background and objectives

Can raise equity	

Emcos designs and develops emission control systems for motor vehicles. The company is based in the United Kingdom. When it was **listed** in 20X0 it forecast trading losses for the first three full years of listing (**20X1 – 20X3**) but then substantial profits from 20X4 onwards.

Including this year	
Intangible asset	
Terms	

Emcos **patents** its designs and receives its income in the form of **royalty payments** from manufacturing companies in the **UK, Spain, Norway and Japan** to which it licenses its designs. The company's main objective is to become the **market leader** in its field, as measured by revenue and **industry quality standards**, by 20X6. To achieve these goals, it spent large sums of capital in the five years up to 20X2. This investment has **yet to yield results** in terms of positive cash flow.

Exchange rate	
Ambitious	
As expected	
Costs	

Forecast financial statements for 20X2

Financial results are available for the first 10 months of the current year (20X2). The accounts departments has produced the following **full-year forecasts** based on these first 10 months' results.

Probably reliable	

FORECAST INCOME STATEMENT FOR THE YEAR TO 31 DECEMBER 20X2

	£'000
Revenues	**261**
Development expenses	5,315
Administration/other expenses (Note 1)	2,615
Operating loss	**(7,669)**
Interest receivable	**140**
Loss before taxation	(7,529)
Taxation	0
Loss after taxation	(7,529)

Minimal compared with costs	
Investment income	

Note 1: Including £1.2 million depreciation.

FORECAST BALANCE SHEET AT DECEMBER 20X2
ASSETS

	£'000	£'000
Non-current assets (net book value)		
Patents and copyright		751
Tangible assets		**7,850**
Investments		58
		8,659
Current assets		
Inventory and work-in-progress	98	
Marketable securities (Note 1)	**2,150**	
Cash and bank	200	
		2,448
		11,107

High base	
Variable	

EQUITY AND LIABILITIES

	£'000
Capital and reserves	
Share capital (ordinary shares of £0.10)	9,985
Share premium account	37,522
Accumulated profits	(37,850)
	9,657
Current liabilities	
Trade payables	1,450
	11,107

> **Wiped out in 12 months time**

Notes

1   Marketable securities are short-term, interest-bearing investments.
2   Today's share price (19 November 20X2) is 85 pence.

> **Conversion**

Forecast receipts for the year to 31 December 20X3

The company's UK licensees pay royalties in £ sterling; those overseas pay in their **domestic currency** . Forecast receipts for the next 12 months are as follows. Assume for simplicity that all receipts are received at the end of the year.

Licensee number	Country	Receipts expected Amount '000s	Currency	Forecast rates at 31.12.20X3
1	UK	260	£ sterling	n/a
2	Spain	425	Euro	**1.664**
3	Norway	1,365	Kroner	**13.502**
4	Japan	25,000	Yen	**174.310**

> **Predictions been made: no need for IRP, PPP**

Other forecast financial information for 20X3

- Development expenses are expected to fall to **£4.5 million** .

> **I & E**

- Administration/other expenses will **rise by 10%** .

> **I & E CFS**

- Interest receivable will be **£140,000** .

- Capital purchases planned during the year will be:
    - Patents **£320,000**
    - Tangible assets **£250,000**

> **B/S CFS**

> **I & E B/S**

- Depreciation on tangible assets will be charged at **20%** on net book value. Patents are **not**

> **B/S**

  depreciated at present. Investments are in shares in unlisted companies and their **value is not expected to change** .

> **Less reliance**

- Inventory and work-in-progress will increase to **£285,000** by the end of the year.

- The value of trade payables will **decrease by 10%** .

> **B/S CFS**

> **B/S**

Other relevant information

- The company has to date agreed with the bank to maintain a minimum **cash balance at bank of £200,000** . **Sales of marketable securities** will be used to help **maintain this balance** .

> **Balancing figure**

- Ignore any interest payable on overdrawn bank balances.

Required

(a) Assume you are the senior management accountant with Emcos and that today is 19 November 20X2. Using the forecast accounts for 20X2 as a base, you have been asked to construct:

(i) A forecast income statement for the year to 31 December 20X3

(ii) A forecast balance sheet at 31 December 20X3

(iii) A cash flow forecast, in £ sterling, for the year to 31 December 20X3 **(17 marks)**

What are they

(b) On the basis of your forecast financial statements, you have some concerns about the financial strategy of the business. Write a report to the company's directors that discusses and recommends a financing strategy for a business such as Emcos that has a requirement for substantial amounts of cash to continue to develop intellectual property whilst maintaining investor confidence. **(8 marks)**

Sources

What will undermine confidence

(Total = 25 marks)

Answer plan

(a) (i) **Income statement**

Workings royalty income, depreciation

(ii) **Balance sheet**

Working depreciation
Securities/overdraft balancing figures

(iii) **Cash flow**

Operations
Working capital
Tax
Non-current assets
Financing

(b) Intro – need to manage finances and currency risks

Funds

Required urgently
Equity – rights issue
Debt – security, interest, financial risk, hedging
Convertible – S/H income and conversion rights
Other sources- sell patents, joint ventures
Recommendations – sell patents/joint venture/borrow abroad

9 KOL

45 mins

It is currently November 20X5. KOL is a privately owned manufacturer of sports equipment. Information about the company is as follows.

(a)   The business is growing modestly at present but faster growth is planned.

(b)   The business is seasonal with sales peaking in the autumn.

(c)   KOL is anticipating cashflow problems as a result of its planned growth. It has prepared a cash budget for 20X6, details of which are given below.

(d)   The current overdraft facility is $150,000. The bank has indicated it would be unwilling to increase this amount.

(e)   The company has 15 shareholders at present. Four of the shareholders are directors of the company, owning 60% of the share capital between them. The other shareholders take no interest in the running of the business and, although the company is unlisted, shares have changed hands on a few occasions.

(f)   None of the director-shareholders will be in a position to invest capital in the business for the next 2 to 3 years.

Cashflow forecast for 20X6 ($'000)

	Jan	Feb	Mar	Apr	May	June	July	Aug	Sept	Oct	Nov	Dec	Total
Receipts from customers	175	135	115	75	50	50	65	75	90	150	215	295	1,490
Other income			45			45			45			45	180
Total inflows	175	135	160	75	50	95	65	75	135	150	215	340	1,670
Payments to trade suppliers	52	41	34	23	15	15	20	22	27	53	75	103	480
Wages and salaries	53	53	53	53	55	57	57	55	55	53	53	53	650
Other operating expenses	25	25	25	30	30	30	35	35	35	35	35	40	380
Capital expenditure			45			35			40				120
Dividends payable		100											100
Tax payable									65				65
Total outflows	130	219	157	106	100	137	112	112	222	141	163	196	1,795
Net cash inflow/ (outflow)	45	(84)	3	(31)	(50)	(42)	(47)	(37)	(87)	9	52	144	(125)
Opg bank bal	50	95	11	14	(17)	(67)	(109)	(156)	(193)	(280)	(271)	(219)	50
Closing bank bal	95	11	14	(17)	(67)	(109)	(156)	(193)	(280)	(271)	(219)	(75)	(75)

The following information is also available.

(g)   All sales are on credit. The company's usual terms of trade allow 60 days' credit. Customers take, on average, 90 days to pay. This has been allowed for in the cash budget. Sales in the three months to the end of December 20X6 are expected to be $660,000. No increases in selling prices are planned.

(h)   Production is evenly scheduled throughout the year and finished goods for stock are stored until the peak selling period. The company estimates stocks of finished goods will be $170,000 higher at the end of December 20X6 than at the beginning of the year.

(i)   The company's premises are all owned by the company. Other income is rental from letting some of its premises.

(j)   Suppliers, on average, allow KOL 6 weeks' credit although the company typically takes up to 90 days to pay. Purchases for the three months to the end of December 20X6 are expected to be $231,000. All other expenses are paid in the month in which they arise.

(k)   The capital expenditure forecast for 20X6 is for the following items of expenditure.

March 20X6	New plant and machinery	$45,000
June 20X6	New motor vehicles	$35,000
September 20X6	Building renovations	$40,000

Further capital expenditure is planned in 20X7.

Required

(a) Calculate the profit before interest and tax excluding depreciation of the company for 20X6. Use whatever reasonable assumptions you think necessary, but state, briefly, what they are. **(10 marks)**

(b) Review the cash budget and write a report to the board of KOL advising on possible actions it may take to improve its budgeted cashflow for the year and the likely effect of these actions on the company's business. Make whatever reasonable assumptions you think necessary. **(15 marks)**

(Total = 25 marks)

10 RJ (11/05)   **45 mins**

RJ plc is a supplier of surgical instruments and medical supplies (excluding drugs). Its shares are listed on the UK's Alternative Investment Market and are currently quoted at 458 pence per £1 share. The majority of its customers are public sector organisations in the UK. RJ plc is doing well and now needs additional capital to expand operations.

The forecast financial statements are given below.

Extracts from the Income Statement for the year ended 31 December 20X5

	£'000
Revenue	30,120
Costs and expenses	22,500
Operating profit	7,620
Finance costs	2,650
Profit before tax	4,970
Tax	1,491

Note: Dividends declared for 20X5 are £1,392,000

Balance Sheet as at 31 December 20X5

	£'000	£'000
Total assets		
Non-current assets		14,425
Current assets		
Inventories	4,510	
Trade receivables	3,700	
Cash	198	
		8,408
		22,833
Equity and liabilities		
Equity		
Share capital	8,350	
Retained earnings	4,750	
		13,100
Non-current liabilities		
(secured bonds, 6% 2008)		4,000
Current liabilities		
Trade payables	2,850	
Other payables		
(tax and dividends)	2,883	
		5,733
		22,833

You have obtained the following additional information:

1. Revenue is expected to increase by 10% per annum in each of the financial years ending 31 December 20X6 and 20X7. Costs and expenses, excluding depreciation, are expected to increase by an average of 5% per annum. Finance costs are expected to remain unchanged.

2. RJ plc expects to continue to be liable for tax at the marginal rate of 30%. Assume tax is paid or refunded the year following that in which the liability or repayment arises.

3. The ratios of trade receivables to revenue and trade payables to costs and expenses will remain the same for the next two years. The value of inventories is likely to remain at 20X5 levels.

4. The non-current assets are land and buildings, which are not depreciated in RJ plc's books. Capital (tax) allowances on the buildings may be ignored. All other assets used by the entity (machinery, cars and so on) are either rented or leased on operating leases.

5. Dividends will be increased by 5% each year.

6. RJ plc intends to purchase for cash new machinery to the value of £6,000,000 during 20X6, although an investment appraisal exercise has not been carried out. It will be depreciated straight line over 10 years. RJ plc intends to charge a full year's depreciation in the first year of purchase of its assets. Capital (tax) allowances are available at 25% reducing balance on this expenditure.

RJ plc's main financial objectives for the years 20X6-20X7 are to earn a pre-tax return on the closing book value of equity of 35% per annum and a year-on-year increase in earnings of 10%.

Required

Assume you are a consultant working for RJ plc. Evaluate the implications of the financial information you have obtained. You should:

(a)   Provide forecast income statements, dividends and retentions for the two years ending 31 December 20X6 and 20X7.   **(6 marks)**

(b)   Provide cash flow forecasts for the years 20X6 and 20X7. Comment briefly on how RJ plc might finance any cash deficit.   **(8 marks)**

Note. This is **not** an investment appraisal exercise; you may ignore the timing of cash flows **within** each year and you should not discount the cash flows. You should also ignore interest payable on any cash deficit.

(c)   Discuss the key aspects and implications of the financial information you have obtained in your answer to parts (a) and (b) of the question, in particular whether RJ plc is likely to meet its stated objectives. Provide whatever calculations you think are appropriate to support your discussion. Up to 4 marks are available for calculations in this section of the question.   **(11 marks)**

(Total = 25 marks)

11 RG

45 mins

The following financial data relate to RG.

Year	Earnings per share Pence	Net dividend per share Pence	Share price Pence
20X1	42	17	252
20X2	46	18	184
20X3	51	20	255
20X4	55	22	275
20X5	62	25	372

A firm of market analysts which specialises in the industry in which RG operates has recently re-evaluated the company's future prospects. The analysts estimate that RG's earnings and dividends will grow at 25% for the next two years. Thereafter, earnings are likely to increase at a lower annual rate of 10%. If this reduction in earnings growth occurs, the analysts consider that the dividend payout ratio will be increased to 50%.

RG is all equity financed and has one million ordinary shares in issue.

The tax rate of 30% is not expected to change in the foreseeable future.

Required

(a)   Discuss whether the dividend policy being considered by the analysts would be appropriate for the company in the following two sets of circumstances.

   (i)   The company's shareholders are mainly financial institutions.
   (ii)   The company's shareholders are mainly small private investors.   **(7 marks)**

DV is a large international company with widespread interests in advertising, media and various consultancy activities associated with sales promotion and marketing. In recent years the company's earnings and dividend payments, in real terms, have grown on average by 15% and 12% per year respectively. The company is likely to have substantial cash surpluses in the coming year, but a number of investment opportunities are being considered for the subsequent two years. The senior managers of the company are reviewing their likely funding requirements for the next two to three years and the possible consequences for dividend policy.

At present the company has a debt:equity ratio of 1:5, measured in market value terms. It does not want to increase this ratio at the present time but might need to borrow to pay a maintained dividend in the future.

The senior managers of the company are discussing a range of issues concerning financial strategy in general and dividend policy in particular.

Required

Assume you are an independent financial adviser to the Board of DV. Write a report to the board which discusses the following issues.

(b)   The repurchase of some of the company's shares in the coming year using the forecast surplus cash, the aim being to reduce the amount of cash needed to pay dividends in subsequent years. Other implications of share repurchase for the company's financial strategy should also be considered.   **(8 marks)**

(c)   The advisability of borrowing money to pay dividends in years 2 and 3.   **(6 marks)**

(d)   The likely effect on the company's cost of equity if the company decides on share repurchase and/or further borrowing.   **(4 marks)**

(Total = 25 marks)

12 AB and YZ (FLFS, 11/04)

45 mins

AB and YZ both operate department stores in Europe. They operate in similar markets and are generally considered to be direct competitors. Both companies have had similar earnings records over the past ten years and have similar capital structures. The earnings and dividend record of the two companies over the past six years is as follows:

| | AB | | | YZ | | |
| | EPS | DPS | Average | EPS | DPS | Average |
Year to 31 March	cents	cents	share price	cents	cents	share price
20X1	230	60	2,100	240	96	2,200
20X2	150	60	1,500	160	64	1,700
20X3	100	60	1,000	90	36	1,400
20X4	−125	60	800	−110	0	908
20X5	100	60	1,000	90	36	1,250
20X6	150	60	1,400	145	58	1,700

Note. EPS = Earnings per Share and DPS = Dividends per Share

AB has had 25 million shares in issue for the past six years. YZ currently has 25 million shares in issue. At the beginning of 20X5 YZ had a 1 for 4 rights issue. The EPS and DPS have been adjusted in the above table.

The Chairman of AB is concerned that the share price of YZ is higher than his company's, despite the fact that AB has recently earned more per share than YZ and frequently during the past six years has paid a higher dividend.

Required

(a) Discuss:

(i) The apparent dividend policy followed by each company over the past six years and comment on the possible relationship of these policies to the companies' market values and current share prices; and

(ii) Whether there is an optimal dividend policy for AB that might increase shareholder value. **(12 marks)**

(b) Forecast earnings for AB for the year to 31 March 20X7 are €40 million. At present, it has excess cash of €2.5 million and is considering a share repurchase in addition to maintaining last year's dividend. The Chairman thinks this will have a number of benefits for the company, including a positive effect on the share price.

Advise the Chairman of AB of

(i) How a share repurchase may be arranged

(ii) The main reasons for a share repurchase

(iii) The potential problems of such an action, compared with a one-off extra dividend payment, and any possible effect on the share price of AB **(13 marks)**

(Total = 25 marks)

A report format is not required for this question.

13 DRY

45 mins

DRY operates in a mature, low-risk industry and has had a stable level of profits for many years. Profits after tax for the current year were £120 million and this level of profit is expected to continue in the future providing the current dividend/retention policy is maintained. The company adopts a dividend policy based on a dividend payout ratio of 80% and it has just paid a dividend for the year that has recently ended. However, a newly-appointed Chief Executive is considering three new investment strategies. Whilst these strategies will have the same initial investment, they will require different levels of future investment but will lead to different future growth rates.

The Board of Directors has agreed that if any one of the three new strategies is decided upon the future investment required will be financed entirely from retained earnings rather than any new issue of equity. This will entail a reduction in future dividends. Alternatively, the business can continue its current strategy of high dividend and no growth.

The Board has arranged to meet again in the near future to decide whether to support one of the proposed strategies or whether to continue with the existing strategy of high dividend payments and no growth. The following figures, which relate to the proposed strategies, will be presented to the Board at this meeting:

Strategy	Dividend payout ratio	Growth rate in profits	Required return by shareholders
	%	%	%
1	10	8	12
2	30	5	10
3	60	3	9

The cost of ordinary share capital for the company is currently 8.0%.

Required

(a)   Recommend, with supporting calculations, which of the proposed strategies is preferable.   **(7 marks)**

(b)   Explain why the proposed change in dividend policy is likely to be regarded as important by shareholders.
(5 marks)

(c)   Explain why a company may prefer to fund investment projects by the use of retained profits rather than by the issue of new equity shares.   **(3 marks)**

The company's chief accountant has recently retired and the chief executive wishes to re-organise the company's financial management function, as he believes that the function is no longer adequate for the size of company that DRY has become.

Required

(d)   Discuss the main factors that should be considered when developing a financial management department in an organisation.   **(10 marks)**

(Total = 25 marks)

14 TED

45 mins

TED, a company looking to gain a listing on its local stock exchange, is considering the implications of various recent accounting developments on its financial strategy and accounting processes. The company is currently considering a number of projects that have substantial environmental implications.

Required

(a)   Explain how environmental costs and benefits might impact upon TED's accounting procedures.   **(9 marks)**

TED has always had a good reputation for developing its staff, and the directors are keen to demonstrate the impact of its human resource investment.

Required

(b)   Discuss the possible consequences for TED of the introduction of human resource accounting.   **(7 marks)**

The directors of TED are aware that if the company gains a listing on the stock exchange, it will have to comply with corporate governance best practice. The chief executive has queried what the implications of compliance are for financial strategy and costs.

Required

(c)   Discuss the main impacts corporate governance may have on TED's financial strategy and costs.

(9 marks)

(Total = 25 marks)

FINANCIAL MANAGEMENT

Questions 15 to 37 cover financial management, the subject of Part B of the BPP Study Text for Paper P9.

15 PJH (FLFS, 11/02)   45 mins

Assume you are the management accountant in PJH. The company manufactures soft furnishings (such as curtains and drapes) for theatres, exhibitions and concert halls. It has been trading for 20 years. 55% of the shares are owned by 10 members of the founding family. There are also 25 other shareholders with holdings of various sizes. PJH is not quoted on a stock exchange.

Two years ago, the company received an offer of £25 million for its entire equity, which the board of directors rejected without conducting any serious evaluation.

The company is forecasting pre-tax earnings of £4.5 million on turnover of £32 million for the current year. These sales and earnings levels are expected to continue unless new investment is undertaken. The managing director, Mrs Henry, who is also a major shareholder, is planning a major expansion programme that will require raising £5 million of new finance for capital investment. This investment yields a net present value of £1.2 million when evaluated at the company's post-tax cost of capital of 9%.

The board is considering two alternative methods of financing this expansion.

(1)   A rights issue to existing shareholders, plus a new issue of shares to employees and trading partners.

(2)   Medium-term (5 years) debt, interest rate fixed at 7%, secured on the company's long-term assets, mainly land and buildings. The company at present has no long-term debt. It has an overdraft facility that is used for short-term financing needs.

The company pays tax at 30%.

Mrs Henry is aware that the method of financing chosen might have an impact on the valuation of the company and also on the company's long-term objectives.

Required

Write a report to Mrs Henry that advises on:

(a)   The factors that need to be considered by the board when deciding whether to raise new equity.   **(9 marks)**

(b)   How each suggested method of financing will increase the valuation of the company. You only need provide some simple calculations here to support your arguments. You do not have enough information to do a detailed valuation.   **(8 marks)**

(c)   Appropriate long-term financial objectives for a company such as PJH.   **(8 marks)**

(Total = 25 marks)

16 RUMP

45 mins

RUMP is an all equity financed, listed company which operates in the food processing industry. The Rump family owns 40% of the ordinary shares; the remainder are held by large financial institutions. There are 10 million €1 ordinary shares currently in issue.

The company has just finalised a long-term contract to supply a large chain of restaurants with a variety of food products. The contract requires investment in new machinery costing €24 million. This machinery would become operational on 1 January 20X2, and payment would be made on the same date. Sales would commence immediately thereafter.

Company policy is to pay out all profits as dividends and, if RUMP continues to be all equity financed, there will be an annual dividend of €9 million in perpetuity commencing 31 December 20X2.

There are two alternatives that are going to be considered at the next board meeting to finance the required investment of €24 million:

(1)   A 2-for-5 rights issue, in which case the annual dividend would be €9 million. The cum rights price per share would be €6.60.

(2)   Issuing 7.5% irredeemable debt at par with interest payable annually in arrears. For this alternative, interest would be paid out of the €9 million otherwise available to pay dividends.

For either alternative, the directors expect the cost of equity to remain at its present annual level of 10%.

One of the directors has been wondering whether the board ought to be considering further options – raising equity finance by means of a placing, a public offer for sale or subscription, or raising unsecured loan finance with warrants attached.

Required

(a)   Calculate the issue and ex rights share prices of RUMP assuming a 2-for-5 rights issue is used to finance the new project at 1 January 20X2. Ignore taxation.   **(4 marks)**

(b)   Calculate the value per ordinary share in RUMP at 1 January 20X2 if 7.5% irredeemable debt is issued to finance the new project. Assume that the cost of equity remains at 10% each year. Ignore taxation.

(3 marks)

(c)   Write a report to the directors of RUMP which:

(i)   Compares and contrasts the rights issue and the debt issue methods of raising finance – you may refer to the calculations in your answer to requirements (a) and (b) and to any assumptions made.

(ii)   Explains and evaluates the appropriateness of the following alternative methods of issuing equity finance *in the specific circumstances* of RUMP:

(1)   A placing
(2)   An offer for sale
(3)   A public offer for subscription

(iii)   Explains and evaluates the appropriateness of issuing unsecured loan stock with warrants attached in the specific circumstances of RUMP.   **(18 marks)**

(Total = 25 marks)

17 XTA (5/05)

45 mins

XTA plc is the parent company of a transport and distribution group based in the United Kingdom (UK). The group owns and operates a network of distribution centres and a fleet of trucks (large delivery vehicles) in the UK. It is currently planning to expand into Continental Europe, operating through a new subsidiary company in Germany. The subsidiary will purchase distribution centres in Germany and invest in a new fleet of trucks to be based at those centres. The German subsidiary will be operationally independent of the UK parent.

Alternative proposals have been put forward by Messrs A, B and C, Board members of XTA plc on how best to structure the financing of the new German operation as follows:

Mr A: 'I would feel much more comfortable if we were to borrow in our base currency, sterling, where we already have long-standing banking relationships and a good reputation in the capital markets. Surely it would be much more complicated for us to borrow in euros?'

Mr B: 'I am concerned about the exposure of our consolidated balance sheet and investor ratios to sterling/euro exchange rate movements. How will we be able to explain large fluctuations to our shareholders? If we were to raise long-term euro borrowings, wouldn't this avoid exchange rate risk altogether? We would also benefit from euro interest rates which have been historically lower than sterling rates.'

Mr C: 'We know from our market research that we will be facing stiff competition in Germany from local distribution companies. This is a high-risk project with a lot of capital at stake and we should finance this new venture by XTA plc raising new equity finance to reflect this high risk.'

Assume that today is Saturday 1 October 20X5. A summary of the latest forecast consolidated balance sheet for the XTA Group at 31 December 20X5 is given below. It has been prepared BEFORE taking into account the proposed German investment:

	£m
Assets	
Total assets	<u>450</u>
Equity and liabilities	
Equity	250
Long-term borrowings (there were no other non-current liabilities)	150
Current liabilities	<u>50</u>
Total equity and liabilities	<u>450</u>

The proposed investment in Germany is scheduled for the final quarter of 20X5 at a cost of £60 million for the distribution centres and £20 million for the fleet of trucks when translated from euros at today's exchange rate of £1 = €1.50. The directors believe that the euro could weaken against sterling to £1 = €2.00 by 31 December 20X5, but it can be assumed that this will not occur until after the investment has been made. The subsidiary's balance sheet at 31 December 20X5 will only contain the new distribution centres and fleet of trucks matched by an equal equity investment by XTA plc and will only become operationally active from 1 January 20X6.

Required

(a) Write a memorandum to the Board of XTA plc to explain the advantages and disadvantages of using each of the following sources of finance:

(i) A rights issue versus a placing (assuming UK equity finance is chosen to fund the new German subsidiary)

(ii) A euro bank loan versus a euro-denominated eurobond (assuming euro borrowings are chosen)

(8 marks)

(b) Evaluate EACH of the alternative proposals of Messrs A, B and C for financing the new German subsidiary and recommend the most appropriate form of financing for the group. Support your discussion of each proposal with:

(i) A summary forecast consolidated balance sheet for the XTA group at 31 December 20X5 incorporating the new investment; and

(ii) Calculations of gearing using book values using year end exchange rates of both £1 = €1.50 and £1 = €2.00. **(17 marks)**

(Total = 25 marks)

18 EFG (5/06)

45 mins

EFG is a South American entity specialising in providing information systems solutions to large corporates. It is going through a period of rapid expansion and requires additional funds to finance the long-term working capital needs of the business.

EFG has issued one million $1 ordinary shares, which are listed on the local stock market at a current market price of $15, with typical increases of 10% per annum expected in the next five year period. Dividend payout is kept constant at a level of 10% of post-tax profits. EFG also has $10 million of bank borrowings.

It is estimated that a further $3 million is required to satisfy the funding requirements of the business for the next five-year period beginning 1 July 20X6. Two major institutional shareholders have indicated that they are not prepared to invest further in EFG at the present time and so a rights issue is unlikely to succeed. The directors are therefore considering various forms of debt finance. Three alternative structures are under discussion as shown below:

- Five-year unsecured bank loan at a fixed interest rate of 7% per annum;

- Five-year unsecured bond with a coupon of 5% per annum, redeemable at par and issued at a 6% discount to par;

- A convertible bond, issued at par, with an annual coupon of 4-5% and a conversion option in five years' time of five shares for each $100 nominal of debt.

There have been lengthy boardroom discussions on the relative merits of each instrument and you, as Finance Director, have been asked to address the following queries:

Sr. A: 'The bank loan would seem to be more expensive than the unsecured bond. Is this actually the case?'

Sr. B: 'Surely the convertible bond would be the cheapest form of borrowing with such a low interest rate?'

Sr. C: 'If we want to increase our equity base, why use a convertible bond, rather than a straight equity issue?'

Required

(a) Write a response to Sr. A, Sr. B and Sr. C, directors of EFG, discussing the issues raised and advising on the most appropriate financing instrument for EFG. In your answer, include calculations of:

- Expected conversion value of the convertible bond in five years' time;
- Yield to maturity (redemption yield) of the five-year unsecured bond.

Ignore tax. **(18 marks)**
(including up to 8 marks for calculations)

(b) Advise a prospective investor in the five-year unsecured bond issued by EFG on what information he should expect to be provided with and what further analysis he should undertake in order to assess the creditworthiness of the proposed investment. **(7 marks)**

(Total = 25 marks)

19 AIR

45 mins

The directors of ER have decided to concentrate the company's activities on three core areas, bus services, road freight and taxis. As a result the company has offered for sale a regional airport that it owns. The airport handles a mixture of short-haul scheduled services, holiday charter flights and air freight, but does not have a runway long enough for long-haul international operations.

The existing managers of the airport, along with some employees, are attempting to purchase the airport through a leveraged management buy-out, and would form a new unquoted company, AIR. The total value of the airport (free of any debt) has been independently assessed at £35 million.

The managers and employees can raise a maximum of £4 million towards this cost. This would be invested in new ordinary shares issued at the par value of 50p per share. ER, as a condition of the sale, proposes to subscribe to an initial 20% equity holding in the company, and would repay all debt of the airport prior to the sale.

EPP Bank is prepared to offer a floating rate loan of £20 million to the management team, at an initial interest rate of LIBOR plus 3%. LIBOR is currently at 10%. This loan would be for a period of seven years, repayable upon maturity, and would be secured against the airport's land and buildings. A condition of the loan is that gearing, measured by the book value of total loans to equity, is no more than 100% at the end of four years. If this condition is not met the bank has the right to call in its loan at one month's notice. AIR would be able to purchase a four year interest rate cap at 15% for its loan from EPP Bank for an up-front premium of £800,000.

A venture capital company, AV, is willing to provide up to £15 million in the form of unsecured mezzanine debt with attached warrants. This loan would be for a five year period, with principal repayable in equal annual instalments, and have a fixed interest rate of 18% per year.

The warrants would allow AV to purchase 10 AIR shares at a price of 100 pence each for every £100 of initial debt provided, at any time after two years from the date the loan is agreed. The warrants would expire after five years.

Most recent income statement for the airport

	£'000
Landing fees	14,000
Other revenues	8,600
	22,600
Labour	5,200
Consumables	3,800
Central overhead payable to ER	4,000
Other expenses	3,500
Interest paid	2,500
	19,000
Taxable profit	3,600
Taxation (33%)	1,188
Retained earnings	2,412

ER has offered to continue to provide central accounting, personnel and marketing services to AIR for a fee of £3 million per year, with the first fee payable in year one. All revenues and cost (excluding interest) are expected to increase by approximately 5% per year.

Required

Prepare a report for the managers of the proposed new company AIR which:

(a) Discusses the advantages and disadvantages for the management buy-out of the proposed financing mix.

(16 marks)

(b) Discusses whether or not the EPP Bank's gearing restriction in four years' time is likely to be a problem.

(9 marks)

All relevant calculations must be shown. State clearly any assumptions that you make. **(Total = 25 marks)**

20 DDD

45 mins

DDD, a listed company, runs a chain of 26 garden centres which sell plants, gardening implements and a range of other gardening products. It is listed on an international stock exchange and it has an accounting year end of 30 June.

The company plans to open three new garden SuperCentres in 20X4. Unlike existing stores, they will also sell garden furniture.

Each of the three new stores will cost £6 million to build and each will carry £3.5 million of stocks. The following budgeted summary balance sheet at 30 June 20X3 (which *excludes* the three new SuperCentres) was presented at a meeting of the board:

	£m
Land and buildings	26
Other non-current assets	13
Inventory	16
Receivables	1
Cash	1
	57
Share capital (£1 shares)	10
Accumulated profits	20
Loans	24
Trade creditors	3
	57

The balance sheet valuation for land and buildings reflects their current market values.

Chief Executive

'I believe that we should raise new equity to finance the new SuperCentres. Our share price has risen from £4 a year ago to £6 today. I believe that we should take advantage of this high share price and issue shares now in case the share price falls again. Moreover, our dividend yield is only 3% – this is cheap finance at low risk.'

Non-Executive Director

'I am not keen on raising new external finance. We should use our retained profits of £20 million to finance most of the new land, buildings and inventory. To finance the remaining amount, we should sell the least profitable of our existing garden centres. This approach will save all the issue costs and all the uncertainty involved in raising new external finance.'

Finance Director

'I am in favour of raising new debt to finance the expansion. The return on these new SuperCentres is bound to be greater than the cost of debt, so a profit is assured, and thus the risk is minimal.'

There are two alternatives:

Alternative 1: Issue £30 million of 7% corporate bonds. These would be issued on 1 July 20X3 at a 5% discount and would be repayable on 30 June 20X8 at their nominal value. Interest would be payable annually in arrears on 30 June each year.

Alternative 2: Raise a bank loan of £28.5 million on 1 July 20X3. The interest rate would be 5% per annum for the first 3 years and 10% per annum for the following 3 years. The loan would be repayable on 30 June 20X9.

Interest would be payable annually in arrears on 30 June each year. Assume that interest paid can be relieved for tax at a rate of 30%. Assume tax is payable at the end of the year in which the taxable profits arise and sufficient profits exist to set off all interest payments.

Required

(a) Calculate the after-tax cost of debt for each of the two alternatives.

Briefly discuss any further factors that would need to be considered, other than the cost of debt, before choosing between these two alternatives. **(11 marks)**

(b) Write a memorandum to the board, as a member of DDD's treasury department, which discusses the financing options for expansion put forward at the board meeting. In so doing, evaluate the comments of the Directors. **(14 marks)**

(Total = 25 marks)

21 BAC   45 mins

BAC is classified as a small unquoted company for tax purposes and is liable to tax at 21%. The company is considering the purchase of a new computer system. The Chief Executive has been advised that it might be advantageous to lease the computer system rather than buy with a secured bank loan. The before-tax cost of a bank loan to BAC would be 11½%. Apart from the possible financial benefits which might arise, he has been told that leasing provides a hedge against obsolescence.

The capital cost of the computer would be £50,000. The leasing company, which is not the supplier or manufacturer of the equipment, has offered what it considers to be very favourable terms for the lease of the computer. Payments would be £15,000 per annum for five years. The first payment would be made at the beginning of the lease contract. This would be followed by four further payments at the beginning of each of the next four years. Insurance and maintenance of the computer would be the responsibility of the lessee. At the end of year 5, the second-hand value of the computer is expected to be £5,000.

The leasing company pays tax at the marginal rate of 31%. Tax is paid the year after the related cash flows arise. Lease payments are allowable in full for tax purposes. Tax allowances are available on the computer at 25% on a reducing balance basis. The company's required rate of return on equity is 15% and it considers this deal to be of about the average risk of its commercial ventures. The lessor will be able to finance the purchase of the computer from retained earnings.

BAC is currently all equity-funded, with a share capital of 150,000 £1 shares. You can assume its current cost of equity is 14%.

Required

(a) Evaluate the financial decision concerning the lease from the point of view of both the lessee and the lessor. **(10 marks)**

(b) Write a report to the Chief Executive of BAC explaining the purpose and conclusions of your evaluation. Include in your report an explanation of the claim that leasing provides a hedge against obsolescence. **(5 marks)**

(c) The Chief Executive of BAC claims that the evaluation is basically a capital budgeting exercise and that the company's weighted average cost of capital is a more appropriate rate to use as a discount rate.

Discuss the validity of the Chief Executive's comments. **(3 marks)**

(d) Demonstrate the effect on the cost of equity of taking out the loan and calculate the company's new weighted average cost of capital. **(7 marks)**

(Total = 25 marks)

22 XYZ

45 mins

You are a management accountant working for XYZ, a large company whose 200 million £1 shares are listed on a major international stock exchange. It manufactures a variety of concrete and clay building materials. The company's year-end is 31 December.

You have received this memorandum from the Finance Director

To:	Management Accountant
From:	Finance Director
Date:	14 October 20X3
Subject:	Grinding machines

The board has resolved to replace 100 of its grinding machines with 100 of a new type of machine that has just been launched. I need you to provide various pieces of information and guidance for the Board on this decision, as I am hard-pressed on other work, and Simon, who was helping me, has been called away to visit a sick aunt.

The board has decided that the company cannot issue any further equity. Simon has therefore suggested a number of other methods of financing the new machines.

Option 1 – Issue debt to purchase the machines

The machines are expected to cost £720,000 each on 31 December 20X1 and on average are expected to have a useful economic life of 10 years. After this time, the company expects to scrap the machines, but it has no idea what proceeds would be generated from the sale.

If XYZ issues debt, it would do so on 31 December 20X1 for the full purchase price of the machines in order to finance the investment. The debt would be issued at a discount of 10% of par value (that is, at £90 per £100 nominal) being redeemable at par on 31 December 20Y1 (in ten years' time) and carrying a coupon annual interest rate of 6%. Debt interest is tax allowable and the corporation tax rate can be assumed to be 30% (ignore any tax on the redemption). If this option is chosen, the share price on 31 December 20X1 is expected to be £1.50, and the cost of equity 10%.

The debt would be secured by fixed and floating charges.

Option 2 – Long-term lease

The machines can be leased with equal annual rentals payable in arrears. The lease term would be eight years, but this can be extended indefinitely at the option of the company at a nominal rent. The lease cannot be cancelled within the minimum lease term of eight years. The company would need to pay its own maintenance costs.

Option 3 – Short-term leases

The machines can be leased using a series of separate annual contracts. Maintenance costs would be paid by the lessor under these contracts but, even so, the average lease rentals would be much higher than under option 2. There is no obligation on either party to sign a new annual contract on the termination for the previous lease contract.

I shall do the full appraisal of the three options, but I need you to provide a couple of figures

(a) Please can you calculate the after tax cost of debt at 31 December 20X1 to be used in assessing Option 1.

(6 marks)

(b) Please can you calculate the weighted average cost of capital for Option 1. **(3 marks)**

(c) I'd also like you to prepare some notes discussing the appropriateness of using the after tax cost of debt or the weighted average cost of capital to evaluate XYZ's investment in grinding machines. **(5 marks)**

(d) Finally, please can you draft a memorandum to the directors which identifies the factors that should be considered when deciding which of the three methods of financing the grinding machines is the most appropriate. The memo needs to cover operational and financial issues, and highlight the most important factors. **(11 marks)**

(Total = 25 marks)

23 TFC

45 mins

The Translavian Ferry Company (TFC) operates four ferries. It wishes to acquire a further new ferry due to high demand for its services from passengers.

At a Board meeting, proposals were put forward for three different methods of financing the new ferry. It was made clear at the meeting that the company is unable to raise any further equity finance.

The ferry being acquired is identical under all three methods of financing. The price of the ferry will be $10 million at 1 January 20X4 and it will have a ten year life. After this time, the terms of the operating licence given by the Transalvian government require that the ferry be scrapped for health and safety reasons. The net proceeds are expected to be zero.

The company's accounting year end is 31 December. The company uses an annual after tax discount rate of 7% to evaluate financing projects.

Method 1 – Long-term lease

The ferry can be leased with equal annual rents of $2.8 million payable in arrears. The lease term would be 5 years, but this can be extended indefinitely, at the option of the company, at a nominal rent. The lease cannot be cancelled within the minimum lease term of 5 years. TFC would incur all the maintenance costs of $200,000 per year, payable at the end of each year of the life of the asset.

Method 2 – Short-term leases

The ferry can be leased using a series of separate annual contracts. The annual expected lease rental would be $1.7 million payable annually in advance, with the first payment being on 1 January 20X4. Maintenance costs would be paid in full by the lessor. There is no obligation on either party to sign a new annual contract on the termination of the previous lease contract.

Method 3 – Loan

TFC's bank is willing to make a four-year loan of $10 million so that the ferry can be purchased. Annual repayments would be $3.154 million including both capital and interest. These payments are to be made at the end of each of the four years. The loan would be secured by fixed and floating charges over the company's assets.

Taxation

Taxation payments are made a year after the relevant transaction occurs. The tax rate is 30%. All lease payments, interest payments, and maintenance charges are allowable in full for tax. Similarly, the purchase price of the ferry is allowable in full as a tax deduction in the year in which the expenditure is incurred. The company has sufficient profits from the existing ferries to ensure that tax allowances can be offset immediately.

The Marketing Director's view

After the meeting, the *Marketing Director* expressed concerns about the Board's decision to consider only the three funding methods proposed. He argued that 'All three methods involved financing charges. Yet we can obtain just about enough cash to fund the new ferry from our own resources, even though we may need to sell some of our short-term investments. Why should we pay interest and other finance charges to outsiders when we can fund the new ferry for free ourselves?'

Required

(a)   Calculate the rate of interest implicit in the four-year loan under financing Method 3 above.   **(3 marks)**

(b)   Calculate the net present values at 1 January 20X4 of Method 1 and Method 2 for financing the new ferry. Use an annual after tax discount rate of 7%.   **(6 marks)**

(c)   As a consultant, write a memorandum to the Board of TFC which:

     (i)   Discusses the non-quantitative factors that should be considered when deciding which of the three methods of financing the new ferry is the most appropriate; and

     (ii)   Evaluates the concerns of the Marketing Director.   **(16 marks)**

(Total = 25 marks)

24 Question with helping hand: RZ (Pilot paper)   45 mins

RZ is a privately-owned textile manufacturer based in the UK with sales revenue in the last financial year of £68 million and earnings of £4.5 million. The directors of the company have been evaluating a cost saving project, which will require purchasing new machinery from the USA at a capital cost of $1.5 million. The directors expect the new machinery to have a life of at least 5 years and to provide cost savings (including capital allowances) of £240,000 after tax each year. Cash flows beyond 5 years are ignored by RZ in all its investment decisions. The discount rate that the company applies to investment decisions of this nature is its post-tax real cost of capital of 9% per annum.

RZ at present has no debt in its capital structure. The directors, who are the major shareholders, would be prepared to finance the purchase of the new machinery via a rights issue but believe an all-equity capital structure fails to take advantage of the tax benefits of debt. They therefore propose to finance with one of the following methods:

(i)   Undated debt, raised in the UK and secured on the company's assets. The current pre-tax rate of interest required by the market on corporate debt of this risk is 7% per annum. Interest payments would be made at the end of each year.

(ii)   A finance lease raised in the USA repayable over 5 years. The terms would be 5 annual payments of US$325,000 payable at the *beginning* of each year. The machinery could be bought by RZ from the finance company at the end of the five year lease contract for a nominal amount of $1. Assume the whole amount of each annual payment is tax deductible.

(iii)   An operating lease. No cost details are available at present.

Other information

- The company's marginal tax rate is 30%. Tax is payable in the year in which the liability arises.

- Capital allowances are available at 25% reducing balance

- If bought outright, the machinery is estimated to have a residual value in real cash flow terms, at the end of five years, of 10% of the original purchase price.

- The spot rate US$ to the £ is 1.58

- Interest rates in the USA and UK are currently 2.5% and 3.5% respectively.

Required

(a)   Discuss the advisability of the investment and the advantages and disadvantages of financing with either (i) undated debt, (ii) a finance lease or (iii) an operating lease compared with new equity raised via a rights issue and comment on whether the choice of method of finance should affect the investment decision.

        Provide appropriate and relevant calculations and assumptions to support your discussion.   **(18 marks)**

(b)   Discuss the benefits and potential problems of financing assets in the same currency as their purchase.

                                                                                                    (7 marks)

                                                                                            (Total = 25 marks)

Helping hand

(a)   **Acquisition decision using WACC**

        Buy decision using debt (are there tax allowances on the asset)

        Features to discuss

        - Tax shield (perpetuity or limited number of years, calculations)
        - Control
        - Costs/Commitments
        - Risks

Finance lease decision (need to calculate yearly exchange rates?)

Features to discuss

- Flexibility
- Repayments
- Risks
- Tax

Operating lease (no calculations)

Features to discuss

- Flexibility
- Accounts disclosures
- Responsibilities
- Costs

(b) **Consider the following**

- Impact of matching
- Long-term risks
- Interest rate parity

25 FLG (5/05)   45 mins

FLG Inc is an airline operator based in the United States, operating a wide network of both domestic and international flights. It has recently obtained a new licence to operate direct flights to a new European destination which will necessitate the acquisition of four identical secondhand aeroplanes at a total cost of $100 million. The aeroplanes are expected to be in service for five years and each one is expected to have a residual value of $12.5 million at the end of the five years. However, the residual value is highly dependent on the state of the airline industry at the end of the five-year period and there is a risk that the residual value could be much lower if there is a general reduction in air travel at that time.

The company has been offered a lease contract with total lease payments of $15 million per annum for five years, payable in advance, with all maintenance costs being borne by the lessee.

Alternatively, the aeroplanes could be purchased outright and the bank has offered the company a five-year loan with variable interest payments payable semi-annually six months in arrears at a margin of 1% per annum above a reference six-month $ inter-bank rate. The reference six-month $ inter-bank rate is forecast to be at a flat rate of 2.4% for each six-month period, for the duration of the loan.

The company pays tax at 30% and expects to make taxable profits in excess of the lease payments, interest charges and tax depreciation allowances arising over the next five years. Tax depreciation on the purchase of the aeroplanes can be claimed at a rate of 20% at the end of each financial year on a written-down value basis, with a delay of one year between the tax depreciation allowance arising and the deduction from tax paid.

Required

(a) Calculate:

(i) The compound annualised post-tax cost of debt

(ii) The NPV of the lease versus purchase decision at discount rates of both 4% and 5%

(iii) The breakeven post-tax cost of debt at which FLG Inc is indifferent between leasing and purchasing the aeroplanes **(10 marks)**

(b)　Recommend, with reasons, whether FLG Inc should purchase with a loan or lease the aeroplanes.

Your answer should include appropriate calculations of the sensitivity of the lease versus purchase decision to changes in EACH of the following:

(i)　The reference $ inter-bank rate for the duration of the loan

(ii)　The residual value of the aeroplanes

(15 marks)

(Total = 25 marks)

26 GREBE　　　　　　　　　　　　　　　　　　　　　　　　　45 mins

GREBE operates a chain of cellular telephone stores in the UK. An abbreviated profit and loss account and balance sheet of the business for the year that has just ended is as follows:

Abbreviated income statement for the year ended 31 May 20X3

	£'000
Sales	6,450
Operating profit for the year	800
Interest payable	160
Net profit before taxation	640
Tax (20%)	128
Net profit after taxation	512
Dividends proposed	256
Accumulated profit for the year	256

Abbreviated balance sheet as at 31 May 20X3

	£'000
Assets	
Non-current assets at written down values	3,500
Current assets	1,800
	5,300

	£'000
Equity and liabilities	
£0.50 ordinary shares	600
Accumulated profits	1,600
Long-term liabilities	2,000
Current liabilities	1,100
	5,300

The company is expecting a surge in sales following advances in cellular telephone technology that should translate into additional operating profits of £180,000 per year for the foreseeable future. However, the company will need to invest £1,200,000 immediately in expanding the asset base of the business if it is to achieve these additional profits.

The business has approached a large supplier that already has an equity investment in the business to see whether it would be prepared to provide further funds for the business. The supplier has indicated it would be willing to provide the necessary funds by either:

(i)　An issue of £0.50 ordinary shares at a premium of £1.50 per share; or

(ii)　An issue of £1,200,000 10% debt at par, repayable in 10 years' time.

One of the directors has contacted the bank and has received an indication that the bank might be prepared to lend on more generous terms, but on a short-term basis.

The Board of Directors of GREBE has already announced that it will maintain the same dividend payout ratio in future years as in the past and that this policy will be unaffected by the form of finance raised.

Required

(a) For each of the financing options:

    (i)   Prepare a forecast income statement for the forthcoming year
    (ii)   Calculate the forecast earnings per share for the forthcoming year
    (iii) Calculate the projected level of gearing at the end of the forthcoming year   **(9 marks)**

(b) Calculate the level of operating profit at which the earnings per share will be the same under each financing option.   **(4 marks)**

(c) Evaluate each of the financing options from the viewpoint of an existing shareholder.   **(4 marks)**

(d) Discuss the main factors that will influence whether GREBE would be financed by debt or equity, or long-term or short-term debt.   **(8 marks)**

                                                 (Total = 25 marks)

27 UR (FLFS, 11/03)   **45 mins**

UR is a privately-owned machine tool manufacturing company based in the Republic of Ireland. For the past five years, it has operated an aggressive policy in respect of the management of its working capital. The following information concerns the company's forecast end-of-year financial outcomes if it continues with this type of policy.

	€'000
Receivables	5,200
Inventory	2,150
Cash at bank	350
Total current assets	7,700
Non-current assets	14,500
Trade payables	4,500
Sales	17,500
Operating costs	14,000
Operating profit	3,500
Earnings	2,625

There are 2.5 million shares in issue.

The company has been experiencing a series of problems because of the type of working capital management policy it has been following and is considering an alternative approach to working capital management.

The percentage figures shown below are changes to the above forecast. These changes are anticipated to occur if a more conservative policy is adopted.

Receivables	– 40%
Inventory	+ 20%
Cash (figures in €000)	Increase to €1,000
Non-current assets	No change
Trade payables	– 30%
Forecast sales	– 5%
Operating profit and earnings	+ 5%

Required

Evaluate the two working capital management policies described above and recommend a proposed course of action. Include in your evaluation a discussion of the problems that might have arisen as a result of operating aggressive working capital management policies and the key elements to consider and actions to take before making a decision to change.

You should calculate appropriate and relevant ratios or performance measures to support your arguments. *[The calculations will earn up to 8 marks]*   **(25 marks)**

28 MNO (5/06)
45 mins

MNO is a private toy distributor situated in the United States of America (US) with a US customer base and local suppliers. There is a central manufacturing base and several marketing units spread across the US. The marketing units are encouraged to adapt to local market conditions, largely acting independently and free from central control. These units are responsible for all aspects of local sales, including collecting sales revenues, which are paid across to Head Office on a monthly basis. Funding is provided by Head Office as required.

Figures for last year to 31 December 20X5 were as follows:

Revenue	$10 million
Gross profit margin	40% of revenue
Accounts receivable days	minimum 20, maximum 30 days
Accounts payable days	minimum 40, maximum 50 days
Inventories	minimum 50, maximum 80 days
Non-current assets	$8 million

Accounts receivable, accounts payable and inventories can all be assumed to be the same on both 31 December 20X4 and 31 December 20X5, but fluctuate between those dates.

The Financial Controller is carrying out an analysis of MNO's working capital levels, as requested by the Treasurer. He is assuming that the peak period for accounts receivable coincides with the peak period for inventories and the lowest level of accounts payable.

MNO is currently in consultation with a potentially significant new supplier in Asia, who will demand payment in its local currency.

Required

(a) (i) Calculate the minimum and maximum working capital levels based on the Financial Controller's assumption regarding the timing of peaks and troughs in working capital variables and discuss the validity of that assumption. **(6 marks)**

(ii) Using the figures calculated in (i) above, calculate and draw a chart to show the short-term and long-term (permanent) financing requirements of MNO under each of the following working capital financing policies:

- Moderate policy, where long-term financing matches permanent net current assets;

- Aggressive policy, where 30% of permanent net current assets are funded by short-term financing;

- Conservative policy, where only 40% of fluctuating net current assets are funded by short-term financing. **(7 marks)**

(b) Discuss the advantages and disadvantages of an aggressive financing policy and advise whether or not such a policy would be appropriate for MNO. **(6 marks)**

(c) Advise MNO whether a profit or cost centre structure would be more appropriate for its treasury department. **(6 marks)**

(Total = 25 marks)

29 LE International

45 mins

The following is an extract from the balance sheet of LE International at 30 June 20X2.

	£'000
Ordinary shares of 50p each	5,200
Reserves	4,850
9% preference shares of £1 each	4,500
14% debt	5,000
Total long-term funds	19,550

The ordinary shares are quoted at 80p. Assume that the market estimate of the next ordinary dividend is 4p, growing thereafter at 12% per annum indefinitely. The preference shares, which are irredeemable, are quoted at 72p and the debt is quoted at par. Tax is 33%.

Required

(a) Use the relevant data above to calculate the company's weighted average cost of capital (WACC), ie the return required by the providers of the three types of capital, using the respective market values as weighting factors. **(6 marks)**

(b) Explain how the capital asset pricing model would be used as an alternative method of estimating the cost of equity, indicating what information would be required and how it would be obtained. **(7 marks)**

(c) Assume that the debt has recently been issued specifically to fund the company's expansion programme under which a number of projects are being considered. It has been suggested at a project appraisal meeting that because these projects are to be financed by the debt, the cutoff rate for project acceptance should be the after-tax interest rate on the debt rather than the WACC. Discuss this suggestion. **(6 marks)**

(d) Assume that instead of raising £5 million of 14% debt, the company had raised the equivalent amount in preference shares giving the same yield as the existing preference capital.

　　(i) Explain why the pre-tax yields on preference shares and debt reflect the risk levels of these investments.

　　(ii) Calculate how LE International's equity earnings would have been affected if the preference shares had been issued instead of the loan capital.

　　Assume income tax at 25% where relevant. **(6 marks)**

(Total = 25 marks)

30 WZ (11/05)

45 mins

WZ is a manufacturer of specialist components for the motor trade. It is based in Zafran, a country in the Far East. The entity's capital structure is as follows:

(i) 5 million ordinary shares of Z$1 each, currently quoted at Z$12·5 per share.

(ii) 10 million preference shares of Z$1 each, currently quoted at Z$0·80 per share, paying a dividend of 7% per annum.

(iii) Z$20 million, 8% undated debt, secured on the entity's non-current assets. This debt is currently trading at Z$90 per Z$100 nominal.

To finance expansion, the directors of WZ want to raise Z$5 million for additional working capital. Cash flow from trading, before interest and tax is currently Z$15 million per annum. If the expansion goes ahead, this is expected to rise to Z$17 million. The current rate of tax, which is expected to continue for the foreseeable future, is 30%.

Assume for the purposes of simplicity:

(i)   That profit after interest and tax equals cash flow

(ii)   The required rate of return on equity will remain at the current rate of 12% per annum irrespective of the type of finance raised

(iii) There are no transaction costs

The directors of WZ are considering three forms of finance:

(i)   Equity via a rights issue at 15% discount to current market price

(ii)   9% bonds repayable in 20X9 secured as a floating charge on the entity's current assets

(iii) Factoring the entity's trade receivables. This is likely to provide a one-off release of funds of approximately Z$5 million

Required

(a)   Calculate for the current situation and financing alternatives (i) and (ii) the expected

      (i)   Earnings per share
      (ii)   Market value of equity, using the capitalisation of earnings at the cost of equity
      (iii) Market value of the entity
      (iv) Gearing ratios (debt to total value of the entity), using market values
      (v)   Weighted average cost of capital

    State whatever assumptions you consider necessary.

(12 marks)

(b)   Assume you are a Financial Manager with WZ. Advise directors of WZ of the issues to be considered before deciding on which form of finance to choose, including factoring, and make your own recommendation.

(13 marks)

(Total = 25 marks)

31 IML   **45 mins**

IML is an all equity financed listed company. It develops customised software for clients which are mainly large civil engineering companies. Nearly all its shares are held by financial institutions.

IML's chairman has been dissatisfied with the company's performance for some time. As a result a major new investment in a European country is proposed, which will introduce £10 million 10% irredeemable debentures into the company and result in a debt-equity ratio of 1:3. The investment is expected to generate annual returns of £5 million for the foreseeable future. One of the directors is concerned that IML's current cost of equity of 12% will rise significantly as a consequence of undertaking this investment.

The finance director has found out that the required annual rate of equity return for a company operating in similar markets in Europe that has a debt-equity ratio of 1:2 is 17%.

The new finance director has proposed using the capital asset pricing model and the adjusted present value method to evaluate the investment. However the chairman is unhappy with using market data. He has argued that the company should not take too much notice of stock market data. Last year the company had to announce a loss and its share price went up.

Assume that the risk-free rate in the local and European stock markets is 5%, the expected rate of return on the market portfolio is 15% and the tax rate is 30%.

Required

(a)   Calculate the adjusted present value of the proposed investment.   **(7 marks)**

(b)   Calculate the revised cost of equity of IML.   **(3 marks)**

(c)   As the new finance director, write a memorandum to the chairman which explains, in language
       understandable to a non-financial manager, the following:

   (i)   The assumptions and limitations of the capital asset pricing model; and
   (ii)   An explanation of why IML's share price could rise following the announcement of a loss.

   In so doing, discuss the observations and concerns expressed by the chairman. You may refer, where
   appropriate, to your calculations in (a) and (b) above.   **(15 marks)**

(Total = 25 marks)

32 CAP   **45 mins**

CAP is a listed company that owns and operates a large number of farms throughout the world. A variety of crops
are grown.

Financing structure

The following is an extract from the balance sheet of CAP at 30 September 20X2.

	£m
Ordinary shares of £1 each	200
Reserves	100
9% irredeemable £1 preference shares	50
8% loan stock 20X3	250
	600

The ordinary shares were quoted at £3 per share ex div on 30 September 20X2. The beta of CAP's equity shares is
0.8, the annual yield on treasury bills is 5%, and financial markets expect an average annual return of 15% on the
market index.

The market price per preference share was £0.90 ex div on 30 September 20X2.

Loan stock interest is paid annually in arrears and is allowable for tax at a tax rate of 30%. The loan stock was
priced at £100.57 ex interest per £100 nominal on 30 September 20X2. Loan stock is redeemable on 30 September
20X3.

Assume that taxation is payable at the end of the year in which taxable profits arise.

A new project

Difficult trading conditions in European farming have caused CAP to decide to convert a number of its farms in
Southern Europe into camping sites with effect from the 20X3 holiday season. Providing the necessary facilities for
campers will require major investment, and this will be financed by a new issue of loan stock. The returns on the
new campsite business are likely to have a very low correlation with those of the existing farming business.

CAPM and arbitrage pricing theory

One of the directors has read a report that arbitrage pricing theory may be more useful for some companies than
the capital asset pricing model, and wonders if this is true for CAP.

Required

(a)   Using the capital asset pricing model, calculate the required rate of return on equity of CAP at 30 September
       20X2. Ignore any impact from the new campsite project. Briefly explain the implications of a Beta of less
       than 1, such as that for CAP.   **(3 marks)**

(b)   Calculate the weighted average cost of capital of CAP at 30 September 20X2 (use your calculation in answer to requirement (a) above for the cost of equity). Ignore any impact from the new campsite project.

(10 marks)

(c)   Without further calculations, identify and explain the factors that may change CAP's equity beta during the year ending 30 September 20X3.   **(5 marks)**

(d)   Explain the limitations of the capital asset pricing model and discuss whether the arbitrage pricing model would be more suitable for CAP.   **(7 marks)**

(Total = 25 marks)

33 DEA   45 mins

DEA is a listed company which manufactures quality cut-glass products. The company's sole manufacturing site and 95% of its sales are in the United Kingdom. The company is, however, currently considering entering into a contract to sell a specialist range of glass ware to a Japanese retailer. The revenues from the Japanese contract are expected to amount to 25% of all future sales and 15% of future profit. It will require a significant initial investment, but it is expected that the money could be borrowed from the company's bank.

The Deaton family and other directors own the majority of the equity share capital, the remainder being held by employees and small shareholders. The total share capital amounts to 12 million £1 ordinary shares and has been unchanged for many years. Dividends per share paid on 31 May each year have been

20X2	20X3	20X4	20X5
35.64 pence	37.78 pence	40.05 pence	42.45 pence

The dividend for 20X6 will be 45.00 pence per share.

The company also has £12.5 million of 8% loan stock to be redeemed at par on 31 May 20X7, £11 million 10% loan stock to be redeemed at a 10% premium on 31 May 20X9 and 8 million £1 6% preference shares. Interest on loan stock is payable annually in arrears on 31 May.

At 31 May 20X6 the company's ordinary shares were quoted at £5.50 (cum div), the 20X7 loan stock at £98 per £100 nominal (ex-interest), the 20X9 loan stock at £103 per £100 nominal (ex-interest) and the 6% preference shares at £1.05 (ex-div).

The tax rate can be assumed to be 30% for the foreseeable future.

Interest is allowable for tax purposes.

Ignore any taxation of dividends.

The directors' meeting

The directors of DEA were uncertain whether to proceed with the Japanese contract and in particular they were concerned about the discount rate that should be used for assessing the project.

The *marketing director* argued: 'We should use the weighted average cost of capital. This is the rate we have used in the past and it reflects the average cost of acquiring funds.'

The *production director* disagreed: 'If we are going to borrow to finance this project, then we have to pay interest. So long as the cash flows from the project cover the interest payments, we will make a profit on the contract. Common sense dictates that we should therefore simply use the interest rate charged to us by the bank as the discount rate.'

The *finance director* argued: 'The real issue in deciding the relevant discount rate is the finance that we use. I suggest that instead of paying more and more dividends each year, largely to ourselves as individual shareholders, we should reduce dividends and use the cash saved to decrease the company's debt. If the company can earn a better rate of return than individual shareholders then the cash should be retained in the company. As it is, the company is in effect borrowing to pay a dividend. Also this project is high risk and therefore demands a high-risk premium in the discount rate.'

Required

(a)   Calculate DEA's weighted average cost of capital at 31 May 20X6.   **(12 marks)**

(b)   As a member of the treasury team, write a memorandum to the directors of DEA which discusses the views expressed by the directors. In so doing, and so far as the information permits, describe the factors to be considered in determining a discount rate for the Japanese project.   **(13 marks)**

(Total = 25 marks)

34 AB (FLFS, 5/02)   45 mins

AB manufactures products for children. The company's turnover and earnings last year were $56 million and $3.5 million respectively. Its shares are not listed but they occasionally change hands in private transactions. AB's weighted average cost of capital (WACC) is 13% net of tax. The directors believe that an appropriate gearing ratio (debt to debt + equity) for a company such as AB is 30%, which is the industry average. Currently, AB's gearing ratio is slightly higher than this at 35%. Its debt comprises two secured long-term bank loans and a permanent overdraft, secured by a floating charge on the company's current assets. The current cost of debt to a company such as AB is 10% before tax.

The company is considering expansion abroad, in particular in an Eastern European (EE) country where its products have become popular. The EE government has offered AB plc a financing deal to establish a manufacturing operation. The financing would take the form of an EE marks 30 million 6-year loan at a subsidised rate of only 2.5% each year interest. The current exchange rate is EE marks 20 to the $.

Interest would be payable at the end of each year and the principal repaid at the end of 6 years. The exchange rate of EE marks to the $ would be fixed at the current rate for the whole 6-year period of the loan. The marginal tax rate in both countries is 25%.

Required

(a)   Calculate the company's present cost of equity and the present value of the EE government subsidy implicit in the loan. Comment briefly on the method used and any assumptions you have made in your calculations.
                                                                                                         (7 marks)

(b)   Discuss the relevance of both the cost of equity you have calculated in answer to (a) above and the WACC given in the scenario, to the company's investment decision. Include comment on an alternative discount rate that could be used appropriately in the scenario's circumstances.   **(6 marks)**

(c)   (i)   Discuss the advantages and disadvantages of using the EE government subsidy in AB's international investment decision.

        (ii)   Recommend alternative methods of financing that might be suitable for AB in the circumstances of the scenario.   **(12 marks)**

(Total = 25 marks)

35 MAN

45 mins

MAN is a UK-based manufacturer of navigation equipment for the aviation industry. The company is currently considering whether or not to establish a new manufacturing division in Spain, which will produce passenger safety equipment for ships. The Board of Directors has asked the Finance Department to conduct a financial appraisal of the proposal. The company employs net present value analysis for the appraisal of all its long-term projects.

The following information has been taken from the balance sheet of the company for the year that has just ended:

	£m
Share capital and reserves	
£1 ordinary shares	200
Accumulated profits	800
	1,000
Loan capital	
6% loan stock	500

The ordinary shares have a current market value of £5.35 per share and the equity beta of the company is 1.2. The returns to the market are 10.4% and the risk-free rate is 5.1%. The loan stock is irredeemable and currently trading at £106 per £100 nominal value. It can be assumed that loan stock is risk free. The company will not need to raise new finance for the new venture.

The Finance Department has identified a Spanish company which manufactures passenger safety equipment for ships. The company is financed 50% by equity and 50% by loan capital, based on market values, and has an equity beta of 1.6.

The effective tax rate is 25% in both the UK and Spain.

Required

(a) Identify and discuss three key assumptions that underpin the use of the weighted average cost of capital as an appropriate discount rate for investment appraisal purposes. **(5 marks)**

(b) Explain why the existing weighted average cost of capital of MAN should be adjusted when evaluating the new investment proposal and what problems may be encountered in making any adjustment. **(3 marks)**

(c) Calculate the weighted average cost of capital that should be used as the discount rate when evaluating the new proposal. **(7 marks)**

(d) 'Capital structure can have no influence on the value of the firm.'

Discuss this statement and identify the practical factors which a company may take into account when determining capital structure. **(10 marks)**

(Total = 25 marks)

36 KM

45 mins

KM is a company that has expanded overseas over a number of years and now has operations in many countries. KM is organised in a divisionalised structure and historically the divisions have enjoyed considerable autonomy, including deciding what specialists they should employ. Head office functions are categorised as support functions such as the financial control and accounting function that has overseen all financial activity, and profit centres such as the information technology function that are required to charge divisions with a full market price for their services.

The directors have recently become concerned about various aspects of financial management within the group as one division has recently lost considerable money through trading on the derivatives market. The returns from the investment of surplus funds by other divisions appear to be unsatisfactorily low. There has also been criticism that the financial control function lacks resources to supervise all aspects of the group's financial management satisfactorily.

The finance director is therefore considering removing certain responsibilities from the financial control function, and establishing a separate treasury function, based at Head Office.

Required

(a) Describe the main responsibilities of the treasury function, and explain why the director is considering separating the treasury and financial control functions. **(11 marks)**

(b) Explain the advantages and disadvantages of operating the treasury function as a profit centre rather than a cost centre. **(6 marks)**

(c) Explain the advantages of centralisation of the treasury function. **(8 marks)**

(Total = 25 marks)

37 HH (FLFS, 11/02)   **45 mins**

Assume you are a financial manager with HH, a multinational company based in the USA with subsidiaries in Germany and the UK. One of your responsibilities is cash management for the group of companies. You have received the following forecasts of surplus funds for the next 30 days from the financial managers in the two subsidiaries:

Germany   Euros (€) 10.5 million
UK   £ sterling 5.5 million

The US operation is forecasting a cash deficit of US$10 million.

You obtain the following exchange rate information from the financial press:

	€/US$	£/US$
Spot	1.131	0.695
30-day forward	1.126	0.700

Annual borrowing/deposit rates available to the group are:

US$ 30-day	1.7%/1.6%
£ sterling 30-day	4.1%/3.9%
€ 30-day	3.1%/3.0%

You are considering introducing a system of cash pooling whereby all funds are converted into US$ and the net balance invested or borrowed in US$ in the USA.

Ignore taxes and transaction costs.

Required

(a) Calculate the cash balance at the end of the 30-day period, in US$, for each company in the group (including the US parent) under each of the following two scenarios:

   (i) Each group company acts independently and invests/finances its own cash balances/deficits in its local currency.

   (ii) Cash balances are pooled immediately in the USA and the net $ balance invested/borrowed for the 30-day period.

   Based on your calculations, comment on which method is the most favourable in financial terms from the US parent's point of view.

   You should assume simple interest rates based on a year of 360 days. **(13 marks)**

(b) Discuss the benefits and possible drawbacks to the parent company and to each subsidiary if a system of pooling were to be introduced as a general policy for the group. **(12 marks)**

   A report format is not required in answering this question. **(Total = 25 marks)**

38 CD (FLFS, 5/03)   45 mins

CD is a private company in a computer-related industry. It is based in India and has been trading for 6 years. It is managed by its main shareholders, who are the original founders of the company. Most of the employees are also shareholders, having been given shares as bonuses in 20X2. None of the shareholders has attempted to sell shares in the company so the problem of placing a value on them has not arisen.

Turnover last year, the 12 months to 31 December 20X5, was 356 million Rupees.

The table below shows earnings and dividends for CD since its creation:

| Year | Earnings after tax | | Dividend declared |
	Million Rupees	Rupees per share	Rupees per share
20X0	25	8.33	0
20X1	120	40.00	20.0
20X2	145	48.33	24.2
20X3	185	52.86	26.4
20X4	195	55.71	27.8
20X5	203	58.00	26.3

Between 20X0 and 20X2 there were 3 million shares in issue. This was increased to 3.5 million by the issue of bonus shares at the end of 20X2. The par value of the shares is 1 Rupee. The company is all-equity financed. The company pays tax at 30%.

In the current year (20X6), earnings are likely to be slightly below 20X5 at around 200 million Rupees. The company's directors have decided to pay a maintained dividend for 20X6.

They are now evaluating investment opportunities that would require all the company's free cash flow for 20X6 plus borrowings of 150 million Rupees of undated debt. If the company does not borrow to invest, growth in earnings and dividends will be zero for the foreseeable future. If the company does borrow and invest, then it expects growth in earnings and dividends of 5% in 20X7 (from the 20X6 base). The company's expected post-tax cost of equity capital is estimated at 14% per annum, assuming the borrowing takes place. Ignore the effects of inflation.

Required

(a)   Discuss the relationship between dividend policy, investment policy and financing policy in the context of the scenario and recommend a course of action for the directors of CD.   **(10 marks)**

(b)   Calculate an estimated company value, share price and P/E ratio for CD using Modigliani and Miller's theory of capital structure, assuming the company does borrow and invest.   **(6 marks)**

(c)   Discuss the relevance of the figures you have just calculated in answer to requirement (b) above in placing a value on (i) a small parcel of shares, for example the shareholding of one employee, and (ii) the entire company.   **(9 marks)**

Note: A report format is NOT required in answering this question.

                                                                            (Total = 25 marks)

39 Synergy

45 mins

(a) It is 20X8. OA, a company quoted on the London Stock Exchange, has cash balances of £23 million which are currently invested in short-term money market deposits. The cash is intended to be used primarily for strategic acquisitions, and the company has formed an acquisition committee with a remit to identify possible acquisition targets. The committee has suggested the purchase of ML, a company in a different industry that is quoted on the AIM (Alternative Investment Market). Although ML is quoted, approximately 50% of its shares are still owned by three directors. These directors have stated that they might be prepared to recommend the sale of ML, but they consider that its shares are worth £22 million in total.

Summarised financial data

	OA	ML
	£'000	£'000
Revenue	480,000	38,000
Pre tax operating cash flow	51,000	5,300
Taxation (33%)	16,830	1,749
Post tax operating cash flow	34,170	3,551
Dividend	11,000	842
Non-current assets	168,000	8,400
Current assets	135,000	4,700
Current liabilities	99,680	3,900
	203,320	9,200

	OA	ML
	£'000	£'000
Long-term finance		
Ordinary shares (25 pence par)	10,000 (ML 10 pence par)	500
Reserves	158,320	5,200
12% Debentures 20Y6	20,000	
10% Bank term loan	15,000	
Recent 11% bank loan		3,500
	203,320	9,200

	OA	ML
Current share price	785 pence	370 pence
Earnings yield	10.9%	19.2%
Average dividend growth during the last five years	7% p.a.	8% p.a.
Equity beta	0.95	0.8
Industry data:		
Average P/E ratio	10:1	6:1
Average P/E of companies recently taken over, based upon the offer price	12:1	7:1

The risk free rate of return is 6% per annum and the market return 14% per annum.

The rate of inflation is 2.4% per annum and is expected to remain at approximately this level.

Expected effects of the acquisition:

(i) 50 employees of ML would immediately be made redundant at an after tax cost of £1.2 million. Pre-tax annual wage savings are expected to be £750,000 (at current prices) for the foreseeable future.

(ii) Some land and buildings of ML would be sold for £800,000 (after tax).

(iii) Pre-tax advertising and distribution savings of £150,000 per year (at current prices) would be possible.

(iv) The three existing directors of ML would each be paid £100,000 per year for three years for consultancy services. This amount would not increase with inflation.

Required

Calculate the value of ML based upon:

(i)   The use of comparative P/E ratios
(ii)   The dividend valuation model
(iii)   The present value of relevant operating cash flows over a 10 year period

and discuss the advantages and disadvantages of *each* of the three valuation methods.

Recommend whether or not OA should offer £22 million for ML's shares.

(20 marks; approximately 8 marks for discussion)

(b)   Discuss the factors that might influence whether or not OA uses its *cash balances* rather than shares or bonds, to make payment for ML. **(5 marks)**

(Total = 25 marks)

40 Question with student answer: MC   45 mins

MC provides a range of services to the medical and healthcare industry. These services include providing locum (temporary) cover for healthcare professionals (mainly doctors and nurses), emergency call-out and consultancy/advisory services to government-funded health organisations. The company also operates a research division that has been successful in recent years in attracting funding from various sources. Some of the employees in this division are considered to be leading experts in their field and are very highly paid.

A consortium of doctors and redundant health-service managers started the company some years ago. It is still owned by the same people, but has since grown into an organisation employing over 100 full-time staff throughout the UK. In addition, the company uses specialist staff employed in state-run organisations on a part-time contract basis. The owners of the company are now interested in either obtaining a stock market quotation, or selling the company if the price accurately reflects what they believe to be the true worth of the business.

Summary financial statistics for MC and a competitor company, which is listed on the UK Stock Exchange, are shown below. The competitor company is broadly similar to MC but uses a higher proportion of part-time to full-time staff and has no research capability.

	MC Last year end: 31.3.20X0	Competitor Last year end: 31.3.20X0
Shares in issue (m)	10.1	20
Earnings per share (pence)	75	60
Dividend per share (pence)	55	50
Net asset value (£m)	60	75
Debt ratio (outstanding debt as % of total financing)	10	20
Share price (pence)	N/A	980
Beta coefficient	N/A	1.25
Forecasts:		
Growth rate in earnings and dividends (% per annum)	8	7
After tax cash flow for 20X0/20X1 (£m)	9.2	N/A

Notes

1   The expected post-tax return on the market for the next twelve months is 12 per cent and the post-tax risk-free rate is 5 per cent.

2   The treasurer of the company has provided the forecast growth rate for MC. The forecast for the competitor is based on published information.

3   The net assets of MC are the net book values of land, buildings, equipment and vehicles plus net working capital.

4   Sixty per cent of the shares in the competitor company are owned by the directors and their relatives or associates.

5   MC uses a 'rule-of-thumb' discount rate of 15 per cent to evaluate its investments.

6   Assume that growth rates in earnings and dividends are constant per annum.

7   Debt is assumed to be risk-free.

8   The tax rate is 30%.

Required

Assume that you are an independent consultant retained by MC to advise on the valuation of the company and on the relative advantages of a public flotation versus outright sale.

Prepare a report for the directors that:

(a)   Produces a range of share prices at which shares in MC might be issued. Use whatever information is available. Explain the methods of valuation that you have used and discuss their suitability for providing an appropriate valuation of the company.   **(16 marks)**

(b)   Discusses the relative advantages of flotation and direct sale of shares.   **(6 marks)**

(c)   Recommends a course of action that the company should take.   **(3 marks)**

(Total = 25 marks)

41 PP   **45 mins**

The directors of PP, a food retailer with 20 superstores, are proposing to make a takeover bid for VE, a company with six superstores. PP will offer four of its ordinary shares for every three ordinary shares of VE. The bid has not yet been made public.

SUMMARISED ACCOUNTS
BALANCE SHEETS AS AT 31 MARCH 20X6

	PP		VE	
	£m		£m	
Non-current assets				
Land and buildings (net)		483		42.3
Other non-current assets (net)		150		17.0
		633		59.3
Current assets				
Inventory	328		51.4	
Receivables	12		6.3	
Cash	44		5.3	
		384		63.0
		1,017		122.3

EQUITY AND LIABILITIES

	PP £m		VE £m	
Capital and reserves				
Ordinary shares	(25 pence par) 75		(50 pence par) 20.0	
Accumulated profits		147		34.7
		222		54.7
Non-current liabilities	200		–	
14% loan stock				
Floating rate bank term loans	114		17.5	
		314		17.5
Current liabilities				
Payables	447		46.1	
Dividend	12		2.0	
Taxation	22		2.0	
		481		50.1
		1,017		122.3

INCOME STATEMENTS FOR THE YEAR ENDING 31 MARCH 20X6

	PP £m	VE £m
Revenues	1,130	181
Earnings before interest and tax	115	14
Net interest	40	2
Profit before tax	75	12
Taxation	25	4
Available to shareholders	50	8
Dividend	24	5
Retained earnings	26	3

The share price of PP is currently 232 pence, and of VE 295 pence. The loan stock price of PP is £125.

Recent annual growth trends

	PP	VE
Dividend	7%	8%
EPS	7%	10%

Rationalisation following the acquisition will involve the following transactions (all net of tax effects).

(a)   Sale of surplus warehouse facilities £6.8 million
(b)   Redundancy payments £9.0 million
(c)   Wage savings of £2.7 million per year for at least five years

PP's cost of equity is estimated to be 14.5%, and weighted average cost of capital 12%. VE's cost of equity is estimated to be 13%.

Required

(a)   Discuss whether or not the bid is likely to be viewed favourably by the shareholders of both PP and VE. Include discussion of the factors that are likely to influence the views of the shareholders. (All relevant calculations must be shown.)   **(17 marks)**

(b)   Discuss the possible effects on the likely success of the bid if the offer terms were to be amended to a choice of one new PP 10 year zero coupon debenture redeemable at £100 for every 10 VE shares, or 325 pence per share cash. PP could currently issue new 10 year loan stock at an interest rate of 10%. (All relevant calculations must be shown.)   **(8 marks)**

(Total = 25 marks)

42 PR (FLFS, 5/02)

45 mins

PR is listed on the London Stock Exchange. The directors have made a bid for its main UK competitor, ST. ST's directors have rejected the bid. If the bid eventually succeeds, the new company will become the largest in its industry in Europe. However, it will still be smaller than some of its US competitors. The directors of PR are aware that the company must continue to expand if it is to remain competitive in a global market, and avoid being taken over by a larger US company.

	PR	ST
Share price as at today (21 May 20X2)	671 pence	565 pence
Shares in issue	820 million	513 million
P/E ratios as at today	14	16
Debt outstanding (market value)	£2.2 billion	£1.8 billion

- The average P/E for the industry is currently estimated as 13.

- The average debt ratio for the industry (long-term debt as proportion of total funding) is 30% based on market values.

- 40% of PR's debt is repayable in 20X5; 30% of ST's in 20X6.

- PR's cost of equity is 13% net of tax.

- PR has cash available of £460 million following the recent disposal of some subsidiary companies. ST's cash balances at the last balance sheet date (31 December 20X1) were £120 million.

PR's directors made an opening bid one week ago of 10 PR shares for 13 ST shares. They are aware that they might have to raise the bid in order to succeed and also may need to offer a cash alternative. Their advisors have told them that, typically, 50% of shareholders might be expected to accept the share exchange and 50% the cash alternative.

Required

Assume you work for PR's financial advisers. You have been asked to write a report advising the directors of PR. Your report should cover the following issues:

(a) A discussion of the implications that the current share prices of the two companies have for the bid. Recommend terms of a revised share exchange. **(8 marks)**

(b) The advantages and disadvantages of offering a cash alternative and how the cash alternative might be financed, based on your revised bid terms recommended in answer to (a) above. Your discussion should include an evaluation of the impact of the proposed finance on the merged group's financial standing. Assume a rights issue is not appropriate at the present time. **(17 marks)**

(Total = 25 marks)

43 BA (FLFS, 11/02)

45 mins

BA is a firm of recruitment and selection consultants. It has been trading for 10 years and obtained a stock market listing 4 years ago. It has pursued a policy of aggressive growth and specialises in providing services to companies in high-technology and high-growth sectors. It is all-equity financed by ordinary share capital of $50 million in shares of $0.20 nominal (or par) value. The company's results to the end of June 20X2 have just been announced. Profits before tax were $126.6 million. The chairman's statement included a forecast that earnings might be expected to rise by 4%, which is a lower annual rate than in recent years. This is blamed on economic factors that have had a particularly adverse effect on high-technology companies.

YZ is in the same business but has been established much longer. It services more traditional business sectors and its earnings record has been erratic. Press comment has frequently blamed this on poor management and the company's shares have been out of favour with the stock market for some time. Its current earnings growth forecast is also 4% for the foreseeable future. YZ has an issued ordinary share capital of $180 million in $1 shares. Pre-tax profits for the year to 30 June 20X2 were $112.5 million.

BA has recently approached the shareholders of YZ with a bid of 5 new shares in BA for every 6 YZ shares. There is a cash alternative of 345 cents per share.

Following the announcement of the bid, the market price of BA shares fell 10% while the price of YZ shares rose 14%. The P/E ratio and dividend yield for BA, YZ and two other listed companies in the same industry *immediately prior* to the bid announcement are shown below. All share prices are in cents.

20X2				
High	Low	Company	P/E	Dividend yield %
425	325	BA	11	2.4
350	285	YZ	7	3.1
187	122	CD	9	5.2
230	159	WX	16	2.4

Both BA and YZ pay tax at 30%.

BA's post-tax cost of equity capital is estimated at 13% per annum and YZ's at 11% per annum.

Assume you are a shareholder in YZ. You have a large, but not controlling, shareholding and are a qualified management accountant. You bought the shares some years ago and have been very disappointed with their performance. Two years ago you formed a 'protest group' with fellow shareholders with the principal aim of replacing members of the board. You call a meeting of this group to discuss the bid.

Required

In preparation for your meeting, write a briefing note for your group to discuss. Your note should:

(a) Evaluate whether the proposed share-for-share offer is likely to be beneficial to shareholders in *both* BA and YZ. You should use the information and merger terms available, plus appropriate assumptions, to forecast post-merger values. As a benchmark, you should then value the two companies using the constant growth form of the dividend valuation model. **(13 marks)**

(b) Discuss the factors to consider when deciding whether to accept or reject the bid and the relative benefits/disadvantages of accepting shares or cash. **(8 marks)**

(c) Advise your shareholder group on what its members should do with their investment in YZ, based on your calculations/considerations. **(4 marks)**

(Total = 25 marks)

44 PDQ (FLFS, 11/03) 45 mins

PDQ is a software company and Internet provider that was established in the dot-com boom of the late twentieth century.

The three founding shareholders, who are still directors and managers of the company, own 30% of PDQ. Employees, friends and relatives of the founders own a further 15%. The majority 55% shareholding is owned by a venture capital company that bought a stake in PDQ four years ago for £12 million. The venture capital company now wishes to dispose of the holding. The 45% minority shareholders and non-shareholding employees are considering a management buyout.

PDQ has sustained losses for the past three years but believes it is now moving into profit. Because of these losses, no liability to tax will arise in 20X4 but the company will begin to pay tax at 30% per annum from 20X5. It has not declared or paid a dividend since the company was formed. A summary of forecast key financial information for the current year and for 20X4 is as follows:

Income statement for the year ended:	31 December 20X4	31 December 20X3
	£ million	£ million
Revenues	15.25	14.52
Direct costs and expenses	12.50	16.97
Profit/(loss) before tax	2.75	(2.45)

Balance sheet at	31 December 20X4		31 December 20X3	
	£ million	£ million	£ million	£ million
Non-current assets (NBV)		0.50		0.50
Current assets				
Inventory	1.25		1.25	
Receivables	4.25		3.25	
Cash and marketable securities	0.50		0.00	
		6.00		4.50
		6.50		5.00
Ordinary share capital (Ordinary shares of £1)		0.25		0.25
Total reserves		3.45		0.70
Equity shareholders' funds		3.70		0.95
Current liabilities				
Trade payables	2.80		3.20	
Bank overdraft	0.00		0.85	
		2.80		4.05
		6.50		5.00

The directors expect growth of 20% each year for the three years 20X5 to 20X7 inclusive, falling to 5% each year after that. The average P/E ratio for established listed companies in the industry is currently 28.4 but there is a wide range of between 7.5 and 51.5. The average post-tax cost of equity capital for the industry, according to a recent survey, is 15%.

Required

Assume today is 31 December 20X3.

Advise the founders/employees on the following.

(a)   The price they might have to offer the venture capitalist to succeed with a management buyout. You should include in your discussion the various methods of share valuation that might be suitable in the circumstances. Make and state whatever assumptions you feel are necessary and appropriate.   **(18 marks)**

(b)   The advantages and disadvantages of pursuing a management buyout at the present time compared with the possibility of a sale of the venture capitalist's shareholding to another investor.   **(7 marks)**

Note: A report format is NOT required in answering this question.   **(Total = 25 marks)**

45 PCO (Pilot paper)   45 mins

PCO plc operates in oil and related industries. Its shares are quoted on the London International Stock Exchange. In its retailing operations the company has concentrated on providing high quality service and facilities at its service stations rather than competing solely on the price of petrol. Approximately 75% of its revenue and 60% of its profits are from petrol, the remainder coming from other services (car wash and retail sales from its convenience stores which are available at each service station).

The company has been highly profitable in the past as a result of astute buying of petroleum products on the open market. The company does not enter into supplier agreements with the major oil companies except on very short-term deals. However, profit margins are now under increasing pressure as a result of intensifying competition and the cost of complying with environmental legislation.

The managing director of the company is assessing a possible acquisition that would help the company increase the percentage of its non-petroleum revenue and profits. OT plc specialises in oil distribution from the depots owned by the major oil companies to their retail outlets. Its shares have been quoted on the UK Alternative Investment Market for the past 2 years. It operates a fleet of oil tankers, some owned and some leased. PCO plc has used its services in the past and knows it has an up to date and well-managed fleet. However, a bid for OT plc would almost certainly be hostile and, as the directors and their families own 40% of the shares, a successful bid is far from assured.

Extracts from PCO plc's Balance Sheet at 31 December 20X3

	£m
Assets Employed	
Cash and marketable securities	105.00
Accounts receivable and inventories	95.00
Less current liabilities	(75.00)
Working capital	125.00
Property, plant and equipment	160.00
Less long term liabilities	(80.00)
Secured loan stock 7% repayable 20X9	205.00
Shareholders' equity	
Share capital (Authorised £50 million)	
Issued	40.00
Accumulated profits	165.00
Net Assets Employed	205.00

PCO plc's financial advisors have produced estimates of the expected NPV and the first full year post-acquisition earnings of PCO plc and OT plc:

	Estimated post-acquisition earnings in first full year following acquisition	*Estimated NPV of combined organisation*
PCO plc plus OT plc	£70 million	£720 million

Summary financial statistics		
	PCO plc	*OT plc*
Last year end	31 December 20X3	31 December 20X3
Shares in issue (millions)	40	24
Earnings per share (pence)	106	92
Dividend per share (pence)	32	21
Share price (pence)	967	1,020
Book value of non-current assets and current assets less current liabilities (£ million)	285	145
Debt ratio (outstanding debt as % of total market value)	17.0	14.0
Forecast growth rate %(constant, annualised)	5	9
Beta co-efficient	0.9	12

Required

(a) Calculate, for PCO plc and OT plc *before* the acquisition:

   (i)   The current market value and P/E ratio.

   (ii) The cost of equity using the CAPM, assuming the return on the market is 8% and the return on the risk free asset is 4%.

   (iii) The prospective share price and market value using the dividend valuation model.   **(6 marks)**

(b)   Discuss and advise on the following issues:

(i)   The price to be offered to the target company's shareholders. You should recommend a range of terms within which PCO plc should be prepared to negotiate.

(ii)   The most appropriate form of funding the bid and the financial effects (assume cash or share exchange are the options).

(iii)   The business implications (effect on existing operation, growth prospects, risk and so on).

(19 marks)

Marks are split roughly equally between sections of part (b) of the question.   **(Total = 25 marks)**

46 BiOs (Pilot paper)   45 mins

BiOs Limited (BiOs) is an unquoted company that provides consultancy services to the biotechnology industry. It has been trading for 4 years. It has an excellent reputation for providing innovative and technologically advanced solutions to clients' problems. The company employs 18 consultants plus a number of self employed contract staff and is planning to recruit additional consultants to handle a large new contract. The company 'outsources' most administrative and accounting functions. A problem is recruiting well qualified experienced consultants and BiOs has had to turn down work in the past because of lack of appropriate staff.

The company's two owners/directors have been approached by the marketing department of an investment bank and asked if they have considered using venture capital financing to expand the business. No detailed proposal has been made but the bank has implied that a venture capital company would require a substantial percentage of the equity in return for a large injection of capital. The venture capitalist would want to exit from the investment in 4-5 years' time.

The company is all-equity financed and neither of the directors is wholly convinced that such a large injection of capital is appropriate for the company at the present time.

Financial information

Revenue in year to 31 December 20X3	£3,600,000
Shares in issue (ordinary £1 shares)	100,000
Earnings per share	756p
Dividend per share	0
Net asset value	£395,000 (Note 1)

Note. The net assets of BiOs are the net book values of purchased and/or leased buildings, equipment and vehicles plus net working capital. The book valuations are considered to reflect current realisable values.

Forecast

- Sales revenue for the year to 31 December 20X4 – £4,250,000. This is heavily dependent on whether or not the company obtains the new contract.

- Operating costs, inclusive of depreciation, are expected to average 50% of revenue in the year to 31 December 20X4.

- Tax is expected to be payable at 30%.

- Assume book depreciation equals capital allowances for tax purposes. Also assume, for simplicity, that profit after tax equals cash flow.

Growth in earnings in the years to 31 December 20X5 and 20X6 is expected to be 30% per annum, falling to 10% per annum after that. This assumes that no new long-term capital is raised. If the firm is to grow at a faster rate then new financing will be needed.

This is a niche market and there are relatively few listed companies doing precisely what BiOs does. However, if the definition of the industry is broadened the following figures are relevant:

P/E Ratios

Industry Average:	18
Range (individual companies)	12 to 90

Cost of Equity

Industry average	12%
Individual companies	Not available

BiOs does not know what its cost of equity is.

Required

(a)   Calculate a range of values for the company that could be used in negotiation with a venture capitalist, using whatever information is currently available and relevant. Make and state whatever assumptions you think are necessary. Explain, briefly, the relevance of each method to a company such as BiOs.   **(15 marks)**

(b)   Discuss the advantages and disadvantages of using either venture capital financing to assist with expansion or alternatively a flotation on the stock market in 2-3 years' time. Include in your discussion likely exit routes for the venture capital company.   **(10 marks)**

(Total = 25 marks)

47 BST (FLFS, 11/04)   45 mins

BST Motors plc (BST) is a long-established listed company. Its main business is the retailing of new and used motor cars and the provision of after-sales service. It has sales outlets in most of the major towns and cities in the UK. It also owns a substantial amount of land and property that it has acquired over the years, much of which it rents or leases on medium-long term agreements. Approximately 80% of its fixed asset value is land and buildings.

The company has grown organically for the last few years but is now considering expanding by acquisition. The Chief Executive is not in favour of hostile bids as he believes the bidder always pays too much to acquire the target. Any acquisition that BST makes will therefore need to be an agreed bid.

SM Limited (SM) owns a number of car showrooms in wealthy, semi-rural locations in the North of England. All of these showrooms operate the franchise of a well-known major motor manufacturer. SM is a long-established private company with the majority of shares owned by the founding family, many of whom still work for the company. The major shareholders are now considering selling the business if a suitable price can be agreed. The Managing Director of SM, who is a major shareholder, has approached BST to see if they would be interested in buying SM. He has implied that holders of up to 50% of SM's shares might be willing to accept BST shares as part of the deal.

The forecast earnings of BST for the next financial year are £35 million. According to the Managing Director of SM, his company's earnings are expected to be £4 million for the next financial year.

Financial statistics and other information on BST and SM are shown below:

	BST	SM
Shares in issue (millions)	25	1.5
Earnings per share (pence)	112.5	153
Dividend per share (pence)	50.6	100
Share price (pence)	1237	N/A
Net asset value attributable to equity (£m)	350	45
Debt ratio (outstanding debt as percentage of total market value of company)	20	0
Forecast growth rate percentage (constant, annualised)	4	5
Cost of equity	9%	N/A

SM does not calculate a cost of equity, but the industry average for similar companies is 10%

Required

Assume you are a financial manager working with BST. Advise the BST Board on the following issues in connection with a possible bid for SM:

(a)   Methods of valuation that might be appropriate and a range of valuations for SM within which BST should be prepared to negotiate.   **(10 marks)**

(b)   The financial factors relating to both companies that might affect the bid.   **(5 marks)**

(c)   The most appropriate form of funding the bid and the likely financial effects on BST.   **(5 marks)**

(d)   The advantages and disadvantages of growth by agreed acquisition as compared with growth by internal (or organic) investment.   **(5 marks)**

(Total = 25 marks)

A report format is not required for this question.

48 FS (11/05)

45 mins

FS provides industrial and commercial cleaning services to organisations throughout a country in the European Union. Its shares have been listed for 15 years and, until two years ago, the entity followed a policy of aggressive growth, mainly by acquisition.

However, in the last two years, there have been few suitable takeover opportunities and, as a consequence, growth has slowed. The market has downgraded FS's shares and they are currently trading at €3·57, the lowest price for five years. The market as a whole has declined in value, but not to the same extent as FS's shares. FS's bank has recently informed FS's directors of a possible takeover opportunity of another of its clients, MT. This is a large private entity in the same industry as FS. MT's directors have indicated to the bank that if the price is right they may be prepared to sell the entity. MT's directors have made their financial forecasts and other strategic documentation available to the bank on a strictly confidential basis, requesting that this information only be released to a serious potential bidder. After much discussion between the bank and the two companies, MT agrees that FS should have the information.

MT's results for the past three years and the directors' estimates for the current year are as follows:

Year to 30 June	Revenue	Earnings
	€million	€million
20X3	925	55.5
20X4	1,020	62.7
20X5	1,150	71.5
20X6 (forecast)	1,350	88.9

For 20X7 onwards, growth in earnings and dividends is likely to fall to 4% per annum, according to MT's directors. MT has paid a dividend of 50% of its earnings for the past 10 years.

Summary balance sheets as at 30 June 20X5 for both FS and MT are as follows:

	FS	MT
	€million	€ million
Total assets		
Non-current assets	1,944	1,040
Current assets*	796	375
	2,740	1,415
Equity and liabilities		
Equity		
Share capital (shares of €1)	420	
(shares of 50 cents)		220

	FS € million	MT € million
Retained earnings	1,080	680
	1,500	900
Non-current liabilities		
Secured bonds, 6% 20X9	750	
Unsecured bonds, 7% 20X9		300
Current liabilities	490	215
	1,240	515
	2,740	1,415
* Includes cash of	250	65

FS's revenues and earnings for the year ended 30 June 20X5 were €2,250 million and €128·5 million respectively.

After thoroughly examining the information on MT, financial managers in FS have identified a number of savings and potential synergies that would arise if the takeover were to go ahead. These synergies are estimated to have a net present value of €200 million. However, the FS directors believe MT's forecast earnings are over-optimistic and think earnings growth for 20X6 onwards is likely to be in the range 2% to 4%. The bank advisers disagree, but they are in a delicate situation trying to balance the interests of two clients.

FS's cost of equity is 8·5%. MT has not provided information on its cost of capital, but the two entity's asset betas are likely to be the same. FS's equity beta is quoted as 1·1. The expected risk free rate of return is 3% and the expected return on the market is 8%. Assume that the debt beta for both companies is 0·2 and that FS's debt is trading at par.

Ignore tax in your calculations.

Required

Assume you are a Financial Manager with FS. Advise the directors of FS on:

(a) The appropriate cost of capital to be used when valuing MT. Accompany your comments with a calculation of the cost of equity for MT. **(6 marks)**

(b) A bidding strategy; that is the initial price to be offered and the maximum FS should be prepared to offer for the shares in MT. Use whatever methods of valuation you think appropriate and accompany each with brief comments on their suitability in the circumstances here. In calculations of value that require a discount rate, use the cost of equity you have calculated in (i) above. Your answer should consider the interests of both groups of shareholders. **(13 marks)**

(c) The most appropriate form of consideration to use in the circumstances. Assume the choice is either a share exchange or cash. Your answer should consider the interests of both groups of shareholders. **(6 marks)**

(Total = 25 marks)

ADVANCED INVESTMENT APPRAISAL

Questions 49 to 60 cover advanced investment appraisal, the subject of Part D of the BPP Study Text for Paper P9.

---

49 VEN
45 mins

VEN produces a wide range of educational toys for children. Recently, it has developed a new type of activity centre for very young children and the directors of the company are now considering whether this product should be put into production. The following information has been produced to help evaluate the commercial viability of the new product.

(a) The cost of developing the new product was £125,000. In addition, market research was carried out by a firm of marketing consultants at a cost of £80,000. The development costs have all been paid and the market research costs are due for payment next month.

(b) The company expects to sell 10,000 activity centres per year for each of the next five years. The selling price of each centre will be £65.

(c) Machinery which originally cost £1,500,000 and which has a written down value of £950,000, will be required to produce the activity centres. If production does not go ahead, the machinery will be sold immediately for £790,000. If, however, production goes ahead, the machinery will be sold at the end of five years for £70,000.

(d) Additional working capital of £150,000 will be required immediately in order to support production of the new product. This can be released at the end of the production period.

(e) To produce the new product, two types of material will be required. Type A material is used throughout the product range of the business and 20,000 kilos are already in stock at a purchase cost of £14 per kilo. The company intends to maintain stocks of type A material at their current level. Recently, however, the supplier of this material has raised the price to £15 per kilo. Type B material is also in stock although there is no further use for this material except for use in the production of the new product. There are 12,000 kilos in stock at a purchase cost of £2 per kilo, however, the replacement cost is £2.50 per kilo. If production does not go ahead, the existing stock will be sold immediately for £1.50 per kilo. Year-end stock levels of type B material will be zero. Each activity centre requires one kilo of Type A material and three kilos of Type B material.

(f) Labour costs are estimated at £12 per activity centre. If the new product is not produced, some existing employees will be made redundant immediately at a cost of £50,000 to the company. If, however, the new product is produced, these employees will be used to produce the new product and will be made redundant at the end of the production period at a cost of £80,000 to the company.

(g) Total fixed costs apportioned to the new product will be £200,000 per annum of which £60,000 per annum is estimated to arise as a direct result of the decision to produce the new product.

The company has a cost of capital of 12 per cent.

Ignore taxation.

Required

(a) Calculate the incremental cash flows arising from a decision to produce the activity centre. **(6 marks)**

(b) Calculate:

(i)   The net present value (NPV), and
(ii) The approximate internal rate of return (IRR)

of the activity centre and state whether or not VEN should produce this product. **(6 marks)**

(c)   Calculate the modified internal rate of return on the project on the basis that VEN can reinvest the net cash inflows each year at its cost of capital and explain whether it changes your recommendation in (b). **(4 marks)**

As well as considering investing in the new activity centre, the board of VEN are also considering a longer-term investment in a new computerised production monitoring system that they believe should have financial benefits across their whole product range.

(d)   Explain in a memo to the board how an investment in information technology can help to increase contribution and reduce fixed costs.   **(9 marks)**

(Total = 25 marks)

50 Canada   45 mins

PG is considering investing in a new project abroad in Canada which involves developing a new product that will have a life of four years. The initial investment is C$150,000, including working capital. The net after-tax cash flows which the project will generate are C$60,000 per annum for years 1, 2 and 3 and C$45,000 in year 4. The terminal value of the project is estimated at C$50,000, net of tax.

The current spot rate of C$ against the euro is 1.7. Economic forecasters expect the euro to strengthen against the Canadian dollar by 5% per annum over the next 4 years.

The company evaluates projects in its own country of similar risk at 14%.

Required

(a)   Calculate the NPV of the Canadian project using the following two methods:

   (i)   Convert the currency cash flows into euros and discount the euro cash flows at a euro discount rate

   (ii)   Discount the cash flows in C$ using an adjusted discount rate which incorporates the 12-month forecast spot rate

   and explain briefly the theories and/or assumptions which underlie the use of the adjusted discount rate approach in (ii).   **(8 marks)**

(b)   The company had originally planned to finance the project with internal funds generated in its own country. However, the Finance Director has suggested that there would be advantages in raising debt finance in Canada.

   Discuss the advantages and disadvantages of matching investment and borrowing overseas as compared with local-sourced debt or equity.

   Wherever possible, relate your answer to the details given in this question for PG.   **(8 marks)**

(c)   Explain the main stages of the process for developing new products.   **(9 marks)**

(Total = 25 marks)

51 IT (FLFS, 11/01)   45 mins

HS and IT are both manufacturing companies which trade in similar industries. However, HS is a much larger company with more diversified interests, and trades internationally. By comparison, IT trades solely in its domestic market. Comparative data on these two companies is as follows.

	HS	IT
Turnover	US$2.5 billion	US$1.2 million
Gross profit margin	28%	17%
Debt: equity	40%	10%
Shares in issue	200 million	2,000
Number of shareholders	Many	Few
Share price	US$12.60	not available

Required

Compare and evaluate the usefulness or impact of the following variables in the investment appraisal process for these two companies:

(a)   The use of weighted average cost of capital (WACC) as a discount rate
(b)   The use of certainty equivalents compared with using an adjusted discount rate in evaluating the cash flow
(c)   The use of payback or accounting rate of return compared with DCF techniques
(d)   The influence and effects of taxation on their investment decisions

(Each item carries up to 7 marks to a maximum of 25 for all four

(Total = 25 marks)

52 GH (FLFS, 5/01)   45 mins

GH is a USA-based retailing company. The company is evaluating the potential for expansion into Europe, starting in Denmark. A detailed assessment of the costs and likely incremental revenues of opening stores in two major Danish cities has been carried out. The initial cost of the investment is 80 million Danish Kroners. The nominal cash flows, all positive and net of all taxes, are summarised below.

	Year 1	Year 2	Year 3
Cash flow (DKr million)	35.50	42.50	45.00

The company's treasurer provides the following information.

- The expected inflation rate in Denmark is 4% each year and in the USA 3% each year.

- Real interest rates in the USA and Denmark are the same. They are expected to remain the same for the foreseeable future.

- The current spot rate is DKr8.5 to $1.

- The risk-free annual rate of interest in Denmark is 6% and in the USA 5%. These nominal rates are not expected to change in the foreseeable future.

- The company's post-tax weighted average cost of capital (WACC) is 15%, which it uses to evaluate all investment decisions.

The expansion will be financed by a combination of internal funds generated in the USA and long-term fixed interest rate debt raised in Denmark. The company plans to purchase in Denmark the majority of its goods for resale.

Required

(a)   Calculate the $ net present value of the project, using both the following methods:

(i)   By discounting annual cash flows in $
(ii)   By discounting annual cash flows in DKr, using an adjusted discount rate

and explain, briefly, the reasons why the two methods give almost identical answers.   **(9 marks)**

(b)   Assume that the company's management is considering purchasing from *outside* Denmark a substantial proportion of its goods to be sold in the Danish stores. Approximately 50% of total goods for resale might be purchased in the Far East and a further 25% in the USA. Discuss how a decision to change buying patterns might affect the evaluation and funding of the investment.   **(8 marks)**

(c)   Assume that inflation in Denmark turns out to be higher than forecast for the whole period of evaluation, with corresponding impact on the other economic factors. Inflation in the USA is slightly less than forecast. Discuss how the financial returns on the investment might be affected, and advise on a funding strategy that could minimise the impact of such inflationary effects.   **(8 marks)**

Note. Parts (b) and (c) are independent – that is, part (c) is not dependent upon the answer to part (b).

(Total = 25 marks)

53 Question with student answer: QE   45 mins

QE is a medium-sized food manufacturing company. It has recently sold a subsidiary that traded in what the company considered to be non-core business. The sale raised £1.4 million in cash.

The company's long-term debt to equity ratio is relatively high compared with other companies in the industry and the directors have ruled out further borrowing at the present time. In fact, one of the directors thinks the cash raised from the sale of the subsidiary should be used to repay some of the company's outstanding debt.

This is not a view shared by the other directors who are evaluating three small but potentially profitable acquisition opportunities. The directors believe that the shareholders of all three target companies would not be opposed to a bid at this time, especially to a cash offer. However, to acquire all of them would require £2.3 million. The share price is standing at an all-time high – a level considered unsustainable by the directors based on the company's projected earnings. The directors therefore intend to limit their expenditure to the £1.4 million cash raised by the sale of the subsidiary.

Expected after-tax cash flows

Company	Year 1 £'000	Year 2 £'000	Year 3 £'000	Acquisition price £'000
AB	(100)	750	1,100	(1,100)
CD	125	275	380	(550)
EF	200	325	450	(650)

Note. The cash flows are in real terms, ie they do not include inflation. QE plc's shareholders currently require a real return of 12% on their investment in the company. The company uses this rate to evaluate all its investment decisions, including acquisitions.

Required

Assume you are a financial manager with QE. Write a report to the directors evaluating the potential acquisitions. You should include the following information in your report.

(a)   The expected net present value and profitability indexes of the three projects. Based solely on these calculations, discuss which company(ies) should be chosen for acquisition and discuss the use of 12% as a discount rate in the circumstances here.   **(10 marks)**

(b)   Recommendation of uses for any cash that is left over after the acquisitions have been made.   **(4 marks)**

(c)   Discussion of the directors' decisions

       (i)   To invest rather than repay debt, and

       (ii)   To limit their investment for the current year to cash purchases rather than raise new capital in the form of debt or equity   **(6 marks)**

(d)   Discussion of the advantages and disadvantages of growth by acquisition as compared with growth by internal (or organic) investment.   **(5 marks)**

(Total = 25 marks)

54 KH (FLFS, 11/01)

45 mins

KH is a large food and drink manufacturer and retailer based in the United States of America. To date, the company has operated only in the US but is planning to expand into South America by acquiring a group of stores similar to those operated in the US. Projected cash flows in the US and South America for the first three years of the project, in real terms, are estimated as follows.

	Year 0	Year 1	Year 2	Year 3
Cash flows in the USA:				
In US$'000	−10,000	−300	−400	−500
Cash flows in the South American country:				
In SA currency'000	−1,000,000	+250,000	+350,000	+450,000

US$ cash flows are mainly incremental administration costs associated with the project. SA currency cash flows are cash receipts from sales less all related cash costs and expenses.

The exchange rate for the South American country's currency is extremely volatile. Inflation is currently 40% a year. Inflation in the US is 4% a year. Best estimates by KH's treasurer suggest these rates are likely to continue for the foreseeable future. The current exchange rate is SA currency 30 to US$1.

The following information is relevant

- KH evaluates all investments using nominal cash flows and a nominal discount rate.

- SA currency cash flows are converted into US$ and discounted at a risk-adjusted US rate.

- All cash flows for this project will be discounted at 20%, a nominal rate judged to reflect its high risk.

- For the purposes of evaluation, assume the year 3 nominal cash flows will continue to be earned each year indefinitely.

Note. Ignore taxation

Required

Assume that you are the financial manager of KH. Prepare a report to the finance director that evaluates the proposed investment. Include in your report the following.

(a)   Calculation of the net present value of the proposed investment and a recommendation as to whether the company should proceed with the investment, supported by your reasons for the recommendation.

(12 marks)

(b)   Discussion of the main political risks that might be faced by the company and provision of advice on management strategies that could be implemented to counter those risks. **(13 marks)**

(Total = 25 marks)

55 DAC

45 mins

DAC is a manufacturer of expensive, built-to-order motor cars. The company has been trading for 25 years and has seen year-on-year growth of sales and profits. Whereas most of the large, mass-production motor manufacturers have experienced over-capacity and falling profit margins in recent years, DAC has a waiting list of six months for a new car. All cars are manufactured in the UK, but there are sales outlets throughout Europe and the Far East. The chief executive of the company, who is still the major shareholder, is considering extending the distributor network into the USA where there is a rising demand. At present, American customers have to order direct from the UK.

A detailed assessment of the costs and likely incremental revenues of opening distributorships into major US cities has been carried out. The initial cost of the investment is US$4.5 million. The cash flows, all positive and net of all taxes, are summarised below.

Year	1	2	3	4
Cash flow (US$million)	1.75	1.95	2.50	3.50

The following information is available.

- The expected inflation rate in the USA is 2 per cent a year.

- Real interest rates in the UK and USA are the same. They are expected to remain the same for the foreseeable future.

- The current spot rate is US$1.6 per £1 sterling.

- The risk-free rate of interest in the USA is 4 per cent per annum and in Britain 5 per cent per annum. These rates are not expected to change in the foreseeable future.

- The company's post-tax WACC is 14 per cent per annum, which it uses to evaluate all investment decisions.

- The company is financed by £10 million shareholders' funds (book values) and £2 million long-term debt which is due to be retired in two years' time.

The company can finance part of the investment from cash flow but, as it is also expanding operations in the UK, the chief executive would prefer external finance if this is available on acceptable terms. He has noted that borrowing rates in the euro-debt market appear very favourable at the present time. At 3 per cent they are below the rates in both the UK and the USA.

Required

(a) Calculate the *sterling* net present value of the project using both of the following methods:

    (i) By discounting annual cash flows in sterling.
    (ii) By discounting annual cash flows in US$. **(10 marks)**

(b) Discuss:

    (i) The use of WACC as a discount rate in an international investment decision, in general terms and as it applies to DAC.

    (ii) The main risks to be faced by a company such as DAC when it moves into a new international market, and how it might manage those risks.

    (iii) The main methods of financing overseas operations and the factors that the company should consider before making a decision about borrowing in euro debt. **(15 marks)**

(Total = 25 marks)

56 CTC (5/05)

45 mins

CTC Technology College (CTC) is a non-profit making institution located in Ireland, where the national currency is the euro. The college is funded by a combination of student fees and government grants.

The number of students enrolled on the part-time Information Technology course at CTC has fallen over recent years due to competition from other colleges and the wide range of different courses available. The number of students enrolling on the current course, ITS (IT Skills) has stabilised at around 150 students per annum and there are currently 20 computers surplus to requirements which CTC plans to sell for an estimated €100 each; the current book value of each computer is €200. However, this sale will not occur if the college goes ahead with its plan to replace the current ITS course with an updated course, as it is expected that a new course would result in a significant increase in student numbers.

CTC realises that the financial viability of switching courses is highly dependent on the number of students that the college can attract onto the new course and has commissioned some market research, at a cost of €10,000, into the best course content and likely increase in student numbers. The results of this research indicate that an ITC (IT Competence) course would be the most popular and lead to a significant increase in student enrolments at the college. It is also estimated that there could be an additional benefit to the college of average net revenues of €20 per additional student over and above 150 as a result of those students being attracted to the college and taking other courses at the college at the same time as the ITC course.

The new ITC course would be run by existing staff currently working on the ITS course at a cost of €50,000 per annum. If, however, the numbers of students on ITC were to rise above 200 per annum, an additional part-time member of staff would be needed at a cost of €10,000 per annum, payable in advance. If ITC is adopted, several computers would need to be upgraded at a total one-off cost of €15,000.

Other relevant data is as follows:

	ITS	ITC
	€	€
Fee for the course (per student, payable in advance)	350	360
Directly attributable course costs (per annum, payable in arrears)	1,000	2,000
Books and consumables per student, payable in advance	50	60
Apportionment of college overheads (excluding staff costs) (per annum, charged at the end of the year)	20,000	25,000
Staff training and course development (initial set-up cost)	0	30,000

The planning horizon for the college is four years and projects are evaluated using a discount rate of 8% and on the basis of a zero terminal value at the end of the four-year period. Each course is of one year duration and student enrolments should be assumed to remain constant throughout the four-year period, with ITS attracting 150 students each year.

Taxation and inflation should be ignored.

Required

(a) Evaluate the number of student enrolments required on the ITC course in order for it to be financially beneficial, on a net present value of cash flow basis, for the college to replace the ITS course with the ITC course. **(15 marks)**

(b) Advise the governing body of the college on the following issues:

(i) How to monitor and control the costs and revenues of the project from the decision to introduce the new course to the start date of the course. **(5 marks)**

(ii) Options available if only 150 students enrol on the new ITC course by the enrolment deadline two weeks before the beginning of the course by which time all other course preparations will have been completed. **(5 marks)**

(Total = 25 marks)

57 XZ (FLFS, 5/01)   45 mins

The shares of XZ are quoted on a stock market. Two of the directors are also major shareholders in the company. They have been evaluating investment in a project which will require €3.9 million capital expenditure on new machinery. The directors expect the capital investment to provide annual cash flows of €600,000 indefinitely. This figure is net of all tax adjustments.

The company is at present all equity financed. The discount rate, which it applies to investment decisions of this nature, is 14% net. The directors believe that the current capital structure fails to take advantage of the tax benefits of debt, and propose to finance the new project with undated debt secured on the company's assets. The current annual gross rate of interest required by the market on corporate undated debt of similar risk is 10%. The after-tax costs of issue are expected to be €162,000. The company intends to issue sufficient debt to cover the cost of capital expenditure and the after-tax costs of issue.

The company's marginal tax rate is 30%.

You should use a sensible approach to rounding your answers throughout the question.

Required

(a)   Calculate the adjusted present value of the investment and the adjusted discount rate, and explain the circumstances in which this adjusted discount rate may be used to evaluate future investments.   **(10 marks)**

The company is considering three other investment opportunities. The initial capital investment required, the NPVs and the duration of these three projects are as follows.

	Initial investment € million	NPV € million	Duration Years
Project 1	3.85	0.85	3
Project 2	4.25	0.90	4
Project 3	2.95	0.68	2

However, resource constraints mean that the company cannot invest in all three projects. It wishes to restrict investment to €7.5 million.

Notes

- The projects are not divisible.
- The company has used its cost of capital of 14% to evaluate all three investments.
- Any surplus cash could be invested in the money market at 6%.
- Assume all rates in this part of the question are net of tax.

Required

(b)   Discuss and recommend, with reasons, which project(s) should be undertaken.   **(15 marks)**

(Total = 25 marks)

58 Question with helping hand: REM (FLFS, 11/02)　45 mins

REM is a family-owned business. The family owns 80% of the shares. The remaining 20% is owned by four non-family shareholders. The board of directors is considering the purchase of two second-hand (that is, previously used) freight planes to deliver its goods within its key markets in the USA. The managing director, an ex-pilot and one of the non-family shareholders, commissioned an evaluation from the company's accountants and was advised that the company would save money and be more efficient if it performed these delivery operations itself instead of 'outsourcing' them to established courier and postal services. The accountants built into their evaluation an assumption that the company would be able to sell spare capacity on the planes to other companies in the locality.

The managing director has decided that the accountants' recommendation will be conducted as a 'trial' for 5 years when its success or otherwise will be evaluated. The net, post-tax operating cash flows of this investment are estimated as:

Year 0　　　–$12.50 million (the initial capital investment)
Years 1 to 4　$3.15 million each year
Year 5　　　$5.85 million

Year 5 includes an estimate of the residual value of the planes.

The company normally uses an estimated post-tax weighted average cost of capital of 12% to evaluate investments. However, this investment is different from its usual business operations and the finance director suggests using the capital asset pricing model (CAPM) when determining a discount rate. REM, being unlisted, does not have a published beta so the finance director has obtained a beta of 1.3 for a courier company that is listed. This company has a debt ratio (debt to equity) of 1:2, compared with REM whose debt ratio is 1:5.

Other information:

- The expected annual post-tax return on the market is 9% and the risk-free is 5%.
- Assume both companies' debt is virtually risk-free.
- Both companies pay tax at 30%.

Required

(a)　Using the CAPM, calculate:

　　(i)　An asset beta for REM

　　(ii)　An equity beta for REM

　　(iii)　An appropriate discount rate to be used in the evaluation of this project

　　(iv)　The NPV of the project using the discount rate calculated in (iii); and comment briefly on your choice of discount rate in part (iii). **(11 marks)**

(b)　Evaluate the benefits and limitations of using a proxy company's beta to determine the rate to be used by REM in the circumstances here, and recommend alternative methods of adjusting for risk in the valuation that could be considered by the company. **(9 marks)**

(c)　Advise the managing director on the benefits of a post-completion audit. **(5 marks)**

A report format is not required in answering this question. **(Total = 25 marks)**

Helping hand

(a)　(i)　–　Asset beta = ungeared beta
　　　　　–　Have geared beta for a similar company
　　　　　–　See formula sheet

　　(ii)　–　Equity beta = regeared beta, using REM's gearing
　　　　　–　Rearrange formula used in (a)(i)

(iii)   –   Use answer (a)(i) + CAPM formula
           – k_{adj} = ? in formula sheet

(iv)   Use precise discount rate and calculate discount factors using $\dfrac{1-(1+r)^{-n}}{r}$

(b)   Advantages

     (i)   Information required
     (ii)   Nature of investment

     Disadvantages

     (i)   The same circumstances
     (ii)   Debt levels
     (iii) β reliability
     (iv)   CAPM assumptions

     Other methods

     (i)   Certainty equivalents
     (ii)   Arbitrage pricing theory
     (iii)   Project-specific rates

(c)   Post-completion audits

     Consider impact on future decision-making and control

---

59 GHI (5/06)

45 mins

GHI is a mobile phone manufacturer based in France with a wide customer base in France and Germany, with all costs and revenues based in euro (€). GHI is considering expanding into the UK market and has begun investigating how to break into this market and is designing a new phone specifically for it. A small project committee has been formed to plan and control the project.

After careful investigation, the following project cash flows have been identified:

Year	£million
0	(10)
1	5
2	5
3	4
4	3
5	3

The project is to be funded by a loan of €16 million at an annual interest rate of 5% and repayable at the end of five years. Loan issue costs amount to 2% and are tax deductible.

GHI has a debt : equity ratio of 40 : 60 based on market values, a pre-tax cost of debt of 5.0% and a cost of equity of 10.7%.

Tax on entity profits in France can be assumed to be at a rate of 35%, payable in the year in which it arises. UK tax at 25% is deductible in full against French tax in the same time period under the terms of the double tax treaty between the UK and France. The initial investment of £10 million will not qualify for any tax relief.

Assume the current spot rate is £1 = €1.60 and sterling (£) is expected to weaken against the euro by 3% per annum (so that in year 1 it is worth only 97% of its value in euro (€) in year 0).

Required

(a) Advise GHI on whether or not to proceed with the project based on a calculation of its adjusted present value (APV) and describe the limitations of an APV approach in this context. **(15 marks)**

(b) Explain the function of the project committee of GHI in the following stages of the project:

    (i) Determining customer requirements and an appropriate product design for the UK market; and

                                         (5 marks)

    (ii) Controlling the implementation stage of the project. **(5 marks)**

                                         (Total = 25 marks)

60 RST (5/06)   **45 mins**

RST is a publicly-owned and funded health organisation based in the Far East. It is reviewing a number of interesting possibilities for new development projects in the area and has narrowed down the choice to the five projects detailed below. RST is aware that government budget restrictions may be tighter in a year's time and so does not want to commit to a capital budget of more than $30 million in year 1. In addition, any project cash inflows in year 1 may be used to fund capital expenditure in that year. There is sufficient capital budget remaining in year 0 to enable all projects to be undertaken. Under government funding rules, any unused capital in year 0 cannot be carried over to year 1 and no interest may be earned on unused capital. No borrowings are permitted.

RST assesses capital projects at a hurdle rate of 15% based on the equity beta of health-based companies in the private sector.

	Cash outflows		*Cash inflows*	
	Year 0	Year 1		
Project	$ million	$ million	$ million	
A	9	16	4	from year 1 in perpetuity
B	10	10	4	from year 2 in perpetuity
C	10	12	5	in years 1 to 10
D	8	5	6	in years 3 to 7
E	9	8	2 ⎫	in years 1 to 5
			5 ⎭	in years 6 to 15

Notes:

- The projects are not divisible
- Each project can only be undertaken once
- Ignore tax

Required

(a) Advise RST on the best combination of projects based on an evaluation of each project on the basis of both:

    (i) NPV of cashflows;

    (ii) A profitability index for use in this capital rationing analysis. **(15 marks)**

(b) Discuss

    (i) Whether or not capital rationing techniques based on NPV analysis are appropriate for a publicly-owned entity such as RST. **(5 marks)**

    (ii) As a publicly-owned entity, what other factors RST should consider and what other analysis it should undertake before making a final decision on which project(s) to accept. **(5 marks)**

                                         (Total = 25 marks)

61 Casarina

90 mins

Background to the company

It is currently May 20X0. Casarina operates a chain of fast food outlets. Some are company-owned and some are operated under franchise. Two colleagues who were made redundant from one of the major fast food companies started the company 15 years ago. Initially they opened outlets in smaller UK towns and cities where there was limited competition. The company experienced rapid growth in the first 10 years of operations. Over the past five years, growth has stabilised and the company may now be facing a downturn in business caused primarily by increased competition.

Financing history and current situation

The original owners obtained a listing on the UK stock market 8 years ago when 40% of the 20 million £1 shares in issue were offered for sale at 260 pence per share. Further capital was raised 4 years ago by means of a 1 for 4 rights issue. As a result of a series of share disposals, the original owners' combined shareholding has fallen to 35% of the shares currently in issue. Institutional investors now own the majority, although a number of employees are shareholders as a result of the company's share option scheme. A summary of the company's most recent financial statements is shown in Table 1. The company's shareholders have, historically, required a return on their equity of 15%.

Financing alternatives

At a recent meeting between the company's directors, financial analysts and institutional investors, it was suggested that the company should consider a programme of expansion by extending the franchise to other UK locations if it is to return to growth. However, it is unlikely to be able to undertake major expansion out of cash surpluses and the company must now consider raising new finance. Two alternatives are being considered:

Alternative 1

A rights issue of 1 for 5 at 500 pence.

Alternative 2

A floating rate loan of £25 million at an initial rate of 8% per annum. The loan would be for 8 years, repayable at maturity and secured against the freehold land and buildings owned by Casarina. However, the bank has imposed a condition that the company's gearing, measured by the book value of total debt to total debt plus equity, is no more than 50% throughout the period of the loan. If this condition is infringed then the bank has the right to call in the loan at 3 months' notice. Casarina can purchase a 4-year interest cap at 10% for an immediate premium of 2% of the initial amount of the loan. This expense will be amortised over the life of the cap.

Profit improvement scheme

The directors recognise that raising new capital, especially if it is by means of a rights issue, will need to be justified in terms of benefits to shareholders. The costs and benefits of the proposed expansion have yet to be fully evaluated but as a broad objective the directors aim to increase turnover by 10% per annum for the foreseeable future. It is expected that direct costs other than depreciation will, on average, increase by only 8% per annum as a result of a cost-reduction programme and new supplier contracts. Indirect expenses are expected to hold constant as a result of internal restructuring. Other relevant information is as follows.

- The ratios of *receivables to sales* and *payables to direct costs* (excluding depreciation) will remain the same as in the year to 30 April 20X0.

- Depreciation on assets existing at 30 April 20X0 is forecast to be £9 million in the year ending 30 April 20X1 and £7 million the year after that. New non-current assets will be purchased to the value of £25 million in the year to 30 April 20X1 and £20 million in the year to 30 April 20X2. Depreciation on these new assets will be 20% per annum straight-line starting in the year of purchase. Assume tax allowances are available at the same rate.

- £10 million of additional inventory will also be purchased in the year to 30 April 20X1. Assume this is the only change in the inventory level for 20X0/20X1.

- Tax is payable at a marginal rate of 30% per annum in the year in which the liability arises.

- Dividends are payable the year after they are declared. Assume the company maintains the 20W9/20X0 payout ratio in 20X0/20X1.

Table 1 – Summary financial statements

Income statement year to 30 April 20X0

	£'000
Revenue	135,000
Direct costs (note 1)	85,500
Indirect costs	20,000
Interest payable	2,500
Profit before tax	27,000
Tax on profit at 30%	8,100
Profit after tax	18,900
Dividends declared	11,340

Balance sheet at 30 April 20X0

	£'000	£'000
Non-current assets (NBV)		117,000
Current assets		
Inventory	17,500	
Receivables	24,500	
Cash at bank	5,250	
		47,250
		164,250
Capital and reserves		
Ordinary shares (£)		25,000
Reserves (note 3)		81,410
		106,410
Non-current liabilities		
10% debentures 20X5		25,000
Current liabilities		
Payables	21,500	
Others (note 2)	11,340	
		32,840
		164,250

Notes

1   Includes depreciation of £9,500,000.

2   Other payables are dividends payable.

3   Includes revaluation reserve of £25,000,000.

4   Share price movements during the year:

High	630p
Low	550p
As at today (23 May 20X0)	560p

Required

(a)   For the two financing alternatives being considered by the directors of Casarina, prepare forecast

   (i)   Income statements for the year to 30 April 20X1
   (ii)   Balance sheets at 30 April 20X1, and
   (iii)   Cash flows for the year to 30 April 20X1

   Notes

   1   Ignore transaction costs on the issuing of new capital and returns on surplus cash invested short term.

   2   You are not required to adopt the IAS 7 format for the cash flow forecasts, but may do so if you wish.

   (18 marks)

(b)   Assume you are a management accountant with Casarina. Write a report to the Directors that evaluates the proposed methods of financing. You should:

   (i)   Base your evaluation on the forecast you have provided in part (a) of the question but include whatever additional calculations you think necessary and appropriate to aid the evaluation

   (ii)   Discuss the advantages and disadvantages of the two methods of financing being evaluated and comment briefly on alternative types of finance which might be considered suitable in the circumstances

   (iii)   Identify any additional information which would be useful before the Directors can make an informed decision   **(32 marks)**

   (Total = 50 marks)

62 Spearhead   **90 mins**

Background to the company and selected financial information

Spearhead, a company based in the United Kingdom, manufactures high-technology landing and airport control equipment which it sells worldwide, mainly to government departments. The company was owned by the government of the United Kingdom until 19X8 and has demonstrated strong growth since privatisation, although it is not the market leader in the industry.

In its last financial year, the company had earnings of £360 million and earnings per share (EPS) of 60 pence. The current share price is 950 pence compared with 825 pence a year ago. The company's equity beta is quoted at 1.5.

Company objectives

Financial objectives

(i)   Investing in projects which yield a positive NPV when discounted at an appropriate discount rate
(ii)   Maintaining an annual return on assets at 25%

Other objectives

The company aims to be the leading UK supplier of airport control equipment within the next 10 years and retains a large proportion of its earnings for future investment. It pays a relatively low annual cash dividend and aims to top this up with a scrip dividend each year.

Information on major contracts

Spearhead is examining two potential contracts which will each require substantial capital investment. The timing of the bids, the amount of capital investment required, and the need for highly-specialised design staff mean that it can bid for only one of the two contracts. Details are as follows.

CONTRACT 1

The customer is the Swiss government. The contract is for the supply of radar-controlled landing equipment over a period of four years to a value of SFr2,000 million. Spearhead must agree a fixed price in Swiss Francs for the duration of the contract.

The forecast cash flows, in nominal terms, are:

Initial capital expenditure	£300 million
Estimated residual value at the end of the project	£50 million
Income from sales	SFr 500 million per annum
Contract costs	£75 million per annum

The bidding for this contract was expected to be fiercely competitive. Despite the need for a fixed-price clause in the contract, the company classifies this investment as low risk.

CONTRACT 2

The customer is the government of a country in the Middle East. The contract is in two stages. The first stage is for the provision of a single delivery of a major piece of equipment worth US$2,000 million. The terms are that a 50% deposit is to be paid when contracts are signed: the balance will be paid on delivery at the end of year 2. Payments for stage 1 will be in US$. A penalty of 10% of the contract value is payable if the contract overruns.

The second stage of the contract, starting in year 3, involves the supply of a large number of smaller pieces of equipment over a 3-year period. No additional capital investment will be required for this work, which is estimated to be worth £600 million. Payment for stage 2 will be in pounds sterling.

The second stage of the contract is relatively low risk, but there are high risks associated with the first stage. For example, the initial piece of equipment is state-of-the-art technology. This requires the full-time involvement of many of the company's design staff, and will mean the loss of some other business currently being considered by Spearhead. The incremental cash flows (net of any saving in capital outlay) associated with this lost business are estimated at £175 million in year 1 and £150 million in year 2.

The forecast cash flows, in nominal terms, are:

Stage one of contract 2

Initial capital expenditure	£500 million. This can be used on the second stage of the contract if it is awarded, but otherwise there is no residual value.
Sales income	As per contract details above.
Contract costs	£350 million in year 1 and £150 million in year 2.

Stage two of contract 2 (starting in year 3)

Sales income	£200 million per annum
Contract costs	£100 million per annum

Other information

- Estimated inflation rates per annum: UK 3%; Switzerland 2%; USA 4%.

- The risk-free rates are currently: UK 6%; Switzerland 5%; USA 7%. You have been instructed to assume that these remain the same for the duration of the contract.

- The expected return on the market is 12% per annum.

- The current spot rates are SFr3 to £1 and US$1.6 to £1.

- All cash flows occur at year end except where otherwise indicated.

- All raw materials and other costs associated with the supply of the equipment are sourced and paid for in the UK.

- The evaluation method used by Spearhead is to translate the foreign currency income into sterling and discount the cash flows at the appropriate sterling opportunity cost of capital.

- The company depreciates capital equipment on a straight-line basis over the life of the equipment, after adjusting for any estimated residual value.

- The company calculates its costs of equity using the CAPM and uses this to evaluate all sterling-denominated investments. However, because of the difficulties in determining discount rates for international investments, it uses a 'rule of thumb' approach and adjusts its cost of equity by a percentage for the estimated amount of risk involved, as follows.

High risk projects	cost of equity plus 5%
Medium risk	cost of equity plus 2%
Low risk	cost of equity

Ignore taxation throughout this question, including the calculation of capital allowances, in all aspects of your calculations.

Required

(a) Calculate, using the information given in the case:

   (i) The cost of equity
   (ii) The exchange rates to apply to the foreign currency cash flows of each of the contracts
   (iii) The net present value and annual return on assets of each of the contracts

   Make (and state in your answer) whatever assumptions you think necessary.

   Work to the nearest million units of currency (pounds sterling, SFr, US$). **(22 marks)**

(b) Assume you are a financial manager with Spearhead. Write a report to the board of Spearhead which recommends, with reasons, which contract, if either, should be chosen. You should include in your report comments on:

   (i) How each contract might contribute to the achievement of the company's objectives

   (ii) How the company has incorporated risk into its evaluation, and alternative methods of risk management which could be considered by the company

   (iii) The difficulties involved in evaluating mutually-exclusive projects of unequal risk and unequal lives

   (iv) The risks associated with international investment. **(28 marks)**

Note. If you have not been able to complete part (a) of this question, or think you have arrived at incorrect NPVs, answer part (b) in general terms but relate your answer to the company details in the case wherever possible.

(Total = 50 marks)

62 Question with analysis: Spearhead

90 mins

Background to the company and selected financial information

IT risk

Spearhead, a company based in the United Kingdom, manufactures **high-technology** landing and airport control equipment which it sells **worldwide**, mainly to **government departments**. The company was owned by the government of the United Kingdom until the 1980's and has demonstrated **strong growth** since privatisation, although it is **not the market leader** in the industry.

Trading risk

Growth potential

Political risk

Objectives

In its last financial year, the company had earnings of £360 million and earnings per share (EPS) of 60 pence. The current share price is **950** pence compared with **825** pence a year ago. The company's **equity beta is quoted at 1.5**.

CAPM

Growth

Company objectives

Financial objectives

Risk adjusted

Yearly not average

(i)   Investing in projects which yield a positive NPV when discounted at an **appropriate discount rate**

(ii)   Maintaining an **annual return** on assets at 25%

Hi-tech market share

Other objectives

The company aims to be the **leading UK supplier of airport control equipment** within the next 10 years and **retains a large proportion of its earnings for future investment**. It pays a relatively low annual cash dividend and aims to top this up with a **scrip dividend** each year.

Dividend and investment

↓ EPS

Spearhead is examining two potential contracts which will each require substantial capital investment. The timing of the bids, the amount of capital investment required, and the need for highly-specialised design staff mean that it can bid for **only one** of the two contracts. Details are as follows.

Mutually exclusive

Information on major contracts

CONTRACT 1

Low risk

The customer is the **Swiss government**. The contract is for the supply of radar-controlled landing equipment over a period of **four years** to a value of **SFr2,000 million**. Spearhead must agree a **fixed price in Swiss Francs** for the duration of the contract.

Period

Exchange risk

The forecast cash flows, in **nominal terms**, are:

Inflation

Initial capital expenditure	£300 million
Estimated residual value at the end of the project	£50 million
Income from sales	SFr 500 million per annum
Contract costs	£75 million per annum

Low NPV

The bidding for this contract was expected to be **fiercely competitive**. Despite the need for a fixed-price clause in the contract, the company classifies this investment as **low risk**.

Foreign exchange risk

Political

CONTRACT 2

Higher risk

The customer is the government of a **country in the Middle East**. The contract is in two stages. The first stage is for the provision of a single delivery of a major piece of equipment worth **US$2,000 million**. The terms are that a 50% deposit is to be paid when contracts are signed: the balance will be paid on delivery at the end of year 2. Payments for stage 1 will be in US$. **A penalty of 10% of the contract value is payable if the contract overruns**.

NPV impact

| Year 0 only |

The second stage of the contract, starting in year 3, involves the supply of a large number of smaller pieces of equipment over a 3-year period. **No additional capital investment** will be required for this work, which is estimated to be worth £600 million. Payment for stage 2 will be in **pounds sterling**.

| No foreign exchange risk |

| Cost of capital |

The second stage of the contract is **relatively low risk**, but there are **high risks associated with the first stage**. For example, the initial piece of equipment is **state-of-the-art technology**. This requires the full-time involvement of many of the company's design staff, and will mean the **loss of some other business** currently being considered by Spearhead. The incremental cash flows (net of any saving in capital outlay) associated with this lost business are estimated at £175 million in year 1 and £150 million in year 2.

| Meets objective |

| Opportunity cost |

| Inflation |

The forecast cash flows, in **nominal terms**, are:

Stage one of contract 2

| Initial capital expenditure | £500 million. This can be used on the second stage of the contract if it is awarded, but otherwise there is no residual value. |

| Sales income | As per contract details above. |

| Contract costs | £350 million in year 1 and £150 million in year 2. |

Stage two of contract 2 (starting in year 3)

| Sales income | £200 million per annum |
| Contract costs | £100 million per annum |

Other information

| PPP |

- **Estimated inflation rates** per annum: UK 3%; Switzerland 2%; USA 4%.

| CAPM R$_F$ |

- The risk-free rates are currently: **UK 6%; Switzerland 5%; USA 7%**. You have been instructed to assume that these remain the same for the duration of the contract.

| CAPM R$_M$ |

- The **expected return on the market is 12% per annum**.

| Year 0 |

- The current **spot rates** are SFr3 to £1 and US$1.6 to £1.

| No exchange risk, but no matching |

- All cash flows occur at year end except where otherwise indicated.

- All raw materials and other costs associated with the supply of the equipment **are sourced and paid for in the UK**.

| Need future exchange rate |

- The evaluation method used by Spearhead is to **translate the foreign currency income** into sterling and discount the cash flows at the appropriate **sterling opportunity cost of capital**.

| ROI |

- The company depreciates **capital equipment on a straight-line basis** over the life of the equipment, after adjusting for any estimated residual value.

- The company calculates its costs of equity using the CAPM and uses this to evaluate all sterling-denominated investments. However, because of the difficulties in determining discount rates for international investments, it uses a 'rule of thumb' approach and adjusts its cost of equity by a percentage for the estimated amount of risk involved, as follows.

  High risk projects – cost of equity plus 5%
  Medium risk – cost of equity plus 2%
  Low risk – cost of equity

| No tax |

Ignore taxation throughout this question, including the calculation of capital allowances, in all aspects of your calculations.

Required

(a)   Calculate, using the information given in the case:

(i)   The cost of equity
(ii)   The exchange rates to apply to the foreign currency cash flows of each of the contracts
(iii)   The net present value and **annual return** on assets of each of the contracts

ROI

Make (and state in your answer) whatever assumptions you think necessary.

Format

Work to the nearest million units of currency (pounds sterling, SFr, US$).   **(22 marks)**

(b)   Assume you are a financial manager with Spearhead. Write a **report** to the board of Spearhead which

Recommend

recommends, with reasons, which contract, if either, **should be chosen**. You should include in your report comments on:

(i)   How each contract might contribute to the achievement of the **company's objectives**

Above

(ii)   How the company has incorporated risk into its evaluation, and **alternative methods of risk**

Sensitivity

evaluation which could be considered by the company

Equivalent annual cost

(iii)   The difficulties involved in evaluating **mutually-exclusive projects** of unequal risk and unequal lives

(iv)   The risks associated with **international trade**.   **(28 marks)**

Note. If you have not been able to complete part (a) of this question, or think you have arrived at incorrect NPVs, answer part (b) in general terms but relate your answer to the company details in the case wherever possible.

(Total = 50 marks)

Answer plan

(a)   (i)   CAPM

–   Rf 6%
–   Rm 12%
–   Beta 1.5

(ii)   PPP

–   Francs/sterling 1.02/1.03
–   US dollars/sterling 1.04/1.03

(iii)   Use PPP to translate sales

Contract 1

NPV

–   ARR adjust assets for depreciation and take average
–   Profits = Sales – contract costs – Depreciation

Contract 2

Sales net of penalty

NPV

–   Include costs of lost business
–   COC 20% Years 1–2
–   Calculate without penalty

ARR

- Exclude costs of lost business
- Calculate without penalty

(b)   (i)

	Contract 1	Contract 2
Risk	Low political Realisable value?	High political initially Year 2 payment?
Discount rate	Cost of equity	Cost of equity + premium
NPV	Breakeven?	Breakeven with or without penalty
Foreign exchange exposure	Sales in Francs	Year 2 $ payments
Return on assets	25%?	25%

Other non-financial factors

- Reputation
- Technology
- Opportunity costs
- Other objectives – further business

(ii)   **Other risk methods**

- Payback time limit
- Sensitivity analysis
- Certainty equivalent
- Probability estimates
- Simulation

(iii)   – ROI – unequal lives
        – Use risk-adjusted NPV

(iv)   – Political
        – Economic
        – Transaction

Conclusion

(i)   Preferred option
(ii)   Fulfil objectives?

63 Premoco

90 mins

Background information

It is currently November 20X7. Premoco operates in oil and related industries. Its shares are quoted on the London Stock Exchange. In its retailing operations the company has concentrated on providing high-quality service and facilities at its service stations rather than competing solely on the price of petrol. Approximately 75% of its revenue and 60% of its profits are from sales of petrol, the remainder coming from other services (car wash and retail sales from its convenience stores which are available at each service station).

The company has been highly profitable in the past as a result of astute buying of petroleum products on the open market. The company does not enter into supplier agreements with the major oil companies except on very short-term deals. However, profit margins are now under increasing pressure as a result of intensifying competition and the cost of complying with environmental legislation.

Future strategy

The managing director of the company, David Wong, is assessing three possible acquisitions which would help the company increase the percentage of its non-petroleum revenue and profits.

Option 1. Nafco owns fifteen service stations in the south of England. These sites are of poor image, the company having, in the past, aimed at selling petrol at the lowest possible prices and providing little in the way of other services. However, the sites are in good locations and therefore suitable for renovation and development. The institutional investors in Nafco are known to be dissatisfied with the company's recent performance and can be expected to support a bid if the terms are right. Nafco's service stations are too small for the major oil companies to want to operate, so Premoco foresees little competition from alternative buyers. One of Premoco's suppliers of petroleum products has indicated it might be willing to provide development finance for up to 50% of the acquisition cost at only 5% interest per annum, repayable over ten years. However, this would involve Premoco entering into a long-term supply agreement for all fifteen sites.

Option 2. Oiltrans specialises in oil distribution from the depots owned by the major oil companies to their retail outlets. Its shares have been quoted on the stock market for the past two years. It operates a fleet of oil tankers, some owned and some leased. Premoco has used Oiltrans' services in the past and knows it has an up-to-date and well-managed fleet. However, a bid for Oiltrans would almost certainly be regarded as hostile and, as 40% of the shares are owned by the directors and their families, a successful bid is far from assured.

Option 3. Carsals owns six car showrooms in prestige locations, all of which operate the franchise of a major motor manufacturer. It is a long-established family-owned business which is not listed on a stock market. The managing director and major shareholder is planning to retire shortly and his children have shown no interest in taking over the business. He has therefore approached David Wong, whom he has known for some years, asking if Premoco would be interested in buying Carsals.

Premoco's financial advisors have produced estimates of the expected NPV and the first full-year post-merger earnings of Premoco with each of the three acquisition options. These are as follows.

	Estimated post-merger earnings in first full year following merger £ million	Estimated NPV of combined organisation £ million
Premoco plus Nafco	32	512
Premoco plus Oiltrans	35	595
Premoco plus Carsals	23	368

Financial statistics and other information on Premoco and the three possible acquisitions are shown below.

Extracts from Premoco's balance sheet at 30 June 20X7

	£ million	£ million
Non-current assets (NBV)		140.00
Current assets:		
Inventory and receivables	120.00	
Bank and cash	80.00	
		200.00
		340.00
Ordinary £1 share capital:		
(authorised £30 million)		
Issued		20.00
Reserves		180.00
Secured loan stock 8% redeemable in 8 years time		50.00
Current liabilities		90.00
		340.00

Summary financial statistics

	Premoco	Nafco	Oiltrans	Carsals
Last year end	30.6.X7	30.6.X7	30.6.X7	31.3.X7
Shares in issue (millions)	20	10	12	0.5
Earnings per share (pence)	103	75	85	160
Dividend per share (pence)	31	55	42	112
Share price (pence)	1,648	675	1,530	N/a
Net asset value (£ million)	250	60	65	6
Debt ratio (outstanding debt as				
% of total market value)	13.0	30.0	15.0	0
Forecast annual growth rate %	11	5	14	9
Beta co-efficient	1.2	0.9	1.3	1.25

(1) The forecast growth rates have been provided by Premoco's financial advisors. They are based on **publicly available information** and assume all companies continue to operate independently and that dividend policies, capital structure and risk characteristics remain unchanged.

(2) The beta shown for Carsals is the **equity beta** of a **larger**, **quoted company** in a similar line of business. This company has a gearing ratio (debt : debt + equity) of 20%. Assume a debt beta of zero.

You should ignore any taxation issues throughout this question.

Required

(a) Calculate, for Premoco and, where relevant, for the three acquisition options before the merger:

    (i)   The current market value and P/E ratio

    (ii)   The cost of equity using the CAPM

    (iii)   The prospective market value using the constant growth dividend valuation model

    assuming the return on the market is 12% and the return on the risk-free asset is 6%.   **(10 marks)**

(b) You now have up to three values for each company as an independent entity. These are the current market value and the value using the dividend valuation model (as you have calculated for part (a)), and asset value (given in the scenario).

Discuss the usefulness and limitations of each of these methods of company valuation to Premoco in its acquisition decision.   **(12 marks)**

(c)   Assume you are working as one of Premoco's financial advisors. Write a report to David Wong, the managing director, which discusses the following issues for *each* acquisition option:

(i)   The price to be offered to the target company's shareholders. You should recommend a range of terms within which Premoco should be prepared to negotiate

(ii) Whether cash or a share exchange would be the most appropriate method of financing the bid

(iii) The business implications (effect on existing operation, growth prospects, risk etc)

You should recognise that there is no single correct solution to the issues raised in this part of the case. The exercise is to assess and analyse the information available (state any assumptions you make), and then use your judgement to offer credible advice.   **(28 marks)**

(Total = 50 marks)

64 Garden World   90 mins

Garden World is a company specialising in horticultural and botanical products. It has two wholly product-centred divisions and a corporate head office. Its business to date has concentrated mainly on supplying retailers of garden products (garden centres), landscape gardeners and other major users and retailers of its products.

A summary balance sheet at 31 December 20X3 for the company is as follows.

	£m
Non-current assets (net of depreciation)	50.0
Net current assets	20.0
Total assets less current liabilities	70.0
Capital and reserves	
Called-up share capital – 50 million shares of 50p each	25.0
Reserves	25.0
12% debentures 20X9	20.0
	70.0

The debentures are secured on some of the company's land and buildings.

The shares are currently trading at 250 pence per share. The company's shareholders currently require a return of 15% on their investment.

Garden World is now considering a major investment programme. This will involve the creation of a new wholly owned retail subsidiary to operate a chain of garden centres in selected locations throughout the United Kingdom.

As Chief Accountant you have been asked to evaluate the proposed investment. You ask your Assistant Accountant to prepare a schedule of expected cash flows and total working capital requirements as a starting point for your appraisal.

	Year	0	1	2	3	4
		£'000	£'000	£'000	£'000	£'000
Land and buildings		5,000				
Fittings and equipment		1,000				
Working capital		500	600	750	800	800
Gross turnover			1,750	3,250	5,250	6,250
Direct costs			1,500	2,300	3,100	3,300
Marketing/advertising			300	450	400	400
Office overhead			250	250	250	250

Note. All expenditure should be assumed to take place at the end of each year, with the exception of capital expenditure and opening working capital which will take place immediately.

You discuss these figures with your assistant and ask her to obtain further information which you will need before you proceed with your investment appraisal. The following day she provides you with the following notes.

(a) Taxation is at present 33% and is expected to remain at this rate for the foreseeable future. The company will claim tax allowances on fittings and equipment at 25% on a reducing balance basis. Tax allowances are not available on land and buildings. Tax is paid one year in arrears.

(b) The company also depreciates its fittings and equipment at 25% on a reducing balance. It does not depreciate land and buildings.

(c) 50% of office overhead is an allocation of head office operating costs which will be charged to the new subsidiary.

(d) The cost of land and buildings includes £250,000 which has already been spent on surveyors' and other advisors' fees.

(e) The parent company expects to be able to sell the subsidiary at the end of year 4. It would expect to receive a sum equal to the book value of land and buildings, the written-down value of fittings and equipment and working capital plus three times year 4's post-tax profits.

(f) Forecast inflation for trading income and all costs and expenses is 4% per annum.

(g) The risk-free rate of interest is at present 8%. You may assume this rate will not change during the life of the project.

You are keen to provide the worth of the investment as you have been told by the Managing Director that the company intends to promote you to be Finance Director of the new subsidiary if the investment goes ahead. However, you are aware that your appraisal must be realistic as it will be judged not only on the actual performance of the subsidiary but also on the comparison of actual with your forecasts.

You are therefore concerned that the appraisal should take adequate account of the risks of the new venture. After assessing the various methods available for incorporating risk into the investment decision, you decide to use the certainty equivalent approach. Based on the probabilities used to estimate the expected cash flows for each year of the project's life, and your estimates of the rates of return which investors require for investments of different levels of risk, you calculate the following certainty equivalents.

Year	Certainty equivalent
1	0.90
2	0.85
3	0.80
4	0.75
5	0.70

Required

(a) Advise the board of Garden World whether to proceed with this new venture. Base your advice solely on the information presented so far in the case and ignore any possible group tax effects such as rollover relief or capital losses brought forward. **(16 marks)**

(b) The information provided for part (a) of this question is necessarily simplified for examination conditions.

(i) Describe how your appraisal might differ in real life from the one you have just produced.

(ii) Identify any judgmental factors which should be taken into account by the board before it takes the investment decision. **(8 marks)**

(c) The use of certainty equivalents is one method of adjusting for investment risk.

Discuss, two other methods which you might have used. **(6 marks)**

The company decides to proceed with the venture and the directors discuss how it will be financed. The Managing Director would like to finance it with equity because he believes this minimises the overall risk. The Finance Director agrees with the Managing Director's comment on risk but suggests that, as the company is substantially equity-financed at present, an increase in the amount of debt in the capital structure would be quite acceptable to the market and could have a favourable effect on the share price. The Finance Director produces the following table of types of medium to long-term debt and the associated average costs.

	%
Medium-term borrowing (1 to 5 years)	8.5
Long-term borrowing (over 5 years)	9.5
Convertibles with conversion dates between 5 and 10 years	9.0
Preference shares	9.5

Required

(d)   Discuss the suitability of each of these types of borrowing in the circumstances of this case.   **(8 marks)**

During the period of the company's evaluation of the investment and method of financing, interest rates start to rise as a result of economic and political factors. The equity market however appears strong and set to improve further over a period of 12 to 18 months. The company is now undecided about whether to issue debt or equity and calls in a merchant bank to advise on the decision.

Required

(e)   Explain what services a merchant bank might provide to Garden World in connection with an issue of new capital.   **(6 marks)**

(f)   Describe the factors which should be considered in establishing:

(i)   The method of issue
(ii)   The issue price

if the company decides to finance the investment with equity.   **(6 marks)**

(Total = 50 marks)

65 Almond Arts   90 mins

Almond Arts manufactures and distributes paint and related products to the building trade. It has traded for over 40 years and has been listed on the UK stock market for a number of years. The shares are now widely held, with approximately 75 per cent in the hands of institutional investors. Draft, abbreviated financial statements for the year to 31 December 20X1 are attached. The company's directors are considering a rights issue to help finance an expansion programme. The first phase of the expansion will involve expenditure of £3 million on non-current assets and £1 million on inventory in 20X2. Additional capital expenditure of £2 million will be required in 20X3.

Assume you are assistant to the finance director. You have been asked to provide some key financial data and supporting evidence for discussion by the board. You have so far obtained the following information based on the assumption that the expansion will go ahead. *Using the draft accounts for the year to 31 December 20X1 as a base:*

- Revenues are expected to grow by 5 per cent in the financial year ending 31 December 20X2. This increased level of sales is expected to be at least maintained in 20X3 and beyond.

- The ratio of cost of sales excluding depreciation to sales (revenues) will improve in 20X1 by 2.6 percentage points as a result of improved buying procedures.

- Operating expenses in 20X2 are expected to be held constant at the year 20X1 level as a result of organisational restructuring and efficiency measures. However, this will involve a one-off charge of £125,000 during the year for redundancy payments.

Other relevant information is as follows.

The company's tax accountant estimates that tax payable for 20X2 will be £850,000. Assume tax is paid in the year in which the liability occurs.

The ratios of *receivables to sales* and *payables to cost of sales less depreciation* are expected to remain the same in 20X2 as in 20X1. Operating expenses are paid in the year in which they occur.

No sales of non-current assets are planned for the next two years. Depreciation on existing and new assets will be £1.2 million in 20X2.

Dividends are payable in the year after they are declared. The company plans to maintain the 20X1 payout ratio in 20X2.

The company's cost of equity is 14 per cent per annum. It uses this rate to evaluate new investments but a full appraisal has not yet been carried out for the expansion proposals.

Assume interest charges for 20X2 will relate only to payment on existing fixed rate debt (ie no overdraft interest will be payable).

Inflation is anticipated at between 2 per cent and 3 per cent per annum for 20X2. Interest rates on long-term bonds suggest that inflation is likely to rise above 3 per cent in 20X3.

Financial objectives

The company's financial objectives are stated as follows.

- To earn an annual after tax return on shareholders' funds (as at the end of each financial year) of at least 25 per cent

- To increase earnings per share and dividends per share by at least 10 per cent per year

- To increase share price year on year without taking undue risk

DRAFT INCOME STATEMENT FOR THE YEAR TO 31 DECEMBER 20X1

	£'000
Revenues	16,500
Cost of sales (note 1)	11,600
Operating expenses	1,750
Operating profit	3,150
Interest	200
Tax	885
Net profit	2,065
Dividends declared	1,136
Retained profits	929

DRAFT BALANCE SHEET AT 31 DECEMBER 20X1

	£'000
Assets	
Non-current assets (net book value)	7,500
Current assets	
Inventory	2,850
Receivables	1,675
Cash and bank	55
	12,080

EQUITY AND LIABILITIES

	£'000
Equity	
Ordinary share capital (ordinary shares of £1)	5,000
Net retained earnings	2,194
	7,194
Long-term liabilities	
10% loan stock 20X6	2,000
Current liabilities	
Trade payables	1,750
Other payables	1,136
	12,080

Notes

1   Including depreciation of £925,000.

2   *Share price information (pence)*

As at 31 December 20X0:	465p	Range for year (1.1.X0 – 31.12.X0)	425p-535p
As at today (31 December 20X1):	525p	Range for year (1.1.X1 – 31.12.X1)	515p-565p

3   *Other financial information for 20X0*

EPS	37.2p
DPS	20.5p
After tax return on shareholders' funds	26.2%

Required

Assume that today is 31 December 20X1. Prepare:

(a)   (i)   A forecast income statement for the year to 31 December 20X2

(ii)   A forecast balance sheet as at 31 December 20X2

(iii)   A cash flow forecast for 20X2 (this is not an investment appraisal and you do not need to discount your cash flows)

(iv)   Calculations of after tax return on shareholders' funds, earnings per share and dividends per share for the two years 20X1 and 20X2.

Notes

Work to the nearest £'000 for parts (i) and (ii).

Assume that the expansion is to be part-funded by a rights issue of 1 for 10 at 475 pence. Ignore issue costs.   **(20 marks)**

(b)   Write a report to the finance director of Almond Arts in which you:

(i)   Discuss the key aspects and implications of the financial information you have obtained in your answer to part (a) of the question, in particular whether the company is likely to achieve its financial objectives in the years to 31 December 20X1 and 20X2. Include in your discussion comments on the suitability of the financial objectives for the company in its present circumstances and advise on alternative objectives which the directors could consider.

(ii)   Explain the need for financing in 20X2 and discuss alternative types of finance that might be suitable for the company at the present time. Use relevant data from the scenario and your answers to part (a) of the question, plus any additional calculations you think appropriate and relevant. Make whatever assumptions you think necessary. If you have been unable to complete your calculations for part (a), use your assumptions as the basis for discussions.

(iii) Discuss the difficulties of incorporating inflation into forecasts and comment on how a rate of inflation exceeding the 2-3 per cent anticipated for 20X2 might affect the achievement of the objectives (you are not expected to rework your figures).

(iv) Recommend a course of action for the board to consider. **(30 marks)**

(Total = 50 marks)

66 Eros (FLFS, 5/01) 90 mins

Company's business and background

Eros is an unquoted company that specialises in corporate design products, including web page designs. It was formed and has been trading for 4 years and has obtained a reputation for being one of the most innovative and technologically advanced operators in this particular field.

The company was formed by Eric Dee and Oscar George. The company borrowed £50,000 from the bank, secured on the two shareholders' personal property. It is repayable in 20X7. Interest is paid at 10% each year.

When the company was launched, it operated from rented premises and leased much of its computing equipment. It has subsequently bought additional and replacement equipment and other assets such as furniture and fittings. It has also moved premises and has taken out a 25-year lease on office premises that are large enough to allow for significant expansion.

The company now employs 15 people and is planning to recruit additional designers and programmers to handle a large new contract it is hoping to obtain from a supermarket group. Eros 'outsources' most administrative and accounting functions.

Future plans

The company's two owners/directors have been approached by the marketing department of an investment bank and asked whether they have considered using venture capital financing to expand the business. No detailed proposal has been made but the bank has implied that a venture capital company would require a substantial percentage of the equity in return for a large injection of capital. The venture capitalist would want to exit from the investment in 4 to 5 years' time.

Neither Eric nor Oscar is wholly convinced that such a large injection of capital is appropriate for the company at the present time. Their objective has been to obtain a stock market listing in 2 to 3 years' time if their most optimistic expectations are realised. This would allow them to get some money back on their investment by selling some of their shares at the same time as raising additional funds for the company's expansion. However, the two directors have little financial expertise and have decided to take some independent advice from their accountants before responding to the investment bank.

Assume you are employed by Eros's firm of accountants. You have been asked to advise Eric and Oscar about the company's current financial position and the various financing alternatives available to maximise Eros's growth potential. You spend some time reviewing the company's financial affairs and discussing future prospects with the directors and staff. You have managed to obtain the following information.

Financial information

Past data

Turnover has grown from £50,000 in the first year of operations to £750,000 last year, the year to 31 March 20X1. However, the company sustained losses in the first 3 years of operations and made only a small operating profit last year. The apparent poor results are primarily because of high research costs relative to sales. These were written off during the year. Expenditure on research and development will continue but not at such high levels. Other financial data for the year to 31 March 20X1 is as follows.

Shares in issue (ordinary £1 shares)	10,000
Earnings per share	125 pence
Dividend per share	0
Net asset value	£385,000

Note

The net assets of Eros are the net book values of purchased and/or leased buildings, equipment and vehicles plus net working capital. The book valuations are considered to reflect current realisable values

Forecasts

The company's forecast sales turnover for the year to 31 March 20X2 is heavily dependent on whether or not the company obtains the new contract from the supermarket group. If it does, forecast sales turnover is £1.8 million for the year. The company's directors think they have a 50% chance of getting this contract. Although this contract will be prestigious for Eros and should lead to a long-term business relationship, the terms will prevent Eros from undertaking work for the supermarket's competitors, a number of whom have also shown interest in the company's designs. If Eros does not get this contract, it will bid for other work which is likely to be less profitable.

Sales turnover for the following year, to 31 March 20X3, is dependent to some extent on the outcome of the year to 31 March 20X2. Estimated turnover and probabilities are as follows.

	Estimate for year to 31 March 20X2		*Estimates for year to 31 March 20X3*	
Probability	*Turnover*		*Probability*	*Turnover*
	£'000			£'000
0.5	1,800	(Outcome 1)	0.8	2,500
			0.2	3,000
0.3	1,200	(Outcome 2)	0.5	1,700
			0.5	1,400
0.2	800	(Outcome 3)	0.5	1,000
			0.5	800

Operating costs, inclusive of depreciation, are expected to average 35% of turnover in the year to 31 March 20X2, reducing to 30% in the year to 31 March 20X3 as a result of economies of scale. Interest costs will remain at the present level for both years.

Tax is expected to be payable at 30%. Assume book depreciation equals tax allowances for tax purposes. Also assume that profit after interest and tax equals free cash flow.

Growth in earnings in each of the years to 31 March 20X4 and 20X5 is expected to be 40%, falling to 10% each year after that. This assumes that no new long-term capital is raised. If the firm is to grow at a faster rate, then new financing will be needed.

Competitors/industry information

This is a niche market and there are relatively few listed companies doing precisely what Eros does. However, if the definition of the industry is extended to include all companies involved in electronic design and associated products, the following figures are relevant.

P/E ratios

Industry average	27
Range (individual companies)	12 to 82

Increase in market capitalisation over the past 24 months

Industry average	22%
Range (individual companies)	−10% to +2,000%

Cost of equity

Industry average (net of tax)	16%
Individual companies	Not available

Share price movements of competitor companies are extremely volatile. Recently, two similar companies, one listed two years ago and one unquoted, have gone into liquidation. These and other failures of Internet-style companies have caused widespread concern. Calls for improved regulation of 'new economy' companies have been made, largely because of the huge potential debts involved in some cases and suspicions of trading irregularities. Tougher regulatory controls might address the composition of boards of directors and require more substantial trading history before flotation can be considered.

Required

(a) Write a report to the directors of Eros that explains the various methods by which the company might be valued and the alternative types of financing available for expansion. You should include in your report:

  (i) Calculation of a range of values for the company that could be used in negotiation with a venture capitalist, using whatever information is currently available and relevant. Make and state whatever assumptions you think are necessary. **(15 marks)**

  (ii) Discussion of the methods of valuation you have used. Explain, briefly, the relevance of each method to a company such as Eros. **(9 marks)**

  (iii) Discussion of the advantages and disadvantages of using either venture capital financing to assist with expansion or alternatively a flotation on the stock market in 2 to 3 years' time. Include in your discussion likely exit routes for the venture capital company. **(9 marks)**

  (iv) Discussion of alternative types of financial support that could be used by Eros to assist the company to expand. Advise on the issues that the directors should consider before deciding on the most appropriate type of finance. **(9 marks)**

(b) Advise the company's directors on what actions/measures the company might take to protect itself against the risk of loss of key staff with technical expertise. **(8 marks)**

(Total = 50 marks)

67 Margate (FLFS, 11/01)   90 mins

Margate Group is a large, long-established company whose primary interests are in transport and distribution within the United Kingdom. It is considering a bid to acquire Hastings, a company also in the transport and distribution industry. Hastings, however, has a strong operations base in Europe as well as in the UK. Both companies are listed on a recognised stock exchange. They both have a wide share ownership including many institutional investors.

Hastings has recently fought off a bid from a company based in the United States of America and has made a public statement that it will defend itself against any future bids. The company has recently won a fiercely contested five-year contract to undertake transport and distribution services for a major supermarket group. Margate Group also tendered for this contract. Press comment suggests this contract will allow Hastings' earnings to grow at 10% a year for at least the next five years. However, some industry experts believe Hastings tendered a price that was so low that the contract could result in very little profit, or even losses.

If the acquisition were to succeed, it would create the largest company of its kind in the UK. A concern is that this would attract the interest of the competition authorities. However, as both companies have recently restructured their operations, redundancies are likely to be few and concentrated mainly in central administration.

Financial Statements

Key financial information for the two companies for the latest financial year is given below. All figures are in £ million unless otherwise stated.

INCOME STATEMENTS
FOR THE YEAR TO 31 AUGUST 20X1

	Margate Group £m	Hastings £m
Revenues	2,763	1,850
Operating costs	1,950	1,380
Operating profit	813	470
Net interest	125	85
Profit before tax	688	385
Tax	185	85
Earnings	503	300
Dividends declared	201	135
Retained profit for the year	302	165
Earnings per shares (pence)	47.90	35.29
EPS for year to 31 August 20X0 (pence)	34.85	29.50

BALANCE SHEETS AT 31 AUGUST 20X1

	Margate Group £m	Hastings £m
Non-current assets (net book value)	3,250	2,580
Current assets		
Inventory	125	175
Receivables	550	425
Cash at bank	450	45
Net assets	4,375	3,225
Equity and liabilities		
Equity		
Issued share capital (ordinary £1 shares)	1,050	850
Revaluation reserve	220	150
Retained earnings	750	450
Total shareholders' funds	2,020	1,450
Non-current liabilities		
Debenture	1,450	950
Taxation	150	40
	1,600	990
Current liabilities		
Bank loans and overdrafts	0	420
Other	755	365
	755	785
Total liabilities	2,355	1,775
Total equity and liabilities	4,375	3,225

Note. Margate Group's debenture is 8%, repayable 20X5. Hastings' is 9%, repayable 20X4.

Share price information (prices in pence)

	Margate Group	Hastings
Share price movements: High for last financial year	705	590
Low for last financial year	470	440
Share price today (20 November 20X1)	671	565
P/E ratios today	14	16
Equity betas	1.1	1.2

Other information

- The average P/E for the industry is currently estimated as 13.

- The return on the market is currently estimated as 12%, the risk-free rate as 6%. These rates are expected to remain constant for the next 12 months and are post-tax.

- The average debt ratio for the industry (long-term debt as proportion of total long-term funding) is 30% based on book values

- Economic forecasts provided by Margate Group's financial advisors expect inflation and interest rates to remain at their current levels for the foreseeable future. Inflation is currently 2% a year.

Terms of the proposed bid

Margate Group's directors are planning to offer a share exchange to Hastings' shareholders.

Required

(a) Calculate and discuss briefly three key ratios for both companies that are relevant to the evaluation of the proposed acquisition. **(9 marks)**

(b) Calculate a range of possible values that Margate Group could place on Hastings.

Accompany your calculations by brief comments or explanations. Where necessary, explain any assumptions you have made **(9 marks)**

(c) Assume you are the Financial Manager with Margate Group. Write a report to the directors of the group that evaluates the proposed acquisition.

You should use the figures you have calculated in answer to parts (a) and (b) to support your recommendations/advice where relevant. If you have not been able to do the calculations for parts (a) and (b), you should make, and state, appropriate assumptions.

Your report should include the following.

(i) Recommend to the directors a bid price and offer terms, assuming a share-for-share exchange.

(ii) Advise on a strategy for making the offer to Hastings to minimise the likelihood of outright rejection by the Hastings board, and discuss the other risks involved in making the bid.

(iii) Discuss the strategic and financial advantages that might arise from the acquisition by Margate Group of Hastings.

Support your discussion with calculations of the post-acquisition value of the combined group and how the estimated gains are likely to be split between the shareholders of Margate Group and Hastings. **(32 marks)**

(Total = 50 marks)

68 KL (FLFS, 5/02)

Background of company

KL Group provides a range of products and services for sale in the United Kingdom and overseas. Its shares are listed on the London Stock Exchange and are widely held, although institutions hold the majority of shares. The company is structured as a group of wholly-owned subsidiaries. Each subsidiary specialises in a particular product or service.

Financial data

Key data for the year to 31 December 20X1 is as follows:

Turnover	£850 million
Earnings	£105 million
Shares in issue	250 million
Share price as at today (21 May 20X2)	331 pence
Weighted average cost of capital (WACC) for the Group	14% (nominal net of tax rate)

Company objectives

The company has two stated objectives:

- To increase operating cash flow and dividends per share year-on-year by at least 5%.

- To increase the wealth of our shareholders whilst respecting the interests of our employees, customers and other stakeholders and operating to the highest ethical standards.

Future plans

The directors are considering establishing a new subsidiary company, KL15, to process industrial waste. The subsidiary will require a factory. The directors have identified that the factory used by a long-established subsidiary, KL3, is currently operating at only 50% capacity. This factory could be converted for use by the new subsidiary at a cost of £1.3 million. KL3's annual net (after-tax) earnings are £1.5 million. This subsidiary's operations would cease immediately the decision to proceed with KL15 is taken, as it will take some months to convert the factory.

However, the company is aware that the government is reviewing the environmental controls currently in operation for waste processing and it is possible that tougher regulations will be introduced. Industry spokesmen are attempting to argue that current controls are adequate. Nevertheless, the directors of the KL Group wish to consider the situation should these tougher controls be introduced and two alternative methods of equipping the new subsidiary have been proposed by the company's technical advisers.

The company has sufficient cash available from a recent disposal to finance the capital costs of the new subsidiary under either alternative.

Alternative 1

This alternative will equip the factory to process waste to the highest environmental standards that the government regulations might impose. This would require the purchase of very expensive, specialised machinery from the USA. This machinery would have to be ordered and delivery time is approximately 6 months, which would coincide with completion of the factory conversion. The cost of this machinery is currently US$12 million but the price of the equipment is likely to rise by 5% over the next 6 months. If an order is placed immediately (year 0), together with a 50% deposit, the supplier will hold today's price. The balance of the purchase price is payable 6 months after installation. The current exchange rate, US$ to £1 sterling, is 1.45. Inflation in the USA is forecast to be 4% over the next 12 months. In the UK it is forecast to be 2.5%.

This equipment is not likely to need replacement for at least 8 years.

Forecast revenues for KL15 under this alternative are as follows. The probabilities are based on forecasts of the economy in the UK and the main overseas trading areas where the KL Group plc hopes to sell its services.

	Year 1 (6 months of operating)			Year 2			Year 3		
Revenues (£m)	0.5	2.5	3.5	8.5	10.5	12.5	10.5	13.5	16.0
Probability	0.4	0.5	0.1	0.4	0.5	0.1	0.4	0.5	0.1
Expected revenues (£m)	1.8			9.9			12.55		

The probabilities of sales for year 2 or 3 and beyond are assumed to be independent of the achievement of the previous year's sales.

The costs are as follows:

- Cash operating costs are expected to have a fixed element of £1.5 million each year starting as soon as the factory starts work, plus a variable element of 30% of sales revenue. A full year's fixed costs will be charged to production in year 1.

- Redundancy payments of £1.2 million will be necessary for staff from the KL3 subsidiary. These would be payable immediately.

- The costs of the factory conversion will be incurred during the 6 months following the decision to proceed but, for simplicity, it can be assumed that these are paid at the end of year 1.

- The availability of tax allowances and other tax reliefs mean that no tax is likely to be payable until year 4. For year 4 onwards a rough estimate suggests 20% of annual net cash flows (revenue less cash operating costs) will be payable in tax.

Alternative 2

To plan for a continuation of, or modest improvement to, current regulations and produce accordingly. This alternative has greater flexibility as there is a much larger market, worldwide, for processing waste at a lower and therefore much cheaper specification. The capital cost to the KL Group would also be much lower at £2.5 million. Equipment for this alternative is readily available in the UK and can be bought when the factory conversion is completed. However, the equipment is likely to need to be replaced in 6 years' time from the date of purchase.

The revenues shown below are forecast using similar methods as used in Alternative 1. However, sales will be made to a wider range of customers, many in developing countries.

	Year 1 (6 months of operating)			Year 2			Year 3		
Revenues (£m)	3.5	4.5	5.5	4.5	6.5	7.5	8.5	9.5	11.5
Probability	0.2	0.6	0.2	0.2	0.6	0.2	0.2	0.6	0.2
Expected revenues (£m)	4.5			6.3			9.7		

Costs are as follows:

- Fixed cash operating costs will be £1.2 million each year; variable costs will be 15% of sales revenue.

- With this alternative, there will be fewer redundancies from KL3 and the associated costs will be only 20% of those for Alternative 1.

- Costs of factory conversion are as Alternative 1.

- Tax relief will be similar to Alternative 1, that is, no tax will be payable until year 4 when tax will become payable at 20% of annual net cash flow (revenue less cash operating costs).

Required

(a)   Calculate net present values for the new subsidiary (KL15) under the two alternatives, using whatever assumptions you think are appropriate. Include brief comments on your assumptions.   **(15 marks)**

(b)   Assume you are the company's financial manager. Write a report to the directors that:

  (i)   Discuss how the new subsidiary and the two alternatives might contribute to the attainment of the Group's objectives. Refer to the figures you have calculated in answer to part (a) where appropriate
.   **(10 marks)**

  (ii)   Analyses and discusses the various types of risk and limitation involved in each alternative.
   (10 marks)

  (iii)   Recommends, which, if either, of the alternatives should be chosen. Your recommendation should take into account all aspects of your evaluation as discussed in parts (b) (i) and (b) (ii) of this question.   **(5 marks)**

  You should provide any additional calculations that you consider appropriate to support your discussion and analysis.

(c)   Option pricing theory was originally developed to apply to share prices. The theory can also be applied to capital investment options, sometimes known as 'real options'.

  Discuss the option features involved in the KL Group's decision and explain, briefly, the benefits of including such options in the investment appraisal process.   **(10 marks)**

  (Total = 50 marks)

69 Dobbs (FLFS, 5/03)   90 mins

Dobbs is an international publishing company based in the United Kingdom. It has recently sold a subsidiary that publishes technical journals, a field the company considered to be non-core business. The sale raised £30 million in cash. The directors are evaluating what they consider to be a very promising acquisition opportunity and the cash raised from the sale of the subsidiary would be used as part of the financing arrangement.

Potential investment in a new subsidiary

Alice Jain is an American publisher that has two main divisions. One division publishes books, mainly 'blockbuster' type fiction, and the other publishes 'lifestyle' magazines. Both divisions have seen strong growth over the past five years as a result of changes in the public's magazine-buying habits and also because of two high-selling authors whom the company contracted before they became popular. These contracts have between three and five years to run before they are re-negotiated. Many industry observers think Alice Jain has been successful because of good luck rather than good judgement and that with stronger management the company could become a major international publisher.

Alice Jain is privately owned (that is, it does not have a listing on a stock market). There are approximately 50 shareholders although 60% of the shares are owned by the husband and wife partnership that started the business 25 years ago. Dobbs' directors have already made an informal approach to Alice Jain's directors and believe they will be receptive to an offer if terms can be agreed. No announcement has yet been made to the press or to Dobbs' shareholders about their intentions.

On the basis of industry information and private sources, Dobbs' directors forecast the following cash flows from Alice Jain:

Year	1	2	3	4
Net cash flows ($ millions)	35.5	43.5	46.5	52.5

Notes

(1) The spot $US / £ exchange rate is 1.45. Forecast economic data relevant to the USA and the UK is as follows:

	USA	UK
Risk-free rates for each year	3.5%	4.5%
Inflation rates for each year	2.5%	3.2%

Assume the theory of interest rate parity applies when forecasting exchange rates.

(2) The cash flows are in real terms. Dobbs evaluates all its investment decisions at its domestic, post-tax cost of capital, which is a nominal 11%. It evaluates international investments by converting the foreign currency cash flows to sterling and applying its domestic cost of capital of 11%. The cost of capital for Alice Jain is not known. Dobbs' Finance Director has used the capital asset pricing model to assist in the calculation of a discount rate based on the published information about a quoted British company with a similar commercial and financial profile to Alice Jain. He has calculated that the proxy company's nominal, post-tax cost of capital is 13%.

(3) When evaluating investments, Dobbs ignores cash flows beyond four years and terminal values.

Financing of the acquisition

Dobbs' directors are considering offering Alice Jain's shareholders either shares in Dobbs or a cash alternative. The two majority shareholders are likely to take 50% shares, 50% cash as there are tax advantages to a share exchange. This will use up most of the cash from the sale of the subsidiary. The cash for the remaining shareholders will have to be raised by Dobbs increasing its borrowing. The 'worst case' scenario is that the remaining shareholders (that is, those except the two major shareholders) will all opt for cash.

Finance Director's concerns

Dobbs' long-term debt to equity ratio is relatively high compared with other publishing companies of similar size. The Finance Director thinks some of the cash raised from the sale of the subsidiary should be used to purchase a small British publishing company at an approximate cost of £15 million. The remaining cash should then be used to repay some of Dobbs' outstanding debt. The other directors disagree and believe the financial risk of investing in Alice Jain will be justified by substantial value enhancement strategies that can be put in place following the acquisition.

Summary financial information on bidder and target companies

	Dobbs £ million	Alice Jain $ million
Profit and loss account for 12 months to December 20X2		
Revenues	251.5	75.8
Operating profit	65.6	20.9
Interest payable	12.0	2.0
Profit before tax	53.6	18.9
Taxation	15.0	7.0
Balance sheet at 31 December 20X2		
Non-current assets	195.0	45.0
Net current assets	75.0	25.0
Total assets less current liabilities	270.0	70.0
Net assets	145.0	55.0
Ordinary share capital		
Ordinary shares of £1	45.0	
Common stock of $1		15.0
Total reserves	100.0	40.0
Equity shareholders' funds	145.0	55.0
Long-term debt	125.0	15.0

Current share price for Dobbs is 885 pence. High and low share prices for the past 12 months were 925 pence and 755 pence respectively.

No share price is available for Alice Jain.

Assume you are a financial manager with Dobbs.

Required

(a) (i) Calculate the present value of the investment/acquisition's cash flows and explain your method of evaluation, including your choice of discount rate.

(ii) Calculate the number of shares Dobbs might need to issue and the amount of debt that might need to be raised in the 'worst case' scenario. Include brief comments to explain your calculations.

(16 marks)

(b) Write a report to the directors of Dobbs, evaluating the potential acquisition. You should include in your report:

(i) A recommendation, with reasons, of whether the investment should proceed and at what price

(ii) Advice on strategies for enhancing the value of the combined company following the acquisition

(iii) Discussion of the Finance Director's recommendation to acquire a smaller company and repay some debt

(iv) Advice on Dobbs' directors' responsibilities to ensure fair and equal treatment for all shareholders in accordance with current takeover regulation

Use additional calculations to support your arguments wherever relevant and appropriate.

Note: Marks are distributed roughly equally between these four sections of the report.   **(34 marks)**

(Total = 50 marks)

70 C&C Airlines (FLFS, 11/03)   90 mins

Background to company

C&C Airlines operates a small fleet of aeroplanes from an airport in the United Kingdom. Its business is aimed at low-budget travellers on short-haul flights. The company was formed some years ago by a group of private investors who continue to own the company. Two of these investors take an active role in the management of the company as executive directors.

The shareholders' objective is long-term capital growth. They have taken relatively low dividends out of the company since its incorporation. The strategy has been to accept low, or no, profits, and build the brand name and market share in its niche market. Their 'exit strategy' is eventually to sell a majority holding in the company following either a stock market flotation or private sale of shares to another company.

Assets and turnover

C&C Airlines currently owns 12 planes, mainly Boeing 737s. It has bought all of them second-hand from the major airlines.

The company's total net assets are currently, and realistically, valued at £130 million. It is all-equity financed. The turnover in the last full financial year was £85 million. The forecast turnover for the current year is £98 million. Profits after tax are forecast as £18 million.

Proposed investment

The company's directors are examining a proposal for a strategic move into the long-haul market. The initial investment involves the purchase of a five-year-old Boeing 757, which will be used to fly to and from the Caribbean. Negotiations to buy this plane are already underway. C&C Airlines plans to operate the plane for three years and replace it at the end of this time with a newer model.

When fully loaded, this type of plane will carry 220 passengers. The company estimates an average return fare of £300 per passenger on this route. All income will be received in £ sterling. The company's estimates of average passenger loading are as follows:

	Probability of load being achieved	
Load	Year 1	Year 2-3
100% (all seats taken)	10%	15%
80% full	50%	60%
50% full	30%	20%
40% full	10%	5%

The plane is expected to make 6 return trips every week and be operational 48 weeks of the year.

The capital costs of the purchase of the plane are US$ 30 million. To date, C&C Airlines plc has spent £500,000 on market research and purchase negotiations. Other financial data associated with the venture are:

- Capital allowances are available at 25% on a reducing balance of the total capital cost.
- The estimated resale value of the plane 3 years after purchase, in nominal terms, is $16 million.

Cash operating costs (per annum)

Sterling-denominated costs such as maintenance, insurance, crew wages, salaries and training	£2.9 million
US$-denominated fuel costs	US$ 4.2 million

Overheads and other costs (per annum)

Administration and office space	£0.3 million
These costs include a £50,000 re-allocation of current head office costs.	
Advertising and promotion	£0.35 million

Estimates of increases in income and income costs

The figures given above are all in nominal terms as at today. Because this is an increasingly competitive market, the company is unlikely to be able to increase fares in line with inflation. The best estimate is an annual increase of 2%. Operating costs (excluding fuel) are expected to increase by the annual UK rate of inflation (3%). Forecasting fuel costs is very difficult but best estimates are that they will rise by 5% each year over the next 3 years. Assume these inflationary increases commence in the first year of operations. Overheads and other costs are expected to be held constant in nominal terms.

Currency and inflation rates

- Current spot exchange rate is US$ 1.53/£1

- Estimated per annum inflation rates are as follows:

UK	3%
USA	4%

  Inflation rates in the UK and USA are expected to remain at these levels.

Allowing for risks

The company evaluates investments by discounting cash flows at 9% per annum nominal and applying certainty equivalents to net after-tax cash flows. The estimates for the proposed investment are shown below:

Year	Certainty equivalent
1	0.90
2	0.85
3	0.80

The company's new Finance Director would prefer to use a risk-adjusted discount rate. A competitor company to C&C Airlines has a quoted equity beta of 1.3 and a debt : equity ratio (based on market values) of 1 : 4. This is unlikely to change in the foreseeable future. The post-tax return on the market is expected to be 12% and the risk-free rate 5%. Assume a debt beta of 0.15.

Assumptions:

- Capital costs are paid immediately but all other cash flows occur at the year-end

- Taxation at 30% is paid or repaid at the end of the year in which the liability/repayment arises (that is, no time lag)

- The plane is acquired and becomes operational immediately

Required

(a) Calculate the discount rate to be used in the investment decision using the CAPM and comment, briefly, on the limitations of using the CAPM in the circumstances here.

The relevant formula here is:

$$\beta u = \beta g \left[\frac{V_E}{V_E + V_D(1-t)} \right] + \beta_d \left[\frac{V_D(1-t)}{V_E + V_D(1-t)} \right]$$ **(5 marks)**

(b) Calculate the £ sterling NPV of the proposed investment in the new plane using:

(i) The discount rate calculated in (a) above, rounded to the nearest 1%; and

(ii) A discount rate of 9% per annum nominal and adjusting for the company's estimated certainty equivalents,

and recommend, briefly, whether to proceed with the investment, based solely on your calculations above.

NPV should be calculated in sterling, converting US$ cash flows to sterling. Assume the theory of purchasing power parity applies when calculating exchange rates. **(20 marks)**

(c) Assume you are the assistant to the Finance Director. On his behalf, draft a report to the board that critically evaluates the following:

(i) The major economic forces that might impact on, or influence, the success of the investment
(ii) Commercial aspects of the investment that involve the greatest uncertainty and risk
(iii) Strategies for managing the risks discussed in parts (c)(i) and (c)(ii)

The report should conclude with a recommendation of a course of action. **(25 marks)**

(Total = 50 marks)

71 RGB (FLFS, 11/04)   90 mins

Background

RGB is a computer technology business based in the UK. It was listed until 4 years ago but following disagreements between the Board and major shareholders, the directors and senior managers bought out the external shareholders, effectively re-privatising the company.

RGB sells its products and services worldwide, but its main market outside the UK is in North America. To date, all its manufacturing and administrative functions have been conducted from the UK.

Summary Financial Statements for last financial year

	£m
Turnover	840
Earnings (post-tax)	76
Non-current assets	650
Net current assets	90
Less: Long term liabilities (8% Secured loan repayable 2010)	(320)
Total net assets	420

Shareholders' equity (120 million £1 shares in issue) = £420,000,000

The average P/E ratio of listed companies in a similar industry is 10.53.

Company objectives

The company has three stated objectives. These are:

- Increase earnings per share by 5% per annum
- Post-tax accounting rate of return on shareholders' funds of 20% per annum
- Maintain a leading global presence in its operating markets

New Capital Investment

The company is evaluating establishing a new manufacturing plant, marketing and administration facility in either the South of England or North America. Ideally, it would like to open the new UK facility as well as expanding into North America, but it does not believe it has the financial or management resources to do both at the same time.

RGB has a policy of limiting capital investment in any one financial year to £50 million. Last year the company did not spend up to this limit, however capital investments have already been approved in the current year that require total capital expenditure of £17 million. None of these can be postponed without loss of money spent on set up costs such as feasibility studies.

The estimated cost for the UK investment is £30 million. These initial investment costs will be written off over a period of 5 years. To establish operations in North America will cost an estimated US$75 million. This US investment, combined with capital expenditure already committed, would exceed the company's capital investment limit if it were to be enforced.

Forecast pre-tax operating nominal cash flows for the first three years of operations are as follows:

	Year		
	1	2	3
North America Investment US$m	22.25	24.25	26.25
UK £m	6.30	9.00	10.50

- All operating cash flows may be assumed to occur at the end of each year. The initial capital investment will be made at the beginning of year 1 (year 0).

- Estimated cash flows beyond year 3 are highly uncertain, but for purposes of evaluation, the company assumes 5% per year growth on year 3's pre-tax operating sterling cash flows until the end of year 5. Cash flows beyond year 5 are ignored.

The investments this year will be financed by cash. The company has built up cash reserves of £50 million over the past 2 years and has also recently agreed the cash sale of some surplus assets.

Exchange rate information

	Forecast inflation rates per annum constant %
USA	1.5
UK	2.5

The spot $/£ exchange rate as at today is 1.70.

Taxation

Corporate tax rates in the two countries are as follows:

	%
USA	25
UK	30

Assume for the purposes of evaluation:

- Both countries allow 100% first year allowance tax relief on capital investments of this type.
- There is a double taxation treaty in existence.
- Tax is payable (or refundable) at the end of the year in which the liability or refund arises.
- RGB pays tax at the national tax rates.

Cost of capital and adjustment for risk

For domestic investments RGB uses a risk-adjusted discount rate using the CAPM where possible. The expected nominal, post-tax risk free rate in the UK is 5% and the return on the market is 9%. The quoted equity beta of a suitable proxy company with similar capital structure to RGB is 1.3.

However, RGB's Finance Director recognises that the risks involved in the overseas proposal are different. Determining an appropriate discount rate to reflect risk is difficult in the circumstances. She has therefore recommended that the post-tax cash flows for the North American venture be adjusted using estimates of probability applied to sterling cash flows, discounted at the risk free rate. These estimates of probability are as follows:

	Year		
	1	*2*	*3*
Probability	0.9	0.87	0.82

Beyond year 3, a probability factor of 0.7 is estimated.

Methods of investment appraisal

RGB uses NPV analysis in the investment appraisal process, but the company also expects new investments to contribute to all the company's objectives.

Required

Assume you are the Capital Investment Analyst at RGB.

(a) Estimate the discount rate to be used in the evaluation of the UK investment and comment briefly on the limitations of using this rate in the investment being proposed here for RGB. Assume RGB's debt is trading at par and has a beta of zero. **(5 marks)**

(b) Calculate the NPV, Profitability Index and estimated Accounting Rate of Return on Capital Employed (ROCE) for each investment. For the purposes of calculating the ROCE, assume that cumulative sterling post-tax cash flows at the end of year 5 equal cumulative post-tax profits before depreciation. **(20 marks)**

(c) Write a report to the board evaluating the proposed investments. Include the following sections in your report:

    (i) An evaluation of how each of the two investments will contribute to the achievement of the company's stated objectives. **(10 marks)**

    (ii) An analysis of the various types of risk involved in these investments and advice on a strategy for managing those risks. Include comments on the methods the Finance Director has recommended to adjust the cash flows for risk. **(8 marks)**

    (iii) A recommendation as to whether the company should invest in either or both projects. Include comments on the appropriateness of RGB limiting investment to £50 million in the current financial year. **(7 marks)**

(Total = 50 marks)

72 JHC (Pilot paper)

90 mins

Background of company

JHC Group manufactures and distributes a wide range of food products for sale throughout Europe. It also provides advisory services to retailers. Its shares are listed and are widely held, although institutions hold the majority. The company is structured as a group of wholly-owned subsidiaries. Each subsidiary specialises in a particular product or service.

Financial data

Key data for the year to 31 December 20X3 is as follows:

Revenue	€1,750 million
Earnings	€215 million
Shares in issue	350 million
Share price as at today	€8.31
Weighted Average Cost of Capital (WACC) for the Group	9% (nominal net of tax rate)

Company objectives

The company has two stated objectives:

- To increase operating cash flow and dividends per share year-on-year by at least 4%, which is 2.5% above the current rate of inflation.

- To increase the wealth of shareholders while respecting the interests of our employees, customers and other stakeholders and operating to the highest ethical standards.

Future plans

The directors are considering establishing a new subsidiary company, SP, to manufacture and distribute health food products. The subsidiary will require a factory. The directors have identified that the factory used by a long-established subsidiary, CC, is currently operating at only 60% capacity. This factory could be converted for use by the new subsidiary at a cost of €2.8 million. CC's annual net (after-tax) earnings are €2.2 million and are expected to remain at this level in nominal terms for the foreseeable future. This subsidiary's operations would cease immediately the decision to proceed with SP is taken as it will take some months to convert the factory.

However, the company is aware that the European parliament is discussing legislation that would introduce more stringent controls on the manufacture of health food products than are currently in operation. Industry spokesmen are attempting to argue that current controls are adequate. Nevertheless, the directors of the JHC Group wish to consider the situation should these tougher controls be introduced and two alternative methods of equipping the new subsidiary have been proposed by the company's technical advisers.

The company has sufficient cash available from a recent disposal to finance the capital costs of the new subsidiary under either alternative.

Alternative 1

This alternative will equip the factory to manufacture to the highest food safety standards that new regulations might impose. It would require the purchase of specialised machinery, which would have to be ordered. Delivery time is approximately 6 months, which would coincide with completion of the factory conversion.

Capital costs

The cost of this machinery is currently €8 million but its price is likely to rise by 5% over the next 6 months. If an order is placed immediately (year 0), together with a 40% deposit, the supplier will hold today's price. The balance of the purchase price is payable 6 months after installation (that is, 12 months after payment of the initial deposit). This machinery is not likely to need replacement for at least 8 years.

Revenues

Forecast revenues for SP for the first three years of operation have been provided by JHC Group's planning department as follows. The probabilities are based on forecasts of the economies of JHC Group's main trading areas.

	Year 1 (6 months of operating)			Year 2			Year 3		
Revenues (€m)	2.5	4.5	7.4	7.5	12.5	16.5	13.5	18.5	21.5
Probability	0.3	0.5	0.2	0.3	0.5	0.2	0.3	0.5	0.2
Expected revenues (€m)		4.48			11.80			17.60	

The probabilities of sales for year 2 or 3 and beyond are assumed to be independent of the achievement of the previous year's sales revenues.

Operating and other costs/reliefs

- Cash operating costs are expected to have a fixed element of €2.5 million each year, plus a variable element of 35% of sales revenues. A full year's fixed costs will be charged to production in year 1. Variable costs will be much higher under this alternative because the new regulations are likely to require more expensive ingredients in the products.

- Redundancy payments of €2.1 million will be necessary for staff from the CC subsidiary. These would be payable immediately.

- The costs of the factory conversion will be incurred during the 6 months following the decision to proceed but, for simplicity, it can be assumed that these are paid at the end of year 1.

- The availability of capital allowances and other tax reliefs mean that no tax is likely to be payable until year 4. For year 4 onwards, a rough estimate suggests 20% of annual net cash flows (revenues less cash operating costs) will be payable in tax.

Alternative 2

To plan for a continuation of, or modest improvement to, current controls and regulations. This alternative has greater flexibility, as there is a much larger market, worldwide, for cheaper products.

Capital costs

The capital cost to JHC Group would also be much lower at €4.5 million. Equipment for this alternative is readily available and can be bought when the factory conversion is completed.

However, the equipment is likely to need to be replaced in 6 years' time from the date of purchase.

Revenues

The revenues shown below are forecast using similar methods as used in Alternative 1. However, sales will be made to a wider range of customers, many in developing countries.

	Year 1 (6 months of operating)			Year 2			Year 3		
Revenues (€m)	4.5	7.5	9.5	7.1	9.4	11.1	9.5	12.5	15.6
Probability	0.1	0.6	0.3	0.1	0.6	0.3	0.1	0.6	0.3
Expected revenues (€m)		7.80			9.68			13.13	

Costs are as follows:

- Fixed cash operating costs will be €1.5 million each year; variable costs will be 20% of sales revenue.

- With this alternative, there will be fewer redundancies from CC and the associated costs will be only 20% of those for Alternative 1.

- Costs of factory conversion are as Alternative 1.

- Tax relief will be similar to Alternative 1, that is, no tax will be payable until year 4 when tax will become payable at 20% of annual net cash flow (revenue less cash operating costs).

The revenues and costs for both alternatives are in nominal terms.

Required

Assume you are JHC Group's financial manager.

(a) (i) Calculate the net present value for the new subsidiary (SP) under each of the two alternatives. Make, and comment on, appropriate assumptions about cash flows beyond year 3, including terminal values, and the discount rate to use in the evaluation. **(15 marks)**

(ii) Explain, without doing any additional calculations, the appropriateness and possible advantages of providing modified internal rates of return (MIRRs) for the evaluation of the two alternatives. **(5 marks)**

(b) Write a report to the directors that discusses how the new subsidiary and the two alternatives might contribute to the attainment of the Group's objectives and recommends which, if either, of the alternatives should be chosen. Refer to the figures you calculated in part (a) where appropriate. You should provide any additional calculations that you consider relevant to support your discussion and analysis. **(22 marks)**

(c) Discuss the option features involved in the JHC Group's decision and explain, briefly, the benefits of including such options in the investment appraisal process. **(8 marks)**

(Total = 50 marks)

73 Groots (5/05)   90 mins

Scenario

Business background – The Groots Group

The Groots Group (Groots) is a retailer of clothing for women and children. The group started as a single store in France in the early 1900s. The business grew by acquisition of new premises and, occasionally, by buying out small competitors. Expansion outside France started fifty years ago and the group now has stores in most European cities. The parent company obtained a listing thirty-five years ago, although at that time the founding family still owned the majority of the shares. It is no longer controlled by the family although the grandson of the founder is a board member and owns 2% of the share capital. The company's other directors and senior managers own a further 8% between them. *90% outside*

The style of clothing sold in the Group's stores has changed over the years and its main theme now might be described as 'ethnic'. Most of its goods are manufactured outside Europe, predominantly in India and other parts of Asia.

Corporate objectives

Groots has two financial objectives and one non-financial objective. These are:

- To increase earnings and dividends per share year on year by 5% per annum

- To maintain an optimal debt/equity ratio within the range 25-30%

- To adhere to ethical trading policies and recognise the interests of its various stakeholder groups in all our business activities

Proposed acquisition

The directors of Groots believe they have exhausted possibilities for further expansion in Europe unless they are to diversify into different products such as men's clothing or household goods. They have, therefore, been reviewing opportunities for investment further afield for the past year. They have identified a small group of clothing stores trading in the East Caribbean and parts of South America, Cocomos Limited (Cocomos).

Cocomos is a listed company whose shares trade on an East Caribbean Stock Exchange. It has 18 stores as outlets for its products. Twelve of them are operated by the company itself and six are operated by franchisees. The clothing is at the expensive end of the market and aimed mainly at tourists.

Cocomos has followed a policy of buying locally-made clothing from within the Caribbean, Cuba or Puerto Rico, mainly from small co-operative-type manufacturers. The advantage of this policy is that the cost base is low, allowing for a substantial mark-up to retail. The disadvantage is that the quality is variable. If the acquisition proceeds, Groots would aim to review the product sources to improve the quality and expand the range. One alternative would be to supply the stores from sources in India, which already supply some of the European stores.

The directors of Cocomos and their families own 51% of the shares. A further 15% of the shares are owned by a local pension fund. The remaining 34% are owned by a number of wealthy individual investors, including a few who live most of the time in Europe or Canada.

Cocomos' directors are believed to be interested in opening discussions about a bid from Groots, but the franchisees are likely to be hostile. Although the franchisees are not shareholders, they will use the 'stealing our national assets' argument to agitate the press, local politicians and, ultimately, the local population.

On the basis of published accounts, industry information and discussions with Cocomos' directors, the Groots' directors have forecast the following post-tax cash flows for Cocomos:

	Year			
	1	2	3	4
Net cash flows (C$millions)	31.5	37.5	41.5	47.2

Post-tax cash flows beyond year 4 are estimated to grow at 2% per annum.

The cash flows are in real terms; that is they do not include inflation. Groots evaluates all its domestic investment decisions at a nominal, post-tax discount rate of 10%. Cocomos' directors estimate their company's cost of capital as 12%. However, Groots' directors think this rate of 12% does not adequately reflect the risk of Cocomos' cash flows.

Summary of financial statements of bidder and target companies

	Groots Group €m	Cocomos Ltd Caribbean C$
Income statement for the year ended 31 March 20X5		
Revenue	1,051.5	215.8
Operating profit	241.5	63.6
Finance costs (including overdraft interest)	48.0	15.0
Profit before tax	193.5	48.6
Taxation	46.9	11.5
Balance sheet as at 31 March 20X5		
Assets		
Non-current assets		
Property, plant and equipment	895.0	245.0
Current assets		
Trade receivables and inventories	275.0	88.0
Cash and cash equivalents	45.0	12.0
Total assets	1,215.0	345.0

	Groots Group €m	Cocomos Ltd C$
Equity and liabilities		
Equity		
Share capital (Nominal value of €1 and C$1 respectively)	245.0	55.0
Retained earnings	290.0	100.0
Total equity	535.0	155.0
Non-current liabilities		
Secured loan stock 7% repayable 20X9	475.0	
Secured loan stock 10% repayable 20X8		135.0
Current liabilities		
Trade and other payables	205.0	55.0
Total liabilities	680.0	190.0
Total equity and liabilities	1,215.0	345.0

Other financial information

	€	C$
Share price today	6.85	6.95
Shares last traded on	19 May 20X5	31 January 20X5
High-Low share prices in past 12 months	9.25–6.25	7.50–5.50
Debt value (market) per €100	105.50	N/A
Debt last traded on	30 December 20X4	N/A

Notes

Exchange rate €/C$, interest and inflation rates

The spot exchange rate is 0.30 (C$1 = €0.30). Forecast economic data relevant to the Caribbean, the US and the European Common Currency Area (ECCA) are as follows:

	ECCA %	Caribbean %
Risk-free interest rate per annum	3.5	6.5
Inflation rate per annum	2.5	4.5

You should assume the theory of interest rate parity applies when forecasting exchange rates.

Taxation

Both companies will pay tax at an average of 25% from next year for the foreseeable future. Assume a double taxation treaty is in existence between France and the Caribbean country.

Debt agreement

There is a clause in Cocomos' debt agreement that says the whole of the C$135 million debt is repayable immediately in the event of a successful takeover bid.

Required

(a) (i)   Calculate the maximum price that Groots would be prepared to pay for Cocomos based on the present value in euros of the forecast cash flows. Using appropriate discount rates, you should calculate present value using *both* the recognised methods of evaluating international investments.

                                                                                 (7 marks)

    (ii)   Comment briefly on why, in theory, these two methods should give the same answer and why, in practice, the answers might be different.   **(3 marks)**

    (iii) Calculate the number of shares Groots might need to issue if it offers its own shares in exchange for Cocomos using the higher of the values for the company you have calculated in (i). Comment briefly on your calculations and/or assumptions.   **(4 marks)**

(b)   Assume you are a financial manager with Groots. Write a report to the directors of Groots which should include the following:

(i)   A recommendation of the maximum price to be offered to Cocomos. You should base your recommendation on the figures you calculated in part (a) and *other* suitable methods of company valuation.

(ii)   Identify and discuss alternative methods of financing the acquisition and make a recommendation of the most appropriate method in the situation here.

(iii)   An analysis of strategies for enhancing the value of the combined company following the acquisition.

(iv)   Advice on the benefits and limitations of a post-completion audit and review in the context of the acquisition.

Use additional calculations to support your arguments, wherever relevant and appropriate, for which up to 10 marks are available. Marks are distributed roughly equally between sections of the report.

(36 marks)

(Total = 50 marks)

74 GAS (11/05)   90 mins

Scenario

Description of the business

GAS plc is an international energy entity with a head office in the UK. Through its principal operating subsidiaries based in the UK and elsewhere in Europe, it generates electricity and supplies gas and electricity via energy supply networks across Europe.

GAS plc's strategy is to generate future growth through investment in new power stations, energy supply networks and gas storage assets. Its current focus for new investment is Bustan, a large Asian country that is in urgent need of major improvements in its electricity generation and supply systems to support the recent rapid increase in industrial production.

Group profile

On 31 December 20X4, GAS plc had 1,200 million 50 pence ordinary shares in issue and a share price of 335 pence ex-dividend. Shareholders expect a return on equity of 9·4%. Dividends for GAS plc for the year ended 31 December 20X4 were 14 pence a share, maintaining the 5% annual increase in dividends that has been achieved in recent years. For simplicity, dividends should be assumed to be declared and paid on 31 December each year.

Investment project

The new investment in Bustan has been at the planning stage since the beginning of 20X4 when the government of Bustan first invited proposals for a large construction project from interested parties.

The project was evaluated over a 10-year period beginning January 20X5 and the project net operating cashflows in B$, the local currency of Bustan, were estimated to be as follows:

Year	B$ million
1	20
2	150
3	250
4–10	300

$20 + 150 + 250 + (350 \times 7)$

All cash flows should be assumed to arise on 31 December of each year. It should also be assumed that annual cash flows, less tax, are paid across to the UK on the final day of each year.

The cost of the initial investment in plant and other equipment at the beginning of January 20X5 was B$700 million and this is subject to depreciation charged in the subsidiary accounts on a straight line basis at 5% per annum. An additional B$50 million was required to finance working capital at the beginning of January 20X5.

Tax

Bustan charges entity tax at a preferential rate of 20% for the first 10 years of such investment projects, rather than the normal rate of 40%. In Bustan, tax depreciation allowances are calculated on the same basis as accounting depreciation allowances. The tax rate in the UK is 30%, but a double tax treaty allows taxes charged in Bustan to be deducted from UK taxes charged in the same period. Assume that Bustan taxes are payable in the year in which they are incurred and that UK taxes are payable one year in arrears.

Exchange rates

At 31 December 20X4, the spot exchange rate was £1 = B$0.7778. The B$ is expected to weaken against the British pound (sterling) in line with the differential in long term interest rates between the two countries over the life of the project. Long term interest rates are expected to remain stable at 4.8% per annum in the UK and 10% per annum in Bustan for the foreseeable future.

Financing the project

The total initial investment of B$750 million was funded by GAS plc at the beginning of 20X5. The B$700 million investment in plant and equipment was funded by a rights issue and the B$50 million working capital requirement out of surplus cash.

GAS plc evaluated the project on the basis of a realisable residual value of B$350 million for the plant and equipment and that 80% of the investment in working capital would be realised at the end of the project. Both these amounts are to be repaid in full to the UK without any taxes payable in either Bustan or the UK.

Press statements

In June 20X4, GAS plc issued a press statement announcing its intention to submit a proposal for the project. On the same day, it announced its plans to use a 1 for 4 rights issue to fund the B$700 million capital investment in the event of the proposal being accepted. GAS plc's proposal was accepted on 1 January 20X5 and a press release issued to announce the acceptance of the proposal and GAS plc's intention to proceed with the project without delay. The press statement also announced GAS plc's intention to temporarily reduce dividend growth rates during the development stage of the project. Revised dividend plans are as follows:

20X5-20X7 Dividend per share to be frozen at December 20X4 levels

20X8 onwards 7% per annum growth

Investment criteria

Criterion 1

GAS plc requires overseas projects to generate an accounting rate of return in the overseas country, which is Bustan in this instance, of at least 25% per annum. Accounting rate of return is defined as:

$$\frac{\text{average annual accounting profit before interest and taxes}}{\text{average annual (written down) investment}}$$

Criterion 2

GAS plc also assesses investment projects based on the net present value of the cashflows and applies a risk-adjusted sterling discount rate of 10.5% to overseas projects of this nature.

Required

(a) Show, by calculation, that the proposed investment project in Bustan met the two minimum investment criteria set by GAS plc. **(18 marks)**

(b) Discuss the major risk issues that should have been considered by GAS plc when evaluating the project

(7 marks)

(c) The board of GAS plc has been concerned about the unusually volatile movements in the entity's share price in 20X4 and 20X5 and has asked you, an external management consultant, to draft a report to the board of GAS plc that critically addresses the issues detailed below. Assume a semi-strong efficient market applies.

(i) Explain the possible reasons for the unusually volatile movements in GAS plc's share price in the twelve months up to and including 1 January 20X5. No calculations are required. **(6 marks)**

(ii) Advise what would have been a fair market price for GAS plc's shares in January 20X5 following the announcement of the acceptance of the proposal and after adjusting for the proposed rights issue. As part of your answer, calculate GAS plc's share price on each of the bases listed below and discuss the relevance of each result in determining a fair market price for the entity's shares:

- The theoretical ex-rights price *before* adjusting for the project cashflows
- The theoretical ex-rights price *after* adjusting for the project cashflows
- Directors' dividend forecast issued in January 20X5 **(14 marks)**

(iii) Advise on how and to what extent directors are able to influence their entity's share price.

(5 marks)

Within the overall mark allocation, up to 4 marks are available for structure and presentation.

(Total = 50 marks)

75 PM (5/06)   90 mins

Scenario

Background

PM Industries plc (PM) is a UK-based entity with shares trading on a UK Stock Exchange. It is a long established business with widespread commercial and industrial interests worldwide. It had a modest growth and profitability record until four years ago when a new Chief Executive Officer (CEO) was appointed from the United States of America (US). This new CEO has transformed the business by divesting poor performing, or non-core, subsidiaries or business units and focusing on volume growth in the remaining units. Some of this growth has been internally generated and some has come about because of financially sound acquisitions. A particular area of strength is in non-drug pharmaceutical materials such as packaging. PM now controls the largest share of this market in the UK and Europe.

Financial objectives

PM's current financial objectives are:

- To increase EPS by 5% per annum;
- To maintain a gearing ratio (market values of long-term debt to equity) below 30%;
- To maintain a P/E ratio above the industry average.

Proposed merger

The senior management of PM is currently negotiating a merger with NQ Inc (NQ), a US-based entity with shares trading on a US Stock Exchange. NQ is an entity of similar size to PM, in terms of revenue and assets, with a similar spread of commercial and industrial interests, especially pharmaceutical materials, which is why PM originally became attracted to NQ.

NQ has had a less impressive track record of growth than PM over the last two years because of some poor performing business units. As a result, PM's market capitalisation is substantially higher than NQ's. Although this will, in reality, be an acquisition, PM's CEO refers to it as a 'merger' in negotiations to avoid irritating the NQ Board, which is very sensitive to the issue.

NQ holds some software licences to products that the CEO of PM thinks are not being marketed as well as they could be. He believes he could sell these licences to a large software entity in the UK for around £100 million. He does not see the commercial logic in retaining them, as information technology is not a core business. The value of these licences is included in NQ's balance sheet at $US125 million.

Both entities believe a merger between them makes commercial and financial sense, as long as terms can be agreed. The CEO of PM thinks his entity will have the upper hand in negotiations because of the share price performance of PM over the last 12 months and his own reputation in the City. He also believes he can boost the entity's share value if he can convince the market his entity's growth rating can be applied to NQ's earnings.

Summary of relevant financial data

Extracts from the Income Statements for the year ended 31 March 20X6

	PM	NQ
	£ million	$ million
Revenue	1,560	2,500
Operating profit	546	750
Earnings available for ordinary shareholders	273	300

Extracts from the Balance Sheets as at 31 March 20X6

	PM	NQ
	£ million	$ million
Total net assets	2,000	2,100
Total equity	850	1,550
Total long term debt	1,150	550

Other data

Number of shares in issue

	PM	NQ
Ordinary shares of 10 pence	950,000,000	
Common stock of $1		850,000,000
Share price as at today (24 May 20X6)	456 pence	450 cents
High/low share price over last 12 months	475 pence/326 pence	520 cents/280 cents
Industry average P/E ratio	14	13
Debt traded within last week at	£105	Par

Five-year revenue and earnings record

	PM (£m)		NQ (US$m)	
Year ended 31 March	Revenue	Earnings	Revenue	Earnings
20X2	1,050	225	1,850	250
20X3	1,125	231	1,950	265
20X4	1,250	245	2,150	280
20X5	1,400	258	2,336	290
20X6	1,560	273	2,500	300

The two entities' revenue and operating profits are generated in the following five geographical areas, with average figures over the past five years as follows:

	PM		NQ	
Percentage of total:	Revenue	Profits	Revenue	Profits
UK	30	28	20	17
US	22	23	75	76
Mainland Europe	20	17	5	7
Asia (mainly Japan)	18	20	0	0
Rest of World	10	12	0	0

Economic data

PM's bankers have provided forecast interest and inflation rates in the two main areas of operation for the next 12 months as follows:

	Interest rates Current forecast	Inflation rate Current forecast
UK	4.5%	2.0%
US	2.5%	1.5%

Terms of the merger

PM intends to open the negotiations by suggesting terms of 1 PM share for 2 NQ stock units. The Finance Director of PM, plus the entity's professional advisors, have forecast the following data, post-merger, for PM. They believe this is a 'conservative' estimate as it excludes their estimate of value of the software licences. The current spot exchange rate is $US1.85 = £1.

Market capitalisation	£6,905 million
EPS	31.65 pence

A cash offer as an alternative to a share exchange is unlikely, although the CEO of PM has not ruled it out should the bid turn hostile. However, this would require substantial borrowing by PM, even if only 50% of NQ's shareholders opt for cash.

Except for the potential profit on the sale of the licences, no savings or synergies from the merger have as yet been identified.

Required

Assume you are one of the financial advisors working for PM.

(a) (i) Explain, with supporting calculations, how the Finance Director and advisors of PM have arrived at their estimates of post-merger values. **(10 marks)**

(ii) Calculate and comment briefly on the likely impact on the share price and market capitalisation for each of PM and NQ when the bid terms are announced. Make appropriate assumptions based on the information given in the scenario. **(4 marks)**

(iii) If NQ rejects the terms offered, calculate

- the maximum total amount and price per share to be paid for the entity; and

- the resulting share exchange terms PM should be prepared to agree without reducing PM's shareholder wealth.

(6 marks)

(Total for part (a) = 20 marks)

(b) Write a report to the Board of PM that evaluates and discusses the following issues:

(i) How the merger might contribute to the achievement of PM's financial objectives, assuming the merger goes ahead on the terms you have calculated in (a) (iii). If you have not managed to calculate terms, make sensible assumptions; **(12 marks)**

(ii) External economic forces that might help and/or hinder the achievement of the merger's financial objectives. Comment also on the policies the merged entity could consider to help reduce adverse effects of such economic forces; **(8 marks)**

(iii) Potential post-merger value enhancing strategies that could increase shareholder wealth. **(10 marks)**

(Total for part (b) = 30 marks)

Up to 4 marks are available for structure and presentation in Question One.

(Total = 50 marks)

145

Answers

1 Goals

(a)   REPORT

To: Managing Director
From: Finance Director
Date: 17 November 20X5
Subject: Definition of corporate objectives

Introduction

1   This report has been drafted for use as a discussion document at the forthcoming board meeting. It deals with the validity of continuing to operate with the single major goal of **shareholder wealth maximisation**. The remaining sections of the report contain an analysis of the advantages and disadvantages of some of the alternative objectives that have been put forward in recent discussions.

Maximisation of shareholder wealth

2   The concept that the **primary financial objective** of the firm is to **maximise** the **wealth** of shareholders, by which is meant the **net present value** of estimated future cash flows, underpins much of modern financial theory.

3   While the relevance of the wealth maximisation goal is under discussion, it might also be useful to consider the way in which this type of objective is defined, since this will impact upon both parallel and subsidiary objectives. A widely adopted approach is to seek to **maximise the present value of the projected cash flows**. In this way, the objective is both made measurable and can be translated into a yardstick for financial decision making. It cannot be defined as a single attainable target but rather as a criterion for the continuing allocation of the company's resources.

4   There has been some recent debate as to whether wealth maximization should or can be the only true objective, particularly in the context of the multinational company. The **stakeholder view** of corporate objectives is that **many groups** of people have a stake in what the company does. Each of these groups, which include suppliers, workers, manager, customers and governments as well as shareholders, has its own objectives, and this means that a compromise is required. For example, in the case of the multinational firm with a facility in a politically unstable third world economy, the directors may at times need to place the **interests of local government and economy** ahead of those of its shareholders, in part at least to ensure its own continued stability there.

Cash flow generation

5   The validity of **cash flow generation** as a major corporate objective depends on the timescale over which performance is measured. If the business maximises the net present value of the cash flows generated in the medium to long term, then this objective is effectively the same as that discussed above. However, if the aim is to **maximise all cash flows**, then decisions are likely to be disproportionately focused on **short-term performance**, and this can work against the long-term health of the business. Defining objectives in terms of long-term cash flow generation makes the shareholder wealth maximisation goal more clearly definable and measurable.

Profitability

6   Many companies use **return on investment (ROI)** targets to **assess performance** and **control the business**. This is useful for the comparison of widely differing divisions within a diverse multinational company, and can provide something approaching a 'level playing field' when setting targets for the different parts of the business. It is important that the **measurement techniques** to be used in respect of both profits and the asset base are very clearly defined, and that there is a clear and consistent approach to accounting for inflation. As with the cash flow generation targets discussed above, the selection of the time frame is also important in ensuring that the selected objectives do work for the long-term health of the business.

Risk adjusted returns

7   It is assumed that the use of **risk adjusted returns** relates to the criteria used for investment appraisal, rather than to the performance of the group as a whole. As such, risk adjusted returns cannot be used in defining the top level major **corporate goals**; however they can be one way in which corporate goals are made **congruent** with operating decisions. At the same time, they do provide a **useful input** to the goal setting process in that they focus attention on the company's policy with regard to making risky investments. Once the overall corporate approach to risk has been decided, this can be made effective in operating decisions, for example by **specifying the amount** by which the **cost of capital** is to be **augmented** to allow for risk in various types of investment decisions.

Performance improvement in non-financial areas

8   As discussed in the first section of this report, recent work on corporate objectives suggests that firms should take specific account of those areas which impact only indirectly, if at all, on **financial performance**. The firm has responsibilities towards many groups in addition to the shareholders, including:

    (i)   **Employees:** to provide good working conditions and remuneration, the opportunity for personal development, outplacement help in the event of redundancy and so on

    (ii)   **Customers:** to provide a product of good and consistent quality, good service and communication, and open and fair commercial practice

    (iii)   **The public:** to ensure responsible disposal of waste products.

9   There are many **other interest groups** that should also be included in the discussion process. Non-financial objectives may often work indirectly to the financial benefit of the firm in the long term, but in the short term they do often appear to compromise the primary financial objectives.

Conclusions

10   It is very difficult to find a comprehensive and appropriate alternative primary financial objective to that of **shareholder wealth maximisation**. However, achievement of this goal can be pursued, at least in part, through the setting of specific **subsidiary targets** in terms of items such as return on investment and risk adjusted returns. The definition of non-financial objectives should also be addressed in the context of the overall review of the corporate plan.

Signed: Finance Director

(b) **Factors affecting remuneration policy**

(i) **Cost:** the extent to which the package provides value for money.

(ii) **Motivation:** the extent to which the package motivates employees both to stay with the company and to work to their full potential.

(iii) **Fiscal effects:** government tax incentives may promote different types of pay. At present there are tax benefits in offering some types of share option schemes. At times of wage control and high taxation this can act as an incentive to make the 'perks' a more significant part of the package.

(iv) **Goal congruence:** the extent to which the package encourages employees to work in such a way as to achieve the objectives of the firm - perhaps to maximise rather than to satisfice.

Option (i)

In this context, Option (i) is likely to be **relatively expensive** with no payback to the firm in times of low profitability. It is unlikely to encourage staff to maximise their efforts, although the extent to which it acts as a motivator will depend on the individual psychological make-up of the employees concerned. Many staff prefer this type of package however, since they know where they are financially. In the same way the company is also able to budget accurately for its staff costs.

Option (ii)

The costs of this scheme will be **lower**, though not proportionately so, during a time of low profits. The effect on motivation will vary with the **individual** concerned, and will also depend on whether it is an **individual** or a **group performance calculation**. There is a further risk that figures and performance may be manipulated by managers in such a way as to maximise their bonus to the detriment of the overall longer term company benefit.

Option (iii)

A share option scheme (Option (iii)) carries **fiscal benefits** in the same way as the performance related pay above. It also **minimises the cost to the firm** since this is effectively borne by the existing shareholders through the dilution of their holdings. Depending on how pricing is determined, it may assist in **achieving goal congruence**. However, since the share price depends on many factors which are external to the firm, it is possible for the scheme to operate in a way which is unrelated to the individual's performance. Thus such a scheme is **unlikely to motivate directly** through links with performance. Staff will continue to obtain the vast majority of their income from salary and perks and are thus likely to be more concerned with maximising these elements of their income than with working to raise the share price.

2 Educational Institution

Text references. Chapter 1 looks at objectives of organisations and performance measures are revised in Chapter 3.

Top tips. The key to (a) was recognising the range of requirements that the Institution now has to fulfil – the needs of different stakeholders and the different objectives that should be met. You would have limited the marks you could earn if you had not discussed publicity of objectives. In (b) we have provided answers for all the measures, although you were only asked to discuss a selection. You need to think carefully about what could distort the measures used and how they might prompt action.

Easy marks. More a tip on avoiding throwing marks away. The examiner's comments indicated candidates did not discuss how measures should be used. Separate headers for the measures and then the use of measures makes clear to the examiner that you have taken account of the question requirements. Headers and mention of the question requirements in your answer also makes sure that you stay focused on what the examiner wants you to do.

Examiner's comments. The main weakness in (a) was poor discussion. In (b) discussions were often limited to the purpose of the measures used and failed to discuss **how** they would be used in the context of the question.

(a) **Different stakeholders**

At present the government is the most important **external stakeholder**. However the government will become less important and private sector users more important as the proportion of income derived from private sector courses increases. In addition the Institution will also have to take into account the interests of staff (internal stakeholders) and public sector students.

Links between financing and objectives

The cash limits set by the government relate to the **effectiveness** of the Institution's operations. The limits that the Institution has to meet are determined by what its outputs are in terms of research publications and quality. The Institution will have to take into account the methods of **measuring** these non-financial objectives.

Use of finance

Fulfilling the government's requirements (and therefore obtaining finance) is the most important current objective. However the Institution should also consider how it makes the best use of the finance it obtains, and here financial objectives become important. It should be looking to **minimise costs** as far as possible. The Institution should have the objective of choosing the **most economical** option that does not compromise the achievement of the non-financial objectives. The Institution should also have the objective that the **expenditure** it undertakes produces the **maximum return** in terms of meeting the non-financial objectives.

Level of investment

The Institution also needs to consider how much to spend on **long-term investment** rather than spend its entire budget on short-term requirements. If the Institution does not invest in upgrading facilities, over time teaching and research quality will suffer as the best staff move to other institutions with better facilities, and the Institution fails to fulfil more demanding expectations of quality.

Advantages of publicising objectives

Publicising the above objectives seems unexceptionable, as the Institution will be demonstrating that it is trying to achieve **value for money** from its operations. Likewise publicising an **investment target** will indicate to prospective teachers and students the Institution's recognition that it needs to allocate resources to ensure that it keeps up with changing views on what constitutes **excellence.**

Disadvantages of publicising objectives

The main problem with publicising objectives is that the Institution may be judged on the basis of objectives which it does not have the freedom to set. As well as fulfilling government requirements on effectiveness, the Institution may also need to take into account **other government guidelines**, for example those relating to mix of students. In addition publicising objectives may **highlight conflicts** between serving the needs of the public sector and serving the needs of private sector clients.

(b) **Value added**

Value added can be defined in financial terms as **sales revenues** less **the cost of running courses** (lecturers' fees, costs of producing material, costs of facilities used). Sales revenues is not however the only measure of the success of an Educational Institution. Better measures may be percentages of students **passing their exams**. For non-exam private sector courses the measure should ideally relate to **enhanced job performance**.

Use of value added

The Institution will undoubtedly pay attention to revenues, but it will also need to measure the benefits students have gained from its courses. Benefits can be measured in a variety of ways; for non-exam courses they could take the form of students demonstrating improved skills or knowledge at the end of the course, for example by giving a presentation. Data about all the **costs directly related** to the courses will also be needed. Sophisticated measures such as **shareholder value added** can be used to measure the impact of **fixed and working capital investment**, and the Institution's **required rate of return**.

Profitability

Profitability can be used to **measure the returns** that the **resources input** are generating, **relative** to the **sales** made. Measured in these terms, profit measures by themselves do not take account of the **investment** used to generate the profits.

Use of profitability

Profits may be distorted by the **accounting policies**, the **method** used for **allocating the costs** of running the Institution or depreciation. Depreciation charges may be particularly problematic if many of the assets have not been purchased on the open market but provided by the government, and have **no resale value**. Provided though that profits are calculated on a **consistent basis** over the five year period, the **trend of profits** should indicate the Institution's progress towards its targets.

Profits should also be used in conjunction with measures of **quality**. If profits have been **increased** by **cutting costs** and running poorer quality courses, in time the increase may be negated by the **fall in turnover** resulting from customers looking elsewhere for higher quality training.

Profitability measures can also influence the **range** and **frequency** of courses run, with the **most profitable** courses being run more often. However past profits may not be the **best indication** of future prospects, and focusing on the performance of individual courses may **not highlight** the **links** between them.

Return on investment

Return on investment is calculated by **dividing profits** by the **value of assets used**.

Use of return on investment

Again the profit figures used may be subject to distortion, but return on investment does at least take into account the **resources needed** to generate profits. However the figures might be distorted by the methods used to **allocate assets**. Provided though the methods used are consistent, return on investment can be used as an indication of changing efficiency levels over time. Its use may however **restrict investment**, as managers seek to keep down levels of capital employed; this may not be in the Institution's best interests as it is trying to expand its courses programme.

Competitive position

There are various measures of competitive position that may be valuable to the Institution. These include the **number and variety of courses** offered by competitors, also the extent to which competitors are introducing **new courses,** the **standard of courses** offered and the **pricing structure** of courses.

Use of competitive position

The Institution can **benchmark** competitors by sending its **staff** on **competitors' courses**, and getting them to report on the standards of teaching, material and facilities. The feedback provided should indicate the Institution in what areas its **own courses** need to be **improved** to match those offered by competitors. Benchmarking may also highlight **strengths** of the Institution's courses compared with its competitors, and these **strengths** can be **emphasised** in **marketing literature.**

Customer satisfaction

Customer satisfaction is likely to be a key measure for the Institution. If customers are satisfied with the courses provided, they are likely to **book further courses** and also **recommend the courses** to others.

Use of customer satisfaction

The Institution can obtain feedback from customers **by review forms** at the end of every class. These should allow participants to **rank different aspects** of the courses (quality of teaching, quality of material, facilities provided). **Targets** could be set for the marks that should be achieved. These targets could be increased over time, and also improvements made to courses that failed to reach the targets. Alternative methods of assessing how customers' needs have been met include **internal peer reviews**, **quality audits**, and obtaining **feedback** from **private sector participants' employers.**

Another way of measuring satisfaction is to track the **level of bookings** from **previous participants** on Institution courses. In a competitive market, customers will only book again if they are happy with what they have received in the past.

Market share

Market share measures the **percentage share** that an organisation has in the **total market** for a good or service. It measures the **success** of the **sales performance**, **pricing strategy** and **product quality**.

Use of market share

The Institution will need to research who offers similar courses and **ascertain numbers** who go. The courses offered by others need to be tracked over time. In order to achieve its growth targets, it may be better for the Institution to concentrate on expanding courses in areas in which it currently has **low market share**, since there may be potential to attract customers away from competitors. **Market share targets** may be set as **subsidiary targets** to **growth targets**.

3 Objectives

Text references. Chapter 1 looks at the inter-relationship between investment, financing and dividend decisions. The Treasury function is discussed in Chapter 14.

Top tips. (a) is a straightforward question about the links between the different types of decision. In the exam you may be expected to bring out these links without being prompted, for example when discussing the wider issues relating to an investment.

(b) is a good test of your knowledge of the distinctions between financial control and treasury function. In particular the treasury function is responsible for strategic and specialist advice, whereas financial control is responsible for the management and financial accounting functions.

Easy marks. A very straightforward question; if this had come up in an actual exam, undoubtedly most candidates would have chosen it.

(a)   **The three types of policy decision**

Investment policy

Investment policy is concerned with the types of capital investment that a company makes in order to develop its business (such as **replacement of non-current assets**, **new investment projects** concerned with generating organic business growth, and acquisitions of other businesses). Investment policy will stipulate the types of investment that are targeted and any restrictions over investment choices.

Return on investment

From a financial point of view the company's investments will normally need to earn a **sufficient return** to cover the cost of funds used to finance them. A successful investment will earn a surplus over this minimum required rate of return, which will therefore increase the value of the firm by increasing the present value of its projected cash flows. The minimum required rate of return of an investment project is dependent on its **systematic risk** (that is the part of its risk that depends on general market factors). The higher the systematic risk, the higher the minimum required return for the investment.

Other criteria

There will be exceptions to this general rule. Investment policy may stipulate types of investment that do not have to cover their cost of funding because they generate **other benefits** to the company or to other stakeholders.

Financing policy

Financing policy is concerned with the **sources of funds** used to finance capital investments and working capital. The general principle is that funds should be obtained at the **cheapest possible cost** of capital (so that the present value of the firm's cash flows is maximised), but again this is dependent on the **risk** the company suffers when it uses the funds.

Cost of finance

The **more risky** a source of funds is to the providers of finance, the **more expensive its cost of capital** will be. Thus equity funds are more expensive than debt. If there is a cash crisis, interest has to be paid, but dividends do not. Unsecured debt is more expensive than secured debt, and so on.

Targets and limits

Financing policy will normally place **targets and limits** on the different types of funds used by the company: the ratio of debt to equity (gearing), the amount of floating rate debt, the proportion of short term to long term debt and so on. These ratios will also be affected by the needs of lenders, who may stipulate maximum gearing levels or minimum liquidity ratios. Financing policy will also consider the **extent** to which foreign currency finance is used, as well as hedging instruments to reduce currency and interest rate risk.

Dividend policy

Dividend policy is concerned with the pattern of dividend payments to shareholders. This implies more than the principle that the present value of dividends should be maximised – it is concerned with practical matters.

Retention policy

A key issue is whether the dividends paid should be a **high proportion of equity earnings** that will result in the company needing to seek external finance more often) or a **low proportion of earnings** (which will leave more funds available for reinvestment). Although in a perfect market these decisions would result in identical present values for the firm, the existence of **taxation** can cause groups of shareholders to favour differing dividend policies, and the company's dividend policy must attempt to find an appropriate balance.

Pattern of dividend payment

The business must also decide whether dividends should be **paid** in a **smooth trend** (eg 5% growth per year) or **allowed to fluctuate** as much as **equity earnings**. Again, although in a perfect market this would not be important, in practice the lack of perfect information to shareholders makes the 'signalling content' of dividends more significant.

Inter-relationship between the policies

Investment, financing and dividend policies are all inter-related. Investments must earn sufficient to cover the cost of funds used. The risk of these investments will influence the cost of these funds. Planning of investment and finance must go hand in hand, otherwise the ability to start an investment may be delayed by lack of available funds.

Cash surpluses generated by investments are equity funds, and **dividend policy** determines how much of these surpluses are available for **reinvestment** and how much are to be paid as **immediate rewards** to the fund providers.

(b) **Treasury and financial control departments**

CIMA Official Terminology describes the treasury function as 'the function concerned with the provision and use of finance'. Broadly, the treasury department **raises and manages company funds** and liquid assets while the financial control department is responsible for **financial control** over receipts and payments, accounting for all financial transactions and regular reporting on the company's financial position.

Role of treasury function

The treasury department will usually be responsible for:

- Strategic financial planning, as an input into the company's overall strategic plan

- Identifying sources and types of funds and appraising their cost and risk

- Raising funds, managing service payments and repayment of funds

- Managing the company's liquid assets, cash, marketable securities etc, currency management

- Managing risk associated with short and long term funds and currencies, using financial instruments where appropriate

- Financial appraisal of potential capital investments and other strategic opportunities

- Tax planning

- Pension fund investment

Role of financial control function

The financial control department's main planning role centres around **annual and shorter term budgets**. The company's annual budget is the responsibility of top management, but the financial control department will be used to carry out much of the preparation and evaluation work, including evaluation of alternative proposals.

The operational roles of the financial control department include:

- Management of receipts, expenditures and payroll

- Management accounting and reporting of financial position against monthly and annual budgets

- Budgetary control feedback to company managers at all levels

- Financial accounting and periodic financial statements for external stakeholders, including statutory accounts

- Computation of corporate taxation (but this may be handled by treasury)

- (Sometimes) internal financial audit

As part of its control role, the department will also carry out **analytical assignments**, including cost reviews and post-appraisal of capital projects.

Contribution to financial objectives and policies

As a broad distinction, the treasury department has more responsibility for setting **financial objectives** and **policies**, whereas financial control has more responsibility for implementing the policies and ensuring the achievement of objectives.

Inter-relationships of roles

In reality, however, the roles of treasury and financial control in these areas are inter-related, for example:

(i) Planning and policy setting are **iterative processes**, in which feedback from **annual budgets** or **actual results** may show that longer term policies need to be revised. It is important that the financial control department plays a **proactive role** in determining how effective existing policies are and making suggestions for their improvement.

(ii) Treasury department is responsible for **achieving and reporting** on its **own financial objectives** (eg on interest rates, cash control, exchange rate risk management etc) and relies on information from the financial control department to help it.

4 JS

(a) **Evaluation of the Cost Benefit Analysis**

Hardware and software

Hardware and software costs should be reasonably accurate as these should be relatively easy to obtain from suppliers.

However, the CBA should be amended to specify (in supporting notes) exactly what the hardware and software figure includes.

Implementation including data conversion

There is no indication of how this figure was arrived at, for example whether the vendor would be performing all installation tasks and how many hours data conversion are budgeted.

More detail showing how these figures were obtained is required.

Lost sales while staff train

Again, there is no detail provided such as number of hours training per person. The figure seems very conservative and also only includes 'on-the-job' training. Most training must be performed before the system is used 'on-the-job' – which will increase costs considerably.

The CBA should be amended to take into account a more realistic training figure.

Benefits

There is no supporting evidence explaining exactly how the system will lead to increased sales – and how the original increase will be improved upon by 10% for each of the following four years. On the surface at least, the £100,000 figure appears to have been somewhat conveniently 'plucked out of thin air'.

The CBA should be amended to include justification for the benefits figures.

Maintenance, support and running costs

The CBA excludes the on-going costs associated with running the new system.

These costs should be calculated and included in an amended CBA.

Intangible costs and benefits

The CBA also excludes intangible costs and benefits. For example, the new system may cause resentment among sales staff, with a follow-on reduction in motivation and sales. On the other hand, improved knowledge sharing may facilitate more effective telemarketing lead to improved sales.

Some attempt should be made to quantify these intangible costs and benefits, and these figures should be included in an amended CBA.

No accounting for inflation or cost of capital

The CBA has not been adjusted for the effects of inflation or JS's cost of capital. As this investment has been assessed over five years, these factors could be significant. The CBA should be amended and future income discounted appropriately.

(b) (i) **Regulatory intervention**

Where there is competition in the supply of a service, efficient producers will be able to undercut the prices of less efficient competitors, ensuring that customers get the best possible price and that the industry remains competitive and efficient.

Where the provision of a service is in the hands of a monopoly, the firm can **maximise its profits** at a higher price level than where there is competition, despite the fact that its unit cost should be lower than if it had a lower share of the market. The result is that either the **shareholders gain super-profits** or that the organisation can operate inefficiently with above-average returns going to its managers and employees. These gains are all at the expense of the consumer.

The objective of the **regulatory body** is to intervene on behalf of the consumer, forcing the monopoly provider to lower its prices and hence to operate more efficiently. Often the regulatory body is only a first step, preceding genuine deregulation of the industry and the opening of the service to competition.

(ii) **Methods of regulation**

(1) **Price control**: the regulator agrees the output prices with the industry. Usually the price is progressively reduced in real terms each year by setting price increases at a rate below that of inflation as measured by the Retail Prices Index (RPI). This has been used with success by regulators in the UK but can be confrontational.

(2) **Profit control**: the regulator agrees the maximum profit which the industry can make. A typical method is to fix maximum profit at x% of capital employed, but this does not provide any incentive to making more efficient use of assets: the higher the capital employed, the higher the profit.

In addition the regulator will be concerned with:

(1) Actively **promoting competition** by encouraging new firms in the industry and preventing unreasonable barriers to entry

(2) **Addressing quality and safety issues** and considering the social implications of service provision and pricing

(iii) **Retention of regulator**

Even when **competition** enters an industry, the regulator is still needed because the original monopolist will still command enough market power to main high prices in the absence of such regulation until the market is completely open to international competition. In addition the regulator is needed to supervise industry-wide matters such as the policy on identification and issue of telephone numbers.

In addition the regulator will be concerned with a **monopoly supplier exploiting its position** to offer other products, for example here an infrastructure provider also selling mobile phones. The supplier can impose barriers to entry by restricting the access of other suppliers or using its position to drive down its own costs.

5 PQD

(a) (i) **Analysis of PQD's performance**

A numerical analysis of the **financial performance** of PQD is shown below. The figures provide the basis for making a traditional evaluation of the performance of the company from the point of view of the shareholders. However, there is only limited information on which to assess performance from the standpoint of the other stakeholders.

Calculation of key variables

		Year 1	2	3	4	5
Shareholders' ratios						
(1)	Payout ratio (%)	40.38	39.39	40.00	40.00	50.00
(2)	Dividend per share	£0.35	£0.43	£0.50	£0.43	£0.60
(3)	Share price					
	P/E × earnings/no of shares in issue	£6.93	£9.35	£11.25	£9.78	£11.40
(4)	Dividend yield (%)	5.05	4.60	4.44	4.40	5.26
(5)	Earnings/share	£0.87	£1.10	£1.25	£1.06	£1.20
(6)	Market capitalisation (£'000)	41,580	56,100	67,500	78,240	91,200
Profitability						
(1)	Post tax profit/sales (%)	10.16	11.32	11.74	11.30	12.28
(2)	ROCE					
	(PBIT: total assets) (%)	22.33	25.22	26.77	20.54	21.76
(3)	Sales growth (%)		13.87	9.61	17.68	3.99
(4)	PBIT growth (%)		23.91	9.65	4.00	12.31
(5)	Interest: debt (%)	10.00	10.67	10.83	8.57	8.00
Working capital						
(1)	Receivable days	75	73	76	72	71
(2)	Payable days					
	(based on cost of sales)	68	69	77	81	83
	Average wages/person	£8,953	£9,600	£9,451	£9,186	£8,994

Shareholders

(1) **Payout ratio**

From the point of view of the shareholders, financial performance has been good. The **payout ratio** has been maintained at 40% and in year 5 increased to 50%.

(2) **Dividend per share**

Dividend per share has increased throughout the period with the exception of year 4 when their was some **dilution** due to the rights issue. This reflects the overall trend of growth in sales and profits, albeit somewhat less erratically.

(3) **Return on capital employed**

Return on capital employed fell after the rights issue although it shows signs of renewed improvement in year 5.

(4) **Sales**

It appears that in the earlier part of the period under review, growth in earnings was achieved from growth in sales. The figures suggest that the part of the proceeds of the rights issue not used to redeem debt was **invested in assets** which may have been used to generate the further sales growth in year 5.

(5) **Workforce**

At the same time there was a **significant reduction** both in the **number of people employed** and the **average level of remuneration** in years 4 and 5, which may suggest that PQD has been replacing labour by capital to achieve both sales growth and cost savings. The drop in the average earnings level could also suggest either a switch to more part-time working (assuming that the number employed figure is not a full-time equivalents figure) or that there has been rationalisation in the management structure which has reduced the proportion of more highly paid employees.

(6) **Return to shareholders**

The actual **return to the shareholders** over the period can be calculated as follows.

	£m
Increase in market capitalisation (£91.2m – £41.58m)	49.62
Less cost of rights issue	(20.00)
Dividends (Yrs 1-4)	11.10
	40.72

This equates to a total return over four years of 98%.

Stakeholders

Other stakeholders in the business include customers, suppliers, employees, providers of debt finance and the tax authorities. The performance of PQD from their points of view can be evaluated as follows.

(1) **Customers**

The **volume of goods and services provided** has increased by 52.7% over the period, presumably to their benefit. However, the period of credit allowed has **reduced from 75 to 71 days**.

(2) **Suppliers**

The **volume of business** has also increased by 48.8% based on the **cost of goods sold**. However, the period of credit taken by PQD has increased from 68 to 83 days, presumably to the detriment of the suppliers.

(3) **Employees**

The **numbers employed increased** from years 1 to 3 before being cut back. **Average earnings** similarly increased to year 3 before falling back. Assuming that there was some degree of wage inflation in the economy during the period, the employees do not appear to have fared particularly well. Possible reasons for the movement in the figures were outlined above.

(4) **Providers of debt finance**

There has been a steady **repayment of debt** capital during the period with the major repayment being made at the same time as the rights issue in year 4. At the same time the average rate of interest paid has reduced from 10% to 8%.

(5) **Tax authorities**

They have benefited from **payments** of £18.4m over the five year period.

Shareholders' position

In conclusion, it can be seen that the major benefit over the period has accrued to the **ordinary shareholders**. Some assessment of the position of the other stakeholders has been made but it is not possible to make a full evaluation of their relative position from the information given. Since the objective is not expressed in quantitative terms it is not possible to provide a definitive appraisal as to whether or not it has been successfully met.

(ii) The other financial information that would be helpful include the following areas.

(1) **Financial projections and investment proposals**

The wealth of the shareholders as represented by the **market value** of the shares is very dependent upon **future earnings** and **dividend projections**. It would therefore be helpful to have access to more detailed information on these areas in order to assess the likely movements in both financial performance and the share price. The fact that the P/E ratio has been increasing at a faster rate than the industry average suggests that the market takes a positive view of PQD's current performance and projections.

(2) **Factors external to the firm**

These include factors such as the **current rates of interest and inflation** which would allow a better appraisal to be made of the performance of the company in real terms from the point of view of the shareholders. It would also be helpful to have information on the **size and projected growth of the markets** in which PQD operates, its current and projected market share and the competitive structure of the industry.

(3) **Detailed management accounts and reports**

It would be helpful to have access to a more detailed analysis of the customer and supplier base, the breakdown of the sales figures by market sector, volume and price, credit policies etc. Similar information on the status of the fixed asset base would also be helpful. Human resources information on the grading, turnover and salary levels of the various groups of employees would enable a better analysis to be made of the position of this particular stakeholder group.

Internal targets

The objective as stated is not expressed in terms of **measurable targets**. It would therefore be helpful to have any internal information relating to any internal targets that are set, as well as discussion documents relating to this process. A further stakeholder group that has not been mentioned so far is the **wider community** and the **environment**; details of charitable giving, social and environmental projects would allow an appraisal to be made of performance in this area.

(b) **Role of financial management**

(i) The financial managers must understand the **listing requirements** and be able to liaise with the banks and institutions advising on the flotation.

(ii) The financial managers must also be **able to provide information** on the likely valuation of the shares and to advise on the proposed capital structure of the quoted company.

(iii) If the flotation is being made due to the need for **access to a wider pool of funds** to finance expansion, then many of the points made in part (a) will also be relevant.

(iv) If the purpose of the flotation is to enable the owners to realise the value of their investment then the financial managers must be able to **persuade potential investors** that the company will be as successful under a new ownership and control structure as it was as a private company.

(v) The managers must be good at **communicating information** about the company to the wider public, and must be able to present **financial information in a clear and accessible format**.

6 HG

> **Text references.** Chapter 1 covers objectives of organisations and financial management decisions.
>
> **Top tips.** (a) requires detailed analysis of stakeholders but also a realisation that the primary objective must be maximisation of shareholder wealth. Hopefully you discussed the lack of a strategic plan. It is possible to use other frameworks in (b), such as grouping the decisions under what is acceptable, suitable and feasible; our answer focuses on the key decisions that have to be made. You must make sure that your discussion is applied to the specific circumstances of HG not a vague waffle.
>
> **Easy marks.** Hopefully you found plenty to say in (b) whatever framework you used.
>
> **Examiner's comments.** The main areas of weakness were providing vague and insubstantial discussion and not concluding with valid recommendations.

(a) **Corporate objectives for HG**

HG has two main objectives at present:

- To treat all stakeholders with fairness and equity
- To increase dividends each year

(i) **Fairness and equity**

Stakeholders

There will always be a number of **stakeholder groups** interested in a company's operations, including shareholders, loan creditors, directors and managers, other employees, customers, suppliers, government (including tax authorities), and the communities in which the company is based.

Shareholders

The primary stakeholders are the **shareholders,** who are the owners of the company. They appoint **directors as agents** to run the company on their behalf. In a private company like HG the directors will almost invariably also be shareholders. Thus private sector companies **must** have a primary objective that is related to the needs of shareholders.

Stakeholders with legal rights

Some of the stakeholder groups (e.g. loan creditors and the national and local tax authorities) have **clear legal rights** to payments by the company, and the concept of 'equity and fairness' will not really apply. For the most part these are stakeholders whose sole need is for the law to be satisfied, that is they expect to be paid on time, and any negotiations start from this premise.

Other stakeholders

For the other stakeholders, the concept of fairness and equity is a good general approach to adopt. Even those who assert that a company's **sole objective** should be to benefit shareholders will agree that this is best done by considering the needs of other stakeholder groups. For example:

(1)   **Customers** should **not be cheated** on the quality of goods (or they will buy elsewhere).

(2)   **Suppliers** should **not be made to wait unduly** for payment (or they will increase their prices).

(3)   **Directors and key managers** should be given **fair rewards** for their successes (or they will lose motivation, divert benefits to themselves or leave the company); however they should not be allowed to take the same rewards if they are unsuccessful.

(4)   **Other employees** should **not only be paid fair market rates** but also encouraged to participate in company plans.

(5)   **The local community** should **not be subjected** to **unnecessary noise or pollution**, and can provide powerful good publicity for the company.

(ii)   **Increasing dividends each year**

Although it correctly focuses on shareholders, the objective of increasing dividends each year is unsatisfactory as a primary objective for HG. This is because the pattern of dividends may need to be **varied** to take advantage of **investment opportunities**. In some years it may be wise to restrict dividends in order to reinvest in the company for growth.

Finance director's suggestion

The finance director suggests that 'maximisation of shareholder wealth' should be the **sole objective**. As stated above, the **primary objective** of a **private sector company** must be to **benefit its owners**, taking into consideration the fact that this cannot be properly done without also satisfying the legal needs of other shareholders and treating them with equity and fairness. Whether or not equity and fairness is viewed as a set of objectives or conditions is not particularly important in practice, provided it is acknowledged.

The question then turns to whether 'maximisation of shareholder wealth' is something that can actually be achieved, and if so, how? Some writers would say that 'satisficing' (i.e. paying a **minimum required rate of return**) is the closest that can be achieved, with surpluses generated by the company being the subject of bargaining between stakeholders. Also, in a private company like HG, where the boundary between shareholders and directors is blurred, the **remuneration paid to directors** usually contains some element of shareholder rewards.

A range of performance objectives

The other directors propose a range of 'objectives' which are probably best described as **targets,** designed to help achieve the main objective of shareholder wealth creation. Thus a target return on investment is a way of trying to increase shareholder wealth. In setting these financial targets, however, it is vital to recognise the **relationship between risk and return** and to put boundaries on risks taken in pursuit of the targets.

The problem with **financial targets** is that they **depend on non-financial actions,** such as increases in sales or productivity. Hence non-financial performance improvement measures are vital as a component of the set of targets the company should seek.

Strategic plan

This leads to the most important criticism of all. The company appears to have **no strategic plan**, but appears to working on the basis that its **current success** will continue unchanged. In particular it is likely to be outflanked by some of its competitors that have relocated production facilities to low cost East European countries.

Conclusions

The company's main objective should be to **pay shareholders a minimum rate of return** consistent with the **risk** they are prepared to accept. The company should investigate attitudes to risk among its main shareholders.

The main objective should be presented in conjunction with statements that that the company will **fulfil its legal obligations** and will **treat other stakeholders with equity and fairness.**

The main objective should then be accompanied by a set of **financial and non-financial targets,** based on the **strategic plan**.

(b) Financing or refinancing strategies

The treasury department should develop a **financing strategy** based on its ongoing business and investment plans, and the cash requirements forecasts that come out of these plans. The financing strategy should consider:

(i) Debt or equity

Treasury should **evaluate the project plans** in conjunction with the **gearing ratio** and decide whether it is **worthwhile taking out more debt or redeeming it with surplus cash** instead of paying dividends. Some investments will provide **good security** for borrowing and may allow gearing to be increased without taking undue financial risk. Other investments are **less certain** in the development stage and are **better financed with equity.** The directors may also wish to consider **ownership** implications, the tax shield effects of debt, and the **interest commitment** made if debt is taken out.

(ii) Short and long term debt

It is best to obtain a **satisfactory mix** of short and long term debt, in order to manage financing risk at the minimum interest cost. In general **long term debt** will be **more secure** but **more expensive** because the lender does not have the option to withdraw it so soon. The policy should consider **financing assets out of funds** from the **same type of duration**. For example non-current assets and the permanent part of working capital can be financed from equity and longer term loans, whereas fluctuating working capital should be financed from overdraft or other short term funds.

(iii) Fixed or floating rate loans

Interest on fixed rate debt is **easier to forecast** but **may be more expensive** in the long run that floating rate debt. The fact that interest rates are predicted to fall is an indicator that floating rate debt may be beneficial at the moment but interest rate risk must be acknowledged. There may be **cash flow problems** in the event of rising interest rates.

(iv) Foreign currency loans

A foreign currency loan should probably only be considered as a **hedge against income received** in that currency. For example a euro loan can be **matched** against **expected euro receipts**. Foreign currency loans should not be taken out simply because the interest rate appears cheap, because unhedged exchange rate movements can cause significant losses.

Financing and overall strategy

Financing strategies will be reflected in the company's overall strategic plan. In general the aim should be to **trade off** the **cost and risks** of finance. The decisions taken on financing will be reflected in some of the target figures accompanying the corporate objectives – for example gearing, cost of capital and duration of finance.

7 CBA

Text references. The preparation of forecasts is revised in Chapter 3 and working capital management is also covered in this chapter.

Top tips. Changes in working capital management and the effect on cash flow are significant areas in the syllabus. (a) emphasises the key points for and against overdraft finance (flexibility v frequent re-negotiation), and also touches on strategic aspects of working capital finance that are important in this paper.

In (b) a clear layout is essential. It is not enough to just show changes to assets and liabilities, you have to demonstrate clearly the effect on cash flow. Although you do not have to follow IAS 7 in every detail, a similar layout will generally be useful. Complications that you should have watched for include time lags on dividend and tax, and changes in inventory.

As (c) offers only 6 marks for a report, you do not have time to develop any of the points in too great a depth. Your answer should have referred to the calculations in (b).

Easy marks. (a) is a straightforward lead in to this question.

(a)   **Uses of overdrafts**

The overdraft is a **key source of finance** for **working capital** because of its flexibility: the finance **varies automatically** up to the **agreed limit**, enabling the company to handle **peaks and troughs** in cash flows without incurring excess interest charges with the company's cash flow. The potential disadvantage for an expanding company is that the **overdraft limit** may have to be **frequently renegotiated**. There is also a tendency for expanding companies to ignore the need to underpin their growth with **longer term finance.**

Need for other funds

When considering alternatives to the bank overdraft, it is essential to consider the need for **longer term funds** (loans or equity funds) to finance the **permanent element** of working capital. Although such funds may be more expensive than short term finance, they provide a longer term stability for planning.

(b)   **Cash flow forecasts**

(i)   **No change in policies**

		£'000
Operating profit		1,326
Add depreciation		225
Less: increase in inventory		(275)
increase in receivables		(230)
Add: increase in trade payables		144
Net cash flow from operating activities		1,190
Finance payments		
Interest	54	
Dividends	339	
		(393)
Tax paid		(283)
Acquisition of non-current assets		(550)
Reduction in cash/increase in borrowings (25 + 11)		(36)

(ii) **Proposals are implemented**

	£'000	£'000
Original operating profit		1,326
Add reduction in cost of sales (W3)		150
Less 2% sales discount (W1)		(52)
Revised operating profit		1,424
Add depreciation		225
Less increase in inventory (W4)		(213)
Add decrease in receivables (W2)		74
Less decrease in trade payables (W5)		(86)
Net cash flow from operating activities		1,424
Finance payments		
Interest	45	
Dividends	339	
		(384)
Tax paid		(283)
Acquisition of fixed assets		(550)
Increase in cash		207

Workings

1   2% discount on 50% of sales = (£'000) 2% × 50% × 5,200 = 52.

2   Revised receivables will be (£'000): 750/2 + (2,600 × 10/365) = 446. Annual decrease in receivables = 520 – 446 = 74.

3   Cost of sales (excluding depreciation) is reduced by (£'000): 5% × (3,224 – 225) = 150 reduction to 2,849.

4   Inventory is reduced to (£'000): 90% × 625 = 563. Annual increase in inventory = 563 – 350 = 213.

5   Trade payables fall to (£'000): 2,849 × 30/365 = 234. Annual decrease in trade payables= 320 – 234 = 86.

(c)   To: Ms Smith, Financial Manager
       From: Assistant
       Date: 21 November 20X0
       Subject: Evaluation of working capital management proposals

Receivables

Although customers are supposed to pay within 30 days, they are currently taking **45 days** and are predicted to take 53 days next year. The discount scheme offered to customers who pay within 10 days is predicted to reduce the average payment period to (10 +53)/2 days = 31.5 days. The **discount cost**, estimated at £52,000, will be partially paid for by interest savings on the reduction in average receivables of from £625,000 to £446,000. There is also the possibility of bad debt savings, which have not been quantified. A rough cost of this scheme is 17% per annum (see below) which is fairly expensive, and before implementing it, we should consider **tightening up** on our **credit control** procedures to speed up payments. This must be done with care and tact, in order to preserve customers' goodwill.

Trade payables and inventory

Our original plans showed an **increase in credit** from suppliers from 50 to 56 days. The revised proposals will require us to pay in 30 days, but enable a 5% reduction in cost of sales through reduced prices and other purchasing costs. On the basis of our assumptions for the 'just in time' policy, the projected financial effects are extremely good. Cost of sales is reduced by £150,000 and there are interest savings on inventory reductions of £62,500, and although these are offset by interest costs on the cash requirement to reduce trade payables from £464,000 to £234,000, the overall effect is beneficial. However, our predictions may be optimistic as suppliers are likely to **require higher prices** to deliver 'just in time'. Also, this system will increase our dependence on fewer suppliers and will greatly increase the likelihood of production breakdowns due to lack of stock unless we implement higher quality processes.

Profitability and cash flow

Overall, on the basis of our projections, the scheme will improve profitability before tax by £'000 (150 – 52 + 9) = £107,000, a factor of 8%, and cash flow will be improved by £36,000 + £207,000 = £243,000 although there will be an impact on tax payable the following year. Despite some of the reservations above, the proposals are worth implementing.

Workings

	Next year	*Current year*
Average receivables payment period: receivables/sales × 365	53 days	45 days

Approximate cost of discount is 2% for (53 – 10) = 43 days, that is 2% × 365/43 per year = 17% per year.

	Next year	*Current year*
Cost of purchased goods (cost of sales less dep'n): £'000	2,999	2,345
Average credit from suppliers:		
trade payables/cost of purchased goods × 365	56 days	50 days

8 Question with analysis: Emcos

Text references. Forecasting is revised in Chapter 3, equity finance is covered in Chapter 5, debt finance in Chapter 6.

Top tips. Computation of the forecasts in (a) is best approached in the order of the question requirements: income statement, followed by balance sheet (in which you can put bank overdraft as the balancing figure), and finally the cash flow forecast.

Step 1 Set out the major items/balance sheet headings in your proformas, but leave some gaps just in case you have to insert extra items.

Step 2 Work down the accounts and the notes, inserting figures that don't need any calculations or just require simple calculations. Note those items that will require workings, but don't do them at this stage.

Step 3 Calculate the items that require workings (in particular here the royalty income).

Step 4 Include the overdraft figure as the balancing figure in your balance sheet and ensure it balances.

If the overdraft figure is not the same as current cash + movement in cash per cash flow statement, don't spend a lot of time trying to reconcile it. You will get more marks attempting the report in (b).

- Depreciation needs to be separated out of administration expenses: the 20X3 depreciation charge will be based on the NBV of tangible assets including new acquisitions. In doing this, you will have completed non-current asset workings for the balance sheet and simply need to follow the notes to slot in the other figures.

- To make it balance, you will need to assume that all the marketable securities are sold and that an overdraft facility is used, the value of which is the balancing figure on the balance sheet. This figure can be confirmed when you construct the cash flow forecast.

This forecast can be laid out in any (reasonable) way you like.

Easy marks. Because (a) is so time-pressured, you may think the easier marks are in (b). Whilst you need to allocate your time so that you spend the 14 minutes on (b), you shouldn't really attempt it first, as your answers will depend on your calculations in (a).

Examiner's comments. In general most answers to (a) were satisfactory, with the structure and presentation of calculations being of a higher standard than previous exams. The balance sheet tended to be the worst prepared, with candidates keeping cash and marketable securities at the same levels and wrongly calculating the balance on equity shareholders' funds. Some candidates ignored the fact that their balance sheets did not balance! Other mistakes included not adjusting for administration and depreciation correctly, and failing to reconcile the cash flow statement with the balance sheet.

The main weakness in (b) was a lack of focus in answers, with many candidates taking a saturation bombing approach, throwing in everything they knew of any relevance, and ignoring the specific requirements of the question and the figures they had calculated in (a). Worryingly, some candidates did not appear to know what financial strategy was, confusing it with general business strategy.

Overall time management could have been improved. Many candidates appeared to have spent a long time on part (a), with the results that their answers to part (b) were too brief.

(a) (i)   EMCOS
           FORECAST INCOME STATEMENT
           FOR THE YEAR TO 31 DECEMBER 20X3

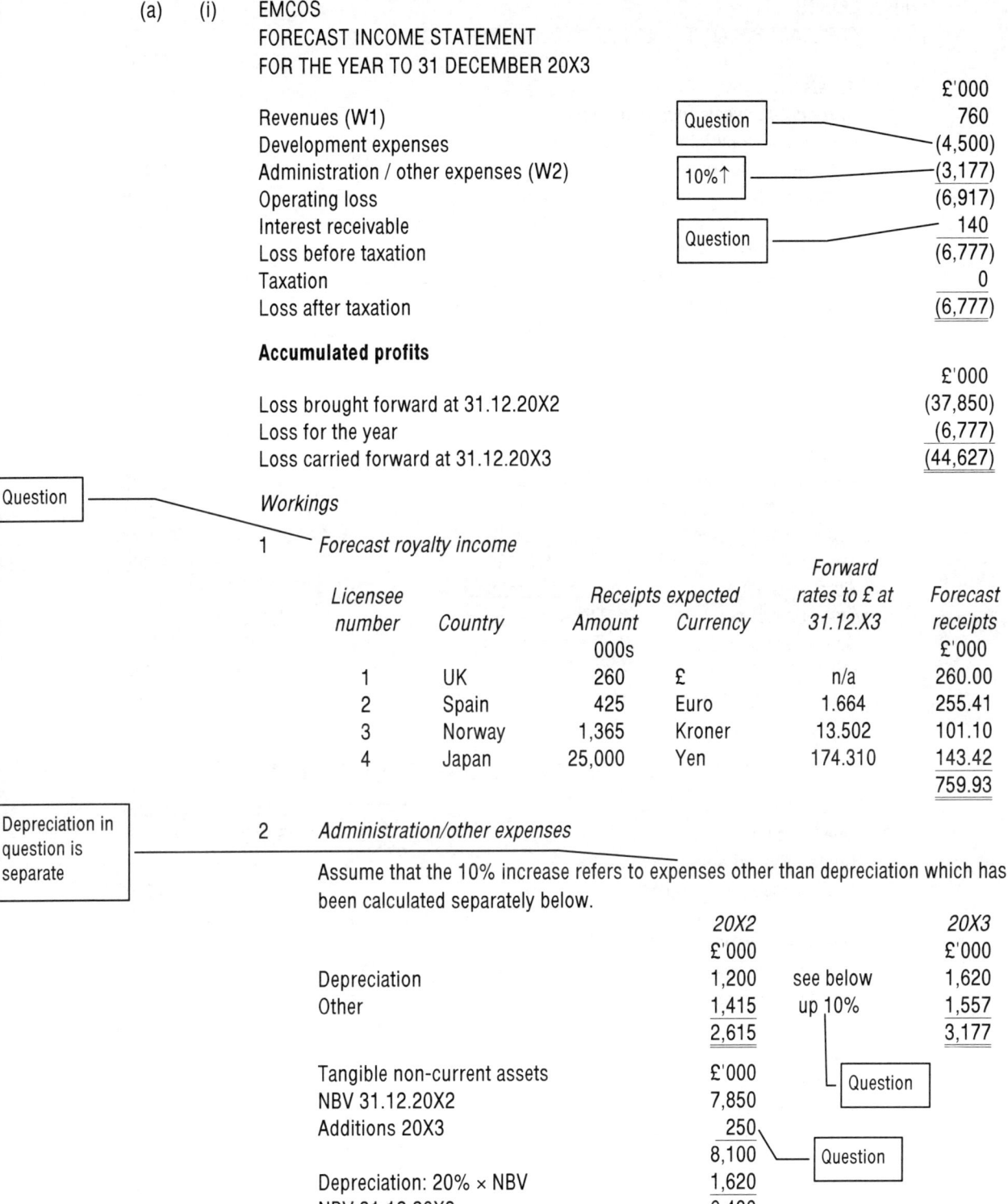

		£'000
Revenues (W1)	Question	760
Development expenses		(4,500)
Administration / other expenses (W2)	10%↑	(3,177)
Operating loss		(6,917)
Interest receivable	Question	140
Loss before taxation		(6,777)
Taxation		0
Loss after taxation		(6,777)

Accumulated profits

	£'000
Loss brought forward at 31.12.20X2	(37,850)
Loss for the year	(6,777)
Loss carried forward at 31.12.20X3	(44,627)

Question

Workings

1   *Forecast royalty income*

Licensee number	Country	Amount 000s	Currency	Forward rates to £ at 31.12.X3	Forecast receipts £'000
1	UK	260	£	n/a	260.00
2	Spain	425	Euro	1.664	255.41
3	Norway	1,365	Kroner	13.502	101.10
4	Japan	25,000	Yen	174.310	143.42
					759.93

Depreciation in question is separate

2   *Administration/other expenses*

Assume that the 10% increase refers to expenses other than depreciation which has been calculated separately below.

	20X2 £'000		20X3 £'000
Depreciation	1,200	see below	1,620
Other	1,415	up 10%	1,557
	2,615		3,177

Tangible non-current assets	£'000	
NBV 31.12.20X2	7,850	Question
Additions 20X3	250	
	8,100	Question
Depreciation: 20% × NBV	1,620	
NBV 31.12.20X3	6,480	

(ii) EMCOS
FORECAST BALANCE SHEET AT 31 DECEMBER 20X3

	£'000	£'000
Assets		
Non-current assets (net book value)		
Patents and copyright (751 + 320)		1,071
Tangible assets (W2)		6,480
Investments	Question	58
		7,609
Current assets		
Inventory and work in progress	Question — 285	
Marketable securities	–	
Cash and bank	Bank — 200	
		485
		8,094
EQUITY AND LIABILITIES		
Capital and reserves		
Called up share capital (ordinary shares of 10p)		9,985
Share premium account		37,522
Accumulated profits		(44,627)
	1,450 × 90%	2,880
Current liabilities		
Trade payables	Balancing figure — 1,450	
Bank overdraft	3,909	
		5,214
		8,094

(iii) EMCOS
CASH FLOW FORECAST FOR THE YEAR ENDED 31 DECEMBER 20X3

	£'000	£'000
Operating loss	I & E (6,917)	
Depreciation of non-current assets	1,620	
Funds consumed by operations	W2	(5,297)
Increase in working capital		
Inventory increase	285 – 98 — 187	
Decrease in trade payables	145	
	1,450 × 10%	(332)
Net cash outflow from operating activities		(5,629)
Taxation	Question	0
Capital expenditure		
Payments to acquire patents	(320)	
Payments to acquire tangible non-current assets	Question — (250)	
		(570)
Financing	Question	
Interest received		140
Sale of marketable securities	All sold as need overdraft	2,150
Decrease in cash and bank balances		(3,909)
	Overdraft in B/S	

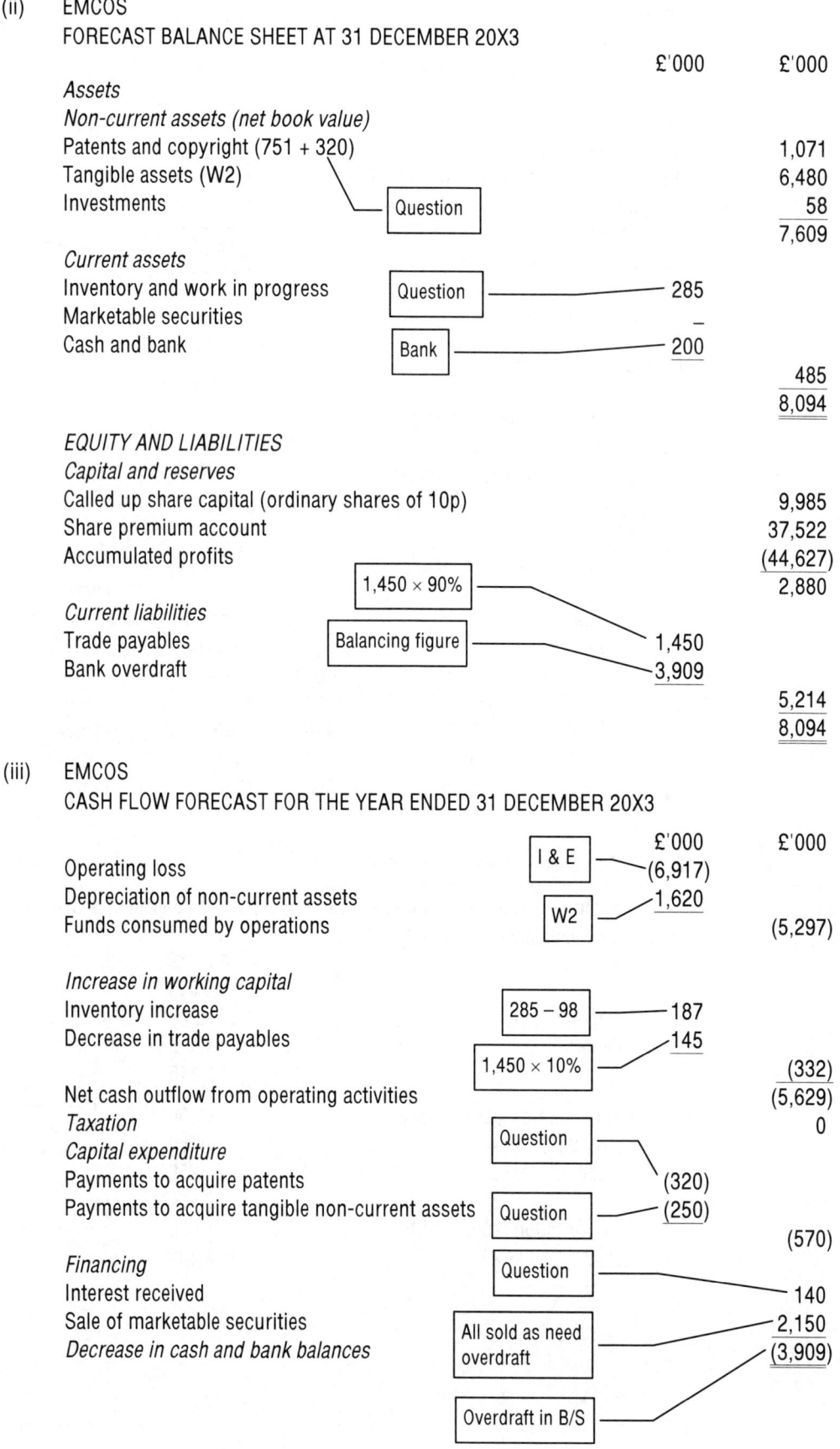

BPP
LEARNING MEDIA

(b) To: The Board of Directors, Emcos
From: Senior Management Accountant
Date: 9 December 20X2
Subject: Report on financial and risk strategies

a(i)

This report is written after preparation of the first draft of our financial forecasts for the year to 31 December 20X3, which show a forecast loss of £6.8 million, matched by a £6.1 million depletion in our cash and liquid investment resources. As you know, when we became listed in 20X0, we forecast losses until 20X3, followed by substantial trading profits thereafter. This report presents recommendations on strategies for **managing our future finances**, including a currency risk strategy.

3,909 + 2,150

Financing strategy

Need for funds

Next 12–24 months

New as well as existing

If we continue with our existing policy of designing, developing and owning the patents for a range of products, our financing strategy needs to take account of the likelihood that we will need to raise substantial sums of cash from investors before our current products **reach their full market potential**. We will also have a continuing need for investment funds to **develop new designs**, in order to maintain our competitive position.

Equity finance

Rights issue

No debt

Won't buy necessarily

These funds could be raised by further issues of equity funds or by borrowing. To raise **equity funds**, we would be required to offer shares to existing shareholders in a rights issue. The success of such an issue would depend on the evidence we can present for the profitability of future operations. If the issue is fully subscribed, our company would have succeeded in **minimising its financial risk**. However, shareholders may be **reluctant to subscribe** if they fear that our profit forecasts are unjustified, and this may lead to a collapse in our share price.

Alternative issue

If our shareholders agreed to **forego** their pre-emption rights, we could offer shares in a new issue on the stock exchange. Again however there is the risk that the issue will not be a success, and a new issue would **dilute the control of existing shareholders**.

Debt finance

Limits EMCOS

Long-term investment

Doesn't reduce risk

Investors may be more willing to **lend** funds than to subscribe for shares. We could decide to take out a **term loan** (of say 5 years) to give ourselves a stable source of finance. However, to make the interest rate acceptable, the loan would need to be **secured** on our **tangible assets** and **patents** and would introduce a high level of **financial risk** into our business. We would also increase our losses (or reduce our profits) by the amount of **interest payable**, and would not be able to gain the benefit of tax relief on debt interest while we were making losses.

Commitment

Using debt to hedge

Matching

Borrowings in the currency of our customers would enable us to **hedge** against the **currency risk** associated with our royalty receipts (see (ii) below).

Convertibles

Equity and loans

Less cost

More flexibility

A compromise choice would be to issue **convertible loan stock** (that is, loan stock with the right to convert to ordinary shares after a given time). Investors would have the **security of a fixed income** but would have the **option of exchanging** that for a **shareholding** when we become profitable. In return for this option, we might be able to **borrow at a lower interest rate** and without offering the security of our assets.

Realise assets	**Other options**

An alternative policy would be to **sell** some of our **patents** at a stage before they are fully developed. This would raise cash that we could **invest** in our **other products**. A further alternative would be to engage in **joint ventures** with our customers to develop some of our products.

Funds suppliers	

Recommendation — Mix

This report recommends that the company explores opportunities for **selling patents** and **entering into joint ventures** with customers, and makes plans for raising further investment funds by means of **limited borrowings in foreign currencies** (see (ii) below) and an issue of convertible loan stock.

9 KOL

Text references. Forecasts are revised in Chapter 3 and working capital management is also discussed in this chapter.

Top tips. (a) demonstrates the assumptions that you may have to make in this type of question.

In (b) calculation of the outflow of funds backs up the point emphasised at the start of the report, that cash flow difficulties are imminent. The outflow calculation also provides a structure to the subsequent discussion. To earn high marks for this discussion you needed to discuss the effects of the actions you propose and also make sensible suggestions; suggesting that a company which has less than £2 million annual revenues be floated on the stock exchange is not realistic. Note the answer to (b) concludes by discussing immediate solutions and also strategic issues.

Easy marks. Generally a fairly straightforward question. As always, don't get bogged down in the numbers, but leave plenty of time for the discussion.

(a) KOL
     ESTIMATED INCOME STATEMENT FOR 20X6

	$'000	$'000
Sales (W1)		1,725
Purchases (W2)	(584)	
Wages and salaries (W3)	(650)	
		(1,234)
Inventory movement		170
Gross profit		661
Other operating expenses	(380)	
Other rental income	180	
		(200)
Profit before interest and tax excluding depreciation		461

Workings

1   *Sales*

	$'000
Receipts for year	1,490
Less: January	(175)
February	(135)
March	(115)
Add: October to December sales	660
Total	1,725

2   *Purchases*

It is assumed that the actual amount of credit taken (90 days) has been used in the calculation of the cash flow.

		$'000
Payments for year		480
Less:	January	(52)
	February	(41)
	March	(34)
Add:	October to December purchases	231
Total		584

3   *Wages and salaries*

Since KOL is a manufacturing company, it is assumed that the wages and salaries are primarily direct costs. It is further assumed that they are all paid in the month in which they arise.

(b)   REPORT

To:	Board of Directors, KOL
From:	Management Accountant
Date:	21 November 20X5
Subject:	Review of 20X6 cash budget

Introduction

The purpose of this paper is to highlight those areas arising out of the **recent cash budgeting exercise** which need to be addressed by the Board, in particular the short-term financing requirements for 20X6. Some possible courses of action to address these areas will also be discussed.

Funding requirements

The cashflow forecast for 20X6 shows that the current **cash surplus will disappear** during the first quarter of the year and be replaced by a **rapidly growing deficit** that peaks in September. Although the projections suggest that the situation should improve thereafter, a cash deficit of $75,000 is still forecast for the end of the year. At its worst, the deficit is likely to be nearly twice the size of the existing overdraft limit, and therefore urgent action needs to be taken to address this issue.

Outflow of funds

Over the course of the year, the total **net outflow of funds** is $140,000 (reduction in cash balance, plus estimated interest). This movement comes about as follows.

	$'000
Profit generated from operations	448
Increase in inventory	(170)
Increase in receivables ((175 + 135 + 115) − 660)	(235)
Increase in payables ((52 + 41 + 34) − 231)	104
Dividends	(100)
Taxation	(65)
Capital expenditure	(120)
	(138)

Possible strategies for addressing the funding need

(i)   **Improve control of working capital**

The **net increase** in **working capital** for the year is forecast at $301,000 which is significant in terms of the amounts involved. The item showing the **largest increase is receivables**, and there should be scope for improvement in this area since customers are currently taking on average 30 days more than their normal terms of trade. The normal terms of trade of 60 days does not seem to be an unreasonable target to aim at, and if the **collection period** could be **reduced** by only 15 days during the year, the closing receivables would fall by $110,000. **Inventory** is also **forecast to increase** by the end of the year, and this increase should be fully justified in terms of additional sales before it is accepted as a budget figure.

The main disadvantage is a **potential loss of customer goodwill** because of increased pressure being put on them, and the possibility of loss of sales to competition. However it is unlikely that the competition will have much more generous credit terms than 60 days.

(ii) **Change production scheduling**

The **major increase in sales** is not forecast to take place until the second half of the year, with **increased receipts** from **customers** not being seen until the final quarter. However, **production** is **scheduled evenly** throughout the year. If production could be planned to **mirror demand** more closely, then the cash flow situation would be improved since the average inventory level would be reduced, and payments to suppliers would not increase until the second half of the year.

However cash flow over the whole year may suffer as a result of increased labour costs because of **overtime** or the need to **employ extra labour** to meet the demand.

(iii) **Defer capital expenditure**

If the investment in new plant and machinery is required in order to increase the level of production to meet increases in demand then it may be difficult to put off this item. However, it may be possible to **delay the purchase of new motor vehicles** and the **building renovations**, or alternatively to acquire the vehicles on a lease or hire basis and thus spread the cost of these assets more evenly over their useful lives. Again though the **ultimate cost of leasing** may be greater than that of purchasing.

(iv) **Defer the dividend**

It may be possible to defer or **stage the payment of the dividend**, or perhaps to offer a **scrip alternative**. Whether this is possible depends on anticipated shareholder reaction; although the shareholders cannot **force the directors to recommend a dividend,** in a private company there may be a few dominant shareholders against whose wishes the board cannot go for long.

(v) **Take on some medium-term debt**

KOL appears to be 100% equity financed at present. It should therefore be able to negotiate some form of **medium-term loan** given that the company is both growing and currently shows a good profit margin (26% before depreciation and tax). Although this would probably need to be secured on the assets, it is likely to be less risky than the overdraft which is repayable on demand. Again however **shareholders may react adversely** to the need to make interest payments and hence the increased risk to their dividend levels.

(vi) **Asset refinancing**

Although rental income is currently generated from some of the premises, KOL might consider raising additional cash by **selling part** of the **premises** assuming that this is practicable and that they are not required for future expansion plans. Alternatively the company could consider some form of **sale and leaseback** of the property and/or some of the other assets. However the terms of the sale and leaseback arrangement may mean that the company **loses flexibility** in the future if for example it wants to expand or change the use of the premises.

(vii) **Venture capital**

Although the company might be a little small for this source of development funds, KOL may be able to attract a **venture capital investment**. However, it would have to be able to get the **agreement of the shareholders** to this and the directors would have to **relinquish some degree of control** to the venture capital organisation. Alternatively, some of the other shareholders may be able to make a further investment in the company.

Conclusions

(i) **Immediate plan**

The directors need to put a plan in place now to meet the **forecast mid-year financing problems**. Any changes to the credit and stockholding policies or to the production scheduling must be evaluated in terms of their effect on sales, and the budget reworked to take account of the revised figures.

(ii) **Other issues**

It is suggested that the directors should also consider two more fundamental questions in the course of their review.

(1) Is the **proposed expansion justified** in terms of the amount of value added to the business? If the NPV of the incremental cashflow is low then slowing down the expansion programme would benefit the cashflow.

(2) The directors could **consider selling all or part of the business** to a larger company with the desire and the resources to fund the expansion plans.

Signed: Management Accountant

10 RJ

Text references. Forecasting and performance measures are revised in Chapter 3.

Top tips. Tax is complicated in part (a) by the difference between depreciation and tax allowances. You need a working for payables and receivables although a full balance sheet is not required. Note (b) is quite similar to a question in the May 2005 exam; the fact that the finance is only needed short-term is significant.

Easy marks. You would get some marks for the more straightforward figures.

Examiner's comments. Part (a) was generally well answered except for the impact of capital allowances in the taxation calculation. In Part (b), the presentation of figures could have been improved.

(a) **Forecast income statements**

Year	20X5	20X6	20X7	
	£'000	£'000	£'000	
Revenue	30,120	33,132	36,445	Up 10%
Cash based costs and expenses	(22,500)	(23,625)	(24,806)	Up 5%
Depreciation	–	(600)	(600)	10% straight line on £6 million.
Operating profit	7,620	8,907	11,039	
Finance costs	(2,650)	(2,650)	(2,650)	Unchanged
Profit before tax	4,970	6,257	8,389	
Tax	(1,491)	(1,607)	(2,359)	W1
Profit after tax	3,479	4,650	6,030	
Dividend	(1,392)	(1,462)	(1,535)	Up 5% Paid following year
Retained profit for the year	2,087	3,188	4,495	
Retained earnings b/f		4,750	7,938	
Retained earnings c/f		7,938	12,433	

Working 1: Tax payable

	20X6	20X7
	£'000	£'000
Plant value at start of year	6,000	4,500
Tax allowance (25% reducing balance)	(1,500)	(1,125)
Profit before tax	6,257	8,389
Add back depreciation	600	600
Less tax allowance	(1,500)	(1,125)
Taxable profit	5,357	7,864

(b) **Cash flow forecasts**

Year ended

	20X6	20X7	
	£'000	£'000	
Cash from sales (33,132 + 3700 – 4070) (W2)	32,762	36,038	Up 10%
Cash on costs and expenses (23,625 + 2,850 – 2,993)	(23,482)	(24,656)	Up 5%
Cash from operations	9,280	11,382	
Finance costs	(2,650)	(2,650)	Constant
Dividend paid	(1,392)	(1,462)	Previous year's div.
Tax paid	(1,491)	(1,607)	Previous year's tax
Purchase of plant and machinery	(6,000)	-	
Net cash flow	(2,253)	5,663	
Balance brought forward	198	(2,055)	
Balance carried forward	(2,055)	3,608	

Working 2: Trade receivables and payables

	20X5	20X6	20X7
	£'000	£'000	£'000
Trade receivables (grow by 10% p.a.)	3,700	4,070	4,477
Trade payables (grow by 5% p.a.)	2,850	2,993	3,143

Financing of cash deficit

The cash deficit in 20X6 could be financed by **increasing the company's overdraft; by taking out a medium term loan**; by **reducing the dividend** (would only finance part of the deficit); or by using a **source of short term finance** based on its **receivables** (factoring or invoice discounting). The deficit is not large enough and does not last long enough to consider a longer term source of funds such as a share issue or long term loan. The situation may be complicated if there are **restrictive covenants** in the company's borrowing based on **liquidity and/or gearing levels**, in which case equity funds would be needed unless the company can renegotiate terms with its bankers.

Reducing the dividend would require **careful explanation to shareholders** and most quoted companies would probably opt to increase borrowings rather than reduce the dividend when the profitability trend is firmly upwards.

(c) **Key aspects of the company's performance**

Pre-tax return

The company's stated targets are concerned with profitability and growth. On the basis of above forecasts, the pre-tax return on closing book value of equity is forecast to stay consistently above the target of 35% p.a. and to show steady growth:

20X5: 4,970 / (8,350 + 4,750) = 37.9%
20X6: 6,257 / (8,350 + 7,938) = 38.4%

20X7: 8,389 / (8,350 + 12,433) = 40.4%

Growth in equity earnings

At the same time, the forecast annual growth in equity earnings (profit after tax) is much higher than the company's target.

20X6: 4,650 / 3,479 – 1 = 33.7%

20X7: 6,030 / 4,650 – 1 = 29.7%

These results are excellent, especially as an **increase in sales** (or reduction in cost) specifically from the investment in plant has not been **factored** into the forecasts.

Liquidity position

However, the results cannot be looked at in isolation of the company's liquidity position. The investment and rapid growth will cause a significant drop in the cash resources during 20X6, though this is predicted to turn round in 20X7.

The liquidity ratios will change as follows:

	20X5	20X6	20X7
	£'000	£'000	£'000
Inventories	4,510	4,510	4,510
Trade receivables	3,700	4,070	4,477
Cash	198		3608
	8,408	8,580	12,595
Current liabilities			
Trade payables	2,850	2,993	3,143
Other payables: Tax and dividends	2,883	3,069	3,894
Overdraft		2,055	
	5,733	8,117	7,037
Current ratio (current assets/ current liabilities)	1.47	1.06	1.79
Quick ratio (current assets – inventory / current liabilities)	0.68	0.50	1.15

Although the liquidity position is only bad for one year, the company will need to increase its overdraft facility with its bankers, or use one of the other sources of funds mentioned in part (b) above.

The 6% bonds will need to be **redeemed in 20X8** and there will probably be enough cash by then to do this, although an alternative would be to refinance with more long term debt at that stage.

11 RG

Text references. Dividend policy is discussed in Chapter 4.

Top tips. (a) provides the opportunity to display your knowledge of recent developments in the discussion of dividend policy. Examples of the more extreme policies can be given, together with examples of pronouncements made by some of the institutions.

(b) starts by explaining an important point – that cash does not have to be given back to shareholders but can be retained in the business for investment. (b) brings out the importance of signalling, suggesting that markets are not always strongly efficient. Hence they may not be able to recognise a large payment as being one-off, they may instead view the payment as a sign that the directors have run out of ideas for investments. Because markets are not strongly efficient, a steady stream approach may be best, supported on occasions by short-term borrowing as brought out in (c). Note in (d) that an increase in financial risk caused by higher gearing is likely to be outweighed by the benefits of obtaining cheaper finance provided gearing levels are not too great.

Easy marks. The parts look fairly even in terms of difficulty, so marks are maximised by ensuring you make some reasonable comments for each part, and don't miss any out.

(a)   **Dividend policy**

The policy being put forward is consistent with the basic accounting concept that dividends should only be paid if there are **sufficient distributable profits** available to cover the payout. However, profits vary from one accounting period to the next, and companies face the conflicting demands of maintaining a **constant payout ratio** and level of dividend cover against maintaining a **consistent level of actual dividend payments**. In recent recessions some firms adopted a conservative policy and severely cut the dividend, while others maintained the level of payments in line with their view of longer term future prospects rather than short-term current performance.

(i)   **Financial institutions**

Financial institutions tend to prefer **dividend income** to **capital growth** because cash flows are required to meet their liabilities and, if these cash flows are in the form of dividend payments, they can **avoid the transaction costs** involved in realising capital gains. It is therefore likely that institutional shareholders would prefer the increased payout ratio in the period of reduced growth. Institutions often put pressure on companies to ensure that dividend levels are maintained during periods of reduced profit performance.

(ii)   **Small private investors**

The **position of small private investors** will vary. Where they **fall below the income tax threshold** then they too are likely to express a preference for an **increased payout ratio**. However these tax advantages are not available to other investors, who will **prefer capital gains** if they can take advantage of any exemption from tax on capital gains below a certain limit. They will also be able to time their realisation of capital gains in order to minimise their tax liability.

(b)/(c)/(d) REPORT

To: The Directors of DV
From: IFA Financial Advisers
Date: 15 May 20X7
Subject: Dividend policy and share buybacks

We set out below our comments on the matters we talked about at our recent meeting.

(b)   **Implications of share repurchase**

Before deciding on a **share repurchase**, you must clarify the company's overall cash requirements for the foreseeable future. Our assumption in this discussion is that the company will have a substantial temporary surplus of funds this year but that, if this is distributed to shareholders, additional funds will be needed for the subsequent two years.

Cash retention

Your first decision is whether to retain the cash until it is needed next year, or to distribute it to shareholders, or to retain a proportion, distributing the balance. **Retained cash** could be placed on deposit or invested in a suitable **financial portfolio**. Secondly, if you decide to distribute the cash to shareholders, this can be done either as a dividend or by buying back some shares.

Deciding level of cash retention

The argument against retaining too much cash is that it can give the impression that the directors have 'run out of ideas' for expanding the company's operations. This may cause the **share price to drop** and attract unwanted takeover bids. On the other hand, the retention is logical if the company can **invest the cash short term** at a higher interest rate than individual shareholders. Any such retention of cash must be accompanied by careful explanations to the market of the company's investment plans over the following two years.

Implications of dividend payment

If the surplus cash is distributed to shareholders as a **dividend**, this will cause a big percentage increase in dividend this year. Shareholders will be happy with the cash received but, in the absence of further explanations, will become confused by what the company is trying to **'signal'** by this dividend increase. Some may assume that further large increases in dividend can be expected in future years, and may develop over-optimistic expectations of the company's prospects.

Buyback as use for surplus cash

Most finance directors take the view that it is best to increase dividends at a steady rate which **signals the company's long-run growth prospects**. If you agree with this view and you wish to make an **above-average distribution** to shareholders, you may consider using the balance of surplus cash to buy back some of the company's shares. For example, GEC, which for many years was criticised for holding too much cash, has more recently adopted a policy of share buy-backs.

Mechanism of buyback

The share buy-back requires provision in the company's constitution and approval in general meeting. It can be arranged as a series of purchases on the open market or as a **private purchase** from a number of large shareholders. Assuming that the buy-back is at **market price**, the **share price** should be **unaffected**, whereas if a dividend payout is made, the share price will fall (from cum div to ex div). With a buy-back, the remaining shares will effectively be worth more, reflecting the higher future earnings per share.

Strategic share buybacks

Share buy-backs are sometimes made for **strategic reasons** separate from the dividend policy considerations outlined above. These include:

(i)   The wish to **re-privatise a business**; in this case all the shares were bought back from investors
(ii)   To make **shares available for employee share option schemes**
(iii)   As a **defence** against a **hostile takeover bid**
(iv)   To **increase** the **company's gearing**

(c)   **Advisability of borrowing money to pay dividends in years 2 and 3**

Borrowing money to pay dividends is legal provided that the dividends are **covered by the accumulated balance of distributable profits**. The question is whether it is financially advisable.

Maintaining dividend growth

In theory, if cash is invested and dividends are reduced, this should not worry shareholders provided that they can see the prospect of **increased future dividends.** In practice, for 'signalling' reasons mentioned above, it is believed that shareholders are happiest when they receive a steady stream of dividends increasing from year to year. This is an argument in favour of borrowing in order to maintain the dividend growth. Shareholders receive more cash in years 2 and 3 but less in future years because of the need to repay the loans with interest.

Recommendation

Given that the company is not highly geared we recommend that the company borrows as much as is needed to **maintain dividend growth** in line with long-term earnings growth.

(d) **Effect on the company's cost of equity**

If shares are repurchased, the **total value of equity goes down** by the amount of cash paid out while debt remains unchanged. This **increase in gearing** will cause the **cost of equity to rise** because of the increased financial risk (volatility of equity earnings) experienced by the shareholders. In the same way, if the company increases its borrowings in order to pay dividends, the gearing will increase and the **cost of equity capital** will rise.

Effect on cost of debt

However, DV is operating at a **low level of gearing**. The increase in the **cost of equity** is likely to be **outweighed** by the **cheap after-tax cost of debt** compared with equity. The tax savings resulting from debt interest will mean that, even though the cost of equity goes up, the weighted average cost of capital will be reduced.

I hope these notes address the points you have raised with us. If you require any further clarification please contact us at any time.

Signed: IFA Financial Advisers

12 AB and YZ

Text references. Dividend policy is discussed in Chapter 4.

Top tips. On inspection you can see that AB is paying out the same dividend, and you may have been able to see that YZ's payout ratio is also constant; a quick calculation would show you in any event. The other information and the hints given in the question about share price should have helped you realize that you needed to calculate the price-earnings ratio. You don't have time to say very much about other factors that may affect market value but these certainly should be briefly mentioned.

(a) (ii) discusses the main points of the Modigliani and Miller theory; when planning you should have noted these and then thought how each might relate to the two companies.

(b) is a good summary of the main issues on a share repurchase. The question requirements helpfully detail the principal points.

Easy marks. Whether you choose a question in the exam will depend on how well you know share repurchases. You could score close to full marks on (b) if you know share repurchases well, but would probably avoid the question if you weren't confident.

Examiner's comments. Discussions on the actual dividend policy in (a) tended to be rather better than discussions of the optimal dividend policy. Some candidates were confused when answering (b) between share repurchases and reprivatisations.

(a) (i) **Dividend policies followed by AB and YZ**

Payout and price earnings ratio

	AB		YZ	
	Payout % DPS/EPS	P/E	Payout % DPS/EPS	P/E
20X1	26	9.1	40	9.2
20X2	40	10.0	40	10.6
20X3	60	10.0	40	15.6
20X4	–	–	-	–
20X5	60	10.0	40	13.9
20X6	40	9.3	40	11.7

AB's dividend policy

Over the past six years, AB and YZ have had virtually identical earnings per share (after adjusting for YZ's rights issue), but have had **different dividend policies.** AB has paid **constant dividends per share**, maintaining its dividend during the period of falling profits from 20X1 to 20X4, but not increasing them when profits recovered in 20X5 and 20X6. This has resulted in an overall average dividend payout ratio over the six year period of 60% of earnings.

YZ's dividend policy

By contrast YZ has maintained a **consistent dividend payout ratio of 40%** of equity earnings each year, the only exception being in 20X4 when losses were made and no dividend was paid.

Both companies operate in the same industry and have **similar capital structures** and, as stated above, virtually identical earnings records. However, throughout the six year period YZ has had a **consistently higher share price** (and hence lower cost of capital) than AB. On average, YZ's share price has been **17% higher**. This seems to provide evidence that the constant payout ratio policy of YZ has been superior to the constant dividend policy of AB. This may also be confirmed by events in 20X4, when YZ made a loss, failed to pay a dividend and its share price declined by 35%, whereas AB's share price only fell by 20%.

Other factors

The share price will **not only** be **determined** by dividend policy. If the market is well informed about investment policy, it may value YZ higher, because AB has, by paying a constant dividend, reduced the amount of funds invested and therefore limited future earnings. The market may also feel generally that YZ's overall strategy is superior, for example that the rights issue was a good decision despite being launched just after YZ had made a loss.

(ii) **Is there an optimal dividend policy?**

Modigliani and Miller's theory

Modigliani and Miller's theory of **dividend irrelevance** suggests that the value of the two companies' shares should be identical, because share value depends on the present value of future cash surpluses generated, not on the manner in which they are distributed. This theory has been criticized because of its unrealistic assumptions:

- Perfect capital markets, with no transaction costs
- Investor indifference between dividends and capital gains
- Full information about future investments

In theory companies either have positive NPV investments that they should **finance** by **retained earnings,** thus paying zero dividends, or they have no investments, in which case all earnings should be paid as dividends. In practice they do not do this.

Signalling

The traditional view that dividends act as a signal to shareholders has led to **widespread adoption** by companies of policies of constant dividends or constant growth in dividends. Under such policies, dividends are **never reduced** unless it is really unavoidable. Yet although AB has followed such a policy, it has led to a lower share price than that of YZ, thus offering some evidence against the effectiveness of this strategy.

Agency theory

Agency theory predicts that payment of dividends helps to **reduce the agency conflict** between shareholders and managers. This might work in several ways. In general, the **higher the dividend, the lower the agency costs** (favouring AB over YZ), but it may be that in paying a dividend which is a fixed percentage of profits, YZ's managers are demonstrating that they are aware that profits belong to the shareholders. This may result in **lower agency costs for YZ** than for AB, and hence a lower cost of capital and higher share price.

To maximize share values, AB's directors should ensure that they always **keep shareholders informed** about company plans and results. Their current policy of constant dividends could be regarded as an attempt to hide operations from shareholders.

Taxation

Tax regimes where **dividends** are **taxed at a higher effective rate** than **capital gains** tend to make high dividend pay-outs disadvantageous.

Conclusion

In summary, there is no simple solution to an optimal dividend policy. Some shareholders are likely to prefer dividends, some eventual capital appreciation.

(b) **Share repurchase**

(i) **How a share repurchase may be arranged**

Special resolution

If permitted by its articles, AB may pass a special resolution to **authorise the company** to **buy back some of its shares**, but it cannot do so if this would leave only redeemable shares in issue. The terms of the special resolution will depend on whether it is a 'market purchase' (that is, an open market purchase made on the stock exchange), a tender offer to all shareholders or an individual arrangement with certain shareholders.

Treatment of shares purchased

Generally, when a company purchases its own shares, the **shares are cancelled** on their return to the company. However, a listed company may be able to hold the shares 'in treasury' for resale or **transfer to an employees' shares scheme** at a later date.

(ii) **Main reasons for a share repurchase**

Use of surplus cash

AB will have more cash than is needed for its investments and must therefore choose **what to do with its surplus cash.** The cash could be used to **increase the dividend.** However, companies like AB, which maintain a steady dividend policy, usually take the view that when a dividend is increased this will lead the shareholders to expect a similar increase in future years.

If AB is not sure that this increase can be maintained, it will **keep the dividend constant** and use one of a number of alternative actions including **purchasing own shares** or **repaying debt.** Repayment of debt is the most common approach used by companies like AB, but if this is not feasible (e.g. because of high termination costs) they may choose to repurchase shares. The repurchase of shares will signal a 'one-off special payment' to shareholders rather than trigger expectations of a permanent increase in dividend.

Reduction of future total dividends

If the company is maintaining levels of dividend per share, then **fewer shares** will mean **smaller total dividends.**

Enhancement of earnings per share

Fewer shares will mean an **enhancement of earnings per share,** perhaps resulting in an increased market price per share.

Control

By buying out problem shareholders, those **currently in control of the company** can improve their position. One consequence may be that **AB** becomes **less vulnerable** to a hostile takeover bid.

Tax position of shareholders

Shareholders may be better off tax-wise than if they **receive a higher dividend.** A share repurchase may lead to a capital gains tax liability; however a special dividend will attract a (possibly higher) income tax liability.

Effect on cost of capital

Repurchase of shares will **increase the company's gearing,** possibly ensuring that the company is nearer an optimal gearing level, thus lowering the cost of capital.

(iii) **Potential problems**

Lack of new ideas

Purchase of own shares may be interpreted as a sign that the company has **no new ideas** for **future investment strategy.** This may cause the share price to fall. Other shareholders may, of course, be thankful that the management is not gambling shareholder funds in areas it knows little about. They may consider that they can diversify more effectively than AB.

Costs

Compared with making a one-off extra dividend payment, purchase of shares requires **more time and transaction costs** to arrange. It may require more cash than the company has available.

Shareholder consent

Shareholders will have to pass a **special resolution** and it may be difficult to obtain their consent. Determining the right price may be difficult.

Agency theory

Agency theory would explain a preference for dividends by saying:

(1) Shareholders need a **commitment by company management** that they will distribute free cash flow and not invest it in unprofitable activities

(2) In this regard **dividends are perceived as a stronger commitment** than the repurchase of shares.

Gearing

If the equity base is reduced and gearing is increased, then **shareholders' financial risk** may be **increased.**

(iv) **Effect on share price**

In theory in a **perfect market** shareholders should be **indifferent** between a repurchase of own shares and a dividend.

However in practice the **market's reaction** may be **difficult to predict,** depending on how the market views an **increase in earnings per share,** versus the market believing that a **repurchase** demonstrates a **lack of future opportunities** and hence **limited prospects of future increases in earnings per share**. If the cash is not reinvested for growth the share price will fall and/or the company may be subject to a takeover bid.

13 DRY

Text references. Dividend policy is discussed in Chapter 4 and the role of the finance function is covered in Chapter 13.

Top tips. Part (a) is a simple matter of plugging the various numbers into the formula and seeing which gives the best result. Income preferences, tax position and signalling are key points in (b), costs, resource usage and risk in (c).

(d) doesn't just focus on the finance function's role in compliance, it also covers other important strategic issues, how the department contributes to the business and how its performance is measured.

Easy marks. (b) and (c) are little more than tests of knowledge, and you should revise these areas if you struggled with these parts.

(a) Using the dividend growth model the overall market value of the company can be assessed under the current dividend policy and under each of the three new proposed strategies.

$$P_0 = \frac{d_0(1+g)}{(r-g)}$$

Current policy

Market value = (£120m × 80%)/0.08 = £1,200m

Strategy 1

Market value = ((£120m × 10%) × 1.08)/(0.12 − 0.08) = £324m

Strategy 2

Market value = ((£120m × 30%) × 1.05)/(0.10 − 0.05) = £756m

Strategy 3

Market value = ((£120m × 60%) × 1.03)/(0.09 − 0.03) = £1,236m

The recommendation therefore would be to follow investment strategy 3 as this increases the overall market value of the shareholders by £36m (or 3%).

(b) The dividend policy of a company and any proposed changes to that policy are important to the shareholders of the company for a number of reasons.

(i) Many investors will have invested in a company **solely because** of its **dividend policy**. For example investors who need regular income such as insurance companies might choose to invest in companies with relatively high and stable dividend payout ratios.

(ii) Investors will often have a preference between **income and capital gains**. If they have invested in a company with a high dividend payout ratio then they may wish to disinvest if the company aims for high capital growth and lower dividend payments.

(iii)   Different types of investors will have **different tax profiles**. Some may like high dividend payments whilst others may prefer capital gains. Either way they will tend to invest in companies whose dividend and retention policies suit their own tax profile.

(iv)   Many investors prefer **current dividends** to the promise of future capital gain as the dividend being paid now is more certain than capital gains and/or higher dividends in future.

(v)   A change in dividend policy is often perceived by the market in general, and by shareholders in the company in particular, to have an **informational content**. The change may be perceived to signal an **upturn or downturn** in the success of the company.

(c)   There are a number of reasons why a company may prefer to use retained profits to fund an investment project instead of raising new equity funds.

(i)   An issue of new shares is a **costly** business with the payment of **legal** and merchant **bank** fees, **prospectus** costs etc. The use of retained profits avoids the need to incur these additional costs.

(ii)   An issue of equity shares will require a great deal of **management time** in discussions with financial advisors and merchant banks etc.

(iii)   There is an element of **uncertainty** when issuing new equity shares. The entire process of organising an issue takes a considerable period of time and the share price at the time of the issue and the overall success of the issue are by no means guaranteed.

(iv)   An issue of equity shares will generally mean a **change in earnings per share** as there are new shares in issue and the profits from the new investment may not be fully operational. If there is a risk of a short-term decrease in earnings per share due to the issue then managers may prefer to use retained profits as earnings per share is viewed as one of the most **important market indicators** for a company.

(d)   **Evaluation of strategic opportunities**

The board needs to decide the extent to which it wishes the finance function to be involved in the **evaluation of strategic opportunities** including expansion of existing businesses, product/market diversification and merger and acquisition work. However too great an involvement in operational concerns may mean that the finance function no longer has the **independence** to be able to exercise a control function.

Thus many organisations have adopted a **business partner model** where operational departments are responsible for the **creation** of ideas, and the finance function is responsible for the **assessment** and **validation** of these ideas. The finance function's role is to review and challenge plans if necessary.

Statutory requirements

If the company is a listed company, or intends to seek a listing, much of the finance function's time will be spent ensuring compliance with **statutory and listing requirements**. This includes fulfilling the requirements of relevant corporate governance codes, including operating internal controls and perhaps providing an internal audit presence. The function must also be able to **communicate well** with investors, and present financial information in a clear and accessible format.

Treasury expertise

If DRY is seeking finance for investment, **strong treasury skills** will be required to secure both the short and long-term financing of the company and to contribute to capital structure decisions. A **separate treasury function** may need to be established.

Cost control

If growth is slow due to market constraints, there is likely to be a higher degree of attention paid to the improvement of profit by means of cost control. Therefore the finance function must be able to select and implement **appropriate budgetary and control systems**, and to provide management information in a concise and relevant form.

Measurement of the finance function's performance

The board will need to decide what measures should be used to measure the finance function's effectiveness.

(i) **Reliable information** is likely to be a key indicator, particularly because of the recent tightening up of the accountancy regulations.

(ii) Similarly the finance function's role in **introducing new financial accounting standards** will need to be assessed.

(iii) The **speed** with which information is produced will also be significant. This includes statutory information, where reporting time limits are prescribed by law, and internal management accounting information, where business imperatives will be important.

(iv) Efficiency measures, such as transactions processed per employee, will be needed to gain an idea of the **value for money** of the function.

A **balanced scorecard approach** may be used, focusing on the **value enhancements** provided by the department and the satisfaction expressed by the function's internal 'customers'.

14 TED

Text references. Current issues in financial reporting are discussed in Chapter 4 and corporate governance is covered in Chapter 1.

Top tips. You are unlikely to get a full question on topical financial accounting issues in the exam. However this question highlights the fact that emerging and current issues are in the syllabus, and you must be aware of their significance. The question highlights the ways in which the areas discussed impact upon financial strategy, influencing the decision-making process, the information that managers will use and the impact on relations with stakeholders.

Easy marks. Keeping your answer focused timely on strategic issues (what decisions do managers make and what information do they require to make them) will help you score well here. You don't need detailed knowledge of any of those areas to pass this question, just a broad overview of key issues.

(a) **Impact of environmental costs**

Investment appraisal

The way in which **environmental costs and benefits** are included in the appraisal process will depend on the nature of the environmental implications, and the way in which the company intends to approach them. One method is to include in the appraisal only those elements of **environmental cost** that are **directly attributable** to undertaking the project, and to evaluate any further actions that the company may wish to undertake as a separate issue. In some cases, this may be relatively simple, particularly if legislation exists that defines the environmental standards to be applied.

Problems with investment appraisal

The problems arise where the company sees the opportunity to go beyond its statutory duties and to act in such a way as to **maximise the environmental benefits**. In this situation, the higher cost option may become more attractive, although this is not a direct requirement of the project being undertaken. The benefits that arise are difficult to quantify and will not accrue directly to the company undertaking the investment.

In this situation, two approaches are possible.

(i) The company could decide that its own environmental standards form a financial constraint upon the project, and thus that the project should be **evaluated at its full environmental cost**.

(ii) Alternatively, it could decide that the additional costs of on-site treatment over and above the cost of meeting the statutory requirements represent a **separate environmental investment**. If the company sets aside a budget for environmental and social issues, these excess costs could then be taken away from the project and allocated against this environmental budget.

Both approaches are valid and will depend on the objectives and policies of the company with regard to environmental issues.

Accounting systems

Increasing concern with environmental costs will have various impacts upon the accounting systems, including the way in which production is measured (energy used and disposal of waste being more significant) and analysis of the impact of **variances**.

Annual accounts

As well as the impact upon specific investments, organisations have to consider the effect on the accounts as a whole. This includes **expenditure** on for example **cleaner technology** that affects all operations. Organisations also have to consider the potential costs of non-compliance such as **legal fees and fines**.

As well as affecting the numbers, environmental considerations will impact upon the disclosures made in the accounts. External pressures mean shareholders and other **stakeholders** will be looking for measurement of social cost and environmental performance

(b) **Impact on accounts**

Human resource accounting aims to **assist decision-making** by valuing how managers and employees and human resource practices **add value** to the organisation. In a acquisition for example an important reason for buying a company can be its human expertise, and reliable human resource accounting methods can help ensure that this premium is calculated fairly.

Problems with valuation methods

However there are problems with possible valuation methods. One method would be to **capitalise** all **human development costs** such as recruiting and training and amortising these costs over the employee's expected career. An alternative method is to **calculate** the **replacement cost**, the costs of obtaining and training another employee if the current one leaves. However the problem with both these methods is that the value of the benefits generated by an employee may not bear much relation to training, development or replacement costs. Replacement costs may also be difficult to estimate. Other methods, such as discounting future wages by a factor corresponding to effectiveness, are very subjective.

In addition it may be difficult to compare the performance of organisations because of their **different circumstances**. Organisations may concentrate on performing well according to measures that are easy to operate, as opposed to trying to improve in more important areas that are less easy to assess.

Impact on stakeholders

Human resource accounting can be a means of **demonstrating success to external shareholders**. It can show that the organisation is able to recruit, retain and develop good people who can contribute to high performance. It can also demonstrate to staff as **internal stakeholders** the value the organisation puts on their contribution.

However human resource accounting may highlight conflicts between stakeholders, particularly staff who are interested in their long-term career and shareholders whose interests are more short-term.

(c) **Corporate governance**

Decision-making

The corporate governance codes require certain matters to be **reserved** for decision by the board. This includes **major issues of financial strategy** such as mergers and acquisitions and acquisitions of major assets. The reports also require the board to have a **sufficient range of expertise** including financial expertise. This implies not only having a suitably-qualified financial director but appropriate knowledge amongst the non-executive directors, particularly those who staff the audit committee

Directors' remuneration

Directors' remuneration can have a significant impact upon financial strategy because of the **amounts involved**, how effective the packages are in obtaining directors of sufficient calibre to take major decisions and also relations with stakeholders. The corporate governance reports try to help companies balance up these perhaps conflicting factors by allowing companies to set **appropriate levels** provided there is a **clear remuneration policy**, **independent scrutiny** by a remuneration committee of non-executive directors and **full disclosure** in the accounts.

Risk management

Recent reports require companies to have in place **appropriate risk management procedures** including reviews by the board, audit committee and internal audit. These reviews are likely to take a particularly close interest in the activities of the treasury department, because of the potential for major losses in certain of its activities, for example dealing on the derivatives markets.

Internal audit

Most corporate governance reports either **require** the **establishment of an internal audit function** or require companies to consider the need for one annually. This impacts upon the work of the **financial control function** in terms of the resources they require and also their priorities, with more stress on control and compliance work and less stress on adding value to operational departments.

Relationships with stakeholders

The reports suggest a number of methods for **improving relations** with stakeholders, including clear disclosure in the annual report not just of financial accounting issues, but of **performance**, **financing and future strategy** in the operating and financial review, and of how internal controls, including internal financial controls, are operated.

The reports also stress the importance of treating other stakeholders fairly in accordance with the law, in particular **suppliers of finance** such as trade creditors.

15 PJH

Text references. Equity finance is covered in Chapter 5 and debt finance in Chapter 6.

Top tips. Make sure your answer is laid out as a report. When discussing the raising of new equity, don't forget to mention cash retained as a source of equity funds, and compare raising equity with raising debt. Also, don't forget this is an unquoted company (so for example rights to new shares cannot be sold on the market). Financial objectives are difficult to describe for an unquoted company, because they depend on the wishes of the shareholders, and tax can distort the way in which shareholder-directors take their benefits. In any discussion of this nature you should make some mention of profitability, gearing and liquidity.

(b) emphasises that the value of the company increases by the finance brought in, in addition to the net present value of the investment. With debt, you have the further amount of the tax shield; as debt is redeemable here you have to discount the amount received over five years.

Easy marks. Make sure you remember the key points in (c) if you didn't score well on this part. Although it's not necessarily easier than the other two parts, the points included are fundamental strategic points which may well need to be included in discussion parts of questions, particularly of compulsory Question 1.

Examiner's comments. This question was less popular than expected, and many candidates failed to take into account the factors that applied to a family-owned company. In (a) candidates discussed debt v equity rather than new equity, and then repeated much of their answer in (b). Valuation techniques were often poor, and in some cases no calculations were shown. In general there was too much emphasis on Modigliani and Miller's calculations and general long – term objectives.

To: Mrs Henry, Managing Director, PJH
From: Management Accountant
Date: 9 December 20X2
Subject: Report on financing the proposed expansion programme

This report is written in the light of the need to raise finance for the proposed new expansion programme. It covers general matters concerning the **raising of equity finance**, an **appraisal** of **different financing alternatives** for the expansion, and discusses **appropriate long-term financial objectives** for the company.

(a)   **Factors to be considered when raising new equity**

   Equity funds can be raised in two ways:

   (i)   **Restricting the company's dividend** and **retaining the cash for investment** (retained earnings)
   (ii)   **Making a share issue**

   Retained earnings

   Using the **cash from retained earnings** is the cheapest and simplest method of raising equity funds. It avoids the **administrative costs** of making a **share issue**. Also, some tax-paying shareholders prefer this source of funds as it effectively **substitutes capital gains** (increase in share value) for their dividends. However, there are **insufficient retained profits** to finance the proposed expansion entirely with cash from retained earnings.

   Rights issue

   A **rights issue** is an **issue to existing shareholders** in proportion to their **existing holdings**, unless a shareholders' resolution is passed overriding these legal requirements. In a rights issue, shareholders do not change their **proportional shareholdings** if they all take up the rights.

Issue price

If shares are issued in any other proportions, or to new shareholders, the **issue price** will need to be **carefully determined** and agreed, and care must be taken to examine the disposition of shareholdings after the issue, as this can **affect the control** of the company. In this case, the family may lose control if its shareholdings fall below 50% as a result of issuing shares to employees and trading partners. In practice however this is unlikely to affect practical control as there will be more than 25 outside shareholders.

Flotation

The board could consider making PJH a **listed company** and raising finance from the market by means of a placing, possibly using a quotation on the **alternative investment market** to facilitate this. This would be fairly expensive and would dilute all shareholdings.

Borrowing

Given that the use of retained earnings cannot provide enough funds for the expansion, any decision to make a share issue must first be weighed against the possibility of borrowing the funds. **Issue costs** for a loan can be **relatively cheap** and some good fixed interest loans can be secured at present. Debt has the advantage that interest is an **allowable expense** for **tax purposes**. Although debt **increases** the company's **financial risk**, the company's current lack of debt means that this type of risk will remain low.

(b) **Comparison of debt and rights issue effect on value of company**

Increase in value due to equity

	£m
Equity invested	5.0
Net present value of investment	1.2
Increase in value of company	6.2

Increase in value of company due to debt

	£m
Debt invested	5.00
Net present value of investment	1.20
Tax shield	0.43
Increase in value of company	6.63

Value of tax shield

Debt interest = 7% × £5m = £0.35m
Tax saved = £0.35m × 30% = £0.105m

Value of tax shield = £01.05 million for 5 years, discounted at cost of debt. Assume risk and cost of capital does not change because gearing is low, around 7%.

Value of tax shield = £0.105m × 4.100 = £0.43 million

Assumptions

This assumes that risk, and hence the cost of capital do not change. In practice the introduction of debt will mean that **financial risk increases**, although the effect on the cost of capital may not be great, as debt levels are small compared with equity.

Issue costs

Both the share issue and the issue of debt will have **issue costs**, as yet undetermined. These can be ignored as they are not likely to be large in the context of the project NPV.

The **issue price** of the shares and the **number of shares issued to employees and trading partners** will **affect the value per share** and the relative wealth of existing shareholders, but will not affect the total value of the company.

(c) **Appropriate long term financial objectives for the company**

Strategic objectives

The long-term financial objectives of our company will depend in part on its strategic objectives. Since this is an unlisted company, the strategic objectives are set by **formal and informal negotiation** between shareholders, managers, employees and other stakeholders. However there appears to be a consensus for **long term growth in company value**, while keeping financial and operational risks within limits, thereby benefiting all stakeholders.

Remuneration packages

Because this is an unlisted company, **shareholder value** is difficult to estimate, and is **distorted** by the **trade-off** between **remuneration packages** and **dividends** for directors and employees who are also shareholders. This trade-off is affected by corporate and personal taxation rules. We therefore need to **estimate notional salaries** based on reasonable market rates, and hence forecast notional annual cash surpluses for the company. Our basic long-term financial objective is then to **maximise the present value** of these surpluses, when discounted at the company's cost of capital.

Choosing finance

Finance should be chosen so as to assist the maximisation of company value. As noted in part (ii) above, this implies that we should raise funds by borrowing to gain the benefit of the **tax relief.** However, borrowing should not be so high as to put the company at risk of **financial distress** in the event of a downturn in the market.

Working capital management

Working capital and cash should be managed so that there is sufficient to keep the business running smoothly, but not excess, which would be expensive to finance.

Other stakeholders

The company may set certain financial objectives that take account of the interests of other stakeholders, for example paying **competitive remuneration** to employees who are not shareholders, and **not exceeding credit terms** with suppliers.

Targets

After appraising the company's business opportunities, these basic financial objectives can be translated into **long run targets** for:

- **Profitability** (sales growth, profit, return on capital employed, earnings per share)
- **Gearing** (debt/equity ratio, interest cover)
- **Working capital** and liquidity ratios

16 RUMP

Text references. Equity finance is covered in Chapter 5 and debt finance in Chapter 6.

Top tips. In (a) you can either do the calculation for the whole company or for individual shares. In (b) it is easier to do the calculation for the whole company. The technique is to deduct the debt interest and use a perpetuity cash flow which you can do because the debt is irredeemable.

In (c) it is not enough to describe the various alternatives although you will have scored some marks if you focused on costs and share buyers. You must compare and contrast the merits of the rights issue and the debt, and ensure that all your discussions are related to the particular circumstances of RUMP.

> **Easy marks.** As the examiner's report stresses, some candidates saw (c) as an easy general discussion. and failed to relate it to the scenario.
>
> **Examiner's comments.** Many answers to (c) failed to refer to financial risk or use the calculations in (a) to support their argument. Candidates confused different types of share issue.

(a)   There are currently 10m shares in issue. A 2 for 5 rights issue would mean that **4m additional shares** would have to be issued (10m × 2/5).

The rights issue must raise €24m. Therefore the new shares must be **issued** at a price of **€6 per share** (€24m/4m).

Assuming that all the rights are taken up, the share capital in issue will be made up as follows:

	€'000
10m existing shares at €6.60	66,000
4m new shares at €6.00	24,000
Total market capitalisation	90,000

Total number of shares in issue = 14m

Theoretical ex rights price = **€6.43**

Alternative solution

Alternatively using the formula

Theoretical ex rights price $= \dfrac{1}{N+1}\,((N \times \text{rights price}) + \text{issue price})$

$\qquad\qquad\qquad\qquad = \dfrac{1}{2.5+1}\,((2.5 \times 6.60) + 6.00)$

$\qquad\qquad\qquad\qquad = 6.43$

(b)   If the debenture issue is made, the number of equity shares in issue will be unchanged at 10m.

The **profit available** for **dividend** will be reduced by the amount of the debenture interest, which is €1.8m per year (€24m × 7.5%), giving an annual dividend of €7.2 million.

The theoretical share price can be found using the dividend valuation model:

$k_e \quad = d/p_0$
$10\% \quad = €0.72/p_0$
$\mathbf{p_0} \quad = \mathbf{€7.20}$

(c)   To: Chairman
From: Finance Director
Date: 20 November 20X1
Subject: Financing alternatives for the new investment

Introduction

The new contract is large in relation to the size of the company, and therefore the new external source of finance could have a **significant effect** on the existing **capital structure** of the business, and on its **ownership and control**. There are two main sources of finance that are being considered, namely a rights issue and a debt issue, and these will be considered in more detail below. The final section of the report will consider some further methods of raising equity finance that are available to RUMP.

(i) **Rights issue versus debenture issue**

Ownership

The rights issue is large in relation to the **existing equity** in issue, and requires a **significant additional investment** on the part of the shareholders. If shareholders are likely to be unwilling or unable to exercise their rights, the company should consider underwriting the issue. The **underwriters** will then take up any shares that remain unsold, but this could result in a change in the balance of control. A debt issue by contrast would result in no change in control.

Problems with all equity financing

The company is currently 100% equity financed, and this would continue to be the case in the event of a rights issue. This means that the level of **financial risk** faced by the shareholders is **low**. However, it also means that the company cannot take advantage of the **lower cost** and **tax benefits** of debt finance, and that therefore the potential returns to equity are lower than they might be if some debt were to be used.

Introduction of gearing

A debt issue of this size would introduce a significant element of **gearing into** the company. The value of debt in the company structure would be €24m, and the value of equity would be €72m (10m × €7.20). This gives a gearing ratio of 25% (ratio of prior charge capital to total capital). This represents a significant change in the level of financial risk faced by shareholders, and their attitude to this must be taken into account in making the financing decision.

Issue costs

The calculations ignore **issue costs**. These may be significant for a rights issue, amounting on average to 4% of the finance raised, although this percentage rises for small issues. The issue costs of debt would be less than for a rights issue.

Flexibility

Debt issues are commonly linked to **restrictive covenants** that limit the company's further ability to borrow. The effect of such covenants on the future needs of the company must be taken into account. Equity funding would impose no such restriction.

(ii) **Further methods of raising equity finance**

(1) **A placing**

This is an arrangement whereby the shares are not all offered to the public, but instead, the sponsoring market maker arranges for **most of the issue** to be **bought by a small number of investors**, usually institutional investors such as pension funds and insurance companies. The **issuing costs** would be **lower** than for a **rights issue**, but the position with regard to **pre-emption rights** of the existing shareholders may have to be resolved. There could be a significant effect on the **control** of the business if the new shares are concentrated in the hands of a small number of institutional investors.

(2) **Offer for sale**

This means that RUMP would **allot new shares** to an **issuing house**. The issuing house would then offer the **shares for sale** on the basis of a prospectus, either at a **fixed price** or by **tender**. The **issuing costs** would be significantly **higher** than for a rights issue. This is particularly true for fixed price offers where there is a higher risk that not all the shares will be subscribed. However, the **effect** on the **control of the company** is likely to be less than for a placing.

(3) **Public offer for subscription**

This is the **direct offer** of shares to the **public** by the company using a **prospectus**. **Issuing costs**, **underwriting** and **publicity costs** are **high**. It is only appropriate for **large issues** of shares.

(iii) **Loan stock with warrants**

A warrant is a right given by a company to investors, allowing them **to subscribe for new shares** at a future date at a **fixed pre-determined price**. Warrants are usually **issued** with **unsecured loan stock** to make the stock more attractive.

RUMP's position

From RUMP's viewpoint warrants themselves do not involve the **payment of any interest or dividends**. Issuing stock with warrants could be a means of avoiding supplying security or having restrictive covenants imposed on the company. Debt issued with warrants will run to its full maturity, and so the company will be able to **deduct interest** from taxable profits. Warrants can also be a means of **raising extra equity capital** at some time in the future, although the period of exercise of the warrants may not coincide with a time when RUMP needs further equity capital. However the lack of security may well be a deterrent for many lenders.

Conclusion

Although alternative routes are available for raising equity, in this case the choice is really between a rights issue and a debenture issue. The key factors influencing the decision have been summarised above, but probably the major consideration will be the company's **attitude to financial risk**. This will be significantly increased if the debenture is used, but on the other hand, the **cost** of this will be **less** than if more **equity** is issued, and the potential returns to equity are greater.

17 XTA

Text references. Equity finance is covered in Chapter 5 and debt finance in Chapter 6. International debt finance is also covered in Chapter 6.

Top tips. It's worth summarising briefly in (a) what these different forms of finance are. The advantages and disadvantages need to be a direct comparison between the forms.

In (b) although the question does not specifically require you to calculate what happens if the Euro strengthens, the calculations add an extra perspective. You need to work through the scenario systematically as there are a number of comments made that you have to discuss, some right, some wrong.

Easy marks. The examiner's report indicated that candidates who knew the features of the sources of finance discussed in (a) scored well.

Examiner's comments. Some candidates unnecessarily compared a share issue to debt; that was not what (a) required. A few misunderstood what a placing was, incorrectly suggesting it was more expensive than a rights issue and required underwriting. Some candidates also misunderstood what a euro bank loan was. In (b) some candidates failed to adjust the balance sheet and only presented it at one exchange rate. Many believed wrongly that a sterling loan would eliminate exchange risk.

(a)
Memorandum

To: Board of directors of XTA plc
From: Management Accountant
Date: 13 December 20X5

Rights issues versus placings

Rights issue

In a **rights issue,** existing shareholders are given the right to **subscribe to new shares** in the company at a given issue price. They can either action these rights or sell them to other parties. A **placing** can only be made if existing shareholders pass an **ordinary resolution** to allow it, but it opens the issue up to a wider potential shareholder base. In a placing a bank, or other agent acting on behalf of the company, arranges for a limited number of its clients or other contacts to subscribe for the new shares being issued by the company.

Advantages of rights issue vs placing

(i)   Existing shareholders need not fear that their **holdings** will be **diluted.**

(ii)   The **issue price** is **relatively unimportant** because shareholders who subscribe will end up with the same proportional shareholding and those who do not can sell their rights to make cash equivalent to any loss of value in their shareholding. With a placing, the **issue price** is **important:** if the price is too low, existing shareholders will lose out.

Disadvantages of rights issue vs placing

(i)   The number of potential subscribers to a rights issue is **limited** to the current shareholder base.

(ii)   A rights issue may be **more time-consuming, costly** and **complicated to arrange** than a placing. A placing is the **cheapest way** of issuing new equity shares because the costs of advertising, publicity and printing are much less than for rights issues or other forms of public issue.

Euro bank loan versus euro denominated eurobond

Euro bank loan

A **euro bank loan** is arranged directly from a bank and the **terms** (including the nature and pattern of interest payments and repayment of the principal) can be **tailored** to the exact needs of the borrower. Euro eurobonds are **loan certificates**, denominated in euros, issued by the company direct to lenders, who might be banks or large corporates. Issuing eurobonds can only be done if the company wishes to raise large amounts. They can be issued to **raise long term debt** (up to 20 years).

Advantages of Euro bank loans vs Eurobonds

(i)   Bank loans can be more **quickly arranged.**

(ii)   **Issue costs** are **not high.**

(iii) Bank loans can be arranged on **flexible terms;** Eurobonds are **less versatile** in **interest and repayment schedules** than bank loans.

(iv)   **Syndicated credit arrangements** mean that there is **access to a wider pool** of **funds.**

(v)   Bank loans are **not dependent** on a good **credit rating**.

Disadvantages of Euro bank loans vs Eurobonds

(i)   The **amount of funds** banks are **prepared to advance** is limited and may be insufficient for larger investments.

(ii)   Bank loans **cannot be obtained for long maturities**: 5 years would be a long term.

(iii) Eurobonds may be available at **lower costs of finance.**

195

(b) **New investment**

The new investment costs £80 million, which at today's exchange rate, is €120 million.

There appear to be two possible scenarios for the pound/euro exchange rate, either £1 remains at €1.50 or £1 strengthens to €2. For the sake of completeness we also need to consider what happens if the **pound weakens**, say to €1.20. The company has current long term gearing of debt/(debt + equity) = 150/400, i.e. 37.5%.

Mr A's proposal: Borrowing in sterling

Mr A is may be **incorrect** in saying that **borrowing in sterling** is **easier** than borrowing in euros Long-standing banking relationships should enable the company to borrow easily in euros in today's global markets.

However the sterling loan offers **no protection** against **currency risk.** As seen from the balance sheet below the company is risking a **translation loss** of €20 million if the pound strengthens to £1 = €2. Although it would make an equivalent translation gain if the pound weakens, the company's embarrassment at a significant currency loss may weigh heavier than the advantage of a currency gain.

	€m	£m £1 = €1.50	£1 = €2	£1 = €1.20
UK assets		450	450	450
German assets	120	80	60	100
		530	510	550
Equity: original value		250	250	250
Equity: translation gain / (loss)		–	(20)	20
Long term £ borrowings		230	230	230
Current liabilities		50	50	50
		530	510	550

Under this method of financing we get the disadvantage of **no currency hedge**, and **gearing** is **highest** when the **euro weakens**, at 230/460 = 50%.

Mr B's proposal: Euro borrowings

Mr B is correct in thinking that the euro loan will help the company **avoid currency risk**, as seen from the balance sheets below. There is **no translation risk** because if the euro weakens, the declining value of the foreign assets is offset by the declining value of the euro loan.

The same consideration applies to **economic risk.** If the euro weakens, the declining stream of income from Germany will be offset by the reduced interest payments on the euro loan.

However, with Mr B's proposal **gearing** may still be a problem. Debt/(debt + equity) is highest if the **euro strengthens,** when it moves to 250/500 = 50%.

	€m	£m £1 = €1.50	£1 = €2	£1 = €1.20
UK assets		as above		
German assets				
Equity: original value		250	250	250
Equity: translation gain / (loss)		–	–	–
Long term £ borrowings		150	150	150
Long term € borrowings	120	80	60	100
Current liabilities		50	50	50
		530	510	550

Mr B is wrong in his last two statements. Borrowing in euros will not eliminate all currency risk. There can still be **short term transaction losses** which can create embarrassing losses if not properly hedged. Many aspects of **economic risk cannot be eliminated** by the matching investment-borrowing strategy.

Also the fact that **euro interest rates** have been **lower in the past** is **no guarantee** that they will **remain low.** And even if an interest rate remains low, **interest rate parity** will predict that the currency will strengthen and hence the repayment cost will be high.

Mr C's proposal: UK equity funding

Mr C is correct that equity funding is better if a project bears **high risk** because in the event of cash flow difficulties, **dividends** do not need to be paid, whereas interest does.

However, equity capital, like a sterling loan, **does not provide any hedge** against exchange rate risk and is thus inferior to the euro loan in this respect.

	€m	£1 = €1.50	£m £1 = €2	£1 = €1.20
UK assets		as above		
Equity: original value		250	250	250
New equity finance		80	80	80
Equity: translation gain / (loss)		–	(20)	20
Long term £ borrowings		150	150	150
Current liabilities		50	50	50
		530	510	550

Gearing under this form of finance remains **relatively low,** rising to a maximum of 150/460 = 33% if currency losses are made.

Summary of gearing movements under the three forms of finance

In the figures below, gearing is measured by long term debt / (long term debt + equity). The starting value before investing in the project was 37.5%.

Currency movement	£1 = €1.50	£1 = €2	£1 = €1.20
A: Borrowing in sterling	48%	50%	46%
B: Borrowing in euros	48%	46%	50%
C: Equity funds	31%	33%	30%

Recommendation

The most appropriate form of finance would be **euro borrowings, raised by the German subsidiary** to the extent that it is possible. The parent company will need to give a **guarantee** if the assets of the German subsidiary are insufficient as security for the loan.

If borrowing restrictions prevent the full amount being raised as a euro loan, the balance should be raised using **equity funds** (a rights issue).

18 EFG

Text references. Debt finance is covered in Chapter 6.

Top tips. Set out your calculations clearly and make sure you recommend the most appropriate financing instrument in part (a).

Easy marks. The calculations are quite straightforward if you are well prepared and the discussion in part (b) requires general financial knowledge and common sense.

Examiner's comments. This was the least popular question on the paper but those who attempted it tended to score well on the calculations.

(a) *Workings*

Conversion value of convertible bond

Current market price = $15
Share price in 5 years = $15 × $(1.1)^5$ = $24.16
Conversion value = 5 shares for each $100 nominal @ $24.16 = $120.80
Capital gain = $(24.16 − 15) = $9.16
Yield = $(120.8/100)^{1/5}$ − 1 = 3.85%

Yield to maturity of five-year unsecured bond

Year	Cash flow $m	Discount factor 5%	Present value $m	Discount factor 7%	Present value $m
0	(94)	1.000	(94.00)	1.000	(94.00)
1-5	5	4.329	21.64	4.100	20.50
5	100	0.784	78.40	0.713	71.30
		NPV	6.04	NPV	(2.20)

Yield to maturity = 5% + $\left(\dfrac{6.04}{(6.04 + 2.20)} \right)$ × 2% = 6.47%

Response to Sr A

The bank loan is indeed more expensive than the unsecured bond, but not by as much as might have been expected. The true cost of the bond is given by its **yield to maturity**, which is 6.47%, compared to the 7% annual interest rate of the bank loan. The yield to maturity allows for the **time value** of money and is effectively the internal rate of return of the cash flows. However, the bond may have **issue costs** which need to be accounted for.

Response to Sr B

The coupon rate on the convertible bond is 4.5% and does look to be the cheapest form of borrowing. However, the predicted share price increase of 10% per annum would create a $9.16 **capital gain** on each bond after 5 years. This is equivalent to an additional yield of 3.85% per annum and makes the bond significantly **more expensive** than the alternative structures. Furthermore, the shares created on conversion will be entitled to dividends, increasing further the cost of capital.

Response to Sr C

A straight equity issue is **unlikely to succeed** due to the influence of major institutional shareholders, and so would generate less funds and incur heavy underwriting costs. The convertible bond will be more attractive to investors as they can make the decision whether or not to convert after reviewing the entity's performance over the next 5 years. EFG benefits from **lower finance costs** for 5 years.

In conclusion, the convertible bond is the most appropriate type of finance structure for a **rapidly growing** entity such as EFG. It will benefit from lower finance costs for 5 years and can hopefully increase its equity base at the end of this period.

(b) An unsecured bond is **riskier** than a secured loan as it does not carry a charge on assets. The investor will therefore benefit from a higher rate of interest to compensate for the increased risk but will need to obtain information on the following.

- Cash flow forecasts – are the revenues and costs forecast realistic?
- Past financial statements
- Rating agencies' long- and short-term ratings of this bond and similar bonds
- Prospects for the business and its markets

Further analysis to be undertaken will include:

- Ratio analysis of gearing, liquidity, interest cover, dividend cover
- Free cash flow
- Risk analysis of the business and the markets it operates in

19 AIR

Text references. Equity issues are covered in Chapter 5 and the weighted average cost of capital is discussed in Chapter 9.

Top tips. Don't fall into the trap of discussing the advantages and disadvantages of buyouts; the question asked for an assessment of the financing mix.

The answer starts by:

- Quantifying the financing mix
- The main features and conditions attached to the leveraged buy-out
- It then, as directed by the question, spends most time considering the advantages and disadvantages in the context of gearing.

The discussion starts by:

- Showing the initial effect on gearing
- Then showing how gearing will be reduced, quantifying the effects of each method.

However the answer then goes on to show that these methods will not be enough, and the limited effect they do have is dependent upon certain assumptions. The appendix details these **assumptions** but you also need to discuss the key ones in the main body of the report.

As the report has identified a problem, it needs to conclude by assessing:

- How serious the problem will be
- What can be done to solve it.

Easy marks. It's best to do the calculations first, but don't spend more than around 10 minutes on them. That should give you enough to make sufficient reasonable points in the discussion to pass.

To: The Managers of the proposed AIR company
From: Management Consultant
Date: 29 November 20X1
Subject: Report on the financing mix for the proposed leveraged buy-out of the regional airport

(a)   **Financing mix**

If the airport can be purchased for £35 million, **the financing mix** is proposed as:
Equity: 50 pence ordinary shares

	£m
8 million purchased by managers and employees	4
2 million purchased by ER	1
EPP Bank: secured floating rate loan at LIBOR + 3%	20
AV: mezzanine debt with warrants (balancing figure)	10
Total finance	35

Up to £15 million of the mezzanine debt is available, which could be used to replace some of the floating rate loan. However, this possibility has been rejected because its cost is 18% compared with 13% and the warrants, if exercised, could dilute the manager/employee shareholding.

Leveraged buyout

A **leveraged buyout** of the type proposed allows managers and employees to own 80% of the equity while only contributing £4m out of £35m capital (11%). However, it is important that the managers and employees agree on the company's strategy at the outset. If the shareholders break into rival factions, **control** over the company might be **difficult to exercise**. It would be useful to know the disposition of shareholdings among managers and employees in more detail.

Gearing

The initial **gearing** of the company will be extremely **high**: the **debt to equity ratio** is 600% (£30 million debt to £5 million equity). Clearly one of the main medium-term goals following a leveraged buyout is to **reduce gearing** as rapidly as possible, sacrificing high dividend payouts in order to repay loans. For this reason EPP Bank, the major creditor, has imposed a covenant that capital gearing (debt/equity) must be reduced to 100% within four years or the loan will be called in.

Repayment of mezzanine finance

The gearing will be reduced substantially by steady repayment of the unsecured mezzanine finance. This carries such a **high interest** rate because it is a very risky investment by the venture capital company AV. A premium of 5% over secured debt is quite normal. The debt must be repaid in five equal annual instalments, that is £2 million each year. If profits dip in any particular year, AIR might experience cash flow problems, necessitating some **debt refinancing**.

Warrants

If the **warrants** attached to the mezzanine debt are exercised, AV will be able to purchase 1 million new shares in AIR for £1 each. This is a cheap price considering that the book value per share at the date of buyout is £3.50 (£35m/10 million shares). The **ownership** by managers and staff will be **diluted** from 80% to approximately 73%, with ER holding 18% and AV holding 9%. This should not affect management control provided that managers and staff remain as a unified group.

(b) ### Gearing at period-end

Using these assumptions and ignoring the possible issue of new shares when warrants are exercised, the **gearing** at the end of four years is predicted to be 132%, which is **significantly above the target** of 100% needed to meet the condition on EPP's loan. If warrants are exercised, £1 million of new share capital will be raised, reducing the year 4 gearing to 125%, still significantly above the target.

No dividends

A key assumption behind these predictions is that **no dividends are paid** over this period. This may not be acceptable to managers or employees. It is also assumed that cash generated from operations is sufficient to repay £2 million of mezzanine debt each year, which is by no means obvious from the figures provided.

Increase in LIBOR

Results will be worse if **LIBOR rises** above 10%, over the period. However the purchase of the cap will stop interest payments on EPP's loan rising above 15%. Conversely if **LIBOR falls**, the **increase in profit** could be **considerable**, but it is still very unlikely that the loan condition will be met by year 4.

Problems in meeting loan condition

There will therefore definitely be a problem in meeting the EPP's loan conditions. However, if the company is still showing steady growth by year four, and there have been no problems in meeting interest payments, EPP bank will probably **not exercise its right** to recall the loan. If the loan condition is predicted to be a problem, the directors of AIR could consider:

(i) Aiming for **continuous improvement** in **cost effectiveness**

(ii) **Renegotiating** the **central services** contract with ER, or providing central services in-house, in order to save costs

(iii) **Renegotiating** the **allowed gearing ratio** to a more realistic figure

(iv) Going for further expansion after, say, one or two years (eg extension of a runway in order to handle long-haul flights); financing this expansion with an **issue of equity funds**. However, this may affect control of the company

(v) Looking **for possible alternative sources** of debt or equity finance if the EPP loan is recalled, including the possibility of flotation on the stock market

APPENDIX

AIR: forecast income statements for the first four years and computation of debt/equity gearing ratios

	Estimates from				
	Year 0	Year 1	Year 2	Year 3	Year 4
	£'000	£'000	£'000	£'000	£'000
Landing fees	14,000				
Other revenues	8,600				
	22,600				
Labour	5,200				
Consumables	3,800				
Other expenses	3,500				
	12,500				

	Estimates from				
	Year 0	Year 1	Year 2	Year 3	Year 4
	£'000	£'000	£'000	£'000	£'000
Direct operating profit growing at 5% pa	10,100	10,605	11,135	11,692	12,277
Central services from ER		(3,000)	(3,150)	(3,308)	(3,473)
EPP loan interest at 13% on £20m		(2,600)	(2,600)	(2,600)	(2,600)
Mezzanine debt interest at 18%					
on £10m		(1,800)			
on £8m			(1,440)		
on £6m				(1,080)	
on £4m					(720)
Profit before tax		3,205	3,945	4,704	5,484
Tax at 33%		1,058	1,302	1,552	1,810
Profit after tax		2,147	2,643	3,152	3,674
Reserves b/f		0	2,147	4,790	7,942
Reserves c/f		2,147	4,790	7,942	11,616

	Year 0	Year 1	Year 2	Year 3	Year 4
	£'000	£'000	£'000	£'000	£'000
Share capital + reserves		7,147	9,790	12,942	16,616
Total debt at end of year		28,000	26,000	24,000	22,000
Gearing: debt/equity		392%	266%	185%	132%

If warrants are exercised, £1 million of new share capital is issued, reducing the gearing at year 4 to 22,000/17,616 = 125%.

Assumptions

(a)   The **central services** will be **provided** by ER for the full 4-year period.

(b)   **No dividend** will be paid during the first four years.

(c)   **Sufficient cash** will be **generated** to repay £2 million of mezzanine finance each year and to fund increased working capital requirements.

(d)   **LIBOR** is **assumed to remain at 10%**.

(e)   Tax is **payable one year** in **arrears**.

20 DDD

Text references. Debt finance is covered in Chapter 6. The capital structure decision is discussed in Chapter 10.

Top tips. Do **NOT** assume in (a) that the cost of debt is 7% for Alternative 1, and a weighted average of 5% and 10% for Alternative 2. You need to do an internal rate of return calculation for both. 7% is a reasonable starting point for the calculation in Alternative 1, and you can use the same two test rates in Alternative 2 as the answers are unlikely to be very far apart. Don't forget the tax! You would probably say that by inspection the IRR for Alternative 1 is close to 6% and for Alternative 2 it is close to 5%. This would mean you would avoid the interpolation calculations and save time.

Easy marks. The IRR calculation hopefully provided you remembered to use it because the debt is **redeemable**.

Examiner's comments. Although (a) was answered quite well, some answers were plainly unrealistic, for example costs of debt over 50%. Other candidates:

- Treated the debt as irredeemable
- Ignored tax
- Failed to calculate the cost of debt as a percentage return
- Took a mean average of the two instruments

Answers to (b) were poor, with discussions not being adequately focused on the circumstances of the question. Candidates failed to question the use of retained profits when there was an obvious lack of cash in the balance sheet. Other points that were not adequately considered included:

- The size of the project in relation to existing operations
- The need for additional finance
- The effect on gearing
- Risk
- The efficient market hypothesis
- Dividend yield
- How to adjust the returns on capital

(a)   *Alternative 1*

Year		Cash flow £'000	Discount factor 7%	PV £'000	Discount factor 5%	PV £'000
0	Bond issue (£30m×0.95)	(28,500)	1.000	(28,500)	1.000	(28,500)
1-5	Interest (£30m × 7% × 70%)	1,470	4.100	6,027	4.329	6,364
5	Repayment	30,000	0.713	21,390 (1,083)	0.784	23,520 1,384

Using the IRR Formula : Cost of capital $= a + \left[\dfrac{A}{A-B} \times (b-a) \right]$

Cost of capital $= 5 + \dfrac{(1,384(7-5))}{1,384 - (-1,083)}$

$= 6.12\%$

Alternative 2

Year		Cash flow £'000	Discount factor 7%	PV £'000	Discount factor 5%	PV £'000
0	Loan	(28,500)	1.000	(28,500)	1.000	(28,500)
1-3	Interest					
	(£28.5 m × 5% × 70%)	998	2.624	2,619	2.723	2,718
4-6	Interest					
	(£28.5 m × 10% × 70%)	1,995	2.143*	4,275	2.353*	4,694
6	Repayment	28,500	0.666	18,981	0.746	21,261
				(2,625)		173

* Cumulative discount factor yrs 4 − 6 =

Cumulative discount factor yrs 1 - 6 − Cumulative discount factor yrs 1-3

For 7%, 4.767 − 2.624 = 2.143

For 5%, 5.076 − 2.723 = 2.353

$$\text{Cost of capital} \quad = 5 + \frac{(173(7-5))}{173 + 2,625}$$

$$= 5.12\%$$

The bank loan has the lower cost of debt.

Other factors to be considered

Arrangement costs

DDD will incur **issue costs** if it issues the bonds, whereas the arrangement fees for the bank loan should be much smaller.

Cash flow during the loan period

The bank loan requires a **lower rate of interest** during the **first three years** of the loan, and **higher interest** subsequently. This pattern of payments may match better with the income from the new garden centres, lower in the first few years and higher subsequently as their customer base builds up.

Repayment of loan capital

DDD will need **sufficient funds** for repayment of the capital at the end of the period of the loans. The extra year it has to raise funds to repay the bank loan may be significant.

Renewal

DDD's directors should consider whether there is a **possibility of renewal** of either or both loans, and if so what the terms are likely to be.

Security

Security is likely to be required both on the **bonds** and on the **bank loan**. The directors should take into account the nature of the security demanded, and whether any **onerous restrictions** will be placed on DDD's ability to operate as a result of giving the security.

(b) To: Board
     From: Treasury department
     Date: 22 May 20X3
     Subject: Financing of new garden centres

Introduction

The purpose of this memo is to discuss the various **financing options** that have been put forward to fund the **very significant expenditure** of £28.5 million on the planned new centres. The expenditure is almost equal to current net assets. It is assumed that the finance required is £28.5 million, In practice additional finance may be needed to fund further fittings and equipment purchases, but it is assumed that existing sources such as current cash balances or extension of trade credit can be used to finance these.

(i) **Chief Executive's comments**

Gearing

Assuming the market value of debt in the balance sheet is equal to its book value, the company's current gearing on market values can be calculated as $\dfrac{\text{Loans}}{\text{Loans} + \text{Share capital}}$ ie $\dfrac{24}{(10 \times 6) + 24} = 29\%$

Assuming £28.5 million is raised from a share issue, gearing would fall to:

$$\frac{24}{(10 \times 6) + 24 + 28.5} = 21\%$$

The fall in gearing would mean that DDD's **financial risk** would fall. This may be desirable because currently the security provided, land and buildings, is only just greater than long-term loans (£26.5 million versus £24 million). A decrease in financial risk might also be weighed against a **possible increase in overall business risk**, because the investment involves some diversification into new products.

Level of share price

The chief executive's comments appear to imply that share prices may go up or down at any time, that the market is not very rational. If however the stock market is efficient, share prices will be influenced by available information about a company's **future prospects**. Hence if the market believed that the expansion would lead to greater profits, shares would not lose their value for that reason. The chief executive may be making the remark as he has **inside information** not available to the market, but acting on this may be doubtful legally.

Dilution of share capital

However if more shares were issued to finance the development, the **value of individual shares** would **fall** according to the laws of supply and demand as more shares would be available. However if the market had a positive view of the new development, the **market value** of **total share capital** would **rise**.

Dividend yield

Dividend yield is the dividend expressed as a % of the share's market price, representing the shareholder's rate of return. However the dividend yield is measured using **current dividends**, not the future dividends that will be important for this project. Also the dividend yield does not reflect the **total reward** that may be demanded by shareholders, since they may also require a **capital gain**. In addition for shareholders **equity finance** is not necessarily **low risk**; it would carry a higher risk than providing **debt finance**.

Other issues

The directors should consider which method of share issue would be best, an **issue** to **new shareholders** or a **rights issue** to existing shareholders. They should also consider whether there is likely to be a significant change in the pattern of **share ownership**.

(ii) **Non-executive director's comments**

Issue costs and uncertainty

The director is right in stating that use of internal sources will **avoid issue costs**. He is also correct in raising the issue of **uncertainty**; however as DDD is an established, listed company whose share price has recently risen significantly, it should be possible to raise the external finance required on reasonable terms.

Use of retained profits

However the director has misunderstood the nature of retained profits. Retained profits **do not reflect cash balances** that can be drawn on for capital expenditure; they reflect the amount of equity capital tied up in the whole business, not just cash. The business only has £1 million, not £20 million, surplus cash.

Sale of least profitable garden centres

Certainly a sale of garden centres would raise some cash. However a sale of the least profitable centres is **unlikely to raise much cash**, because of their poor current performance. Sale will also involve **transaction costs**. Sale of a number of centres might mean that overall the company has **less long-term assets** to secure debt.

You will also need to be confident that the new centres are likely to perform significantly better than the current poorest performers, since any loss of profits on the centres disposed of will represent an **opportunity cost**. A more cost-effective option may be to spend money to **improve** the **poor performance** of some of the current centres.

(iii) **Finance director's comments**

Gearing

If more debt is issued, gearing would rise from 29% to:

$$\frac{24 + 28.5}{(10 \times 6) + 24 + 28.5} = 47\%$$

This will mean **increased financial risk**, along with the possible **increase in business risk**. The security that the company provides compared with the debt it has will also not improve.

Return on investment

There appears to be a confusion in the finance director's remarks between the **investment** decision and the **financing** decision. To establish whether it is worthwhile to open the new garden centres, DDD should **appraise** the future returns using a **weighted average cost of capital (WACC)** based on the different costs of all the sources of finance the company uses. WACC should be calculated using a **revised cost of equity** that takes account of the increases in business and financial risk. The **cost of other forms of debt** may also rise because of the increased risks.

Cost of debt

The cost of debt capital should be compared with the costs of other sources of finance (equity shares). In addition (as illustrated in (a)) there is no single cost that applies to all types of debt. **Different forms of debt** themselves have **different costs**.

Pattern of cash flows

The finance director's comments also fail to take into account the **time scale of cash flows**. Ultimately the garden centres may **make** significant profits, but may have generated insufficient cash to pay back the loans when they fall due for repayment.

21 BAC

Text references. Leasing is discussed in Chapter 7. The calculations of cost of equity and cost of capital are illustrated in Chapter 9.

Top tips. The calculations in (a) are quite straightforward but you do need to be able to do them for this paper. You could have presented the times as the columns and the expenses as the rows, but that would have meant your using more columns, which you may not have had space to do.

Tax allowances on a reducing balance basis are x% × (Cost - tax allowances already utilised). Because you are including tax, you need to use the **after tax** discount rate.

You will have thrown away marks in (b) if you did not use the report format of introduction, main sections and conclusion. **Risk** and **flexibility** are very important considerations.

(c) is important; you need to understand and make sure you can explain the two-stage nature of the capital investment process. When carrying out the net present value **investment** appraisal, you should not take the financing costs into consideration. These become important when you carry out a net present value analysis of **financing.**

In (d) remember k_d in the pre-tax cost of debt in the formula.

Easy marks. (c) represents basic knowledge in this area.

(a)   **Lessee**

Discount rate

The discount rate to be used is 9% which is the approximate **after tax cost of borrowing** at 11.5% (11.5 (1 − 0.21)). It is assumed that tax is paid in the year after the related cash flow arises. It is also assumed, in the absence of information about depreciation policies, that the **lease payments** are allowable in full for tax purposes.

Lease

Time	Lease payments £	Tax at 21% £	Cash flow £	Discount at 9%	PV cost £
0	(15,000)		(15,000)	1.000	(15,000)
1	(15,000)	3,150	(11,850)	0.917	(10,866)
2	(15,000)	3,150	(11,850)	0.842	(9,978)
3	(15,000)	3,150	(11,850)	0.772	(9,148)
4	(15,000)	3,150	(11,850)	0.708	(8,390)
5		3,150	3,150	0.650	2,048
	NPV cost of leasing				(51,334)

The NPV cost of leasing exceeds £50,000. Because of tax allowances, the NPV for the purchase option will be less than £50,000. On financial grounds purchasing is therefore the preferred option.

Lessor

The situation from the point of view of the leasing company is as follows.

Time	Revenue £	Capital Costs £	Tax (W) £	Net cash flow £	Discount at 15%	PV £
0	15,000	(50,000)		(35,000)	1.000	(35,000)
1	15,000		(775)	14,225	0.870	12,376
2	15,000		(1,744)	13,256	0.756	10,022
3	15,000		(2,470)	12,530	0.658	8,245
4	15,000		(3,015)	11,985	0.572	6,855
5		5,000	(3,424)	1,576	0.497	783
6			2,128	2,128	0.432	919
	NPV of leasing agreement					4,200

Working: tax computation

Time	Revenue	WDA	Taxable	31% tax	Time of tax flow
	£	£	£	£	
0	15,000	(12,500)	2,500	775	1
1	15,000	(9,375)	5,625	1,744	2
2	15,000	(7,031)	7,969	2,470	3
3	15,000	(5,273)	9,727	3,015	4
4	15,000	(3,955)	11,045	3,424	5
5		(6,866)	(6,866)	(2,128)	6

The leasing company makes a net gain on the deal of £4,200 in present value terms. This is much less than the savings that BAC could make if it purchased rather than leased the equipment.

(b) REPORT

To: Chief Executive
From: Management Accountant
Date: 12 May 20X4
Subject: Computer system financing options

Introduction

This report deals with the **relative merits of buying and leasing** the new computer system. Detailed supporting calculations can be found attached [see (a)].

Financial position

The calculations show that purchase of the equipment is a much **more financially advantageous** option than leasing. This assumes that it will **continue** to be possible to **borrow** at 11½% to finance the purchase. If we feel that it is likely that interest rates will rise, then the possibility of taking out **a fixed rate loan** should be considered. Alternatively it may be possible to **hedge** through a mechanism such as an interest rate swap or by the use of futures.

Other factors

We are effectively **locked into the deal** for the duration of the lease. We are therefore **exposed to the risk** that the equipment becomes obsolete during this period. To terminate the lease and to switch to new equipment is likely to carry **heavy financial penalties**. This sort of flexibility could only be found by taking out an **operating lease**, and this is almost certain to be even more expensive than a finance lease. A further alternative would be a turnkey operation involving facilities management, but this too would be very expensive.

Conclusions

The calculations show that the **relative financial loss** to us in the leasing situation is very great when compared with the financial gain that would be made by the leasing company. There is therefore little point in trying to negotiate a better deal. The discrepancy arises due to the **different tax position** of the two companies and our ability to use all our **capital allowances**. It is therefore recommended that the system should be **purchased outright** although we may need to do further work to identify the best way to finance the transaction.

Signed: Management Accountant

(c) **Decision-making**

It is important to appreciate that there are effectively two stages in the decision making process.

(i) The first step is to **evaluate the benefit to the company** of acquiring the system. This involves calculating the marginal cash flows that will result from the use of the system and then discounting these at the weighted average cost of capital.

(ii) Once the fact that the investment in the system should be undertaken has been established, the next step is to **evaluate the alternative methods of financing the acquisition**. This involves calculating the relative costs of the different methods of finance which are available.

Lease or buy example

In the calculations above, it is taken as given that the system will add value to the business and should be acquired. It is the second stage of the process that is being undertaken, and therefore it is the relative costs of finance which are important and not the weighted average cost of capital.

(d) **Cost of equity**

$$k_{eg} = k_{eu} + [k_{eu} - k_d] \frac{V_D[1-t]}{V_E}$$

using nominal value of shares as value of equity

$$k_{eg} = 14 + (14 - 11.5) \frac{50(1-0.21)}{150}$$

$$= 14.7\%$$

Weighted average cost of capital

$$k_0 = k_{eg}\left[\frac{V_E}{V_E + V_D}\right] + k_d(1-t)\left[\frac{V_D}{V_E + V_D}\right]$$

$$= 14.7\left[\frac{150}{150+50}\right] + 11.5(1-0.21)\left[\frac{150}{150+50}\right]$$

$$= 13.3\%$$

22 XYZ

Text references. Leasing is covered in Chapter 7 and cost of debt in Chapter 9.

Top tips. In (a), the actual values relating to the debt being raised have been used in the suggested solution. It would be equally appropriate to use values based on a £100 unit of debt. The exceptions to the rule about using WACC to appraise investments should be noted in (c). In (d) you should take into account operational as well as financial factors.

A table format for comparisons will not always be appropriate, but in (d) it provides a clear way of giving the detail needed on each option.

In (b) you would have been given credit for using the cost of debt that you calculated in (a) and using market values of share capital and debt. In (c) most of the marks were available for explaining the importance of capital structure and financial risk. Answers to (d) needed to be quite broad, covering cash flow, risk and security, but also mentioning financial reporting implications.

Easy marks. However, because the requirements are broad in (d) there are plenty of points you can bring out. Make sure also your answer is in report format.

Examiner's comments. In (a) many candidates treated debt as if it was irredeemable, and omitted tax charges. Those who tried to carry out calculations often could not complete them, or used too wide a spread of rates; 6% should have been one of the rates used. In (c) many candidates showed a lack of understanding of discount rates, claiming that the after tax cost of debt was an appropriate rate to use. Some answers solely discussed whether the before or after tax rate should be used. Answers to (d) were reasonable, although some contained too much detail on financial reporting, and not enough on finance and risk implications.

(a) The **after tax cost of debt equates** to the **discount rate** at which the cost of the debt over the ten year period is zero. This can be estimated by trying different discount rates and then interpolating.

In order to raise £72m, XYZ must issue £80m of debt, since the debt is to be issued at a **discount** of 10% on par value (£72m ÷ 0.9 = £80m).

The **annual interest cost** net of tax will be £80m × 6%(1 − 0.3) = £3.36m.

The cash flows will be as follows:

Year		Cash flow £m	5% discount factors	PV £m	6% discount factors	PV £m
0	Issue proceeds	(72)	1.000	(72)	1.000	(72)
1-10	Interest	3.36	7.722	25.95	7.360	24.73
10	Capital repayment	80	0.614	49.12	0.558	44.64
				3.07		(2.63)

Calculate the cost of debt using an IRR calculation.

$$IRR = a\% + \left[\frac{A}{A-B} \times (b-a)\right]\%$$

$$= 5\% + \frac{3.07(6\% - 5\%)}{3.07 + 2.63} = 5.54\%$$

The **after tax cost of debt** is therefore 5.54%

(b) $$k_0 = k_e\left(\frac{V_E}{V_E + V_D}\right) + k_d\left(\frac{V_D}{V_E + V_D}\right)$$

V_E = 200 million × £1.50

= 300 million

$$= 10\left(\frac{300}{300 + 72}\right) + 5.54\left(\frac{72}{300 + 72}\right)$$

= 9.14%

(c) **Cost of debt**

The cost of debt is an inappropriate rate to use, as if fails to recognise **any impact** on **existing providers** of finance.

Return in excess of cost of capital

Any new investment undertaken by a company should generate a return in **excess** of the **overall cost of capital** to the company. This is the **minimum return** that a company should make on its own investments, to earn the cash flows out of which investors can be paid their return.

Use of WACC

The current **weighted average cost of capital** should generally be used to **evaluate projects**. This is because the **marginal cost of new capital** should be **roughly equal** to the **weighted average cost of current capital**, provided that the **company's capital structure changes slowly** over time.

Exceptions to use of WACC

(i)   Where the new investment has **different business risk characteristics** from the company's existing operations, and thus the **return required** by shareholders (**the cost of equity**) might **change** as a result of undertaking the investment

(ii)   Where the **finance** that is raised to fund the new investment **substantially changes** the **capital structure** and the perceived **financial risk** of investing in the company.

Implications for XYZ

XYZ is a large listed company, and therefore the **size** of this **investment**, although large, is unlikely to have a significant impact on the capital structure. The project itself is concerned with the **replacement** of **existing assets**, and is therefore unlikely to change the level of business risk faced by the company. There is therefore no reason why the weighted average cost of capital should not be used in this case, and the after tax cost of the new debt should not therefore be used to evaluate the investment.

(d)

To:	Board of Directors, XYZ
From:	Management Accountant
Date:	11 December 20X1
Subject:	Choice of financing method

Introduction

This memorandum deals with the factors that should be considered when deciding which of the three methods of financing the grinding machines is the most appropriate.

Operational effects

(i) **Use of the machines**

With Options 1 and 2 use of the machines is **guaranteed for the full 10 years' useful life,** whereas with Option 3 use of the machines has to be **re-negotiated annually**.

(ii) **Technology**

With Options 1 and 2, XYZ is **tied** into the **technology** for the full ten year life of the machines. If the **technology is superseded**, change could be **difficult and expensive**. However for Option 3, annual contracts mean that in the event of technological change, XYZ would be able to adapt quickly.

(iii) **Maintenance**

XYZ will **bear the maintenance costs** under Options 1 and 2; the lessor will do so under Option 3, but XYZ may need guarantees on quality.

(iv) **Security**

Under Option 1, **creditors' security** is a **fixed charge** over the machines and a **floating charge** over the assets. The lessor's security is over the **machines alone** under Options 2 and 3.

Financial effects

(i) **Tax**

The **interest payments on the debt interest** would be tax allowable under Option 1. Only the **interest element** of the annual payments would be allowable against tax under Option 2. With Option 3, although the **lease rentals are higher** than under Option 2, they would be fully allowable for tax.

(ii) **Tax allowances**

XYZ would be able to claim **tax allowances** on the purchase of the machine only under Option 1.

(iii) **Interest**

Under Option 1, annual interest costs would only be the **interest payments on the debt.** Annual interest costs would be higher than Option 1 for the first eight years of Option 2, but would be insignificant for the last two years. Annual costs would be the highest for each of the ten years under Option 3.

(iv) **Debt repayment**

XYZ would have to find £80 million to **repay the debt** at the end of the 10 year period. Some of this might be recoverable from (uncertain) machine sale proceeds. There would be no terminal costs under Options 2 and 3.

(v) **Impact on accounts**

Key balance sheet ratios may be **affected** including assets and debt on the balance sheet under Options 1 and 2. However assets and finance will be **off balance sheet** under Option 3.

Conclusions

The key factors to be considered are:

(i) **Operational**

Technological flexibility may be important, and **responsibility for maintenance** could prove expensive.

(ii) **Cash flow**

The different options have **different cash flow patterns**.

(iii) **Cost**

The total cost of the different options over the ten year life of the project should be evaluated using **discounted cash flow techniques**.

(iv) **Taxation**

The company should consider whether it could use all the **capital allowances** available under option 1, and whether it has sufficient annual income to benefit from the tax savings on expenses under options 2 and 3.

Signed: Management Accountant

23 TFC

Text references. Leasing is covered in Chapter 7.

Top tips. (a) involves manipulation of discounted cash flow figures. You can save yourself a lot of time in (b) by using annuity factors rather than single year discount factors. With the short-term lease, although the payment takes place at time 0 in the calculation, its date is actually the first day of year 1. Therefore tax relief will be given in year 1 and this will affect payment in year 2.

(c) calls for a discussion of the 'non-quantitative' factors. This is slightly ambiguous, but presumably does not preclude the discussion of broader financial implications, such as the effect of the financing method used on the company's gearing and cash flow.

Easy marks. (c) covers a combination of general factors relating to finance and lease specific issues such as maintenance and provides quite a few points to discuss.

Examiner's comments. Answers to (a) were disappointing. Some candidates ignored the time value of money entirely, others took the fourth root. In (b) the tax relief was often ignored and the maintenance cost on the long-term lease was spread over 5 years. In (c) discussion of maintenance and quality of service was generally limited, and discussion of the Marketing Director's viewpoint was poor. Few candidates saw that the lost interest was an opportunity cost.

(a) Method 3 is a **four year loan** of $10m, with **annual repayments of $3.154m** including both capital and interest made at the end of each of the four years.

10 = 3.154 × Annuity factor yrs 1 − 4

Annuity factor yrs 1 − 4 = 3.170

From annuity tables, 3.170 is yrs 1 − 4 annuity factor for 10%, so the **equivalent annual rate of interest** is 10%.

(b) **Method 1 Long-term lease**

Year		Cash flow	Discount factor	Present value
		$'000	7%	$'000
1-5	Rental	(2,800)	4.100	(11,480)
2-6	Tax saving on rental (30% × 2,800)	840	*3.832	3,219
1-10	Maintenance	(200)	7.024	(1,405)
2-11	Tax saving on maintenance (30% × 200)	60	**6.564	394
	Net present value			(9,272)

* Cumulative present value factor Yrs 1 – 6 – Yr 1 Factor = 4.767 – 0.935 = 3.832

** Cumulative present value factor Yrs 1 – 11 – Yr 1 Factor = 7.499 – 0.935 = 6.564

Method 2 Short-term lease

Year		Cash flow	Discount factor	Present value
		$'000	7%	$'000
0-9	Rental	(1,700)	7.515	(12,776)
1-10	Tax saving on rental (30% × 1,700)	510	7.024	3,582
	Net present value			(9,194)

(c)

To:	TFC Board of directors
From:	A Consultant
Date:	4 December 20X3
Subject:	Issues relating to the acquisition of the new ferry

In addition to making a financial appraisal of the financing options, the following factors should also be taken into account when deciding the best method of making the acquisition.

Maintenance

Options 1 and 3 mean that the **costs of maintaining the vessel** are borne by TFC. If these costs varied from forecast, this would **affect** the **financial projections**.

Option 2 **transfers responsibility for maintenance** to the **lessor**. We need to be confident that the ferry will be **maintained** to the **standards** that we require, and that we will not experience unforeseen periods of downtime. Under Options 1 and 3, we are able to control maintenance directly.

Security

The two leasing options effectively use the ferry itself as **security** for the **lessor**. The loan would be **secured** by **fixed and floating charges** over the company's assets. Given that the company is at present unable to raise any further equity finance, the directors should be aware that taking out this loan might **restrict the security available** to lenders in the future, and hence the company's ability to borrow to finance other future developments.

Flexibility

The long term lease and the loan effectively **tie the company** into the use of the ferry for the whole of its projected 10 year life. The short term lease is **renewable annually** with no obligation to renew. This means that if technological or market conditions change during the next ten years, TFC can **stop using** this ferry and incur no further cost. This would be a positive benefit to TFC.

Effect on the balance sheet

If option 3 is used, the loan will have to **appear** in TFC's **balance sheet.** This is also likely to be a requirement with option 1. This would **increase the gearing ratio**, and possibly **restrict the company's ability to borrow** in the future. The short term loan would have no balance sheet implications.

Cash flow situation of TFC

Options 1 and 3 involve a **greater outlay of cash** in years 1 to 5, although payments do not start until the end of the first year. Option 2 has an **initial payment** at the start of the project, but thereafter **lower annual payments** over a longer period. TFC should consider the payment patterns in the context of the overall cash flow situation of the company.

Other alternatives

A mix of internal and external funding may be most appropriate for investment. Other forms of lease or hire purchase finance, or debt, may also be considered.

Suggestion of Marketing Director

The Marketing Director has suggested that the purchase should be financed out of retained earnings and the liquidation of short term investments due to their lower cost.

However, this source of finance has an **opportunity cost,** which is the income foregone from alternative investments. The **cost of retained earnings** is normally taken to be equivalent to the **cost of equity**, which may well be higher than the discount rate of 7% used to evaluate financing projects, depending on the capital structure of the company. Purchasing the ferry using retained earnings therefore requires a similar financial evaluation to that applied to the other three options.

24 Question with helping hand: RZ

Text references. Leasing is covered in Chapter 7 and debt finance in Chapter 6.

Top tips. It's important to use the correct discount rate when evaluating a lease or buy decision. When evaluating whether to obtain the asset at all, cash flows should be discounted using the investment cost of capital (generally the WACC). The different financing options are then evaluated using the financing cost of capital, the after-tax cost of debt.

You need to read the question carefully to identify the relevant costs that you will need to take into account when considering whether to take out the loan or lease. These are (i) The purchase price (ii) The lease payments (net of tax) (iii) The trade-in value (only available if you buy) (iv) The capital allowances.

The reason why the tax shield is discussed in detail is that you are asked to compare using debt finance with using equity finance.

Easy marks. The general advantages and disadvantages of debt and lease finance are basic core knowledge.

(a)   **Acquisition decision**

If the investment is financed with equity funds, the project can be appraised by finding its net present value at a discount rate of 9% per annum, the post-tax cost of existing capital, which is all equity.

	$'000	Ex. Rate	£'000	9% factors	PV £'000
Machine capital cost	1,500	1.580	(949.37)	1.000	(949.37)
After tax annual cost savings 5 years including capital allowances			240.00	3.890	933.60
Residual value year 5			94.94	0.650	61.71
NPV					45.94

The residual value at the end of year 5 is estimated as 10% of the original purchase price. We assume that the balancing allowance on sale is included in the capital allowances.

On the basis of these figures, the machinery is marginally worthwhile if financed by equity funds, having a net present value of **£45,940**. This ignores the value of the tax shelter.

Financing decision

(i)   **Undated debt**

Discount differential cash flows at after-tax cost of debt:

	0	1	2	3	4	5
	£'000	£'000	£'000	£'000	£'000	£'000
Machine cost (W1)	(949.37)					
Trade-in value						94.94
Tax credits (W2)		71.20	53.40	40.05	30.04	61.63
Cash flows	949.37	71.20	53.40	40.05	30.04	156.57
Discount factors 5%	1.000	0.952	0.907	0.864	0.823	0.784
Discounted cash flows	(949.37)	67.78	48.43	34.60	24.72	122.75

Net cash flows = £(651,090)

Workings

1   Machine capital cost in £ = $\dfrac{\$1,500,000}{1.48}$ = £949,370

2   *Capital allowances*

Year	Written down value	25% writing down allowance	30% tax saving
0	949.37		
1	712.03	237.34	71.20
2	534.02	178.01	53.40
3	400.51	133.51	40.05
4	300.38	100.13	30.04
5*	94.94	205.44	61.63

* The 'writing down allowance' in the last year is a balancing allowance to arrive at the residual value of £94,940.

Conclusion

The main advantages of using debt are:

- The **present value of buying** is **lower than that of leasing**
- Because RZ is equity-financed, it will **benefit** from the tax shield

The main disadvantage is that gearing will increase.

Advantages of debt

Tax shield

Debt interest is an allowable expense against corporate taxation, which RZ pays at the rate of 30% of taxable profits. 7% perpetual debt on £949,370 will require interest payments of 7% × £949,370 per year, and will allow tax savings of 7% × £949,370 × 30% per year in perpetuity.

Tax shield in perpetuity

The present value of these tax savings (known as the tax shield) can be found by discounting at the cost of debt, 7% (because the tax savings have the same risk level as the interest payments, i.e. they are virtually certain).

For a perpetuity, this simply means dividing by 7%:
The PV is 7% × £949,370 × 30%/7% = £949,370 × 30% = £284,811.

(*Note*. This is the Modigliani-Miller formula for the tax shield on perpetual debt: TBc.)

Provided the company can earn taxable profits to perpetuity, this tax shield will be reflected in an increased company value. However, it is not fair to attribute all of this increased value to the new cost saving project. How much is attributable depends on the extent to which the new project assets enable the company **to borrow**.

Tax shield for borrowing

Assuming the new equipment represents a replacement of a major part of the company's assets, a better assumption might be that all the tax relief for the duration of the project (5 years) is attributable to the project.

The present value of tax savings for 5 years is found as follows:

Annual tax savings = 7% × £949,370 × 30% = £19,937
PV of 5 years' savings at 7% = 4.100 × £19,937 = £81,742

Thus borrowing can be argued to increase the project's base case net present value to an adjusted present value of £45,940 + £81,742 = **£127,682**

Other advantages of debt

(1)   Debt will **not change** the **pattern of ownership** of the company or earnings per share.
(2)   The cost of debt is **lower** than that of equity.

Disadvantages of debt

(1)   Because of the gearing effect, **equity earnings** become **more volatile** in response to changes in operating cash flows.

(2)   In an extreme case of low earnings the company may be forced into **bankruptcy** by its loan creditor. This latter is unlikely, however, given the current earnings level of £4.5 million and expected interest cost of only £66,000 per year.

(ii)   **Finance lease**

A 5 year finance lease on an asset with a useful life of 5 years, and with a right to buy for $1 at the end, is **effectively equivalent to a 5 year loan** enabling RZ to buy the asset. It can there be appraised by comparison with a loan. The after tax cash flows associated with the lease can be appraised by discounting at the after tax cost of borrowing, 5%.

Year	0	1	2	3	4	5
Annual lease payment $'000	(325.00)	(325.00)	(325.00)	(325.00)	(325.00)	
	£'000	£'000	£'000	£'000	£'000	£'000
Converted to £'000 (W1)	(205.70)	(207.71)	(209.73)	(211.78)	(213.84)	
Tax savings 30%		61.71	62.31	62.92	63.53	64.15
	(205.70)	(146.00)	(147.42)	(148.86)	(150.31)	64.15
5% factors	1	0.952	0.907	0.864	0.823	0.784
PV	(205.70)	(138.99)	(133.71)	(128.62)	(123.71)	50.29

The net present value of the finance lease is £(680,440) compared with borrowing of £(651,090) showing that borrowing is cheaper.

Working

Exchange rates

Using the formula for interest rate parity, the dollar can be expected to strengthen against the pound each year by the factor $(1 + 2.5\%) / (1 + 3.5\%) = 0.99034$. Thus, year 1 exchange rate = $1.58 \times 0.99034 = 1.5647$, etc.

Year	0	1	2	3	4	5
Exchange rate	1.5800	1.5647	1.5496	1.5346	1.5198	1.5051

Other factors

Advantages of finance lease

(1) The lease may be **easier to organise** than a loan, particularly if the machinery vendor assists in organising it as an incentive to buy the machinery.

(2) The **lease** is paid off **within five years**.

Disadvantages of finance lease

(1) The lease is **riskier** than a **sterling loan**, because it is denominated in a foreign currency. A higher discount rate may need to be used because of this.

(2) RZ will **not be able** to **claim capital allowances** or take advantage of the trade-in value.

(iii) **Operating lease**

With an operating lease the lessee (RZ) does **not receive** the **rights and benefits** of ownership of the asset. It is akin to a rental agreement.

Advantages of operating lease

(1) There would normally be **break points** in the contract that allowed the lessee to terminate the contract if the asset is no longer required.

(2) **Disclosure** in financial accounts is **less onerous**. However this is unlikely to concern the shareholders of a private company.

(3) Unlike the other methods, the lessor will be responsible for **servicing and maintaining the lease**.

Disadvantages of operating lease

The **main disadvantage** is the cost, which is likely to be **more expensive** than the other forms of finance discussed.

(b) **Benefits and problems of financing assets in the same currency as their purchase**

Income and finance in foreign currency

If an asset **generates income** in a foreign currency, it is advantageous to **finance its acquisition** in the same currency. In this way, if the foreign currency depreciates, the loss in income is offset by **lower financing costs**. Thus assets of foreign subsidiaries are best financed in the currency of the country of operation.

Existence of long-term currency risk

However, if, as in the case of RZ, the asset is **purchased** and **financed** in a foreign currency but used to **generate *home* currency income** or savings, there is a long term currency risk over the period of the finance. For example if RZ negotiates a dollar lease and the dollar then strengthens by 10%, the costs of acquiring the asset will rise by 10% whereas the benefits of owning it in the UK will be unchanged. This factor significantly reduces the attractiveness of RZ's dollar lease.

Of course, if the dollar weakened, the company would make exchange gains on its finance. On balance, however, investors are risk averse and tend to fear exchange losses more than they welcome the chance of exchange gains.

Significance of interest rate parity

A loan raised in a foreign currency often **carries a lower interest rate** than a **home currency loan**. This is true in the example, where US interest rates are lower than sterling rates. However, the principle of interest rate parity suggests that the **foreign currency** will **strengthen** to compensate for this, resulting in an **increased home currency value** of loan or lease repayments. The general principle is 'there are no free gifts in finance'. The exception would be if the foreign government subsidised loans in order to assist exporters, but this is contrary to the principles of the World Trade Organisation.

25 FLG

Text references. Leasing is covered in Chapter 7.

Top tips. It's worth revising your financial mathematics notes if you got (a) (i) wrong. The fact that you don't need the answer for (a) (i) in parts (ii) and (iii) is surprising. Note how the answer on the cost of debt is worked through. Although the question doesn't specifically require a discussion of practical issues, you would have gained credit for these.

Easy marks. 6 marks were available in (a) for the NPV calculations, and you could have obtained these even if you got the cost of debt calculation wrong. However some of the other calculations were unusual, and this would have been a question to avoid if you weren't sure what to do.

Examiner's comments. Most candidates answered (a) (i) incorrectly. In (ii) many answers wrongly **excluded** the tax on lease payments and **included** interest and loan principal cash flows. Residual value was either omitted from capital allowance computations or calculated as for a single plane. Many answers to (b) did little more than repeat the question, and lacked quantitative and qualitative analysis.

(a) (i) **Compound annualised post-tax cost of debt**

The **6 month reference rate** is 2.4% and the company's rate is 1% p.a. above this, which is 0.5% per six month period, giving a six month rate for the company of 2.9%.

The after tax rate for 6 months will therefore be 2.9% $(1 - 0.3)$ = 2.03%.

This gives a compound annualised post tax cost of $1.0203^2 - 1$ = 4.10%.

(ii) **NPV of lease versus purchase decision at 4% and 5%**

The PV of the **lease payments** after tax relief, at 4% and 5%, is shown below. The lease is assumed to be an operating lease because the lessor retains the risk of loss on the residual value of the aircraft.

	Year	$m	4% factors	PV $m	5% factors	PV $m
Lease payments	0 - 4	(15.0)	4.630	(69.45)	4.546	(68.19)
Tax relief	1 - 5	4.5	4.452	20.03	4.329	19.48
				(49.42)		(48.71)

The planes cost $100m and their **residual value** is estimated as 4 × $12.5m = $50m. If they are bought, the tax savings from capital allowances will be as computed below. It is assumed that a balancing charge is made in year 5 because the assets are depreciated below their residual value.

Year	Value at start of year $m	20% writing down allowance $m	30% tax saved $m
1	100.0	20.0	6.0
2	80.0	16.0	4.8
3	64.0	12.8	3.8
4	51.2	10.2	3.1
5	41.0	(9.0)	(2.7)
		50.0	15.0

The **PV of purchasing the planes** can then be estimated at 4% and 5%.

Year	$m	4% factor	PV $m	5% factor	PV $m
0 Purchase	(100)	1.000	(100)	1.000	(100)
5 Residual value	50	0.822	41.10	0.784	39.20
2 Tax	6.0	0.925	5.55	0.907	5.44
3 "	4.8	0.889	4.27	0.864	4.15
4 "	3.8	0.855	3.25	0.823	3.13
5 "	3.1	0.822	2.55	0.784	2.43
6 "	(2.7)	0.790	(2.13)	0.746	(2.01)
			(45.41)		(47.66)

Thus the **additional present value** of cost expected if the planes are leased rather than purchased is expected to be:

At 4% cost of borrowing: 49.42m - 45.41m = $4.01m.
At 5% cost of borrowing: 48.71m - 47.66m = $1.05m.

(iii) The **breakeven post tax cost of debt** at which there is no difference between the cost of leasing and the cost of purchasing will be just higher than 5% and can be estimated by extrapolating these results.

Break-even cost of borrowing = 5% + [1.05 / (4.01 − 1.05)] × 1% = **5.35%**.

(b) **Purchase or lease**

On the basis of the above figures, if the company's post tax borrowing rate is 4.1%, **purchasing is cheaper than leasing**, but this needs to be investigated further by looking at the sensitivity of the decision to some key variables.

Sensitivity to the reference 6-month $ inter-bank rate

Leasing is more expensive unless FLG's post tax cost of debt rises to 5.35% p.a. This is a pre-tax rate of 5.35% / 0.7 = 7.643% p.a.

This implies a 6-month rate of $1.07643^{0.5} - 1$ = 3.75% per 6 month period.

Taking off FLG's risk premium of 0.5% gives a maximum reference 6-month $ inter-bank rate of **3.25%**, compared with the present figure of 2.4%.

Thus if interest rates rise more than 85 basis points, leasing will be cheaper.

Sensitivity to the residual value of the aeroplanes

PV of additional cost of leasing @ 4% = $4.01m
@ 5% = $1.05m

By interpolation, PV of additional cost of leasing @ 4.1% = $4.01m $- \left[(4.01m - 1.05m) \times \dfrac{(4.1\% - 4\%)}{(5\% - 4\%)} \right]$

$$= \$3.71m$$

The PV of the residual value of the aeroplanes $= \dfrac{\$50m}{1.041^5}$ = $40.9 m

The sensitivity of the calculation to changes in the residual value $= \dfrac{3.71}{40.9}$ = 9.07%

Thus although purchasing is expected to be cheaper, it carries **interest rate risk** and the risk of a fall in the planes' residual value. Neither of these variables need to move far before the lease is a better option.

Other factors

Other factors affecting the decision include:

(i)   It is assumed that the **planes** are **identical** whether leased or purchased.

(ii)   It is assumed that there will be **no restrictions** put on fittings, conversions or upgrades to the aircraft if they are leased (e.g. refitting of passenger seats).

(iii) It may be **more difficult to break the lease early** than to sell the planes if business suffers a downturn. On the other hand if the planes are kept for the full 5 years, leasing avoids the risk of a drop in residual value.

(iv)   Purchasing becomes a **progressively better option** the longer the planes can be kept in service beyond 5 years.

Recommendation

In expected value terms, leasing is only **slightly more expensive** than purchasing. Assuming the planes will be replaced after 5 years, no earlier and no later, leasing is likely to be the **better choice of finance**, as it avoids the significant risk attached to residual value. If the period of use is uncertain, then purchasing may still be a better option.

26 GREBE

Text references. Forecasts are revised in Chapter 3 and the capital structure decision is discussed in Chapter 10.

Top tips. (a) requires preparation of forecasts covering alternative scenarios, something which you may be asked to do in other syllabus areas. You may also be asked to manipulate formulae so work carefully through our answer to (b) if you struggled.

Easy marks. (d) should have been straightforward. Remember the mix should be suitable, acceptable and feasible.

Examiner's comments. (a) was often answered well with many candidates scoring high marks. This section also required forecast earnings per share and forecast levels of gearing to be calculated for each financing option. These calculations were usually completed less well. Many candidates failed to calculate the correct number of shares for the earnings per share calculations and many failed to calculate correctly the equity element for the gearing calculation. These were fairly straightforward calculations and a little more preparation for these types of questions would have helped candidates to gain valuable marks.

(b) required a calculation of the level of operating profit at which the earnings per share would be the same under each financing option. This section was not answered well. Many candidates struggled with the calculations and some avoided answering this section. (c) was completed reasonably well.

(a)   (i)   **Forecast income statement for the year ending 31 May 20X4**

	Shares £'000	Debentures £'000
Operating profit (800 + 180)	980	980
Interest (160 + 120)	160	280
Profit before tax	820	700
Tax (20%)	164	140
Profit after taxation	656	560
Dividend (PAT $\times$ 50%)	328	280
Retained profit for the year	328	280

(ii) **Forecast earnings per share**

Share issue – number of shares current in issue 1,200,000
           – new shares issued (1,200,000/2)   600,000

$$1{,}800{,}000 = \frac{£656{,}000}{1{,}800{,}000}$$

$$= 36.4 \text{ pence}$$

Debt issue

$$= \frac{£560{,}000}{1{,}200{,}000}$$

$$= 46.7 \text{ pence}$$

(iii) **Projected level of gearing**

$$\text{Share issue} = \frac{2{,}000}{600+1{,}200+1{,}600+328+2{,}000} \times 100\%$$

$$= 34.9\%$$

$$\text{Debt issue} = \frac{2{,}000+1{,}200}{600+1{,}600+280+2{,}000+1{,}200} \times 100\%$$

$$= 56.3\%$$

(b) Operating profit is profit before interest and tax. The operating profit level at which earnings per share under each financing option would be equal is calculated as follows:

x = operating profit

Shares		Debt
$\dfrac{(x-\text{interest})(1-\text{tax rate})}{\text{Number of shares}}$	=	$\dfrac{(x-\text{interest})(1-\text{tax rate})}{\text{Number of shares}}$
$\dfrac{(x-£0.16m)(1-0.2)}{1.8m}$	=	$\dfrac{(x-£0.28m)(1-0.2)}{1.2m}$
$\dfrac{0.8x-£0.128m}{1.8m}$	=	$\dfrac{0.8x-£0.224m}{1.2m}$
$0.96mx-£0.1536m$	=	$1.44mx-£0.4032m$
$0.48mx$	=	$£0.2496m$
x	=	$£0.52m$

(c) **Impact on EPS**

The calculations in part (a) show that for the existing shareholders the issue of the debt would lead to a **significantly higher level of earnings per share** than the share issue and also increase their earnings per share above the current level of 42.7 pence.

Impact on risk

However the debt issue would significantly increase the gearing level from the current level of 47.6%. Therefore the debt issue, although increasing earnings per share will increase the **level of risk faced** by the equity shareholders. The attitude of the existing shareholders to this increase in risk must therefore be considered.

Ownership

The share issue although reducing the gearing level has risks of its own in that the share capital is to increase by 50%, and this one third holding will be held by the **supplier** who already has an **equity investment** in the business. This change of ownership power may not be acceptable to the existing shareholders.

(d) **Equity and debt**

(i) The **cost of debt capital**. Tax relief will be available to GREBE on interest costs, but not on dividends. Debt capital is therefore cheaper than equity, and is consequently often preferred by management.

(ii) GREBE's board of directors might try to **keep gearing** within a **target range** that shareholders and lenders might regard as 'normal' or **'acceptable'** for the company.

(iii) Gearing policy might be affected by board policy on **retained profits**. When retained profits are fairly high, a company might have little recourse to external financing, and so would have a very low gearing level.

(iv) Gearing might be influenced by **management's views on interest rates**. Borrowing might be avoided when market interest rates are considered high, or in the case of variable rate borrowing if interest rates are expected to rise.

Long-term and short-term debt

(i) **Non-current assets** should normally be **financed** by **long-term sources** of **finance** and **current assets** by a **mixture of long-term and short-term sources**. If a company finances illiquid assets from short-term debt it faces the risk of insolvency in the event of its being unable to renegotiate the loans when they fall due.

(ii) **Transaction** costs **vary** according to the type of finance being raised, for example it will be cheaper for GREBE to arrange a medium-term bank loan than a public issue of dated loan stock. Short-term debt will need to be renegotiated more frequently and this will give rise to recurring transaction costs.

(iii) The **relative interest rates** carried by long-term and short-term debt will **vary over time** according to supply and demand and to market expectations of interest rate changes. Rates are generally higher on long-term loans than on short-term since the level of risk faced by the lender that interest rates may rise before repayment is due is higher.

(iv) GREBE's directors may find it easier to **raise short-term finance** with **low security** than long-term finance.

(v) In opting for short-term debt, GREBE would face the risk that it may **not** be able to **renegotiate the loan** on such good terms, or even at all, when the repayment date is reached. Long-term loans are thus less risky.

(vi) Long-term debt may carry **early repayment penalties** if it is found that the loan is no longer needed or a more attractive form of finance becomes available. Short-term debt is **more flexible** since it allows the firm to react to interest rate changes and to avoid being locked into an expensive long-term fixed rate commitment at a time when rates are falling.

27 UR

> **Text references.** Working capital management is discussed in Chapter 3.
>
> **Top tips.** This may appear to be similar to the types of question that you may have come across in lower level papers, and indeed the calculations are similar to those often required at lower levels. However the examiner has made it clear that she expects answers to concentrate on higher level policy decisions rather than going into a lot of detail about day-to-day working capital management.
>
> The key distinction is between **investing** in current assets and **financing** that investment through a mix of short and long-term finance. Perhaps surprisingly we are not told anything about the long-term finance the company has, but this means the discussion on finance has to concentrate on trade payables (even under the current aggressive policy the company doesn't have a bank overdraft).

Current policy

Investing

(a) UR has made a significant investment in debtors, the **credit period for customers** being **108 days** (see workings below). This is costly to finance and exposes the company to an **increased risk of bad debts**. However, the policy appears to have played a role in increasing sales revenue.

(b) Investment in inventory has been less significant than investment in receivables, with **relatively low inventory levels (less than two months worth of inventory in stores)** (see workings below). This **reduces financing costs**, and also **reduces the likelihood of obsolescence** of machine parts, but the risk of running out of inventory is high unless **customer demand** is very **carefully monitored**.

(c) UR has maintained **low levels of cash (less than 8% of trade creditors)**. This is a risky policy: if some suppliers decided to **enforce payment**, the company could be forced into financial difficulties.

Financing

(a) UR appears to be financing its investment in receivables by the use of trade credit as a source of finance, 117 days (see workings below) being a very long period. UR may have believed that this source of short-term credit has low or zero direct costs, and was **much cheaper** than sources of longer-term finance. However the problems UR is currently facing may include difficulties with suppliers, such as suppliers **suing for payment**, refusing to do further business, or increasing their prices.

(b) However trade credit appears to be the only significant source of short-term finance. UR has not utilised any borrowing capacity.

Impact of current policy

The overall effect on working capital does not look particularly risky. There is no overdraft or other borrowing. The **current ratio** (1.71) and **quick ratio** (1.23) (see workings below) appear reasonable for this type of business. The **cash operating cycle** (period between paying suppliers and being paid by customers) is 47 days, which does not appear to be too long or short. **Profitability** appears to be good: **operating profit margin** and **return on net assets** are both 20% (see workings below).

The main risk UR faces, a risk that the change in policy may be trying to mitigate, is that if a **market downturn** forces non-payment by debtors, the company would need to take quick action to obtain sufficient funds.

Changes to the working capital policy

Investing

(a) The **receivables' collection period** will be reduced from 108 days to 68 days (see workings below). **Financing costs** will be substantially reduced. UR needs to consider whether this will be achieved by tightening credit monitoring procedures and putting more pressure on slow-paying customers, or **tightening limits and controls** on **all customers**. The risk particularly of taking measures that affect all customers is that sales may be reduced as some customers obtain **better terms**. The reduced sales estimate indicates the danger, and UR will need to pay particular attention to industry norms for credit periods.

(b)   Inventory in stores **will be increased from 56 days to 73 days** (see workings below) **worth of production**. This will **increase the financing cost** but will **reduce the probability of running out of inventory**. This policy however appears to go against the trends in many businesses which are using modern production management to minimise inventory levels.

(c)   **A higher cash balance will be maintained.** Cash will increase from 8% to 32% of payables. This will reduce the **likelihood of needing to borrow** in the event of financial difficulties. However it is important that the surplus cash is earning a proper return and not lying idle in the bank.

Financing

(a)   **Suppliers will be paid more promptly**. Payment period will be reduced from 117 days to 89 days (see workings below). To a significant extent this matches with the reduction in debtors and will **reduce financial risk**. However three months is still a significant period, and is rather in excess of the debtor collection period. Trade payables could be further decreased by a **corresponding decrease** in cash balances.

(b)   UR does **not** appear to be **drawing** on any other **sources of finance**.

Effects of changes

The proposed new policies would have a beneficial effect on **liquidity ratios**, but would increase the cash operating cycle slightly by 5 days.

The directors are aiming to **improve profit margins**. Some improvement in profit will come from the **reduced financing cost of receivables** and, it is presumed, **reduction in bad debts,** This will be **partially offset** by the **increased stock financing requirement** and the **decision to pay suppliers more promptly**. The **5% increase in profit** implies a **2% increase in profit margins** which may imply **further cost efficiencies** (eg reduced prices paid to suppliers as a result of quicker payment) or an increase in sales price. Return on net assets will not be materially affected.

Recommended action

The change in working capital policy will produce an **increase in profitability** and an **improvement in liquidity.** It should therefore be explored, subject to the recommendations below.

Centralisation of asset management

UR needs to explore **how efficiently** working capital is being **managed**. In particular it needs to consider whether the **credit control function** should be expanded. If more efforts are made to speed up debt collection from slow-paying customers, this may eliminate the need to impose **unpopular tighter controls** on all customers.

The **efficiency of inventory management** should also be reviewed. Stock levels should only be increased if there is clear evidence that **stock-outs** have been a **problem** under the existing policy and, if so, only for those product lines which have been subject to stock-outs. For other lines **just-in-time and other modern supply chain** procedures should be introduced to minimise stock levels.

Similarly cash should be **carefully managed**, with any surpluses not required for immediate needs invested. Careful prediction of cash needs should mean that surpluses are invested in instruments of varying lengths that between them offer the maximum returns subject to limited investment risk.

Relationships with suppliers

As suppliers will be paid earlier, relationships should improve and could improve further if some of the predicted cash surplus was used to pay off suppliers. UR should consider whether the improvements mean that it could seek **further benefits** from its relationships with suppliers, maybe **reduced prices for prompter payment, possibly supplier co-operation** if just-in-time stock management procedures are introduced.

Borrowing facilities

The company should anticipate any possible short-term problems caused by a financial downturn in the market by **arranging borrowing facilities** with its bankers, if it has not already done so. Although the cost of these facilities may be greater than the cost of trade credit as a source of credit, the facilities would only have a cost to the extent that they are used.

Workings

	Original €'000	% change	Revised €'000
Receivables	5,200	−40%	3,120
Inventory	2,150	+20%	2,580
Cash at bank	350	given	1,000
Total current assets	7,700		6,700
Trade payables	4,500	−30%	3,150
Net current assets	3,200		3,550
Non-current assets	14,500	no change	14,500
Net assets	17,700	+2%	18,050
Sales	17,500	−5%	16,625
Operating costs	14,000	−7.5%	12,950
Operating profit	3,500	+5%	3,675
Earnings	2,625	+5%	2,756
No of shares million	2.5		2.5
Ratios			
Current ratio: current assets / current liabilities)	1.71		2.13
Quick ratio: (current assets − inventory)/current liabs	1.23		1.31
Cash/payables	7.8%		31.7%
Operating profit margin: operating profit /sales	20.0%		22.1%
Earnings per share	1.05		1.10
Return on net assets: operating profit/net assets	19.8%		20.4%
	Days		*Days*
Receivables collection: receivables/sales × 365	108		68
Credit period taken: trade cr./cost of sales × 365	(117)		(89)
Inventory: inventory/cost of sales × 365	56		73
Cash operating cycle	47		52

28 MNO

> **Text references**. Working capital management is covered in Chapter 3 and treasury departments are discussed in Chapter 14.
>
> **Top tips**. In part (a) make sure you base your calculations for accounts payables and inventories on **cost of sales** and recognise that maximum accounts payable coincides with minimum working capital. Do not forget to discuss the validity of the Financial Controller's assumptions.
>
> **Easy marks**. Parts (b) and (c) are a straightforward discussion of textbook knowledge but you must make sure you **apply** your discussion to MNO.
>
> **Examiner's comments**. This question was avoided by the majority of candidates even though it was a standard working capital and financing question. Many candidates ignored the financing aspects and the main weaknesses was the inability to provide the calculations required.

Workings

	Minimum ($m)	Maximum ($m)
Accounts receivable	20/365 × 10 = 0.55	30/365 × 10 = 0.82
Accounts payable Cost of sales (60% × 10 = 6)	40/365 × 6 = 0.66	50/365 × 6= 0.82
Inventories	50/365 × 6 = 0.82	80/365 × 6 =1.32

Maximum level of working capital

= peak accounts receivable + peak inventories – lowest accounts payable

= 0.82 + 1.32 – 0.66 = $1.48m

Minimum level of working capital

= lowest accounts receivable + lowest inventories – peak accounts payable

= 0.55 + 0.82 – 0.82 = $0.55m

(a) (i) The Financial Controller has assumed that the peak period for accounts receivable coincides with the peak period for inventories and the lowest level of accounts payable. However, if sales have been **particularly high** resulting in accounts receivable peaking, it is likely that inventories will be lower. If inventories are high it is likely that there has been increased spending on purchases and accounts payable will be higher.

Working capital levels will be affected by many factors and monitoring the fluctuations over a year in order to identify any **relationships** and **cyclical patterns** would produce a more **accurate** forecast.

(ii) Permanent net current assets = $0.55m
Fluctuating net current assets = $(1.48 – 0.55) = $0.93m
Non-current assets = $8m

	Moderate ($m)	Aggressive ($m)	Conservative ($m)
Short-term financing	0.93	(30% × 0.55) + 0.93 = 1.09	40% × 0.93 = 0.37
Long-term financing	0.55 + 8 = 8.55	(70% × 0.55) + 8 = 8.39	(60% × 0.93) + 8 + 0.55 = 9.11

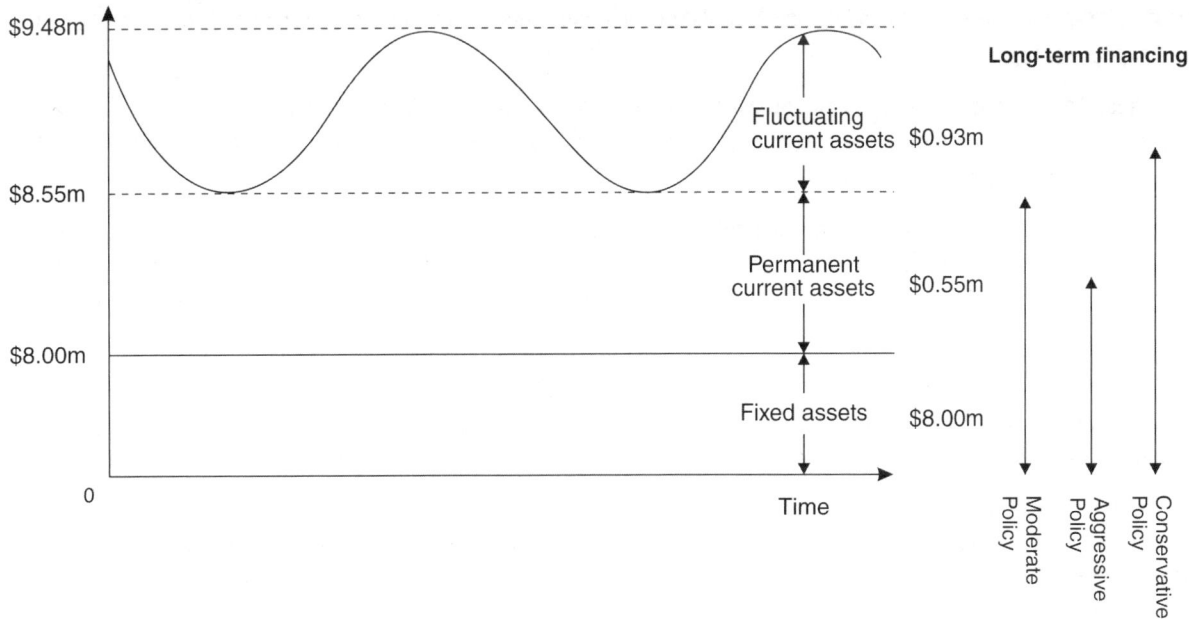

(b) The **advantages** of an aggressive financing policy are that it carries the greatest returns. It aims to reduce the financing costs, as short-term financing is cheaper than long-term, and increase profitability by cutting inventories, speeding up collections from customers and delaying payments to suppliers. It also enables greater flexibility in financing.

BPP
LEARNING MEDIA

However, there is an increased risk of **illiquidity** and managers will need to spend a significant amount of time managing and renewing short-term sources of finance. Short-term finance may not always be easily available.

MNO is likely to have **large fluctuations** in its levels of working capital requirements and would therefore find the **flexibility** of an aggressive financing policy beneficial.

(c) The treasury department is usually run as a **cost centre** if its main focus is to keep costs within budgeted spending targets. In a cost centre, managers have an incentive only to keep the costs of the department within budgeted spending targets. The cost centre approach implies that the treasury is there to perform a **service** of a certain standard to other departments in the enterprise. The treasury is treated much like any other service department.

It may be run as a **profit centre** if there is a high level of foreign exchange transactions, or the business wishes to make speculative profits. Treating the treasury department as a profit centre recognises the fact that treasury activities such as **speculation** may earn revenues for the company, and may as a result make treasury staff more **motivated**. It also means that treasury departments have to operate with a greater degree of commercial awareness, in for example the management of working capital, by reducing interest and bank spreads. The profit can also be made by charging individual business units a **market rate for services** with a lover cost of provision.

In MNO, the treasury department is unlikely to be run as a profit centre as it is a relatively **small entity** so finance savings will be limited. There are currently no foreign exchange dealings, and, although this is due to change, there will be no opportunity to make a profit by netting cash flows as there will be only payments in the Asian currency. MNO **is de-centralised** which makes it harder to impose central finance policies although Head Office does provide funds as required.

In conclusion, a cost centre structure is probably the most appropriate for the treasury department of MNO.

29 LE International

Text references. The cost of capital basic calculations are explained in Chapter 9 and Chapter 10 looks in detail at the capital asset pricing model.

Top tips. This question is testing your knowledge of the different theories relating to the cost of capital, as well as testing your ability to calculate the cost of capital correctly taking into account the effects of taxation and the market values of each element.

The answer to (b) starts with the rationale behind the capital asset pricing model before discussing each element. As you are asked about the use of CAPM as an alternative to using the dividend valuation model, you need to bring out the significant differences between the two. Don't worry if you couldn't remember the formula for calculating the beta factor.

In (c) you are required to demonstrate the way in which the cost of capital should be used by the company in assessing individual projects. You should approach this from the point of view of the effect of the new funding and investments on the overall capital structure of the firm, and the implications of this for raising finance in the future.

In (d) don't forget that you need to adjust the return on preferred shares for tax. It would be possible (company constitution permitting) to issue different types of preferred share with different nominal values and interest rates. Don't however give the impression that the company can issue £1 preferred shares at 72p; that would be illegal in most regimes.

Easy marks. (b) is a fairly straightforward test of knowledge of the capital asset pricing model.

(a)   It is assumed that the market prices of the shares and debt are quoted **excluding dividend and interest**. Since the WACC is to be calculated based on market values, the cost of reserves can be ignored.

Cost of equity

The dividend valuation model taking into account growth will be used.

$$k_e = \frac{d_1}{P_0} + g$$

where: k_e = cost of equity
         d_1 = annual level of dividends
          g = annual rate of growth in dividends
         P_0 = market price of shares (ex div)

In this case: k_e = 4/80 + 0.12
                    = 17.0%

Cost of preference shares

$k_{pref} = d_1/P_0$
where: k_{pref} = cost of preference shares
              d_1 = preference dividend (9p)
             P_0 = market price of shares (72p)
        k_{pref} = 9 / 72
                 = 12.5%

Cost of debt

It is assumed that the debt is irredeemable. The after tax cost to the company will be calculated.

$$k_{dnet} = \frac{i(l-t)}{P_0}$$

where: k_{dnet} = cost of debt
              i = annual interest payment (14p)
             P_0 = market price of debt (100p)
              t = rate of tax (33%)
        k_{dnet} = $\dfrac{14(1-0.33)}{100}$
                  = 9.4%

Weighted average cost of capital (WACC)

	No in Issue	Market price £	Market value £	Cost %	Weighted cost
Equity	10,400,000	0.80	8,320,000	17.0	1,414,400
Preference shares	4,500,000	0.72	3,240,000	12.5	405,000
Debt (£ stock)	5,000,000	1.00	5,000,000	9.4	470,000
			16,560,000		2,289,400

WACC (2,289,400 / 16,560,000) = 13.82%

(b)   **CAPM**

The **capital asset pricing model** (CAPM) provides an alternative to the dividend valuation model in calculating the cost of equity. Unlike the dividend valuation model, the CAPM seeks to **differentiate** between the **various types of risk** faced by a firm and to allow for the fact that new projects undertaken may carry a different level of risk from the existing business.

(i)   The model focuses on the level of **systematic risk** attaching to the firm, in other words, that element of risk which is common to all investments and which cannot be avoided by diversification.

(ii)   The model uses the **beta factor** as a measure of an individual share's volatility of expected returns as against the market average. A beta factor of less than 1.0 indicates that the expected volatility is less than that of the market as a whole, and vice versa.

The model can be formulated as follows:

$$k_e = R_f + (R_m - R_f] \beta$$

where: k_e = cost of equity capital
         β_j = beta factor for the firm
         R_m = market rate of return
         R_f = risk free rate of return

Thus the additional information that would be required is as follows.

Beta factor

This can be calculated statistically from historical records of:

(i)   The returns earned by the share in terms of capital gains/losses and dividends
(ii)   The overall returns earned by the market

Market rate of return

The average annual rate of return on the securities market as a whole. This can be calculated from historical records.

Risk free rate of return

This is generally taken to be the rate of return on short-dated government stocks.

(c)   **Cost of funds**

It is not usually correct to regard the **required rate of return** for an individual project as the cost of the actual source of funds that will be used to finance it, even where the funds can be traced directly. Debt is cheaper than equity only because there is an **equity base** which **takes the risk** - if the equity funds were not there then the company could not borrow. Each year some profits should be retained to increase the equity base, thus allowing further borrowing to take place. The borrowing is not independent of equity funds, and thus it is appropriate to combine the two in arriving at the cost of capital to be used in project appraisal.

WACC

The WACC reflects the company's long-term capital structure, and therefore capital costs. The **capital structure** generally **changes** only very **slowly** over time, and therefore the marginal cost of new capital should be approximately equal to the WACC. The **WACC** is therefore a more appropriate yardstick for the evaluation of new projects.

(d)   (i)   **Risk**

As calculated above, the existing preference shares are yielding 12.5% net. Based on the single income tax rate given in the question of 25%, this represents a gross yield of 16.67%, as compared with 14% on the debt. In the event of LE International being wound up, the **debt holders** would **rank above** the **preference shareholders** for repayment of capital. Similarly, preference dividend will only be paid in a given year if sufficient funds are available after the debt holders have been paid. Thus holders of preference shares carry a greater burden of risk than do the debt holders, and it is consistent that they should expect to receive a higher rate of return in compensation for this.

(ii)   **Equity earnings**

The net payment made by the company on the debt is:

£5m × 14% × 0.67 = £469,000

In order to raise the £5m through a preference share issue, the company would need to offer the shares at a discount. To yield 12.5% to the investor, the shares would therefore need to be priced at the same level as the existing preferred shares ie 72p per share. The nominal value would have to be 72p or below. 6,944,445 shares would need to be issued at 72p in order to raise £5m. The annual cost in terms of dividends can be calculated either as 12.5% of £5m, or as 9.0% of the nominal value (£6,944,445). In either event, the cost to the company is £625,000. Thus if preferred shares are issued instead of debt, the annual equity earnings would be reduced by £156,000 (£625,000 − £469,000). This would be partly compensated by the preference shareholders taking on some of the ordinary shareholders' risk.

30 WZ

Text references. Cost of capital calculations are explained in Chapter 9 and the capital structure decision is discussed in Chapter 10.

Top tips. (a) is a good example of a numerical question, which if you think about the framework of the calculations at the planning stage, you should be able to present your answer in a framework that's helpful to you and clear to the marker. The point that market value of a company equals the sum of all its long-term sources of finance (ie you have to consider loan and preference capital as well as equity capital) is something that's often missed.

(b) is a good illustration of the points that will be considered when choosing between different sources of finance.

Easy marks. (b) raises a number of issues which will very often have to be considered when assessing finance.

Examiner's comments. Part (a) was not as well answered as expected given it required fairly straightforward calculations. Common errors included not recognising that the dividend on preference shares does not attract tax relief; not calculating earnings; incorrectly calculating the market value of equity; assuming the market value of the entity was the same as the market value of equity; using coupon rates instead of calculating the cost of preference shares and cost of debt.

In part (b) it was important to relate the discussion to the specific circumstances of the question.

(a) **Alternative 1**

For Alternative 1, the **rights issue** price will be 85% of **current market price** Z$12.50 = Z$10.625 per share. Number of shares issued = 5 m / 10.625 = 0.471 million.

	Current situation	Alternative 1	Alternative 2
	Z$m	Z$m	Z$m
Earnings before interest	15.00	17.00	17.00
Interest on 8% debt	(1.60)	(1.60)	(1.60)
Interest on Z$5m 9% bonds	–	–	(0.45)
Profit before tax	13.40	15.40	14.95
Tax @ 30%	(4.02)	(4.62)	(4.49)
Profit after tax	9.38	10.78	10.46
Preference dividend	(0.70)	(0.70)	(0.70)
Equity earnings	8.68	10.08	9.76
No. of shares (million)	5	5.471	5
(i) **Earnings per share (Z$)**	**1.74**	**1.84**	**1.95**
Market value per share (Z$) (eps / 12%)	14.50	15.33	16.25
(ii) **Total market value of equity (Z$m)**	**72.50**	**83.87**	**81.25**
Value of preference shares (10m × Z$0.8)	8.00	8.00	8.00

		Current situation Z$m	Alternative 1 Z$m	Alternative 2 Z$m
	Value of 8% debt (Z$20m × 0.9)	18.00	18.00	18.00
	Value of 9% bonds			5.00
(iii)	**Market value of the entity**	**98.5**	**109.87**	**112.25**
(iv)	**Gearing (debt / total value)**	**18.3%**	**16.4%**	**20.5%**

(v)   **Weighted average cost of capital**

The after tax cost of the 8% debt is 8/90 (1 − 0.3) = 6.22% p.a.

The cost of the preference shares is 7/80 = 8.75% p.a.

Current situation

	MV Z$ m	Cost %	MV × Cost/98.5
Equity	72.50	12.00	8.83
Preference shares	8.00	8.75	0.71
8% unsecured debt	18.00	6.22	1.14
	98.50		10.68

WACC = 10.68%.

Alternative 1

	MV, Z$ m	Cost %	MV × Cost/109.87
Equity	83.87	12.00	9.16
Preference shares	8.00	8.75	0.64
8% unsecured debt	18.00	6.22	1.02
	109.87		10.82

WACC = 10.82%.

Alternative 2

	MV, Z$ m	Cost %	MV × Cost/112.25
Market value of equity	81.25	12.00	8.69
Preference shares	8.00	8.75	0.62
8% unsecured debt	18.00	6.22	1.00
9% bonds	5.00	6.30	0.28
	112.25		10.59

WACC = 10.59%.

The above calculations ignore issue costs.

(b)   **Issues to be considered**

Period of finance

The **injection of working capital** is needed to **underpin general expansion**. This implies it is a **permanent increase** and should be financed from **permanent** or **long term funds.** In this respect, the best is **equity capital,** followed by the **10-year bond**. Factoring should not really be used as a source of permanent funds. It is best held in reserve for short term funding needs.

Cost of the funds

From the calculations above, the 10 year bond (Alternative 2) is **cheaper than equity** (Alternative 1). The bond **lowers WACC** whereas the equity issue **raises it.** Although these calculations ignore the fact that as **gearing increases** the **cost of equity** will rise to compensate for increased financial risk, the **over-riding effect** will still be that debt attracts **tax savings** on interest whereas **equity dividends** are **not tax allowable.** Furthermore the debt will probably have **lower issue costs** than the equity. Rates of interest for factoring the receivables can be very competitive and might be cheaper than the bond issue.

Gearing and liquidity

The equity issue **reduces gearing** whereas the **debt issue increases** it. In terms of economic substance, factoring debtors would also increase gearing, as it is a form of borrowing. The gearing of the company is not unduly high, so this consideration would probably be outweighed by the cheaper cost of debt funds than equity.

The only source of funds to affect liquidity would be the **factoring**. Insufficient information is available to test the result, but the effect of using short term sources of funds to finance long term needs will usually strain liquidity.

Flexibility of funding

It is possible that the **debt** can be **'drawn down'** as needed, though this is **more difficult** for **bonds** than for a bank loan. The equity is a one-time issue. Factoring is very flexible, automatically varying with the size of the receivables ledger.

Ease of raising the funds

Factoring is easy to arrange. The ease of raising funds through bonds and share issues depends on the **state of the market,** but if bonds are difficult there is always the alternative of a **bank loan,** though this might have to be at floating rate interest. Share issues require a prospectus and a lot more administrative time than loan issues.

Recommendation

Because the gearing of the company is not unduly high, and a relatively permanent source of funds is needed, the **loan** is **recommended.** This is likely to reduce the overall cost of capital.

31 IML

Text references. Chapter 12 covers the capital asset pricing model and Chapter 8 includes a discussion of the efficient market hypothesis.

Top tips. Although this looks like a question on the CAPM, the final part of the question requires a discussion of the efficient markets hypothesis, so you should be confident in both these areas.

(a) takes you through the stage-by-stage process of calculating the adjusted present value. Often you will be given the proxy company's beta, but here calculating it provides an additional test of your ability to use the capital asset pricing model. The tax benefit is a straightforward debt value x tax rate calculation; on other occasions it might only be available for a number of years and you'd be required to discount the tax relief over that period.

You're not given the formula used in (b) on the formula sheet, but you should have recognised that it's just a simple rearrangement of the formula used in (a).

Note the requirement for the discussion in (c) to be comprehensible to a non-financial manager. Discussion of the assumptions and limitations of CAPM carried most marks in (c), although to score heavily the efficient markets hypothesis and the chairman's assertions also needed to be discussed, and the calculations carried out in (a) and (b) used in support.

> **Easy marks.** The limitations of CAPM are core knowledge in this paper, and should represent easy marks if you're asked to discuss them.
>
> **Examiner's comments.** The main weakness in this question was discussion of the efficient markets hypothesis; the key point here was the market's expectations re the company's loss.

(a)   The first stage is to calculate the geared beta of the other company.

Using $k_e = R_f + [R_m - R_f] \beta_g$

$17\% = 5\% + \beta(15\% - 5\%)$

$$\beta_g = \frac{(17\% - 5\%)}{(15\% - 5\%)}$$

$$= 1.2$$

Substituting in the formula

$$\beta_u = \beta_g \left[\frac{V_E}{V_E + V_D[1-t]} \right]$$

$$= 1.2 \left(\frac{2}{2 + 1(1 - 0.3)} \right)$$

$$= 0.89$$

So the ungeared cost of equity $= 5 + (15 - 5)\, 0.89$
$$= 13.9\%$$

To calculate the adjusted present value of the investment

(i)   Calculate base case NPV

$$NPV = -£10m + \frac{5}{0.139} = £26 \text{ million}$$

(ii)   Add tax shield effects

Tax benefit $= £10m \times 0.3 = £3$ million

Adjusted present value $= £29$ million

(b)   Calculate equity beta

$$\beta_g = \beta_u \times \frac{V_E + V_D(1-t)}{V_E}$$

$$= 0.89 \, \frac{3 + 1(1 - 0.3)}{3}$$

$$= 1.10$$

New cost of equity $= 5 + (15 - 5)\, 1.1$
$$= 16\%$$

(c) To: The Chairman
From: Finance Director
Date: 20 November 20X1
Subject: The Capital Asset Pricing Model (CAPM) and stock market reactions

(i)   **Assumptions and limitations of CAPM**

Diversification

Under the CAPM, the return required from a security is **related** to its **systematic risk** rather than its total risk. Only the risks that **cannot** be **eliminated** by diversification are **relevant.** The assumption is that investors will hold a **fully diversified portfolio** and therefore deal with the unsystematic risk themselves. However, in practice, markets are **not totally efficient** and investors do not all hold fully diversified portfolios. This means that total risk is relevant to investment decisions, and that therefore the relevance of the CAPM may be limited.

Excess return

In practice, it is difficult to determine the excess return ($R_m - R_f$). **Expected rather than historical returns** should be used, although historical returns are used in practice.

Risk-free rate

It is similarly difficult to **determine the risk-free rate**. A risk-free investment might be a government security; however, interest rates vary with the term of the debt.

Risk aversion

Shareholders are risk averse, and therefore **demand higher returns** in compensation for increased levels of risk.

Beta factors

Beta factors based on historical data may be a **poor basis** for future **decision making**, since evidence suggests that beta values fluctuate over time.

Unusual circumstances

The CAPM is **unable** to **forecast accurately returns for companies** with **low price/earnings ratios,** and to take account of **seasonal 'month-of-the-year' effects** and **'day-of-the-week'** effects that appear to influence returns on shares.

(ii) **Efficient markets hypothesis**

The way in which the stock market responds to information released by a company can be understood with reference to the **efficient markets hypothesis** (EMH). It is generally accepted that the UK stock market demonstrates a **semi-strong form** of **market efficiency**. This means that share prices **respond immediately** to all **publicly available information**, but not to information available only to insiders.

Implications of efficient markets hypothesis

- It is **not possible** consistently to **beat the market** (on a risk-adjusted basis) without the use of inside information.

- **Past share prices** are **not** a **predictor** of future share prices.

- The price of a share reflects **market expectations** of future performance.

- Investors behave **rationally** and are not deceived by manipulation of accounting figures.

IML's position

This can help to explain the situation of IML. The effect of an announcement of either profit or loss on the share price will not depend simply on the **magnitude** of the profit or loss, but in the relationship between the **announcement** and what the **market was expecting**. In this case, the company announced a loss and the share price rose. The market might have been expecting the **loss** to be **much larger** than it actually was, and the share price therefore adjusted in response to what was effectively good news. Alternatively, it could be that investors looked not simply at the loss, but at the **future prospects** of the company and decided that these were better than had been expected. The share price would then rise accordingly.

32 CAP

Text references. The capital asset pricing model is discussed in Chapter 8.

Top tips. In (a) you should give a brief definition of the beta factor and what it measures. This will help you to explain the implications of a beta factor of less than one. Preference shares do not count as equity and should be ignored at this stage of the calculations.

In (b) there are a number of valid approaches that can be used to find the cost of the loan stock. The most usual of these, using the internal rate of return, is described in the suggested solution. Using 5% as we have means you only need to calculate one rate. It is equally correct to use a higher and lower rate, say 7% and 4%, and then to use interpolation to find the discount rate at which the NPV approaches zero.

Another possible approach is to calculate the net cash flow at the end of year 1 (£105.60) and divide this into the initial cash flow (£100.57). The result is 0.952. You can then look at the discount tables, where you will see that this is the 5% discount factor for year 1.

In (c) you may find it helpful to think in terms of financial factors and factors affecting the level of business risk when structuring your answer.

Easy marks. Limitations of CAPM should always represent straightforward marks.

Examiner's comments. A number of candidates failed to complete the calculation correctly; a common mistake was using 0.8 as a to the power of function. Candidates also failed to explain the link between risk and returns, and what a beta of 0.8 meant in relation to the market as a whole.

Many candidates did (b) well but poorer candidates made various basic mistakes.

- Stating the preference share denominator as 1000
- Giving tax relief on the preference dividend
- Treating the debt as irredeemable
- Omitting the tax relief on the interest
- Adding reserves onto the market value of equity
- Ignoring the cost of preference shares in the WACC calculation
- Amalgamating preference shares with equity or debt in the WACC calculation
- Using book values rather than market values for weighting in the WACC calculation

Answers to (c) were generally poor, and were insufficiently focused on correlation and systematic risk. Few candidates discussed the significance of gearing levels.

(a) The cost of equity can be found using the following formula:

$$k_e = R_f + (R_m - R_f)\beta$$

where k_e is the cost of equity capital – expected equity return
          R_f is the risk-free rate of return
         R_m is the return from the market as a whole
          β is the beta factor of the individual security

Here: R_f = 5% (annual yield on treasury bills)

R_m = 15%

β = 0.8

k_e = 5% + (15% − 5%)0.8

     = 13%

The required rate of return on equity of CAP at 30 September 2002 is therefore 13%.

Beta factor levels

The beta factor is a measure of **systematic risk**, that is, the element of risk that cannot be avoided by **diversification**. The beta factor measures the **variability in returns** for a given security in relation to the variation in returns for the market as a whole.

A beta factor of 1.0 means that if the market goes up by x%, all other things being equal, one would expect the return on the security to go up by x% as well. A beta factor of less than 1.0 means that the return on the security is likely to be less variable than the return on the market as a whole. A beta value of 0.8 means that if the market returns go up by 5%, the return on the security would only be expected to go up by 4% (5% × 0.8). Similarly, if the market returns fall by 5%, the return on the security would only be expected to fall by 4%.

(b)   **Weighted average cost of capital**

The weighted average cost of capital (WACC) is the **average cost** of the **company's finance** weighted according to the proportion each element bears to the total pool of capital. Weighting is usually based on market values, current yields and costs after tax. Where market values can be used, as in this case, reserves can be ignored.

Equity

The cost of equity has already been calculated at 13%.

The market value of equity (V_E) is the number of shares in issue multiplied by the market price (ex div):

V_E = 200m × £3

    = £600m

Preference shares

Preference shares are irredeemable. The interest on preference shares is not tax deductible. The cost of the preference shares (k_{pref}) is therefore:

k_{pref} = d/P_0

where: d = annual dividend in perpetuity

        P_0 = current ex div price

     k_{pref} = 9%/0.90

          = 10%

The market value of the preference shares (V_P) is the number of shares in issue multiplied by the market price (ex div):

V_P = 50m × £0.90

    = £45m

Loan stock

The loan stock pays interest of 8%, which is allowable against tax. Tax is paid at the end of the year in which taxable profits arise, in other words, at the same time as the interest payment at the end of year 1.

Since the net cost of the interest is 5.6% (8% × 0.7), and the current market price of the stock is just above par, we will try an initial rate of return of 5%.

Year		Cash flow £	5% disc factors	Present value £
0	Market value	(100.57)	1.000	(100.57)
1	Interest	8.00	0.952	7.62
1	Tax saved	(2.40)	0.952	(2.28)
1	Redemption	100.00	0.952	95.20
	Net present value			(0.03)

This net present value is virtually zero, and therefore the effective cost of the loan stock is 5%.

The market value of the loan stock (V_D) is the number of units in issue multiplied by the market price:

V_D = 250m × £100.57/100.00
   = £251.4m

WACC

Total market value = 600.0 + 45.0 + 251.4 = 896.4

$$WACC = k_e \left[\frac{V_E}{V_E + V_P + V_D} \right] + k_{pref} \left[\frac{V_P}{V_E + V_P + V_D} \right] + k_d \left[\frac{V_D}{V_E + V_P + V_D} \right]$$

$$= 13 \left[\frac{600.0}{896.4} \right] + 10 \left[\frac{45}{896.4} \right] + 5 \left[\frac{251.4}{896.4} \right]$$

$$= 10.6\%$$

Alternative working

	MV £'000	Cost %	Weighted average (MV × cost/896.4)
Equity	600.0	13	8.70
Preference shares	45.0	10	0.50
Loan stock	251.4	5	1.40
	896.4		10.60

(c) **Factors affecting equity beta**

CAP's equity beta will be affected by factors that change the perceived **volatility in returns** to the ordinary shareholders. These will include **financial factors**, such as the **change in gearing**, and other factors related to effect of the new investment on the systematic risk of the company's activities.

Rise in gearing

Following the new issue of loan stock, the **gearing will rise**. This in turn is likely to affect the **volatility** of the returns to equity in relation to the market index. As a consequence, the beta may rise.

Effect of diversification

Since the returns on the campsite business are likely to have a very **low correlation** with those of the existing farming business, the effect of the new investment will be to **smooth out the earnings pattern**. This will reduce the volatility of the returns to equity. However the beta value will be affected by how the **campsite returns vary** in relation to **returns on the market portfolio**, and they may **vary more or less** than the **returns from the farming activities**. The equity beta will be the weighted average of the betas of the two sorts of activity.

Refinancing

As well as raising new debt, the company also has to redeem its existing debt in 20X3. If it replaces existing debt with similar debt, there will be little or no effect on the beta. However, if the debt is **replaced by equity** and gearing reduced, volatility of returns on equity and hence the **beta factor** are likely to fall.

Investor perceptions

This is a major diversification by CAP, and investors may perceive this to be a **risky strategy**. As a consequence in the short-term, the beta could rise to reflect this. Investors may feel that CAP's managers **lack the skills required** to manage campsites, as managing camping sites is a very different job from farming. As a consequence this will increase the risk of the new investment, and hence the equity beta may rise. There are also **start-up costs** associated with the new investments. These may depress the profits in the first year of trading, which in turn may cause investors to perceive the new business to be riskier than it really is. The effect of this will be to cause a short-term rise in the beta value.

Industry

Events within the farming and tourism industries, and perceptions of how they are doing, may also affect the beta levels.

(d) **Limitations of CAPM**

Diversification

Under the CAPM, the return required from a security is **related** to its **systematic risk** rather than its total risk. Only the risks that **cannot** be **eliminated** by diversification are **relevant.** The assumption is that investors will hold a **fully diversified portfolio** and therefore deal with the unsystematic risk themselves. However, in practice, markets are **not totally efficient** and investors do not all hold fully diversified portfolios. This means that total risk is relevant to investment decisions, and that therefore the relevance of the CAPM may be limited.

Excess return

In practice, it is difficult to determine the excess return $(R_m - R_f)$. **Expected rather than historical returns** should be used, although historical returns are used in practice.

Risk-free rate

It is similarly difficult to **determine the risk-free rate**. A risk-free investment might be a government security; however, interest rates vary with the term of the debt.

Risk aversion

Shareholders are risk averse, and therefore **demand higher returns** in compensation for increased levels of risk.

Beta factors

Beta factors based on historical data may be a **poor basis** for future **decision making**, since evidence suggests that beta values fluctuate over time.

Unusual circumstances

The CAPM is unable to forecast accurately returns for companies with low price/earnings ratios, and to take account of seasonal 'month-of-the-year' effects and 'day-of-the-week' effects that appear to influence returns on shares.

Arbitrage pricing theory

Arbitrage pricing theory may be more suitable for a company like CAP, since it is based on the assumption that returns are determined by a number of **independent factors**, to which a particular risk premium is attached. These could include the various economic factors that have impacted on the conditions CAP has been facing.

If arbitrage pricing theory is used, there will be no need to identify the market portfolio. However CAP will then face the problem of identifying what **factors are relevant**, and what their **risk premiums** are.

33 DEA

Text references. The calculation of the weighted average cost of capital is explained in Chapter 9 and financial strategies are discussed in Chapter 4.

Top tips. This question tests both your ability to calculate the cost of equity, debt and the WACC, and your understanding of the issues surrounding choice of a discount rate for investment appraisal. You also need to be able to discuss the relationships between dividends, retentions and financing policy.

In (a) you need to adjust the market value of equity to take account of it being quoted cum div. You can carry out the calculation we have used for the 20X7 debt as it is only discounted one year into the future, but you need to use the IRR approach for the 20X9 debt. A tabular approach is the best way to tackle the WACC calculation.

Easy marks. The preference share calculation should have been the easiest calculation. The calculation of the 20X9 redeemable debt should have been fine provided you remembered to use the IRR approach. You can use IRR for the 20X7 calculation as well, but our method saves time.

Examiner's comments. In (a) many candidates failed to calculate the cost of debt correctly, some treating the cost of debt as irredeemable. Answers to (b) were often too general, failing to focus on the comments made by the directors.

(a) **Cost of 20X7 debt**

Payments to be made over the next year prior to redemption

	£'000
Interest net of tax (£12.5m $\times$ 8% $\times$ (1 – 0.3))	700
Payment on redemption	12,500
	13,200

The current market value of the debt is £12.25m (£12.5m $\times$ 98%)

The cost of debt (k_d) can be found as follows:

$$\frac{£13.2m}{(1+k_d)} = £12.25m$$

$$1 + k_d = \frac{£13.2m}{£12.25m}$$

$$k_d = 7.76\%$$

Cost of 20X9 loan stock

Year		Cash flow £	Discount factor 10%	Discounted cash flow £	Discount Factor 5%	Discounted cash flow £
0	Market value	(103.00)	1.000	(103.00)	1.000	(103.00)
1–3	Interest (10 $\times$ (1 – 0.3))	7.00	2.487	17.41	2.723	19.06
3	Redemption	110.00	0.751	82.61	0.864	95.04
				(2.98)		11.10

$$\text{Cost of 20X9 stock} = 5 + \left(\frac{11.10}{11.10-(2.98)}\right)(10-5)$$

$$= 8.94\%$$

Cost of preference shares

$$k_p = \frac{d}{P_0}$$

$$= \frac{6}{105}$$

$$= 5.71\%$$

Cost of equity

This can be estimated using the dividend growth model.

$$
\begin{aligned}
\text{20X2 dividend} \times (1+g)^4 &= \text{20X6 dividend} \\
35.64 \times (1+g)^4 &= 45.00 \\
(1+g)^4 &= 45.00 \div 35.64 \\
\sqrt[4]{(1+g)} &= 1.2626 \\
1+g &= 1.06 \\
g &= 6\%
\end{aligned}
$$

The dividend growth model can now be used:

where: P_0 = £5.50 − £0.45 = £5.05

$\quad\quad\quad d_0$ = £0.45

$\quad\quad\quad g$ = 6%

$$k_e = \frac{d_0(1+g)}{P_0} + g$$

$$k_e = \frac{0.45(1+0.06)}{5.05} + 0.06$$

$$k_e = 15.45\%$$

Weighted average cost of capital (WACC)

Weightings will be based on market values.

	Market value £m	Cost of capital %	Weighted average $\dfrac{\text{Market value} \times \text{Cost of capital}}{92.58}$
Equity	60.60	15.45	10.11
20X7 loan stock	12.25	7.76	1.03
20X9 loan stock	11.33	8.94	1.09
Preference shares	8.40	5.71	0.52
	92.58		12.75

WACC is 12.75%

(b) To: Directors of DEA
From: Treasury team member
Date: 17 November 20X1
Subject: Selection of a discount rate and dividend policy

This memorandum addresses the issues raised by the individual directors at the recent meeting.

(i)   **The Marketing Director**

Assumptions of WACC

The weighted average cost of capital (WACC) does reflect the **average cost** of acquiring funds. Use of the WACC as the **discount rate** is the normal approach in appraising potential new investments. However, this is based on the assumption that the new investments are **small** in relation to the size of the company, and that they carry a **similar level of risk** to the existing business.

Japanese contract

The Japanese contract does not fulfil these conditions. First of all, it is **large** in relation to the size of the company, with revenues expected to amount to 25% of sales. Secondly, since this represents a **diversification** into a **new market**, it is possible that it will have **higher operating risk** than alternative investments. There is also **foreign currency risk** associated with the project, and, due to the size of the contract, the company will need to raise additional finance.

Risk analysis

It is therefore recommended that a **more detailed analysis of the risks and sensitivities** associated with the investment be made. If this suggests that the level of risk is significantly greater than for alternative UK projects, then the discount rate used should be adjusted to reflect this.

(ii) **The Production Director**

Cost of finance

The cost of finance used for a specific project should not be used as the discount rate. This approach ignores the effect of both undertaking the project, and the new source of finance, on the company as a whole. **Bank borrowings** are **cheaper** than **equity finance**, but an increase in borrowings will lead to an increase in the **level** of **financial gearing**, and therefore to an **increase in the financial risk** of the company. This will cause the **cost of equity** to **rise**, and this will be reflected in the weighted average cost of capital.

Investment and financing

If the project has a higher level of risk than the existing business of the company, then this will magnify the effect on the cost of capital. It is a good principle to **separate** the **investment decision** from the **financing decision** in project evaluation. The project should be evaluated from the point of view of its effect upon the cash flows of the company as a whole, while the financing decision will involve different considerations of the effect of the new funds upon the financial structure of the company.

(iii) **The Finance Director**

Retentions and dividends

It is true that if the company cannot earn a better return than could be made by individual investors, then funds should be returned to the shareholders. However it is incorrect to turn this statement round and to argue that retentions should be preferred to dividends. Investors require **dividends** to provide a **return** on their investment. They may lose confidence in the company if there are **wide fluctuations** in the level of dividends from year to year. Substituting small individual share sales for dividends has a **high transaction cost**, and may **increase** investors' **tax liabilities**.

Cost of retentions

The Finance Director also implies that there is no cost of finance associated with retentions. However, this is not the case – the **cost of retentions** is in fact the **same** as the **cost of equity**. It is not therefore cheaper to finance new investment using retentions rather than debt.

Need for both

In practice, the company needs cash both for **new investment** and to **pay dividends**. The best way in which to finance the cash requirements will depend on the financial structure and tax position of the company.

Investment and financing

The appropriate discount rate to use for evaluating the contract has been discussed above. However, the cost of raising new finance should be looked at **separately** from the **investment decision** itself, and the effect of the project upon the business risk profile of the company must also be taken into account.

Signed: Treasury team member

34 AB

(a) Using the formula

$$k_0 = k_{eg}\left[\frac{V_E}{V_E + V_D}\right] + k_d\left[\frac{V_D}{V_E + V_D}\right]$$

where k_0 = weighted average cost of capital

k_{eg}, k_d = cost of equity, cost of debt (post-tax)

V_E, V_D = value of equity, value of debt

$13 = k_{eg}\, 0.65 + 10(1 - 0.25)\, 0.35$

$k_{eg} = 16.0\%$

Annual interest savings = $(30,000,000/20)\, (0.1 - 0.025)\, (1 - 0.25)$

= \$84,375

Discounted at pre tax cost of debt 10%

Interest savings = $84,375 \times$ Year 1-6 cumulative present value factor

= $84,375 \times 4.355$

= 367,453

Assumptions

The method assumes:

(i)   The **cost of debt** on additional borrowing will be 10%.

(ii)   The **cost of equity** remains static.

(iii)   The company has **sufficient profits** against which to set interest charges.

(iv)   The **debt ratio** will **remain unchanged**.

Use of WACC

Instead of being **discounted** at the **cost of debt**, the subsidy could be **discounted** at the **weighted average cost of capital** as this would be used to discount the benefits of alternative scenarios.

(b)   **Cost of equity**

The **cost of equity** would not be appropriate as:

(i)   Equity is **only one** of the **sources of finance** for the new project.

(ii) The **cost of equity** may change as equity shareholders desire different returns as a result of the company expanding into Eastern Europe.

The **weighted average cost of capital** given in the question would not be appropriate.

(i)   It does not take into account the **cost of the subsidised EE government loan**.

(ii) The **capital structure** and thus the **financial risk** of the company will change. As the company already has a gearing ratio in excess of the industry average, the additional risk may be significant.

(iii) **AB's overall business risk** may change as a result of investing in Eastern Europe. Whether it will increase or decrease is difficult to say. Returns from Eastern Europe may be more uncertain than from current sales areas; on the other hand, **diversification** into Eastern Europe may lower business risk if returns from that area are not positively correlated with returns from other areas.

Marginal cost of capital

AB should use a **marginal cost of capital** to appraise the investment. This should be based on the risks and incremental cost of investing in Eastern Europe. AB could find the beta of a similar company that invested into Eastern Europe and use CAPM to **calculate the discount rate**, taking into account the **differences in gearing**.

(c)   (i)   **Advantages of using subsidy**

1   The loan represents **long-term finance** matched against the returns from a long-term manufacturing project.

2   AB does not need to **provide security** for the loan.

3   Government involvement may mean that AB **faces fewer administrative problems** when setting up its investment, such as planning permission.

Disadvantages of using subsidy

1   There may be **onerous conditions** attached to the subsidy, for example a requirement to have **local managers** involved in directing the project.

2   A change of government may lead to a **change** in the **terms** of the loan.

3   The **exchange rate** may **move adversely;** if EE marks become more expensive, the interest costs will be greater.

4   The interest savings will be **less attractive** if domestic rates decrease over the **six year period.**

5   If the investment quickly proves **unviable**, AB will be **locked into interest and repayment commitments** for some years afterwards.

(ii) **Other possible methods of finance**

1   **Rights issue**

An issue of shares to existing shareholders would have the advantages of **maintaining the existing ownership structure** and **reducing** the **company's gearing levels.** The main problem may be whether **sufficient funds** can be raised by this method.

2   **Stock market**

AB could seek a **listing on a stock exchange** in order to be able to offer its shares to the general public. It should be able to raise the money it needs by this means and the share issue would **reduce gearing;** however the current shareholders would face a **loss of influence** on the company's affairs and **publicity and disclosure requirements** will be greater. These drawbacks may imply that the amount of funding required is too small to justify seeking a listing.

3   **Debt finance**

Although more debt finance would **worsen AB's gearing**, the directors should investigate the possibility of issuing **loan stock** secured on fixed assets. The **cost of loan stock** may be **lower** than the current cost of bank finance, and AB would not have to fulfil the onerous conditions that the overseas government might impose.

4   **Asset disposal**

AB may be able to raise significant sums of money by selling off surplus assets or spinning off for sale certain parts of its business.

5   **Venture capital**

Venture capitalists may well be interested in this type of new venture. However if they provide debt finance, **gearing** will be **worse**; if they provide equity finance, AB will have to consider the **level of return** they require. Either way venture capitalists are likely to demand a **degree of control** (perhaps a seat on the board) and AB may have to **match the finance** that the venture capitalists provide by obtaining funding from other sources.

Recommendations

AB should consider obtaining a **mix of finance** to finance the project, as no single source seems to be completely suitable. A combination of debt and equity finance, with the aim of at least maintaining current gearing levels, would be best.

35 MAN

Text references. Weighted average cost of capital is covered in Chapter 9 and the capital structure decision is discussed in Chapter 10.

Top tips. Parts (a) to (c) are a good guide to the technique of gearing and ungearing betas. See how the steps are taken and you will be able to handle questions in this area. (d) covers the main points you need to know about Modigliani and Miller, the key difference being that under the traditional view there is an optimal level of gearing that produces the lowest WACC and highest view. This is not true under M and M's basic theory, and company value only increases by the tax relief under the with tax version of M and M. The practical factors are discussed under the key criteria for strategic decisions – feasibility, acceptability and suitability.

Easy marks. If you struggled in discussing practical factors, revise Chapter 10 of the text, as these issues are very important when a company determines its sources of finance.

Examiner's comments. Candidates answering this question usually performed better in the narrative sections than in the computational section. (a) required candidates to discuss the key assumptions underpinning the use of the WACC in investment appraisal. This section was answered reasonably well with many candidates identifying at least two key assumptions.

(b) required a discussion as to why the existing WACC of a company was inappropriate for evaluating a new investment proposal. Once again, this section was answered reasonably well. (c) required the calculation of the WACC and this section often produced poor answers. Most candidates seemed unfamiliar with the way in which the key formulae should be used to produce the correct results. Once again, a lack of practise in answering such questions was apparent.

(a) Three key assumptions have to be made if the current weighted average cost of capital of a company is to be the appropriate discount rate to use for investment appraisal purposes.

Capital structure

If new finance is to be raised for the project that is being discounted then it must be raised in the proportions of the **current capital structure**. If this is not the case then the capital structure will change and this will in turn affect the weightings that are used in order to calculate the weighted average cost of capital. If the weights used are changed then the weighted average cost of capital will change as well.

Risk

The weighted average cost of capital is based upon the **systematic risk** of the company. The discount rate used to appraise a project should be based upon the systematic risk of the project. Therefore if the systematic risk of the project is different from that of the company the weighted average cost of capital will not be an appropriate discount rate.

Size of investment

If the weighted average cost of capital is to be used to appraise a project then the project itself must be **small in relation** to the overall size of the company. The costs of debt and equity and therefore the derived weighted average cost of capital are all marginal costs and therefore the weighted average cost of capital is only appropriate when there is an issue of relatively small amounts of capital.

(b) **MAN's situation**

If the current weighted average cost of capital is to be used to appraise this new project then the project must have the **same level of systematic risk** as the company itself. In this case this is unlikely as MAN is entering into a new line of business, passenger safety equipment for ships, and also in a new geographical area. Therefore it is likely that the project being appraised will have a different level of systematic risk from that of MAN.

Adjusting beta factors

However it is still possible to use the weighted average cost of capital once it has been adjusted for the **differing systematic risk of the new project**. This is done by using the **beta value** for a similar company in the same line of business in the same geographical area. However there may also have to be adjustments to reflect the different capital structures of the two companies.

(c) As the Spanish company has a different capital structure from MAN the first stage is to take the equity beta of the Spanish company and ungear it by finding the asset beta.

$$\beta_u = \beta_g \left(\frac{V_E}{V_E + V_D(1-t)} \right)$$

$$= 1.6 \left(\frac{50}{50 + 50(1 - 0.25)} \right)$$

$$= 0.914$$

The gearing structure of MAN based upon market values:

	£m
Equity – 200m × £5.35	1,070
Debt – 6% loan stock £500m × 106/100	530

Using the formula

$$\beta_g = \beta_u \left(\frac{V_E + V_D(1-t)}{V_E} \right)$$

$$= 0.914 \left(\frac{1,070 + 530(1 - 0.25)}{1,070} \right)$$

$$= 1.254$$

$$k_{eg} = R_f + (R_m - R_f)\,\beta_g$$

$$= 5.1 + (10.4 - 5.1)\,1.254$$

$$= 11.7\%$$

$$k_{dnet} = \frac{i(1-t)}{P_0}$$

$$= \frac{6}{106}(1 - 0.25)$$

$$= 4.2\%$$

$$k_0 = k_{eg}\left(\frac{V_E}{V_E + V_D} \right) + k_{dnet}\left(\frac{V_D}{V_E + V_D} \right)$$

$$= 11.7\left(\frac{1,070}{1,070 + 530} \right) + 4.2\left(\frac{530}{1,070 + 530} \right)$$

$$= 9.2\%$$

Therefore 9.2% is the weighted average cost of capital that should be used to appraise this investment.

Alternative answer

We can now use the capital asset pricing model to determine the cost of equity for this ungeared or asset beta:

$$k_e = R_f + (R_m - R_f)\,\beta_u$$

$$k_e = 5.1 + (10.4 - 5.1)\,0.914$$

$$= 9.9\%$$

This gives us the cost of equity in a company similar to the Spanish company but which is ungeared. Using MM we can now find the WACC of a similar company which is geared in the ratio of Mansfield's capital structure.

$$k_{adj} = k_{eu}(1 - tL)$$

$$k_{adj} = 9.9\% \left(1 - \frac{530 \times 0.25}{1,070 + 530} \right)$$

$$= 9.1\%$$

Therefore 9.1% is the weighted average cost of capital that should be used to appraise this investment.

(d) **Capital structure**

The contention that capital structure is irrelevant to the value of the firm was first put forward by **Modigliani and Miller**. Until that point the **traditional view** was that there is an optimal mix of debt and equity that minimises the weighted average cost of capital (WACC).

Traditional view

The key difference between these two approaches is related to the behaviour of the **rate of return** required by shareholders as the gearing level rises. The traditional view is that the **cost of equity** remains at a constant level at low levels of gearing, causing the WACC to fall. Beyond a certain point however, the shareholders begin to demand a higher rate of return in compensation for the higher level of financial risk and the WACC begins to rise, and the value of the company to fall.

Modigliani and Miller

Modigliani and Miller showed that the value of the firm was determined by the **income generated** from its **business activities**, and that the way this income was split between the providers of capital was irrelevant. If the shares of two firms with the same level of business risk but different gearing levels were traded at different prices, then shareholders would move from the overvalued to the undervalued firm and adjust their level of personal borrowing through the market to maintain their financial risk at the same level. This **arbitrage process** would force the total price of the two firms to a common equilibrium value. Tax is a possible complication, acting to increase the value of the geared firm by the tax relief on debt.

Influence of capital structure

The above discussion would suggest that capital structure is irrelevant. However in practical terms this is not the case and other factors come into play.

Financing is seen as a key strategic decision and as such must be **acceptable, suitable,** and **feasible.**

Acceptable

Balance of control

In the UK there is often a preference for **retained earnings** over debt finance and equity issues. This is partly due to the **transaction costs** involved in raising the finance, but has also to do with the balance of ownership and control. The use of retained earnings causes the minimum disruption to the existing balance of control and is often preferred for this reason.

Debt providers

It is increasingly common for covenants to be placed on loans. Examples include **restricting the level of dividend payments** to prevent the capital base being run down and thereby increasing the risk of the lenders, and **preventing the company taking on further loans**. Thus not only do the directors have to consider whether loan holders will accept further loans, they have also to consider whether shareholders will **accept restrictions** being placed on their income.

Shareholders

In any event shareholders may not be prepared to accept the **risk** that their dividend levels will decrease in poor years because the company is committed or the ultimate threat of bankruptcy if debt levels are too high.

Constitution

There may be a **clause in the company's constitution** that restricts the ability of the firm to borrow.

Suitable

Taxation

Both **corporate and personal taxation** distort the theory and can cause a bias in **favour of debt** into the capital structure.

Interest rate fluctuations

Interest rate fluctuations may deter firms from taking on a high level of borrowings.

International operations

If the firm has significant **international operations**, it may need to take on **loans denominated in foreign currencies** in order to **minimise its exchange exposure**.

Signalling

Some investors may see the issue of debt capital as a sign that the directors are confident enough of the future cash flows of the business to be prepared to commit the company to making **regular interest payments** to **lenders.** However this depends on the view that market efficiency is not very high. The argument would be that an efficient market would have sufficient information to be able to make its own mind up about the debt issue, without needing to take the directors' views into account.

Feasible

Asset base

Companies with a **high level** of **tangible assets** find it easier to take on debt since they are able to offer better security in the event of bankruptcy than firms with a high level of intangible assets such as a software house.

Variability of cash flows

The **nature of the projected cash flows** will affect the ability of the firm to raise debt. The greater the **potential variability in the cash flows**, the less easy it will be for the firm to borrow.

Excessive costs

The directors may believe that the **costs of the debt** that the company is taking on are more than it can bear.

Availability of share capital

If the **stock market** is **depressed**, it may be difficult to raise cash through share issues, so major amounts will have to be borrowed.

36 KM

Text references. Chapter 14 discusses the work of the treasury function.

Top tips. This is a fairly comprehensive question on the role of the treasury department, covering the major areas that you are likely to be asked about. Questions in this area tend to demand breadth of knowledge, so you will need to make a good number of points in order to pass the question. Note what exactly the treasury department does manage. Ideally your answer should refer to the circumstances of KM.

Easy marks. If you revised this area this should have been a straightforward question.

(a) **Definition**

Treasurership has been defined as 'the function concerned with the provision and use of finance. It includes provision of capital, short-term borrowing, foreign currency management, banking, collections and money market investment'.

Responsibilities of treasury function

The main responsibilities of the treasury function include:

(i) **Strategic decisions**

Treasury is likely to be consulted on the **establishment of corporate financial objectives, aims and strategies** and be responsible for establishing policies and systems (outlined further below).

(ii) **Liquidity management**

This involves making sure that the organisation has the **liquid funds** it needs and invests any surplus funds, even for very short terms. The treasurer should maintain a good relationship with one or more banks to ensure that negotiations are as swift as possible, and that rates are reasonable. It includes **working capital and money transmission management, banking relationships** and **arrangements** and **money management**.

(iii) **Funding management**

Funding management is concerned with all forms of **borrowing**, and alternative sources of funds, such as leasing and factoring. The treasury function includes **establishing funding policies and procedure, obtaining the right types of funds** from the **best sources**.

(iv) **Currency management**

The treasury department should have the expertise to be able to deal with the problems and substantial risks involved in trading abroad and in particular dealing in foreign exchange markets. Treasury should establish **exposure policies and procedures** and have responsibility for exchange dealing, including futures and options.

(v) **Corporate finance**

The treasury department will be involved with major **equity funding decisions** and **dividend policies**, and **major investment decisions** including business acquisitions and disposals, project finance and joint ventures. It will also be involved in attempts to obtain a **stock market listing**.

(vi) **Other functions**

Treasury may also be responsible for a variety of decisions including effective management of the organisation's **tax liability**, **risk management and insurance** and **pension fund investment management**.

Reasons for separating the financial control and treasury functions

(i) **Different roles**

As indicated above, the treasury department's role is concerned developing financial strategy and fund management, functions demanding specialist skills. The finance function's role is focused on **recording and reporting skills**, which requires management and financial accounting knowledge. The financial control function may also be responsible for managing the **payroll** and **internal audit** functions and hence will require specialist skills in these areas.

(ii) **Relationships with stakeholders**

The financial control function is concerned with **determining whether** the **various activities** of the organisation are meeting their **financial objectives**. This function will therefore be interested in a **wide variety of stakeholder relationships**, for example, with customers, suppliers and employees. By contrast, the treasury function is mainly concerned with the relationship of the company to the **providers of finance**.

(iii) **Geographical dispersion**

In a geographically dispersed company such as KM, it is likely that financial control functions will exist at a variety of local levels, while the **treasury department** will be centralised at the head office.

(b) **Advantages of operating treasury department as profit centre**

(i) This approach recognises the fact that some companies are able to make **significant profits** from their treasury activities. Treating the department as a profit centre may make treasury staff more motivated to achieve the best possible return for the company.

(ii) If it is treated as a profit centre, the department will have to **charge for its services** to other parts of the organisation. This may make the subsidiaries more aware of the true cost of the services they use, and encourage them to use the department more efficiently.

Disadvantages of operating treasury department as profit centre

(i) Treasury staff may be tempted to **speculate**, and to ignore the risk criteria that they should be using. The company may suffer **large losses** as a result.

(ii) **Internal charging** may mean that **some subsidiaries go outside the** organisation for treasury services and thus reduce the overall benefit to the organisation of having a centralised treasury function.

(iii) **Performance evaluation** may be difficult. The success of the function may sometimes involve the avoidance of costs rather than the maximisation of profits.

(iv) **Administrative costs** may be **increased**.

(c) **Advantages of a centralised treasury department**

(i) Centralised liquidity management avoids having a **mix of cash surpluses and overdrafts in different localised bank accounts**, particularly in a company such as KM, which now includes a number of overseas operations.

(ii) **Bulk cash flows** are possible, allowing lower bank charges to be negotiated.

(iii) **Larger volumes of cash** are available to invest, giving better **short-term** investment opportunities.

(iv) Any borrowing can be arranged in **bulk**, at **lower interest rates** than for smaller borrowings.

(v) **Foreign currency risk management** should be improved, with matching of cash flows in different subsidiaries being possible. This means that there should be less need to use expensive hedging instruments such as option contracts. This is particularly valuable in a company such as KM plc where there are a number of overseas operations.

(vi) A large centralised department can employ **staff with a greater level of expertise** than would be possible in a local, more broadly based, finance department.

(vii) Centralisation will allow the company to benefit from the use of **specialised cash management software**.

(viii) Access to treasury expertise should improve the quality of **strategic planning and decision making**.

37 HH

(a) **Cash balances for group companies**

    (i) **Group companies act independently**

        Interest rates for a 30 day period

Germany €	deposit rate	$30/360 \times 3.0\% = 0.25\%$
UK £	deposit rate	$30/360 \times 3.9\% = 0.325\%$
US $	borrowing rate	$30/360 \times 1.7\% = 0.14167\%$

        Cash surpluses / (deficits) after 30 days

Germany	10.5m × 1.0025	= €10.5263m
UK	£5.5m × 1.00325	= £5.5179m
US	($10m × 1.0014167)	= ($10.0142m)

        If the German and UK surpluses were converted to US$ at the 30 day forward rate, and netted off against the US$ borrowings, the balance would be as follows:

Germany	10.5263m/1.126	= $9.3484m
UK	5.5179m/0.700	= $7.8827m
US		($10.0142m)
Net balance	**$7.2169m**	

    (ii) **Cash balances are pooled in US$**

        Converting the euros and pounds at the spot rate yields the following:

Germany	10.5m/1.131	= $9.2838m
UK	5.5m/0.695	= $7.9137m
Less: US		($10.0000m)
Net balance	$7.1975m	

        The US$ deposit rate for 30 days is $1.6\% \times 30/360 = 0.1333\%$

        Cash on deposit in US$ after 30 days is $7.1975m × 1.001333 = **$7.2071m**

        From the US parent's point of view the first method is more favourable in financial terms, because it results in a higher overall cash balance.

(b)   **Benefits of pooling of subsidiaries' cash balances**

Netting surpluses and deficits

For the parent company, the main benefit of pooling cash balances is that **surpluses** can **be netted off** against deficits, thus reducing the amount of interest payable. Because borrowing rates are higher than deposit rates, it is better to use surplus cash to **reduce borrowing** than to put it on deposit. A central treasury could lend funds to subsidiaries at better rates than they would be able to borrow.

Unfortunately when cash balances are in different currencies this tactic does not necessarily work, as shown by the figures in this question. If the **forward rates** are **not in equilibrium** with the interest rates, then there may be opportunities for making gains by keeping cash in other currencies.

Greater control

Pooling balances means that it is easier for a central treasury department to exercise control over funds, and use its **expertise** to ensure risks are managed and opportunities exploited effectively.

Greater investment opportunities

Better rates may be available for pooled funds, and the central treasury function that holds the pooled funds may have **access to markets** such as offshore markets that are not available to local operations.

Elimination of exchange risk

Another benefit to the parent company of pooling all resources in the home currency (dollars) is that **currency exchange risk** is **eliminated** for the net surplus.

Drawbacks of pooling of subsidiaries' cash balances

Need for cash

Operating subsidiaries need **cash balances** as part of their working capital in order to make payments. If these payments are higher than expected, there may be insufficient cash in the subsidiaries. Local managers may try to ensure that they have the maximum amount of cash possible to make the payments, leading to disharmony within the group.

Local decision-making

Local managers may feel **demotivated** if the responsibility for investing funds is taken away from them. They may not therefore provide **full co-operation** to the centralised department.

Transaction costs

Transferring cash surpluses to the parent company and then back to the subsidiary again when required incurs **unnecessary transaction costs**, which can be relatively high compared with any interest saving, particularly when interest rates are low.

Matching

Good currency risk management will attempt to **minimise risk** by **matching receipts and payments**, and assets and liabilities, in the same currency. For example, the German subsidiary might have borrowed in euros. If the euro then strengthened against the dollar, the increased loan liability could be offset by cash surpluses kept in euros. However if the surpluses had been converted to dollars, the **loss** would have been **higher**.

38 CD

Text references. The relationship between investment, financing and dividend decisions is discussed in Chapters 1 and 4. Valuation using Modigliani and Miller is explained in Chapter 15.

Top tips. Your answer to (a) needed to bring out clearly the links between dividend and financing policy, including links with the cost of capital. The 0.5 deducted at the end of the calculation is the bonus issue. In (b) you need to make clear how you calculate the value of the ungeared company as it is not clear from the question which method is appropriate. However even if you used an inappropriate method, you should only have lost one mark provided you followed the other stages of the calculation through correctly. The value of the geared company is the market value of equity **and** the market value of debt. In (c) you need to discuss the problems with the assumptions made, and will get credit for coming up with a reasonable alternative estimate of your own.

Easy marks. You should score the majority of marks you need to pass on (c), provided you applied your discussion to the scenario.

Examiner's comments. This question proved surprisingly unpopular. Few candidates commented in (a) on the payout ratio and related their answer to the circumstances of the company. In (b) candidates failed to use the correct formula despite it being given on the formula sheet. Many answers did not include calculations of the value of the ungeared company or the tax shield. The main problem in (c) was focusing too heavily on the general difficulties of valuing an unquoted company, rather than linking answers into the circumstances of this specific company.

(a) **Dividends or finance**

A possible argument would be that CD should not pay roughly half its earnings out as dividends, and retain half its earnings to finance future investment. If **investment opportunities with positive present values** exist, the interests of shareholders are best served by retaining all earnings and using the cash surpluses to take up the opportunities. Alternatively if there are **no opportunities** for investment, **all earnings** should be **distributed as dividends.** However other practical considerations will apply as well.

Dividend policy

As CD is a private company, shareholders may expect rewards to be mainly in the form of **dividends**. Disposal of shares and hence realisation of a capital gain may be difficult, and indeed no shareholders have attempted to sell their shares in the last four years. In addition, employees' bonuses have been in the form of shares, so effectively dividends are part of their remuneration. Hence there may be pressure to maintain dividends levels to keep employees happy. Over the last few years, CD has mainly followed a **consistent dividend policy**, paying out roughly half the earnings per share as dividends, so the dividend policy is in line with the **company's performance**.

Insufficiency of retained earnings

However it appears that the level of earnings that CD is retaining is **inadequate** to **support the investments** that CD needs to undertake to grow further. If the company is to remain equity-financed, shareholders face the choice of zero growth in income, or less dividend income for a few years until returns are generated from the (possibly uncertain) investments.

Debt and equity

As the company is all equity-financed, it should have **scope** to **introduce debt finance** at a **cheaper cost than the cost of equity.** The cost of equity will rise as shareholders require higher returns for the **increased financial risk**, the increase in variability of returns due to the need to pay interest to debt providers. However if predictions are correct, the new investments should provide an increase in income that will compensate equity shareholders. In addition shareholders may be unwilling or unable to **subscribe** for **further equity** in the form of a **rights issue**.

Gearing

Level of debt = R150 million

Nominal value of shares = R3.5 million

Assume 20X6 dividend is the same as 20X5 as dividends have been maintained despite the expected fall in earnings.

Retained earnings = 3 (8.33 + 40 + 48.33 − 20.0 − 24.2) + 3.5 (52.86 + 55.71 + 58 + (58 × 200/203) − 26.4 − 27.8 − 26.3 − 26.3) − 0.5

= R566.1 million

$$\text{Gearing} = \frac{\text{Debt}}{\text{Debt} + \text{Equity}}$$

$$= \frac{150}{150 + 3.5 + 566.1}$$

$$= 0.21$$

Debt constitutes about a fifth of the company's total capital, so its introduction does not appear to lead to excessive gearing.

Recommendation

In order to maintain growth levels, CD can reasonably introduce the proposed loan finance without incurring excessive financial risk. It may also help to reduce its weighted average cost of capital due to tax relief on interest payments.

(b) **Company value**

Using the formula $V_g = V_u + TB_c$

V_u is calculated using the expected **earnings figure** in 20X7 (200 × 1.05 = 210), assuming that after 20X7 earnings **remain constant** in **perpetuity** and that Modigliani and Miller's dividend irrelevance theory applies (ie that all earnings are paid out as dividends). As no further information is given about the cost of equity prior to borrowing taking place, we use the geared company's cost of equity.

$$V_u = \frac{210}{0.14}$$

= R1,500.0m

V_g = 1,500 + 150(0.3)

= R1,545.0m

Value of equity = 1,545.0 − 150

= R1,395.0m

Share price

$$\text{Share price} = \frac{1,395.0}{3.5}$$

= R398.6m

Price earnings ratio

$$\text{P/E ratio} = \frac{398.6}{58 \times 200 / 203}$$

= 7.0

(c)   **Limitations of Modigliani and Miller**

The assumptions of the theory have been subject to various criticisms including **differences** in the **risk** of **personal and corporate gearing**, **differences** in the **cost of borrowing** between **individuals and companies**, and the impact of **transaction costs** on investor behaviour. Modigliani and Miller also assume that investors act rationally which may not be completely true in practice.

In addition the theory implies that the only difference between the ungeared company's value (which is based on the assumption of constant earnings after 20X7), and the geared company's value is the value of the debt shield. This appears to go against expectations, which are that introducing debt will allow investment that will generate increased earnings.

Small parcel of shares

Dividend

The dividend valuation model, implying that the main concern of small shareholders is **dividends,** would appear to be appropriate here. Employees cannot control decisions affecting the company's profits and earnings, and, as discussed above, dividends are effectively part of their remuneration.

If we use the dividend valuation model to calculate V_u, assume that the 5% growth of dividends in 20X7 is maintained in subsequent years, and that 26.3 is paid out as dividends in 20X6.

$$V_u = \frac{D_1}{k_e - g}$$

$$= \frac{26.3 \times 1.05 \times 3.5}{0.14 - 0.05}$$

$$= R1,073.9 \text{ m}$$

$$V_g = 1,073.9 + 150(0.3)$$

$$= R1,118.9m$$

Value of equity $= 1,118.9 - 150$

$$= 968.9$$

Lack of marketability

The MM equations do not take into account the fact that the shares are **not quoted** on a stock exchange and cannot easily be traded. This may **depress** their **price.**

Business risk

The equations ignore the **risk** that **earnings and dividends** may **not grow** at the predicted rates. Potential shareholders may be particularly sensitive to this risk, as they may not be able to sell their shares if returns fail to reach expected levels.

Financial risk

Again the equations do not include the **risk** to the company of the significant financial commitment of **extra debt.**

Simplicity

In practice, if a single shareholder sells his or her shares, they may be valued using a **net asset valuation** for the company plus a **premium.** CD may feel that this method is simpler and perhaps less controversial.

Entire company

Reasons for sale

The directors may be seeking to sell the company for different reasons to individual shareholders selling their shares. If for example a shareholder wanted a **quick sale** and ready cash (say an employee leaving the company), he might be prepared to accept a lower price per share.

Lack of marketability

As above, the fact that CD is an **unquoted company** may depress the price of the shares.

Debt burden

The predator would have to take on the burden of any debt that CD issued. This could be significant if the predator needed to take on an **extra debt burden** itself to fund the purchase of CD.

Other factors

Use of a model based on expected dividends will not be appropriate for a predator seeking to take CD over, since all the earnings will accrue to the predator. The price the predator agrees to pay is likely to be determined by a number of factors.

- General economic and financial conditions

- **Industry conditions** and the **status** of CD within the computer industry

- **CD's record** within the industry. The company has shown consistent growth in what over the last few years has been a troubled sector.

- The **asset backing.** Because of technological advances, CD's assets may have a limited break-up value.

- The extent to which CD has been dependent on its **main shareholders** and **managers**. A predator may wish to ensure that it retains these individuals' services as part of a takeover deal.

39 Synergy

Text references. Business valuations are covered in Chapter 15. Payment methods are discussed in Chapter 16.

Top tips. Read the question in (a) carefully – you are required to provide critical comment on each of the valuation methods used, not just that in part (iii), and you must also make a reasoned recommendation as to whether OA should make the bid for ML. Comparability of 'similar' companies is a frequent problem.

The calculations in (a)(iii) can appear confusing. You must work out which figures and discount rates are real rates excluding inflation, and which are money rates including inflation. You must be particularly careful with the consultancy fees; firstly, you will need to adjust for tax, and then for inflation. Although the fee is fixed at £100,000 per year, and does not increase with inflation, the amount that the directors receive will be reducing each year in real terms due to the effects of inflation. Therefore, if you choose to base your calculations on real rather than inflated figures (which is the quickest approach) you will need to deflate these figures before discounting.

In (b), remember that the form of the bid has yet to be agreed with ML and that the views of the ML shareholders are just as relevant as the financial position of OA.

Easy marks. Spending eight minutes first on (b) should yield 4-5 marks, and will mean that you can leave (a) (iii), the most complicated calculations until last. If you struggle with the (a) (iii) calculations remember that you can earn certainly 3 marks on the discussion part, so make sure you leave five minutes for the written part.

(a)   (i)   **P/E ratio**

Since ML operates in a different industry, the comparative P/E ratio valuation must be based upon the average P/E ratios in that industry. The P/E ratio of 7:1 will therefore be used.

Current share price	370 pence
Earnings yield	19.2%
Earnings per share	71.04 pence (370 × 19.2%)
Price per share	497.28 pence (71.04 × 7)
Value of ML	**£24.864m** (£4.9728 × 5m shares)

255

Problems with calculations

The problem with this approach is that P/E ratios are based on historic performance, and take no account either of the likely impact of the takeover on the performance of the company, or of its current earnings projections.

Comparability of companies

In this case, there is a further problem in that it is not known whether the recently taken over companies on which the ratio is based were sufficiently similar to ML in terms of size, rate of growth, type of activities and overall level of risk. It may well be that the average should be adjusted to take into account the particular situation of ML.

(ii) **Dividend valuation model**

The dividend valuation method (including growth) for share valuation is:

$$p_0 = \frac{d_0(1+g)}{k_e - g}$$

In the case of ML:

$d_0 = £842,000$

$g = 8\%$, assuming that this rate of dividend growth will continue

$k_e =$ can be estimated using the Capital Asset Pricing Model (CAPM):

$$k_e = R_f + (R_m - R_f)\,\beta$$

where
k_e = cost of equity
R_f = risk free rate of return (6%)
β = beta factor (0.8)
R_m = market rate of return (14%)
k_e = 6% + 0.8(14% − 6%) = 12.4%

$$p = \frac{£842,000(1+0.08)}{(0.124-0.08)} = £20.667m$$

Weakness of dividend valuation model

The main weakness of this approach is the **method used** to **estimate the growth** rate. This assumes that the **historic rate of dividend growth** will **continue** at a constant rate into the future, but the current rate of dividend growth is different from that of OA, and could well change following the acquisition. However, the model does attempt to relate the share price to the future stream of earnings from the business, and in this sense is more realistic than the comparative P/E ratio basis of valuation.

(iii) **Operating cash flows**

The first stage is to estimate what the operating cash flows will be following the acquisition.

	£'000
Current pre-tax operating cash flow	5,300
Post acquisition adjustments:	
Annual wage savings	750
Advertising/distribution savings	150
	6,200
Taxation (33%)	2,046
Annual post tax cash flow	4,154

The other cash flows to be taken into account are:

		£'000
Year 0:	Redundancy costs (after tax)	(1,200)
	Sale of land and buildings (after tax)	800
Years 1-3:	Consultancy payments of £201,000 (£300,000 × 0.67) per year after tax	

Discount rate

The discount rate used will be the existing weighted average cost of capital (WACC) for ML, although it must be recognised that this could be **different** after the **acquisition** since OA is a much larger company and its shares are quoted on the main market rather than the AIM. The cost of equity has already been calculated above as 12.4%, and the cost of debt is 11% as per the balance sheet. The following expression will be used.

$$WACC = k_{eg} \frac{V_E}{(V_E + V_D)} + k_d(1 - t) \frac{V_D}{(V_E + V_D)}$$

where: k_{eg} = cost of equity in geared company

k_d = cost of debt

t = tax rate (33%)

V_E = market value of equity (5m × £3.70 = £18.5m)

V_D = market value of debt (£3.5m)

$$WACC = 12.4\% \frac{18.5}{(18.5 + 3.5)} + 11\%(1 - 0.33) \frac{3.5}{(18.5 + 3.5)}$$

WACC = 11.60%

This discount rate has been calculated on the basis of market values, and therefore will incorporate **inflation**. The cash flows (with the exception of the consultancy fees) all exclude inflation, and therefore either the **nominal discount rate** that has been calculated must be **adjusted to the real rate**, or the **cash flows** must be **adjusted to include inflation**.

If we adjust the discount rate to exclude the expected 2.4% rate of inflation: 1.116 ÷ 1.024 = 1.0898, ie the real discount rate to be used is 8.98%, say 9.0%.

PV of cash flow

The present value of the cash flows can now be found.

	Year 1 £'000	Year 2 £'000	Year 3 £'000	Total £'000
Gross payment to directors (after tax)	201	201	201	
11.6 say 12% discount factors	0.893	0.797	0.712	
PV cash flow	179	160	143	(482)
Ongoing cash flows for 10 years at 9% (4,154 × 6.418)				26,660
Income from land and buildings				800
Redundancy costs				(1,200)
Total PV of relevant operating cash flows				25,778

Problems with calculations

Although this is theoretically the best method of valuation to use, the calculations are in reality quite crude. Any likely **changes** in the pattern of the **cash flows** following the acquisition are **ignored**, as are any strategic plans that the company may have for such a long time frame. Ten years is a long period over which to estimate cash flows, inflation rates and discount rates, and there will inevitably be a large margin for error in the figures.

End of period

In addition, the question of what happens at the end of the ten year period is not addressed. Is there an **appropriate terminal value** that could be used in the calculations to reflect the ongoing value of ML as a business?

Comparison with offer price

Two of the valuation methods used, including the present value of the operating cash flows (which is possibly the best of the three approaches) give a valuation greater than the proposed offer price of £22m. If OA can successfully complete negotiations at this price, and if the acquisition of ML would be in line with OA's long-term strategic objectives, then it is **recommended** that the **offer** should go ahead.

(b)   **Factors that will influence the form of the payment**

(i)   **Cash offer**

A cash offer would effectively **use up** all of OA's **cash deposits**. OA must therefore consider its **overall cash flow projections** when deciding the form of the bid, so as to avoid possible liquidity problems.

(ii)   **Desired long-term capital structure**

OA must also consider what its **desired long-term capital structure** should be in terms of **gearing level**, **type of debt** used etc, and try to structure the bid to fit these requirements.

(iii)   **Long-term costs**

Both the **long-term costs** of the different sources of finance, and the **transaction cost** of raising the finance in relation to the size of the bid must be taken into account.

(iv)   **Requirements of ML shareholders**

The **requirements** of the **ML shareholders** must also be considered. Since three individuals own 50% of the shares, it is **unlikely** that they would be **happy with a 100% cash offer** since this would mean that they would incur a large capital gains tax liability.

40 Question with student answer: MC

REPORT

To: Directors of MC
From: Independent Consultant
Date: May 20X0
Title: Valuation of MC

Introduction

This report will discuss the advantages and disadvantages of a flotation compared to the direct selling of shares.

It will analyse a range of potential share prices that could be used, explaining how they have been arrived at and any assumptions used or drawbacks to the method/

Finally an appropriate course of action will be recommended.

Flotation

Advantages

One of the key advantages of floating the company is that the profile and public image of the company may be raised, and arguably it could be _viewed more favourably_.

There is also the ability to increase growth through mergers or takeovers of other listed companies once MC has been floated.

Floating on the stock market rather than selling shares directly may lead to a much more diverse range of shareholders and therefore limit the dilution of control that may be experienced through a direct sale.

Disadvantages

There is substantial increased pressure for short-term results once a company is floated with shareholders demanding quick results which could be detrimental to the company's long-term prospects.

There are huge costs involved with floating a company. There are lawyers and accountants fees, as well as lots of criteria to meet and it can be very lengthy process taking up considerable time. There is also likely to be underwriting costs involved.

Direct sale

Advantages

This option would have much lower transaction costs, and it would also limit the restrictions and regulations placed on the company, such as those required by corporate governance.

Disadvantages

It may be difficult to find an appropriate buyer for the business that wishes to invest such a large amount. It is also likely to be more difficult to agree an appropriate price, as will be discussed later. On the stock market using an offer for sale. The company has a more straightforward method of determining the "right" price.

A new purchaser would undoubtedly have considerable control in the company and this could lead to managers being demotivated and could negatively affect staff morale and productivity.

Valuations

Assets method

Appendix A shows that based on the net assets in the business, the company can be valued at £6.00 per share.

This method is relatively straightforward and simple to calculate. However, the values used are book values and therefore due to the subjectivity and valuation in depreciation, may not provide a true and fair reflection of the company's real worth.

This method also does not reflect the value of human capital within the business. Many staff are the leading experts in their field and their expertise is helping the business to add value.

Overall, this method may be undervaluing the business.

P/E method

This method values a company based on its current earnings multiplied by the price earnings ratio.

MC is not listed and does not have a share price and this can therefore not properly be calculated.

An assumption has been made that MC's P/E ratio would be similar to that of a competitor and this results in a share price of £12.25.

Despite the P/E method being the most common approach, it is not prudent to use this figure due to considerable differences between MC and the competitor, such as a lower forecast growth rate, lower earnings and dividends per share last year and differences in the nature of operations, eg the competitor has no research capability.

NPV method

The NPV method values a company based on the discounted future value of dividends (although cash flows or profits after tax can be used).

This method has produced a value of £8.49 per share.

Theoretically this is the most superior method, with it reflecting the time value of money and reflecting all future cash flows. True of cash flow, not dividend method.

There are still several limitations of this approach though. A beta co-efficient was required during calculation and a proxy number from the competitor had to be used which is likely to be inaccurate for the previously stated reasons and due to different gearings.

Also constant growth had o be assumed which may change and the cost of equity was also a "rule of thumb" rather than completely accurate.

APPENDIX A

Valuations

Assets method

$$\text{Net asset value} = £60m$$

$$\text{Value per share} = \frac{£60m}{10m} = 600p$$

P/E method

Based on last year:

$$\text{Earnings} \times \text{P/E ratio} = £0.75 \times 10m \text{ shares} = £7.5 \times 16.3 = £122.25m$$

$$\text{Value per share} = £122.25m \div 10m = £12.25$$

$$\text{P/E ratio of competitor} = \frac{\text{Market price of share}}{\text{EPS}} = \frac{980}{60} = 16.3$$

NPV method

$$\frac{D_1}{k_e - g} = \frac{£0.55 \times 1.08}{0.15 - 0.08} = £8.49 \text{ per share}$$

Total company value = 8.49 × 10m = £84.9m

$$K_{eg} = R_F + (R_m - R_F) \beta_G$$

$$= 5\% + (12\% - 5\%) \times 1.25$$

$$= 13.75\%$$

Recommendations

If the Directors decide that a floatation is the most appropriate course of action then an offer for sale can be used to determine the relevant share price that will be accepted by the market, however as discussed earlier and floatation is by no means the easier or cheaper option.

If a direct sale is chosen then a price will need to be negotiated with the buyer, likely to at last 600p per share.

BPP answer

Text references. Business valuation is covered in Chapter 15 and equity issues in Chapter 5.

Top tips. This lengthy question addresses a number of areas of knowledge, including share valuation, and the issues surrounding a stock market flotation. The answer is required in a report format, and you should map out an appropriate structure that will allow you to address all the key issues as succinctly as possible.

Important points brought out by the discussion are when each method is useful and the **problems** with the figures used (for example balance sheets not including intangible assets, difficulties with figures of comparable companies).

Note that the discussion in (b) focuses on the aims of shareholders and management. A conclusion, recommending a method and price, would be essential even if the question had not required it.

Student answer. The student answer would have scored a very comfortable pass with 16 or 17 marks, although tackling the question in the wrong order would have irritated the marker. The direct comparison that BPP uses to answer (b) is a better technique than discussing each in turn. The student's answer needed to consider stakeholder viewpoints more as CIMA has stressed their importance.

It is reasonable, if pessimistic, to use the competitor's P/E ratio, although BPP's answer explains why a more optimistic answer may be better and suggests a possible figure, which the student doesn't do; doing a calculation and then saying it's not a very good guide is a limited approach, when you could do better.

The main weakness in the student answer is the confusion of the dividend valuation model with the cash flow (NPV) model; the two may give very different results depending on the company's dividend policy.

Easy marks. Knowing the advantages and limitations of each valuation method always earns marks in this question.

Marking scheme

		Marks
(a)	3-4 marks for each method discussed. Max 10 for discussions not supported by calculations	16
(b)	Up to 2 marks for each advantage/disadvantage/point of comparison	6
(c)	Reasonable conclusions based on previous analysis	3
		25

To: Board of Directors, MC
From: Independent Consultant
Date: 31 December 20X0
Re: Valuation of MC

Introduction

This report deals with the alternative methods available for the valuation of the shares in the company. It also seeks to highlight some of the key issues to be addressed in arriving at an appropriate valuation for this type of company, and looks at the relative merits of public flotation versus an outright sale of the business.

(a)   **Company valuation**

There are four main valuation techniques that could be appropriate in this situation:

- Net assets basis
- Price/earnings ratio
- Dividend valuation model
- Discounting the future earnings stream

These will be discussed in more detail below.

(i)   **Net assets basis**

This method arrives at a price for the business on the basis of the **market value** of the **asset base**. It is most commonly used to arrive at a **break-up value** for businesses with a significant amount of fixed assets. However, it is **less appropriate for service businesses**, and in particular for those in which the majority of the value is in the form of human and/or intellectual capital. In the latter type of company, a net assets valuation can be attempted if the intangibles are included as assets in the balance sheet. However, a significant part of the value of MC resides in its research division, and this is not reflected at all in the company's present balance sheet.

Although it could be argued that items such as brands should be included in the balance sheet so as to make the market more aware of the true value of the company, in reality it is extremely difficult both to **arrive** at and to **retain** an appropriate measure of these types of items.

A further argument against the incorporation of this type of intangible is that if the company is **publicly quoted**, and if the market shows **semi-strong or strong form efficiency**, then the market price of the shares should reflect this information in any case.

In view of these points, there is little point in attempting a net assets valuation for MC at the present time. The inappropriateness of this can be illustrated with reference to the competitor, which would have a theoretical net assets based valuation of £75m as compared with a market capitalisation of £196m (£9.80 share price × 20m shares in issue).

(ii) **Price/earnings ratio**

This method **compares the earnings information** of the company with that of other **companies of similar size** and characteristics that operate in the same markets, to arrive at an appropriate market price for the shares. The information that has been provided for the quoted competitor will be used to arrive at an initial price, but this will need to be adjusted to reflect the fact that the competitor lacks MC's research capability.

The **price/earnings (P/E) ratio** is calculated by **dividing the market price of the shares** by the **earnings per share**. The competitor has a P/E ratio of 16.3 (980p/60p). Although this is likely to be above the average for quoted industrial companies as a whole, it does not appear to be unreasonably high for the medical sector. Given that MC is forecasting better growth prospects than the competitor, and also has a research capability, it seems reasonable to value the company on a P/E of around 18 times. This would value MC at £135m (18 × 75p × 10m shares in issue). However, if the shares were to be offered on the open market, it would be prudent to price them at a discount to this to reflect the fact that the company would be a new entrant to the stock market, despite an eleven year trading history. Pricing at a discount will also make the issue more attractive to investors and thereby help to obtain a good take-up of shares.

Valuation on a P/E of 18 implies a price of £13.50 per share. If the shares were to be offered at a discount of, say, 15%, this would result in an offer price of around £11.50 per share, and a market capitalisation of £115m.

(iii) **Dividend valuation model**

The dividend valuation model has the central assumption that the **market value** of shares is **directly related** to the **expected future dividends** on those shares. It can be expressed as:

$$P_0 = \frac{d_0(1+g)}{(k_e - g)}$$

Since the shares are not yet quoted, it is **not possible to say** exactly what the **shareholders' net cost of capital** is likely to be. However, given the comments about comparability above, it might be reasonable to use the competitor's data to obtain an estimate.

$$\beta_u = \beta_g \left[\frac{V_E}{V_E + V_D(1-t)} \right]$$ can be used as debt is risk-free, and $\beta_d = 0$

$$\beta_u = 1.25 \left[\frac{80}{80 + 20(1-0.3)} \right]$$

$$= 1.064$$

Regearing for MC

$$\beta_g = \beta_u \times \left[\frac{(V_E + V_D(1-t))}{V_E} \right]$$

$$= 1.064 \left[\frac{90 + 10(1-0.3)}{90} \right]$$

$$= 1.147$$

Substituting in CAPM

$$k_e = 5\% + (12 - 5) \, 1.147$$
$$= 13.03\%, \text{ say } 13\%$$

This cost of equity can now be used in the dividend valuation model to estimate the market value of MC:

$$P_0 = \frac{d_0(1+g)}{(k_e - g)}$$

$$P_0 = \frac{(55p \times 10m) \times (1+8\%)}{(13\% - 8\%)}$$

$$P_0 = £118.8m$$

The dividend valuation model values the company at £118.8m, or £11.88 per share. This assumes a growth rate of 8%, however in reality the **potential growth** rate may be **higher** since the company is currently evaluating investments at a discount rate that is above the estimated cost of capital. This means that it may be turning down investments that would in fact add value to the company.

The same method of valuation can be applied to the competitor for comparative purposes:

$$P_0 = \frac{(50p \times 20m) \times (1 + 7\%)}{(13.75\% - 7\%)}$$

P_0 = £158.5m or £7.92 per share

(iv) **Discounting the future earnings stream**

This method involves **discounting the future long-term earnings stream** at the shareholders' cost of capital to **arrive at a value for the company**. However, there is insufficient information available to use this approach here; much more information about the long-term cash flow projections and estimates of terminal values is needed before this method could be attempted.

(b) **The relative advantages of flotation and direct sale**

The following points should be considered when deciding which option is to be preferred.

(i) **Aims of existing owners**

The **aims of the existing owners** are important in determining the best course of action. If a significant number of the existing consortium wish to **maintain control** over the business in the future, then they are more likely to be able to achieve this if the company is floated rather than sold.

(ii) **Market for shares**

Flotation will create a **wider market** for the **company's shares**. This has the twin benefits that it will be **easier** for the company to **raise additional capital** to finance expansion, and that the existing shareholders will be able to realise all or part of their holding. However, if MC is to achieve a good price, the existing owners should aim to retain the major part of their holding for a reasonable period following the flotation.

(iii) **Share option schemes**

Flotation will allow the company to offer **share option schemes** to its employees, which should **assist** in the **recruitment** and **retention of good staff**. This is particularly important in a company such as MC, where a significant part of the value in the company is linked to the knowledge base and research capability. Retaining a high proportion of the key staff will be vital to the success of any change in ownership, and must be taken into account in the structuring of either the sale or the flotation.

(iv) **Costs of flotation**

Flotation will be an **expensive process** and will mean that the company has to comply with the stringent Stock Exchange regulations. It will put extra administrative burdens on the management and will cost more to organise than would a direct sale of the business.

(c) **Conclusions and recommendations**

(i) **Sale price**

The calculations suggest that the company should achieve a **sale price** of at least £120m. This compares with a **market capitalisation** of the **competitor** of £196m. Since MC has better growth prospects and also has a research base, which the competitor lacks, it may be able to achieve a better price than this, but £120m should be regarded as the base price in any negotiations.

(ii) **Stock market quotation**

It is also recommended that the company should opt for a **Stock Market quotation** rather than for a direct sale. Given the current state of the market for this type of stock, it should be able to achieve a good price, and flotation will also give flexibility to the owners in allowing them to realise a part of their investment, while at the same time retaining control over the future direction of the business.

41 PP

(a)   **Factors influencing the views of shareholders**

    (i)   **Premium**

        The PP offer of four shares for every three of VE equates to a **bid price** of 309.3 pence per share (232 $\times$ 4/3). This compares with the current market price of 295 pence for VE shares, giving a premium of 14.3 pence per share, or 4.8%.

        Shareholder response

        On the face of it, a premium should be attractive to shareholders. However, VE's shareholders will have to consider how highly they value the PP shares, the **future prospects** of the group and **integration costs**.

        Dividend growth model

        When evaluating the bid price VE's shareholders may also wish to consider the **theoretical market price** of their shares. Using the dividend growth model:

$$P_0 = \frac{d_1}{k_e - g}$$

        where: P_0 = theoretical market share price
                    d_1 = dividend in year 1 (£5m $\times$ 1.08/40m)
                    k_e = cost of equity
                    g = annual rate of dividend growth

$$P_0 = \frac{13.5p}{13\% - 8\%} = 270 \text{ pence per share}$$

        The implication of this is that the shares are currently overvalued in the market (possibly due to bid speculation) and that the 'true' premium is closer to 39.3 pence per share, or 14.6% of 270 pence. While still relatively low, this is likely to be more acceptable to the shareholders.

(ii) **Directors' views**

VE's shareholders are also likely to take into account the **views of the directors**, and whether or not the bid is likely to be contested. If the directors are of the view that the offer is likely to be in the **best long-term interests** of the company then the shareholders are more likely to view it favourably. If however the bid is likely to be contested, the shareholders will probably **reject the offer**, either in support of the directors or in the hope of a more lucrative offer being made.

(iii) **Control**

	No of shares m	shareholding %
PP	300.0	85
VE shareholders (40 × 4/3)	53.3	15
	353.3	100

PP shareholders are clearly in control of the combined entity, whereas VE shareholders own a 15% minority. VE's shareholders may be concerned that they have too little influence over the future direction of the group.

(iv) **Risk**

If the shareholders are intending to hold the PP shares after the acquisition, then they will be concerned with the **security** of the new shares. Since both companies trade in the food retailing sector, the **operational gearing** and **asset betas** are likely to be similar. However, VE's shareholders should also consider the **relative financial risk** of the two companies which can be measured by the **capital gearing** and the **interest cover**.

Gearing

The **gearing** can be defined as the ratio of the prior charge capital (loan stock and term loans) to shareholders' funds. Using book values, the ratios are as follows.

	PP £m	VE £m
Loan stock	200	–
Term loans	114	17.5
Total	314	17.5
Capital and reserves	222	54.7
Gearing ratio	141%	32%
EBIT (£m)	115	14
Net interest (£m)	40	2
Interest cover (times)	2.9	7.0

It can be seen that the gearing level of PP is high, being in excess of 100%, and the interest cover is relatively low, being less than 3 times. The level of financial risk is therefore significantly higher than for VE, and the shareholders must take this into account when considering the offer.

(v)   **Dividend policy**

Dividend policy can be evaluated by considering the **payout ratio** and the **dividend yield**.

	PP	VE
Profit available to equity (£m)	50	8
Dividend (£m)	24	5
Payout ratio	48%	62.5%
Number of shares in issue	300m	40m
Dividend per share (pence)	8	12.5
Share price (pence)	232	295
Dividend yield	3.4%	4.2%

The payout ratio for VE is higher than that for PP, so shareholders in VE who are intending to hold on to their new PP shares are therefore likely to receive a lesser dividend stream to that which they currently obtain.

(vi)   **Earnings per share**

Pre-merger

	PP	VE
Earnings £m	50	8
Shares m	300	40
Earnings per share	16.7p	20p

Post-merger

	£m
Combined earnings	58.0
Labour savings per annum	2.7
	60.7

Shares m	353.3
Earnings per share PP shareholders	17.2p
Earnings per current share VE shareholders 17.2 × 4/3	22.9p

Both sets of shareholders will see an improvement in earnings, though PP's less so than VE's.

(vii)   **Synergies**

The extra value generated from the rationalisation to be undertaken following the acquisition is as follows.

	£m
Proceeds of warehouse sale	6.8
Redundancy costs	(9.0)
Annual labour cost savings (PV):	
5 yrs at 12% = 2.7 × 3.605	9.73
Total synergistic benefits	7.53

The market value of the PP shares after the acquisition is as follows.

	£m
Value of company PP before combination is: 300m × 2.32	696.00
Value of company VE before combination is: 40m × 2.95	118.00
Value of synergies: (as above)	7.53
Value of combined entity (assuming no value destroyed)	821.53
Number of shares in combined entity:	353.33m
Value per share: 821.53/353.33	£2.325

The value attached to each current V share will be 2.325 × 4/3 = £3.10. Thus V shareholders will gain value compared with the £2.95 their shares are currently worth. PP's shareholders will not gain anything.

Conclusion

The improvements in earnings and capital value are limited for both sets of shareholders. VE's shareholders may choose to accept the bid and liquidate their shareholdings, obtaining the premium of 14p per share. They are unlikely to hold on to their shareholdings unless they feel management can generate more synergies.

As a consequence, the shareholders of PP will probably feel neutral towards the acquisition unless their directors can convince them that it will provide additional long-term benefits in terms of growth and earnings stability, for example through cost reductions, access to a wider customer base or superior buying power.

(b) **Redemption yield**

The merits of the debenture offer can be evaluated by calculating the **redemption yield** if the debentures are held to maturity, or the alternative capital gain if they are taken up and then surrendered. The effective price at which the debentures are being offered is the VE share price of 295 pence times 10 = £29.50 per £100 debenture.

The redemption yield can be calculated using the following expression, where 'r' = the redemption yield (this gives the same result as calculating the internal rate of return):

$$£29.50 = \frac{£100}{(1+r)^{10}} \quad \therefore \ (1 + r)^{10} = 3.390 \text{ and } (1 + r) = 1.130$$

The **redemption yield** is thus 13%. The current yield on ten year stock is only 10%, and therefore this effective premium of 3% could be very attractive to the VE shareholders. However, they would probably have to hold the stock for the ten year period to realise the gain.

Problems with debentures

A potential problem for some shareholders who are holding the VE shares, in part for their regular dividend income, would be that the debenture would pay **no interest** during that period and would not therefore meet the requirements of their portfolio.

Realising a capital gain

An alternative would be for the VE shareholders to take up the stock and then **sell it to realise a capital gain.** The expected market price (MV) of the new debenture at the time of issue can be estimated if it is assumed that it will have the same level of risk as new ten year loan stock:

$$MV = \frac{£100}{(1+0.10)^{10}} = £38.55$$

This is a premium of £(38.55 – 29.50)/10 = £0.905, ie 90.5 pence per VE share (30.7%). This too is likely to be attractive to the shareholders, although they would have to take into account the effect of such a course of action on their **individual capital gains tax** positions, and the transaction costs of selling.

Cash offer

The cash offer of 325 pence per share equates to a premium of 30 pence per share or 10.2% above the current market price. Although this is an improvement on the original share offer, it is not as good as the **debenture offer**, and the shareholders would also have to take into account the **effect** on their **capital gains tax positions** since the payment in cash would precipitate an immediate capital gains tax liability.

42 PR

Text references. Acquisition issues are covered in Chapter 16.

Top tips. A variety of approaches are possible in (a) and your suggested price will probably have differed from ours. Don't worry if you didn't spot that the directors were using the combined P/E ratio of the two companies, although it would have helped your answer to calculate the P/E ratio they were using. Certainly an answer that stated the ratio should be close to or even at 16 and calculated what the revised terms of the offer should be should have scored a comfortable pass. You need to keep control over your answer to (b) and make sure you cover the points mentioned in the question. Some discussion (4 to 5 marks) worth was needed on the various types of debt that could be used, but you needed to concentrate on the advantages and disadvantages for **PR** rather than discussing the features of each type of debt in detail.

Easy marks. The advantages/disadvantages of the cash alternative is a general summary that would earn a few marks. More significant in terms of marks available was the discussion on sources.

Examiner's comments. The least popular question. Generally answers were quite good, although some answers discussed rights issues (excluded in the question) and did not cover revised bid terms. A few candidates stated incorrectly that retained earnings were a source of finance, rather than the cash retained and not paid out as dividends.

Answer plan

(a)   Valuation calculations – offer cf market price
       P/E ratios used to calculate offer
       Advantages to PR
       Appropriate revised terms

(b)   Advantages of cash (shareholders)
       Disadvantages of cash (shareholders, risk, costs)
       How much
       Financing source – Impact on gearing and consequences
                        – Types of debt

       Other costs

REPORT

To: Directors
From: Financial advisers
Subject: Bid for ST
Date: 8 October 20X2

This report covers various issues relating to the bid for ST.

(a)   **Valuation of existing bid**

       PR has offered $10/13 \times 513$ million = 394.6 million shares for the shares of ST. At a market price of 671 pence, the offer is worth £2.65 billion. However the market currently values ST's shares at 513 million × 565 = £2.9 billion. PR's bid indicated that it sought to acquire ST on a P/E ratio of $16 \times 2.65/2.9 = 14.6$. This is the weighted average of the P/E ratios of the two companies, as shown below. The earnings figures used in the weighted average calculation are:

       PR 820 million × 6.71/14 = 393.0 million
       ST 513 million × 5.65/16 = 181.2 million

       Combined P/E ratio $= \dfrac{(393.0 \times 14) + (181.2 \times 16))}{(393.0 + 181.2)}$

       $= 14.6$

This calculation assumes that there are no benefits from the merger. The directors of ST would appear to be arguing that the merger would bring considerable benefits for PR. It would eliminate its main competitor in the UK, it would make the company the largest in Europe, and it would reduce the risk of the company being taken over in the USA.

These advantages would appear to indicate that the terms for ST should be much closer to those suggested by its P/E ratio. Using a P/E ratio of 15.4 would suggest terms of 10.5 shares in PR for 13 shares in ST (10 × 15.4/14.6). However the market situation is changing quickly, and we are not sure how **efficient** the market's valuation of ST is.

(b)   **Advantages of cash alternative**

(i)   The more shareholders of ST take up the cash alternative, the less shares in PR and the less the **balance of control** in PR **will alter**.

(ii)   A greater proportion of the **gains resulting from the merger** will be enjoyed by PR's current shareholders.

Disadvantages of offering a cash alternative

(i)   Shareholders who take up the cash alternative may face an **immediate liability** to **capital gains**.

(ii)   The amount of cash that will be **required** is **uncertain**.

(iii)   If PR has to issue debt to fund the cash alternative, its **financial risk** and therefore **its cost of equity** will **increase**.

Amount of cash to be raised

Assuming the terms are as above, and assuming 50% of shareholders will take the cash alternative, PR will need 10.5/13 × 0.5 × 513 × 6.71 = £1.39 billion.

Financing of offer

If PR was to exhaust the cash reserves of itself and ST, it would need extra finance of 1.39 – 0.46 – 0.12 = £0.81 billion. This amount would have to be financed by issue of **additional debt**, unless PR could raise further sums through selling subsidiaries. At the opposite end, PR could fund the whole cash alternative by the issue of debt finance.

Effect on debt/equity ratios

To calculate the effect, an assumption is needed about the market price of PR's shares after the merger. Assuming PR's P/E ratio rises to 15.4,

Market value of shares = (820 + (0.5 ×10.5/13 × 513)) × 6.71 × 15.4/14
                                     = £7.58 billion

Assuming the lower figure of £0.81 billion is needed,

$$\text{Debt/equity ratio} = \frac{(2.2+1.8+0.81)}{(2.2+1.8+0.81+7.58)}$$

$$= 38.8\%$$

Assuming the higher figure of £1.39 billion is needed,

$$\text{Debt/equity ratio} = \frac{(2.2+1.8+1.39)}{(2.2+1.8+1.39+7.58)}$$

$$= 41.6\%$$

Both figures are rather larger than the industry average of 30%. In addition PR currently has £880 million worth of debt repayable in three years time compared with current cash balances of £460 million, and ST has £540 million worth of debt repayable in four years time compared with current cash balances of £120 million.

Equity shareholders may require a **higher return** for the increased financial risk they are being asked to bear, and this may **depress the price-earnings ratio**. The additional financial risk may also mean that new debt carries a **higher rate of interest** than existing debt.

Different types of debt

Various types of debt could be used to finance the bid.

Ordinary debt

An issue of **debentures** should be **attractive** to investors if they are **secured** on the company's assets. From the company's viewpoint **debenture interest** is **tax deductible**, but it will represent a significant financial commitment. Money will have to be found ultimately to redeem the debentures if they are **redeemable**. Because of the need to redeem a significant proportion of debt in the near future, a **long date to maturity**, maybe fifteen years, should be considered.

Convertible bonds

The main advantage of convertible bonds are that PR should be able to avoid a **large cash outflow** if **bondholders convert to shares**. Most companies issuing convertible securities expect them to be converted. Companies are generally able to issue convertible debt at a slightly lower rate than equivalent ordinary loan stock, because bondholders are acquiring the option of being able to buy into the equity of the group.

If conversion takes place, there may however be a **significant change in the balance of shareholding**. In addition **setting the terms of conversion** may be **difficult** given the **uncertainties** in the **prospects** of the merged group.

Debt with warrants

As with convertible debt, debt with warrants can be issued on **more advantageous terms** than straight debt. PR will also be able to raise money in the future if the users **exercise their warrants**.

Costs of acquisition

The analysis above has ignored the costs of the acquisition process. In practice the costs of a contested takeover bid are likely to be substantial including **professional services, advertising** and **underwriting costs**. These are likely to require considerable cash expenditure in the short-term.

Conclusion

An improved offer and a cash alternative is likely to enhance significantly the chances of the takeover being successful. However the proportion of debt in total financing that is likely to result will be high compared with industry averages.

43 BA

Text references. Acquisition issues are covered in Chapter 16.

Top tips. A briefing note need not be as formally laid out as a report. In (a) you need to compute the values of both companies before the announcement, which you can do by using their earnings and P/E ratios. You are then told how the share prices react to the announcement: good news for YZ shareholders but not for BA. As you have the information needed for a dividend valuation calculation, it's helpful to carry out a comparison.

The normal arrangement on a cash or shares offer is that the cash equivalent is lower, because cash is less risky. This does not appear to be the case here, though, for reasons that are difficult to understand. When discussing the factors to consider, you should include BA's motives and plans for the merger, and whether large shareholders in YZ plc wish to retain their influence on the board of directors.

Easy marks. (a) is a tough question, and it's useful to work through the stages to see how our answer fits together. (b) is a fairly mainstream discussion, but it does need to be tailored to the needs of shareholders to secure a good mark.

Examiner's comments. This question proved to be the least popular question on the paper, surprisingly because it covered familiar ground and a key syllabus topic. In general calculations were either non-existent or confused; although candidates did use the dividend valuation model, they failed to use any other model that would have provided a basis for comparison. EPS calculations were also poor. Many candidates ignored the requirement in (c) to give advice.

Briefing note on proposed offer by BA for the shares of YZ

Prepared by: A. Shareholder
Date: 9 December 20X2

(a) **Evaluation of the share-for-share offer from BA**

Value of the companies' shares before the announcement

	BA $m	YZ $m	Combination
Earnings before tax	126.60	112.50	
Tax (30%)	(37.98)	(33.75)	
Earnings after tax	88.62	78.75	
P/E immediately before announcement	11	7	
Total value of equity shares before announcement:			
(= earnings after tax × P/E): $m	974.82	551.25	$1526.07m
No. of shares (= share capital/par value): million	250	180	
Value per share before announcement (cents)	390c	306c	

These share prices are in within the range of the 20X2 maximum and minimum share prices given. The value of the two companies together, before the announcement of the share offer, is $1,526 million.

Value of shares if merger takes place

Assuming the companies are fairly valued and that there is no hidden synergy in the combination (which is unlikely), the value of the combination will remain unchanged by the merger, at $1,526 million. If we accept the merger terms of 5 shares in BA for every 6 shares in YZ, the number of shares in BA will increase by 5/6 × 180 million = 150 million. This will give a total of 250 +150 = 400 million shares in BA, giving a share price for BA after the merger of $1,526/400 = 381 cents.

This values YZ shares at 5/6 × 381 cents = 317 cents. On the basis of these computations shareholders in BA lose (down 2.3%), while those in YZ gain (up 3.6%).

However, these computations are made redundant by the extreme reaction of the stock market against BA's offer:

	BA	YZ	Combination
Change in share price on announcement of offer:	−10%	+14%	
Value per share after announcement: cents			
BA: 390 × 0.9	351		
YZ: 306 × 1.14		349	
No of shares m	250	180	
Total value of equity shares after announcement: $m	877.50	628.20	1505.70m
Total value of shares before announcement: $m	974.82	551.25	1526.07m
Total gain/(loss) by shareholders: $m	(97.32)	76.95	(20.37m)
Gain/(loss) per share: cents	(39)	43	

The shareholders of BA have lost more than the shareholders of YZ have gained, creating a net loss in the total value of the two companies.

Valuation using the dividend valuation model

As a benchmark, we can value both companies using the dividend valuation model

	BA	YZ
Dividend yield just before announcement	2.40%	3.10%
Share price before announcement	390c	306c
Therefore, latest dividend, d	9.36c	9.49c
Growth forecast, g	4%	4%
Cost of equity capital, k_e	13%	11%
Thus, value per share by DVM: $d(1+g)/(k_e - g)$	108c	141c

The share values obtained by the dividend valuation model are significantly lower than the current market prices. We need to consider carefully what future **dividend policy** would be if we accepted shares.

(b) **Factors to consider when deciding whether to accept or reject the bid**

Raising the offer

We need to assess the chances that BA will make a **better offer** if we reject their current offer. We should assess whether there are other potential targets for which BA might bid.

The value of the offer

An alternative to accepting the offer is to sell our shares on the market. Although we will probably not be able to sell our large shareholdings at the current market price, the **comparison** of the two values is of prime importance.

Our influence as shareholders

As we hold large blocs of shares, we are in a position to influence the board of YZ through our 'protest group'. Our shareholdings will be **diluted** if we accept the share-for-share offer by BA and we may prefer to reject the offer.

BA's motive for the merger

BA has developed a reputation **for rapid growth**, but appears to have slowed down recently. If we accept the offer, it should be because we believe that BA can achieve the results that we have been seeking for YZ. There is a danger, however, that BA is merely seeking to **increase its earnings per share** by acquiring us – this can be easily done because our P/E is lower than BA's. BA may also be hoping to take advantage of our share price being near its lowpoint for the year.

BA's plans for the merged companies

We need to examine the plans for **management** of the combination and strategic plans which justify the combination, and to determine whether long-term gains are likely for shareholders in the merged company.

Market viewpoint

The market gives us a low **price-earnings ratio compared** with our competitors. We should consider whether the market has **underestimated the value in the company,** particularly the **intellectual expertise** or whether the market does not believe in YZ's ability to turn the company around.

Shares or cash?

Cash is **more certain in value** than shares because, as we have seen, shares in listed companies can fall very quickly. BA's shares dropped by 10% following announcement of the merger, illustrating the potential risk involved. To compensate us for accepting the risk, BA should have offered a higher value in shares than the cash alternative. However, their share offer to us was worth $5/6 \times 390c = 325c$ for each of our shares, which is *less* than the cash offer to us (unless the 345c cash is per BA share).

A disadvantage of accepting the cash offer is that this counts as **a disposal of shares**, resulting in a charge to capital gains tax, whereas accepting a share-for-share offer does not count as a disposal.

If we accept shares that we intend to keep in the long-term, the likely **dividend policy** of the group will be significant.

(c) **Advice on action to take**

On the basis of my calculations, I make the following recommendations:

(i) **Do not accept the current share-for share offer** made by BA. Our share price is now standing at 349c, against BA's 351c. At 5 of their shares for 6 of ours you would make a clear loss.

(ii) You should consider **accepting the cash offer** of 345 cents per share. Although our share price is slightly higher, you would be unlikely to be able to sell large shareholdings at full market price. Since our share price appears high compared with the company's fundamental valuation (as shown by the dividend valuation model calculation), it may be a good time to accept the cash offer and take your profit.

(iii) If you do not wish to sell at the moment, then **reject BA's offer**. The market appears to be signalling that the **proposed terms** were **not good enough**. BA may yet return with a better offer, or another offer may come elsewhere.

(iv) You should consider a **fall-back strategy** if BA do not improve their offer of trying to appoint a new board who are more likely to unlock the value in YZ.

44 PDQ

Text references. Business valuations are explained in Chapter 15. Management buyouts are discussed in Chapter 16.

Top tips. You may have suggested equally plausible valuations to the ones we have suggested in (a). To score good marks, you would need to suggest various measures, and examine critically their limitations, (assumptions, lack of information, range of values suggested, further factors) considering how useful they would be in the circumstances described in the question.

(b) needs to be examined from the viewpoints of the managers/employees, and also the venture capitalists. The venture capitalists will be looking to obtain a good price if possible.

Easy marks. Remember that the calculations in (a) will only account for a small number of marks; it's equally important to discuss the non-financial factors and to provide a reasonable recommendation.

Examiner's comments. Generally (a) was not answered well, as candidates struggled to place a value on a company that was lossmaking. Most DCF calculations did not go beyond 20X4. Common weaknesses included failing to allow for tax, failing to estimate cash flows beyond 20X7, and not bringing the value of the perpetuity calculated back to the present. Generally (b) was answered well, except by those candidates who ran out of time after (a).

(a) **Offer price for management buy-out**

Bases of valuation

The shares in the company can be valued by various methods, which fall into two main categories: **assets** and **expected income**.

Assets basis

For a going concern, using the value of the **net assets** will normally understate the value of PDQ, as there is no clear way of valuing the intangible asset of **goodwill**, other than by examining expected future income. The figures obtained should therefore be seen as providing a **minimum value**.

Using **net assets**, after deducting all liabilities, this method gives a book value of:

£0.95 million, or £3.80 per share as at 31 December 20X3 and
£3.70 million, or £14.80 per share as at 31 December 20X4.

Expected income – dividend valuation model

The value of a going concern is the **discounted value** of **future income** to be generated by that concern, where the discount rate reflects the appropriate risk. One method of estimating the value of the company's shares is to **estimate future dividends** and to **discount them at the shareholders' cost of capital**, using the dividend valuation model.

However no dividends have yet been paid, and will not be paid in 20X3, and we lack information about what the future dividend policy might be. Because of this lack of information it is unrealistic to use the dividend valuation model, as too many doubtful assumptions would be involved. There is also the problem of potential differences between the dividends the shareholders might desire, and the limits on dividends that the company may face so it can retain enough cash for investment to achieve the predicted levels of growth.

Expected valuation – earnings

Using earnings rather than dividends has the advantage that we do not need to speculate about dividend policy. It may also be a more realistic reflection of the venture capitalists' viewpoint since they hold the majority of shares.

Capital growth

A number of calculations can be made using the dividend valuation formula, but substituting Eo, earnings, for Do, dividends:

$$P_0 = \frac{E_0(1+g)}{(r-g)}$$

The problems of using this method in the initial few years is that the growth rate 20%, exceeds the cost of capital.

Hence the calculation has to be in two parts

	Post tax cash flow £ million	Discount factor 15%	Discounted cash flow £ million
20X4	2.75	0.870	2.39
20X5	2.31	0.756	1.75
20X6	2.77	0.658	1.82
20X7	3.33	0.572	1.90
			7.86

20X5 figure = 2.75 (1.2) (1 – 0.3); 20X6 and 20X7 earnings increase by 20% and for 20X8 onwards:

$$\frac{3.33(1+0.05)}{0.15-0.05} \times 0.572 = \text{£20 million, where 0.572 is the year 4 discount factor for 15\%.}$$

Combining the two gives a company valuation of £27.86 million and a valuation of the venture capitalists' shares of £15.32 million.

A more pessimistic calculation would be to take the 20X4 earnings figure, adjust for tax in subsequent years $(2.75 \times (1 - 0.3)) = 1.925$, assume that 5% rather than 20% was a more realistic growth rate after 20X4, and use the formula:

$$P_0 = \left(\frac{1.925(1.05)}{0.15 - 0.05} \times 0.870 \right) + 2.39$$

giving a valuation for the company of approximately £20 million and a valuation for the venture capitalists' shareholding of around £11 million.

Expected income – p/e ratio method

An alternative method based on expected income is the p/e ratio method. Using the (notional) post tax earnings for 20X4 of £1.925m, we can multiply by a p/e ratio that is regarded as suitable for PDQ. The **industry average p/e** is 28.4, which would give a company value of £54.67 million. If the venture capitalists share was to be valued at the original purchase price, £12 million, this would imply use of a p/e ratio of

$$\frac{(\text{£12 million} / 0.55)}{\text{£1.925 million}} = 11.3$$

However, the p/e method is **simplistic** and takes **no specific account of growth expectations** or **risk** of the specific company. P/es for listed companies in the industry vary from 7.5 to 51.5, which would value PDQ at anywhere between £14 million and £99 million, if it was an established listed company. However, as the company is unlisted, a p/e ratio lower even than 7.5 may therefore be appropriate. We would need to know what sort of expectations of growth were generating the higher p/e ratios in the sector, and the reasons for those expectations.

Other considerations

The venture capitalists may well be unwilling to accept a **price lower** than the £12 million they initially paid, and may be looking for a **premium** on their initial investment.

The venture capitalists should have a **good knowledge** of the company, and may well be in a good position to assess the likely accuracy of the directors' forecasts. They will not necessarily assume that the directors are being over-optimistic in their predictions. Particularly in the later years, it is possible that the directors are being over-conservative, as a forecast of lower growth would imply a lower purchase price.

They will also examine **market data** on listed companies that are similar in profile to PDQ, and base their valuation on the share prices of such companies, with perhaps some allowance for the fact PDQ is unlisted.

If the finance can be raised quickly, the venture capitalists may be willing to accept a lower price in return for a sale to a willing buyer.

Offer terms

The founders and employees may wish to start by offering the price of £12 million that the venture capitalists paid, since the earnings method suggests this figure is reasonable and it can also be calculated using a p/e ratio above the sector minimum. The venture capitalists' attitude will be determined by the alternatives available and current market conditions for similar companies. The founders/employees' attitudes will be determined by the **available finance** (discussed further below).

(b)   **Management buy-out versus sale to another investor**

Advantages of management buy-out

(i)   The management team already **knows** the **strengths and weaknesses** of the business and does not need time to evaluate it. The managers may be better able to focus the business on its **core activities**.

(ii)   Assuming finance is available, the buy-out may be **arranged quicker** than a sale to another party.

(iii) Widening the equity ownership to employees of the company gives them the opportunity of **participating in large equity gains**. This is likely to increase motivation and strengthen the commonality of objectives with top management during the crucial growth period of the next few years.

(iv) The company's **independence** will be **preserved**, whereas a sale to a competitor may result in effective closure of the business to eliminate competition.

Disadvantages of management buy-out

(i) The statement that a management buy-out will be speedy is based on the assumption that the **necessary finance** will be **readily available**. Managers and employees may find it difficult to contribute enough equity, and any lender would be influenced by the **limited security available** and the fact that PDQ has not yet actually **moved into profit**. Obtaining the funds may thus prove problematic.

(ii) The main disadvantages of a buyout to existing equity shareholders is that the **price** obtained from the **sale of shares** may be **lower** than that **obtainable from another buyer** for various reasons. Another buyer may overlook various problems with the company that are fully perceived by the management team.

(iii) Another buyer may be able to **create synergetic gains** by combining the company with their own business, which would not be available to the management team.

(iv) From the **employees' viewpoint**, the main disadvantage of a buyout is that their **savings**, in the form of shareholdings in the company, are subject to the same risks as their job. It is safer to save in a **diversified portfolio** than to put 'all one's eggs in one basket' in the company.

(v) Although they suffer from the risks resulting from lack of diversification, many employees will not be in a position to **exercise influence** on company decisions. It appears that the founding shareholders will remain in charge. This can create substantial tension if the outcome of company plans is not successful.

45 PCO

Text references. Acquisition issues are covered in Chapter 16.

Top tips. This question covers most of the significant areas on mergers and acquisitions and includes a mix of calculations and discussion of non-financial issues. Remember when doing the calculations that you are not looking for a single right answer but different possibilities to use to suggest a range of possible offers.

You may well see a very similar question to this in Section B of your paper. Mergers and acquisitions may also be set as a compulsory question, including the themes discussed here, but perhaps with more complicated calculations and expanded discussions (maybe for example on takeover defences) as well.

(a) covers the main methods which are covered in many other questions in this kit. Don't be surprised incidentally if the dividend growth rate exceeds the cost of equity capital, as it does here. If this happens, you need to suggest how to adjust the valuation.

In (b) remember that the target is a listed company, so the results of (a) should be compared with the current market values (which rules out the net asset valuation method as providing any sort of guide). Once you've decided the rough offer price, funding that offer needs to be considered. As we're not told anything here, you have to consider both a cash and shares offer, and calculate the effect on gearing if a cash offer is made and borrowing is required.

Easy marks. (b) (iii) is a discussion of the main points you'll need to consider if asked to discuss the impact of any merger; the chances of synergies weighed against possible post-acquisition problems.

(a) **Pre-acquisition data**

		PCO	OT
(i)	Shares in issue (million)	40	24
	Share price (pence)	967	1,020
	Market value of shares (£m)	386.8	244.8
	Earnings per share (pence)	106	92
	P/E ratio	9.12	11.09
(ii)	Beta of equity	0.9	1.2
	Cost of equity [4% + (8% - 4%)β]	7.6%	8.8%
(iii)	Dividend per share (pence)	32	21
	Growth rate	5%	9%
	Prospective share price (pence) $\dfrac{\text{Dividend per share} \times \text{Growth rate}}{\text{Cost of equity} - \text{Growth rate}}$	1,292	See below
	Prospective market value of company (£m)	516.8	See below

For OT, the dividend growth model is not valid as the forecast growth rate, 9% is higher than its cost of equity 8.8%. The formula would give an infinite value to the shares. A forecast of lower growth after an initial high-growth period would be more realistic.

(b) (i) **Price to be offered to target company's shareholders**

As noted above, it is impossible to use the dividend valuation model to value OT based on the current forecast data. The current market value (£244.8m, at 1,020 pence per share) is probably the **minimum value** that OT's shareholders will accept for their company. This is significantly higher than its net tangible asset value of £145 million, which is not a realistic going concern value.

Maximum price

Because the bid is likely to be treated as hostile by OT's directors, PCO will probably need to offer a premium over OT's current market value. In doing so, they must be careful not to offer too high a price, thus gaining a subsidiary at the expense of creating a loss in value for their own shareholders. The estimates made by PCO's financial advisors are key to determining the **maximum price** that PCO can offer. This data can be analysed as follows:

	Share value £m	Earnings £m
Pre-acquisition figures:		
PCO	386.8	42.4
OT	244.8	22.1
Total	631.6	64.5
Financial advisors' post acquisition estimate	720.0	70.0
Estimated gain from merger synergy	88.4	5.5

The **maximum price** that PCO could offer for OT's shares would be if it gave away the whole of the synergetic gains from the merger to OT. This would imply a premium of £88.4 million over the current market value of £244.8m, representing a bid price of (£244.8m + £88.4m) / 24m = 1,388 pence per share. At this maximum price PCO's shareholders would expect to make no gain or loss from the merger.

Fair price

Clearly both parties need to negotiate within the minimum and maximum offer prices of 1,020 and 1,388 pence per share for OT. PCO should make an initial offer towards the low end of this range and be prepared to negotiate upwards. A 'fair' price might be where the synergetic gains from the merger are split in proportion to the existing market values of the companies:

	PCO	OT	Total
	£m	£m	£m
Current market value	386.8	244.8	631.6
Proportion	61%	39%	100%
Gain, split in same proportion	53.9	34.5	88.4

This would value OT at £244.8m + £34.5m = £279.3 million, that is 1,164 pence per share.

Conclusion

PCO should initially offer a price in the region of 1,100 pence per share, and be prepare to negotiate up to about 1,164 pence, with an absolute maximum of 1,388 pence.

(ii) **Funding the bid**

PCO would consider offering either cash or shares as purchase consideration for the acquisition.

Cash offer

To OT shareholders the advantage of receiving a cash offer is that the price, once offered, is **not subject** to **stock market fluctuations**. Because of this relative certainty, PCO may feel that it need not offer such a high price as it might if it were offering shares. However, the disadvantage of a cash offer to the OT director-shareholders is that they will **no longer have** an **equity stake** in their business. This may cause them to reject a cash offer unless the price is very high. A cash offer will also fail if the market bids the price of OT's shares above that of the cash offer.

Need for borrowing

Assuming PCO is going to pay approximately £279 million for OT, it can only make a cash offer if it borrows most of these funds. The existing cash balance is £105 million, so PCO will need to borrow, say, £200 million to finance the acquisition and leave some cash in the bank. This will cause gearing to rise significantly.

Existing gearing by market values is given in the data:

		PCO	OT
Current market value of equity	£m	386.8	244.8
Debt ratio		17%	14%
Debt market value (Equity market value × 17/83)	£m	79.2	39.9

Thus the total debt in the firm following the merger would be approximately £79m + £40 + £200 = £319m. **The value of equity** is estimated by the advisors as £720m. This would give a debt ratio $V_D/V_D + V_E$) of 319/1039 = 31%. In other words gearing will nearly double if the acquisition is made with cash.

There is a possible advantage in increasing gearing (**tax relief** on debt interest). However the likelihood is that the large gearing increase needed to finance the acquisition of OT would result in **excessive financial risk** and cause a **significant rise in the cost of capital** and **reduction in share value**.

Share offer

To PCO, a share offer has the advantage that it need not borrow cash and the disadvantage that existing shareholdings will be diluted. To OT, there is the chance of remaining as shareholders (and as directors) but the effective price offered varies with the market's valuation of PCO's shares.

Increase in authorised capital

A share offer by PCO will require it to increase its authorised share capital. At present there are only 10m shares left unissued, and any reasonable offer will require more shares than this. Note that the increase in authorised share capital is likely to act as a **signal to the market** that an acquisition is being contemplated.

Terms of offer

If PCO (share price 967p) initially values OT shares at, say, 1,100 pence, the initial offer would be 1,100/967 = 1.14 shares in PCO for every share in OT.

If this is rejected, and PCO allows itself to be negotiated up to the price of 1,164p per OT share (see (i) above), the revised offer would be 1,164/967 = 1.2 shares in PCO for every share in OT (ie 6 for 5).

Suppose this offer is eventually accepted. PCO would need to issue 1.2 × 24 million = 28.8 million new shares.

The total number of PCO shares in issue would then be 40 + 28.8 = 68.8 million in a company with a value of £720 million. In theory the PCO share price would move up to 720/68.8 = 1,047 pence per share.

OT shareholders would then hold shares worth 1.2 × 1,047p = 1,256p in exchange for their original OT shares which were worth 1,020p. Thus both sets of shareholders would gain from the share exchange.

Effect on earnings per share

Predicted earnings per share in the company would however fall to £70m / 68.8m = 102 pence, from 106 pence. A careful statement would need to be made to the market, possibly attaching longer-term predictions.

Cash and shares

In reality, the choice may not just be between a purely cash offer and a purely shares offer. PCO could consider offering a combination of cash and shares, also an element of debt as well.

(iii) **Business implications**

Comparability of companies

Both PCO and OT appear to be **well-managed**, **efficient** companies. They are of comparable order of magnitude, at present PCO being roughly 60% bigger than OT in terms of market value.

Future prospects

Existing prospects differ between the two companies. OT is younger and appears at present to have **greater growth opportunities** in its business of wholesale distribution of oil products from depots to retail outlets. OT could probably continue to grow quite well on its own, but might gain from a merger with PCO, especially if this enables the combination to achieve a 'critical mass' and enhance its competitive power.

Synergies

PCO is a well-established operator of retail petrol stations, but is at the moment suffering **pressure on its profit margins** as a result of new legislation. Its growth rate is likely to decline unless it takes steps to broaden its activities. However whether acquiring another company in the oil industry represents much of a widening of activities is doubtful.

From the financial analysts' report nevertheless, there appear to be opportunities for fairly significant gains (approximately 14%) if the businesses are combined. Referred to as synergy, these gains may come from a number of areas, including:

- **Economies of scale**. Elimination of duplicated resources, ability to sell surplus land and premises, rationalisation of head office and administration costs.

- **Economies of vertical integration**. Achieving lower operating costs by owning both distribution channels and sales outlets. It may be possible to use OT's distribution expertise to eliminate outside contractor delivery costs for PCO's petroleum and other products, although the flexibility to change supplier will disappear,

In acquiring OT and paying more than the current market price per share, PCO will need to be confident that such synergetic gains are **achievable**. Unless the new organisation effectively translates its plans into actions, profits and share prices will fall below expectations. In particular, the management of the enlarged company will need to ensure that key management and technical skills are retained.

Problems of integration

Because the combination is a form of vertical integration, there is no clear link between the management issues of the two organisations. It may take some time before directors and employees from the two different companies understand each others' business needs. One of the major risks of the merger is that a conflict may emerge between the **management styles and objectives** of employees of the two original companies. For example if the merger is financed by a share exchange, the director-shareholders of OT are likely to become fairly large shareholders of the combined organisation and may all demand seats on the new board, which may then become difficult to control.

More information

The directors need to consider further how the **business** and **financial risks** of the company will change if the merger takes place, and in particular how the costs of capital might alter. They may also wish to investigate whether there are better **targets for takeover**.

46 BiOs

Text references. Business valuation techniques are covered in Chapter 15. Venture capital is discussed in Chapter 16 and flotation in Chapter 5.

Top tips. Questions or parts of questions like (a) are likely to occur in most exams. You could have calculated a more precise P/E ratio based on forecast growth rates but this would be complicated and unnecessary. (b) brings out the sort of knowledge you need to have about different finance sources. However the last paragraph brings out the possibility that there is not a 'right' answer; it may be that what is most **suitable** for the **company** (delaying listing?) may not be so **acceptable** to **shareholders** who wish to realise their investments.

Easy marks. The discussion of the advantages and disadvantages of a stock exchange listing is a standard one that you must be able to reproduce.

(a) **Range of values for the company**

Valuation methods

A company can be valued in terms of:

- The **underlying value** of its assets
- Its **ability to generate future profits** and cash flows (economic value).

Net asset valuation

Asset values are mainly of relevance if the company is to be broken up for disposal. BiOs Ltd's net asset value is **£395,000**, which, we are told, reflects the realisable value of its assets. This gives a 'floor level' value for the company, but is far too low to be of relevance to negotiations with the investment bank, because:

- The company is a **going concern** and is not about to be broken up.

- As BiOs is a consultancy company, most of its **assets** (know-how, skills, contacts) are **intangible** and their value is not included in the net asset value.

It is more relevant to estimate the **economic value** of BiOs, which can be done in a number of ways.

Price/earnings (P/E) ratio method

In this method, which gives a quick approximation to economic value, equity earnings are multiplied by a suitable P/E ratio taken from quoted companies in the same industry.

BiOs' earnings in 20X3 = 756p × 100,000 shares
= £756,000

P/E ratio	12	18	90
Valuation (£'000)	9,072	13,608	68,040

The problem with P/E ratios is that they are affected significantly by the expected growth rate of the company. In the industry examined, P/Es vary between 12 and 90. Given that BiOs is predicted to **grow fast**, we would expect its value to be in the top half of this range, at least, but the P/E ratio method does not adequately allow for the growth rate in the computation.

This approach to valuation is therefore relevant but simplistic and subject to large margins of error.

Present value of future cash flows

This method estimates a stream of future cash flows rather than just one profit figure and discounts the cash flows at a **cost of capital** suitable for the risk of the company's operations.

Using the assumptions that profit after tax equals cash flow, that this will grow in years 2 and 3 at 30% per annum, followed by 10% per annum after that, and that the industry average cost of capital is suitable, we can estimate the company's value as follows:

20X3 = year 0, 20X4 = year 1 etc.

	£'000	12% factor	PV £'000
20X4 earnings	1,487	0.893	1,328
20X5 earnings: 30% higher	1,933	0.797	1,541
20X6 earnings : 30% higher	2,513	0.712	1,789
			4,658
20X7 to perpetuity: 10% growth (Working)	2,764		98,398
Present value of future cash flows:			103,056

Working

20X7 cash flow = 2,513 × 1.1 = 2,764. Present value (at 20X6) of the perpetuity from year 4 onwards, growing at 10% per annum = 2,764/(12% − 10%) = 138,200. To find the PV as at year 0, discount by the 3 year factor: 138,200 × 0.712 = 98,398.

The value of BiOs by this method is **£103 million**. Although there is a substantial margin of error on this valuation estimate, the method is considerably more useful than the P/E approach because it allows for **earnings growth estimates**. The company's growth projections are dependent on the ability to find skilled consultants, who are in short supply.

Conclusion

On the basis of the figures given, the company's value is probably in the range £65 million to £130 million. Further information is needed on the following areas:

- The **assumptions** on which earnings forecasts are based, in particular the assumption that staffing resources can deliver the **predicted growth rates**

- The **company's cost of capital** would help to make a more accurate assessment.

(b)   **Advantages of using venture capital**

Venture capital funding

Venture capital funds specialise in financing **early stage**, **risk-oriented ventures** like BiOs. They will offer finance and assistance once a company has started to generate revenue and shows that it has high growth prospects. The funds offered are typically for **five to seven years**. At the end of this period it is presumed that the company will have grown and will be looking for more permanent sources of funds, at which point the venture capital fund will seek an exit route.

Exit route

The most profitable exit route for a venture capital company is when the company in which it has invested achieves a **stock exchange listing** (see below). Alternatives are to sell their shares to another investor (which might be another venture capital fund, but could be a potential acquirer of BiOs) or back to the original owners.

Disadvantages of using venture capital

Selection of investments

Extensive research is carried out on potential companies for **venture capital investment** and only a very small percentage of applications are accepted. The fact that BiOs has been approached by the marketing department of an investment bank is no guarantee that a venture capital fund will find the company an acceptable proposition.

Participation of venture capitalist

The venture capital fund becomes an equity participant in the company through a structure typically comprised of a combination of a substantial proportion of shares, warrants, options, and convertible securities. It also provides a representative who sits on the **company's board**, offers strategic advice to the management team and assures that the fund's interests are considered. If the directors of BiOs would not welcome this level of **investor involvement**, they should not consider venture capital.

Stock market flotation

The alternative under consideration by BiOs is to continue with existing sources of funds and to go for a stock exchange flotation within two to three years. To achieve a listing, the company needs to demonstrate that, in addition to good growth prospects, it has a **strong management team**, **strong financial controls** and **good management reporting systems**. These last factors will probably need improvement, as most of BiOs' administration systems are currently outsourced.

Advantages of obtaining a stock exchange listing

- Existing owner directors can **realise** some or all of **their investment**
- **New equity finance** is easier to raise
- The company's **status** is **raised**
- The company's shares can be used as **consideration for an acquisition**

Disadvantages of obtaining a stock exchange listing

- **Accountability is increased**: directors must be seen to be accountable to outside shareholders and there is more scrutiny over the company's activities
- **Costs** are incurred for the initial flotation and as ongoing annual fees

The choice

Whichever method is adopted, the end result is probably a **stock exchange flotation**. The directors of BiOs need to decide whether they are happier reaching this end with funding and advice from a venture capital company or whether they are better off seeking an **earlier listing** and thus encouraging equity investors through the stock market. To make their decision they need first to consider their **personal and business objectives**, for example do they wish to realise their wealth in the shortest time or to develop a dominant force in their market sector.

47 BST

Text references. Acquisition issues are covered in Chapter 16.

Top tips. In (a), as often happens in this paper you are not told what methods to use so you have to identify relevant information. You are given the net assets value, given all the information for the price-earnings, market capitalisation calculation, and given an indication of future growth that you can use in the dividend valuation model calculation.

Key factors in (b) are quality of forecasts, assets being purchased, effect on dividend policy and post-acquisition savings.

In (c) the answer adopts the simplest assumptions based on the details in the question (50% want cash, need debt to pay them). However you could have conducted some sensitivity analysis and calculated gearing on the basis that all shareholders required cash.

Easy marks. If you struggled to score marks in (d), take careful note of the issues mentioned, as they will be relevant in the discussion parts of many acquisition questions.

Examiner's comments. Most candidates calculated a range of values, although few commented that the highest value was given with the asset valuation. Discussion of funding methods was often not related to the companies, and few answers calculated what the share exchange might be. Some answers failed to recognise it would be an agreed acquisition and discussed hostile takeover bids.

(a) **Methods of valuation and range of values for SM**

Net assets

The book value of SM's **net assets attributable to equity shareholders** is £45 million. This figure may need to be adjusted for **increased or decreased market values** of assets, particularly SM's property holding. However in any case, for a going concern, the book value of assets is a poor indicator of their economic value, which depends on their **income-generating capacity,** rather than their historical cost or realisable value. Here also SM has a **franchise** generating earnings that will not be reflected in the balance sheet.

Price/earnings model

SM's existing earnings per share is £1.53, and number of shares is 1.5 million, giving total equity earnings of £2.295 million. Taking the 5% growth figure given, next year's earnings would be **£2.410 million.** However, the managing director is estimating £4 million for next year. This figure cannot be accepted at face value and would need to be substantiated.

In the absence of any better information, BST's P/E ratio could be applied to these earnings figures. This is 1237/112.5 = 10.996, say 11.

The range of values for SM's valuation would be between £2.410 million × 11 and £4 million × 11 i.e. between **£26.5 million and £44 million.**

This valuation is dependent upon the **P/E ratio.** Arguably a lower ratio should be used as SM is unquoted, but it is difficult to say how much lower. Also BST's ratio may not be typical of the industry.

Dividend valuation model

Again there is a range of values depending on whether the MD's forecast earnings are believed.

Last year's total dividends were 1.5m × 100 pence = £1.5 m. A 5% increase next year would give £1.575 million. The cost of equity for similar firms is 10% and the expected growth rate 5%.

So on this basis the expected company value = £1.575m / (0.1 − 0.05) = **£31.5 million**.

SM Ltd's dividend payout ratio (dividend / earnings) is 100 /153 = 0.654.

Based on the MD's forecast earnings of £4 million, next year's dividend would be £4m × 0.654 = **£2.616 million.**

The forecast company value would be £2.616 million / (0.1 − 0.05) = £52.3 million.

The **drawbacks** of this method are:

(i)   The assumption that SM's **cost of equity** is the **same as similar firms** may be misleading.

(ii) The **assumption of constant dividend growth** at that rate may be **misleading.** Dividend policy may change on takeover.

(iii) Share price is **not normally** just **a function of dividend policy;** future expected earnings are also a key factor.

Summary

Based on valuation of assets and income earning capacity, SM Ltd appears to have a value **anywhere between £25 million and £52 million**. The higher earnings-based figures are heavily dependent on the MD's forecast of next year's earnings that may well be overstated. Because the net asset value is towards the top end of the valuation range, BST could probably look at a value of between **£40 million and £45 million,** but will need to carry out further investigations on likely asset values.

(b)   **Financial factors that may affect the bid**

Financial factors relating to BST

(i)   Like SM, the **forecast of next year's earnings** may be **overstated.** Current earnings = £1.125 × 25 million = £28.125 million. 4% growth (given) gives £29.25 million, but BST's forecast for next year is £35 million.

(ii) The **total market value of the company's shares** is **below the net asset value.** 25m shares × £12.37 = £309.25.m that is below the £350m net asset value. This may indicate that the company possesses **under-utilised assets**, or alternatively that its assets are overstated in value. On the face of it, the company would be better broken up than operating as a going concern. All these factors will be of interest to any of SM's shareholders who would be considering receiving BST shares. It will also interest the market and BST's low market value may mean that it becomes a takeover target itself.

(iii) BST has a fairly **high gearing ratio.** If BST lacks cash and has to borrow more in order to buy out those 50%+ shareholders of SM who do not wish to have BST shares, this may have the effect of increasing the company's cost of capital.

(iv) BST has a **lower dividend payout ratio** than SM. This may discourage some of SM's shareholders from accepting BST's shares.

(v)   **Strategically** it is **unclear** why BST is buying SM; whilst BST may be trying to diversify, SM may not be a big enough acquisition to make it worth diversifying. There may be better investment opportunities.

Relevant financial factors relating to SM

(i)   Next year's **forecast earnings** may be **overstated.** However, some of the directors may be taking **higher salaries** than **realistic market levels,** and the ongoing future profitability of the company may be higher if these people are replaced with lower cost managers.

(ii) Like BST, **asset value** is **high.** The net asset valuation is in fact higher than some of the other valuations, and SM's shareholders are unlikely to accept an offer below net asset value.

(iii) The company is **ungeared,** which is advantageous, as it enables BST to borrow to fund part of the acquisition.

(iv) The **'quality' of SM's earnings** is probably **higher** than BST's, as it operates in up-market areas.

(v)   Selling SM to a listed company represents a good way for SM's shareholders to **realise the value of their investment**. However, many of the shareholders are likely to lose their jobs and may find it difficult to find equivalent positions. The bid may therefore be opposed by a substantial number of shareholders.

(vi)   There are likely to be many areas where **costs can be saved** as a result of the acquisition of SM. This may make it worthwhile for BST to pay a higher price for SM.

(vii)   BST is likely to have **good access to SM's business documentation** as SM has contacted BST. This should enable BST to calculate a more accurate valuation.

(c)   **Funding the bid**

Need for borrowing

Assume that 50% of SM shareholders will **accept shares in BST**, the remainder will be bought out for cash. This probably means that BST must borrow to raise the cash.

Assume that SM is **valued** as its **net asset value £45m**. This represents a value of £30 per share.

Suppose 50% of these shareholders will accept **new shares in BST** issued at £12.37.

This implies that BST will have to issue £22.5m/£12.37 =1.819 million new shares in exchange for 0.75 million shares in SM (a 2.425 for 1 offer).

BST's **total debt is currently 20% of total market value**; i.e. 25% of the equity market value = £77.3 million. Buying out the remainder of SM's shareholders would mean issuing £22.5m more debt, bringing the total to £99.8 million.

Change in capital structure

BST's capital structure would move as shown below (£m). Gearing would increase from 20% debt to 23% debt.

On the basis of the forecast earnings made by the Managing Directors:

	Before	Acquisition	After	%
Equity	309.3	22.5	331.8	77
Debt	77.3	22.5	99.8	23
Total	386.6	45.0	431.6	100

BST would be showing an **EPS** of £35m / 25m = 140 pence per share, if the acquisition is not made.

If SM is acquired, total earnings would be £39m and total shares 26.819m, giving an EPS of 145.4 pence per share, a 3.9% increase.

(d)   **Advantages of growth by acquisition**

(i)   It **provides economies of scale** by elimination of duplicated resources, combining complementary resources, etc.

(ii)   It enables **increased market power** by eliminating competitors.

(iii)   The acquisition of a going concern business will bring **technical and commercial expertise**, an existing customer base and other aspects of 'goodwill' that will take a long time to achieve through internal development.

(iv)   It provides a **quicker method of entering new or related markets** or acquiring new technology or patents, sometimes enabling very rapid growth. This is especially important when there is the need to achieve a 'critical mass' quickly in order to remain competitive.

Disadvantages of growth by acquisition

(i)   Growth by acquisition **cannot be planned in as much detail** as organic growth.

(ii)   **Quick decisions** sometimes have to be made in response to acquisition opportunities, often without as much information as the acquiring company would like.

(iii)   The acquiring company may **pay too high a price** if the bid is contested, which is why BST prefers uncontested takeovers.

(iv)   Major acquisitions may **change the company's strategic direction**.

(v)   **Staff problems** are more likely to arise as attempts are made to integrate or change the cultures of merged organisations.

48 FS

> **Text references.** The calculation of cost of capital using the capital asset pricing model is explained in Chapter 12. Acquisition issues are discussed in Chapter 16.
>
> **Top tips**. (a) requires use of the more complicated asset beta formula which is now in your formula sheet. (a) is looked at through MT's viewpoint and does not take into account possible changes in the debt-equity ratio. (b) and (c) are fairly standard discussion using the common valuation methods to assess an acquisition, and discussing the main implications of cash vs shares (borrowing vs loss of control).
>
> **Easy marks**. Nothing very surprising in (b) or (c) but you must **relate** your discussion to the scenario.
>
> **Examiner's comments.** This question was generally quite poorly attempted with many not realising the approach that was required. In part (b) most candidates managed to provide some discussion of a range of valuation methods. Common errors included showing net assets as total assets; not recognising that assets will be increased by retained earnings; not providing a range of valuations based on different growth forecasts; providing calculations but inadequate discussion. Discussion must always be **related** to the scenario details.

(a)   **Cost of capital for valuing MT**

FS wishes to make an offer for the share capital of MT and therefore **needs to value MT's shares**. This can be done by **discounting MT's equity dividends** at its cost of equity, which is not provided and cannot be easily observed as it is a private company. MT's cost of equity will therefore be **estimated** from **its asset beta,** which is assumed to the same as FS's.

FS's equity beta is 1.1, its debt beta is 0.2 and its capital structure in market values is:

	€m
Debt (trading at par)	750
Equity (420m × €3.57)	1,500
	2,250

Using $\beta_u = \beta_g \left[\dfrac{V_E}{V_E + V_D} \right] + \beta_d \left[\dfrac{V_D}{V_E + V_D} \right]$

Ignoring tax, FS's β_u is $(1.1 \times 1,500/2,250) + (0.2 \times 750/2,250) = 0.8$.

Thus MT's asset beta is also 0.8, its debt beta is 0.2 and its capital structure is:

	€m
Debt	300
Equity	900
	1,200

MT's equity beta β_g is estimated as $[0.8 - (0.2 \times 300/1200)] \times 1200/900 = \mathbf{1.00}$.

The **cost of equity** for MT is **estimated** from the **capital asset pricing model**. As the equity beta is 1, the cost of equity will be the same as the expected return on the market – 8%.

Note. No adjustment has been made for the fact that MT's bonds are paying a higher interest rate than FS's bonds. This is assumed to be because they are unsecured and MT is a private company. Thus MT's bonds are also assumed to have a fair value equal to their nominal value.

(b) **Bidding strategy for MT's shares**

Valuation by dividend valuation model

The value of MT's shares to FS can be estimated by **discounting MT's expected future dividends** (as a stand-alone company) at 8% and adding on the value of identified synergy from the merger.

Using MT's estimates, earnings are forecast as €88.9 million in 20X6, growing at 4% per year. Assuming dividends remain at 50% of earnings, this gives a 20X6 **dividend** of €44.45 million and a **value of equity** of 44.45 / (0.08 – 0.04) = €1,111 million.

However FS's estimates of MT's growth show 20X6 earnings as somewhere between €71.5 million × 1.02 and €71.5 million × 1.04, that is between €72.93m and €74.36m. Assuming 50% payout, 20X6 dividends will be between and €36.465m and €37.18m.

At 2% growth the **value of MT's equity** is 36.465 /(0.08 – 0.02) = €608 million, and at 4% growth the value is 37.18 / (0.08 – 0.04) = €930 million.

Adding the estimated synergy of €200 million gives a maximum value for MT as **€**1,311 million (based on MT's forecasts) or **€**1,130 (based on FS's forecasts).

Earnings basis valuation

An alternative method of valuing MT is to apply a **suitable P/E ratio** to its latest earnings. FS's earnings per share in 20X5 is 128.5 / 420 = €0.306. The P/E ratio is €3.57 / €0.306 = 11.67.

Applying this ratio to MT's 20X5 earnings gives 11.67 × €71.5 m = €834 million. Adding synergy gives a maximum value of €1,034 million. This method is simpler and less satisfactory as it stands than the discounting method as it does not specifically account for growth expectations. It might be possible to factor in growth using earnings yield, if necessary.

Assets basis valuation

In practice this would need to take into account **revaluation of assets to fair values**, but since no information is available, the value of MT's equity on this basis would equal book value, i.e. €900 million and adding synergy would give €1,100 million. Since this is lower than the P/E valuation, FS should ask for more detail on MT's asset values.

Conclusion

On the basis of the above figures, the maximum FS should be prepared to offer MT would be €1,311 million, but only if it accepts MT's **projections of earnings growth**. More information would be useful, if possible. The initial price to be offered would probably have to be around €1,100 million unless new information showed that some of the company's assets are overvalued.

(c) **Purchase consideration**

Cash offer

FS shares are trading at roughly their book value, €1,500 million. The acquisition of MT would involve purchase consideration nearly as high as this and an offer for cash would therefore have to be financed by **increasing borrowing.** Since FS's gearing is already quite high at D/E = ½, a cash offer for MT can probably be taken as out of the question.

Nevertheless if a cash offer were possible, it would have the advantage to MT's shareholders that it is a **more secure form of purchase consideration** and the advantage to FS's shareholders that there would be no dilution of shareholdings.

Share for share offer

It is far more likely that the FS would offer a **share for share swap.** Thus if MT were valued at €1,200 million, say, giving a value per share of €1,200 / 440 = €2.73, the offer would have to be of the form 2.73 shares in FS for 3.57 shares in MT, i.e. approximately 10 shares in FS for 13 in MT.

The advantage to FS is that there would be no need to borrow, but the great disadvantage is that the **existing shareholders** would **lose control** of the group. There are likely to be large shareholders on the board of MT who would end up as the major shareholders in the combined group. This would have knock-on consequences for the composition of the board of directors and may result in disputes that are impossible to reconcile.

49 VEN

> **Text references.** Relevant costs are discussed in Chapter 17 and NPV, IRR and MIRR are explained in Chapter 18.
>
> **Top tips.** Make sure if you got any items in (a) wrong that you understand why, as in the exam it may not be clear whether all costs are relevant. Our answer to (a) gives explanations in a bit more detail than you'd need in the exam, but they're designed to show clearly why certain figures are relevant.
>
> (b) requires no particular workings so the figures can just be slotted in the NPV calculation. The obvious shortcut as you're calculating the NPV is to use that as the first element of the IRR calculation. We've then added 5% to arrive at the second rate.
>
> The main purpose of the MIRR in (c) is to see what will happen if funds earned are invested. You calculate it by recalculating the cash flows and seeing what rate of interest has the discount factor for the final year that corresponds to Reinvested cash inflows/Cash outflows. You might be asked to calculate MIRR in the exam as well as discussing it.
>
> (d) represents the sort of part question you could get on IT investment, focusing on benefits (including cost savings) and major expenditure.
>
> **Easy marks.** The investment appraisal in (b) doesn't contain any significant complications, (d) can be answered without referring to the rest of the answer.

(a) The cash flows to consider are only those future cash flows arising as a direct consequence of deciding to manufacture the product. Sunk costs (costs already committed or future spending already committed) and costs not involving any cash spending (such as depreciation charges) must be ignored for decision-making purposes.

   (i) **Development costs** are **irrelevant** because they have already been incurred, and future marketing costs are irrelevant because they have already been committed.

   (ii) The only **relevant costs of machinery** are the **amount it could be sold for now** (£790,000) which is a benefit forgone of going into production, and what it could be sold for in five years' time, which would be a cash benefit of going into production.

   (iii) The **relevant cost** of Type A material is its **replacement cost**, £15 per unit.

   (iv) The **relevant cost** of the first 12,000 kilos of Type B material (4,000 units of product) is £1.50 per kilo or £18,000 in total. This is a benefit that would be forgone immediately, ie in Year 0. Further costs of Type B material for units after the first 4,000 are £2.50 per kilo, or £7.50 per unit. Costs are therefore £75,000 per annum except in year 1, when Type B materials for only 6,000 units will be purchased (cost £45,000).

   (v) If the project goes ahead, labour costs will be £12 per unit, with a redundancy cost of £80,000 at the end of year 5. However, there would be a saving in current redundancy costs of £50,000.

   (vi) The only relevant fixed costs are those relating to **incremental expenditure** as a consequence of going into production, £60,000 per annum.

(b) Cash flows

Year	0	1	2	3	4	5	NPV
	£'000	£'000	£'000	£'000	£'000	£'000	
Sales		650	650	650	650	650	
Machinery	(790)					70	
Working capital	(150)					150	
Type A material		(150)	(150)	(150)	(150)	(150)	
Type B material	(18)	(45)	(75)	(75)	(75)	(75)	
Labour costs	50	(120)	(120)	(120)	(120)	(200)	
Fixed costs		(60)	(60)	(60)	(60)	(60)	
Net cash flow	(908)	275	245	245	245	385	
12% factors	1.000	0.893	0.797	0.712	0.636	0.567	
NPV 12%	(908.0)	245.6	195.3	174.4	155.8	218.3	81.4
17% factors	1.000	0.855	0.731	0.624	0.534	0.456	
NPV 17%	(908.0)	235.1	179.1	152.9	130.9	175.6	(34.4)

Approx IRR

$$12\% + \left(\frac{81.4}{(81.4 + 34.4)} \times (17 - 12) \right) \% = 15.5\%$$

The NPV is £81,400 and the IRR is 15.5% (approx). Since the NPV is positive and the IRR exceeds the company's cost of capital, VEN should make the product, subject to the view being taken that the risk is not excessive. Some sensitivity analysis might be carried out on the estimates of cash flows, to assess the sensitivity of the NPV and IRR to realistic potential variations in the estimates.

(c)

Year	Cash inflows £'000	Interest rate multiplier	Amount when reinvested £'000
1	275	1.5735	432.7
2	245	1.4049	344.2
3	245	1.2544	307.3
4	245	1.12	274.4
5	385	1	385.0
			1743.6

MIRR present value factor year 5 = 908/1743.6 = 0.521

MIRR = approximately 14% (0.519 is 14%)

As the MIRR is greater than the company's cost of capital, the recommendation in (b) does not change.

(d) REPORT

To: Board of VEN
From: Management accountant
Subject: Investment in IT system
Date: 14 May 20X4

1 Introduction

This report will attempt to explain some of the benefits of implementing a new computer based production monitoring system.

2 Increase in contribution per unit

Increased contribution per unit will require the lowering of the variable costs of production, and/or an increase in the selling price. VEN's variable costs comprise raw materials, machine usage and labour.

2.1 **Concentrate on more profitable lines**

The system will provide **more accurate costing information** enabling VEN to accurately monitor the contribution obtained from each type of product. Less profitable lines may require an adjustment in price – or if this is not sustainable VEN may consider ceasing production of those types. Production could then be focused on lines that make higher contributions.

2.2 **Improved product**

The use of IT to monitor the input mix and production process will enable the company to increase the **quality of the toys** being produced. Higher quality toys should allow VEN to charge a **higher price** – although some education of customers as to the improved quality and hence better overall value would be required.

2.3 **Reduced waste**

Computer-aided measurement of raw materials will **cut down raw material usage**. This will reduce the cost per unit, and increase contribution per unit.

2.4 **Reduced over-time cost**

The increased automation and accuracy of the production process should **reduce the number of hours** production staff need to produce the same volume of toys. This saving will lower cost per unit.

2.5 **Reduced machine downtime and repair costs**

Machines will be monitored by the computer system which will build up a profile of the history of each machine. **Maintenance schedules** can be more **accurately monitored** reducing break-downs. Any problems should be seem before they develop into costly repairs. Minimising machine downtime and repair costs will decrease the cost per unit.

3 **Fixed costs**

Fixed costs do not change with changes in the level of production. VEN's fixed costs include administration staff, rent, rates, office power etc.

3.1 **Production overheads**

In the long-term **fewer machines** may be required as the efficiency of each machine increases - meaning more machine hours can be obtained from a smaller number of machines. This would reduce the amount of factory space required, reducing the associated fixed costs of rent and rates assuming the freed up space can be sold, or income obtained for its alternate use.

3.2 **Staff**

Additional staff will be required to look after the **computer system**, raising costs. This increase will be more than off-set by the **reduction in production staff** costs referred to earlier.

3.3 **Distribution costs**

The inclusion of customer and distribution details in the system will allow for better **co-ordination of deliveries**. The overall number of delivery vehicles and drivers may fall, reducing fixed costs.

50 Canada

Text references. NPV using foreign exchange cash flows is explained in Chapter 18. International debt finance is discussed in Chapter 6 and new product development in Chapter 17.

Top tips. Both the calculations and the discussion are straightforward, and are well established questions in this paper. The adjusted discount rate is computed in the same manner as converting a real discount rate to a nominal one.

It is important in (b) to relate the discussion to Canada; political risk is unlikely to be a big issue when investing in Canada, so is worth no more than a brief mention.

Business strategy knowledge is handy in (c) although you should have picked up the majority of marks if you demonstrated how product development should be a logical process.

(c)(ii) needs a discussion of internal hedging techniques.

Easy marks. If you remembered the product development cycle, (c) should be straightforward.

(a) **Method (i)**

	0	1	Year 2	3	4
Investment C$'000	(150)				50
After tax cash flows C$'000		60	60	60	45
Net cash C$'000	(150)	60	60	60	95
Exchange rate	1.700	1.785	1.874	1.968	2.066
Net cash €'000	(88.24)	33.61	32.02	30.49	45.98
14% discount factors	1.000	0.877	0.769	0.675	0.592
PV in €'000	(88.24)	29.48	24.62	20.58	27.22
NPV in €'000	**13.66**				

Method (ii)

Adjusted discount rate: equivalent discount rate in C$, allowing for 5% appreciation of the euro, is given by $1 + r = 1.14 \times 1.05 = 1.197$. Discount rate = 19.7%.

	0	1	Year 2	3	4
Net cash C$'000	(150)	60	60	60	95
19.7% discount factors	1.000	0.835	0.698	0.583	0.487
PV C$'000	(150)	50.10	41.88	34.98	46.27
NPV C$'000	23.23				
Exchange rate	1.700				
NPV €'000	**13.66**				

The adjusted discount rate is computed in the **same way** as a **nominal discount rate** is computed from a real discount rate and an inflation rate.

To provide a 14% rate on return and to cope with a 5% annual strengthening of the euro, a dollar invested in Canada would have to grow by 14% to $1.14 and by a further 5% to $1.14 \times 1.05 = $1.197. In other words it would have to show a rate of return of 19.7%. The company's cost of capital, translated into Canadian dollars is therefore 19.7%.

In a system of **free floating exchange rates**, if the C$ depreciates by 5% per year against the euro, the cost of borrowing in C$ is likely to be about 5% more expensive than borrowing in euros.

(b) **Finance by borrowing**

The decision to **finance** a **foreign investment** by **borrowing** in the foreign country's currency is influenced by a number of factors, including:

(i)   Ability of the foreign borrowings to act as a **currency hedge** against currency risk

(ii)   **Cost** of the foreign borrowings compared with borrowing in the home currency

(iii) Other factors, including **political risk**

Loan in the same currency

For any income-generating foreign investment there is a risk that the foreign currency **depreciates**, resulting in a reduced value of income when converted to the home currency. If, however, borrowings are taken out in the **same currency** as that in which the **income** is generated, then the **reduced income** is at least partially offset by reduced **loan interest costs**. It should be noted, however, that this hedging effect also **reduces** the chances of **currency gains**: if the foreign currency appreciates, then the increased value of income is offset by an increased loan interest cost when converted to the home currency.

Unexpected losses

In the example, the Canadian dollar steadily devalues against the euro. Borrowing in Canadian dollars would therefore enable currency risk to be managed better than if borrowing is arranged in euros. However, in a system of free floating exchange rates, if the C$ depreciates by 5% per year against the euro, the cost of borrowing in C$ is likely to be about 5% **more expensive than borrowing** in euros. This **increased interest cost** will take away the advantage of the devaluation of the C$ loan. If currencies always moved in predictable ways, there would be little advantage in financing the Canadian investment with a Canadian loan. However, currency **devaluations** can sometimes be **unexpected** and much larger than predicted. It is to prevent these **unexpected losses** that hedging using a foreign loan is recommended.

Cost of foreign loans

The **cost of foreign loans** may be higher than the theoretical equivalent cost of a domestic loan because the company does not have such a **good credit standing** in the foreign country. Better rates may be obtained from the **euromarkets** or by arranging a **currency loan swap**. Care should be taken to match the duration of the loan with the **expected duration** of the project (4 years in this question), unless further foreign investments are anticipated. A further consideration is the availability of **tax savings** on the loan interest. The effect on the company's **overall tax charge needs** to be included in the decision process.

Impact of political risk

For countries with high political risk, which may impose exchange controls, or even expropriate assets, **borrowing** in the **local currency** is recommended to **offset** investment losses which might result from political action.

(c) **Product development process**

(i)   **Idea generation**

PG should adopt a **systematic procedure** to **generate new product ideas** based on scanning its marketing environment to identify new opportunities. This should be supported by a **programme of marketing research** which is integrated with research and development. New ideas can also be generated from employee suggestions, the R&D function or simply by observing competitive activity and listening to customers.

(ii)   **Screening of new ideas**

This process should analyse each idea in terms of **prescribed criteria** including its potential development, the market potential, its likely product life cycle, financial and other resources required, its contribution and fit relative to overall company strategy, PG's capability to market the product effectively and the likely return on investment.

(iii) **Concept development and testing**

The ideas need to be developed into **conceptual products** which meet identified customer needs and can be packaged to sell to market segments in viable quantities.

(iv) **Marketing strategy**

A **draft marketing plan** then needs to be produced to indicate short and long-term sales, profit and market share objectives, together with details of the marketing mix.

(v) **Business analysis**

Subject to favourable reactions to concept testing, the next step is to undertake **more detailed evaluation**. This would involve more comprehensive marketing research, a detailed competitor analysis and a full analysis of the resources required to launch successfully and achieve the sales targets. The **market analysis** should determine the degree of market attractiveness, the level of competitiveness, growth rates and the longer-term potential. **Sales forecasts** are needed of initial uptakes and the level of replacement sales, to facilitate more accurate operational plans.

(vi) **Product development and finalisation**

Prototypes of the **new product** need to be produced, tested and modified as necessary.

(vii) **Test marketing**

The product can be tested with a **selected customer** or customers and/or in a particular geographic region. It can involve simple trial or be supported by testing various marketing mixes to see which has the most effect on sales.

(viii) **Commercialisation**

Essentially these are decisions taken after successful test marketing on **when to launch, where to launch**, which initial groups should be targeted and **how** it should be launched.

(ix) **Post-launch evaluation**

The **launch** itself needs to be **tracked** and performance against targets evaluated, together with competitors' reactions. **Modifications to the marketing** may be required and decisions will need to be made as to which **further groups/regions** the **new product** should be **marketed**.

51 IT

Text reference. Investment appraisal issues are discussed in Chapters 18 and 19.

Top tips. One problem with this question is that the requirements are inter-related and there is a tendency to repeat points from one section to the next. This should be avoided. Do not forget to give a simple description of the subject of each section (i.e. WACC, certainty-equivalents, payback, etc) as marks for doing this are easier to gain than for discussion of the relevance of the techniques, which should consider assumptions, calculation difficulties and how they deal with risk.

The essential differences between the companies are that HS is a quoted multinational with foreign investments in a range of risk categories and IT is a private single risk category firm with no foreign trade, whose directors are also the shareholders. Note the headings under which tax is discussed in (d).

> **Easy marks.** (a) and (c) represent mainstream discussion topics, and you may expect to comment on the limitations of the techniques even if you're not specifically asked to do so.
>
> The examiner's report included the tip that 'Time management can be used to good effect here ... balance a good discussion of what you know well with a briefer discussion of aspects of which you are less knowledgeable'. Marks for this and many other questions are likely to be 0.5 to 2 or 3 marks **per point** depending upon the depth, quality, **and relevance** of discussion.
>
> **Examiner's comments.** Good answers related the brief company details to the question; the vital point was that the size and circumstances of each company would influence how useful each technique was. Common mistakes included irrelevant detailed calculations of WACC, a lack of understanding of certainty equivalents and adjusted discount rates, and a failure to relate answers to the information given in the question.

(a)   **Use of weighted average cost of capital as a discount rate**

The weighted average cost of capital (WACC) is the average of the company's existing cost of equity and cost of debt capital, using the value of the shares and debt as weights. As a discount rate this is only useful if:

(i)   The project under investigation has roughly the **same risk** as the average for the company's existing business.

(ii)   Finance for the project is raised in roughly the **same proportions** as the existing capital structure.

(iii)   The project is **small** compared with **existing business**.

WACC and HS

For HS, although the WACC is easy to estimate, it is of little use for **appraisal** of **new projects**, which are unlikely to bear average risk because the company has diversified interests. Also, finance raised for projects will often involve **foreign currency loans** which are difficult to handle properly using WACC. A more suitable technique would be to compute a specific cost of equity for the new project based on its **estimated systematic risk** and to use this as a base case discount rate in an **adjusted present value** (APV) computation, which could allow separately for the financing method used.

WACC and IT

The WACC concept is more likely to be appropriate for IT because the company has no foreign **investments or trade** and is more of a **single-product firm**, which implies that most projects will bear similar risk. The problem for IT is that the **cost of equity**, and hence the WACC, is **difficult to estimate** because the company does not have quoted shares. One method of estimating IT's cost of equity would be to use the **figures from quoted companies** which are in IT's precise business. However, such companies are often difficult to find because most of them are more diversified than IT.

(b)   **The use of certainty equivalents compared with using an adjusted discount rate**

When using the certainty equivalent method, **individual cash flows** are **adjusted** to allow for **risk** and then discounted at the risk free rate of interest. The certainty equivalent method is theoretically **sounder** than **adjusting the discount rate** because **increases to the discount rate** have a **disproportionate effect** on later cash flows. Also, the **risk** of different categories of cash flows in a project may **vary**, and this is more likely to be brought into a certainty equivalent calculation than by using the adjusted discount rate method, where several discount rates would be needed.

Usefulness for HS

The method is more appropriate for HS which has **international projects** with **significant variations** to the **systematic risk** of its **cash flows** and where experts are able to appraise projects on behalf of shareholders who have no management role.

Usefulness for IT

As stated above, IT is probably more of a single-product firm in which there are no large variations in project risk. IT does **not need the level of sophistication** offered by the certainty-equivalent method, particularly as it is a private company where most of the shareholders are probably also managers and need to understand the basis on which investment decisions are being made.

(c) **Payback and accounting rate of return compared with DCF techniques**

Payback

The **payback period** is the **time taken for a project to repay** its investment outlay. The method is too simplistic to be used in isolation for investment appraisal because it ignores the time value of money and ignores cash flows after the payback period. If used at all, the payback method is better used as a **constraint on investments** rather than as a prime decision tool. For example, a constraint rule such as 'no project with a payback period of more than 5 years should be considered' is better than a decision rule such as 'choose the project with the shortest payback period', which would favour short-termism in decision making. In effect, the payback method assumes that time is the greatest determinant of risk, which is untrue in many cases.

Accounting rate of return

The accounting rate of return (ARR), which measures **average accounting profits** generated by a project compared with its **investment outlay**, appears at first sight to offer a useful method of computing project return. However, the returns are **not cash-based** and cannot therefore be compared with interest rates or costs of capital, and no allowance is made for the 'time' value of money. Also, **risk analysis** is not a specific component of the calculations and is often **ignored** when using this method.

DCF techniques

Discounted cash flow (DCF) techniques are technically superior in all ways to both payback and ARR because they are **cash based**, and **allow for risk** and the **time value of money**. The only stated advantages of payback and ARR are that they are simple and easy to understand.

HS and IT's position

For HS, this argument is irrelevant as the company employs professional decision makers. For IT, as noted above, it is important that the director/shareholders understand the decision making method, and this factor accounts for the relative popularity of ARR/payback with smaller companies. However, the fact that a method is popular does not necessarily make it useful, and the directors of IT would be better learning how to use DCF appraisal if they do not already do so.

(d) **The influence and effects of taxation on investment decisions**

HS

(i) **Minimisation of liability**

For HS, which trades internationally and probably has foreign subsidiaries, taxation is likely to be payable in several countries. The company will need to **plan tax centrally** and will probably use a number of devices to **minimise its total liability**, including transfer pricing policy, royalty charging and negotiation of concessions with foreign governments.

(ii) **Impact on investment**

When appraising new projects, these factors must be taken into consideration. For example, tax may have a major impact on where a **new investment** is **located** (eg a country may be offering 'tax holidays' for foreign investors), whether a '**tax haven**' country is used to collect dividends from foreign subsidiaries, and the **legal form** in which payments are moved from one country to another (eg as dividends, interest or transfer prices). Methods used by the company to minimise tax may have adverse consequences for other stakeholders, such as minority joint venture partners, and all these factors must be considered.

IT

(i) **Minimisation of liability**

For IT, the **major tax objective** is to **minimise** the **tax liabilities** of the **shareholder/managers**. These people have a choice as to how they take cash from the company for their own use, including salaries, benefits in kind, dividends and services rendered by partnerships or other private businesses they own. These factors will affect all marginal investment decisions in the sense that if tax can be lowered, the cost of equity capital is less, and more investments become worthwhile.

(ii) **Impact on investment**

Specific **tax saving opportunities** may also be available for categories of investment that IT is interested in, for example **tax holidays** or **accelerated tax depreciation** for socially desirable projects. The decision of whether to lease or buy investment assets will also depend partly on the tax implications.

52 GH

Text references. Investment appraisal calculations are explained in Chapter 18.

Top tips. In (a) the correct approach matters more than the exact numerical answers, which will be affected by whether you choose to use interest rate parity or purchasing power parity theory. The main point is that the two discount rates should give the same answer.

(b) brings out a number of important (but sometimes forgotten) points about dealing with international operations risk. Firstly if you are asked about risks in specific countries or regions, try not to make misleading assumptions – it is simply not true for instance that countries outside Europe and North America are automatically subject to political instability. Also important are methods other than derivatives for limiting currency risk. Your answer needs to discuss all elements (receipts and payments) that determine net returns, and describe how each might vary unfavourably **and** favourably.

2-3 marks would be available for each of the main elements in (a) (spot rates, NPV), and a couple of marks would be available for purchasing and interest rate parity.

Easy marks. The discussion on currency risk and the simpler hedging methods in (b) is fairly straightforward. Don't assume that such discussions will be confined to Paper P3 Risk and Control Strategy. Knowledge from that paper is assumed here, and may have to be brought into discussion questions, though not on a much more complicated level than here.

Examiner's comments. In (a) some candidates failed to calculate NPV by dividing the foreign currency cash flows at the spot rate. Some candidates also incorrectly inflated the cash flows. In (b) some candidates failed to realise that not every area outside Europe is highly volatile. Not all candidates recognised that (c) was about funding methods, not hedging strategies.

(a) (i) Using the first method it is necessary to estimate **future exchange rates**. If purchasing power parity is used, the Danish kroner will be expected to depreciate each year by the factor 1.04/1.03, ie 1.00971:

Exchange rates:

Year 0: 8.5
Year 1: $8.5 \times 1.00971 = 8.583$
Year 2: $8.583 \times 1.00971 = 8.666$
Year 3: $8.666 \times 1.00971 = 8.750$

The project cash flows are discounted as follows:

	Year			
	0	*1*	*2*	*3*
Cash DKr million	(80.00)	35.50	42.50	45.00
Exchange rate DKr/$	8.500	8.583	8.666	8.750
Cash $ million	(9.41)	4.14	4.90	5.14
WACC 15% factors	1.000	0.870	0.756	0.658
PV $ million	(9.41)	3.60	3.70	3.38

The project net present value is **$1.27 million**.

> **Top tips.** If interest rate parity were used to predict exchange rates instead of purchasing power parity, the Danish kroner would be expected to depreciate each year by a factor of 1.06/1.05 = 1.009524. Following similar calculations would give a project NPV of $1.28 million.

(ii)   Using the second method, the **adjusted discount rate** needs to be **computed** first.

Using the formula

$$(1 + \text{Kr discount rate}) = 1 + \$ \text{ discount rate} \times \left(\frac{1 + \text{Kr interest rate}}{1 + \$ \text{interest rate}} \right)$$

$$= 1.15 \times \left(\frac{1.06}{1.05} \right)$$

$$= 16.10\%, \text{ say } 16\%$$

Discounting the Danish kroner cash flows at this rate and converting the NPV at today's spot rate gives the following result.

	Year			
	0	*1*	*2*	*3*
Cash DKr million	(80.00)	35.50	42.50	45.00
16% factors	1.000	0.862	0.743	0.641
PV	(80.00)	30.60	31.58	28.85
NPV	11.03			
Exchange rate DKr/$	8.500			
NPV	1.3			

The project net present value is **$1.30 million**, which matches the result in method (i) above.

The two methods are based on related theories:

(i)   **Purchasing power parity**

A country with a **higher inflation rate** will have a currency that tends to **devalue** to maintain purchasing power parity between countries.

(ii)   **Interest rate parity**

This predicts that future exchange rates are influenced by interest rates in the two countries. A country with a higher interest rate will have currency which sells at a discount in the forward markets and this will tend to work towards future **devaluation** of the currency.

Both theories are only approximate in the short term and are dependent on floating exchange rates and markets free of government interference.

(b)   **Currency risk in Denmark**

The original idea of buying and selling goods in Denmark had a natural in-built currency hedge, as only the operating margin is subject to currency risk. If the policy is changed so that some goods are purchased in the USA, the whole DKr sales price for these goods becomes sensitive to **currency fluctuations**, causing the potential for widely fluctuating profits.

Currency risk in Far East

The currency risk becomes even higher if half the goods are purchased in the far east. Not only may the **currency fluctuations be higher** than those of the kroner against the dollar, but there is the potential for a double-negative if the far eastern currency/ies strengthens while the kroner weakens against the dollar. In a mass retail operation, profit margins are very low and currency fluctuations can easily remove them altogether.

Other issues in Far East

The company may not be dealing with just one company in the Far East, but with a number of different regimes. The **legal** and **tax situation** may differ and there may be **differing rates of inflation** and **interest rates**, complicating attempts to use **interest rate and purchasing power parity.**

Hedging

Although the company has the option of accepting currency risk, which has the potential for gains as well as losses, it is safer for shorter term planning to hedge against it. This will mean **matching kroner income against costs** so far as possible and can be done in a number of different ways.

(i)   The cost of the goods purchased in dollars can be financed by **borrowing** an **amount** in kroners equal to the value of goods purchased and **converting** the money immediately **to dollars**. If the kroner declines, the resulting debt will be devalued to offset loss of income.

(ii)   The purchase price of far eastern goods could be **negotiated in kroners**, which would **shift** the **currency risk** onto the **supplier**. Alternatively the price could be negotiated in Japanese yen, or Singapore dollars, say, and forward rate currency contracts could be taken out to purchase that currency. An increase in DKr borrowings could alternatively be used to purchase the far eastern currency and leave it on deposit as a hedge.

The **cost** of **hedging foreign currency transactions** can be **significant**, but hopefully this is paid for by reduced purchase prices from far eastern suppliers. The decision to finance the subsidiary using Danish debt should not be changed, as this is useful for reducing currency risk (see (c) below).

(c)   **Devaluation**

If Danish inflation turns out to be higher than forecast, there would be pressure on the kroner to **devalue against the dollar**. This is the theory of purchasing power parity (see (a)): a country with a higher inflation rate will have a currency that tends to devalue to maintain purchasing power parity between countries.

Effect on NPV

The financial value (NPV) of the Danish subsidiary would therefore tend to fall in pound terms. However, the subsidiary may have scope to **raise prices** in line with **inflation**, which would restore value. **Costs** may also **change** by varying amounts. The practicalities of increasing prices need to considered carefully, taking into account the competition.

Usefulness of loan

In this scenario, the usefulness of **financing the subsidiary** with a DKr loan is demonstrated. The depreciation in the value of income from the Danish subsidiary would be partially offset by **devalued loan interest payments**. If the kroner remained low, the eventual repayment of the loan would also be cheaper in pound terms.

53 Question with student answer: QE

<u>REPORT</u>

To: Directors of QE
From: Finance Manger – QE
Date: 1st May 2005
Subject: Potential acquisitions

This report will aim to evaluate potential acquisitions, and to recommend the most suitable acquisition for QE. It will also discuss the directors decisions and compare growth by acquisition and organic growth.

<u>Acquisition choice</u>

Appendix one and two show the net present values and profitability indexes for all three companies proposed for acquisition.

All three companies show a positive net present value, however the profitability index of company CD is only 9.5%, compared with the shareholders requirement of 12% return on all investments, this acquisition would not be viable.

Companies AB and EF both have a PI above the shareholders requirement and would therefore be viable.

Company AB would require the largest investment of £1.1 million and would leave QE with only £300k cash surplus to re-invest.

On this basis, I think QE would be wise to invest just £650k in company EF, as their cash surplus would be larger and the return would still be 16.6%. This is not much less than the return from company AB of 17.5% and I think it would reduce risk.

<u>12% discount factor</u>

There is little information regarding the markets that the three target companies operate in, therefore it is difficult to tell if they all represent the same business risk as QE.

If the business risk differs the discount factor of 12% should be adjusted to represent the increase or decrease in risk.

However, in these circumstances, the use of 12% provides QE with a rough view of the appropriateness of these three companies using a consistent basis.

I would advise QE, before making a final decision to analyse the rises associated with these three companies and re-evaluate the figures using a more appropriate discount factor.

<u>Surplus cash</u>

QE's long term debt to equity ratio is currently high compared to other companies in the industry.

Debt is usually cheaper to hold than equity, so I think QE should retain an average holding of debt. However, the cash surplus should be used to reduce QE's gearing level in line with the industry average.

It is unclear what value of debt is currently held by QE, and what the industry average would be, but I would suggest that all of the surplus cash £0.75 million (£1.4m – £0.65m) is used to repay debt.

If this is too much, a reasonable amount of debt should be repaid and further investment opportunities should be sought for the balance.

Directors decisions

Invest rather than repay debt

The decision to invest funds rather than repay debt, is focused towards growth of the business, as future cash flows will enable QE to repay it's debts in the long term.

However, in the short term, QE needs to be able to repay interest on it's debts, and QE need to be able to ensure that it is able to keep up the short-term repayments as well as investing .

The debt providers of QE will become concerned if QE's interest cover falls as they will be worried that the debt may become "bad".

QE should consider using the surplus cash to both re-invest and repay some debt as suggested above. I believe this would be the optimum solution for QE.

Limit investment to cash purchases as opposed to raising new capital

QE currently have too high a debt to equity ratio, therefore it would not be sensible for them to raise new capital in the form of debt.

QE currently have two viable investment options that would return 17.5% and 16.6% over the next three years, however, QE do not have enough cash to invest in both projects.

QE would only have to raise a further £350,000 to invest in both projects and this could be done through an equity issue.

However, this is a relatively small value to raise via an equity issue and QE must consider the costs of this issue and the time it would take to raise the funds.

This new issue could also potentially dilute control of the current shareholders of QE.

If QE were to raise this additional finance and acquire both companies, it would be unable to repay any of it's debt. With the current debt to equity ratio being so high. This could hinder shareholders desire to invest any further funds into QE.

Therefore, I think this decision made by the directors is entirely appropriate at this time.

Growth by acquisition v organic growth

Advantages

Growth by acquisition means taking control of an existing company that is currently operating within an existing market. Therefore, it would be much quicker to expand into a new market via acquisition rather than organically.

By acquiring a company, you gain all the expertise and knowledge of the market, as opposed to having to develop these skills internally. This would make it much quicker for the company to gain success in the new market.

Disadvantages

Acquiring a company usually requires a large cash outlay at the start. This may hinder the companies ability to further invest in the company to make changes.

The strategies of the acquired company will have to be brought in line with those of the predator company. This can take time and could create conflict between management and employees.

<u>Appendix one</u>

<u>NPV of three proposed acquisition</u>

<u>AB</u>

Time	Cashflow	12% DF	PV
	£'000		£'000
0	(1,100)	1	(1,100)
1	(100)	0.893	(89)
2	750	0.797	598
3	1,100	0.712	<u>783</u>
			<u>192</u>

<u>CD</u>

Time	Cashflow	12% DF	PV
	£'000		£'000
0	(500)	1	(550)
1	125	0.893	112
2	275	0.797	219
3	380	0.712	<u>271</u>
			<u>52</u>

<u>QE</u>

Time	Cashflow	12% DF	PV
	£'000		£'000
0	(650)		(650)
1	200	0.8	179
2	325	0.7	259
3	450	0.7	<u>320</u>
			<u>108</u>

<u>Appendix two</u>

<u>Profitability index for three proposed acquisitions</u>

	<u>AB</u>	<u>CD</u>	<u>QE</u>
NPV (£'000)	192	52	108
Acquisition price	1,100	550	650
PI (%)	17.5	9.5	16.6

BPP answer

Text references. The profitability index method is explained in Chapter 19 and acquisition issues are discussed in Chapter 16.

Top tips. You would normally get a couple of marks for using an appropriate format, that is the answer should be a report, divided into the four bullet point headings in the question, and including main computations as an appendix.

In (a) the profitability index method would be used to decide which investment to undertake, as capital is rationed for the period in which the decision is taken. (b) represents important knowledge about alternative uses of funds. (c) stresses the importance of finding the right level of gearing. (c) and (d) also bring in non-financial factors (will acquisitions take up too much management time? Will synergies be realised?)

Student answer. The student answer should score well, around 20 marks. The calculations were all correct, the report laid out in correct format, and there's good use of headers and short paragraphs to make points clear to the marker. In (a) the student fails to discuss the importance of (a) having the largest NPV; PI does not represent a return on investment that compares with the required 12%; thus CD is incorrectly rejected and the answer fails to consider therefore the possibility of investing in both CD and EF.

The student limited his mark scoring opportunities in (b) by concentrating too much on the repayment of debt and failing to consider other possibilities. (c) would score well, though the discussion in the second part needed to cover wider organisational issues as well as financing. (d) also would have scored well, despite omitting to mention acquiring the target's customers.

Easy marks. Organic growth vs acquisition should be a very straightforward discussion.

Marking scheme

			Marks
(a)	Calculations	7	
	Discount rate	3	10
(b)	One mark per use		4
(c)	Up to 2 marks per relevant point max		6
(d)	Up to 2 marks per relevant point max		5
			25

To: Board of Directors
From: Financial Manager
Date: 12 May 20X0

(a) **Evaluation of potential acquisitions**

This report reviews the three potential acquisitions which are at present under consideration and comments on aspects relating to them.

Financial appraisal of the investments

Given that there is a ceiling of £1.4 million available for investing in three potential businesses which have a total cost of £2.3 million, the principles of investment appraisal using **capital rationing** should be applied. The following results summarise calculations which are attached in the Appendix:

Company	Initial outlay	Net present value	NPV/outlay
	£'000	£'000	
AB	1,100	192	17.5%
CD	550	52	9.5%
EF	650	108	16.6%

Highest NPV

The goal is to achieve the **highest net present value (NPV)** from a combination of projects that can be afforded. The profitability index (NPV/outlay) shows that AB offers the highest NPV per £ invested. If AB is accepted, both others must be rejected. The only other alternative is to accept both of CD and EF, which would give a total NPV of £160,000, which is significantly less than the £192,000 generated by AB.

Conclusion. Accept the acquisition of AB and reject the other two investments.

Discount rates

In making this decision it is assumed that 12% per annum in real terms is a **valid discount** rate for all the projects. Although this is the normal 'hurdle rate' applied to all our company's projects, in practice the **discount rate used** should vary with each project, depending on its risk. Also, in a situation of capital rationing, the **opportunity cost of capital increases**, representing the rate of return foregone on investment opportunities that must be rejected because of the shortage of cash. The computations may therefore need to be reworked using different discount rates.

(b) **Use of surplus cash not needed for investment**

If AB is acquired, there will be a £300,000 cash surplus left over, which cannot be invested in CD or EF. This should not be left idle, but should be applied in the best possible way(s) from the following:

(i) **Repaying** some of the **company's debt** which, we agree, is at a high level at the moment

(ii) **Placing** some of the **cash on deposit** or in short term investments to produce enough for the required investment in Company AB in one year, which is estimated at £100,000; although an investment in the money market produces a return below the company's cost of capital, this is acceptable if it eases a further cash restriction in one year's time

(iii) **Investing in increased working capital,** if this is thought to be beneficial

(iv) **Increasing the dividend** to shareholders

(c) **Comments on previous Board decisions relating to this investment**

I have been asked to comment on:

(i) **Invest rather than to repay debt**

There is no harm in having a higher gearing ratio than other companies in the industry unless it is thought that there is a significant chance of difficulty in **meeting debt obligations** in the event of a downturn in profits. Debt servicing costs have the advantage of **attracting tax relief**, whereas dividend payments do not. Since you have weighed up the risks involved and have decided that the present gearing level is acceptable, and I have no grounds on which to disagree with your judgement.

(ii) **Reject a further issue of funds to finance the remaining investment opportunities**

All investments with a positive NPV will increase shareholder wealth. There is therefore **no financial reason** for rejecting the acquisition of CD and EF, which could be financed by a further issue of shares or debt. Bearing in mind the company's high level of gearing, the most suitable financing method would be a **share issue**. In this way, the three companies could be acquired by suitable **combinations of cash and shares** offered to their shareholders. However, there are organisational and managerial grounds for rejecting too many acquisitions at the same time. They might **divert management time** and **adversely affect the core business**. I ask you to consider further these investment opportunities in the light of these suggestions.

(d) **Advantages of growth by acquisition**

Acquiring an **existing company** is a speedier method of entering a new business than setting up a project using internal resources, because an acquired business will already have **customers** and, hopefully, **goodwill**. An acquisition also effectively **eliminates a competitor** and may **allow higher profitability**. Other advantages may come from the **combination of complementary resources** of the acquiring and acquired companies.

Problems of growth by acquisition

Frequently a **significant premium** must be **paid** in order to **encourage existing shareholders** to sell, or to outbid a rival. This may make it difficult to show a **respectable return** on the cost of the acquisition.

The acquired company may **not produce the exact product or service** that the acquirer needs, or may need **significant investment** before it conforms to quality requirements.

Management problems are also quite common, particularly when the acquiring and acquired companies have different organisational cultures. **Disputes** may case the loss of key staff members, resulting in reduced quality or even in the establishment of competing businesses.

Appendix – computation of NPV and profitability index

		Year				
	0	1	2	3	NPV	Profitability index*
12% factors	1.000	0.893	0.797	0.712		
AB	£'000	£'000	£'000	£'000		
Cash flows	(1,100)	-100	750	1100		
DCF	(1,100)	-89	598	783	192	17.5%
CD						
Cash flows	(550)	125	275	380		
DCF	(550)	112	219	271	52	9.5%
EF						
Cash flows	(650)	200	325	450		
DCF	(650)	179	259	320	108	16.6%

* Profitability index = NPV/initial outlay.

54 KH

Text references. NPV calculations are explained in Chapter 18 and risks of international investment are discussed in Chapter 17.

Top tips. To conform with the information given in the question bullet points, calculations in (a) must be based on nominal cash flows converted to dollars and discounted at 20%. The recommendation to proceed should be accompanied by a brief description of the purchasing power parity theory of exchange rates and notes on the estimation uncertainties and lengthy project payback period.

The most important elements of the calculations in (a) were the determination of the net present value and the SA cash flows in US $ (worth two marks).

(b) is a fairly typical example of a discussion question where you would be awarded up to three to four marks for every relevant point. However a short list of political risks would not be enough. The examiner will expect you to discuss them in enough detail to show why they're relevant, linking into the scenario (for example it's quite justifiable to suggest that exchange rate volatility indicates potential economic problems), and suggesting appropriate remedies (risk reduction by hedging techniques or borrowing in the country).

Don't be surprised to see a similar question to (b) in the Paper P3 exam, as the risks of international investment is an area where the syllabuses definitely overlap.

Easy marks. You should be able to gain 6-7 marks by discussing common economic and political risks, though you need to think a bit more widely (and use your Business Strategy knowledge) to come up with the other risks.

Examiner's comments. Attempts at (a) were generally satisfactory, although few were completely correct. Some answers had very confused calculations and lacked recommendations; other, more specific mistakes, included failure to inflate South American cash flows to nominal values before conversion, using real rather than nominal rates and failure to consider terminal values. (b) was generally answered better by non-UK candidates; some answers discussed hedging to the exclusion of other risks (a brief mention of hedging would have been fine, but no more.)

To: Finance Director
From: Financial Manager
Date: 4 December 20X1
Subject: Evaluation of potential acquisition of South American stores group

(a)   **Net present value of the investment**

The financial evaluation of the South American project is based on estimates of the future nominal cash flows of the investment, in both South America and USA. All foreign cash flows are **converted to dollars** and the total is **discounted** at a **risk adjusted cost of capital** of 20% per annum. The theory of **purchasing power parity** has been used to estimate future currency exchange rates. This predicts that if currencies are allowed to float freely on the market, they will **adjust in the long run to compensate** for differences in countries' **inflation rates**. The results show that the project has an **expected net present value** of nearly $30 million, which indicates that it is worthwhile and should add to shareholder value.

Risks and uncertainties

However, the risks and uncertainties which need to be appreciated include:

(i)   **Large margins** of **potential error** in the **exchange rate predictions**
(ii)   A **slow payback**: in present value terms the project will probably not break even until year 6 or 7
(iii) The **political risks** discussed below

Calculations

Computation of expected future exchange rates using the theory of Purchasing Power Parity

The current exchange rate is SA30 =$1. If the rates of inflation in South America and the USA are estimated as 40% and 4% indefinitely, future exchange rates will be expected to increase by the factor 1.4/1.04 each year:

	Year			
	0	1	2	3
Exchange rate (previous year × 1.4/1.04)	30.00	40.38	54.36	73.18

Discounted cash flows for first three years

	Year			
	0	1	2	3
South American cash flows (in '000):				
In real terms	(1,000,000)	250,000	350,000	450,000
In nominal terms (40% pa inflation)	(1,000,000)	350,000	686,000	1,234,800
Exchange rate	30	40.38	54.36	73.18
Converted to dollars	(33,333)	8,668	12,620	16,873
US cash flows ($'000)				
In real terms	(10,000)	(300)	(400)	(500)
In nominal terms (4% pa inflation)	(10,000)	(312)	(433)	(562)
Total nominal cash flow ($'000)	(43,333)	8,356	12,187	16,311
20% discount factors	1	0.833	0.694	0.579
Present value	(43,333)	6,961	8,458	9,444
Net present value (0-3)				(18,470)

Years 4 to perpetuity

Taking cash flows from year 4 as a constant $16.311 million, the present value of the perpetuity will be:

Valued as at year 3: $16.311m/0.2 = $81.555m

Discounted back to year 0: $81.555 × 0.579 = $47.220m

Total net present value is therefore $47.22m – $18.47m = **$28.75m**

(b)   **Main political risks**

The main political risks that might be faced by the company in the South American country are discussed below, together with suggested counter-strategies.

(i)   **Political instability**

Extreme **political problems** include civil war, prolonged terrorist activities, or expropriation of private (especially foreign-owned) assets by the government. If these situations are likely, investment is unwise, and an alternative country in the region should be chosen. It is recommended that a **detailed political analysis** is undertaken, covering the stability of the present government and the policies of likely alternatives. To counter the risk of extreme threats suddenly arising, it is wise to negotiate as much **loan finance** as possible from institutions in the South American country. This would allow a **swift bankruptcy** and withdrawal from the country in the event of severe difficulties. To counter this strategy, the host government/institutions may require guarantees from our parent company, however.

(ii)   **Economic sanctions**

If the South American government experiences economic difficulties, it may attempt to solve them by taking short term action which is detrimental to our investment.

(1)   **Raising local taxes**

Our best counter-strategies are to **negotiate tax concessions** in advance and to **use transfer pricing strategies**, including royalties and management charges, to minimise the South American taxable profits and dividends.

(2)   **Imposition of exchange controls**

Examples include non-convertibility of the local currency, or prevention of repatriation of funds. There are a number of measures we can take to minimise this risk, including making **extensive use of local currency loans** for financing, and **arranging currency swaps** and **back-to back loans** with other multinational companies and banks with complementary cash needs.

(iii) **Lack of protection for intangible assets**

As in a number of regions we may experience a **lack of political will** to assist us in enforcement of our intellectual property rights. We need to ensure that **appropriate patents and trade marks** are taken out and to be prepared to take **legal action** against those who attempt to infringe them. However our major strategy in this area should be to build a strong **barrier to entry** by competitors by **promoting our brand image** strongly.

(iv)   **Action groups**

There is also a potential risk posed by the growing number of action groups who are opposed to our company and/or multinational corporations generally. These may succeed in influencing **local public opinion** and/or the host government. Difference in customs, laws and language may also lead to problems. Our counter-strategy should involve **development of a public relations campaign**, including charitable donations, and the appointment of competent local partners to assist us with interpretation of the regulatory and cultural environment.

55 DAC

> **Text references.** NPV calculations are explained in Chapter 18 and risks of investments are discussed in Chapter 17.
>
> **Top tips.** This question tests your ability to evaluate foreign income cash flows and the management of the risks involved.
>
> In (a), as the UK inflation rate is not given, but the risk-free interest rates are given for both countries, you have to use the interest rate parity theory to calculate the year-end exchange rates. The answers to (a)(i) and (ii) should be the same, barring a small difference due to rounding.
>
> A common failing of answers to questions such as (b) is failure to mention DAC at all, and providing a discussion of the risks and management of foreign investment in general terms. DAC's situation is more significant in (ii) as you need to make some sort of an assessment of the level of the risks the company faces. Again a question like (b)(ii) could also crop up in P3. Be careful in (iii) not to repeat in detail what you said in (ii) about risks; you should focus on the risks relating to finance rather than the risks relating to the company's market.
>
> **Easy marks.** Most of the arguments in (b)(i) are fairly standard points about the WACC, but the answer does acknowledge how they relate to DAC.

(a)   (i)   **To calculate the sterling NPV of the project**, it is necessary to estimate the year end US$/£ spot rates for the duration of the project. This can be done using the interest rate parity theory as follows.

	Rate at start of year $/£	Adjust by	Closing rate
Year 1	1.6000	× 1.04/1.05	1.5848
Year 2	1.5848	× 1.04/1.05	1.5697
Year 3	1.5697	× 1.04/1.05	1.5547
Year 4	1.5547	× 1.04/1.05	1.5399
Year 5	1.5399	× 1.04/1.05	1.5252

The US$ cash flow can now be converted to sterling and discounted at the sterling required rate of return (14%):

	Year 0	Year 1	Year 2	Year 3	Year 4
Cash flow in US$m	(4.50)	1.75	1.95	2.50	3.50
Closing spot rate	1.6000	1.5848	1.5697	1.5547	1.5399
Cash flow in £m	(2.813)	1.104	1.242	1.608	2.273
14% discount factors	1.000	0.877	0.769	0.675	0.592
Discounted cash flow	(2.813)	0.968	0.955	1.085	1.346

Net present value   **£1.541m**

(ii)   To discount the annual cash flows in US$, it is necessary to calculate the appropriate discount rate to use. This can be done by

Using the interest rate priority formula

$$(1 + \$ \text{ discount factor}) = (1 + £ \text{ discount factor}) \times \frac{(1 + \$ \text{ int rate})}{(1 + £ \text{ int rate})}$$

$$= 1.14 \times \frac{1.04}{1.05}$$

Discount factor = 12.91%, say 13%

The NPV calculated in US$ is as follows.

	Year 0	Year 1	Year 2	Year 3	Year 4
Cash flow in US$m	(4.50)	1.75	1.95	2.50	3.50
13% discount factors	1.000	0.885	0.783	0.693	0.613
Discounted cash flow	(4.500)	1.549	1.527	1.733	2.146
Net present value ($m)	2.455				

NPV in sterling at $1.6/£   **£1.534m**

(b) (i) The **WACC** is valid for use in investment appraisal, given the following **assumptions**.

(1) **New investments** must be **financed by new sources of funds**.

(2) The **cost of capital** to be **applied** to project evaluation must **reflect the marginal cost of new capital**.

(3) The WACC **reflects the company's long-term future capital structure** and capital costs.

Argument in favour of the use of the WACC in investment appraisal

A company's capital structure **changes only very slowly over time**, and therefore the marginal cost of new capital should be roughly equal to the weighted average cost of current capital. If this is correct, then by selecting investments that offer a return above the WACC, the company will increase the market value of its ordinary shares in the long run.

Arguments against the use of the WACC

(1) New investments undertaken by a company might have **different business risk characteristics** from the existing operations. In this situation, the return required by investors might go up or down as a result.

(2) The new finance raised to fund the project might **significantly change the capital structure** and the perceived financial risk of investing in the company.

(3) Where there is a significant proportion of floating rate debt, the WACC will be **constantly varying**, and therefore the WACC at any one point in time will only be an approximation of the true cost of capital.

In an **international situation**, such as that faced by DAC, the drawbacks arising from variations in risk are likely to become more significant. However, it is always difficult to quantify these types of risks objectively, and it is likely that the WACC will continue to be the most appropriate measure. Where quantifying risk is a problem, the company could use additional measures, such as sensitivity analysis, to direct attention to the key areas of concern surrounding the decision.

(ii) The **main risks** that are likely to be encountered by a company moving into a new international market include the following.

(1) **Foreign exchange risks**

Transaction risk. Costs and revenues may be **more volatile** than predicted due to unforeseen movements in exchange rates between the home country and that in which the investment is located. This can be managed by matching costs and revenues as far as possible, and using hedging techniques such as forward exchange contracts.

Translation risk. The **valuation** of the assets to be included in the consolidated balance sheet may **vary** due to **movements in exchange rates**. This is unlikely to be important in the investment decision unless the company is highly geared and close to breaching any borrowing covenants.

(2) **Economic risks**

These arise when **events** occur in the economy of the country that **impact upon the performance of the investment**. For example, a sharp rise in the level of personal taxation may cause a fall in demand for the project. This risk is unlikely to be significant in DAC's case, and there is little that can be done to manage such a situation.

(3) **Geographical separation**

This causes a number of problems in the areas of **communication and control**, and the **recruitment of the appropriate local specialists**. Since DAC is proposing to invest in the USA, these problems are likely to be less significant than in a more remote, less developed, non-English speaking country.

(4) **Political risk**

Where a multinational invests in another country, it may face political risk of **action by that country's government**, which restricts the multinational's freedom. An example is the import restrictions imposed by the USA on the British cashmere industry in retaliation for the EU restrictions on banana imports in 1999. This can be a risk in any country, and again there is little that the company can do to avoid it.

(iii) **DAC** should consider various options when it decides how to obtain finance for its overseas operations.

Retained cash surpluses

DAC could use retained cash balances for investment. The advantages are that there would be no **formalities or issue costs**. The obvious disadvantage is that cash surpluses may not be large enough to finance the level of expansion the directors wish to undertake. The value of the investment may also decline due to exchange movements.

Borrowing in domestic market

Borrowing in DAC's own market may be a cheap source of finance, and DAC will be able to take advantage of **tax shield effects**, being able to claim loan interest on debt. However the terms and amounts available will depend on DAC's credit rating, and DAC will also be subject to **exchange risk.** DAC may however be able to arrange a **currency swap** to mitigate these problems.

Borrowing in US

The main advantage of borrowing in the US is that DAC will limit exchange risk by **matching,** because the **borrowing** is in the **same currency** as the expected revenues. The directors may wish to gear up quite highly on US borrowing. However the availability and terms of finance may be less favourable as DAC is not a well-known borrower

Borrowing in euro-debt

Borrowing on the euromarkets will be cheaper, and DAC would look to borrow dollars in this market, dealing again with the problem of **exchange risk**. Other terms may also be favourable as often euroloans do **not require any security.** It may be quicker to raise the sums required than on the US market. However DAC will require a **good international credit rating** and must have **access to enough hard currency** to be able to **make repayments.**

56 CTC

Text references. Relevant costs and benefits and project management are discussed in Chapter 17.

Top tips. The examiner's comments emphasise the importance of being able to recognise sunk costs, and it's worth setting these out. Although the unusual form of the question may be offputting, in the end it is breakeven analysis, comparing the extra costs with revenue per student and finding the missing figure which is number of students required. (b) emphasises various important factors in project control including staff support and monitoring.

Easy marks. Using knowledge from earlier management accounting papers together with project control principles should have helped you answer (b).

Examiner's comments. Many candidates included sunk costs and excluded benefits such as students taking other courses. Another fundamental error was misallocating costs to time frames. Many candidates failed to answer the question in (b) and few calculated revised break-even numbers.

(a)   Number of student enrolments on ITC course required for viability

The costs and revenues given can be divided into the following groups:

Costs which are irrelevant to the decision

These are:

- **Book value of computers** (not a cash flow)

- **Market research cost** (sunk cost)

- **Existing staff costs** (common to all alternatives)

- **Apportionment of college overheads** (not an incremental cost, total will be common to all alternatives)

Initial investment costs, year 0

	€
Sale of computers foregone: 20 × €100	(2,000)
Upgrade of computers	(15,000)
Staff training and course development	(30,000)
	(47,000)

Annual incremental revenues/costs for the course as a whole

In advance	€	
Additional fees for the 150 'baseline' students @ 360 – 350 = €10	1,500	
Additional costs for the 150 @ 60 – 50 = €10	(1,500)	
	–	These cancel out

In arrears	
Additional directly attributable course costs	(1,000)

Potential additional cost, in advance	
Additional staff member, if students > 200	(10,000)

Incremental revenues/costs per student over 150

In advance	€
Fees	360
Additional benefits to college (assumed in advance)	20
Books and consumables	(60)
	320

Case 1: Student numbers not > 200

	Years	€	8% factor	PV €
Investment costs	0	(47,000)	1	(47,000)
Annual incremental course costs	1 - 4	(1,000)	3.312	(3,312)
				(50,312)
Incremental benefit per student over a four year period	0 - 3	320	3.577	1,145

The **number of additional students** over 150 to cover the investment costs and annual incremental costs is 50,312 / 1,145 = 43.9.

Thus the number of students required on the ITC course for it to be financially beneficial is 150 + 44 = 194 or more up to 200, when the additional staff cost sets in.

Case 2: Student numbers > 200

	Year	€	8% factor	PV
Investment costs	0	(47,000)	1	(47,000)
Additional staff cost (in advance)	0 - 3	(10,000)	3.577	(35,770)
Annual incremental course costs	1 - 4	(1,000)	3.312	(3,312)
				(86,082)

The **number of additional students** over 150 to cover the investment costs, additional staff cost and annual incremental costs is 86,082 / 1,145 = 75.2.

This is 150 + 76 = 226 students.

Summary

The ITC course will be financially viable if enrolments are between 194 and 200 or greater than 226.

(b) **Advice to the governing body of the college**

(i) **Effective monitoring and control of the costs** requires the following approach:

(1) The course should be the **clear responsibility** of a course director who should account to the governing body for its financial results (as well as quality, success, etc).

(2) The course director will need **proper back-up** from the course enrolments department and the accounting department to provide assistance in budgeting, a check on numbers enrolling, cost collection and control over expenditure.

(3) **Budgeting** should be **realistic, not over-optimistic** or **pessimistic**. The course director should involve all relevant parties to gain their views.

(4) The enrolments department and the accounting department should be prepared to **provide daily information** on enrolments and costs during the run-up to the start of the course. In addition to actual results, periodic **'feed-forward' estimates** of the likely final results would be extremely useful for the course director.

(5) **Possible candidates** for the extra part-time staff member should be identified well in advance, so that recruitment can take place swiftly if numbers warrant it.

(6) The course director should **hold regular meetings** with all relevant parties to assess progress. Swift decisions should be made in response to enrolments above or below targets or other unbudgeted factors.

(ii)   **Options available if enrolments are 150 by the enrolment deadline**

The options available are to **cancel the course** or to **run it.** Cancelling is probably not an option if 150 students have enrolled, as it will cause much bad will. It would be better to run the course for one year only and then review the situation as to whether it should be continued.

By the time the **enrolment deadline** has been reached, the money will already have been spent on the course investment costs: **upgrading the computers** and staff training and development, total €45,000. These therefore become sunk costs, and the number of additional students per year over 150 to cover the remaining costs falls to (50,312 – 45,000) / 1,145 = 4.6 students. Thus enrolments of 155 will now cover relevant costs.

The additional 5 students (and more) can probably easily be found by **extending the enrolment deadline** or by some **low-cost advertising.**

57 XZ

Text references. Adjusted present value and project ranking are explained in Chapter 19.

Top tips. (a) must be solved using the adjusted present value method: that is:

- By computing the base case NPV
- Adjusting it for the PV of the financing side effects (interest and issue costs).

The adjusted discount rate is easiest calculated if the APV is already known.

In (b) note that the projects are **indivisible**, which means the eventual solution is found by trial and error.

Even in this primarily numerical question about one third of the marks would be available for discussion. In (a) you need not only to be able to use the adjusted present value method, but also to discuss how helpful it is. In (b) you should bring in problems with the evaluation method, including the very important issue of the need for more information. Note the point also that you would look to invest surplus funds when projects are indivisible.

Easy marks. The discussion points are mostly fairly standard.

Examiner's comments. Weaknesses in (a) included incorrect treatment of issue costs, calculating tax relief for one year only, and failing to calculate an adjusted discount rate.

(a)   **Adjusted present value**

The base case net present value at the appropriate cost of equity capital, 14%, is:

€(3.9 m) + €0.6m/0.14 = €0.386 m.

The debt issued to finance the project is €3.9m + issue costs €0.162m = €4.062m. The financing side effects of the project are:

	€m
Tax shield (Dt = €4.062m × 30%)	1.219
Issue costs	(0.162)
	1.057

The adjusted present value is: €0.386m + €1.057m = **€1.443 million.**

Working

Annual interest is 10% × €4.062m = €0.4062m.

Annual tax savings are 30% × €0.4062m = €0.1219m.

The debt is irredeemable (undated) and interest will last to perpetuity. The present value at 10% of the perpetuity of tax savings is €0.1219m/0.1 = €1.219m.

The main difficulties with the APV technique are:

(a)   **Establishing** a **suitable cost of equity**, for the initial computation as if the project were all-equity financed

(b)   **Identifying all the costs** associated with the method of financing

(c)   **Choosing the correct discount rates** used to discount the costs

The adjusted discount rate of the project

Using the formula

$$k_{adj} = k_{eu}(1 - tL)$$

$$= 14\% \left(1 - \left(0.3 \; \frac{4,062}{1,443 + 4,062}\right)\right)$$

$$= 10.9\%$$

This rate will give the appropriate accept/reject decision for new projects provided that:

(i)   The **new projects** are of **similar risk characteristics** to this one.

(ii)   Finance is **raised** on the **same terms** and in the **same proportions** (ie 100% debt).

Clearly these two conditions are highly unlikely. Also, the adjusted discount rate will not give meaningful present value figures that can be reconciled with theoretical gains in shareholder wealth. It serves only as a 'hurdle rate'.

(b)   **Profitability index**

In a situation of **single period capital rationing**, the **objective** should be to **maximise the net present value** per pound invested. A computation of net present value / initial investment (often called profitability index) for each project shows the following:

Project	NPV/ initial investment	Ranking
1		2
2	0.2118	3
3	0.2305	1

This implies that the company should choose to invest first in project 3, then in project 1 and finally in project 2. However, there is not enough money to invest in all of them, and the projects are indivisible, which implies that only two can be accepted. The solution must be determined by trial and error between the three different combinations.

Choice of projects

A combination of projects 1 and 2 is impossible because total outlay comes to £8.1 million, which is higher than the maximum €7.5 million. The other two combinations show the following results:

	Projects 3 and 1				Projects 3 and 2	
Project	Outlay	NPV		Project	Outlay	NPV
3	2.95	0.68		3	2.95	0.68
1	3.85	0.85		2	4.25	0.90
	6.8	1.53			7.2	1.58
Surplus	0.7				0.3	
	7.5				7.5	

(i)   The **best result is obtained from projects 3 and 2**, with a total NPV of €1.58 million compared with €1.53 million for 3 and 1.

(ii)   Although 3 and 1 is a **relatively more profitable combination** (in terms of profitability index), it does not use up sufficient of the available funds to maximise NPV. The fact that this combination yields more surplus funds which can be invested at 6% is no help, because NPV can only be increased if investment is at a rate of return above 14%.

Need for more information

More information is required about the projects before making a final decision. It may be that some or all of them could be **postponed**. For example, project 3 has the highest profitability index and the quickest payback. It may be that if this project generates high cash flows quickly, project 1 could be started after only a short delay. Information about **opportunities for further borrowing** would also be helpful.

Problems with evaluation method

A weakness of the evaluation method is that all projects have been **evaluated** at the **same discount rate**, namely the company's **overall cost of capital**. If they have **different risk characteristics**, these should be incorporated into the calculation, most conveniently by adjusting the discount rates used.

58 Question with helping hand: REM

Text references. CAPM calculations are explained in Chapter 12. Post-completion audits are discussed in Chapter 20.

Top tips. (a) requires an application of the formula relating asset and equity betas. We have used the adjusted cost of capital formula in (a) (iii) to reflect the financing effects of undertaking the new investment. This represents a revised WACC, as opposed to the ungeared cost of equity (8.85%) or the geared cost of equity $5 + 1.098 (9 - 5) = 9.36\%$.

The main problem with using a proxy company to find an asset beta is that most quoted companies are diversified and finding one in the same 'industry' as the project is difficult. In the course of your discussion, don't forget to 'work in' some limitations of the capital asset pricing model, which will gain you a few more marks.

Post- completion audits are easier to write about if you think of it as debriefing or post mortem: Did we achieve our objective? What did we do right and what went wrong?

Easy marks. Post-completion audits may come up in this paper or Paper P3, and it's easy to earn half a dozen marks discussing them.

Examiner's comments. (a) was generally done quite well. Errors some candidates made included a failure to adjust for tax, and lack of discussion, including failure to justify use of the equity beta. In (b) answers tended to be stronger on use of a proxy company than the alternative approaches. Candidates appeared unclear on what was meant by use of an adjusted discount rate. The main problem with (c) was that candidates spent too long on this part of the question.

(a)　(i)　We need first to find the ungeared (asset) beta of the courier company, a company with similar business risk to the project REM is undertaking. Its beta is 1.3, at a debt equity ratio (V_D/V_E) of 1:2 and it is assumed this is an equity beta and not an asset beta.

If tax is 30%, and debt is risk free, the beta of debt is zero, and the asset beta β_u for the courier company is given by:

$$\beta_u = \beta_g \left[\frac{V_E}{V_E + V_D[1-t]} \right]$$

Thus $\beta_u = 1.3 \times 2/[2 + 1(1 - 0.3)] = 1.3 \times 2/2.7 = 0.963$

Since REM is considering investing in a courier-type project, the asset beta for this project appraisal can be assumed to be **0.963**. (Note that this will be different from REM's existing asset beta).

(ii) We need to adjust the asset beta to take account of REM's finance risk and hence find its equity beta. REM's debt equity ratio is 1:5.

Equity beta will be given by:

$0.963 = \beta_g \times 5/[5 + 1(1 - 0.3)]$

Therefore $\beta_g = 0.963 \times 5.7/5 = 1.098$

The equity beta for REM when appraising this project is **1.098**.

(iii) Use asset beta to find ungeared cost of equity

$k_{eu} = 5 + 0.963 (9 - 5)$
$\phantom{k_{eu}} = 8.85\%$

We then need to adjust the ungeared cost of equity to arrive at a cost of capital that reflects REM's financial risk.

Use $k_{adj} = k_{eu}[1 - tL]$ to find k_{adj} to be used as discount rate

$k_{adj} = 8.85 [1 - (0.3 \times 1/6)]$
$\phantom{k_{adj}} = 8.4\%$

(iv) NPV of the project

Year	$m	Discount factor 8.4%	PV $m
0	(12.50)	1	(12.500)
1–4	3.15	3.283	10.341
5	5.85	0.668	3.908
			1.749

The net present value of the project is **$1.749 million**, indicating that the project is worthwhile.

Working: 8.4% discount factors

4 year cumulative discount factor $= \dfrac{1-(1+r)^{-n}}{r}$

$= (1 - (1/1.084^4)/0.084 = 3.283$

Five year PV factor $= 1/1.084^5 = 0.668$

(b) **Advantages of using a proxy company**

(i) Beta factors for company's shares can only be **directly measured** if the companies are **quoted** and have **market prices**. For companies that do not have a quoted share price, the use of a proxy company is a reasonably good method of determining a beta factor and hence a cost of capital.

(ii) The betas of proxy companies are also useful if a company decides to invest in a project that is in a **different risk class** from its normal business. The proxy company is chosen because its business is **similar to the new project**, not to the investing company's existing business.

Since both cases are true for REM – it is unquoted and it is investing in a project of a different risk class – the identification of the courier company as a quoted proxy company with a known beta is useful.

Problems with using a proxy company

(i) The courier company is **unlikely** to be **fully representative** of REM's new project.

(ii) Few quoted companies operate in just one business field. **Diversification** affects a company's beta.

(iii) **Beta factors** are affected by **gearing**. To adjust for the different gearing levels of REM and the proxy company requires two computations, as shown.

(iv)   The computations and indeed the CAPM are based on a number of **simplifying assumptions**, and estimates of betas are subject to **large statistical errors**, which mean that the estimates can only be approximate. They are also based on **historical data**.

(v)   The **relevance** of the CAPM to the cost of capital of an unquoted company is doubtful. The CAPM assumes that shareholders **eliminate unsystematic risk** by holding **diversified portfolios**. The shareholders of REM probably do not hold large portfolios outside their investment in REM. Hence the investment's **total risk** may be more relevant than its systematic risk.

Alternative methods of adjusting for risk

(i)   The project cash flows could be **reduced subjectively** to certainty-equivalents, and the project **discounted at the risk free rate**.

(ii)   If sufficient appropriate data could be found, the cost of equity could be estimated using **arbitrage pricing theory**. This assumes that the cost of equity is based on a number of **independent factors,** to each of which a particular **risk premium** is attached. These could include unanticipated inflation, changes in production levels, changes in the risk premium on bonds and changes in the term structure of interest rates.

(iii)   The **marginal cost of new finance** could be used.

(c)   **Post-completion audits**

A **post–completion audit** is a **review** of the project after it is completed to establish whether the **estimated benefits** have been **achieved**, and whether target outputs were achieved to the required quality specifications, and completed on time and within budget.

Benefits of post-completion audits

(i)   **Better forecasting techniques**

The audit can identify **weaknesses** in the forecasting and estimating techniques used to evaluate projects, and should help to improve the **discipline and quality** of forecasting. In particular by **classifying variances** as controllable (for example efficiency of operations) or non-controllable (for example weather, interest rates), the evaluation can be used to improve future project appraisals, and encourage a more realistic approach to project uncertainties.

(ii)   **Better future investment decisions**

Post-completion evaluation of the project will help determine whether a **continuation of the project**, or similar future projects, is likely to be worthwhile. The post-completion audit can also identify where **mistakes** have been made, so that similar mistakes can be avoided in the future. It may also identify **successes** that might be created in future projects.

(iii)   **Better current investment decisions**

Awareness that an audit will be carried out at a later date may encourage managers to be **more realistic** and not unduly optimistic in their judgements. However this might tempt managers towards prudence, which may be counter-productive if it leads to rejection of a good project.

(iv)   **Contribution to performance evaluation**

A post-completion audit can provide feedback to project managers and to senior management which is of use in the process of **management control** and **performance** assessment.

59 GHI

> **Text references**. Adjusted present value is covered in Chapter 19 and project control in Chapter 20.
>
> **Top tips**. Part (a) is a complicated calculation with numerous opportunities to make mistakes! Make sure you use an **ungeared** cost of equity in the NPV calculation and carefully calculate each part of the APV calculation. The examiner also accepted an approach where additional tax of 10% on UK profits is charged after translating £ cash flows into €s.
>
> **Easy marks**. Part (b) is a straightforward discussion where it is relatively easy to pick up marks.
>
> **Examiner's comments**. This was a very popular choice of question to do but many candidates failed to fully understand how to progress from NPV to APV and few candidates used an ungeared cost of equity in the NPV base calculation.

(a)   **Calculation of K_e:**

$$k_{eg} = k_{eu} + [k_{eu} - k_d] \frac{V_D(1-t)}{V_E}$$

$$10.7\% = k_{eu} + [k_{eu} - 5\%] \frac{4 \times (1-0.35)}{6}$$

$$10.7\% = k_{eu} + 0.433\,k_{eu} - 2.167\%$$

$$k_{eu} = 12.867\%/1.433 = 8.98\% \approx 9\%$$

NPV calculation:

Year	0	1	2	3	4	5
	£m	£m	£m	£m	£m	£m
Project cash flows	(10)	5	5	4	3	3
UK tax @ 25%		(1.25)	(1.25)	(1)	(0.75)	(0.75)
After tax cash flow	(10)	3.75	3.75	3	2.25	2.25
Exchange rate (weakening at 3% pa)	1.60	1.55	1.51	1.46	1.42	1.37
	€m	€m	€m	€m	€m	€m
Cash flows in €	(16.00)	5.81	5.66	4.38	3.19	3.08
French tax @ 35%		(2.03)	(1.98)	(1.53)	(1.12)	(1.08)
Add back UK tax converted into €		1.94	1.89	1.46	1.06	1.03
After tax cash flow	(16.00)	5.72	5.57	4.31	3.13	3.03
9% discount factor	1.00	0.917	0.842	0.772	0.708	0.650
Discounted cash flow	(16.00)	5.25	4.69	3.33	2.22	1.97

Net present value   **€1,460,000**

Adjusted present value:

Tax relief on debt interest = €16m × 5% × 35% = €280,000 per annum
Present value of tax relief for 5 years @ 5% (cost of debt) = €280,000 × 4.329 = €1,212,120

Issue costs = €16m × 2% = €320,000
Tax relief on issue costs = €320,000 × 35% = €112,000

Adjusted present value = NPV if all equity financed + PV of the tax shield
APV = €(1,460,000 + 1,212,120 - 320,000 +112,000) = €2,464,120

The project has a **positive** base case NPV but it is not particularly large. After allowing for the tax relief on debt, the NPV is higher and the project could be recommended. However, the limitations of the NPV and APV calculations may make this advice **unreliable**.

The **limitations** of an APV approach in this context are as follows.

- Establishing a suitable cost of equity for the initial DCF computation is difficult and subjective and may not fully reflect the risk of the project

- It is difficult to accurately identify all the costs and benefits associated with the method of financing

- It is assumed in the calculations that all of the €16m loan will be needed for this project

(b) (i) The project committee of GHI will play a vital role in the **planning** of the project. Effective planning, particularly the **design** of the product, is an essential contributor to the success of this project. A good design is a very important way of making products **distinctive**. It not only draws attention to the company's products, it also improves performance and cuts production costs.

The project committee will collect information about the UK market using detailed **market research** of UK customers. The UK phone market is highly **competitive** and **saturated** so the strategic market position must be considered. GHI could **differentiate** their product according to price, design or service, depending on the outcome of the market research.

(ii) The implementation stage is concerned with **co-ordinating** people and other resources to carry out the project plan. The project committee will prepare a plan for implementation, which may first involve a trial implementation in selected areas which are thought to be representative of the total market. They will then plan for the full launch of the product, ensuring that the product is in the right place at the right time and that customers know about it. Launch plans may have to be modified if competitors change their response.

The project committee will be responsible for **evaluating the performance** of the project in terms of costs incurred, sales volumes and sales prices compared to budget. This will feed into a **control mechanism** as deviations from budget are investigated throughout the implementation and action taken as necessary.

On completion of implementation, the project committee will be responsible for carrying out a post-completion appraisal designed to provide information to aid the implementation and control of future projects.

60 RST

Text references. Capital rationing is covered in chapter 19.

Top tips. Be careful with the timing here. The capital rationing is in year 1 so the profitability index should be based on net year 1 cash flows. Make sure you relate your discussion in part (b) to the **public** sector.

Easy marks. The calculations are quite straightforward provided you get the timings right. You can use your common sense and financial knowledge to gain good marks in part (b).

Examiner's comments. This question was generally well answered with most candidates being able to make a reasonable attempt at the NPV calculations and draw basic conclusions from the results. However, few were able to calculate appropriate PI's or identify the best overall combination of projects.

(a) (i) **NPV of cash flows:**

Project		NPV $m
A	$-9 + (-16 \times 0.87) + (4/0.15)$	3.75
B	$-10 + (-10 \times 0.87) + (4/0.15 \times 0.87)$	4.50
C	$-10 + (-12 \times 0.87) + (5 \times 5.019)$	4.66
D	Cumulative discount factor when n is 7 = 4.16, when n is 2 = 1.626	2.85
	$-8 + (-5 \times 0.87) + (6 \times (4.16 - 1.626))$	
E	Cumulative discount factor when n is 15 = 5.847, when n is 5 = 3.352	3.22
	$-9 + (-8 \times 0.87) + (2 \times 3.352) + (5 \times (5.847 - 3.352))$	

On the basis of NPV of cash flows, the **ranking of the projects** is **C, B, A, E, D.**

With the capital constraint of $30m, this will mean that projects **C, B and A** should be **accepted** with a total net cash outflow in Year 1 of $29m (16 + 10 + 12 − 5 − 4) and a total NPV of $12.91m.

(ii) **Profitability index:**

Project	NPV	Year 1 net outflow	Profitability Index
A	3.75	12	0.31
B	4.50	10	0.45
C	4.66	7	0.67
D	2.85	5	0.57
E	3.22	6	0.54

On the basis of the profitability index, the **ranking of the projects** is **C, D, E, B, A.**

With the capital constraint of $30m, this will mean that projects C, D, E and B should be accepted with a total net cash outflow in Year 1 of $28m and a total NPV of $15.23m.

In conclusion, RST should accept projects **C, D, E and B** as this will give the highest possible NPV given the capital constraint in Year 1.

(b) (i) RST is a publicly-owned entity and is therefore subject to debate as to whether capital rationing techniques based on maximising NPV are appropriate.

NPV is a very useful technique for **privately owned** entities whose prime objective is the **maximisation of shareholder wealth**. The NPV of a project produces an estimate of the amount by which shareholder wealth will be increased. A publicly-owned entity will have **other non-financial objectives**, such as maximising service, so maximising NPV may not be the most appropriate prime objective.

However, publicly-owned entities are subject to **capital rationing** as funds, and therefore spending, are restricted. This makes it even more important for them to have an effective way to measure which projects are the most financially attractive, as they are unlikely to be able to borrow additional funds as a private entity could.

(ii) Other factors that RST should consider would be firstly, which are the key variables in the calculations carried out. A **sensitivity analysis** could then be conducted to look at the impact of changes in these key variables. Each project's NPV can be recalculated using alternative assumptions, for example the timing of the cash-flows.

Options theory could be applied to the development projects. For example, there may be follow-on investments as options or an option to wait on some of the projects.

As a publicly-owned entity, RST will need to consider non-financial factors such as targets and priorities for service levels. For example, which geographical areas or types of patients have particular needs. They may also need to be concerned with environmental and human resources issues. There is a significant element of political risk for RST as health care priorities can change.

61 Casarina

Text references. Forecasting is revised in Chapter 3. Debt and equity finance are covered in Chapters 6 and 5 and the capital structure decision in Chapter 10.

Top tips. Questions like (a), requiring income statement, balance sheet and cash flow forecasts, are common in this paper. Although there is quite a lot of calculation, it is not difficult if you perfect an ordered approach.

- Read the narrative in the question, noting references in the financial statements to the narrative notes and extra items that might have be added into the proformas (such as the loan cap)

- Assuming you are doing this during the 20 minutes reading time, mark items that are relevant to (b) and jot down ideas, particularly extra calculations that you will need

- When you start writing set up the income statement and balance sheet proformas, fill in the amounts. The items don't require significant workings, so you can go straight down the two statements for each option. Leave the cash figure in the balance sheet blank.

- Set out the cash flow statements in whatever form you find easiest (here IAS 7 format).

- If you run out of time insert the cash figure that makes both balance sheets balance whatever the state of your cash flow forecasts.

- Start question (b) by carrying out the calculations in the appendix.

- Make sure you have 40-45 minutes left on the question to write the report. Further ideas may have occurred to you while you were doing the calculations in (a) and you should have noted these down.

The end of year cash balance will be the balancing figure in the balance sheet and can also be computed from the cash flow statement. A columnar layout for the two alternatives might have saved you time. Note that the operating cash flows computed for Alternative 1 can be re-used in Alternative 2.

The report in (b) is the main part of this question. A good interpretation of the results of (a) cannot be made unless additional calculations are made, for example earnings per share, gearing and return on equity, which are mentioned as performance targets in the case study description. The discussion centres around the advantages and disadvantages of debt and equity finance. Don't forget to mention different types of debt, and don't throw marks away by, failing to discuss other information.

Easy marks. Most of the themes in (b) (ii) are areas that you'll normally need to consider when assessing which source of finance is appropriate such as control, costs, financial risk, tax shield and other sources of finance (don't forget retained cash earnings)

(a)   **Year ended 30 April 20X1**

      Alternative 1: Rights issue

      INCOME STATEMENT

	£'000
Revenue 135,000 × 1.1	148,500
Direct costs, except dep'n:	
(85,500 – 9,500) × 1.08	(82,080)
Depreciation 9,000 + 20% × 25,000	(14,000)
Indirect costs	(20,000)
Operating profit	32,420
Interest payable (unchanged)	(2,500)
Profit before tax	29,920
Tax at 30%	(8,976)
Profit after tax	20,944
Dividend 60% × 20,944	(12,566)
Retained profit	8,378

SUMMARY BALANCE SHEET

		£'000
Non-current assets		
117,000 + 25,000 − 14,000 depreciation		128,000
Inventory 17,500 + 10,000		27,500
Receivables 24,500 × 1.1		26,950
Cash (see cash flow below)		18,124
		200,574

		£'000
Share capital	25,000 + 5,000	30,000
Reserves	81,410 + 20,000 + 8,378	109,788
10% Debentures 20X5		25,000
Payables	21,500 × 1.08	23,220
Dividend payable		12,566
		200,574

CASH FLOWS

	£'000	£'000
Operating profit		32,420
Add depreciation		14,000
Increase in: inventory		(10,000)
receivables		(2,450)
payables		1,720
		35,690
Net cash flow from operations		
Dividends paid	(11,340)	
Interest paid	(2,500)	
		(13,840)
Tax paid		(8,976)
Acquisition of non-current assets		(25,000)
Net cash outflow before financing		(12,126)
Share issue		25,000
Increase in cash		12,874
Opening cash		5,250
Increase in year		12,874
Closing cash		18,124

Alternative 2: Loan with cap

INCOME STATEMENT

	£'000
Operating profit (same as alternative 1)	32,420
Interest payable: 2,500 + 8% × 25,000	(4,500)
Amortisation of loan cap:	
2% × 25,000 / 4	(125)
Profit before tax	27,795
Tax at 30%	(8,339)
Profit after tax	19,456
Dividend: 60% × 19,456	(11,674)
Retained profit	7,782

SUMMARY BALANCE SHEET

	£'000
Assets, as alternative 1:	
Non-current assets	128,000
Inventory	27,500
Receivables	26,950
Cash (see cash flow below)	16,261
	198,711

	£'000
Share capital	25,000
Reserves 81, 410 + 7, 782	89,192
10% debentures	25,000
Floating rate loan	25,000
Unamortised cap	(375)
Dividend payable	11,674
Payables: as alternative	23,220
	198,711

CASH FLOWS

	£'000	£'000
Net cash flow from operations (as alternative 1)		35,690
Dividends paid	(11,340)	
Interest paid (+ cap amort.)	(4,625)	
		(15,965)
Tax paid		(8,339)
Acquisition of non-current assets		(25,000)
Net cash outflow before financing		(13,614)
New loan (less cap balance)		24,625
Increase in cash		11,011
Opening cash		5,250
Increase in year		11,011
Closing cash		16,261

(b) REPORT

To:	Board of Directors
From:	Management Accountant
Date:	17 May 20X0

Financing the growth of our franchising operations

This report evaluates two possible methods of raising £25 million to finance the expansion of our franchise to more UK locations. These are (i) a **1 for 5 rights issue** at 500 pence per share; and (ii) a **floating rate loan** at an initial interest rate of 8% per annum, backed by an interest rate cap which will ensure that the maximum rate paid over the next four years is 10% per annum.

(i) **Evaluation of the methods**

I attach calculations showing the results of each financing method for the year ending 30 April 20X1. In summary these are as follows:

BPP
LEARNING MEDIA

(1) **Return on assets**

Whichever method is adopted, the company's **return on assets** will fall from 18.6% to 17.8% in the year to April 20X1. It is because of this factor that the **return on equity funds** also **falls** under both options, as shown below. This is to be expected with new investment because the money has been invested in expensive assets but the profits take time to materialise. As the assets age, their value decreases, improving the return on assets ratio.

(2) **Rights issue**

Total equity earnings will increase from £18.9m to £20.9m. However, **earnings per share** will **decline** by 6% from 74.3p in 20X0 (adjusted for rights issue) to 69.8p in 20X1. The company's return on equity funds will fall from 17.8% to 15%, which has been regarded historically as the minimum acceptable for our shareholders. Gearing will decrease from 19% to 15.2%.

(3) **Loan with cap**

Total equity earnings will **increase** from £18.9m to £19.456m. Although this is less than under the rights issue, the number of shares in issue is less, causing EPS to rise by 3% from 75.6p to 77.8p. Although return on equity funds falls from 17.8% to 17.0%, this is not by so much as with the rights issue option and remains comfortably above 15%. Gearing will increase significantly from 19% to 30.3%. However, this is well within the restriction applied by the bankers of maximum 50% gearing.

(ii) **Advantages and disadvantages of the two financing methods and a consideration of alternative methods**

These figures illustrate some of the following characteristics of equity and debt financing.

Dilution of share ownership

A share issue may alter the **disposition of power** in the ownership of the company, reducing the influence of the original shareholders. Because it is risk-bearing capital, and dividend payouts are not tax deductible, **equity finance** is **expensive** compared with the direct cost of debt. It also has **very high issue costs** because of the legal requirements that must be observed. A share issue will often cause a fall in EPS, especially in the early years of a new investment. However, the advantage is that **gearing** is **reduced**, which improves the **stability of equity earnings**, reducing shareholders' financial risk and lowering the return that they demand from their investment.

Direct issue costs

Debt finance will not cause any dilution of shareholding and, because interest payments are more predictable than dividends and are an allowable expense for tax purposes, debt has a **cheaper direct cost** than equity finance. The additional profit generated from the investment will therefore **enhance expected EPS**. However the increase in gearing and interest payments will cause shareholders' returns to drop markedly if profits do not materialise, increasing their financial risk and causing an increased cost of equity capital. Floating rate debt brings the added problem of possible significant increases in future interest rates, referred to as interest rate risk.

Profit uncertainty

In general, if the new project has highly uncertain or volatile predicted profits, **equity finance may be preferred** because **financial risk for existing shareholders may become too high if debt finance is used**. Gearing that is too high may also increase bankruptcy risk, with its attendant costs. Debt finance may be preferred for projects with more stable profit and cash flow profiles, because of its cheap direct cost.

Tax shield

However, **financial theory** shows that the combined effects of the advantages and disadvantages listed above create very little difference between the **effect of equity and debt finance** on company value. If anything, debt has an advantage if the company is not highly geared and can take advantage of interest payments as a tax allowable expense, but it has been argued that this **'tax shield'** effect of debt is overstated, and this will certainly be the case when interest rates are low.

Retained earnings

As a purely practical method of financing projects, **'pecking order theory'** shows that financial managers will normally look to **retained equity earnings** as a first source of capital for expansion. This implies that companies wishing to expand will normally have low dividend payouts. The advantage of using retained earnings is that there are **no issue costs** and **no prospectus** or **other requirements** for reporting to investors. Only when retained earnings have been fully utilised will companies look to the **next source of finance**, which is normally **borrowing**, because of the speed at which it can be arranged compared with share issues, its relatively low issue costs and the many different forms it can take, which can often be tailored to the company's needs. Share issues are reserved for **very large expansions or acquisitions**. Because of their high issue costs and the onerous legal requirements, they cannot be carried out too often.

Variations on borrowing

For example, **convertible debt** gives the holder an option to convert from debt to the company's shares, and **warrants** (options to buy the company's shares at a fixed price) can be **linked to debt** issues. Both of these methods succeed in **reducing the interest cost of debt** to the company but may become more expensive in the long run if the options are exercised, resulting in the effective issue of cheap shares. Types of debt instrument have grown greatly in number in the last few decades. Swaps enable fixed rate debt to be converted to floating rate or *vice versa*. Futures and forward debt contracts can be arranged and, as in our case, options can be purchased to provide caps (maximum interest rates) or collars (maximum and minimum interest rates).

Other sources of finance

We might consider include **acquisition of the new assets by hire purchase or lease finance,** sale and leaseback of existing property, or raising finance from our working capital, for example by factoring our debts or invoice discounting, or by negotiating purchase finance for inventory.

(iii) **Additional information**

The financial analysis in (i) above is based on projections of the company's results for a one year period only. It really needs to be extended into a **proper investment and financial appraisal** covering, say, the next five years and set within the context of the company's strategic plans. The strategy of **expanding the existing business needs** to reviewed in the context of a SWOT analysis and compared with alternatives such as moving into related or unrelated businesses, including acquisition options. Each option needs to be appraised by a proper cost benefit analysis.

More detailed estimates

On the financial side I will attempt to obtain **more detailed estimates of expected movements** in interest and inflation rates over the next few years, will **investigate the costs of early termination** of our existing 10% debenture loan and will keep all options under continuous review.

Appendix: financial computations

Alternative 1: Rights issue: Theoretical ex-rights price

	£m
25 million original shares at 560 pence	140
5 million new shares at 500 pence	25
30 million shares in total	165

Theoretical ex rights price = £165m/30m = 550 pence

Earnings per share

20X0 earnings per share, based on 25 million shares was £18.9m/25m = 75.6 pence.

Alternative 1: Rights issue

For comparison with 20X1, 20X0 EPS needs to be restated as 75.6 × 550/560 = 74.3 pence.

20X1 earnings per share, based on 30 million shares is predicted as £20.944m/30m = 69.8 pence.

This is a 6% fall in EPS.

Alternative 2: Loan

20X1 earnings per share, based on 25 million shares is predicted as £19.456m/25m = 77.8 pence.

This is a 3% rise in EPS from the 20X0 figure of 75.6 pence.

Gearing (ratio of debt to debt + equity)

April 20X0 ratio is 25,000 / 131,410 = 19.0%.

Alternative 1

April 20X1 gearing: 25,000 / (25,000 + 139,788) = 15.2%.

Alternative 2

April 20X1 gearing: 49,625 / (49,625 + 114,192) = 30.3%.

Return on equity (profit after tax/shareholders' funds)

April 20X0: 18,900/106,410 = 17.8%

Alternative 1

April 20X1: 20,944/139,788 = 15.0%

Alternative 2

April 20X1: 19,456/114,192 = 17.0%

Return on assets (operating profit/total assets excluding cash)

20X0: 29,500/(117,000 + 17,500 + 24,500) = 18.6%.

20X1 (under either alternative): 32,420/(128,000 + 27,500 + 26,950) = 17.8%.

(Variations on this ratio could be used, but they would all show a decline in return on assets under both financing options.)

62 Question with analysis: Spearhead

> **Text references**. Investment appraisal calculations are explained in Chapter 18 and risks of investment are discussed in Chapter 17.
>
> **Top tips**. In (a)(ii) the exchange rates could be calculated using either relative interest rates or inflation rates. Since inflation rates are available, this is the preferred method. In (a)(iii) there are a variety of methods that could be used to calculate the return on assets. It is therefore most important that you state clearly the method that you have chosen, and that you calculate an annual rate as required, and not just an average rate for the contract.
>
> When doing the calculations for Contract 2, there are no instructions as to how the penalty clause should be treated, and you should therefore explain your approach to this issue. If time permits, you could adjust the calculations to show the figures for the contract both including and excluding this item.
>
> The report in the final section of the question accounts for 28 marks and you should therefore not neglect this at the expense of the calculation. You could structure your answer around the four sub-sections of the question, but if doing this, you must remember to discuss the non-financial factors and objectives as well as the financial areas.
>
> **Easy marks.** Part (b) of the question could have been answered reasonably, if you had failed to answer part (a) or had arrived at figures you thought incorrect.

(a) (i) The **cost of capital** will be estimated using the **CAPM**. UK interest rates will be used in the calculations:

$$k_e = R_f + (R_m - R_f)\,\beta$$

where
k_e = cost of equity capital
R_f = risk free rate of return (6%)
R_m = market rate of return (12%)
β = equity beta (1.5)
k_e = 6% + 1.5(12% − 6%)
k_e = **15%**

Use if given inflation rates

(ii) The exchange rates can be estimated using purchasing **power parity theory**. This states that an exchange rate varies according to relative price changes, so that:

$$\text{'Old' exchange rate} \times \frac{\text{Price level in country A}}{\text{Price level in country B}} = \text{'New' exchange rate}$$

Francs/Sterling

Year 0 'spot' rate = 3.0 SFr/£

	Opening rate	$\times \dfrac{1.02}{1.03}$	Closing rate
Year 1	3.0000		2.9709
Year 2	2.9709		2.9421
Year 3	2.9421		2.9135
Year 4	2.9135		2.8852

US dollars/Sterling

Year 0 'spot' rate = 1.6 $/£

	Opening rate	$\times \dfrac{1.04}{1.03}$	Closing rate
Year 1	1.6000		1.6155
Year 2	1.6155		1.6312
Year 3	1.6312		1.6470
Year 4	1.6470		1.6630

(iii) It is assumed that all cash flows arise at the end of the year.

Contract 1 cash flows

[Risk-adjusted rate]

This contract will be discounted at the cost of equity of 15% since it is low risk.

	Year 0	Year 1	Year 2	Year 3	Year 4
Sales (SFr million)		500	500	500	500
Exchange rate SFr/£		2.9709	2.9421	2.9135	2.8852
Sales (£m)		168	170	172	173
Contract costs (£m)		(75)	(75)	(75)	(75)
Capital expenditure (£m)	(300)				
Residual value (£m)					50
Annual cash flow	(300)	93	95	97	148
[CAPM value] 15% discount factors	1.000	0.870	0.756	0.658	0.572
PV cash flow (£m)	(300)	81	72	64	85
Cumulative PV cash flow (£m)	(300)	(219)	(147)	(83)	2

The net present value of this contract at the end of four years is **£2m.**

[Must calculate]

The annual return on assets can be calculated using the annual accounting return after depreciation, and the average book value of assets for the year.

[Better than year-end]

The annual depreciation charge will be £62.5m ((£300m – £50m)/4).

	Year 1	Year 2	Year 3	Year 4
	£m	£m	£m	£m
Opening asset value	300	238	175	113
Closing asset value	238	175	113	50
Average asset value	269	206	144	81
Sales	168	170	172	173
Contract costs	(75)	(75)	(75)	(75)
Depreciation	(63)	(63)	(63)	(63)
Accounting return	30	32	34	35
Annual return on assets	11.2%	15.5%	23.6%	43.2%

The average annual return on assets is **23.4%.**

Contract 2 cash flows

[Risk adjustment]

The first stage of this contract will be evaluated at the cost of capital plus a premium of 5% since this is a high risk project - effective discount rate 20%. The 10% penalty will also be included in this part of the calculations to give the worst case scenario.

[Prudence]

The second stage of the contract will be evaluated at the low risk rate of 15%.

	Year 0	Year 1	Year 2	Year 3	Year 4	Year 5
Sales ($m) net of penalty	1,000		800			
Exchange rate $/£	1.6000		1.6312			
	£m	£m	£m	£m	£m	£m
[Opportunity costs] Sales	625		490	200	200	200
Contract costs		(350)	(150)	(100)	(100)	(100)
Cost of lost business		(175)	(150)			
	625	(525)	190	100	100	100
Capital expenditure	(500)					
Net cash flow	125	(525)	190	100	100	100
[Year 1-2] 20% discount factors	1.000	0.833	0.694			
[Year 3–5 as low risk] 15% discount factors				0.658	0.572	0.497
PV cash flow (£m)	125	(437)	132	66	57	50
Cumulative PV cash flow (£m)	125	(312)	(180)	(114)	(57)	(7)

BPP
LEARNING MEDIA

The net present value of this contract at the end of five years is **£7m negative.**

If the penalty clause is excluded, the PV will rise by $200m × 0.694 ÷ 1.6312, = £85m, to **£78m positive.** The annual return on assets can be calculated using the annual accounting return after depreciation, and the average book value of assets for the year. For the purposes of calculation, the contribution in year 0 will be included with year 1.

The annual depreciation charge will be £100m ((£500m – £0m)/5))

	Year 1	Year 2	Year 3	Year 4	Year 5
	£m	£m	£m	£m	£m
Opening asset value	500	400	300	200	100
Closing asset value	400	300	200	100	0
Average asset value	450	350	250	150	50
Contribution (sales – contract costs)	275	340	100	100	100
Depreciation	(100)	(100)	(100)	(100)	(100)
Accounting return	175	240	0	0	0
Annual return on assets	38.9%	68.6%	0.0%	0.0%	0.0%

Opportunity costs not relevant

The average annual return on assets is **21.5%**

If the penalty clause is excluded, the contribution in Year 2 increases by £123 million ($200 million ÷ 1.632) to £463 million. £463m/350m = 132.3% annual return and the average annual return on assets is **34.2%.**

(b)   To: Board of Directors, Spearhead
      From: Financial Manager
      Date: 15 November 20X8
      Subject: Evaluation of potential contracts

(i)   **Contract 1**

Mention as relevant to other contract

      (1)   **Risk**

            Since the contract will be with a European government, political risk should be negligible. A further sensitivity arises in relation to the residual value of the capital equipment. If it proves impossible to realise £50m at the end of year 4, then this too could mean that the contract shows a negative NPV.

      (2)   **Discount rate**

            This contract is classified as **low risk** and has therefore been evaluated at the **cost of equity** with no additional premium.

      (3)   **NPV**

            It is a large project, with a four-year timespan, and requiring an initial investment of £300m. However, at the end of the four-year period it will only just **exceed breakeven** in NPV terms.

      (4)   **Foreign exchange exposure**

Example of sensitivity

            Since all the **sales income is denominated in Swiss Francs**, this means that the contract will be very **sensitive to fluctuations** in the exchange rate of the pound against the Franc. Although it is forecast on the basis of relative inflation rates that the pound will weaken against the mark throughout the life of the contract, if sterling performs better than projected on the foreign exchanges, the contract is likely to show a negative NPV.

(5) Return on assets

The other financial objective of Spearhead is to **maintain an annual return on assets of 25%.** While the absolute level of accounting returns remains relatively stable throughout the contract, the **depreciating asset base** means that the **percentage return increases each year** from 11.2% in year 1 to 43% in year 4. The rate of return only exceeds the target rate in the final year of the project, and the average return for the contract is 23.4%, which is a little below the target return on assets.

Distortion

Contract 2

(1) Risk

This contract carries a higher level of risk than Contract 1, with a level of **political risk** arising from the fact that the deal is with a government in a part of the world that is politically unstable. In addition, 50% of the payment does not fall due until the end of the second year of the contract.

Payment risk

(2) Discount rate

The contract has therefore been classified as carrying **high levels of risk** in the early stages, which have been evaluated at a discount rate with a premium of 5% to the cost of equity. The later, low risk stage has been evaluated at the cost of equity with no additional premium.

Justification for risk adjustment

(3) NPV

In financial terms, provided that Spearhead can deliver on time, the contract shows a **positive NPV** at the end of five years of £78 million. However, the question of delivery is a major sensitivity, and if the penalty clause is invoked, then the NPV of the contract becomes £7 million negative.

Positive NPV dependent on delivery

(4) Foreign exchange exposure

The **foreign exchange exposure** is less than for contract 1, since all $ payments will be complete by the end of year 2, and 50% of the payments will be received at the start of the contract. However, there is still some risk that if the pound strengthens more than expected against the dollar, the value of the second instalment of the payment will be less than expected. Since the second stage of the contract is denominated entirely in sterling, there is no foreign exchange risk in years three to five.

Only risk

(5) Return on assets

Due to the high level of **depreciation**, and the **unevenly phased nature** of the payments, the contract only shows a positive return on assets in years 1 and 2. However, the average return over the life of the contract is 21.5%, which is below Spearhead's target rate of return.

Other non-financial factors

(1) Prestige

Both projects are large government contracts, and it is likely that there will be a good deal of **prestige** attaching to them. Spearhead should therefore consider whether it is worth accepting financial returns that are lower than the targets set in order to enhance the reputation and status of the company.

Reputation

(2) **Technology**

The second contract involves the use of **state-of-the-art technology**. If Spearhead needs to develop this technology in any case so as to maintain competitiveness, it may not be reasonable to allocate the full cost of development to this contract.

(3) **Opportunity costs**

The allocation of design staff to Contract 2 will result in the **loss of other business**. Although the incremental cash flows have been taken into account, the company should also look in more detail at the **financial performance** of the alternative projects that will be foregone, both in NPV and ROI terms.

(4) **Contribution of objectives**

The company should consider **which of these contracts contributes the most** to Spearhead's objective of becoming the UK's leading supplier of airport control equipment within the next ten years.

(ii) **The treatment of risk**

In this evaluation, the problem of differing levels of risk has been dealt with by adding a **pre-determined premium** to the **cost of equity** for each project, depending on its risk classification. This method recognises that risky investments ought to earn a higher return as reward for the risks that are taken, but the size of the risk premium is chosen arbitrarily. Other techniques that could be applied include the following.

(1) **Applying a time limit to the payback period**

Estimates of future cash flows are difficult to make at the best of times, and estimates of cash flows several years ahead are quite likely to be **inaccurate**. A method of limiting the risk on a project is to apply a payback time limit, so that a project should not be undertaken unless it pays back within a given period. There are two ways of applying a payback time limit:

- A project might be **expected to pay back within a certain time limit**, and in addition show a **positive NPV** from its net cash flows.

- Alternatively, a project might be expected to pay back in DCF terms within a certain time period.

(2) **Sensitivity analysis**

One method of applying sensitivity analysis tests to a project is to **recalculate the NPV** in a **number of different situations**. If the NPV is negative when costs are increased a little, or benefits are reduced a little, the project would be rejected on the grounds that it is too sensitive to variations in one or more key cost or revenue items.

(3) **Certainty equivalent approach**

In this method, the expected cash flows of the project are **converted to equivalent riskless amounts**. The greater the risk of an expected cash flow, the smaller the certainty equivalent value (for receipts) or the larger the certainty equivalent value (for payments). One disadvantage of this approach is that the amount of the adjustment made to each cash flow is a subjective decision.

(4) **Probability estimates of cash flows**

It may be possible to **estimate a probability distribution** of expected cash flows, and this may be used to calculate an expected value of the NPV. It can also be used to **measure risk** by calculating the worst possible outcome and its probability, and by calculating the probability that the project will fail to achieve a positive NPV.

Margin labels:
Strategic consequences

Opportunity implications

Strategic implications

Short-term

Change in assumptions

Dealing with risk

Analyse several outcomes

More
sophisticated
analysis

(5) Simulation models

When project cash flows are given probability estimates, it might be more suitable to **use simulation models** to establish a probability distribution of the project's expected NPV, instead of simply calculating an expected value.

(iii) The problem of mutually exclusive projects

Both the NPV and the ROI approaches can be used as a basis for the comparison of mutually exclusive projects. However, the ROI approach runs into problems where the projects have **unequal risk** and **unequal lives**. In this situation, it is better to look at the risk-adjusted NPVs of the projects, and to choose the one with the greater NPV since this will add the most value to the company. In the situation under consideration, this would lead to Contract 2 being selected, given the provisos concerning risk and non-financial factors, already discussed.

Prime objective

(iv) Hedging the risks of international trade

The risks of international trade fall into three main categories.

Relevance to
this contract

(1) Political risk

This is the risk of political action by governments, which **limit a company's freedom of action**, for instance the introduction of exchange controls or a change of government leading to attempts to have the contract cancelled.

(2) Economic risk

This refers to the effect of exchange rate movements on the **international competitiveness** of a company. This arises in both of the contracts under consideration, since the contract costs are **denominated in sterling**, while the **receipts are in foreign currency**.

(3) Transaction risk

This is the risk of **adverse exchange rate movements** occurring in the course of international trading transactions. Since the payments schedule is fixed for both of the contracts under consideration, Spearhead could look at the possibility of using **currency hedges** to reduce the level of exposure.

Conclusions

Neither of the two contracts meets all Spearhead's financial targets, although both can be justified in NPV terms. Contract 1 provides the safest option, and comes close to meeting the ROI target, and is therefore probably the preferred choice in financial terms. However, the final decision must take into account the non-financial factors discussed above, and a more detailed analysis of the various risks involved.

63 Premoco

Text references. Business valuations and acquisition issues are covered in Chapters 15 and 16.

Top tips. This is a wide-ranging case study concerning a company that wishes to diversify by acquisition. It is a good question because it is not unnecessarily complex but it requires a good all-round grasp of the factors involved in the acquisition decision and requires you to explain in words the valuation methods and problems involved.

Important points in (a) are setting out your ratio calculations clearly and recognising the need to ungear and gear betas from the information given in the question.

In (b) you would probably be allocated up to 2-3 marks for each relevant point so you would not need to mention all the points we mentioned. However you would need to comment on each method, otherwise the mark guide would restrict significantly the marks you could score.

In (c) there is, as the question says, no one right or wrong answer. A large amount of financial information could have been generated. The best format for the report is to follow the question requirements directly, that is to use the headings 'price', 'terms of offer' and 'business implications' in a separate commentary on each company.
Our answer to (c) focuses on the most significant points from the viewpoint of valuing the business, but it goes into more detail than would be expected of you under examination conditions, in order to demonstrate the points that you might possibly have made. The answer assumes that 'the estimated NPV of the combined organisation' represents the NPV of shareholders' wealth when the organisations are combined. An alternative interpretation is that the NPV represents equity plus debt, and must therefore be adjusted for the value of debt in the combined company.

Even if the question had not specifically prompted you, your recommendation on price should have been a range of values. The answer highlights the key points (gearing, cost, control) in the debt/equity choice and also how financial strategy interacts with business strategy.

- Is diversification necessary (shareholders can diversify better)?

- What conditions will need to be met if the merger is to be successful?

- What problems will need to be overcome (countering resistance from existing shareholders, post-acquisition difficulties, requirement for additional investment in products and perhaps people)?

Easy marks. The easiest marks will be for breadth, ie providing some discussion on all the points required, so make sure you leave enough time to cover all relevant points.

(a) (i) **Current market values and P/E ratios**

The market value of the company's shares (market capitalisation) is the share price multiplied by the number of shares in issue.

The P/E ratio (price/earnings ratio) is the share price divided by the latest earnings per share.

No figures are available for Carsals, which is a private company.

	Premoco	Nafco	Oiltrans
Share price (pence)	1,648	675	1,530
Number of issued shares (million)	20	10	12
Total market value of shares (£ million)	329.6	67.5	183.6
Earnings per share (pence)	103	75	85
P/E ratio	16	9	18

(ii) **Cost of equity (k_e) using the CAPM (capital asset pricing model)**

This is given by: $k_e = R_f + (R_m - R_f)\beta_g$

The market return, R_m, is 12% and the risk free rate, R_f, is 6%. The equity beta factor (β_g) for the first three companies is given directly, but for Carsals it is estimated by de-gearing the equity beta of a similar quoted company to get the asset beta or ungeared beta, β_u. This is because Carsals has no debt in its capital structure.

The no tax formula is $\beta_u = \beta_g \dfrac{V_E}{V_E + V_D}$

Thus for Carsals $\beta_u = 1.25 \times \dfrac{80}{80+20} = 1.0$

	Premoco	Nafco	Oiltrans	Carsals
Beta factor	1.2	0.9	1.3	1.0
Cost of equity = 6% + (12% − 6%)β	13.2%	11.4%	13.8%	12.0%

(iii) **Prospective market value using the constant growth dividend valuation model**

The formula is $P_0 = \dfrac{d_1}{k_e - g}$ where d_1 (next year's dividend) = $d_0 (1 + g)$.

	Premoco	Nafco	Oiltrans	Carsals
Latest dividend per share (d_0) (pence)	31	55	42	112
Expected growth, g	11%	5%	14%	9%
Next year's dividend, d_1 (pence)	34.41	57.75	47.88	122.08
Estimated value per share $d_1/(k_e-g)$ (£)	15.64	9.02	N/A	40.69
Number of issued shares (million)	20	10		0.5
Total prospective market capitalisation (£m)	312.8	90.2		20.3

> **Top tips.** The dividend growth formula does not work when g is greater than k_e. In practice g, which is supposed to be a growth rate to perpetuity, can never be higher than k_e. In fact, when g is expected to be very close to k_e, as for Premoco, the formula becomes very unreliable.

(b) **Usefulness of the three types of valuation in the acquisition decision**

Summarised values for the four companies

	Premoco	Nafco	Oiltrans	Carsals
	£m	£m	£m	£m
Current market value	329.6	67.5	183.6	N/A
Prospective market value	312.8	90.2	N/A	20.3
Net asset value	250	60	65	6

(i) **Current market value method**

(1) The **current market value** shows the value of each of the listed companies to its existing shareholders. The efficient market hypothesis (semi-strong form) implies that the market value of each company is the best estimate of its fundamental value, based on public information. Despite criticisms of the EMH, there is a large body of evidence which shows that the **semi-strong form** is substantially correct. However, when making an acquisition decision, Premoco is concerned with the value of each target company to itself, not to that company's existing shareholders. Adjustments may therefore be needed

(2) During the negotiations, information which is not known to the public may emerge. This will cause Premoco to adjust its valuations. Premoco may also have plans for **generating synergy** when it combines a new business with its own (eg by elimination of duplicated assets and costs). This will affect the value of the new business to Premoco. However, extreme caution must be exercised when using estimates of synergy to adjust market values, because the market may already have anticipated the merger taking place and may have increased the price of the target company to allow for possible synergy. This effect can make the market values of companies unreliable if takeover rumours start.

(3) Premoco will probably find it necessary to offer a price higher than the **existing market** value in order to induce target company shareholders to sell.

(4) There is, of course, no market value for the private company, which cannot be valued by this method.

(ii) **Dividend valuation method**

The **prospective value based on the constant growth dividend valuation model** is one method of attempting to compute the fundamental going concern value of the business from basic data concerning the company. The model itself is, however, very crude, assuming that dividend growth will be at a constant rate to perpetuity. More complex versions of this model exist where **varying growth rates** can **be postulated**. In particular, the model becomes meaningless if g exceeds the cost of equity and very unreliable when the two figures are close together, as for Premoco itself.

(iii) **Net asset values**

The **net asset values** of the companies are probably based on **historical** cost, although some oil companies do use a current cost basis for reporting.

(1) **Historical cost**

In terms of relevance for an acquisition, historical cost is irrelevant except as an approximation to either net realisable value or current cost.

(2) **Current cost**

Current cost, or replacement cost, is useful in showing the cost of setting up a similar business from scratch but it is *not* a valuation of the business concerned. It ignores goodwill and intangible assets and, if Premoco did decide to set up a competing business from scratch, the original target company would still exist as a competitor.

(3) **Net realisable value**

Net realisable values of the business assets are probably the most useful asset figures which can be provided. This is obviously true if the business is acquired to be broken up but NRV asset values are also useful when viewing the business as a going concern: the break-up value of the business shows the worst-case scenario if the business is acquired as a going concern but fails. In other words, it is NRV which should be used as the basis of the 'asset backing' calculation, not historical cost.

(iv) **Conclusion**

In practice the businesses cannot be valued separately if they are going to be joined together, and a valuation method may well involve a combination of computing the present value of future improved operating cash flows together with the net realisable value of assets which are to be sold. The company will find the 'estimated NPV of the combined organisation' more useful than any of the stand-alone valuations of the businesses.

(c) To: David Wong
From: Financial Adviser
Date: 12 November 20X7
Subject: Report on three possible acquisitions available to Premoco

Introduction

I have examined the information which you have supplied to me on the three potential acquisitions and set out my views on the strategic implications of each, bearing in mind your **wish to diversify away from petroleum**. Relevant calculations are shown in the Appendix. I have assumed that the existing market value of Premoco, £329.6 million, is a fair estimate of its true value.

Nafco

(i) **Price to be offered**

(1) On the basis of the financial advisers' figures (see Appendix), the combination will increase equity earnings by £3.9 million and creates added value (synergy) of £114.9 million (29%). The **absolute maximum price** which can be paid for Nafco is £182.4 million, which is £18.24 per share. The minimum that can be offered is the existing market price of £6.75 per share. You should not of course offer the maximum price. If the shareholders of Premoco are to get their fair share of value added from the merger, they should not pay more than 29% more than the current market price per share of Nafco. This gives a price of **£8.71 per share** (£87.1 million in total).

(2) A **suggested range for negotiation** is therefore £7 to £9 per share. If your intelligence is correct, Nafco's institutional shareholders would be pleased to accept a reasonable offer from a more up-market firm like yours and there should be no reason to go above the figure of £8.71 unless a competing bid emerges.

(ii) **Suggested terms of the offer**

(1) A price of £87.1 million could be financed substantially by cash in the bank but this would leave no investment funds for improving Nafco's operations. If you wish to pursue the cash route, you will need to borrow over the medium or long term. The gearing of Premoco is not high and borrowing will not be a problem, but you must recognise that **group gearing** will **increase** if this acquisition is made, because Nafco's **debt ratio** is much **higher** than your own.

(2) If you intend to borrow, one option is to take up the supplier's offer of cheap loan finance in return for a long-term supply agreement. Acceptance of the offer would reduce Premoco's cost of capital. However, the decision on this source of finance should not be regarded as **part of the acquisition decision**. It is something which needs to be investigated in its own right as it would involve a major **change in strategy** from the existing policy of buying petrol in the open market.

(3) The alternative to increasing borrowing is to **issue shares** in Premoco to the shareholders of Nafco (a share-for-share swap). The share price of Premoco (£16.48) is roughly twice the offer price for Nafco, so the terms of the offer would be approximately 1 for 2. This would have the advantage of **keeping gearing low** and would probably be very acceptable to the disaffected institutional shareholders of Nafco, who would be able to retain their investment in the petroleum industry and maintain the balance of their portfolios. However, the transactions costs of share issues are much higher than for borrowing. Share issues become more obviously advantageous for larger acquisitions.

> **Top tips.** Actually, if the terms of the offer are pitched so that both groups of shareholders gain by 29%, Premoco's share price will rise from £16.48 to £21.26, which is 2.44 times the offer price for Nafco of £8.71. On this basis, the terms of the offer would be approximately 2.44 shares in Nafco for 1 in Premoco, say 5 for 2.

(iii) **Business implications**

(1) The acquisition of Nafco would result in **horizontal integration expanding** the company's operations in **retailing of petroleum** and expanding the company's market share. Large economies of scale could be generated, which accounts for the very high synergy expected from the merger. A choice needs to be made as to whether Nafco's garages should be adapted to run in the same **up-market** way as Premoco's or whether they should concentrate on their existing **low-price** strategy. Whatever the strategy, substantial investment will be needed to improve the image with consumers and hence to improve on the company's existing growth prospects, which are low.

(2) The acquisition of Nafco does not in itself represent a **diversification** away from petroleum products and is therefore not what you appear to be looking for at the moment. However, it appears to be a **good buy** if the price can be kept relatively low and there is much **scope for developing convenience stores** on the Nafco sites.

Oiltrans

(i) **Price to be offered**

Using the same arguments as were put forward for Nafco plc, the **absolute maximum value** of Oiltrans (on the basis of NPV of the combined organisation) is £265.4 million or £22 per share, compared with the current price of £15.30. The added value generated by the merger is 16% which, when added to the current market price, gives £17.75. The suggested **range of prices** for negotiation is **£16** to **£18 per share** but, because the bid is hostile, you might have to be prepared to go higher.

(ii)   **Terms of the offer**

(1)   At £17.75 per share, the total cost of the acquisition is £213 million. This is too large to be financed entirely by cash, and **borrowing** would **increase gearing significantly**. A share issue or a mixture of shares and debt is the most likely route for financing this acquisition. The share-for-share swap would be in the region of 1 for 1 (see tutorial note above) which would mean the issue of 12 million new shares.

(2)   Since only 10 million shares are available for issue, this would mean that the **authorised share capital** would need to be **increased**, and this in turn would signal to the market that something major was about to happen. To avoid an increase in authorised share capital, the company could offer a **choice of shares or a cash alternative**. In cases like this, the cash alternative is usually less than the equivalent share value because it is less risky.

(3)   A **further problem** of a large share issue is that existing share ownership of Premoco will become diluted and large shareholders in Oiltrans may become dominant in the combined company.

(iii)   **Business implications**

(1)   The acquisition of Oiltrans would be a **vertical integration** of an **existing supplier** into the company's business. This represents more of a diversification than the acquisition of Nafco and is therefore more in line with your stated strategy but, judging from the figures, less synergy can be created because of the different nature of the two businesses. Oiltrans has significantly higher growth prospects than the existing business of Premoco.

(2)   Your problem with diversifying into a business of this type is that you **cannot easily demonstrate expertise** and **experience** at managing such companies. In the event of a contested takeover, shareholders will probably back the existing management unless you can demonstrate that they are inefficient in some way. Note that for most large shareholders there is **no benefit** if your company diversifies purely to **reduce risk** because these shareholders will already hold diversified portfolios. Indeed it is quite likely that they already own shares in Oiltrans plc as well as Premoco.

(3)   If the takeover succeeds, the existing management would probably resign, and we lose their skills which appear to have been a **significant influence** on Oiltrans' success.

(4)   When two companies of similar size consider merging there is a real problem as to who will end up running the company. The directors of Oiltrans may turn the tables on you by arranging a **counter-bid** for the shares of Premoco. Alternatively, to agree bid terms, you will need to decide which directors from both sides should head the combined group.

Carsals

(i)   **Price to be offered**

(1)   The **absolute maximum amount** that could be paid for Carsals (on the basis of NPV of the combined organisation) is £38.4 million, which is £76.80 per share. Our dividend valuation model approach gave a figure of £40.69 per share. Synergy generated by the merger is 5%, so to give your own shareholders their fair share of this gain, the price paid should not be more than £42.72 per share, giving a total price of £21.36 million.

(2)   The **price paid** would depend on how quickly the **existing major shareholder needs to make the sale** and on **what other offers** he is likely to receive. One major problem is that other car dealers can generate synergy from the acquisition and can therefore afford to pay more than Premoco. Before agreeing the price, you must be sure of the terms of the franchise, in particular the period for which it lasts and the renewal terms.

(ii)　**Terms of the offer**

This company could be purchased using existing cash in the bank. However a **share-for-share exchange** could be used as a means of tying in the existing managing director, and solving the problem of appointing a suitable managing director (see below). A **generous earn-out arrangement** may also persuade the existing managing director to stay on, and **reduces the risk of loss of customers.**

(iii)　**Business implications**

(1)　Carsals represents a **complete product diversification** from the existing business but maintains the **same up-market image** in prestige locations. There will be no problems of control arising from the acquisition. The business is predicted to show reasonable growth but there will be **no immediate synergy** available from the business combination. The sort of longer term synergy available is in marketing the superior image for both cars, petroleum and other retail services. In addition there may be scope to realise some of the **properties**.

(2)　You will need to appoint a **suitable managing director** from the car sales business if the owner has not groomed a suitable successor. The terms of the franchise must be investigated carefully and, finally, you must be aware that the success of this business depends to a large extent on the continued success of the motor manufacturer.

Conclusions

Despite your wish to diversify, I feel on balance that the opportunity of **expanding the existing business** by the acquisition of Nafco presents much higher wealth-producing opportunities than a contested bid for Oiltrans, which may well drain company resources and come to nothing. The acquisition of Carsals should also be followed up promptly, as a quick purchase may result in a bargain.

Signed: Financial Adviser

APPENDIX

	Premoco £m	Nafco £m	Oiltrans £m	Carsals £m
Total equity earnings	20.6	7.5	10.2	0.8
Existing value of shares*	329.6	67.5	183.6	20.3
Company combination		P+N	P + O	P + C
Sum of existing earnings		28.1	30.8	21.4
Estimated post-merger earnings		32.0	35.0	23.0
Additional earnings predicted		3.9	4.2	1.6
Sum of existing valuations		397.1	513.2	349.9
Estimated NPV of combined organisation		512.0	595.0	368.0
Increase in value from the combination		114.9	81.8	18.1
% increase in value		29%	16%	5%
Maximum price that can be paid for the acquisition**		182.4	265.4	38.4

*Dividend valuation model used for Carsals.

**NPV of combination minus value of Premoco £329.6 million.

64 Garden World

Text references. Investment appraisal techniques are explained in Chapter 18 and equity issues are discussed in Chapter 5. Debt finance is explained in Chapter 6.

Top tips. The best way to approach this question would be to go through the scenario, underlining the key points and thinking not only of complications (are all the costs relevant) but shortcuts (a key shortcut is to adjust for inflation just on operating profit once you've calculated it rather than adjusting all the figures that go to make up operating profit). Then spend the rest of the 20 minutes reading time brain dumping ideas for the other parts. 34 marks are allocated to the discussion section, a high proportion, and a few more than you would normally expect. However this means you will be spending about an hour on the written section so using some of the reading time to jot down ideas on the question paper will be worthwhile.

Once you start writing it's best to set up the proforma and then enter the easy figures. Although contribution is working 1, that is best left until last in your net cash flows calculation. Once you've added up net cash flows, all you then have to do is apply the certainty equivalent factors and discount rates.

Note that the answer to (a) sets out the assumptions clearly and also details the non-relevant costs to enable the examiner to give you credit for recognising these. The complications involved in calculating the tax charge make it worthwhile for you to set out in detail how you carried out the calculation.

(b) is an important test of your ability to recognise the assumptions you are making in an investment appraisal. Our answer contains more points than you would need to score full marks, but make sure you realise the importance of points your answer missed out as you may need to use them in other questions. Questions may not always highlight the simplifications the way (b) does, but nevertheless credit will normally be given for mentioning the important assumptions in an investment appraisal question. (c) might have appeared on P3 as well.

(d) and (f) are a good test of your knowledge of financing sources. Remember also the choice is often not a straight debt v equity decision; different methods of issuing equity and different types of debt must be considered, also the term of borrowing.

Easy marks. The best strategy for getting the easiest marks on the later parts is to make sure you leave yourself enough time. There are plenty of opportunities to score well, but the discussion parts (apart from (e)), do require development which will take time.

(a)   **Garden World – retail investment – cash flow projections**

	Yr 0 £'000	Yr 1 £'000	Yr 2 £'000	Yr 3 £'000	Yr 4 £'000	Yr 5 £'000
Contribution (W1)		(182)	406	1,828	2,837	
Taxation (W1)			143	(72)	(557)	(901)
Land and buildings	(4,750)				4,750	
Fittings and equipment	(1,000)				316	
Working capital	(500)	(100)	(150)	(50)	800	
W/cap inflation (W2)		(24)	(37)	(39)	100	
Disposal proceeds (W3)					5,493	
Disposal – tax						(1,813)
Net cash flows	(6,250)	(306)	362	1,667	13,739	(2,714)
Certainty equiv.	1.00	0.90	0.85	0.80	0.75	0.70
8% discount factor	1.000	0.926	0.857	0.794	0.735	0.681
Discounted certainty equivalent	(6,250)	(255)	264	1,059	7,574	(1,293)
Cumulative PV	(6,250)	(6,505)	(6,241)	(5,182)	2,392	1,099

Workings

1

	Yr 1 £'000	Yr 2 £'000	Yr 3 £'000	Yr 4 £'000	Yr 5 £'000
Sales	1,750	3,250	5,250	6,250	
Direct costs	(1,500)	(2,300)	(3,100)	(3,300)	
Marketing	(300)	(450)	(400)	(400)	
Overhead	(125)	(125)	(125)	(125)	
Cont'n before inflation	(175)	375	1,625	2,425	
After inflation $(1.04)^{yrn}$	(182)	406	1,828	2,837	
Tax allowances	(250)	(188)	(141)	(105)	
Taxable profit	(432)	218	1,687	2,732	
Taxation at 33%		143	(72)	(557)	(901)

2   Working capital inflation is calculated as follows.

$600 (1.04 - 1) = 24$
$750 (1.04^2 - 1) = 61 = 24 + 37$
$800 (1.04^3 - 1) = 100 = 61 + 39$

3   Disposal proceeds will be as follows.

	£
Taxable profit in year 4*	2,732
Tax at 33%	(901)
Post-tax profit	1,831
Post-tax profit × 3	5,493
Tax on disposal proceeds - payable year 5	(1,813)

* This can be used since the depreciation is calculated on the same basis as the tax allowances.

Notes

1   Depreciation is excluded from the calculations since this does not have a cash component.

2   The allocation of head office operating costs is excluded since this will be incurred whether or not the project is undertaken.

3   Surveyors' fees of £250,000 are excluded since these are sunk costs.

4   Since certainty equivalents are being used, the project cash flows will be discounted at the risk free rate of 8%.

5   It is assumed that the tax loss in year 1 can be offset against other group income.

On the basis of the calculations above, the investment should produce a positive net present value of £1.099m. It therefore appears to be financially worthwhile.

(b)   (i)   In reality, the appraisal might differ from that shown above for the following reasons.

(1)   **Terminal value**

A critical element in the calculations is the **terminal value of the project**. In reality there are likely to be a number of **possible exit routes** which would need to be evaluated. The company might also consider the possibility of continuing to operate the retail arm directly for longer than the projected four years.

(2)   **Inflation**

Reality is likely to be much **more complex than the projections suggest**. It is unlikely that all the factors in the cash flow will be subject to exactly 4% inflation and the rates are also likely to vary over time. It would therefore be helpful to carry out a **more detailed sensitivity analysis** in this area, and also to consider the effect of changes in the tax rate.

(3) **Risk free rate**

It is unlikely that **the risk free rate will remain constant** over the period. It would therefore be helpful to consider the effect of **changes in the cost of capital** and perhaps to look at the internal rate of return of the project.

(4) **More choices available**

There are likely to be **more choices available** than a **simple 'go ahead or abandon'** decision. For instance, the scale, degree of specialisation and location could all be varied.

(5) **Markets**

Assumptions about overall market growth and market share would need to be examined and the project evaluated in the light of different operating scenarios.

(6) **Capital**

The availability of capital and the projected contribution of other alternative investments will affect the final choice of projects.

(ii) **Judgmental factors to be considered**

(1) **Other markets**

The **likely effect** of the investment on the **company's other markets**. Since Garden World is considering competing directly with some of its customers, this may **depress sales** of other divisions and cause a deterioration in the relationships with its customers.

(2) **Management skills**

The **technical ability** and **managerial capacity** of the company to achieve the target growth.

(3) **Strategic position**

Where this **investment fits** into the **long-term strategic plan and aims** of the company. If it is crucial to achieving the company's long-term objectives then it will not be looked at on the same basis as an opportunistic diversification.

(4) **Interrelationships**

The **interrelationships** between volume, price, direct costs and fixed overheads, including price sensitivity and the effect of marketing and advertising.

(c) **Two alternative risk adjustment methods**

(i) **Restricting the payback period**

This approach recognises the fact that the level of **uncertainty increases** with the length of the **time horizon**. Therefore the company may decide to set a limit to the amount of time a project will be allowed to pay back. In practice this is often between three and five years. Even if a limit is not set it is helpful to compare the payback period of different projects since this provides some measure of their relative risk.

(ii) **Capital asset pricing model**

This can be used to **quantify** the **effect** on the **cost of equity** to the company due to the **change** in the **level of risk** arising from the new investment. This can then be used to calculate the **new cost of capital** which in turn is used to evaluate the project. Thus the CAPM provides a means of **adjusting the discount rate** to take into account the additional risk which the company will face as a result of undertaking the investment. The advantage of this method is that it allows the **direct comparison** of projects which fall into different risk classes. However the method is **complex to use** in practice and it must be remembered that **estimates of returns and probabilities** will be subjective. In addition, the CAPM is really a **single period model** and thus it should only be used when it is expected that conditions will be stable for the life of the project.

ANSWERS

(d) **Need for capital outlay**

The retail investment project will require a **capital outlay** in the region of £6.5m. The projected cash flows show that the capital outlay should be recouped quickly, with the cumulative net present value becoming positive in year 4. This implies that any loan could be repaid in year 4. However, this is very dependent on Garden World achieving a successful sale of the business at that time. The calculations are also sensitive to the accuracy of the **certainty equivalents** and the way in which they reflect the relationship between **risk and return** in the capital market.

Choice of debt

The **type of debt to be selected** will depend on:

(i) Whether the directors are actually **intending to sell** the subsidiary in year 4, or whether the sale price has only been calculated for the **purpose of providing a terminal value** to enable the investment to be evaluated over four years

(ii) The way in which **interest rates** are **expected to move** in the **medium term**

Medium-term borrowing

If the directors are **intending to sell** the **subsidiary**, then the **medium-term borrowing option** looks attractive. This offers the **lowest rate** and could be **repaid** at the end of year 4 from the proceeds of the sale. Thus the company is not left with debt which it no longer requires. On the face of it this is also the **cheapest option**, although it is not stated whether the rates quoted are fixed or floating. Assuming that the rates are fixed, and in the situation where a sale of the subsidiary is not being seriously considered, this option would also be attractive if the directors expect that interest rates are set to fall. The investment could then be refinanced at a lower rate within the next five years since the company would not be locked into long-term borrowings.

Long-term borrowing

Long-term borrowing becomes attractive in the situation where **interest rates are expected to rise**. This would allow maximum advantage to be taken of the existing low level of rates. It is also a better option if the company is intending to continue to operate the subsidiary directly for the foreseeable future since the need to roll over debt at the end of a shorter term is avoided.

Convertibles

Convertibles will also be attractive if the company is not intending to sell the new business in year 4. They provide a means of **taking advantage** of the **lower cost of debt** and the **tax advantages of debt** in the **medium term**, and have the **added benefit** of being **self-liquidating**, provided that the share price increases in line with expectations at the date of issue. The long-term borrowing capacity of the company is therefore not impaired.

Preference shares

Preference shares are less attractive. Although they possess many of the features of loan stock, the preferred dividend is not allowable for tax and therefore they are relatively **expensive to service**. Since the dividend can be passed in the event of the company having a poor year, and since they rank behind other debt for repayment, they are also relatively unattractive to investors.

(e) **Services provided by merchant banks**

Merchant banks provide companies with a point of access to the capital markets. Companies can take advantage of their knowledge of and technical ability in the markets to achieve the most suitable and efficient form of financing. The services which they offer include the following.

(i) They can **advise Garden World** on the **current view of interest rates** and suggest to them particularly appropriate financing opportunities which are currently available.

342

(ii) They can **advise** on the **procedure** to be followed in **making the issue** and help the company to ensure that all legislative and regulatory requirements are complied with.

(iii) They can **advise** on the **timing and pricing** of any issue.

(iv) They may **offer an underwriting service** to ensure that the offer is adequately subscribed.

(f) (i) **Existing shareholders**

A key factor for an established company in deciding on the method of issue is the **effect of the choice on the existing shareholders**. Shareholders normally have **pre-emptive rights** which means that any new issue of shares must first be offered to them. However it is possible for the company to obtain a waiver of the pre-emptive rights in general meeting. This can be done up to a year in advance in the AGM.

Rights issue and placing

In practice, the choice of issue method for an established company is generally between a **rights issue** and a **placing**. One of the main advantages of the rights issue is that the existing structure of ownership and control remains unchanged. In a placing, the shares are sold in large blocks to a small number of large, usually institutional investors. As a result, no underwriting is needed since a purchaser for the shares is arranged as a part of the issue process. It may also be possible to obtain a higher price than could be obtained from a rights issue.

(ii) **Setting issue price**

In setting the issue price, the directors will be aiming to obtain the required amount of capital for the minimum number of shares. Although in theory, any number of shares could be issued provided that the authorised capital is not breached, in practice the number will be kept to a minimum. The **new shares will have to be priced at a discount** to the current market price of the existing shares in order to make them attractive to investors. However if the discount is too large this could result in a significant dilution in earnings per share which could in turn impact on the share price.

65 Almond Arts

Text references. Forecasting and performance measures are revised in Chapter 3.

Top tips. The question is divided into two parts, calculations and discussions. However, it is impossible to attempt the discussion section competently without having first completed the calculations. When attempting the calculations, be sure to take account of all the information provided in the question, since the way in which certain figures are to be calculated is actually quite closely defined. Underline and cross-reference the question paper whilst you're reading the question during the reading time. Although the majority of the calculations fall in the first part of the question, you will need to undertake further numerical analysis within the main body of the report.

In (a) don't forget setting up proformas, calculating the easy figures first and marking off the figures as you use them in the statements. Quick workings will help the examiner confirm your understanding even if you do make a slip in your calculations. Workings are particularly important in the calculation of ratios.

It's best to complete your income statement and balance sheet before tackling the cash flow, as you can go straight down the cash flow statement for most of the items, comparing the current and forecast income statement and balance sheet.

In (b) you will need to undertake some further numerical analysis to see if the company has achieved its objectives and to project the situation further forward. As it happens (b) emphasises the company's objectives and highlights the need to consider the funding issue. In a question with less helpfully worded requirements earnings per share, dividends and share price impact, also how financing and earnings interact, are all likely to be important elements; calculations are likely to include valuations using the dividend valuation model. Note that the answer clearly states the assumptions made. You may not be told explicitly to use the dividend growth model, so you should be able to recognise when you have sufficient information to be able to use it. However don't spend all your time on the calculations, as the bulk of the marks will be available for discussion of limitations and shareholder interests. The calculation of the needs beyond 20X2 will have a significant impact on the source of finance chosen; the company needs to think very carefully about whether it is worth making a rights issue.

The answer also explains the importance of the assumption that the rate of inflation is constant for all items.

The best recommendation is to use a range of methods giving a more rounded view of the company. However, you would have gained credit for any reasonable recommendation – assuming you remembered to make one.

Easy marks. Make sure you gain the marks in (b) for putting your answer in a report format and making a reasonable recommendation. The discussion on inflation may be the most straightforward as it doesn't require supporting calculations.

(a)　(i)　ALMOND ARTS: FORECAST INCOME STATEMENT FOR THE YEAR TO 31 DECEMBER 20X2

	Note	£'000
Revenues	1	17,325
Cost of sales	2	10,759
Depreciation		1,200
Operating expenses		1,750
Operating profit		3,616
Interest	3	200
Redundancy payment		125
Tax		850
Net profit		2,441
Dividends declared	4	1,343

Notes

1　Turnover is expected to grow by 5% from £16,500,000 to £17,325,000.

2

	£'000
Cost of sales y/e 31.12.X1	11,600
Less depreciation	925
	10,675
As a percentage of sales	64.7%
Expected reduction in percentage	2.6%
Percentage of sales for y/e 31.12.X2	62.1%
Cost of sales for y/e 31.12.X2	10,759

3　Loan stock interest = £2,000,000 × 10%

4　The existing payout ratio is 1,136/2,065 = 55%.

This payout ratio will be applied to the net profit for the year of £2,441,000.

(ii)   ALMOND ARTS
       FORECAST BALANCE SHEET AS AT 31 DECEMBER 20X2

	Note	£'000
Non-current assets (net book value)	1	9,300
Current assets		
Inventory	2	3,850
Receivables	3	1,759
Cash and bank	4	865
		15,774
Equity and liabilities		
Equity		
Ordinary share capital	5	5,500
Share premium account	6	1,875
Reserves	7	3,292
		10,667
Non-current liabilities		
10% loan stock 20X6		2,000
Current liabilities		
Trade payables		1,764
Other payables (dividends)		1,343
		15,774

Notes

1

	£'000
Opening non-current assets	7,500
Additions for year	3,000
Less depreciation	1,200
Closing non-current assets	9,300

2   Inventory will increase by £1,000,000 on the 31 December 20X1 figure.

3   The ratio of receivables to sales at 31 December 20X1 is 1,675/16,500 = 10.15%.

    Increases by 5% as for revenues.

4   This can be calculated most quickly as the balancing figure:

	£'000
Shareholders' funds	10,667
Net assets excluding cash	9,802
Closing cash balance	865

    Note. This figure can be cross checked once the cash flow forecast has been completed.

5

	£'000
Share capital at 31.12.X1	5,000
1 for 10 rights issue	500
Share capital at 31.12.X2	5,500

6   The rights issue will raise 500,000 × 4.75 = £2,375,000. The nominal value of the new shares is £500,000. The balance of £1,875,000 must be credited to the share premium account.

7

	£'000
Opening reserves	2,194
Add net profit for year	2,441
Less dividend	1,343
Closing reserves	3,292

8   The ratio of trade payables to cost of sales at 31 December 20X1 is 1,750/10,675 = 16.39%.

  If this is applied to the 20X2 cost of sales of £10,759,000, the closing payables will be £1,764,000.

9   From forecast income statement.

(iii)   ALMOND ARTS
CASHFLOW FORECAST FOR THE YEAR TO 31 DECEMBER 20X2

	Note	£'000	£'000
Income arising from operations:			
Operating profit			3,616
Add back depreciation			1,200
Increase in receivables	1		(84)
Increase in payables	2		14
Total			4,746
Less			
Investment in non-current assets		3,000	
Investment in inventory		1,000	
Interest paid		200	
Tax paid		850	
Dividends paid		1,136	
Redundancy payment		125	
Total			6,311
Net cash flow from operations			(1,565)
New capital from rights issue			2,375
Total cash flow for the year			810
Opening cash balance			55
Closing cash balance			865

Notes

1   1,675 – 1,759 = (84)

2   1,750 – 1,764 = 14

3   The dividend paid in the year to 31 December 20X2 is the dividend declared for the previous year.

(iv)   The **after tax return on shareholders' funds** can be found by dividing the profit available for dividend by the total shareholders' funds as at the year end.

Note: there is an argument for using the **average** level of shareholders' funds in the calculation, but the financial objective of the company defines shareholders' funds as the **year end** figure.

	20X1	20X2
	£'000	£'000
Profit available for dividend	2,065	2,441
Shareholders' funds	7,194	10,667
Return on shareholders' funds	**28.7%**	**22.9%**

Earnings per share can be found by dividing the profit available for dividend by the total number of shares in issue at the end of the year.

	20X1	20X2
Profit available for dividend (£'000)	2,065	2,441
Number of shares in issue	5,000	5,500
Earnings per share	**41.3p**	**44.4p**

Dividend per share can be found by dividing the dividend declared for the year by the total number of shares in issue at the end of the year.

	20X1	20X2
Dividend declared (£'000)	1,136	1,343
Number of shares in issue	5,000	5,500
Dividend per share	**22.7p**	**24.4p**

(b)

To:	Finance Director, Almond Arts
From:	Assistant to Finance Director
Date:	31 December 20X1
Re:	Review of forecast financial performance for the period 1 January 20X1 to 31 December 20X2

1   Introduction

1.1   Forecast financial performance

This report is concerned with the forecast financial performance of the company for the years 20X1 and 20X2. There are a number of points that the board should consider in its planning for the next year, and which will be discussed in more detail below.

- The **likely level of performance** in relation to the stated financial objectives
- The **need for additional financing** during 20X2
- The **effect of inflation** on the forecast figures
- **Alternative measures** of financial performance that could be introduced

2   Performance against stated financial objectives

2.1   After-tax return on shareholders' funds

Almond Arts has the objective of earning an annual after-tax return on shareholders' funds of at least 25%. The forecasts suggest that this **target** will be **met** for the year to 31 December 20X1, with a return of 28.7%. However, the forecast for 20X2 indicates a **rate of return** of 22.9%, which is **below** the **target level**. The main reason for the shortfall is the significant level of investment that is planned for the year, since net profits are forecast to increase by 18% during the same period.

It is a weakness of using this type of accounting measure that the **calculated returns do go down** at the start of **a period of investment**. This can translate into a temptation to cut back on entirely necessary investment as a means of improving short-term performance.

2.2   Annual 10% increase in earnings per share

The forecast performance against this measure is as follows.

	20X0	20X1	20X2
Earnings per share (pence)	37.2	41.3	44.4
Annual increase (pence)		4.1	3.1
Annual increase (percent)		11.0	7.5

This performance target should be met in 20X1, but the company will fall well short of this in 20X2. There are two main reasons for this:

- The **rights issue will increase** the **number of shares** in issue before the benefits of the new investment are reflected in the earnings figure.

- The **one-off payment** of **redundancy costs** will depress the earnings figure.

Once again, this is more a problem of the measure used than of the likely long-term performance of the company. This situation is likely to persist, even when the EPS is adjusted for comparability due to the change in the number of shares in issue.

2.3 Annual 10% increase in dividend per share

The forecast performance against this measure is as follows.

	20X0	20X1	20X2
Dividend per share (pence)	20.5	22.7	24.4
Annual increase (pence)		2.2	1.7
Annual increase (percent)		10.7	7.5

As with EPS, this **performance target** should be met **in 20X1**, but the company will fall well short in 20X2. Maintenance of the payout ratio at 55% means that the **growth in dividend per share** will directly **reflect** the rate of **growth in earnings per share**. The company would need to make a significant change to the payout ratio to meet this target, largely due to the increase in the number of shares in issue. Although in theory shareholders should be indifferent between capital appreciation and dividends, in practice there is often a preference for dividends at the expense of capital growth. This is because investors will usually opt for certain cash now in the form of dividends, rather than waiting for capital growth to be achieved.

The **payout ratio** is the crux of a **major tension** in **company investment policy**. Shareholders desire a good level of dividends that increase year on year, while companies often prefer to retain earnings as a simple way of financing future investment. Restricting dividends may cause a loss of confidence by the markets and impact upon the share price, and for this reason companies will often prefer to finance new investments by means of debt.

2.4 To increase share price year on year

The share price provides a **measure** of the **value** of the company. Although in theory this is determined by the present value of future cash flows, discounted at the cost of capital, in practice other factors will also influence the **share price**. The overall level of **market confidence**, **interest rates** and **takeover activity** will all affect the price of the company's shares. For this reason, it would be more helpful to specify the target as the level of the share price in relation to the overall level of the market, rather than considering it in isolation.

Given these provisos, the **share price** at the end of 20X1 is **higher** than that at the end of 20X0 (525p as compared with 465p), and thus the company appears to have **met** this **target** for the **current year**. The closing share price for 20X2 can be estimated using the dividend valuation model and on the basis of the P/E ratio:

Dividend valuation model:

$$P_0 = \frac{d_0(1+g)}{(k_e - g)}$$

The cost of capital is 14%, and a 10% rate of dividend growth will be assumed. The net dividend per share will be taken as the dividend forecast of £1,343,000 for 20X2.

$$P_0 = \frac{1,343(1+0.10)}{(0.14 - 0.10)}$$

P_0 = £36.9m

Price per share = £36.9m ÷ 5.5m = £6.71

P/E ratio:

The current P/E ratio can be found by dividing the share price of 525p by the EPS of 41.3p = 12.7. If this is applied to the earnings forecast for 20X2 of £2.441m, the estimated market capitalisation is £31m. This equates to a price per share of £5.64.

Both these approaches suggest that the share price will **increase by the end of 20X2**, with the dividend valuation model predicting the largest increase. This is because this model incorporates the expected growth rate that is expected to result from the investment programme, whereas the P/E ratio method does not.

3 **The need for additional financing during 20X2**

3.1 The cash flow forecast shows that in the absence of any additional financing, there will be a **negative cash flow** during the year of £1.565m. This is due to the **significant investment** of £4m in **non-current assets and inventory** that will take place during the period. However, if profits growth continues at 5% per annum the cash flow for 20X3 and 20X4 should be roughly as follows:

	Notes	20X3 £'000	20X4 £'000
Cash flow from operations	1	4,983	5,232
Less Interest	2	200	200
Dividends	3	1,343	1,477
Taxation	4	935	1,029
Non-current assets		2,000	
Net cash flow from operations		505	2,526
Opening cash balance		865	1,370
Closing cash balance		1,370	3,896

Notes

1 It is assumed that the income arising from operations will continue to grow at 5% per year, and that efficiency savings will offset inflationary increases in costs.

2 It is assumed that there will be no interest payments beyond those due on the debentures.

3 The dividend for 20X3 is that forecast to be declared at the end of 20X2. It is assumed that dividends will increase by 10% per year in line with the performance targets.

4 It is assumed that tax will increase at 10% per year in line with earnings.

3.2 In the absence of the rights issue being made, the cash position would be as follows.

	20X2 £'000	20X3 £'000	20X4 £'000
Opening cash balance	55	(1,510)	(1,005)
Cash flow for year	(1,565)	505	2,527
Closing cash balance	(1,510)	(1,005)	1,522

3.3 While it is acknowledged that these figures are very rough, they do seem to indicate that the company will only have a **cash deficit for two years**, with the cash balance becoming positive during the first half of 20X4. This raises the question as to whether the company should be making a **large rights issue** to finance the investment, particularly given the effect of this on the performance indicators highlighted above. If the cash shortage is only a temporary situation, the company should consider using some form of short or medium-term finance to cover the deficit. The issue of additional permanent capital should only be made if there are further profitable investments in the pipeline.

3.4 Alternative sources of funds in this situation include:
- A **medium-term bank loan**
- Financing the new assets by the use of **hire purchase agreements** or a finance lease
- **Staging the expenditure more** gradually and using short-term finance
- **Retaining a higher proportion of earnings** for the next one or two years - this would require a significant change in the company's existing dividend policy

4 The effect of inflation upon the forecast figures

4.1 At present, **low inflation** is **forecast** for the period in question, and therefore the **effect** upon the **forecast figures** is likely to be **low**. However, this assumes that all the elements of the cost base will be subject to the general level of inflation. In practice, there is considerable **variability in the level of inflation** between different cost factors, and if there were to be a significant increase in the cost of key raw materials for example, this could have a major impact upon the forecasts. In addition, there are signs that wages are increasing at a higher level than prices, and this could have a significant impact upon a manufacturing company such as Almond Arts.

4.2 The figures in the forecasts appear to be in **nominal terms**, ie with an allowance for inflation. The true situation might be clearer if figures were restated in real terms for comparison.

4.3 If inflation began to rise at a level above the 3% forecast, the impact would depend upon the way in which the **different variables** were **affected**, and the **extent to which Almond Arts** would be able to **recover its costs** through increases in selling prices. However, higher inflation would be likely to result in an improvement in the reported ratios on which performance is judged. This is because the dividend and earnings ratios are calculated on the basis of the book value of the assets, and it is unlikely that the entire asset base would be revalued immediately in the event of a rise in the level of inflation.

5 Conclusions and recommendations

5.1 The forecasts suggest that the proposed investment will be beneficial in terms of **both returns and cash flow**. However, the following issues should be addressed before final decisions are taken regarding the investment and its financing.

5.2 **All new investments** are **evaluated at the cost of capital** of 14%. Since this is a major new investment for the company, the specific risks attaching to the project should be investigated and compared with the risk profile of the existing operations. If necessary, the discount rate should be adjusted to reflect any significant differences.

5.3 The **sensitivity of the project outcome to changes** in the key variables should be analysed.

5.4 The **method of financing the project should be re-evaluated**. It appears that the company will become cash positive again within three years if no new capital is raised, and therefore the possibility of using medium-term finance rather than additional permanent capital should be investigated.

5.5 There should be a **review of the company's financial objectives** and the way in which they are measured.

It has become apparent throughout the foregoing discussion that there are **weaknesses** in the **use of the current financial performance targets**. The main area on which attention should be focussed is the extent to which the company is achieving an **increase in the level of shareholder wealth**, and the use of proxies for this such as dividend per share can be misleading. It would perhaps be more helpful to focus on the market capitalisation and P/E ratio of the company in relation to the sector as a whole.

Another approach would be to **take a wider view** of the company's activities and direct attention to performance against a **basket of ratios** that would measure performance in the key areas of:

- Profitability and return
- Liquidity and working capital management
- Debt and gearing
- Shareholders' investment ratios

66 Eros

(a)　To:　　　Directors of Eros
　　　From:　　XYZ & Co, Accountants
　　　Date:　　30 November 20X1
　　　Subject:　Report on possible methods of valuation of Eros and alternative types of finance for expansion

(i)　**Determination of a range of possible values for the shares of Eros Ltd**

Three methods of valuing the company's shares have been used: net asset valuation, and two methods based on expected future earnings/dividends.

Method 1 Net asset valuation

Net asset valuation has been taken as the **realisable value** of **tangible fixed assets** (buildings, equipment and vehicles) plus net working capital (current assets less current liabilities). On this basis the value of the business is £385,000. After deducting the longer term loan liability of £50,000, the net asset valuation of the company's share capital is only **£335,000**.

Method 2 Value of expected future equity dividends by discounting at the cost of equity capital

The calculations below show the estimation of expected turnover, profit and equity earnings in each of the years 20X2 and 20X3, based on the scenarios you have given us concerning the potential new contract with the supermarket group. Equity earnings beyond that point have been estimated by simple growth rates, and it is assumed that:

- In each year equi**ty earnings** are **equal** to **distributable cash**: for example, depreciation is equal to cash reinvested in fixed assets and adjustments for accruals are negligible; and

- **Equity earnings** are **fully distributed** as **cash dividends** to **shareholders**.

The expected future equity dividends to perpetuity are discounted at 16% per annum, which is the estimated average **after-tax cost of equity capital** for the companies involved in electronic design and associated products.

Outcome	Year to 31 March 20X2			Year to 31 March 20X3		
	Probability	Turnover	Expected value	Probability	Turnover	Expected value
		£'000	£'000		£'000	£'000
1	0.5	1,800	900	0.5 × 0.8	2,500	1,000
				0.5 × 0.2	3,000	300
2	0.3	1,200	360	0.3 × 0.5	1,700	255
				0.3 × 0.5	1,400	210
3	0.2	800	160	0.2 × 0.5	1,000	100
				0.2 × 0.5	800	80
Total expected turnover			1,420			1,945
Operating costs		35%	(497)		30%	(584)
Interest (10% × £50,000)			(5)			(5)
			918			1,356
Tax at 30%			(275)			(407)
Expected equity earnings /dividends			643			949

Present value of expected future equity dividends

Year		Expected growth rate	Expected equity dividend	16% factors	Present value
			£'000		£'000
1	(20X2)		643	0.862	554
2	(20X3)		949	0.743	705
3	(20X4)	40%	1,329	0.641	852
4	(20X5)	40%	1,861	0.552	1,027
					3,138

Year 5 onwards

Year 5 expected equity earnings is 1,861 × 1.1 = 2,047, growing at 10% per year.

Present value at year 4 of this stream of cash flows is given by $D_1/(k_e - g)$; ie 2,047/(0.16 – 0.10) = 34,117.

Therefore present value at year 0 = 34,117 × 0.552 = 18,833.

Therefore, by this method, the value of the shares is the expected present value of all cash flows from year 1 to perpetuity, which is (£'000) 3,138 + 18,833 = £21.971 million, or nearly **£22 million**.

Method 3 Value of expected future equity earnings using the P/E ratio of the industry

This method **multiplies** the company's **expected future earnings** by a **suitable P/E ratio** based on market data for companies involved in electronic design and associated products.

Future earnings

On the basis of the above calculations, equity earnings in 20X2 are expected to be £643,000. Earnings in 20X1 were only £12,500 (10,000 × 125p EPS) and can be argued to be irrelevant to the valuation of the company based on future earnings.

Suitable P/E ratio

The average P/E for the industry is 27, but the range extends from 12 to 82. A company's P/E ratio is influenced fundamentally by the expected future growth rate of its earnings. Eros's expected earnings growth is 48% in 20X3 (ie 949/643 –1) and 40% for the two following years. This is likely to be substantially more than average for the industry. A range of possible P/Es could therefore be taken as 27 to 40, say.

Possible values

This gives a possible value to the shares of between:

£643,000 × 27 = £17.4 million; and
£643,000 × 40 = £25.7 million.

This is in the same 'ball-park' as the calculations based on discounted future dividends.

(ii)   **Discussion of the valuation methods**

Net assets

The main asset determining the company's value is the **intellectual capital of its owners** and **employees** (ie knowledge and skills and ability to apply them to create products valued by customers). Since it is impossible to value intellectual capital directly, the net assets valuation is significantly **understated** and can only give the company's value in the '**worst case scenario**' of failure and sale of assets. Since this scenario has been given a zero probability when estimating future performance, it can be ignored for the purposes of negotiating a price for the business.

Discounted value of expected future dividends

This method is the probably best of the three calculations shown because it takes into account most of the key determinants of value as separate estimates: **future cash flows** in the **foreseeable future**, **longer term growth rates**, and the **investors' required rate of return** for companies in this risk category. Nevertheless the method relies on very broad estimates of all these factors, which are subject to great uncertainties for a company like Eros. Criticisms that can be raised are:

(1)   The **expected value** of turnover and profit are **not figures** that will **actually happen**: they are simply an **average** based on the likelihood of different scenarios, with hugely varying success rates. The calculations only really make sense if an investor has many such risky investments.

(2)   Future growth rates are **very broad estimates** and, for long run growth, probably overstated. 10% annual growth may seem small in comparison with the current growth of the business, but it is highly unlikely that this rate can be maintained **to perpetuity.**

(3)   The **cost of capital** is **based** on the **average figure** for the '**electronic design**' sector, which contains many different types of company with different risk attributes.

P/E applied to future equity earnings

This method is really a simplified version of the second method, but suffers from the **lack of a clear methodology** to handle expected growth in earnings. Because of this and because the 'electronic design' sector includes a wide range of companies, P/E ratios vary enormously, making the method highly inaccurate. Nevertheless it has the advantage for negotiation purposes of **simplicity** and of being based on **clearly observable market data**.

Conclusion

The future dividends/earnings methods are both more relevant to the valuation of Eros than the net assets method, but they are highly inaccurate and subject to great uncertainties.

(iii)   **Comparison of financing by venture capital with flotation on the stock exchange**

Venture capital

Venture capitalists assist companies' growth by **providing finance** in the form of **equity interests** and **loans**. The suggestion made by the investment bank centres around an issue of new share capital at a high price, in order to provide funds for accelerated expansion. They would therefore own a **substantial minority interest** and would also require **representation** on the board of directors. You need to consider whether such a **loss of total control** over your business is acceptable to you. In

return, however, the investment bank may bring new ideas for expansion, based on its experience and contacts. Venture capital funds look for **medium term equity investments** (say 5 to 8 years) and need an '**exit route'** for their investment. This can be achieved by various means including:

- Flotation of the company's shares
- Sale to another investor or fund
- Sale back to the original owners, i.e. yourselves

Flotation

The other alternative considers waiting two years until the company has achieved an ex**pected turnover** and **earnings** of approximately £2 million and £1 million respectively, and then **floating the company** on the Stock Exchange by selling some of the owners' shares and **raising new share capital.** The listing would **dilute your shareholdings** and, again, you would need to decide whether this was acceptable. You need to trade off your ownership preferences against the economies of scale of selling a high proportion of the shares. The listing has the advantages over the venture capital route of:

- **Providing a market-determined value for the company's shares**
- **Raising permanent funds**
- Allowing you to **realise** some of your **capital**

(iv) **Alternative types of financial support for expansion and issues to be considered before choosing**

There are a number of other methods of obtaining finance in addition to the routes suggested above. These include:

(1) **Borrowing**

The company's existing borrowings are very low and this method has the advantage of being **relatively cheap** and causing **no dilution of ownership**. However, **tangible assets** available for security are **low** and unsecured loans carry a **higher interest rate**. Also high borrowings can cause appreciable levels of financial risk.

(2) **Issue of shares to selected private investors**

The government operates various schemes to encourage private investment in new and growing businesses. Investors would usually be hoping for an eventual **listing** of the company.

(3) **Working capital**

The increased working capital requirements resulting from rapid expansion could be funded by **factoring**, **invoice discounting** and **supplier finance**. Tightening up control of working capital would ensure optimum cash flow.

(4) **Flotation**

The proposed flotation could be **brought forward** to raise cash earlier.

(5) **Revenue sharing agreements**

The company could **enter** into **revenue sharing agreements** with customers to increase expansion.

Need for cash

The question of how much cash is needed should be determined by what **investment opportunities** are available and the **ability** of the company to manage those opportunities. It would be illogical to raise cash for expansion now if growth is already as high as can reasonably be managed. In this respect it may be better to await the outcome of the bid for the supermarket contract before deciding on raising any further funds.

Choice of methods

Assuming cash is needed now, you should consider the various methods listed above and choose between them, bearing in mind particularly:

(1)   **The amount of cash needed**

(2)   Your **attitudes to dilution of ownership**, and possibly having a venture capitalist on the board

(3)   Whether your own involvement in the company is likely to be **short or long term**: if shorter term, a flotation provides the best exit route

(4)   Your attitudes to the **financial risks of borrowing**

(b)   **Protection against the risk of loss of key staff with technical expertise**

The main risks are that:

- Key staff **fall ill or die**.
- Key staff **leave the company** and **set up on their own** or join a competitor.

Illness or death

The first can be insured against to a certain extent, through **medical insurance** and life insurance, though these are unlikely to provide sufficient compensation if the employee is no longer able to work. The company may also need to consider the advisability of **introducing contracts** and/or **rules to limit health and life risks**, for example banning dangerous sports or limiting the extent to which key employees travel in the same vehicle, train or plane.

Leaving the company

The second risk is more dangerous, since it is more likely to occur. Staff can be asked to sign contracts that **restrict their activities** when they leave the company. However, some may refuse to sign, and in any case such contracts can be **difficult to enforce**. It is better to adopt a proactive approach and to foster a working environment in which staff are **content** and feel **properly rewarded** for their work and creativity. Profit sharing and share option schemes have a useful role to play, particularly when the company's shares are likely to be publicly listed.

67 Margate

Text references. Acquisition issues are discussed in Chapter 16.

Top tips. In this case study there are *many* alternative answers for all parts of the question, but the main requirement throughout the question is to demonstrate your knowledge of the principles involved by writing explanatory notes and comments.

In (a), try to choose three ratios with different purposes (e.g. profitability, liquidity, gearing) - but the P/E ratio is already given - so presumably no marks for calculating it, even though it is a relevant ratio!

In (b), there is a huge range of justifiable values for the company, even without estimating possible merger gains, on which no information is given. Again, the key is to justify the assumptions you make.

The main methods you should have used in (b) were, typically, the dividend valuation model and P/E ratios. Net asset values is not included as it is unlikely to be of any relevance to Hastings' shareholders. Note how the capital asset pricing model is used, and remember that if you're given market and risk-free rates, you would expect to use the capital asset pricing model somewhere. Don't worry too much if you didn't think of the adjusted present value method, though note how it is used, and the justification for using it (to calculate an investment specific cost of capital).

For the report in (c), the most sensible figure to choose for a bid price would be something with a premium over current market value. The 'offer terms' means suggesting how many shares of Margate would be exchanged for a given number of Hastings' shares (eg 7 for 8). The bulk of the discussion marks can be earned by considering principles of takeover defences and reasons for merger synergy. Your calculation for the value of the combined company should show how much would be owned by the original shareholders of Margate and how much by former Hastings shareholders.

Easy marks. Hopefully in (a) you chose relevant ratios, calculated them correctly – and remembered to comment on them.

Examiner's comments. The examiner was disappointed that in (a) 'Students are unable to choose appropriate ratios or calculate them in the correct manner.' Mistakes included inappropriate choice of ratios (P/e ratio was given in the question), choosing very similar ratios or including incorrect variables (calculating the return on capital employed on shareholders' funds). Comments in a number of answers just consisted of statements that one ratio was higher or lower than another without giving further details.

The main error in (b) was failure to calculate a range of values. Some answers assumed Hastings would have zero growth without stating why; this would make it an unlikely takeover target.

(c) discriminated well between stronger and weaker candidates. Common weaknesses included assuming the share exchange had to be 1:1, suggesting an offer price below current market price, and failing to discuss the advantages of the acquisition or estimate post-acquisition values.

(a)   **Three key ratios**

Profitability: Return on shareholders' funds

	Margate Group	Hastings
Earnings £m	503	300
Shareholders' funds £m	2,020	1,450
Return on shareholders' funds	25%	21%

This ratio shows the **rate of return of equity earnings** compared with the book value of shareholders' funds. Margate Group plc has a **higher return** at present, a fact that is consistent with its lower P/E ratio, but inconsistent with its lower equity beta. The measure is **limited** by the fact that **book values** are used.

Gearing: Debt ratio

	Margate Group	Hastings
Long term debt £m	1,450	950
Shareholders' funds £m	2,020	1,450
Total long term funds	3,470	2,400
Debt ratio	42%	40%

Both companies have **higher debt ratios** than the industry average (30%), indicating that use of **debt finance** for the merger would probably be **inadvisable**. The figure for Hastings could be understated if its substantial overdraft is effectively used as long-term debt. Including the overdraft of £420 million, the debt ratio becomes 1,370/2,820 = 49%.

Liquidity: Current ratio

	Margate Group	Hastings
Current assets £m	1,125	645
Current liabilities £m	755	785
Current ratio	1.490	0.822

At less than 1, the current ratio of Hastings looks low. This is despite the fact that it carries **higher inventory levels** than Margate. The high overdraft probably needs restructuring into long term funds, otherwise a period of rapid growth may cause severe liquidity difficulties.

(b) **Range of possible values for Hastings**

P/E ratios

Hastings's **current P/E ratio** is 16, giving its equity shares a current market value of 16 × equity earnings £300 million = £4,800 million. It is highly unlikely that any offer below this figure would be attractive to shareholders, who would have no incentive to sell. Measured by the industry average P/E of 13, Hastings would be worth 13 × £300 million = £3,900 million. The higher value that Hastings enjoys at present is because of its **above-average growth expectations** and, probably, expectations of gains from a merger with another company.

The dividend valuation model

> **Top tips.** Many different calculation assumptions may be offered here. Two or three valuations would be sufficient.

The current dividend is £135 million. The cost of equity for Hastings can be estimated from the **Capital Asset Pricing Model**, k_e = 6% + (12% − 6%) 1.2 = 13.2%.

Possible valuation method

Using this cost of equity in the dividend valuation model, we obtain the following possible valuation figures:

(i)   If, as some experts believe, the **supermarket contract results in zero growth**, the company's equity value would be 135/0.132 = £1,023 million, well below current market value.

(ii)   On the optimistic side, if there was **dividend growth of 10% per year to perpetuity**, the equity value would be 135 × 1.1 / (0.132 − 0.10) = £4,640 million. This is more in line with current market value.

(iii) Dividend growth of 10% per annum for 5 years followed by a period of lower growth would result in a **valuation figure between these two values**.

Adjusted present value method

Hastings is relatively highly geared, which has the effect of increasing its equity beta. Since the acquisition would be financed by equity shares, the Adjusted Present Value method would use a discount rate based on the **cost of ungeared equity** to value Hastings, and there would be no gearing side effect. The beta of ungeared equity for Hastings would be lower than 1.2, let us say 1.0, giving a cost of equity of 12%. The computations above would then lead to higher figures:

(i)   **No dividend growth**: 135/0.12 = £1,125 million
(ii)   **Growth of 10% p.a. to perpetuity**: 135 × 1.1 / (0.12 − 0.10) = £7,425 million
(iii) **Growth of 10% for 5 years**, followed by slower growth: a figure between these two values

Summary

Based on existing information, the value of Hastings' equity can be calculated as somewhere between £1,023 and £7,425 million, with its **current market value** at £4,800 million.

(c) To: Board of Directors, Margate Group
     From: Financial Manager
     Date: 13 December 20X1
     Subject: Report on the proposed acquisition of Hastings

Introduction

This report provides a financial evaluation of the proposed acquisition, recommends offer terms and discusses strategic issues.

(i)   **Recommended bid price and offer terms**

Our calculations show that the intrinsic value of Hastings as a stand-alone company is somewhere in the **range** £1,000 million to £7,400 million. On the basis of the efficient market hypothesis, the **current market value** of £4,800 million is probably as good a guide to the company's value as any, but it should be remembered that the market will undoubtedly have factored some expected merger gains (see below) into the share price as a result of the recent bid by the US company.

Premium

However, if we are to make a bid, we will not be successful unless we offer a **premium over current market value**, giving the Hastings' shareholders an incentive to sell. An offer price of approximately £5,000 million is suggested.

Synergy

It should be noted that if the possibility of merger gains is already factored into Hastings' share price, this offer price can only be justified if we have clear **plans** for **creating synergy** from the combination. Before going ahead, I suggest that we thoroughly investigate the possibilities, as indicated below.

Consideration

A share-for-share exchange should be offered as the terms for this merger, because:

(1)   We have **insufficient cash**.

(2)   As the **debt ratios** of both companies are above the industry average, I do **not recommend** any further **increase in borrowings** to finance this deal.

(3)   Our company's shares have an **above average P/E ratio** that, though not as high as Hastings', indicates that they are a relatively good 'currency' at the moment.

I recommend that we offer **7 of our own shares for every 8 in Hastings.** At our current share price this would value Hastings' shares at $7 \times 671p / 8 = 587.125$ pence, giving a total market value for Hastings' equity of £4,991 million, a premium of 3.9% over the current market value of £4,800 million.

Workings

Our share price is currently 671 pence.

Hastings' total number of shares in issue are £300m/35.29p EPS = 850.1 million. At a total value of £5,000 million, Hastings' share price would be 588 pence.

The terms of the offer should be 588 of our shares for 671 of Hastings, 0.876 of our shares for every one of theirs, or approximately 7 of ours for 8 of theirs.

Revised bid

When we make our initial bid, the market will assess it. The effect on the share price will depend on whether the market anticipated the sort of bid that we shall be making, but it is possible that we may have to make a revised offer.

(ii)   **Strategy for making the offer**

To minimise the **risk of outright rejection** by the Hastings board, our strategy needs to take the following factors into account.

(1)   We must follow the Stock Exchange regulations and the law, especially that on **insider dealing**. We are allowed to approach the board of directors of Hastings for informal talks, but must maintain **absolute secrecy** until we make a formal offer.

BPP
LEARNING MEDIA

(2)   We will need to ensure that Hastings' directors are given **key roles** on the board of the combined company. This bid is most likely to succeed if management arrangements are those of a genuine merger rather than a takeover by ourselves.

(3)   We need to **emphasise the similarities** between the management styles of our companies, and the advantages of joining forces to compete effectively in Europe against world competition.

Risks in making the bid

(1)   The American company may decide to make a **counter offer**, resulting in an auction for Hastings' business, bidding up the price to an unrealistic level.

(2)   Hastings may appeal for an **investigation** by the competition authorities, on the grounds that our bid is against the public interest.

(3)   Hastings' board may decide to **counter our offer** by making an offer to acquire us.

(4)   Hastings' staff may decide to **mobilise public opinion** against us. Some key members may leave (see below).

(5)   Hastings' directors may have strengthened their **contract termination terms**: this needs to be investigated.

Risks of post-merger failure

(1)   There may be a **conflict of cultures** between the management of the two companies. Disagreements at board level may lead to widespread loss of morale. Key staff of Hastings may leave and set up on their own or join another competing company. For example the American company may decide to poach staff rather than making an increased offer for Hastings' business.

(2)   Our objective of achieving synergy may not be realised because of **poor planning**, lack of resolve to tackle the key issues, or shortage of funds for necessary capital investment.

(3)   **Incompatibility of information systems** between the companies is a common merger problem.

(iii)   **Strategic and financial issues**

The rationale for the bid depends on the advantages that a combination of our companies would have over the existing 'stand-alone' businesses. Such combinations can create synergetic merger gains (the whole is worth more than the sum of the parts) by a number of mechanisms.

Increased market power

Elimination of Hastings as a major competitor might allow us to charge **more realistic prices** to customers on some of our less profitable operations. We are also likely to be able to negotiate **more favourable deals** with suppliers in terms of costs and payment terms. However, in this respect we must be careful to avoid the accusation that we have become a monopoly. Our combination will have more than a 25% share of the UK market and the competition authorities may decide to mount an investigation.

Access to new market

The merger would enable us to **grow more rapidly** in Europe, where Hastings already has a strong base.

Combining complementary resources

Hastings's **superior knowledge of markets in Europe** fits well with our dominant position in the UK.

Achieving critical mass to enable effective competition

As trade barriers fall, our competition is worldwide rather than just the UK. Our defence to the potential monopoly accusation is that our **market share** in the **European Union** is still relatively small and we need this merger in order to be able to compete effectively in international markets.

Elimination of duplicated resources

Our research shows that recent restructuring of both our companies does **not** leave **much scope** for **staff reductions** except at the head offices, but there will be possibilities for rationalising our warehouse and depot locations, for example.

Elimination of management inefficiencies

For example, Hastings' **financial management** could be **improved** with savings in financing costs.

Post-acquisition value of combined group

Our company has 1,050 million shares in issue and Hastings has 850 million.

Offer terms of 7 Margate shares for 8 Hastings shares would give each holder of 8 Hastings shares 7 Margate shares (worth 671p each, in total £46.97) in exchange for 8 Hastings shares (worth 565p each, in total £45.20). The premium of roughly 4% on the existing value of Hastings shareholders should help persuade Hastings' shareholders to agree to the offer.

At offer terms of 7 for 8, we will issue $7/8 \times 850m$ new shares in Margate = 743.8m.

Total Margate shares in issue would then be 1,050 +743.8 = 1,793.8m shares.

To maintain our existing share price, the value of the combined company would need to be 1,793.8 $\times$ 671p = £12,036m, shared as follows:

	No of shares	Share price (p)	Value £m
Original Margate shareholders	1,050.0	671	7,045
New shareholders from Hastings	743.8	671	4,991
	1,793.8		12,036

The existing market capitalisation of the two companies is as follows:

		£m
Margate	as above	7,045
Hastings	£300m × P/E16	4,800
		11,845

Size of synergistic gains

To maintain our existing share price, we would need to generate synergetic gains of £191 million (above those gains which have already been factored into the current share prices), which would accrue to the new shareholders from Hastings (£4,991m - £4,800m).

(1) On the down side, if we assume that a more realistic value for Hastings as a stand-alone company is in the region of £4,000 million, the synergy needed is closer to £1,000 million. Clearly we need to start work immediately on evaluating whether this is a **realistic proposition** and, if so, developing plans for implementing our ideas as swiftly as possible.

(2) On the optimistic side, if the market value of Hastings is realistic and our offer is accepted and we can generate an **additional synergy** of **£500 million**, say, the value of the company would be £12,345 million, split as follows:

	No of shares	Share price (p)	Value £m	Original value £m	Gain £m	% gain
Original Margate shareholders	1,050.0	688.22	7,226	7,045	181	2.6%
New shareholders from Hastings	743.8	688.22	5,119	4,800	319	6.6%
	1,793.8		12,345		500	

The gains made by Hastings shareholders would be higher in percentage terms.

Financial advantages

Given that the preferred bid strategy is a **share-for-share exchange**, if the bid goes through the combined group's **debt: equity ratio** will be lower than either of the current companies. We can either accept that this **reduction in financial risk** would be beneficial (as the gearing of both companies currently is high for the industry), or we can take the opportunity to issue further debt. **Perceived business risk** is unlikely to fall because the merger does not involve diversification, and because of the uncertainties surrounding the supermarket project.

Conclusion

Whilst a merger would have some significant benefits, we would need to convince our shareholders that Hastings is not overvalued, before they approve the issue of the consideration shares. Other issues, in particular the reaction of Hastings and the competition authorities, also need to be considered carefully.

68 KL

Text references. Investment appraisal techniques and issues are covered in Chapters 17, 18 and 19.

Top tips. (a) is undoubtedly very time pressurised, emphasising the importance of being able to do NPV calculations quickly and systematically.

In (a) different assumptions about revenues would also be acceptable if clearly stated. You could for example have assumed that the rate of increase between years 2 and 3 was matched in subsequent years; however if you took that view you would have had to calculate revenue and costs for individual years after year 3. The examiner suggests that the net present value calculation for each alternative could have been done from year 4 to perpetuity but that does not take into account the need to replace the machinery after 8 and 6 years. Also for Alternative 2 it would have been acceptable to treat the equipment as being purchased at time 0.

Because of the need to replace the machinery, a net present value calculation does not compare like with like. However there is no need in this question to calculate annualised equivalents (which is technically more correct) as the NPV calculation covering the shorter period had the higher net present value.

Probabilities are not relevant in (a) (a fairly substantial distractor), although they would be brought into the discussion in (b).

To score high marks in (b) you needed to discuss a range of objectives and risks, and relate the alternatives to the objectives of the company. The recommendation needed to cover both objectives and be backed up by discussion. You might have tried a numerical assessment of what would happen if demand figures were at minimum levels for the two alternatives. The problem with doing this is that the calculations will take time to complete and write down, and you may not have had enough time to discuss in sufficient detail the other risks involved.

This demonstrates the importance of care when planning; often in the discussion parts of questions you will have to carry out additional calculations but consider whether the support they give to your discussion will justify the length of time you spend on them.

As with many other Section A questions, you can gain a number of marks through using your risk and control strategy knowledge from P3.

Don't worry too much about the option theory in (c); the key mark-scoring points to learn are the five elements and the main choices.

Easy marks. The answer to (b) (ii) includes most of the main categories of risk that you will have encountered in P3. However to gain the majority of marks, you would have had to have applied these to KL; remember the directors will be looking for analysis that is relevant to the strategic decisions they have to make.

Examiner's comments. Apart from presentation of some calculations in (a) being poor, (a) and (b) were generally attempted very well, 'probably the best performance on the compulsory question I have seen for some time'. However (c) was often not done at all or attempted badly, with discussion focusing on currency or share options, and no attempt being made to relate these to real options.

(a)   **Assumptions for both alternatives**

1   **Revenues**

Revenues for years after year 3 are the same as year 3 revenues.

2   **K3**

K3's cash flows for the next 6/8 years will be a constant £1.5million.

3   **WACC**

The weighted average cost of capital is an appropriate rate to use to discount the project.

4   **Costs and benefits**

Costs and benefits are given in nominal terms.

Alternative 1

Time	Assumptions/Workings	0	1	2	3	4-8
		£m	£m	£m	£m	£m
Revenue	1		1.8	9.9	12.55	12.55
Costs						
Operating costs	2		(2.04)	(4.47)	(5.27)	(5.27)
Redundancy		(1.2)				
Equipment	3	(4.14)	(4.08)			
Factory conversion			(1.3)			
Taxation	4					(1.46)
Opportunity costs KL3			(1.5)	(1.5)	(1.5)	(1.5)
Net revenues		(5.34)	(7.12)	3.93	5.78	4.32
Discount factor	5	1.000	0.877	0.769	0.675	2.317
Present value		(5.34)	(6.24)	3.02	3.90	10.01

Net present value = £5.35 million

Workings/Assumptions

1   **Revenues**

Years 4 – 8 revenues are same as year 3

2   **Costs**

	1	2	3	4-8
	£m	£m	£m	£m
Fixed	1.5	1.5	1.5	1.5
Variable – 30% Sales	0.54	2.97	3.77	3.77
	2.04	4.47	5.27	5.27

3   **Equipment**

Year 0 $12m × 50%/1.45 = $4.14 million

Year 1 Using purchasing power parity Year 1 exchange rate $= 1.45 \times \dfrac{1.04}{1.025}$

$= 1.47$

$12m × 50%/1.47 = 4.08

It is advantageous for KL to accept the supplier's offer.

4 Taxation

	4-8 £m
Revenues	12.55
Costs	(5.27)
	7.28
Tax at 20%	1.46

5 Discount factor

Discount factor 4-8 = 4.639 − 2.322
= 2.317

Alternative 2

Time	Assumptions/Workings	0 £m	1 £m	2 £m	3 £m	4-6 £m
Revenue	1		4.5	6.3	9.7	9.7
Costs						
Operating costs	2		(1.88)	(2.15)	(2.66)	(2.66)
Redundancy		(0.24)				
Equipment	3		(2.5)			
Factory conversion			(1.3)			
Taxation	4					(1.41)
Opportunity costs		___	(1.5)	(1.5)	(1.5)	(1.5)
KL3						
Net revenues		(0.24)	(2.68)	2.65	5.54	4.13
Discount factor	5	1.000	0.877	0.769	0.675	1.577
Present value		(0.24)	(2.35)	2.04	3.74	6.51

Net present value = £9.7 million

Workings/Assumptions

1 Revenues

Assume years 4 – 6 revenues are same as year 3

2 Costs

	1 £m	2 £m	3 £m	4-8 £m
Fixed	1.2	1.2	1.2	1.2
Variable – 15% Sales	0.68	0.95	1.46	1.46
	1.88	2.15	2.66	2.66

3 Equipment

Equipment is assumed to be purchased at Time 1, as it is purchased once factory conversion is completed, and factory conversion costs are assumed to be incurred at Time 1.

4 Taxation

	4-6 £m
Revenues	9.70
Costs	(2.66)
	7.04
Tax at 20%	1.41

5 Discount factor

Discount factor 4-6 = 3.899 − 2.322
= 1.577

(b) REPORT

To: Directors
From: Financial Manager
Date: 28 October 20X2
Subject: Establishment of subsidiary company KL 15

This report covers the expected results if either of the two alternatives are chosen, also the other benefits and risks involved.

(i) **Increase in dividends and cash flows, and creation of wealth**

On the basis of the calculations in the appendix (part (a)), both alternatives will have a **positive net present value**, Alternative 1, £5.35 million, Alternative 2 £9.7 million. Under Alternative 1 the total value of the group will rise from **£827.5 million** to **£832.85 million**, and the share price from **331 pence** to **333 pence**. Under Alternative 2 the group value will rise from **£827.5 million** to **£837.2 million**, and the share price from **331 pence** to **335 pence**.

However both alternatives will have a negative initial impact on cash flows. After year 1, both alternatives will contribute to better cash flows, and facilitate the company increasing dividends, but neither will increase current returns by **5%** or more.

Impact on customers

We may be able to offer the processing of waste as an additional service to many of our existing customers, and this may strengthen relationships between ourselves and them.

Impact on employees

Shutting KL3 will lead to a number of **redundancies**, in some cases of long-established, loyal employees. The increase in unemployment may have a negative impact (and lead to bad publicity) in the community in which KL3 is situated. However in time we shall be able to offer employment when KL15 is fully operational, and we may wish to consider giving priority to former KL3 employees when recruiting for KL15.

Ethical standards

Arguably our moving into the processing of waste shows our commitment to a better environment, by increasing the opportunities for processing of harmful substances.

If we are seeking to operate to the highest possible ethical standards, then arguably we should not need government regulations to impose conditions on us, but choose alternative 1 because it will mean that we work to the highest possible environmental standards. We could gain **good publicity** from publicising our adherence to these standards. The fact that we have followed these standards may also make it more likely that the government imposes stricter regulations (and greater costs) on our competitors.

(ii) **Financial risks**

The **discount rate** being used in the NPV calculation may be misleading. KL's existing weighted average cost of capital may not be appropriate if diversification changes its **levels of business and financial risk**. In addition NPV is a method of assessing **longer-term results**, whereas the company's objectives demand that a shorter-term view is taken. The **payback method** does take account of developments in the immediate future by calculating how long it will take for the alternatives to break even (longer for Alternative 1).

Demand figures

We have used expected values. For Alternative 1, there is a 40% chance for each of periods 1-3 that revenues will be at **least £1 million lower** than anticipated; if this is true of all three periods, it is likely to mean that Alternative 1 will have a **negative present value**. For Alternative 2 the differences between expected values and minimum present values are less for periods 1 and 3 than they are for Alternative 1, and the chances that minimum revenue levels will occur are 20% as opposed to 40%.

The analysis also assumes that nothing can be done to **increase** demand and hence **returns from KL3.**

Price increases

Cost figures may be higher than anticipated. The appeal of both projects may be lessened by **fixed costs** being **higher than projected**, particularly in the first couple of years where the alternatives are due to make a loss.

Exchange risks

For Alternative 1, if KL commits itself to paying for equipment now there is a risk that a **larger deterioration** than forecast in the value of the dollar will outweigh the advantage of setting the price of the equipment at today's prices. However if the company waits to purchase the equipment, there is a risk that it will suffer from **a rise in the value of the dollar**.

In addition, if the company starts trading abroad under Alternative 2, it will be exposed to **exchange risks** that are likely to be complicated given the variety of countries involved.

Political risks

If KL chooses Alternative 2, it faces the risk that government regulations may be stricter than anticipated. **Further expenditure** at higher prices may then be needed if the company is to continue to process waste, and there will also be **disruption** if the factory needs to be shut when conversion takes place.

However if KL chooses Alternative 1 in anticipation of strict regulations, and the standards are such that Alternative 2 would fulfil regulations, then KL will be committed to a **less flexible alternative** probably offering a **lower net present value**.

There may also be **additional political risks** associated with expanding into new countries under Alternative 2.

Technological risks

For both alternatives, the installation and operation of the equipment are assumed to be free of **technological problems**. However for Alternative 1, the specialised nature of the equipment may mean that it is more vulnerable to technological problems; if these occur, it may be difficult to hire expertise to resolve them. However the equipment purchased Alternative 1 has a **longer life** than in Alternative 2, and its life may be even longer than the eight years anticipated. The cheaper equipment purchased in Alternative 2 may be more vulnerable to breakdown as the end of its life approaches. The equipment purchased for either alternative may become **obsolete** some time before the six to eight year period as technology develops.

(iii) **Recommendation**

Alternative 2 appears to be the better choice as its predicted **net present value** is higher, the chances of returns being less than the **expected values** are **smaller** and choosing option 2 will mean **fewer redundancies.**

However neither alternative is likely to make a very positive difference to **dividends** and **returns**, and KL may wish to wait for investment opportunities that yield higher expected returns.

(c) **Benefits of including real options**

Real options can add value to projects, and should be taken into account in investment appraisal. Although the **valuation is difficult**, even a rough estimate is better than no estimate at all. Option theory provides a means for businesses to take into account:

- **Initial costs and benefits** (counterpart to the option exercise price)

- The **present value of future benefits** and costs (share value)

- The **variability of future benefits** and costs (variability of share price)

- The **timescale** directors are allowed to make the decision (time within which options must be exercised)

- The **cost of capital** (the risk-free rate of interest)

Deferral

KL has the option to defer making a decision until the government has decided whether to introduce tougher environmental controls. Deferral is equivalent to a **call option**, with the **timescale** being the period over which the project can reasonably be postponed. One relevant cost would be the **price increase** in the equipment if alternative 1 is chosen, and the equipment not paid for immediately. Deferral might also mean that the company was able to make **better estimates** of **likely returns**; the volatility of currently expected returns would take this into account in option theory.

Abandonment

The option to abandon a project after it has been started is equivalent to a **put option**; the **exercise price** could be the sale proceeds of the project's assets when sold. Abandonment can be valuable for a company if the bulk of the expenditure is not made at the start of the project, and the company can, on the basis of developments after the project starts, decide not to spend any more and realise whatever value assets still have.

Abandonment as an option for KL

A put option may not be valuable for KL, as it is assumed that the probabilities of sales for later years are assumed to be **independent** of what happens at first. If this is true, early sales and costs will not be relevant if the company is considering whether to abandon. However there may be other factors which KL has not taken into account initially (unexpected **economic downturn** in developing countries for example) which may mean the option to abandon becomes more valuable. In addition, if Option 2 is chosen at first, it will take six months for the factory conversion to be completed before KL needs to pay for the equipment. Plans to purchase the more basic equipment could be abandoned if the government brings in tougher regulations which require equipment that fulfils higher standards.

Follow-on investments

These are additional investments that could be made if the initial investment produces good results. In option theory this is equivalent to a **call option**. Again in KL's circumstances you have the problem that initial results are apparently no guide to later results. However again more information may possibly emerge subsequently that affects the assessment of later results, and indicates that further investment will be worthwhile.

69 Dobbs

Text references. Acquisition issues are covered in Chapter 16 and NPV calculations in Chapter 18.

Top tips. (a) requires the use of interest rate parity to calculate forward rates, although you are given sufficient information to be able to use purchasing power parity to calculate forward rates. The discussion part of (a) would be worth about 5 marks.

Calculations like (a) (ii) may appear slightly strange. The best approach is to go through the information in the question thinking about the elements of the consideration and other relevant information (how much cash they've got).

(b) is a typical question where you have to work out what calculations are relevant (here price-earnings and financing mix). Business strategy knowledge can be brought into (b) (ii) and (iii) in particular. In (b) (i) earnings-based methods give the best estimate of value. An asset-based valuation would have to tackle the problem of valuing intellectual capital. You have to use the price earnings ratio of Dobbs in the absence of one for Alice Jain. In (b) (iii) remember that although gearing might be above average, that does not mean that it is excessive.

Easy marks. There are plenty of potential discussion points in this question. (b) (iv) is straightforward if you understand the **principles** of takeover regulation; you don't need to know the detailed rules. If you struggled with (iv), think what a company has to do in order to treat stakeholders **fairly**.

Examiner's comments. In (a) candidates often failed to adjust for inflation, and discounted real cash flows at a nominal cost of capital. Many failed to recognise that shareholders holding up to 70% of shares could opt for cash. Some candidates assumed incorrectly that the cost of the investment was the £30 million raised from the sale of a subsidiary.

The main failing in (b) was simply inadequate discussion. In particular (iv) was answered very badly by many candidates, who discussed corporate governance and the difficulties of merging two companies rather than the issues required by the question.

(a) (i)

	Wkg	1 £000	2 £000	3 £000	4 £000
Dollar cashflows					
Real cashflows		35.5	43.5	46.5	52.5
Nominal cashflows	1	36.4	45.7	50.1	58.0
Forward rates $/£	2	1.44	1.42	1.41	1.40
Sterling cashflows					
Converted		25.3	32.2	35.5	41.4
Discount factor 13%		0.885	0.783	0.693	0.613
Present value		22.4	25.2	24.6	25.4

Present value = £97.6m

Workings

(1) **Nominal cashflows**

Nominal cashflows = Real cashflows × 1.025 in yr 1, Real cashflows × $(1.025)^2$ in yr 2 etc

(2) **Forward rates**

Forward rates = 1.45 × (1.035/1.045) in yr 1, 1.45 × $(1.035/1.045)^2$ in yr 2 etc

Use of earnings

Alice Jain's valuation has been determined by the **value of future cash flows**. This may be more appropriate than an asset-based valuation, since earnings will depend significantly on **intellectual capital** (the abilities of the authors and staff), which is apparently not included in Alice Jain's balance sheet.

Conversion of cash flows

The cash flows must be stated in the same terms as the discount rate, so real cashflows must be **converted** to **nominal cashflows** to match with a nominal discount rate.

Treatment of international cash flows

Dobbs can use two methods.

(1) **Convert Alice Jain's income streams** into **sterling** and then **discount at a sterling discount** rate to calculate the NPV in sterling terms.

(2) **Discount the income streams** in dollars at an **adjusted discount rate** for that currency, and then **convert the resulting NPV to sterling** at the spot exchange rate.

Cost of capital

Ideally the investment should be discounted at a **different cost of capital** to the existing cost of capital, as the **risk associated** with the **investment** will differ from the risk that applies to Dobbs' existing business, Alice Jain will have a different **business risk**, as it is involved in a different market sector to Dobbs and it operates overseas. It would appear in fact that Alice Jain's business risk is higher than Dobbs. It has a lower **financial risk** than Dobbs because of **less gearing**, but a higher overall risk and hence a higher business risk.

To reflect the different considerations, the investment has been **discounted** at the **cost of capital** of the **proxy** of Alice Jain which is somewhat higher than Dobbs.

(ii) **Consideration to husband and wife**

60% × 15 million shares   = 9 million shares

Worth 60% × £97.6 million = £58.6 million

Cash to husband and wife   = £58.6 million × 50%
                           = £29.3 million

Value of shares to husband and wife = £29.3 million

Consideration to others

40% × 15 million shares   = 6 million shares

Worth 40% × £97.6 million = £39.0 million

Worst case scenario

Minority shareholders choose cash alternative.

	£m
Cash required (29.3 + 39.0)	68.3
Less cash available	(30.0)
Debt required	38.3

No of shares to be issued

At current market price $= \dfrac{29.3}{8.85}$

= 3.31 million shares

At low price for the year $= \dfrac{29.3}{7.55}$

= 3.88 million shares

The low price is used as an estimate of how much the share price will fall when new shares are issued.

(b)   To: Directors of Dobbs
      From: Financial Manager
      Date: 29 September 20X3
      Subject: Acquisition of Alice Jain

Introduction

The report below covers various aspects of the acquisition of Alice Jain and the suggestions made by the Finance Director.

(i)   **Methods of valuation**

      Positive returns

      If judged solely by the calculation carried out in (a), the **investment** in **Alice Jain** should proceed subject to a satisfactory negotiation of price. However the calculation takes no account of the **reliability of the sources of information** (how trustworthy are the private sources), and the potential **variability of returns**. This includes how dependent returns are on the **post-acquisition strategies** we introduce being implemented successfully.

      Mix of funding

      There may also be complications involved in obtaining the funds necessary to finance the deal.

      (1)   Our **shareholders** will have to **approve any increases** in **authorised share capital** that are necessary to provide consideration for Alice Jain's shareholders.

      (2)   If **shares** are **issued** to fund the deal, the main shareholders of Alice Jain will own approximately 7-8% of our shares, and would become **significant shareholders** in our company.

      (3)   We cannot tell at present what the precise **impact** will be upon our **share price** when additional shares are used as part of the share-for-share exchange.

      (4)   There may be problems obtaining **debt finance** on **reasonable terms** if a cash offer needs to be financed by extra debt. The debt may only be available at a **higher cost**, and the security demanded may be onerous. In addition we shall also be adding to our debt burden by **taking over** Alice Jain's current long-term debt (valued at $15 million).

      Terms of offer

      We should consider valuing Alice Jain by different methods in order to **ascertain** what a **fair price** would be. The method in (a) indicates a value of £97.6 million, but this only takes into account earnings for the next four years. **Earnings after four years** and **eventual terminal values** may also be significant.

      Price-earnings ratio

      £Value of Alice Jain = $Profits after tax × Price-earnings ratio/Spot rate

      Alice Jain has no P/E ratio as it is not quoted on a Stock Exchange. Assume Dobbs P/E ratio can be used.

      Dobbs P/E ratio   = Price/Earnings per share

      Earnings per share = Profit after tax/Number of shares
                          = (53.6 − 15)/45
                          = £0.858

      Dobbs P/E ratio   = 8.85/0.858
                          = 10.3

      Value of Alice Jain = $11.9m × 10.3/1.45
                          = £84.5m

This method depends on the assumption that the P/E ratio of Alice Jain is approximately the same as Dobbs. This implies that Alice Jain can be successfully integrated, and that the **prospects** faced by the two companies in their current markets are **similar**. This may be pessimistic; Alice Jain might have a higher P/E ratio if it was floated because of its significant potential. Nevertheless £84.5 million may be the best price for an initial offer.

(ii) **Review of operations**

We should carry out a **thorough review** and **position audit** of each aspect of Alice Jain's operations, to see if any parts could be **sold off** or **significantly changed.** Our intentions need to be incorporated into a **clear and workable plan**, ideally agreed with Alice Jain's key staff, but which must be **finalised** before the merger takes place and **firmly implemented**.

Degree of integration

We need to consider carefully the extent to which Alice Jain should be **integrated** with our existing operations. The differences between our current portfolio and Alice Jain's portfolio and Alice Jain's location being in America suggest that Alice Jain might be allowed a significant degree of autonomy. However we must make the most of opportunities to enhance Alice Jain's value through better management, probably introducing a **new senior management team**.

Staff

We could offer **key staff** below senior management levels **generous service contracts** to **ensure their commitment** to the new set-up. All of Alice Jain's staff should be **kept informed** of our plans for the business.

Authors

We need to check whether the authors are allowed to **treat** their **contracts** as **terminated** if a takeover takes place. We may wish to re-negotiate the contracts with the most successful existing authors, offering them **sufficiently generous terms** to tie them into us for a **longer period** than the **current three to five years**.

Our systems

The integration process should include a **review of our own operations** to help ensure the success of the takeover. In particular we should **review** our **information systems** to ensure they can cope with **enhanced demands**, and our **communication systems** to ensure that all staff will be kept well-informed of developments.

Investment appraisal

We may need to review the procedures we use for appraising investments, since the acquisition of Alice Jain will mean that we shall have new and different opportunities. We should consider whether the **cost of capital** we use should change as a **result** of the **changed business risk** of the new merged company.

(iii) **Acquisition of smaller company**

Greater synergies

Synergies with a UK company in a similar field to our current operations may be **easier to realise** than synergies with an American company in a different field. There may be **fewer cultural differences** to overcome in a UK company.

Lack of candidates

There may however be **no suitable candidate** available that will yield a **positive present value,** or be a better **strategic fit** than Alice Jain.

Risk and return

Our choice of investment will be determined by our attitude to **risk** and **return.** Investing in a UK company may be lower risk, but it may well yield less returns.

Repayment of debt

Improvement of gearing

A repayment would **lessen gearing** and bring it more into line with other companies in the sector. However we need to consider whether our above-average gearing is **excessive**. If we take gearing to be Long-term debt/Long-term debt + Equity, the book value of gearing at 31 December 20X2 is 125/125 + 145, approximately 46%. If gearing is calculated using market values of equity and assuming the market value of debt is at par then gearing = $125/(125 + (45 \times 8.85)) = 24\%$. These levels do not appear to be unduly excessive.

We should assess whether **total interest** is too high, whether there are **onerous covenants** attached to existing debt and whether **current lenders** or **our bank** are concerned about our current debt levels.

Lack of ambition

The market may interpret a repayment of debt as a sign that we have **no better use** for surplus cash and that we cannot identify any major investment opportunities. If the market believes we have a **lack of commitment** to taking the company forward, our **share price** may **fall** as a result.

Effect on cost of capital

Repayment of debt may cause our **weighted average cost of capital to rise,** as cheaper debt finance becomes less important, and dearer equity finance more significant.

(iv) **Responsibilities under takeover regulation**

Making an offer

Regulations require us to make a carefully considered and responsible offer. We need to be sure that we can **implement** the **terms of the offer,** and thus in particular we shall need to be certain that we can raise **sufficient debt** should the worst case scenario arise.

Different terms

The same terms have to be offered to **all shareholders** in Alice Jain. Thus if for example the minority shareholders were happy with our initial offer, but the majority shareholders required a better offer, we would have to offer improved terms to all shareholders.

Supply of information

We need to supply **sufficient and relevant information** that will enable Alice Jain's shareholders to reach a properly informed decision. Again we must offer the **same information** to all shareholders. Relevant information should not be withheld from Alice Jain's shareholders. The information we provide must be prepared to the **highest standards of accuracy**, and must **not mislead shareholders**.

Creation of false market

If we are offering a share alternative, we cannot **artificially enhance the price of our shares** by persuading others to bid for them and hence creating a **misleadingly strong market** for them.

Acting in shareholders' interests

As directors, you have a legal responsibility to act in the **best interests** of the **shareholders of Dobbs**. This includes giving shareholders **appropriate advice** about any decisions that they need to take, and also giving due attention to existing operations while the takeover process is going on.

Other legislation

We shall need to comply with American **legislation** and **takeover rules** in addition to complying with British requirements.

Recommendation

I recommend that an offer be made to purchase Alice Jain. The initial offer price should be the **P/E valuation** of **£84.5 million**, with the eventual price probably lying between **£90 and £95 million**. The bid should be financed by a combination of existing cash resources, new shares and debt.

70 C&C Airlines

Text references. CAPM calculations are explained in Chapter 12, NPV calculations in Chapter 18 and elements of investment appraisal are discussed in Chapter 17.

Top tips. The calculation in (a) involves using a debt beta (often you would assume this to be zero and you should be given the formula if you're expected to calculate it as you were here).

It's worth planning your workings in (b); it's definitely preferable to translate the fuel costs to £ in the workings and have sterling cash flows throughout the NPV calculation. Cash flows need to be in nominal terms as costs are increasing at different rates (including 0%). It is not sufficient just to say that the decision should go ahead based on the positive outcomes of the net present value calculations. The use of expected values should indicate to you that there are a number of possible outcomes, and the variety of outcomes need to be considered before the final decision is made. Although you can earn limited marks through drawing up the proformas and inserting the easier figures, you will have to tackle the sales figures at a reasonably early stage.

(c) covers the types of areas that you could well come across in TOPCIMA. Here, as in TOPCIMA, your answer needs to have **breadth** and **depth**. You need to mention a variety of factors (time spent planning will help you generate ideas), but you also must show why these factors may be important. Bullet points consisting of a one-line phrase will not earn you marks.

Easy marks. (c)(iii) requires fairly basic knowledge of risk management; however it shouldn't be answered in isolation, but linked into parts (c)(i) and (ii); best then to leave it till last but you should make sure you have enough time to attempt it.

Examiner's comments. Many attempts at (a) were inadequate. Problems included ignoring the basic formula given in the paper, failing to take account of tax, assuming debt beta was zero, not ungearing, using the debt beta in the CAPM equation, failing to discuss limitations of the CAPM, not understanding the difference between systematic and unsystematic risk, and not using the proxy company.

(b) was generally done well, although a number of candidates produced poorly presented answers. Weaknesses included failing to treat inflation correctly, ignoring balancing allowances, confusing allowances with tax savings, ignoring the resale value of the plane, mixing currencies and including non-relevant costs.

Discussion in many answers to (c) was insufficiently broad, and not linked in enough to the scenario. Discussions of commercial problems often did not differ from discussion of economic problems. Several answers failed to discuss why the factors listed were important. A number failed to provide any recommendation.

(a) **Discount rate to be used in the investment decision**

The **risk adjusted discount rate** is found from the **capital asset pricing model**, using an estimate of the beta factor suitable for this type of investment. The beta can be taken from the quoted competitor of C&C, and adjusted to remove the effect of this competitor's gearing, since C&C is ungeared.

Using the formula

$$\beta_u = \beta_g\left[\frac{V_E}{V_E + V_D(1-t)}\right] + \beta_d\left[\frac{V_D(1-t)}{V_E + V_D(1-t)}\right]$$

$$= 1.3\left[\frac{4}{4+1(1-0.3)}\right] + 0.15\left[\frac{1(1-0.3)}{4+1(1-0.3)}\right]$$

$$= 1.129$$

Using CAPM

$$k_{eu} = R_f + [R_m - R_f]\,\beta_u$$

$$= 5 + [12-5]\,1.129$$

$$= 12.9\%, \text{ say } 13\%$$

Limitations of CAPM

(i) **Finding a suitable competitor's beta.** Because many quoted companies have **diversified** into several industries, examining the beta of a competitor may not give an appropriate result. In any case, the beta is subject to a very large statistical margin of error.

(ii) **Single period model. Adjusting the discount rate** for a multi-period investment may not be as appropriate as using certainty equivalent cash flows.

(iii) **Assumptions.** CAPM is a **simple model**, based on **perfect capital market assumptions**, and tends to be **biased** in its estimates of **discount rates**. More complex models may produce better results.

(iv) **Shareholder diversification.** CAPM only considers **systematic risk** on the assumption that shareholders will be well diversified. However as C&C is owned by only a small group of shareholders, they may not be well diversified and hence may be **exposed** to the **specific risk** of the company as well as systematic risk.

(b) **Sterling NPV of the proposed investment**

				Year	
		0	*1*	*2*	*3*
	Wking	£'000	£'000	£'000	£'000
Sales revenue	1		13,378	14,832	15,128
Costs					
Fuel costs	2		2,854	2,969	3,088
Sterling costs (increase 3%)			2,987	3,077	3,169
Incremental admin overheads			250	250	250
Advertising and promotion			350	350	350
Costs			6,441	6,646	6,857
Income less costs			6,937	8,186	8,271
Tax at 30%			(2,081)	(2,456)	(2,481)
Tax credit on capital allowances	3		1,471	1,103	261
Investment		(19,608)			10,159
Net cash flow		(19,608)	6,327	6,833	16,210
13% discount factors CAPM		1	0.885	0.783	0.693
Present value		(19,608)	5,599	5,350	11,234
Certainty equivalents		1	0.90	0.85	0.80
Certainty equivalent cash flow (£'000)		(19,608)	5,694	5,808	12,968
9% discount factors		1	0.917	0.842	0.772
Present value		(19,608)	5,221	4,890	10,011

Using **CAPM** and 13% discount rate, present value = £2,575,000

Using **certainty equivalents** and 9% discount rate, present value = £514,000

Workings

1   *Expected sales revenue*

	Year 1		Years 2-3	
Load	Prob.	EV	Prob.	EV
100%	0.10	10%	0.15	15%
80%	0.50	40%	0.60	48%
50%	0.30	15%	0.20	10%
40%	0.10	4%	0.05	2%
Expected load	1.00	69%	1.00	75%
Maximum passengers		220		220
Expected passengers		151.8		165

	Year		
	1	2	3
Expected passengers	151.8	165	165
Trips per year (6 × 48)	288	288	288
Fare £ (increase 2% p.a.)	306	312.12	318.36
Total income £'000	13,378	14,832	15,128

2   *Fuel costs*

Exchange rates

Using purchasing power parity theory

End of year	Exchange rate $/£
0	1.530
1 × 1.04/1.03 =	1.545
2 × 1.04/1.03 =	1.560
3 × 1.04/1.03 =	1.575

	Year		
	1	2	3
Fuel costs $'000 (increase 5% pa)	4,410	4,631	4,863
Exchange rates	1.545	1.560	1.575
Fuel costs £'000	2,854	2,969	3,088

3   *Capital allowances*

	$m	Ex. rate	£m
Cost of plane (year 0)	30,000	1.530	19,608
Resale value (year 3)	16,000	1.575	10,159

End of year	WDV	CA (25%)	Tax 30%
	£'000	£'000	
0	19,608		
1	14,706	4,902	1,471
2	11,029	3,677	1,103
3 (balancing figure)	10,159	870	261

4   *Non-relevant costs*

The **market research and purchase negotiations costs** are excluded from the appraisal because they are **sunk costs**. The **£50,000 re-allocation of current head office costs** is excluded because it is not directly attributable to the appraisal.

Recommendation

Based on the calculations, the company should proceed with the investments.

However both methods suffer from limitations. Those of CAPM are outlined above, but the calculations appear to indicate that there is a safety margin, and that the internal rate of return of the investment will be a **few percentage points** higher than 13%. The certainty-equivalents **appear** to take into account the need for caution in assessing future cash flows. However the **weightings chosen** and the **discount rate used** appear to be selected arbitrarily and may not represent the **best guess.**

The figures used in both methods are **expected values**, an average of a number of possible outcomes. It is possible that actual results may vary significantly from these. Instead of basing their decision on one calculation, C&C should carry out a variety of calculations, certainly considering the **best and worst possible outcomes** it could face.

(c) To: Board of Directors, C&C Airlines
     From: Finance director
     Date: 8 December 20X3
     Subject: Report on the proposed investment in Boeing 757 for long haul flights

This report addresses the major economic forces and commercial risks affecting our proposed new investment in the long haul flight market to the Caribbean. Some strategies for managing the risks are suggested.

(i) **Major economic forces influencing the success of the investment**

Demand aspects

The success of the project depends on continuing (and hopefully increasing) **demand** from **middle-income population groups** for travel to the Caribbean. This demand depends on:

(1) The **general level of demand** in the world economy. The **demand in regional economies** that will form our main customer-base, the UK and Europe, is also significant.

(2) **Demand for air transport**. This can be adversely affected by unpredictable disasters (eg airline accidents or terrorist activity).

(3) **Demand for the Caribbean as a destination**. Primarily this still depends on the popularity of the Caribbean as a **holiday destination** (which in turn depends on many other factors such as fashion, safety, time of year, and facilities offered compared with competitor regions). It is also influenced by the **demand for low-cost business flights** (which in turn is affected by the level of trade between UK/Europe and the Caribbean).

(4) The **availability of substitute products**. These include **flights offered by competitors** to the Caribbean and elsewhere. The Caribbean as a holiday destination is also easily substituted by **other world regions** (eg South East Asia, African islands). **E-mail and telephone contact** can be a substitute for business meetings in the event of cost problems.

(5) **Currency variations**. The income currency is proposed as sterling. If **sterling strengthens**, this can **reduce demand** from non-UK customers, but may increase unit profitability; the reverse would happen if sterling weakens.

(6) **Interest rate variations** will impact upon demand and exchange rates.

Cost aspects

The most important influences on costs include the following.

(1) The **general level of fuel (oil) prices**. This will affect all competitors but increases will **reduce profitability**.

(2) **Currency variations**. For example, if fuel prices have been agreed in advance in US dollars, a strengthening of the dollar would increase costs.

(3) **Staff costs**. These will be affected by **required manning levels**, which in turn depend on agreements with trades unions and safety regulations.

(4) **Safety and regulatory costs**. These can be influenced by decisions made by governments in the European Union and/or the Caribbean.

(ii) **Risk and uncertainty from commercial aspects of the investment**

Difficulty of predicting passenger capacity

We intend to make the **plane available** for six return flights per week, 48 weeks per year. The demand for flights to the Caribbean is highly **uncertain** (see above) and is likely to be seasonal because of the **high proportion of holiday passengers** and the availability of an increased number of **substitute destinations** at certain times of the year. We therefore run the risk of having **low capacity flights** at certain times of the year and need a strategy to allow for this.

Low cost price strategy

Our strategy is to **maximise demand** by **selling tickets at low prices**. We know that this market is **increasingly competitive**, and we are **vulnerable** to a larger **competitor** matching or undercutting our prices, possibly accepting losses in order to drive us out of business.

Fuel (oil) prices

Fuel is approximately **45%** of the **running costs**, and large variations are possible and uncontrollable.

Currency risk

Fuel costs of this project are in US dollars, while the remainder, and all of the income, are in pounds sterling. As described in (i) above, **uncontrollable changes in the exchange rate** can result in significant uncertainty of income, costs and profitability.

Resale value

The resale value of planes is uncertain as it is dependent upon fluctuating availability.

(iii) **Strategies for risk management**

The risks noted above, and others that board members may identify, need assessing for likelihood of **occurrence** (probability) and **impact** (the magnitude of any potential losses). Our risk assessment could be extended in various ways, through using **sensitivity analysis**, or using **real options** to extend the evaluation of the project beyond three years and consider alternative decisions at that point. We then need to prepare a strategy for each category of risk, which may involve either **accepting it** and **preparing contingency plans**, or **taking action** to lessen the likelihood and/or impact.

As preliminary thoughts, the following strategies for risk management may be considered.

(1) **Insurance**. Insurance should be considered where feasible. However it may not be possible to insure against **economic forces** or **acts of terrorism,** where other security measures would be required.

(2) **Hedging**. Oil price and currency fluctuations can be hedged on the **commodity** and **financial futures markets**. We could consider futures, forward contracts or option contracts if we believe that price variations are a significant threat.

(3) **Co-operation with other operators**. To combat low capacity caused by general factors that affect most airline operators we must consider contingency plans for code sharing of flights with other operators.

(4)   **Diversification**. As a precaution against becoming too affected by risks of the Caribbean region, we should ensure that our existing business is **expanded** and **diversified**. As a precaution against dependency on holiday passengers, we could develop a freight carrying business.

(5)   **Staff flexibility**. Flexible work contracts should be developed with all categories of staff, to minimise fixed staffing costs.

(iv)   **Recommendation**

My recommendation is that the board of directors **approves this project** for more detailed investigation of risks and development of risk management strategies. Subject to this proving satisfactory, the investment should be approved.

71 RGB

Text references. CAPM calculations are explained in Chapter 12, NPV calculations in Chapter 18 and elements of investment appraisal are discussed in Chapter 17.

Top tips. Note the data that is relevant to the calculation in (a), including risk-free rates and price-earnings ratios for the market values. In (b) it's easiest to do the purchasing power parity calculation. Because there is no timing difference between paying tax in USA and UK, it is easiest to convert the pre-tax dollar cash flows to sterling and then to compute the 30% tax liability.

(c) (i) does not specify that you will need calculations; however remember that the discussion parts of Question 1 often require calculations to support the discussion, even if you are not asked to provide them. Certainly here you need to show whether the quantitative objectives have been fulfilled.

(c) (ii) highlights one of the weaknesses of CAPM; the possibly unwarranted assumption that investors are well-diversified. The 7 marks available in (c) (iii) indicates that you needed more than 2-3 lines recommendation. This part brings out the links between funding and investment. Remember that the company's value will increase by the extra funding plus the net present value of the investments that are made possible by that funding, but that supposes extra funding is available. Whether the company is being too conservative and can afford to relax the constraints is the main issue in this part.

Easy marks. (c) (ii) offers plenty of scope to score half a dozen reasonable marks, provided you mention solutions as well as risk.

Examiner's comments. Only a minority of candidates used the correct techniques in (a) of ungearing beta and adjusting for tax. Credit was given for use of a WACC, although some candidates used book values rather than market values.

The calculations for (b) were badly presented; few candidates calculated the return on capital employed and calculations of certainty-equivalents and the profitability index were poor. In addition many forward rate calculations showed a depreciating rather than appreciating US dollar.

Many answers to (c) lacked headings, and whilst discussions on risk were good, few answers contained good discussion of how the investments fulfilled the company's objectives. Some candidates failed to take account of the information in the scenario that RGB was trading in the US.

(a)   **Cost of capital**

The company will use a **risk adjusted weighted average cost of capital** to appraise its UK investment.

The **risk adjusted cost of equity capital** can be found using the **capital asset pricing model**, where R_f is 5% and R_m is 9%. The beta of the proxy company, 1.3, can be used directly, as this company has a similar capital structure to RGB.

Thus $k_e = 5\% + 1.3\,(9\% - 5\%) = 10.2\%$.

Because RGB's debt beta is zero, its after tax cost will be the same as the after tax risk free rate, 5%.

Market values of equity and debt

Total equity earnings = £76 million and P/E can be assumed to be average, 10.53.

Thus value of equity = £76m × 10.53 = £800m.

Debt is at par, value £320m. Therefore total value of equity plus debt = £1,120m.

Weighted average cost of capital $= \dfrac{800}{1{,}120} \times 10.2\% + \dfrac{320}{1{,}120} \times 5\% = 8.71\%$, say 9%.

Limitations of calculation

This computation uses a number of broad approximations, thus:

- The risk adjustment assumes that the new project is of **average risk** for RGB.

- The valuation of RGB's equity assumes that RGB is of **average risk** for its sector.

- The **proxy company's beta may not be appropriate** as there may be important differences impacting upon risks.

- The CAPM itself is only an **approximate model.**

- RGB is a **private company**: its shareholders are likely to have a large proportion of their assets tied up in RGB, and will be more affected by the unsystematic risk of RGB than is predicted by the CAPM.

(b) **Proposed UK investment**

NPV

The after tax operating cash flows are 70% of the pre-tax figures, and the capital allowance results in a tax reduction at the end of year 1. No residual value after 5 years.

	0	1	2	Year 3	4	5	Total profit
	£m	£m	£m	£m	£m	£m	
Initial outlay	(30.00)						
First yr all		9.00					
Operating cash flows (× 0.7 yrs 1–3, 5% growth yrs 4–5)		4.41	6.30	7.35	7.72	8.11	
Cash flows	(30.00)	13.41	6.30	7.35	7.72	8.11	12.89
Discount factor 9%	1.000	0.917	0.842	0.772	0.708	0.650	
Discounted cash flows	(30.00)	12.30	5.30	5.67	5.47	5.27	4.01

The NPV of £4.01 million is positive, indicating the investment is worthwhile.

Profitability index

The profitability index is $\dfrac{\text{PV}}{\text{outlay}} = \dfrac{34.01}{30} = 1.134$

ROCE

Cost of investment = £30m

Average capital employed $= \dfrac{£30m}{2} = £15m$

Cumulative after-tax operating cash flows total £33.89 million (see above). With the capital allowance tax reduction, the cumulative after tax cash flow is £33.89m + £9m = £42.89m

Total accounting depreciation is £30 million, so total accounting profit is £12.89 million (see above). Per year, this is:

$$\frac{£12.89}{5} = £2.58m$$

So, average ROCE is: $\frac{£2.58m}{£15m} = 17.2\%$ per annum

Proposed US investment

Use **purchasing power parity** to compute the predicted exchange rates for US$/£.

Predicted exchange rate next year ($/£) = spot rate ($/£) (1 + i$)/(1 + i£).

Rate in year 0 is $1.70 = £1. Rates in each succeeding year are found by multiplying by: $\frac{1.015}{1.025}$

	Year			
	0	1	2	3
Exchange rate	1.700	1.683	1.667	1.651

NPV

Taxation

Tax is charged on profits at 25% p.a. in USA. The same profits are taxed at 30% in UK, but the 25% paid in USA is offset. Thus the net tax paid is 30% of profits.

			Year				Total
	0	1	2	3	4	5	profit
Capital outlay $m	(75.00)						
Pre-tax operating cash flows $m		22.25	24.25	26.25			
Exchange rate	1.700	1.683	1.667	1.651			
Cash flow £m	(44.12)	13.22	14.55	15.90	16.70	17.53	
Tax – capital all		13.24					
Tax – op cash flows		(3.97)	(4.37)	(4.77)	(5.01)	(5.26)	
After tax cash flows	(44.12)	22.49	10.18	11.13	11.69	12.27	23.64
Probability factor	1.00	0.90	0.87	0.82	0.7	0.7	
5% discount factor	1.000	0.952	0.907	0.864	0.823	0.784	
Risk adjusted PV	(44.12)	19.27	8.03	7.89	6.73	6.73	4.53

Risk adjusted net present value: £4.53m.

Again the net present value is positive, and project appears worthwhile.

Profitability index

The 'profitability index' is $\frac{PV}{outlay} = \frac{48.65}{44.12} = 1.103$

ROCE

Cost of investment = £44.12m.

Average capital employed = $\frac{£44.12m}{2} = £22.06m$

Total accounting profit is £23.64m (see above), giving an average per year of $\frac{£23.64}{5} = £4.73m$

So, ROCE is $\frac{£4.73m}{£22.06m} =$ **21.4% per annum**

(c) To: Board of Directors
    From: Capital Investment Analyst
    Date: 12 April 20X5
    Subject: Report on proposed investments in South of England and North America

I have carried out computations (see attached) to establish the **financial viability** of the two proposed investments. This report uses these results and other factors to evaluate the investments and to assist you in deciding whether to proceed with them.

(i)   **Contribution to the achievement of the company's objectives**

The company has three stated objectives:

(1)   **To increase earnings per share by 5% per annum**

By itself, the **UK investment** fails to achieve this target in any of the five years. Even in combination with the additional £17 million of investments already proposed, it is unlikely that this target can be reached.

> The **US investment** can achieve a **5% increase in earnings** (and hence in EPS, assuming it is financed from retained earnings) from approximately 2 years' time, though next year will not show the required increase.

UK investment

Year	After tax operating cash flow	After tax depreciation	Accounting profit	Company total after tax profit	% increase
0				76.00	
1	4.41	(4.2)	0.21	76.21	0.28
2	6.30	(4.2)	2.10	78.31	2.76
3	7.35	(4.2)	3.15	81.46	4.02
4	7.72	(4.2)	3.52	84.98	4.32
5	8.11	(4.2)	3.91	88.89	4.60
			12.89		

US investment

Year	After tax operating cash flow	After tax depreciation	Accounting profit	Company total after tax profit	% increase
0				76.00	
1	9.25	(6.17)	3.08	79.08	4.05
2	10.18	(6.17)	4.01	83.09	5.07
3	11.13	(6.18)	4.95	88.04	5.96
4	11.69	(6.18)	5.51	93.55	6.26
5	12.27	(6.18)	6.09	99.64	6.51
			23.64		

(2)   **A post-tax accounting rate of return on shareholders' funds of 20% per annum**

The company's **current post-tax accounting rate of return on shareholders' funds** is 76/420 = 18%, which is below the required target. The UK investment, showing an average accounting rate of return of 17.2%, cannot improve this performance. The US investment shows an expected accounting rate of return that is higher than target, at 21.4% per annum, but this in itself will not be sufficient to raise the company's overall performance to a 20% rate of return.

The company should be cautious when using the accounting rate of return as it **uses profits** rather than the preferable alternative of cash flows. It doesn't take into account timing and differences in cash flows, nor the impact of different project length of lives.

(3)   **Maintain a leading global presence in its operating markets**

The computer technology business changes rapidly and a leading global presence is achieved by **maintaining customer-desirable innovations** and quality of production and delivery. This will require a significant investment programme. The two investments should be rated in terms of these qualities rather than by where the products are manufactured. Nevertheless, despite reductions in world trade barriers, the investment in USA may help to build the company's market in that country.

Net present value

As indicated, both investments have a **positive net present value** and both could be undertaken if financed for example by **increased borrowing.** If they are mutually exclusive, the US investment should be selected as it has the higher NPV. However the US investment, together with other investments, will involve expenditure of £61 million, above the capital expenditure limit of £50 million. This will disqualify the US investment if this limit is inflexible.

If the UK project is chosen, it will not exhaust the funds available for investment and the remaining funds will either have to be invested in other projects now, invested in the financial markets until better opportunities arise or be returned to shareholders.

(ii)   **Analysis of risks and strategies for risk management**

Industry risk

Both proposed investments will carry **operating risks** normal for the computer technology industry, including:

(1)   **Competition for innovation**, increasingly by firms that did not appear to be in the same market sector, as technologies converge

(2)   **Brand image** of large market players

(3)   **Cost competition,** often by relocating factories to low-cost countries; competitors may succeed in obtaining tax holidays or grants from developing countries

(4)   **Competition for scarce technical ability** and skills

Political risk

The US investment will involve a small amount of political/cultural risk caused by **differences in laws** (e.g. property, labour, tax) and business custom. Advice must be sought on these matters. The disadvantages may well be outweighed, though, by a positive response from US consumers.

Financial risks

These will include:

(1)   **Credit risk:** the need to ensure that debts are collected and bad debts avoided by a sound credit control policy.

(2)   **Gearing**: in book values this is currently at the high level of 76% debt:equity. If an attempt to maintain earnings per share results in acceptance of both projects and financing by more debt, financial risk for shareholders may become unacceptably high.

(3)   **Interest rate risk**: since the existing loan is fixed interest, this is not an issue unless floating rate debt is raised to finance either investment.

Foreign exchange risk

The US investment carries **foreign exchange risk**, which is the risk that project cash flows are adversely affected by changes in the $/£ exchange rate. For example dollar cash inflows converted to pounds would be eroded by a weakening of the dollar, and this would hit particularly hard if a substantial proportion of costs were in pounds.

Exchange risk can be reduced by various **hedging strategies.** Specific transactions (purchases or sales) can be hedged using **forward contracts, futures or options**. The ongoing (economic) exchange risk of the net operating cash flows is best managed by **matching income against costs** in dollars where possible. This implies sourcing components locally rather than supplying from head office, and borrowing in dollars to finance the capital investment costs.

CAPM

The methods of allowing for risk suggested by the Finance Director are based on the capital asset pricing model (CAPM), which distinguishes between **market risk** and **specific risk** of investments. When investors hold diversified portfolios of shares, only market risk needs to be considered, because the specific risk of investments is neutralized by the other investments in the portfolio. However:

(1)   RGB is a **private company**, financed by some major shareholders whose investment in the company represents a substantial part of their wealth. They do not hold diversified portfolios as assumed by the CAPM and will probably require a higher return to compensate for specific risk of the company's investments.

(2)   Although the US investment carries more foreign exchange risk than the UK investment, and might be financed in a different way, it would perhaps be better to **appraise both investments** by the same technique, i.e. appraise both by the adjusted present value method, either adjusting the discount rate for both, or by using the 'certainty equivalent cash flow' method for both. This would make comparison and sensitivity analysis easier to carry out.

(iii)   **Recommendations**

The financial appraisal of the investments shows the following:

Investment	UK	US
Outlay £m	30.00	44.12
PV £m	34.00	48.65
Profitability index (PV/outlay)	1.133	1.103
ROCE	17.2%	21.4%

The discounted cash flow appraisal of these two investments shows that both have **significant positive expected net present values**, and that consequently they would be expected to increase shareholder value if accepted and properly managed. These indicators therefore suggest that both investments should be accepted.

Capital rationing

The company's policy of rationing capital investment to a ceiling of £50 million per annum will, however, not allow the acceptance of both. If a choice has to be made, then, on financial grounds, the **UK investment** should be accepted because it has the higher NPV and profitability index. Total capital investment, including the £17 million already proposed, would total £47 million, which falls within the policy limit.

The company must balance the need to **invest in growth** (maintaining competitiveness) against its ability to **manage new investments** as well as the existing business, and against the financial risks that come from rapid growth financed by borrowing. It is therefore important that the Board only decides to accept both projects if it believes the company has the necessary resources to manage them properly.

Global presence

If the opportunity of investing in the USA is regarded as **strategically important** (because of the company's stated objective of maintaining a leading global presence), the **US investment** should be accepted. This would result in a total required capital outlay of £61 million, which would require the £50 million capital outlay constraint to be relaxed slightly. Cash sale of surplus assets may raise the £11 million shortfall in finance, but if not, it might be possible to postpone part of the £17 million other proposed investments.

Financing both investments

If both investments went ahead, **significant additional investment** would be required. The total capital investment requirement would be £91 million, for which £50 million cash would be available.

If **borrowing** were used to finance the shortfall, approximately £41 million of debt would be required – more if there are increased working capital requirements, or less if assets are sold as planned. **Gearing** would increase from 76% to 86% debt: equity.

The alternative of **financing by a share issue** would enable the company to **accept both investments** and to reduce gearing. Unfortunately this may not be easy under the current private company set-up: shareholders may not have the resources to increase their equity investments. There are two main alternatives:

- **Make the company public again** and float on the stock exchange; or

- **Seek a capital investment** from a venture capital fund, thereby delaying eventual flotation by, say, five years

Recommendations

The Board should consider the company's capability to proceed with both new investments this year and the Board should explore the possibility of finance from venture capital funds.

72 JHC

Text references. Investment appraisal methods are covered in Chapter 18 and applications of discounted cash flow in Chapter 19.

Top tips. This is a very similar question to one set in 2002 in the old syllabus. It is possible to use the dividend valuation model to calculate values in perpetuity in alternatives 1 and 2 but these are probably not appropriate given the limited useful life of the equipment.

Don't worry too much if you didn't remember the equivalent annual value method; use of it doesn't make any difference to the recommendation. You should be more concerned if you didn't recognise that loss of CC's earnings was an opportunity cost, as you'll often be asked to identify what's relevant in an investment appraisal.

The discussion part would have needed to consider financial and non-financial issues even if the objectives of the organisation had not been specified. How important each objective is (and hence whether alternative 1 or 2 is chosen) is in the end a matter of opinion, and also affected by attitude to risk (here the risk that alternative 2 will be chosen but alternative 1 subsequently forced on the company).

In common with many other Section A questions, (b) requires you to judge which calculations are required; here the choice is possibly easy than with some other questions as you need to determine whether the company has fulfilled its objectives. (c) covers the real options often faced in a investment decision.

Easy marks. If you can describe the real options in general terms, (c) should be fine **provided** you discuss them in the context of JHC's investment.

Answer plan

(a)   (i)   **Alternative 1**

- Time horizon 8 years
- Discount rates: WACC

Years 0-3

- Machinery

Years 4-8

- Assumption – company objectives mean 4% rise in cash flows

Relevance of CC

Alternative 2

As for 1 except time horizon six years and machinery purchase

(ii)   MIRR

- Treatment of outlays
- Treatment of receipts
- Receipts = payments
- Advantages for managers (cf IRR)
- Disadvantages (distortions)

(b)   Report

Introduction

Summary of alternatives and results of (a)

Objectives

Increased cash flows (level required, inflation?)

Net cash flows – overall and opening years (calculation)

Shareholders/stakeholders

Wealth of shareholders (calculation)

Employees – employment, wages

Ethics

Alternative 1 yes, Alternative 2 no

Legislation passed – costs

Legislation not passed – boycott

Recommendation

Health food yes

Close CC

Alternative 1

(c)   Define real options

Types of option – abandonment, timing, follow-up

(a) (i) **Net present values of subsidiary SP**

Alternative 1

Assumptions

The time horizon for this alternative will be taken as eight years, which is the estimated minimum useful life of the equipment.

The discount rate used is the **group's WACC**, which is 9% per year, net of tax. The implicit assumption is that this new project is of average risk for the group.

For the machinery, the alternative of paying 5% extra (€8.4 million), all at the end of year 1, is more expensive in present value terms than paying €8.0 million in two instalments, as shown.

Years 0 to 3

				Year			
		0		1	2	3
		€m		€m	€m	€m
Factory conversion				(2.80)		
Machinery (Note)		(3.20)		(4.80)		
Revenues				4.48	11.80	17.60
Operating costs:	Fixed			(2.50)	(2.50)	(2.50)
	Variable: 35% × sales			(1.57)	(4.13)	(6.16)
Redundancy		(2.10)				
		(5.30)		(7.19)	5.17	8.94
9% factors		1.000		0.917	0.842	0.772
Present value		(5.30)		(6.59)	4.35	6.90

Net present value years 0 to 3: €(0.64 million).

Years 4 to 8

Assumption

Operating profits and net cash flows will increase by 4% each year from year 4 to year 8 (in line with JHC's company objective).

In year 4, pre-tax net cash flow will be €8.94 × 1.04 = €9.298m. After charging tax of 20%, this leaves 80% × €9.298 = €7.438m. This figure increases at 4% per year till year 8. Discounting at 9%:

Year	After tax net cash flow €m	9%	PV €m
4	7.438	0.708	5.266
5	7.736	0.650	5.028
6	8.045	0.596	4.795
7	8.367	0.547	4.577
8	8.702	0.502	4.368
			24.034

Loss of earnings from CC

In addition, the appraisal must take account of the loss of earnings from business CC, which is a constant €2.2 million per year from year 1 to year 8:

PV = €(2.2)m × 5.535 (9% cumulative discount factor years 1-8) = €(12.177 m).

The net present value of the project over the 8 year time horizon is therefore €11.21 million:

	€m
NPV years 0 to 3	(0.64)
NPV years 4 to 8	24.03
Loss of NPV from CC	(12.18)
	11.21

Alternative 2

Assumptions

The time horizon for this alternative will be taken as **six years**, which is the estimated minimum useful life of the equipment.

The discount rate used is again 9%, the group's WACC.

The machinery is assumed to be purchased at Time 1, as it is purchased when factory conversion is completed, and factory conversion costs are assumed to be incurred at Time 1.

Years 0 to 3

	Year			
	0	1	2	3
	€m	€m	€m	€m
Factory conversion		(2.80)		
Machinery		(4.50)		
Revenues		7.80	9.68	13.13
Operating costs: Fixed		(1.50)	(1.50)	(1.50)
Variable: 20% sales		(1.56)	(1.94)	(2.63)
Redundancy	(0.42)			
	(0.42)	(2.56)	6.24	9.00
9% factors	1.000	0.917	0.842	0.772
Present value	(0.42)	(2.35)	5.25	6.95

Net present value years 0 to 3: €9.43 million.

Years 4 to 6

Assumption

Operating profits and net cash flows will increase by 4% each year from year 4 to year 6 (in line with JHC's company objective). In year 4 the pre-tax cash flow will be €9.00 × 1.04 = €9.36m. After charging tax of 20 % that leaves 80% × €9.36 = €7.488m.

Year	After tax net cash flow	9%	PV
	€m		€m
4	7.488	0.708	5.302
5	7.788	0.650	5.062
6	8.100	0.596	4.828
			15.192

Loss of earnings from CC

Loss of earnings from CC, from year 1 to year 6

PV = €(2.2)m × 4.486 = €(9.869m).

The net present value of the project over the 6 year time horizon is therefore €14.75 million:

	€m
NPV to year 3	9.43
NPV years 4 to 6	15.19
Loss of NPV from CC	(9.87)
	14.75

Equivalent annual annuity

A better comparison between the two alternatives (which have different useful lives) is the equivalent annual annuity, that is the annual receipt that would be equivalent to an investment in the project. This is found by dividing the project NPV by the annuity factor for the project life.

Alternative 1: €11.21m / 5.535 = €2.03 million.
Alternative 2: €14.75m / 4.486 = €3.29 million.

Conclusion

On the basis of the calculations and assumptions, both alternatives are worthwhile but Alternative 2 is forecast to have a higher net present value over a shorter time horizon (and hence a higher equivalent annual annuity) and would appear to be the better financial alternative.

These conclusions are further discussed in part (b).

(ii) **Modified internal rate of return**

The modified internal rate of return of a project is calculated by:

- Converting investment outlays into a **single equivalent payment** in year zero, discounting back at the company's cost of financing where necessary.

- Converting net cash flows generated by the project into a **single equivalent receipt** at the end of the project's life, by compounding forward at the company's reinvestment rate.

- **Finding the rate of return** which equates the **single receipt** divided by the **single payment** (by using discount tables and interpolating).

Advantages of MIRR

The advantage of quoting a rate of return when evaluating a project is that non-financial managers find the concept **easier to understand** than net present value. MIRR has the advantage over a straightforward IRR computation that it **does not make** the **assumption** that the company's **reinvestment rate** is equal to the **IRR** of the project. It also eliminates the problem of **multiple IRRs**.

Disadvantages of MIRR

If the reinvestment rate is greater than the cost of capital, the MIRR will **underestimate the true return**. Despite its simplicity it does **not appear** to be **used much in practice**.

Also, MIRR does not solve the problem of how to **choose between projects** with **different lengths of life**. In the case of the investments under consideration, in which the investment assets have different useful lives, MIRR is not as useful as the equivalent annual annuity approach shown above.

(b)   **Report on proposed new subsidiary company SP**

To: Directors of JHC Group
From: Financial Manager
Date: 1 February 20X4
Subject: Effect of new subsidiary

Introduction

This report discusses how the proposed new health food subsidiary SP might contribute to the attainment of the Group's objectives. The report includes financial and strategic evaluations of the two alternative methods of operation identified by the Board and makes recommendations.

Alternative methods of operation

The Board has identified two alternative strategic approaches to setting up SP:

- Alternative 1 involves equipping the new factory to the highest safety and quality standards.
- Alternative 2 assumes that only modest improvements to existing safety measures will be made.

Higher minimum safety standards may become a reality if the European Parliament passes legislation which is currently under discussion.

Summary of financial evaluation of the alternatives

	Alternative 1	*Alternative 2*
Estimated useful life of equipment	8 years	6 years
Expected net present value over useful life	€11.21 million	€14.75 million
Equivalent annual annuity	€2.03 million	€3.29 million

On the basis of the calculations and assumptions:

- Both alternatives appear to be highly worthwhile investments compared with the existing business CC.

- Alternative 2 is forecast to have a **higher net present value** over a shorter time horizon (and hence a higher equivalent annual annuity) and would appear to be the better financial alternative.

These conclusions are further discussed in relation to the strategic objectives below.

Contribution to the Group's stated objectives

(i)   **Increase operating cash flows and dividends per share by at least 4% per year**

The Group's latest overall earnings are €215 million. A 4% increase would be €8.6 million. However, if the Group's existing earnings keep pace with 1.5% inflation, then new projects need to contribute a 2.5% increase in earnings per year, which is €5.38 million.

In this context, the **net cash flows** generated by the new subsidiary are significant. By the time the project is into its 4th year it is estimated to be generating an expected operating cash flow of about €7.4 million net of tax under either alternative.

However, the figures for the opening years of each alternative, shown below, are less favourable, indicating that the investment has a two year 'gestation period' before it can make a good contribution to the Group's results. Machinery and redundancy costs have been ignored, as they are investment cash flows rather than operating cash flows, but would make the figures less favourable if included.

Alternative 1 Operating cash flows (€m)

	Year 1	Year 2	Year 3
Revenues	4.48	11.80	17.60
Operating costs	(4.07)	(6.63)	(8.66)
Cash flow lost from CC	(2.20)	(2.20)	(2.20)
	(1.79)	2.97	6.74

Alternative 2 Operating cash flows (€m)

	Year 1	Year 2	Year 3
Revenues	7.80	9.68	13.13
Operating costs	(3.06)	(3.44)	(4.13)
Cash flow lost from CC	(2.20)	(2.20)	(2.20)
	2.54	4.04	6.80

Conclusion

Although alternative 2 produces the better results, both alternatives would probably increase the Group's operating cash flows significantly after an initial two-year investment period. This is considered acceptable in helping to meet the stated objective. However, firmer estimates of revenue and cash flows beyond year 3 would strengthen confidence in this conclusion.

(ii) **Increase the wealth of shareholders while respecting interests of other stakeholders and operating to the highest ethical standards**

Wealth of shareholders

On the basis of the financial forecasts, both alternatives have **positive expected net present values** and should therefore increase shareholders' wealth. Alternative 2 appears to be the better because it has the higher NPV, in theory creating a 0.5% increase in wealth from the first 6 years of operation:

	€m
Current value of group shares: 350m x €8.31	2,908.50
NPV of alternative 2, first six years	14.75
Value of shares with project alternative 2:	2,923.25
Theoretical increase in value of shares	0.5%

Interests of employees

Both alternatives would hopefully provide **profitable long-term employment** for those staff with appropriate skills. However, both would **create redundancies** among those currently working for subsidiary CC. In this respect, Alternative 2 is more acceptable to employees, creating only one fifth of the redundancies associated with Alternative 1.

Ethical standards

Given that the European Parliament is currently debating the introduction of safety standards that can only be satisfied by the technology of Alternative 1, it follows that Alternative 2 is incompatible with the objective of operating to the highest ethical standards.

There are two related risks of adopting Alternative 2 that could translate into severely reduced cash flows

(1) If the new legislation is passed, there would need to be a relatively swift change to the **technology of alternative 1**. This would be expensive, requiring not only new machinery, processes and training but a complete re-branding of the product image generated by Alternative 2.

(2)   Even if the legislation is not passed, a significant number of customers for this type of health food product are likely to wish to see the **highest ethical standards** in operation, and may mount a campaign with the general public to boycott SP's products if lower safety standards are in use. This risk even applies if the factory in Europe uses high safety standards but another factory (eg set up in a developing country) uses less stringent standards.

Both of these risks imply that the expected cash flows of Alternative 2 may well be over-optimistic and that Alternative 1 should be chosen.

Recommendations

If the decision on subsidiary SP needs to be made in the near future, we recommend the following:

(1)   The **health food project** should be **implemented**.

(2)   **Subsidiary CC** should be **closed**, sold, or moved to another location.

(3)   The health food project should employ the **technology of Alternative 1**. Although Alternative 2 has a better initial financial projection than Alternative 1, it may prove unacceptable to European customers. Given that Alternative 1 has a reasonably good positive net present value, there is a strong case for adopting it, in order to maintain the objective of operating to the highest ethical standards, which is key to the Group's brand image, and to gain experience of working with cutting edge technology.

(c)   **The option features involved in the JHC Group's decision**

Real options

An option is the right to make a choice. This right is usually gained by paying a price in order to 'hold the option open'. As regards this type of investment decision there are three types of options to be considered: abandonment option, timing option and strategic option.

Abandonment option

An **abandonment option** refers to the ability to **abandon the project at a certain stage** (or stages) in its life. If large sums are being spent, and prospects do not appear healthy, an abandonment option may be valuable. This type of option is affected, for example, by the type of equipment needed for the project and the terms on which the equipment is acquired. If equipment is readily resalable this gives a more valuable abandonment option than if the equipment is highly specialised with no prospective second-hand purchasers. On this basis, Alternative 2 may have a higher value abandonment option.

Timing option

A **timing option** is the option to **'wait and see'** before making an investment decision. In the case of Subsidiary SP, the possibility of 'doing nothing for a year' may be more valuable than either of the two stated alternatives 1 and 2, because it will allow the **resolution of the uncertainty** surrounding European legislation. This option has at least one identifiable cost in the example: the 5% increased cost of equipment in Alternative 1 if the decision to start is delayed.

Strategic option

A **strategic option** arises when a strategy opens up a **choice of follow-up activities** for the future. For example, buying the equipment associated with Alternative 1 enables the company to develop experience and skills with the latest technology, which may allow opportunities that would otherwise have been unavailable.

In each case, the value of the option to the company can be assessed and added to the appraisal computation as a benefit.

73 Groots

> **Text references.** Net present value calculations are explained in Chapter 18. Acquisitions issues are discussed in Chapter 16.
>
> **Top tips.** There are a number of issues that you have to work through in (a) (i) and 7 marks seems a fairly low mark allocation. Note the figures have to be inflated because we are using money cost of capital. Note also the examiner's comment about calculation of forward exchange rates. Although purchasing power parity may be a technically better method than interest rate parity, the scenario specifies interest rate parity, so you must use it. Don't worry too much if you used another method for the perpetuity calculation: others are possible and that part would only have been worth 2–3 marks.
>
> (a) (ii) clearly confused a lot of candidates. It is technically correct to say that the two methods should be the same; the approach we take is to try to speculate why in practice calculations might have distortions
>
> There are also problems with the requirements in (a) (iii), if your two answers were the same (as they should have been in theory), but just use whatever your answer was. Also there may be conflict between using the answer in (a) (i) and attempting to maximise shareholder wealth.
>
> The discussions in (b) need to bring out the curious market value that the shares currently have. As Groots is listed it is possible to expand the shareholder base. There are a number of points in the scenario that can be drawn on in the discussion in (b) (iii).
>
> The examiner's comments are lengthier than normal on this question. The examiner was not generally satisfied with performance in this exam, and so is likely to examine the sorts of issues this question raises in future.
>
> **Easy marks.** The easiest part of the discussion should have been post-completion audits, which is a standard question.
>
> **Examiner's comments.** In (a) calculations were often wrong and comments not provided. Forward rates were often calculated using purchasing power parity rather than interest rate parity, and showing the Caribbean $ appreciating rather than depreciating against the Euro. Candidates also failed to use two methods, adjust for inflation and calculate post year 4 cash flows. Some incorrectly deducted tax from post-tax cash flows and added rather than deducted repayment of debt. The most common error in (a) (iii) was to use the nominal value of shares.
>
> Answers to (b) (i) often lacked discussion of the methods used, and most candidates failed to mention the significance of market values. Some answers incorrectly calculated net asset value. Answers to (ii) were better, although some candidates made the basic mistake of stating that retained earnings could be used to finance the acquisition. Other mistakes included suggesting inappropriate methods eg venture capital and factoring, and failing to support answers with calculations. Some answers failed to take into account the fact that both companies were listed.
>
> (b) (iii) was often answered badly or not at all. (iv) was done reasonably well, but candidates often failed to take into account the fact that this was a takeover situation, and suggested incorrectly that the results of the post-completion audit would be publicised to shareholders.

(a) (i)   **Maximum price that Groots would pay for Cocomos**

This is the **present value** of the expected future cash flows of Cocomos.

For each method, the computation involves looking at the cash flows given for years 1 to 4 and a perpetuity from year 5 onwards.

The cash flows for the first 4 years are:

Year	1	2	3	4
Post tax net cash flow C$ mill. (real terms)	31.5	37.5	41.5	47.2
Nominal cash flow (inflate at 4.5% per year)	32.92	40.95	47.36	56.29

Exchange rates

First evaluate the estimated future exchange rates, using interest rate parity:

Year	€/C$	
0	0.300	
1	0.292	[0.300 × 1.035 / 1.065]
2	0.283	[0.292 × 1.035 / 1.065]
3	0.275	
4	0.268	
5	0.260	

Cost of capital

Groot's nominal discount rate in euros k(€) is 10%. Its discount rate in C$ can be found by comparing the differentials on risk free rates using **interest rate parity.**

$$[1 + k\,(C\$)] / [1 + k(€)] \quad = \quad [1 + r_f\,(C\$)] / [1 + r_f\,(€)]$$

Thus: $[1 + k\,(C\$)] / 1.1 = 1.065 / 1.035$

Therefore: $k\,(C\$) = [1.065 × 1.1 / 1.035] - 1 = 13\%.$

This is higher than the 12% which Cocomos estimates as its cost of capital, and which Groots believes is too low.

Method 1

Year	1	2	3	4
Nominal cash flow C$ (as above))	32.92	40.95	47.36	56.29
Exchange rate €/C$	0.292	0.283	0.275	0.268
Nominal cash flow in € million	9.61	11.59	13.02	15.09
10% discount factor (Groots € cost of capital)	0.909	0.826	0.751	0.683
Discounted cash flow	8.735	9.573	9.778	10.306
NPV	38.39			

The present value of the perpetuity as at year 4 = $\dfrac{15.09\,(1.02)}{0.10 - 0.02}$ = €192.40 million

The present value of the perpetuity as at year 0 (using the 4 year discount factor) = 192.40 × 0.683 = €131.41 million.

Total NPV by method 1 = 38.39 + 131.41 = €169.80 million.

Subtracting Cocomos' debt (value converted at spot = 135 × 0.3 = 40.5), gives the maximum price for Cocomos' equity as 169.80 – 40.5 = **€129.3 million.**

Method 2

Year	1	2	3	4
Nominal cash flow C$ (as above)	32.92	40.95	47.36	56.29
Discount factor 13%	0.885	0.783	0.693	0.613
Discounted cash flow	29.13	32.06	32.82	34.51
NPV C$	128.52			
Spot rate	0.300			
NPV €	38.56			

The present value of the perpetuity as at year 4 = $\dfrac{15.09\,(1.02)}{0.13 - 0.02}$ = €139.93 million

The present value of the perpetuity as at year 0 (using the 4 year discount factor) = 139.93 × 0.613 = €85.78 million.

Total NPV by method 2 = 38.56 + 85.78 = €124.34 million.

Subtracting Cocomos' debt (value converted at spot = 135 × 0.3 = 40.5), gives the maximum price for Cocomos' equity as 124.34 – 40.5 = **€ 83.84 million.**

(ii) **Same rates**

The difference between the two results above should be due to **rounding** of the **discount rates** and **growth rates** used in the computations. In theory the two results should come to exactly the same answer because the same interest rate differential between the two countries has been used to predict exchange rates (by the theory of interest rate parity), and to derive Groot's cost of capital in C$ from the equivalent euro cost. Thus the two methods do the same computations, but in a different sequence.

Practical reasons for differences

Methods used

In practice the **estimates of future exchange rates** and **cost of capital** may be made in different ways, resulting in differences between the two answers. For example, the future exchange rates may be estimated using **purchasing power parity** (based on estimates of inflation rates), and the cost of capital for Groots in C$ may be based on data in the East Caribbean stock market.

Assumptions

Because the theories used for making these estimates make **simplifying assumptions**, and because they depend on **statistical analysis** for estimation of parameters, there are in practice bound to be differences between the results of the two different approaches unless they use exactly the same underlying assumptions.

Risk

The methods used may also be amended to take account of risks. It may be difficult to determine in which direction.

(iii) **Value of Cocomos**

From the above calculations, the **value of Cocomos shares** is **€129.3 million**, which is above its current market value, which is 55 million $\times$ 6.95 $\times$ 0.3 = approximately €115 million.

Groots shares are worth €6.85 today, which implies that the number of shares to be issued as purchase consideration is 129.3/6.85 = 18.88 million (i.e. 1 new Groots share for approximately 2.9 shares in Cocomos).

There are many assumptions behind this computation, including:

- There is **no synergy** when the two companies are merged; this would raise the maximum price that Groots might be prepared to pay

- Groots' **share price does not change** as a result of information and rumours concerning the takeover bid

- **New events** do **not change the value of Cocomos**: e.g. new opportunities, currency changes, new bidders

(b) Report to the directors of the Groots Group

From: Financial Manager

Proposed acquisition of Cocomos

This report discusses and makes **recommendations** on the **maximum price** that should be paid for the prospective new acquisition Cocomos Limited and the most appropriate type of financing for the acquisition. In addition, it analyses strategies for enhancing the value of the combined firm and discusses the benefits and limitations of a post-completion audit and review.

(i) **Recommendation on price to be offered to Cocomos**

The table below shows the value of Cocomos per share and for the whole 55 million shares, using four different bases of valuation.

Price	Per share €	All shares € million
(1) Cash flows (see (a) above)	2.35	129
(2) Current earnings Groots P/E ratio (see workings below)	2.32	127
(3) Current market value of shares	2.08	115
(4) Net asset value (book value of equity shares)	0.84	46

(1) **Cash flows**

Methods (1) and (2) show the value of the **future cash flows** and **earnings** of Cocomos to Groots. Method (1) is based on the **discounted value of future cash flows** arising from Cocomos. It **provides the most logical analysis** of the available data and, because the discount rate is the minimum required return for the investment, this gives the **maximum price** that we consider paying.

The value arrived at is of course **only an estimate,** and subject to appreciable estimation error, because the method is based on **simplified assumptions** about future exchange rates and interest rates, and about the **future cash flows** of Cocomos and the risk that the investment carries. In particular, it is **very sensitive** to **estimates of cash flow** beyond year 5. If we are able to gain more information about these factors, we will be able to have more confidence in the figure.

(2) **Earnings-based measure**

Method (2) is a more traditional earnings-based method. The price/earnings ratio of Groots has been used as to multiply the current profitability of Cocomos, resulting in a broad estimate of earnings-based value, as seen in the workings below.

Workings for method (2)

	Groots	Cocomos
Profit after tax	193.5 – 46.9 = €146.6 m	48.6 – 11.5 = C$37.1 m
		× 0.3 = €11.13 m.
Earnings per share	€146.6 m / 245 m. = €0.598	€11.13 m / 55m = €0.202
P/E ratio	€6.85 / €0.598 = 11.455	

Applying Groots' P/E to Cocomos earnings:

11.455 × €11.13 m = €127.5m. (€2.32 per share).

This method is subject to significant inaccuracies because it **fails to recognise the possible difference in growth rates** between Groots and Cocomos, and because it is based on earnings, which contain significant non-cash items such as depreciation.

(3) **Current market value of shares**

Method (3) is simply the **current market value of the shares** on the East Caribbean Stock Exchange. The fact that this is so far below estimates we have made of the value of Cocomos to Groots needs further investigation. At best, it shows the hidden value that be unlocked from Cocomos as part of the Groots Group. At worst it may mean that our estimates of Cocomos' value are over-optimistic.

(4) **Net assets method**

Finally method (4) shows the **value of the net assets** of the company. This is very low compared with the other methods because it does not attempt to value the business as a going concern, but merely shows the value of its assets as a base-line in the event of poor performance.

Other factors affecting valuation

We need to consider the impact of other factors not allowed for above, in particular the impact of **currency changes** and whether the value may be affected if the franchisees object, and the bid in effect has to become hostile.

Conclusion

In summary, we recommend that the **maximum price payable** for Cocomos is €2.35 per share. We should, of course, not offer this price but should offer a premium over current market price that is sufficient to attract the shareholders of Cocomos (e.g. €2.20 per share).

(ii)   **Alternative forms of consideration**

Cash-share issue decision

The shares of Cocomos can be acquired by **cash** or by an **issue of Groots shares**, or by a combination of the two, including allowing the shareholders of the acquired company to opt for shares or cash.

The general principles are:

(1)   If shares are offered, the **expected value of the purchase consideration** will need to be higher than if cash is offered, because cash is risk free to the former owners of Cocomos, whereas shares in Groots may fall in value.

(2)   Whichever method is used, **nearly all of the existing cash balance** will be needed to **repay the €40.5 million debt** of Cocomos when the acquisition is made. Therefore, if cash is offered, Groots will need to borrow, and this will raise company gearing (and hence financial risk for Groots shareholders). If shares are issued, gearing and financial risk will decrease.

(3)   A **share issue** will tend to **dilute shareholdings** whereas a cash acquisition will not. Key shareholders will be interested in the disposition of shareholdings after the merger.

(4)   If borrowing (in order to pay cash) is carried out in the **currency of the acquired company**, this can act as a hedge against exchange rate risk.

Share issue

A **share issue** would require 19 million new shares (i.e. 1 new Groots share for approximately 2.9 shares in Cocomos – see part (a) above). This would increase Groots share capital by nearly 8% to 264 million. Assuming no change in share value, the gearing will drop from 23% debt to 22%, as seen in the table below.

Before issue	No	Price	Value €m	Gearing
Shares	245	6.85	1,678	77%
Loan stock	475	105.5%	501	23%
			2,179	
After issue				
Shares	264	6.85	1,808	78%
Loan stock			501	22%
			2,309	

The major shareholders of Groots will see their shareholdings diluted by about 7%, also a **dilution of earnings per share** and the directors of Cocomos and their families, who own 51% of Cocomos, will end up owning approximately 3.5% of Groots' shares, a proportion comparable with the existing board of Groots, whose holding will drop to approximately 7.4% from 8%. A share issue will therefore probably imply that Cocomos' management are given a significant role on the board of Groots.

Cash purchase

A **cash acquisition** would mean the purchase consideration could be less, say €120 million instead of €130 million. This would have to be financed by borrowing, which would therefore raise gearing significantly to about 27% debt as shown below.

	Value €m	Gearing
Shares	1,678	73%
Loan stock (501+ 120)	621	27%
	2,299	

Use of debt

The advantage of **debt financing** is that it is cheap and attracts **tax relief on interest**, and the disadvantage is that shareholders' financial risk increases. If we follow the **Modigliani-Miller** approach to analysing this problem, at the level of gearing in question (which is not unduly high) the most significant factor is the beneficial one of tax relief on debt, which will create an increase in shareholder value of approximately €120m × 25% (the tax rate), that is €30m. However Modigliani and Miller assume fixed interest debt: a variable rate loan would increase interest rate risk.

If the company can raise Caribbean dollars debt finance, this would be a good way of **reducing the currency risk** of owning a Caribbean investment.

Attitude of shareholders

The different groups of shareholders in Cocomos are likely to have **different attitudes** to the **offer of cash or shares**.

(1) The **local pension fund and most small shareholders in** the Caribbean will probably **not want shares** in a British company, as this will bring currency risk. They will therefore prefer cash.

(2) The **wealthy individual investors** will probably be **less averse to a share issue**, but may prefer to keep this part of their portfolio in the Caribbean.

(3) The **directors of Cocomos** and their families may be **very interested** in a share issue by Groots as this may enable some of them to gain board positions and exert influence on a much larger trading unit. For the acquisition to succeed it is probably necessary that some of the Cocomos directors receive shares in Groots.

On balance therefore, we recommend that Groots makes an offer involving a share issue with a cash alternative, such that investors can choose the method that is beneficial to them.

(iii) **Strategies for enhancing the combined value of the company following the acquisition**

These strategies should be **developed** and **agreed** before the acquisition is finalised. It is essential that the board is able to communicate its plans to all interested parties as soon as possible in order to maintain the confidence of investors and staff.

The strategies that need to be pursued are:

Management of the group

There needs to be **quick agreement** on the **composition of the board of directors** and **action taken where necessary** to prevent any disputes. **Management of the segments** within the business will need to be **agreed**, taking account of the changes introduced, as discussed below. **Corporate objectives** will need to be **agreed** and **harmonised,** and there may be cultural differences in methods of operation that need to be understood, and either welcomed or eliminated.

Elimination of duplicated costs and sale of duplicated assets

These will occur across the **business functions** of the combined organisation – not just in the acquired company - including purchasing, marketing, finance and administration. A list of these **duplicated activities** is needed, together with a plan for **actioning their elimination**, including redundancies, closure of offices, sales of duplicated buildings and other assets. This plan should be carried out in a controlled fashion, especially **redundancies** and **ending of franchises,** where necessary. The importance of this aspect of the merger is that it has a direct 100% effect on the 'bottom line' and will be expected by shareholders.

Decision on the core business: elimination or sale of fringe activities

Sometimes businesses maintain sections of their business simply to increase their **turnover or status** or because of **directors' special interests.** Frequently these activities consume much management time. Because it makes the firm larger, the merger provides an excuse for **eliminating such fringe activities** and provides the opportunity for **focusing on the core business.** Thus, for example, it may be that certain parts of Groots or Cocomos are worth more to other companies and can be beneficially sold at this stage.

Marketing strategy and the business model

This needs so far as possible to be **harmonised** across the group. Specifically in Cocomos' case, a decision needs to be made on whether the **franchising of outlets** will be **continued,** or whether all outlets will be brought in-house. There will be opportunities for cross-selling products between customers of the two companies. In a 'fashion' business, this is very powerful.

Business and risk management strategies

There will be opportunities to **streamline all business strategies** in the group (e.g. supply chain, finance, administration, information technology). These should all be reviewed. The directors also need to carry out a detailed **risk management programme,** assessing the group's revised **risk appetite**, and analysing key risks such as economic, political and cultural.

Stakeholder relationships

All **stakeholder groups** (e.g. investors, employees, customers) should be managed by appointed directors. A communication plan should be produced and actioned for each group.

(iv) **Benefits and limitations of a post-completion audit and review**

Post-completion audits

A post completion audit (PCA) is an independent appraisal of a project after it is completed, with the objective of evaluating the strengths and weaknesses during the various project stages.

Key issues

Specifically in the case of an acquisition decision, the many questions the company will need answered include:

- Were the **estimates and arguments** that led to the **acquisition realistic**? Or were they over-optimistic or pessimistic?

- Were the **budgets** set before and after the **acquisition realistic**? Did managers have a fair chance of implementing the necessary plans?

- Were there **some plans** which managers were too reluctant to carry out and why?

- What factors were **left out of the original plans** that proved to be significant?

- What **positive factors arose** which meant that performance was better than expected?

- Were there **short term gains** which prevented longer term advantages?

397

Information requirements

The success of a PCA depends on the **availability of information** that, in turn, depends on the quality of records that have been kept and on the availability of staff, who may have left if a project turned out a failure.

Advantages of PCAs

(1)   A PCA forces assessment of why actual results might have differed from expected results. This may impact upon how the **acquired company** is **managed.**

(2)   A PCA will **document lessons** that need to be learned and can potentially greatly **assist in improving the appraisal, implementation and control** of future projects.

(3)   A PCA can also evidence for **appraising the performance of managers** and **training** future managers.

Disadvantages of PCAs

(1)   A PCA can be **time-consuming.**

(2)   A PCA can be **costly in terms of the time** of the senior staff needed to carry out the audit, and the time of the managers in responding to the audit.

(3)   A PCA can be sometimes **demotivational** when managers have already learned their lessons and do not want to be reminded of the mistakes they made.

(4)   A PCA may have difficulty identifying **controllable** and **non-controllable** factors.

(5)   The **strategic benefits** of the merger may only **materialise** after the PCA has been carried out.

74 GAS

Text references. Investment appraisal calculations are explained in Chapter 18. Project risk is discussed in Chapter 17, equity issues in Chapter 5 and share markets in Chapter 8.

Top tips. The calculations in (a) don't seem to have much relevance for the rest of the answer. The tax assumption could alternatively have been taking a tax credit for the year 1 loss. (b) is a list of many of the main risks you will have seen in Risk and Control Strategy Paper P3. (c) requires a good knowledge of the efficient markets hypothesis, particularly the semi-strong version, and how share price models can be affected.

Easy marks. Hopefully use of your P3 knowledge should have enabled you to score heavily in (b).

Examiner's comments. In part (a), candidates made a good attempt at scheduling the cash flows and calculating NPV but some had difficulties in differentiating profit and cash flows. Other common errors included omitting the loss on realisation of working capital and timing problems with, or omission of, the UK tax calculations.

Part (b) was generally done quite well but few candidates picked up the key issue of high dependency of the result on the estimated realisable value of the plant and equipment. The calculations in part (c)(ii) were not done well and there was limited discussion.

(a)   **Investment criterion 1: Accounting rate of return**

Year	1	2	3	4 - 10
	B$ m	B$ m	B$ m	B$ m
Net operating cash flows	20	150	250	300
Depreciation	(35)	(35)	(35)	(35)
Accounting profit before interest and tax	(15)	115	215	265

There is no interest associated with the project.

Average accounting profit is [-15 + 115 + 215 + (7 × 265)] / 10 = B$ 217 million.

Project investment	Year 0	Year 10
	B$ m	B$ m
Plant and equipment	700	350
Working capital	50	40
	750	390

Average investment in the project = (opening value + closing value) / 2 = (750 + 390) / 2 = B$ 570 million

Accounting rate of return = 217 / 570 = **38%**. This is well above the minimum investment criterion of 25% per annum.

Investment criterion 2: Net present value at 10.5% discount rate

Tax allowances on the plant and equipment are the **same** as the accounting depreciation. Because GAS plc has no other projects in Bustan, it is assumed that its loss in year 1 will be carried forward to year 2, resulting in the following tax payments (B$ million):

Year 1:	Zero
Year 2:	20% × 100 = 20
Year 3:	20% × 215 = 43
Years 4 – 10:	20% × 265 = 53.

GAS plc's project discount rate in pounds k($£$) is 10.5%. There are two ways of finding the NPV:

1. **Converting cash flows to £ and discounting at 10.5%;** or

2. **Discounting the B$ cash flows at the equivalent discount rate in** B$ and then converting the NPV to £ at the spot rate.

Although the first method sounds easier, it results in the need to treat each of the 10 years separately, because the exchange rate will change each year. The second method will therefore be used, as it allows the use of annuity factors.

GAS plc's **project discount rate in Bustan dollars k(B$)** can be found by comparing the differential on long term expected interest rates (4.8% in UK and 10% in Bustan) and applying to the UK discount rate of 10.5%.

$$[1 + k\,(B\$)] / [1 + k(£)] = [1 + r(B\$)] / [1 + r(£)]$$

Thus: $[1 + k\,(B\$)] / 1.105 = 1.10 / 1.048$

Therefore: $k\,(B\$) = [1.105 × 1.10 / 1.048] - 1 = 15.98\%$, say 16%, which is the discount rate that will be used on the post tax project cash flows in B$.

NPV of Bustan cash flow(B$ million)

Year	0	1	2	3	4 - 10	10
Plant and equipment	(700)					350
Working capital	(50)					40
Net operating cash flows		20	150	250	300	
Tax payable			(20)	(43)	(53)	
Net cash flow	(750)	20	130	207	247	390
Discount rate 16%	1	0.862	0.743	0.641	2.587	0.227
PV	(750)	17.2	96.6	132.7	639.0	88.5
NPV B$	224.0					

The NPV in £ is found by converting at the spot rate, B$ 0.7778 = £1:

NPV of Bustan cash flows in £ million = 224.0 / 0.7778 = 288.0.

The remaining cash flows of the project are the UK tax payments. Because of the double tax agreement, these will be 30% − 20% = 10% of the taxable profits. Thus UK tax will be half of the tax paid in Bustan, but one year later.

For convenience of calculation, the UK tax payments are treated as if they are in B$ and their NPV is converted at the spot rate.

Year	3	4	5 - 11
Additional tax payable in UK	(10.0)	(21.5)	(26.5)
Discount rate 16%	0.641	0.552	2.231
PV	(6.4)	(11.9)	(59.1)
NPV B$	(77.4)		

PV of UK tax payments in £ million = (77.4) / 0.7778 = (99.5)

Thus the net present value of the project in £ million is 288.0 − 99.5 = **£189 million**.

This is a high positive net present value, indicating that investment criterion 2 is satisfied.

(b)   **Major risk issues**

When evaluating the project there is a wide range of risks that need to be considered. Although overlapping, these can be grouped into operating risks, commercial risks, political risks and financial risks.

Operating risks

These are the risks associated with **electricity generation** and **power supply systems**. GAS plc has experience of this business across Europe and will factor in its normal business risks, but there may be **additional operational risks** when working in Bustan, for example from lower skill levels, unknown geographical terrain, non-availability of materials and poor infrastructure. These risks should be **quantified** and **minimised** by carrying out as much research as possible and building appropriate estimates into the analysis where necessary.

Commercial risks

Most of these result from **competition** (both direct and for substitute sources of power) and need to be evaluated. **Pricing estimates** need to be **examined carefully**, particularly because the Bustan dollar is likely to decline (see financial risks below).

Cultural risks

Other commercial risks may result from **differences in the law and culture** of Europe and Bustan. For example, misunderstandings or conflicting business protocols may cause delays.

Political risks

The government of Bustan (or a future government headed by another political party) may take action that is **detrimental to the profitability** of GAS's operations. For example, it may **impose price controls** on electricity supplies, **increase taxation** or **introduce exchange controls** on repatriated profits. These risks should be minimised so far as possible by conducting research and signing agreements with the government (e.g. on tax rates and profit repatriation).

Financial risks

The financial risks that GAS will face will be an extension of what it already faces in Europe: gearing, interest rate risk and currency risk. Since the project is all equity financed, the directors have chosen **not to increase gearing** or **interest rate risk.** This policy increases the **currency risk** of their operations in Bustan, because the whole value of their operating profit from Bustan will vary with fluctuations in the Bustan dollar. Declines in the value of the B$ will need to be countered by **price increases,** which may be politically unacceptable in some circumstances. An alternative method of financing which could hedge some of this currency risk is to take out a **substantial loan** in **Bustan dollars**.

(c) To: The Board of Directors of GAS plc

From: Management Consultants

Report on share price volatility and estimation of a fair valuation of the shares of GAS plc

You have asked us to provide some possible explanations for the increased volatility of GAS plc's share price in 20X4 and 20X5, to advise on a fair market price for the shares, and to explain how and to what extent the directors can influence the price of the company's shares.

(i) **Volatility of share price movements**

No perfect models of share valuation or share price movements exist. The following notes are therefore intended as partial explanations for the share price volatility. They are based on the **efficient market hypothesis** and the **capital asset pricing model**, two areas of theory that, despite their imperfections, have provided useful analyses of many financial management problems.

Efficient markets hypothesis

The **efficient market hypothesis** (semi strong form) postulates that share prices **swiftly and rationally reflect all information** that is **publicly available**. During this whole period, the market has reacted to any favourable or unfavourable information about the Bustan economy by marking GAS shares up or down accordingly. In addition, in the period to June 20X4 there were uncertainties as to the company's future expansion plans.

June 20X4 announcement

The announcement in June 20X4 ended speculation on the company's intentions but added to market uncertainties for many reasons including:

- The **proposed project** was **so large**
- It would require a **major rights issue**, which is unpopular with some shareholders
- There was **no proposed mechanism** for hedging currency risk on the project
- The proposal could have been **rejected or delayed** by the Bustan government. Thus in the period to January 20X5, further sources of information about Bustan or Gas plc had an increased effect on share price

On 1 January 20X5, the Board's press release **clarified the company's success** in winning the project but the accompanying dividend forecast has been treated with some scepticism, resulting in further uncertainties and fluctuations in the share price.

Capital asset pricing model

The **capital asset pricing model** suggests that much of the company's share price volatility that has been experienced is **irrelevant** to investors who hold diversified portfolios, because specific company risks are cancelled out when a broad portfolio of investments is held. Thus you should not be too concerned about overall share price volatility, but base your decisions on the company's systematic risk (represented by its beta factor).

(ii) **Fair market price for GAS plc's shares in January 20X5**

The **fairest** valuation for a company's shares would be based on **all relevant information** at the time. However, the implication of the efficient market hypothesis (semi-strong form) is that the actual share price will be based on **public information only.**

The market does not have the cash flow forecast for the Bustan project and analysts will therefore either use **other available information**, such as the directors' dividend forecast, or else try to use available public information to construct their own cash forecast for the project.

Effect of the rights issue on the share price

The share price at 31 December 20X4 was 335 pence ex div. The effect of the 1 for 4 rights issue on this price (in isolation of any project effects) can be easily computed.

The number of shares issued to fund the plant and equipment (1 for 4 rights issue) is ¼ × 1,200 million = 300 million. This implies an issue price of approximately $\frac{700 \times 0.7778}{300}$ = 181 pence (ignoring issue costs).

The theoretical ex rights price of the shares (ignoring the project NPV which is not public information) is **304 pence**, as shown below (4,563m / 1,500 m).

Shares	Number (million)	Value £	Total £m
Original	1,200	3.35	4,020
New	300	1.81	543
Total	1,500	3.04	4,563

Effect of the project NPV

If the market was told that the **proposed project** has a **positive expected NPV** of £189 million, and if this figure were believed by the market, then the shares should increase in value by £189 million to a total value of £4,909 million, that is a value per share of **327 pence**. This is the closest we can get to a fair value of the shares.

Effect of the directors' dividend forecast

The market can use the revised dividend forecast to estimate a share value, using the company's cost of equity. The estimate you have given us of the shareholders' required return on equity is 9.4% per annum.

Using the **dividend valuation model**, based on the dividend of 14 pence and the company's share price of 335 pence at 31 December 20X4, and assuming that the market expected a 5% growth rate in dividends (equal to the historical growth rate), the company's cost of equity capital can be estimated as:

$\left(\frac{14 \times 1.05}{335}\right)$ + 0.05 = 0.094 or 9.4%. We therefore concur with your estimate.

If the directors' revised dividend forecast on 1 January 20X5 is believed by the market, the revised value per share, based on the dividend valuation model can be estimated in two stages:

Stage 1: PV of first three years' constant dividends

Year	Div (pence)	DF at 9.4%	PV (pence)
1 (20X5)	14	0.914	12.80
2 (20X6)	14	0.836	11.70
3 (20X7)	14	0.764	10.70
			35.20

Stage 2: PV of the perpetuity from year 4 of dividends growing at 7% per year.

The present value as at *end of year 3* = (14 × 1.07) / (0.094 – 0.07) = 624.17 pence.

This has a present value as at year 0 of 624.17 × 0.764 = 476.87 pence.

Thus the total value per share = 35 + 477 = **512 pence**.

Our conclusion is that the dividend forecast provided by the directors is over-optimistic. An estimate of 7% growth *to perpetuity* when the cost of funds is only 9.4% is impossible in practice. The closest figure to the fair market value is **327 pence**.

(iii) **The extent to which directors can influence their entity's share price**

Importance of confidentiality

Directors of public companies cannot make all information about their entities available to the market without running the risk of giving away information to competitors. It is therefore vital that directors can be **trusted to keep information secret** when necessary. However, risk aversion or a sense of management power will often lead directors to withhold company information from the market when it would be better for it to be disclosed.

Consequences for shareholders

In public companies, therefore, shareholders suffer from a **lack of inside knowledge** about company performance and plans, and this can result in decisions to buy or sell shares (and resulting share prices) based on false or partial information.

Impact of directors' statements

In this situation, directors can **greatly influence share prices** by the statements they make to the market, combined with their reputation for accuracy and truth (or otherwise). Because directors are in a position to make far-reaching strategic decisions using information that is not available to shareholders, their reputations can have a significant effect on share value. In some cases a director can improve a company's share price simply by joining the board.

In the situation of GAS plc it would have been better to issue a **forecast NPV** of the new project than to issue a vague dividend forecast that is clearly over-optimistic.

75 PM

Text references. Business valuation is covered in Chapter 15 and post-merger value enhancing strategies in Chapter 16.

Top tips. You must read this question very carefully as it is easier than you might at first think! It is not a general valuation question so only use the earnings and P/E information given to you. In part (b), you must include supporting calculations to your report (in appendices) and there are marks for good presentation and structure.

Easy marks. Look out for the clues in the scenario, especially in (a)(i) where there are easy marks available for the business values.

Examiner's comments. This question presented candidates with particular challenges with many candidates failing to read the question properly and wasting time calculating values for the two entities using incorrect valuation methods. In part (b), attempts at the report were generally very poor with few supporting calculations.

(a) *Workings*

Post merger values: Market capitalisation = £6,905 million
EPS = 31.65 pence

Terms of offer = 1 PM share for 2 NQ stock units

$$= \frac{850m}{2} \text{ new PM shares}$$

$$= 425m$$

Total number of PM shares = 425m + 950m = 1,375m

To get market capitalisation of £6,905m, implies a share price of 6,905/1,375 = 502p

EPS = 31.65p so P/E = $\dfrac{502}{31.65}$ = 15.86

Current EPS:

PM	NQ
273/950 = 28.7p	300/850 = 35.3c
	@ 1.85 = 19.1p

Current P/E ratios:

PM	NQ
456/28.7 = 15.9	450/35.3 = 12.75

An EPS of 31.65 pence implies combined post merger earnings of 31.65p × 1,375 = £435m.

Combined earnings for y/e 31/3/X6 = 273 + (300/1.85) = £435m

Current market capitalisation:

PM	NQ
950 × 4.56 = £4,332	850 × 4.5 = $3,825
	@1.85 = £2,068

Number of shares in merged entity:

PM	NQ	Post-merger
950	425	1,375
69%	31%	100%

(i)   The post merger values are estimated as a **market capitalisation** of £6,905 million and **EPS** of 31.65 pence. As can be seen in the workings, the total number of PM shares after the merger would be 1,375 and combined earnings with a $/£ exchange rate at 1.85 are £435m. This gives the EPS of approximately 31.65 pence.

The market capitalisation of £6,905m implies a **share price** of 502p, which means that a **P/E ratio** of 15.86 has been used. The current P/E of PM is 15.9 and that of NQ is 12.75. It has therefore been assumed that a P/E ratio similar to that of PM rather than NQ will apply post-merger. The total market capitalisation of PM and NQ is £6,400m (£4,332m + £2,068m), giving a difference of £505m between the pre and post merger values. This is approximately equal to the difference in P/E ratios of 3.15 multiplied by NQ's earnings.

(ii)   If we assume that there will be **no synergies** and the current market capitalisation of £6,400 will apply post-merger, the share prices will be:

PM: £6,400 × 69% = £4,416
          £4,416/950 shares = 465p per share (current price is 456p per share)

NQ: £6,400 × 31% = £1,984

£1,984/850 shares = 233p per share (equivalent of current price is $\dfrac{450}{1.85}$ = 243p)

PM's shareholders will therefore **benefit** and NQ's will **suffer** from the merger. It is usually expected that the share price of the target will rise following the announcement of a bid and that of the predator will fall. Much will depend on the market's views of the proposed merger and whether it believes that synergies will result from it.

(iii) The forecast market capitalisation of £6,905m and the sale of the software licences for £100m would produce a total **maximum value** for the merged entity of £7,005m. The value of NQ as part of this entity would be £7,005m – £4,332m (the current value of PM) = £2,673m. This gives a value of 314p for each stock unit, equating to approximately 1 PM share for 1.5 (456/314) NQ shares.

(b) To: The Board of PM
From: Financial adviser
Re: Issues concerning the merger of PM Industries plc with NQ Inc
Date: May 20X6

1 Introduction

This report will evaluate and discuss the merger of PM with NQ. The following issues will be discussed:

- How the merger might contribute to the achievement of PM's financial objectives

- External economic forces that might help or hinder the achievement of the merger's financial objectives

- Post-merger value enhancing strategies that could increase shareholder wealth

2 The achievement of PM's financial objectives

The current financial objectives are:

- To increase EPS by 5% per annum
- To maintain a gearing ratio below 30%
- To maintain a P/E ratio above the industry average

2.1 EPS

Earnings for the past 5 years have increased by 4.95% for PM per annum and by 4.66% for NQ (see appendix 1). If this were to continue after the merger, this objective would not be achieved. However, the expectation from the merger is that higher growth can be achieved. This would presumably come from NQ rather than PM, as PM has already divested the poor performing business units and it is debateable how much more growth can come from volume in a relatively mature market.

PM has higher margins than NQ and the expectation would be that higher margins could be achieved post-merger at NQ. However, earnings as a percentage of revenue have been falling year on year for both companies as would be expected in a mature market, so the 5% growth in EPS looks ambitious.

2.2 Gearing

Appendix 2 shows the calculation of current gearing for the two companies and that of the merged entity. Both companies have gearing below the financial objective level of 30%. A share exchange would reduce the gearing ratio to 21.8%. However, a cash offer would involve substantial borrowing and PM's current gearing percentage of 27.9% does not leave much room for manoeuvre. Any fall in share price as a result of the bid will also endanger the achievement of this objective.

It is however a relatively low level of gearing in today's financial climate and the Board might want to consider changing this financial objective should it become necessary.

2.3 P/E ratio

PM's P/E ratio is currently 15.9 with an industry average of 14 and therefore meets the objective. NQ's P/E ratio is 12.75 with an industry average of 13 and therefore does not meet the objective. However the bid calculations all involve an assumption that the P/E of the combined company will be nearer to that of PM. Appendix 3 shows that the P/E of the merged entity may be a weighted average of approximately 15, still above the industry average. This will depend entirely on the market's perception of the merged company and whether it believes that synergies will be obtained. Potential downside risks include integration problems and exchange rate volatility.

3 **External economic forces**

3.1 **Economic conditions**

PM has widespread commercial and industrial interests worldwide and as such has a diversified portfolio in terms of industrial sectors and geographic regions. This should mean that the risks from downturns in economies should be reduced as not all economies and sectors will be affected to the same extent. However, NQ obtains 75%, and the combined company would have around 50%, of its revenues from the US and would therefore be heavily affected by any problems with the US economy.

A general crash in stock markets could affect the gearing and P/E ratios.

3.2 **Exchange rates**

A globally trading organisation will be subject to the risks associated with movements in exchange rates. Changes in inflation and interest rates can affect exchange rates and cause uncertainty. For example, higher costs or lower revenues and accounting losses as a result of adverse movements in exchange rates may have a serious impact.

A policy to deal with the risks associated with exchange rates needs to be in place. **Economic exposure** from exchange rate movements can be hedged by matching assets and liabilities and by diversification. **Transaction risk** can be hedged by matching receipts and payments, invoicing in own currency and leading and lagging the times that cash is received and paid.

The organisation may decide to use money market hedges and specialist personnel will be needed.

3.3 **Government interference**

The merged entity may be subject to competition controls, particularly in the pharmaceutical materials sector, where PM is already market leader in the UK and Europe.

Strategies to limit the effects of political risk include negotiation with host governments, re-locating production or threatening withdrawal.

4 **Post-merger value enhancing strategies**

Many mergers fail to achieve their full potential because of lack of attention paid to post-acquisition integration. A clear programme therefore needs to be in place, designed to re-define objectives and strategy and take appropriate care of the human element.

The first stage would be to conduct a position audit to enable a clear understanding of the culture and operations of NQ. Both physical and human assets should be examined in order to get a clear picture. An integration strategy should then be devised before the merger is finalised. There needs to be a clear plan for the integration of the two organisations. This plan should deal with problems such as differences in management styles, information technology incompatibilities and resistance to the merger from employees.

Synergies will result from efficiency gains and/or asset sales, which will probably involve redundancies. These will need to be carefully considered and managed in terms of their effect on the workforce. Successful post-acquisition integration requires careful management of the human factor to avoid loss of motivation.

PF Drucker suggested five golden rules for the process of post-acquisition integration:

Rule 1	There should be a 'common core of unity' shared by the acquiror and acquiree. The ties should involve overlapping characteristics such as shared technology and markets, and not just financial links.
Rule 2	The acquiror should ask 'What can we offer them?' as well as 'What's in it for us?'
Rule 3	The acquiror should treat the products, markets and customers of the acquired company with respect, and not disparagingly.
Rule 4	The acquiring company should provide top management with relevant skills for the acquired company within a year.
Rule 5	Cross-company promotions of staff should occur within one year.

Corporate objectives may need to be re-defined and strategic plans developed for the merged entity. The cost of capital should also be re-evaluated as it may be reduced as a result of the merger.

5   **Conclusion**

This report has demonstrated that the three stated objectives will probably be achieved post-merger. Earnings growth may be boosted by synergies and savings achieved from the merger, PM's P/E ratio is likely to stay above the industry average and gearing will fall if shareholders accept a share exchange. However there are significant downside risks relating to all three objectives.

Appendix 1

Earnings growth:

PM	*NQ*
$273 = 225(1 + g)^4$	$300 = 250(1 + g)^4$
$1 + g = 1.0495$	$1 + g = 1.0466$
$g = 4.95\%$	$g = 4.66\%$

Appendix 2

PM	*NQ*	*Merged entity*
Debt = $1.05 \times 1,150 = £1,208$	Debt = $550	Debt = $1,208 + (550/1.85) = £1,505$
Equity = $950 \times 4.56 = £4,332$	Equity = $850 \times 4.5 = \$3,825$	Equity = £6,905
Gearing % = $1,208/4,332 = 27.9\%$	Gearing % = $550/3,825 = 14.4\%$	Gearing % = $\dfrac{1,505}{6,905} = 21.8\%$

Appendix 3

Weighted average P/E:

PM	*NQ*	*Merged entity*
$15.9 \times 69\% = 11$	$12.75 \times 31\% = 4$	15

Mock Exams

BPP
LEARNING MEDIA

CIMA – Strategic Level

Paper P9

Management Accounting – Financial Strategy

Mock Examination 1

Instructions to candidates:

You are allowed three hours to answer this question paper.
In the real exam, you are allowed 20 minutes reading time before the examination begins during which you should read the question paper, and if you wish, make annotations on the question paper. However, you will **not** be allowed, **under any circumstances**, to open the answer book and start writing or use your calculator during this reading time.
You are strongly advised to carefully read the question requirement before attempting the question concerned.
Answer the ONE compulsory question in Section A.
Answer TWO of the FOUR questions in Section B.

DO NOT OPEN THIS PAPER UNTIL YOU ARE READY TO START UNDER EXAMINATION CONDITIONS

SECTION A – 50 marks

Answer this question

Question 1

Background

The Hi-clean Group is a UK-based unlisted company that imports, assembles and distributes laundry and cleaning equipment for hotels and restaurants and for public sector departments, such as hospitals, prisons and the armed forces. The company was formed several years ago with £24 million start-up capital in ordinary shares of £1. No other capital has been raised since then, except from the venture capital company explained below.

The company has seen growth in turnover and post-tax profits of around 20% each year over the past three years in all sectors of its customer base, although sales to the public sector now account for a much higher proportion of the total than five years ago: 38% in 20X4 compared with 18% in 20X0.

Details on major shareholder

A venture capital company owns 20% of the company's shares, bought three years ago for £25 million. The venture capital company also provided a £25 million loan with equity warrants attached. The loan carries a variable rate of interest, LIBOR +3%, and is repayable in 20X6. The warrants allow for the venture capital company to buy 1 share at 400 pence for every £10 of debt at the time the loan is repaid. This shareholder is looking to exit from its investment in Hi-clean in two to three years' time. Unless Hi-clean has obtained a share listing by then, the venture capital company has indicated it is unlikely to exercise its warrants. The venture capital company's usually required return is an average of 50% per annum (dividends plus capital gain as percentage of initial investment) over a five-year investment period.

Although the venture capital company has a seat on the Hi-clean Group board, it has taken a very 'hands-off' approach and had little involvement in the company's direction or management.

Forecast results for the year to 31 December 20X4

The accounts department has produced the following full-year forecasts for 20X4.

Results by sector

	Public sector	Hotels and restaurants	Total
	£ million	£ million	£ million
Revenue	83.60	136.40	220.00
Direct costs	45.98	68.20	114.18
Gross profit margin	37.62	68.20	105.82
Fixed overheads*	26.53	43.29	69.82
Operating profit	11.09	24.91	36.00

* Fixed overheads are apportioned to operating sectors on the basis of turnover.

Summary group income statement

	£ million
Operating profit	36.00
Interest payable	1.75
Profit before taxation	34.25
Taxation	6.17
Profit after tax	28.08
Ordinary dividends	8.43

Summary group balance sheet

	£ million
Non-current assets (net book value)	124.00
Net current assets	48.00
	172.00
Capital and reserves	
Called up share capital (Ordinary shares of £1)	30.00
(Authorised share capital £35 million)	
Share premium account	18.00
Retained earnings	99.00
Loan capital	25.00
	172.00

Future funding and request for study

Hi-clean's directors have, for some time, been considering a public listing for the company's shares to raise new finance and provide an exit route for the venture capital company. Assume you are the Financial Manager with Hi-clean. The directors have asked you for a study that includes a forecast of the company's financial situation at 31 December 20X5. You have spent the last month obtaining the following information from a variety of sources.

Growth in turnover and profits

You expect growth to continue but not at the high levels seen over the past few years. A complication is that a general election will take place shortly and the outcome will have an effect on Hi-clean's business. If Party A wins, it has promised more money for some public sector departments, which may increase Hi-clean's sales to its public sector customers. However, this increased spending would be paid for by an increase in certain taxes that would adversely impact on some of Hi-clean's private customers. If Party B wins, spending on public services will also increase, but not necessarily in areas serviced by Hi-clean. Opinion polls suggest Party A has a 60% chance of winning and Party B 40%.

Based on your informed opinion about prospects for the economy and the industry, you forecast the following range of turnovers and probabilities for 20X5, by sector, depending on which party wins the election.

		Public sector		*Hotels and restaurants*
If Party A wins:	Revenues £ *million*	102.00	112.00	123.00
	Probabilities	0.55	0.45	1
If Party B wins:	Revenues £ *million*	95.00	110.00	143.00
	Probabilities	0.50	0.50	1

Other information/assumptions

- Corporate tax will be payable at the current percentage level of 18% owing to availability of capital allowances. No capital expenditure is planned for 20X5.

- Gross profit margin percentage by sector is expected to remain unchanged irrespective of the election outcome.

- Fixed costs are expected to rise to £71.8 million.

- LIBOR is currently 4%. It is expected to fall to 3% in 20X5.

- Average P/E ratio and cost of equity capital for listed companies in this industry are currently 11 and 9% respectively. It is difficult to forecast how P/E ratios will move over the next 12 months but market professionals are expecting an upturn in the market generally, so anything between 12 and 15 is not unreasonable.

- The dividend payout ratio has been constant at 30% since 20X1.

Required

(a)   For 20X5, calculate forecasts of the following:

(i)   Revenues, gross margin and operating profits by customer sector
(ii)   An income statement and earnings per share for the Hi-clean Group

Assume a full-year effect for all the changes forecast for 20X5. Provide comments to accompany your forecasts that explain any significant changes between 20X4 and 20X5.   **(10 marks)**

(b)   As Financial Manager, write a report to the directors of Hi-clean Group. In your report you should:

(i)   Calculate a range of potential values as at the end of 20X5 for the entire Group and for the venture capital company's shareholding. Base your calculations on the information you have available and assume the Group remains a private, unlisted company. Accompany your calculations with a brief discussion of each valuation method.

(ii)   Comment on the reasons for potential differences between the value of the entire company and the value of the venture capital company's shares (that is, why the value of the venture capital company's shares might not be strictly proportionate).   **(18 marks)**

(c)   Based on your forecasts, estimate whether the venture capital company will achieve its target return on investment in Hi-clean and identify exit strategies that might be available to the investor in 20X6. Evaluate how the venture capital company's situation might affect Hi-clean's future financial strategy.   **(10 marks)**

(d)   Identify the main risks and opportunities facing the company and advise on methods of managing the risks.
                                                                                            (12 marks)

(Total = 50 marks)

SECTION B – 50 marks

Answer TWO questions ONLY

Question 2

VID Inc is a US-based company, which was established 15 years ago. It makes and distributes videos, both for the general market and to customer specifications. Its common stock (shares) have been listed on a US stock exchange for the past 8 years. However, there are relatively few stockholders and the stock is not traded in large volumes. The founders of the company no longer participate in its management but own around 10% of the stock in issue.

VID Inc borrowed US$ 65 million to purchase new premises three years ago, which have recently been valued at US$ 85 million. The company is now considering diversifying into mainstream film production, which will require raising US$ 50 million for additional fixed and working capital. This new business will involve joint ventures with UK partners and much of the filming will be done in the UK or Spain. The new investment is not expected to have a significant effect on profits for at least 18 months.

The three months being considered for raising capital are:

(i)   New equity in the UK, subject to US stockholders' approval
(ii)   Long-term fixed rate US$ debt
(iii)   Floating rate sterling-denominated Eurobonds

Summary financial statistics for the last financial year for VID Inc are as below.

	US$ millions
Turnover	175.00
Operating profit	45.00
Post-tax profits	31.36
Non-current assets (book value)	95.00
Net current assets	58.00
Long-term loans: 8% redeemable 20Z0	65.00
Common stock (in units of US$ 1)	25.00
Retained earnings	63.00
Share price (US$):	
High for year	28.56
Low for year	18.50
As at today (25 May 20X4)	22.58

Current annual fixed interest rates for secured long term borrowing are as follows.

US$ 6%   UK £   7%   European common currency area €   5%

Floating rate sterling Eurobond notes are available at the bank base rate +0.5%. Tax will continue to be payable at 20% per annum.

Required

Assume you are a financial advisor to VID Inc. Evaluate the three methods of finance being considered at the present time and advise the directors of VID Inc. Support your advice with any calculations you consider appropriate. Assume, for the purposes of this evaluation, that the P/E ratio of the company will rise to 20 if equity finance is used, or 19 if fixed or floating rate debt is issued. Make any other simplifying assumptions you think necessary and appropriate. **(Total = 25 marks)**

Notes. Up to 10 marks are available for calculations. A report structure is not required for this question.

Question 3

TDC is a transport and distribution company listed on the New York Stock Exchange. On 14 November 20X3, the directors made a bid for a competitor, UED, that is based in the UK and listed on the UK stock market.

UED's directors are considering the bid but have indicated the terms are inadequate and would have to be improved if they were to feel able to recommend it to their shareholders.

The merger would create the fourth largest company in the industry worldwide, but it would still be substantially smaller than the three largest companies. TDC has suffered from slow growth over the past few years and has long been rumoured by market professionals to be a likely target of a hostile bid from one of the three larger companies, or even a reverse takeover by a smaller company. The bid for UED is therefore being seen by the market as defensive.

	TDC	UED
Market data		
Common stock/share price as at today (18 November 20X3)	US$ 11.36	425 pence
Common stock/share price on 18 October 20X3	US$ 12.45	305 pence
Common stock/shares in issue	120 million	145 million
P/E ratio as at today	11	13.5
Accounting data	US$ millions	£ millions
Forecast profit after tax for the current financial year	98.5	45.5
Net asset values at last balance sheet date (30 June 20X3)	825.2	230.5
Including cash balances of	125.5	65.2
Debt outstanding (market value)	250	75
[Repayable	20X7	20X8]

Other information

- The average P/E ratio for the industry is currently estimated as 10 in the UK and 13 in the USA.

- The average debt ratio for the industry internationally (long-term debt as a proportion of total funding) is 15% based on market values.

- TDC's cost of equity is 12% net of tax.

- The US$/£ exchange rate today is 1.53.

Terms of the bid

TDC's directors have made an opening bid of 1 TDC common stock for 2 UED shares. No cash alternative has been offered so far.

Required

Assume that you are the financial Manager with TDC. Write an internal memorandum for the board that:

(a) Discusses how the recent price movements of the two companies' shares might impact on the bid negotiations. **(6 marks)**

(b) Recommends revised bid terms that might be acceptable to the directors and shareholders of UED and also to your own board. Your recommendation should be fully evaluated. **(12 marks)**

(c) Evaluate the strategic implications of making a hostile bid compared with an aggressive investment programme of organic growth. **(7 marks)**

(Total = 25 marks)

Question 4

TMc is a large cosmetic and toiletries retail organisations based in a country within the European common currency zone. Its current turnover is approximately €1.4 billion and it has an asset base of €750 million.

The company is evaluating opening up to 10 new retail outlets in a country in Asia, to be financed by its existing cash or other highly liquid assets. It proposes to operate these new retail outlets itself for the first two years of operation. After that time, and subject to satisfactory commercial and financial performance, each outlet will be offered as a franchise to either the outlet manager/employees or to a third party.

Forecast nominal cash flows for the first two years of operation for a single outlet are as follows.

	Year 0 Asian $ million	Year 1 Asian $ million	Year 2 Asian $ million
Initial investment	(15)		
Pre-tax operating cash flows		4.5	5.5

Exchange rate information is as follows.

Spot rate as at today €/Asian $	0.65

Forecast inflation rates (% per annum).

European common currency area	1.50
Asian country	3.50

Estimated cash flows beyond year 2 depend on the type of operation. If the company continues to operate the outlet, it assumes zero growth per year on year 2's pre-tax Euro operating cash flows until the end of year 10. Cash flows beyond year 10 are ignored. If the outlet is franchised, there will be a one-off pre-tax payment by the franchisee at the beginning of year 3 of Asian $500,000 plus an annual pre-tax payment in perpetuity of Asian $3.2 million (both figures in today's money), commencing at the end of year 3.

Additional information

- Corporate taxes in the Asian country are 30% per annum, payable or refundable the year in which the liability to tax arises. In the European country, they are 35% payable or refundable twelve months after the liability arises. Double taxation agreements are in force between the two countries. Both countries allow 100% writing-down allowance for investments of this type.

- TMc uses 9% as the discount rate in its investment appraisals.

- All operating cash flows may be assumed to occur at the end of each year. The initial capital investment will be made at the beginning of year 1 and written off over 5 years.

- TMc evaluates international investments by converting the foreign currency cash flows to €s and applying its domestic cost of capital.

Required

Evaluate the proposed investment and recommend whether it should proceed. You should include in your evaluation some discussion of the risks that might be associated with the two alternative methods of operation being considered after year 2 and advise on how these risks might be managed. **(Total = 25 marks)**

Notes. Up to 10 marks are available for calculations. A report structure is not required for this question.

Question 5

A regional police force has the following corporate objectives:

- To reduce crime and disorder
- To promote community safety
- To contribute to delivering justice and maintaining public confidence in the law

The force aims to achieve these objectives by continuously improving its resources management to meet the needs of its stakeholders. It has no stated financial objective other than to stay within its funding limits.

The force is mainly public-funded but, like other regional forces, it has some commercial operations, for example policing football matches when the football clubs pay a fee to the police force for its officers working overtime. The police force uses this money to supplement the funding it receives from the government. The national government is proposing to privatise (that is, sell off) these commercial operations and has already been in preliminary discussions with an international security company. This company's stated financial objectives are:

- To increase earnings per share year on year by 5% per annum
- To achieve a 20% per annum return on capital employed

Arguments put forward by government in favour of privatisation focus on the conflict of objectives between mainstream operations and commercial activities, and savings to the taxpayer. However, the proposals have met with strong opposition from most of the force's stakeholders.

Required

(a)   Discuss the reasons for the differences in the objectives of the two types of organisation given above. Use the scenario details given above to assist your answer wherever possible.   **(12 marks)**

(b)   Discuss the influence the commercial operations might currently have on the police force's ability to meet its stated objectives. Include in your discussion an evaluation the possible effects on mainstream services and the various stakeholder groups if the commercial operations were to be privatised.   **(13 marks)**

(Total = 25 marks)

Answers

DO NOT TURN THIS PAGE UNTIL YOU HAVE
COMPLETED THE MOCK EXAM

Plan of attack

We know you've been told to do it at least 100 times and we know if we asked you you'd know that you should do it. So why don't you do it in an exam? 'Do what in an exam?' you're probably thinking. Well, let's tell you for the 101st time. **Take a good look through the paper before diving in to answer questions.**

First things first

What you must do in the first five or ten minutes of the exam is **look through the paper i**n detail, working out **which questions to do** and the **order** in which to attempt them. So turn back to the paper and let's sort out a plan of attack.

We then recommend you spend the remaining time analysing the requirements of Question 1 and highlighting the key issues in the question. The extra time spent on (a) will be helpful, whenever you intend to do the question, If you decide to do it first, you will be well into the question when the writing time starts. If you intend to do it second or third, probably because you find it daunting, the question will look easier when you come to back to it, because your initial analysis should generate further points whilst you're tackling the other questions.

The next step

You're probably either thinking that you don't know where to begin or that you could have a very decent go at all the questions.

Option 1 (if you don't know where to begin)

If you are a bit **worried** about the paper, it's likely that you believe that case study **Question 1** looks daunting. We therefore recommend that you do one or both of the optional questions before tackling the case study. Don't however fall into the trap of going over time on the optional questions because they seem easier. You will need to spend half the time available on the case study.

- In order to pass **Question 2** comfortably you will need to include a number of ratios, most of which you should hopefully remember not just from this paper but lower level papers as well. Don't though just concentrate on these, as the discussion will be worth more than half marks.

- You will need to use the data given in **Question 3** to carry out calculations in (a) and (b) to support your answer. These calculations will be worth quite a few marks, so it's best to avoid this question if you're not sure how to go about them.

- Key aspects in the calculations in **Question 4** are tax and international cash flows, so if you don't feel confident about dealing with these, it may be best to avoid this question. Even so, there are a number of fairly straightforward marks on risk that you can score, using what you've learnt for the *Risk and Control Strategy* paper.

- You can score very well on **Question 5** if you can bring out the differences between the objectives and can identify the different stakeholders involved.

- Don't be put off if there are one or two aspects of the calculations you struggle with in part (a) of **Question 1**. There are some easier marks available as well. With valuation questions such as (b) it's important to have a go at the calculations; marks will be given for any sort of reasonable attempt. Even if you struggle with the calculations in (c), you would be able to gain about 2/3 of the marks for the discussion. Make sure you leave yourself enough time to answer part (d) as there are plenty of mark-scoring opportunities there; don't be afraid once again to bring in your *Risk and Control Strategy* knowledge.

Option 2 (if you're thinking 'I can do all of these')

It never pays to be over confident but if you're not quaking in your shoes about the exam then **turn straight to compulsory Question 1**. You've got to do it so you might as well get it over and done with.

Once you've done the compulsory question, choose two of the questions in Section B.

- You should find the calculations in **Question 2** fairly straightforward, but remember that the discussion will account for more than half the marks.

- If you're happy with the area of valuations, you may well choose **Question 3,** although bear in mind it does involve some complicated calculations.

- Be careful with the tax and exchange rates if you choose **Question 4,** but the bulk of the marks will be available for the discussion on risks, which isn't too bad at all.

- If you choose **Question 5,** remember that this is a *financial* strategy paper, hence the bulk of the marks will be available for discussion of financial issues. There will be some, but limited, marks, available for general business strategy issues. You also need to spend time discussing stakeholders, as they are highlighted in the question.

No matter how many times we remind you...

Always, always **allocate your time** according to the marks for the question in total and for the parts of the questions. And always, always **follow the requirements exactly**.

You've got free time at the end of the exam.....?

If you have allocated your time properly then you **shouldn't have time on your hands** at the end of the exam. If you find yourself with five or ten minutes spare, however, go back to **any parts of questions that you didn't finish** because you ran out of time.

Forget about it!

And don't worry if you found the paper difficult. More then likely other students would too. If this were the real thing you would need to forget the exam the minute you leave the exam hall and **think about the next one**. Or, if it's the last one, **celebrate!**

Question 1

(a)   **Hi-clean Group: Forecast results for 20X5**

     (i)   *Turnover, gross margin and operating profits by sector*

	Public sector £ million	Hotels and restaurants £ million	Total £ million
Revenues (W1)	104.90	131.00	235.90
Direct costs	57.69	65.50	123.19
Gross profit margin (W3): 45%/50% × turnover	47.21	65.50	112.71
Fixed costs (apportioned on basis of turnover)	31.93	39.87	71.80
Operating profit	15.28	25.63	40.91
Gross profit percentage	45%	50%	47.8%
Operating profit percentage	14.6%	19.6%	17.3%

Comments

Revenues

Based on the forecasts and probabilities given, the group's overall revenues are **expected to increase by 7.2% from 20X4 to 20X5**. These revenues turnover results from a **predicted 25% increase in sales** to the public sector (104.9 compared with 83.6) and a predicted 4% reduction in sales to hotels and restaurants (131.0 compared with 136.4).

Profit margin

Since the public sector has a lower gross profit percentage than hotels and restaurants, the group's **overall gross profit margin** is expected to **fall slightly** from 48.1% to 47.8% (see Working 3). The control of fixed overheads will, however, enable the group's operating profit percentage to rise from 16.4% to 17.3%.

As a result, the group's operating profit is forecast to be 13.6% higher in 20X5 than in 20X4 (£40.91m compared with £36.00m).

The group's turnover is subject to **significant uncertainties**, dependent on general market factors and the result of the forthcoming election. The worst case turnover is £225 million and the best case £253 million (see working 2).

W1: Expected turnover

The expected public sector turnover (£m) is:

If Party A wins: $(0.55 \times 102) + (0.45 \times 112) = 106.5$
If Party B wins: $(0.50 \times 95) + (0.50 \times 110) = 102.5$

Since the probabilities of Party A or Party B winning are 0.6 and 0.4 respectively:

Expected public sector turnover (£m) = $(0.6 \times 106.5) + (0.4 \times 102.5) = 104.9$
Expected hotel/restaurant turnover (£m) = $(0.6 \times 123) + (0.4 \times 143) = 131$

W2: Best and worst case turnover

	If Party A wins	*If Party B wins*	
Best case:	112 + 123 = 235	110 + 143 = 253	Overall best: 253
Worst case:	102 + 123 = 225	95 + 143 = 238	Overall worst: 225

W3: Gross profit percentages for 20X4

	Public sector	*Hotels and restaurants*	*Total*
	£ million	£ million	£ million
Revenues	83.60	136.40	220.00
Gross profit	37.62	68.20	105.82
percentage	45%	50%	48.1%
Operating profit			36.00
percentage			16.4%

(ii) **Income statement and earnings per share**

	£ million
Operating profit	40.91
Interest payable (£25m × 6%)	1.50
Profit before tax	39.41
Corporate tax @ 18% (given)	7.09
Profit after tax	32.32
Ordinary dividends (30% of profit after tax)	9.70
Retained earnings	22.62
Earnings per share (30 million shares)	107.7 pence

Dividends and eps

The expected increase in group operating profit of 13.6% combined with a forecast drop in interest rates will enable group earnings per share and dividends to be approximately 15% higher in 20X5 than 20X4.

(b)   REPORT

To: The Directors of Hi-Clean Group
From: Financial Manager
Date: 31 May 20X4
Subject: Valuation of the Group and the Venture Capitalist's Shareholding

Introduction

The objectives of this report are to:

(i)   **Calculate a range of possible values** for the Hi-Clean Group using generally accepted methods of company valuation.

(ii)   **Comment on the relative value** per share of the venture capitalists' shareholding compared with the value of the whole group.

Valuation methods

(i)   **Net asset value**

The book value of the Group's assets less liabilities is £147 million at 31 December 20X4.

By 31 December 20X5 this will rise by the amount of retained profits in 20X5 to £147m + £22.62m = £169.62m.

Since the company is a going concern, the book value of assets is likely to understate the economic value of the business. This figure of £169.6 million is therefore likely to be a minimum value.

(ii)   **Capitalisation of earnings using industry P/E ratio**

Earnings after tax in 20X5 are forecast to be £32.32 million. It is felt that an **industry-based P/E ratio of between 12 and 15** is reasonable for 20X5. Assuming Hi-Clean is of average risk for the industry, this will value the group at between £32.32m $\times$ 12 and £32.32m $\times$ 15; between **£387.8 million and £484.8 million**.

This value will be affected by:

(1)   The **risk level of Hi-Clean** compared with the **industry average**: higher risk implies a lower value.

(2)   The fact that **Hi-Clean** is an **unquoted company**: since there are fewer options for disposing of an unquoted company's shares, their value may be lower than that of an equivalent quoted company.

(iii)   **Dividend valuation model**

The formula for valuing a business in terms of future dividends is $D_0 (1 + g)/(k_e - g)$.

If Hi-Clean is of **average risk** for the industry, its cost of equity capital will be 9% per annum. It is very difficult to forecast future growth in dividends, which is expected to be lower than the 15% growth of 20X4/X5 or the 20% p. a. growth of the previous three years.

A figure for g of 5% to 'perpetuity' may be reasonable. This would give a value for the group of: (£9.70m $\times$ 1.05)/(0.09 − 0.05) = £254.6 million.

Since this figure is highly sensitive to the subjective figure chosen for 'g', not much confidence can be placed in the result.

Range of values

Based on the limited data available and the methods described above, the value of the Hi-Clean Group is within the range **£170 million to £485 million**.

Since the company is a going concern the values obtained by using the P/E method seem to be the most appropriate: range **£388 to £485 million**, that is a value per share of between £12.93 and £16.17.

To obtain a more precise value of the company and its shares, it would be useful to make **more extensive forecasts of cash flows,** say over the next five years, and to make a more detailed estimate of the company's cost of capital. These estimates could then be used in a discounted cash flow computation to value the business.

Valuation of venture capitalist's shareholding

The venture capitalist's 20% stake in the group may be **worth less** than 20% of the group's total value. The principal reason for this is that there will probably be **fewer potential buyers** for a 20% shareholding than for the entire company. This is in turn the result of a number of factors:

(1)   **Lack of inside information.** Although the venture capitalist is entitled to a seat on the company's board of directors, this may not be **transferable** to a new owner (or owners) of these shares.

(2)   **Lack of control.** A 20% minority holding is not sufficient to control the company. However, if the venture capitalist's options to buy shares at 400 pence each are taken up, this would **increase its shareholding** by 25m/10 = 2.5 million shares, raising its total shareholding to 8.5m shares, which is a percentage holding of 8.5/32.5 = 26%. This would increase the venture capitalist's level of influence, by allowing it to **block special resolutions** under UK rules, and this influence could be passed on to a single purchaser of these shares.

(3)   **The company is unquoted.** Potential buyers must be identified in person. An unquoted company is therefore by its nature a longer term investment and, when the lack of information and control identified above are considered, a minority interest may not be attractive.

(c)   **Venture capital company's targets and strategies**

Target return of 50% per annum

The venture capitalist purchased 20% of the shares (6 million shares) for £25 million three years ago (May 20X1) with a 5 year time horizon to May 20X6.

However, for convenience of calculation (so that we can deal in whole years) assume that the purchase date was January 20X1 with a five year target period lasting until December 20X5.

The return to the venture capitalist will be estimated under two different sets of assumptions.

Assumptions 1: The group does not become listed, and the warrants are not exercised

At 31 December 20X5, the company is forecast to be worth between £388 and £485 million (see (b) above). A 20% shareholding is therefore worth a maximum of 20% of these figures i.e. between £77.6 and £97.0 million.

To be prudent let us assume that the 20% holding in a private company is worth about 20% less, for the reasons argued in (b) above, between £62 and £78 million, or between £10.33 and £13.00 per share.

Over the period 20X1 to 20X5, the dividends paid out by the company would have been as follows:

Year	Dividend
	£m
20X5	9.70
20X4	8.43
20X3	7.03
20X2	5.86
20X1	4.88
Total	35.90

(Note: These dividends are found from the 20X5 forecast already calculated, the 20X4 results given and by reducing the figure by 20% for each year before 20X4.)

The **venture capitalist's share** of the total 5 year dividends is £35.90 × 20% = £7.18 million, say £7 million.

Thus (ignoring compound interest) the approximate rate of return for the venture capitalist can be calculated as follows:

	Low £m	High £m
Value of 20% shareholding 31 Dec 20X5	62	78
Accumulated dividends 20X1–20X5	7	7
Less: Original price of 20% investment	(25)	(25)
Total gain in 5 years	44	60
Gain per year	8.8	12
% Annual return on £25m investment	35%	48%

Under this assumption set, the venture capital company does not achieve its target return of 50% per annum.

Assumption 2: The Group becomes listed and the warrants are exercised

The venture capitalist exercises its warrants and pays £4 each for 2.5 million shares (£10 million) in order to increase its shareholding to 26%.

Again, at 31 December 20X5, the company is forecast to be worth between £388 and £485 million. The 26% shareholding is worth between £101m and £126m (there is no reduction in share value, since the shares would be easily marketable). 26% of the accumulated dividends is £35.90m × 26% = £9 million.

Thus the venture capitalist's return can be calculated roughly (ignoring discounting) as follows:

	Low £m	High £m
Value of shareholding 31 Dec 20X5	101	126
Accumulated dividends 20X1 – 20X5	9	9
Less: Price paid for shares issued for warrants	(10)	(10)
Original price of 20% investment	(25)	(25)
Total gain in 5 years	75	100
Gain per year	15	20
% Annual return on £25m investment	60%	80%

Under this assumption set, the venture capitalist exceeds its target rate of return of 50% per annum.

Exit routes

The best exit route for the venture capitalist would be via a **listing of the Group** on its local Stock Exchange. The Group would make an **initial public offer** of its shares (offer for sale) or a placing with selected institutions, in the course of which some or all of the venture capitalist's shares could be sold at the offer price. Any remaining shares could easily be sold at market prices afterwards.

Other alternatives include:

(1) **Selling the shareholding to another capital fund**, possibly one that specialises in more mature slower growth investments

(2) **Selling to another company** (e.g. a competitor) which is interested in acquiring the Hi-Clean Group

(3) **Selling to managers and staff** of the Hi-Clean Group (a management buy-out)

(d)   **Risks and opportunities facing the company**

Growth in market share and profit margins

Hi-Clean's original market was sales to private sector hotels and restaurants. More recently it has shown **rapidly increasing sales** to the public sector, where growth opportunities appear to be higher but at lower profit margins.

Hi-Clean has the opportunity of influencing sales volume in both public and private sectors by its **pricing policy** and **marketing strategy.** In general though, **growth opportunities** will be **lower in future** than in recent years, unless the company can take advantage of new developments in cleaning equipment technology, or diversify into other lines of business.

It is unlikely that the company will be **easily able to expand** by **developing export sales,** as it is a distributor, not a manufacturer. If it wishes to expand internationally, its best route is probably to acquire similar businesses in various target countries.

The result of the election and effect on sector mix and profitability

If party A wins the election, it will **advance more funds to the public sector** but tax the private sector more, resulting in a large expected increase in Hi-Clean's public sector sales but a likely decrease in sales to hotels and restaurants. If Party B wins the election, there will be a **smaller increase in sales** to the public sector but the higher margin private sector sales will increase.

In general then, Hi-Clean is quite **well 'hedged'** against the result of the election. Its policy of diversifying into both public and private sectors has effectively reduced sales volatility resulting from political risk.

Relationships with suppliers and customers

Hi-Clean is an importer, assembler and distributor: it does not manufacture any of its equipment. It is therefore **dependent on providing a good service and continuing good relationships** with both customers and suppliers. It faces the potential risk of being cut out of the supply chain, for example by a supplier who agrees a better arrangement with another distributor, or a customer who approaches the manufacturer directly.

On the other hand, the company is in an ideal position to **take advantage of new products** that come on to the market and of new customer demands, and can improve its chances of doing so by maintaining active dialogue with both customers and suppliers.

Currency risk

The company **imports the equipment** that it sells in the UK. Since it probably buys in foreign currencies and sells in pounds it is subject to the **risk of the pound weakening** against other currencies, such as the euro, dollar or yen. Various currency hedging techniques are possible, and it is not clear if any of these are being used. For example, if purchases are mainly from the euro zone, opening a euro bank account to pay suppliers will hedge against unexpected short term currency movements.

If the company decides to **expand internationally**, this will have further implications for currency risk.

Loans and interest rate risk

The company is **currently borrowing at floating rate interest** (LIBOR plus 3%) from the venture capitalist. This leaves it exposed to the risk that interest rates may rise. However, **current predictions** are that they will fall, bringing a **reduction in service payments**. The company may wish to **take advantage of any opportunities** that arise for exchanging floating rate for fixed rate debt, although the current loan is complicated by the warrants that are attached to it.

The loan from the venture capitalist is repayable in 20X6 and will then need to be **replaced with new finance**. At the moment this does not appear to be a problem, as results are good and there are no other major loans in the capital structure.

Equity capital and obtaining a flotation

The future management of Hi-Clean is **significantly dependent on decisions** made by the **venture capital company**. Although they have taken an active role on the board so far, this may change, because decisions need to be made as to how they will achieve their exit route, for example by selling to another fund, or by encouraging a flotation of the business.

A flotation will in itself produce a number of **new opportunities and risks**. For example, the company's **public profile** will be **raised** and its **shares** will be **much more marketable**. It will be able to use its shares as consideration for acquisitions, but may find itself the target of takeover bids.

Question 2

> **Top tips.** This question demonstrates the importance of knowing how to calculate ratios; the examiner's comments that these calculations were poor were surprising. Your discussion needed to address the issues of cost, complexity and risk, also effects on profits and gearing. Shareholder and market reaction is important, and this is reflected in the assumption of a lower p/e ratio. A key aspect of planning is to decide which figures to calculate and how long to spend on the calculations. Here to get figures for gearing and returns to shareholders requires the detailed calculations in the appendix; don't worry about spending time on these, but remember to leave 25 minutes for the discussion.
>
> **Easy marks.** A number of points (costs, financial risks) are key points in any discussion on sources of finance, and can be made without reference to the figures provided you leave yourself enough time to do so.
>
> **Examiner's comments.** This question was unpopular, surprisingly as it dealt with the important topics of methods of finance, including international finance. Gearing and earnings per share were often calculated incorrectly, and other calculations were omitted totally.

VID Inc – finance for new investment

New equity funds raised in the UK

Requirements of equity shareholders

Equity capital is suitable for this project, which will not show any appreciable returns for at least 18 months, because, unlike debt, there is **no requirement to make contractual interest payments**. However, in the longer term, equity shareholders expect a **higher return** than lenders precisely because of the uncertainty and volatility associated with their receipt of dividends.

Shareholder approval

For the company to be able to raise new equity funds in UK, existing US stockholders must first **pass a resolution** to allow this. Since there are relatively few of these stockholders, the company's directors have presumably already sounded out their opinion. However, there may be different views among them and if equity funding is needed, some stockholders may prefer a rights issue.

Issue costs

Financing by a public issue of equity is expensive in terms of issue costs because of the requirements for a **prospectus, advertising, underwriting costs, professional fees,** and **stock exchange and other administration costs**. A placing of the company's equity with selected financial institutions would be cheaper but the amount required may be too large to allow this.

Pricing the issue

A problem associated with new equity issues is the price at which the shares will be sold. Ideally the new shares would be issued at the **current market price**, so that new shareholders do not gain at the expense of existing ones. However, because share prices are **volatile** and might fall between the date of announcing the issue price and the date of subscription, it is more practical to issue the new shares at a **discount below the current price**. The calculations attached assume that the new shares are issued at the sterling equivalent of $20, when today's market price is $22.58. This implies that 2.5 million new shares need to be issued.

P/E and EPS

The attached calculations show that the **price/earnings ratio** of the company's shares is assumed to rise from 18 to 20 following the equity issue and that overall the value of the company's equity is predicted to rise from $572 million to $638 million, an increase of $16 million above the $50 million funds injected.

This is mainly because it is assumed that the **positive net present value** of the new project will be **reflected in the share price** but partly because the equity issue will cause a reduction in the company's financial gearing (leverage).

However, the fact that the new project is not expected to generate profits for at least 18 months must be clearly **communicated** at the time the equity is raised, as earnings per share will be diluted in the short term from $1.27 to $1.16 per share and other measures of performance such as return on capital employed and return on shareholders' funds will be similarly reduced.

Long term fixed rate US$ debt

Costs of debt

Compared with an equity issue, debt has **cheaper issue costs** because prospectus and other administration costs are not incurred.

Debt also has a **cheaper direct cost** (of interest compared with dividends) because:

- The **receipt of interest** is **less risky** to the investor than dividends.
- **Interest payments** are a **tax-deductible expense** to the company.

Interest commitment

The disadvantage of debt is that **interest payments** must be **made** even when **profits** are **not earned.** This causes an increase in the cost of equity capital, by making equity dividends more volatile and by increasing the chances of financial distress during loss-making periods. We have reflected this in our calculations by assuming a lower P/E (19) if debt is used than if equity finance is used (20).

Effect of debt finance

The attached calculations show that, until the new project generates profits, the debt finance will cause:

- A **reduction in overall equity earnings and earnings per share**, though EPS will not fall by as much as if equity finance is used.
- An **decrease in the value of the company's shares** from $572 million to $561 million.
- An **appreciable reduction in interest cover** (operating profit/interest).
- The same **reduction in return on capital employed** as when equity finance is used, but almost no fall in return on shareholders' funds.
- A **very large increase in the company's gearing ratio** both in terms of book and market values.

Floating rate sterling-denominated Eurobonds

The same arguments apply as for the use of the long term fixed rate US$ debt, but some key differences between these types of finance are as follows.

Interest rate risk

Interest on floating rate debt will follow **general market interest rates.** A significant increase in rates could damage the project. The possibility of organising a swap into fixed rate debt needs to be investigated.

Currency risk

A **rise in the value of sterling** compared with the US dollar could **create further losses** for shareholders based in USA but would not affect new shareholders based in UK. To allow properly for currency risk, the whole currency profile of the company's expected earnings and costs needs to be considered and the extent to which earnings and costs can be matched in the same currency where possible.

Issue costs

Issue costs of eurobonds can be **cheaper** than those of other forms of debt, principally because of the less onerous regulatory requirements.

Summary

Overall, the **use of debt finance** for this project does **not appear to be as beneficial** as equity funds. It is only if profits are significantly above expectations that the real benefit of using debt is experienced.

Workings

The income statements, balance sheets, market data and ratios for the company can be computed for existing operations and if $50 million of new equity capital or 6% debt capital is raised. No computations have been supplied for the 7% floating rate Eurobonds, as these would be very similar to those for the 6% debt.

		Existing $m		+$50m equity funds $m		+$50m 6% debt funds $m
Revenues		175.00		175.00		175.00
Operating profit		45.00		45.00		45.00
Interest	($65m × 8%)	(5.20)		(5.20)	(5.20 + (50 × 6%))	(8.20)
Pre-tax profit		39.80		39.80		36.80
Taxation (20%)		(7.96)		(7.96)		(7.36)
Post tax profit		31.84		31.84		29.44
No. of shares (m)		25.00	(2.5m new)[2]	27.50		25.00
Earnings per share $	(31.84/25)	1.27	(31.84/27.5)	1.16	(29.44/25)	1.18
Share price $	(PE18 × 1.27)	22.86	(P/E 20 × 1.16)	23.20	(19 × 1.18)	22.42
P/E	(22.58/1.27)	17.78	(given)	20	(given)	19
		$m		$m		$m
Market value of equity	(22.86 × 25m)	571.50	(23.20 × 27.5m)	638.00	(22.42 × 25m)	560.50
MV of debt		86.67		86.67	(86.67 + 50)	136.67
		658.17		724.67		697.17
Balance sheet		$m		$m		$m
Non-current assets		95.00				
Net current assets		58.00				
Net assets		153.00	Increases by 50m	203.00		203.00
Share capital		25.00		27.50		25.00
Reserves		63.00	(63 + 50 − 2.5)	110.50		63.00
		88.00		138.00		88.00
Long term loans 8%		65.00		65.00	(65.00 + 50)	115.00
		153.00		203.00		203.00

Return on capital employed	(45.00/153.00)	29%	(45.00/203.00)	22%		22%
Return on shareholders' funds	(31.84/88.00)	36%	(31.84/138.00)	23%	(29.44/88.00)	33%
Times covered	(45.00/5.20)	8.65		8.65	(45.00/8.20)	5.49
Post tax profit/turnover	(31.84/175.00)	18.2%		18.2%	(29.44/175)	16.8%
Debt/debt +equity:						
Book value	(65.00/153.00)	42%	(65.00/203.00)	32%	(115.00/203.00)	57%
Market value	(86.67/658.17)	13%	(86.67/724.67)	12%	(136.67/697.17)	20%

Note. The market value of debt is calculated as if it were a perpetuity, as it is not redeemable for 25 years. 8% interest on $65 million, divided by the market cost of debt 6% (65 × 0.08/0.06 = $86.67m).

Assume the new shares are issued below existing market price ($22.58) at $20.00. Then the number of new shares issued is $50m/$20 = 2.5 million.

Question 3

Top tips. The key to (a) is doing sufficient calculations to demonstrate that though the bid may have been attractive when made, it isn't now. The main focus of your answer to (b) should be on the earnings valuations, but you also need to consider how these compare with market valuations. Whilst you shouldn't spend too much time on the calculations, applying different p/e ratios to earnings can yield valuable results.

Last year's figures are useful as a comparison for the forecast figures for this year, and they may indicate a large degree of uncertainty in those figures. However it is better to use the current year forecasts in the valuation, as a more reliable indication of the current situation. We state that we are assuming the current year forecasts to be reliable, and there may be uncertainties involved, but whatever figures are used some significant assumptions will have to be made.

Our answer also brings out the importance of other non-quantifiable issues; valuation is not merely about number manipulation.

(c) covers the sorts of issues that may well come up in TOPCIMA. We have used a point by point comparison of acquisition and organic growth, as this is the best way to compare, and bring out the differences between, the two.

As this is a memo, it is better to put the calculations at the end of every part rather than in the body of each.

Easy marks. A number of points made in (c) are quite general, though you should try if possible to relate them to TDC and UED.

Examiner's comments. Answers often failed to include any calculations and showed a lack of understanding of how share exchanges operate. Many answers did not discuss bid strategy or other important considerations such as market reaction and potential dilution of earnings per share. Many answers recommended unrealistic offer prices, for example offer prices below market value.

Memorandum

To: The Board of Directors of TDC
From: Financial Manager
Date: 18 November 20X3
Subject: Bid for UED

(a)   **Possible impact of recent share price movements on the bid**

Position one month ago

One month ago on 18 October, our stock prices were:

TDC: $12.45
UED: £3.05 = $4.67 (at today's exchange rate – actual rate not given).

The offer of 1 TDC common stock for 2 UED shares was intended to value UED shares at approximately $12.45/2 = $6.225 each, that is at a premium of approximately 33% above the market price on 18 October. We assumed that this offer, when made on 14 November, would be attractive to UED shareholders.

Current position

However since 18 October, UED's stock price has climbed 40% (see workings below) and ours has fallen nearly 9% (see workings below), so that as at today our prices are:

TDC: $11.36
UED: £4.25 = $6.50

The 1 for 2 offer would now value UED shares at only $11.36/2 = $5.68, which is nearly 13% below the current market price. This will not be acceptable to UED's shareholders, unless there is a significant improvement in our relative position before the acceptance date.

Reasons

It is difficult to say what has caused the stock price movements over the last month, but the market may believe that we shall grow UED's earnings at a higher rate than currently, or UED will receive a better offer from another bidder. Our p/e is now significantly below the USA industry average, whereas UED's p/e is above the UK average; this may indicate market expectations that we shall ultimately pay more than the company is worth.

Workings

Exchange rate		$1.53 = £1
	TDC $	*UED translated to $*
Stock price 18-11-X3 $	11.36	6.50
Stock price 18-10-X3 $	12.45	4.67
% change in stock price 18 Oct to 18 Nov	−8.8%	+39.2%
P/E 18-11-X3	11	13.5
Industry averages	13	10

(b)   **Revised bid terms that might be acceptable to UED**

Before revising the offer we need to revisit some of the underlying fundamentals of the two companies.

Earnings-based valuation

Based on current forecasts, **our company's earnings** will be **20.5% lower** this year than last, whereas UED's earnings will fall by only 0.3% (see workings below).

Based on **forecast profit and zero growth:**

TDC is worth $98.5m/0.12 = $821m, whereas UED is worth $69.62/0.12 = $580m.

Values per share based on **forecast profit figures**:

TDC = $821m/120m = $6.84 and UED is $580m/145m = $4.00.

On this basis, 1 unit of stock in TDC is worth 6.84/4.00 = approx. 1.71 shares in UED.

Use of the forecast figures assumes that the **predictions are reliable**. The decrease in TDC's profits may indicate significant uncertainty; although the forecast is a best estimate, the spread of possible results may be wide. In any case, we are also making the significant assumption of zero subsequent growth.

Net asset valuation

Net assets per share are: TDC $6.88 and UED $2.43. This is a ratio of 2.83:1, which values UED relatively **lower than income methods**. This is probably a reflection of the fact that TDC does not **utilise its assets as efficiently**.

The **net assets** method is also flawed because it fails to take into account **intangible assets** such as goodwill not included in the balance sheet, and may not take account of differences in valuation policies between the two companies. In addition UED's figures may be distorted by using the exchange rate of 18 November to translate assets as at 30 June. Generally the **net assets value** can be regarded as a minimum basis for negotiation, but in practice the actual price may differ significantly.

Market values

These theoretical values are well below the current market values of both companies' total equity, which are TDC $1,363m and UED $943m, a combined value of $2,306m. This indicates that the market is probably expecting both **growth and synergy** resulting from a merger. Combining the expected figures (98.5 and 69.62, giving 168.12) and multiplying by UED's p/e ratio gives a figure of $2,270m, close to the market valuation. It seems that the market is quite **efficient**, and is taking into account more than previous movements in share prices.

Market analysts may also view the combined operation of being **lower risk**, and hence be using a lower cost of capital than 12% in their calculations.

Other factors

Need for merger

UED's shareholders may hold out for a **higher price** as they see our merger offer as essentially **defensive**. They may perceive us as needing to merge in a hurry, to reduce the threat of a takeover bid for ourselves.

Rival buyers

If the bid is seen as **hostile**, we may have to pay a **higher price** for UED, in an effort to win over its shareholders. This is particularly likely if there is more than one suitor for UED and an auction results.

Relative performance

Our **forecast profits** are **set to fall**, but UED's profits appear to be holding up. In addition UED's **financial leverage** (debt: total funds) is one third lower than ours.

Alternative consideration

Our current **cash reserves** are $125.5 million, a long way below the most pessimistic value of UED above. An offer of debt as **part-consideration** might be possible. However our gearing of 15.5% (see workings) is already above the industry average, and the increase in financial risk that more debt would bring may not appeal to UED or our shareholders. Hence it seems that the bulk of our offer must be in the form of a **share-for-share exchange**. It is unlikely however that all shareholders would be happy with a share-for-share exchange; some UK shareholders would not want $ shares quoted on the US stock market.

Suggested terms

Based on today's stock prices, 1 unit of stock in TDC is now worth 11.36/6.50 = approx. 1.75 shares in UED. This would equate to a **4 for 7 offer**. To give UED shareholders some incentive to hold $ shares, a **2 for 3** offer may be acceptable on this basis.

Workings

	TDC	UED translated to $
Stock in issue (m)	120	145
Stock price 18-11-X3 $	11.36	6.50
Total equity value 18-11-X3 $m	1,363.20	942.5
p/e at 18-11-X3	11	13.5
Equity earnings 30-06-X3 $m (equity value ÷ p/e)	123.93	69.81
Forecast profit after tax (equity earnings) 30-6-X4	98.5	69.62
Annual % change in equity earnings	−20.5%	−0.3%
Net asset values 30-06-X3 $m	825.2	352.67
Net assets per share $	6.88	2.43
Debt outstanding $m	250.0	114.75
Total equity value 18-11-X3 $m	1,363.20	942.50
Total funding $m	1,613.20	1,057.25
Debt/total funding - 18-11-X3	15.5%	10.9%

(c) **Strategic implications of hostile bid compared with aggressive organic growth**

Speed of growth

For the bidding company, **growth by acquisition** is faster than **organic growth**, because **new business opportunities** are **purchased** as **going concerns** rather than having to be nurtured from a zero base. Because of the worries about a potential takeover, speed of growth may appear to be important here. However, as the combined company will still be much smaller than the three largest companies, it may not offer much protection should one of the three bid for the combined group.

In any event a programme of **aggressive organic growth** take longer to achieve results. It may also be more risky than taking over an established business. Some **investments undertaken from scratch may not succeed** and have to be abandoned, others will not be undertaken because of limited resources.

Synergy

Further advantages of **successful takeovers or mergers** stem from the significant synergy that can be created. Total profits and values are greater than those attributable to the two separate organisations. The combination **gains market power, elimination of competition, ability to compete in wider markets**, and **ability to combine complementary resources**. There are also **economies of scale, elimination of duplicated resources** and **economies of vertical integration**. It may be much more difficult to achieve these with organic growth.

Diversion of efforts

Where the **bid is hostile**, however, **both companies' management teams** can be diverted from their core business by the battles that ensue. By contrast managers in an organically growing business can concentrate on maximising the business's value.

Effect on staff

Mergers are **not always good** for **staff morale**. Directors, managers and staff members from both companies may either **lose their jobs** or have personal opportunities blocked by the merger. Consequently **personnel management** after a merger can be a **more costly exercise** than forecast. The effect on **staff morale** of a company which grows organically is **highly positive** and the **motivation** that results can create a momentum which is not found in many companies that have grown by acquisition.

Diversification

Unless the two companies' cash flows are **perfectly positively correlated**, merger will mean some **diversification** and **lowering of risk**.

Inability to realise synergistic gains

There is also evidence that many potential **synergistic gains** from a merger are not realised because the management team does not or cannot take the appropriate action. For the merger to achieve results, a **costly programme** of **integration and change management** will have to be introduced, but it may not be possible to implement it successfully without the consent of managers and employees of both sides. A company growing organically will have to introduce significant changes, and **consider carefully change management**. However the need for integration actions, and perhaps the feeling of 'us and them' will be absent.

Shareholder wealth

Paying a premium to acquire UED's shares will benefit the **shareholders of UED** at the expense of the shareholders of TDC. TDC's shareholders could acquire an interest in UED more cheaply by buying its shares directly themselves. By contrast the benefits from organic growth will accrue solely to the **shareholders of TDC**.

Future acquisitions

If the market perceives a need for further acquisitions to secure TDC's position, TDC's share price may become **more volatile** as the market tries to assess future earnings without knowing what the next acquisition will be. Further **bid rumours** may also increase share price volatility.

Failure of strategy

Unsuccessful bids may give the market a signal that TDC's strategy is failing whereas failed attempts to grow organically may be **less apparent** and less significant to the continuing development of a company.

Question 4

Top tips. This question demonstrates that you will be expected to calculate forward exchange rates in this paper and discuss the risks that may affect investment appraisals, so knowledge from other strategic papers will be useful.

Don't forget to discount the perpetuity and the annuity.

The time delay in the tax is a complication, don't worry too much if you didn't work it through all areas of the calculation, but remember to look out for what the question specifies about tax. The latter half of the question emphasises the importance of commercial risks; many of the factors listed may be relevant particularly in the discussion in Question 1 of your exam or for TOPCIMA.

Easy marks. Hopefully you will have scored quite well in the discussions on political and currency risk, though these should make some reference to the scenario.

Examiner's comments. Common errors included not bringing tax in, not adjusting for differential tax rates and incorrect timing of tax. Some candidates used the spot rates throughout, others were unable to calculate forward exchange rates correctly. A number of candidates inflated the cash flows, and many appraisals used the wrong discount rate.

Evaluation of proposed investment in an Asian retail outlet

A financial evaluation of one of the proposed retail outlets will be carried out by:

- Estimating investment and operating cash flows
- Estimating the net present value of the project.

Cash flows in the Asian country will be estimated in Asian dollars (A$), then converted to euros. Additional tax in euros will be payable in the home country.

The net cash flows will be evaluated by discounting at the **company's cost of capital,** 9%, on the basis that all the company's retail outlets carry the same systematic risk. There are two options for how the project continues after the initial two-year phase.

Use **purchasing power parity** to **estimate the €/A$ exchange rate** for the next three years.

Year 0: Spot rate is 0.650 €/A$.

Predicted exchange rates:

Year 1: 0.650 × (1 + 1.5%)/(1 + 3.5%) = 0.637 €/A$.
Year 2: 0.637 × 1.015/1.035 = 0.625 €/A$.
Year 3: 0.625 × 1.015/1.035 = 0.613 €/A$.

Cash flows for first phase of project

		Year 0	Year 1	Year 2	Year 3
	Asian cash flows in A$	A$m	A$m	A$m	
	Investment and operating cash flows	(15.00)	4.50	5.50	
	Asian tax at 30%		3.15	(1.65)	
	Exchange rate €/A$	0.650	0.637	0.625	
	Asian cash flows in euros	€m	€m	€m	€m
(1)	Investment and operating cash flows	(9.75)	2.87	3.44	
(2)	Asian tax at 30%		2.01	(1.03)	
	European tax at 35% (one year delay)			2.41	(1.20)
	Double taxation credit			(2.01)	1.03
(3)	Net European tax charge			0.40	(0.17)
(1)+(2)+(3)	Net cash flow in euros	(9.75)	4.88	2.81	(0.17)
	9% discount factors	1.000	0.917	0.842	0.772
	DCF in euros	(9.75)	4.47	2.37	(0.13)
	Net present value for first phase:	(3.04)			

Cash flows for remainder of project

Alternative 1: TMc continues to operate outlet

Cash flows years 3 to 10 are the same as year 2 post tax euro operating cash flows.

This is €3.44m × discount factor for years 3 to 10 = €3.44 × (6.418 – 1.759) = €16.03m

The tax on this amount will be paid in years 4 to 11 = €3.44 × 0.35 × (6.805 – 2.531) = €5.15m

Net present value for option 1 is €16.03m – €5.15m – €3.04m = €7.84m

Alternative 2: Outlet is franchised

The one-off payment at the beginning of year 3 (end of year 2), converted to euros and after all taxes (35%) is:

0.5m × 0.625 = €0.31m

The present value is €0.31 m × 0.842 = €0.26 m

The tax on this payment is paid a year later, present value €0.31m × 0.35 × 0.772 = €0.08m

The stream of payments from end of year 3 to perpetuity, converted to euros and after all taxes is:

3.2m × 0.613 = €1.96 m

The present value of this perpetuity, as at end of year 2 is €1.96m/9%, and discounted back to year 0 is €1.96m × 0.842/9% = €18.34m

The present value of the tax payments on the perpetuity from the end of year 4, discounted back to year 0 is:

€1.96m × 0.35 × 0.772/9% = €5.88m

The net present value for option 2 is €0.26m – €0.08m + €18.34m – €5.88m – €3.04m = €9.60m

Conclusion

On the basis of these estimates, the investment in the retail outlet is worthwhile whichever option is taken after year 2, but the franchising option gives the higher net present value of € 9.60m compared with € 7.84m.

The main problem with the estimates is that they are **only detailed** for the **first two years**, following which some very approximate guesses are made. Since the first two years are unprofitable, the whole justification for the investment depends on the estimates from year 3 onwards, and it is recommended that more accurate data is obtained for this phase of the project.

Risks of franchising options

The franchising option is not only more profitable than the option of the company continuing to operate the outlet but it also **shifts** most of the **commercial risk** from the **company** to the **franchisee**. It also frees up central management time and allows a more rapid expansion of the business in the Asian country, which may be important if it is important to penetrate the market quickly.

The main **commercial risks** from franchising the operation are:

(a)　Some of the franchisees may **not have sufficient business expertise** to develop the market for the product. This problem should be countered by **careful training and monitoring**.

(b)　Other franchisees may **not** be **trustworthy**. Effective control systems must be installed.

(c)　Successful franchisees may **acquire sufficient skills** to set up their own businesses marketing a range of products, including those of the company's competitors. **Non-competition agreements** should be signed, although these may be **difficult to enforce.** Brand loyalty should be encouraged by organising regular marketing campaigns from the home country and ensuring that franchisees display all promotional material provided.

Risks of running the business

The commercial risks of running the business directly include the following:

(a)　**Local employees** may be **less motivated** than franchisees. Expatriate supervisors may **cost more than local entrepreneurs** and may achieve less because of lack of local expertise, for example in business relationships, laws, taxation and knowledge of customer preferences. Comprehensive training should be given to managers and staff to minimize these problems.

(b)　The local customer base may **discriminate against** a **foreign business**, although with cosmetics, the reverse may well be true. Special promotional campaigns can help to solve these problems.

Whether run by a franchise or directly, the business can be affected by:

(a)　**Currency risk.** If the Asian currency depreciates against the euro, **profits** made in this country will be **eroded** when converted to euros. Because **predicted inflation** is **not too high** the ongoing effect is unlikely to be significant. **Sudden short term currency fluctuations** are a greater concern. If the outlet is run directly by TMc they could reduce currency risk substantially by financing the outlet with a loan in the local currency. Where a franchise is in operation, TMc should request payment in euros.

(b)　**Political risk.** In some developing countries, governments place **restrictions on the repatriation of profits** or fees to the parent company's home country or tax such remittances very highly, the objective being to **force reinvestment in the developing country** and **prevent currency depreciation.** The main risk is that

such restrictions are suddenly introduced, for example following a change of government or after a financial crisis. TMc should **monitor the political and economic status** of the Asian country and consider ways in which it might **avoid these problems**, for example by negotiating a specific agreement on tax and remittances with the government.

Question 5

Top tips. Be careful not to repeat yourself as there is potential for overlap between different sections of the question.

In (a) a point-by-point comparison is better exam technique than having the first section dealing with the police force, the second section with the private sector security company. The headers used (objectives, stakeholders and limiting factors) are key considerations if you have to discuss what any organisation is trying to achieve.

(b) deals with the key question of resource utilisation; there is no clear answer as the force may concentrate too much on income-generating services at the expense of other work, but the income generated could be used to fund extra resources. Using a private sector company may not have the simple impact of freeing up all police time formerly spent on policing matches. Bear in mind also that the stakeholders will have non-financial objectives that must be considered. The stakeholders are grouped internal (police) connected (customers, suppliers), external (local community, government).

Easy marks. Hopefully you were able to identify all the stakeholder groups.

Examiner's comments. Answers were generally good, with candidates recognizing how the differences in objectives would influence performance. The most common fault in (b) was failing to discuss the impact on stakeholder groups, whilst some answers were insufficiently focused on finance – candidates provided answers more suited to the Business Strategy paper.

(a)   **Reasons for differences in the objectives**

Objectives

Objectives of government organisations are **set by statute** and are concerned with providing effective public services to their 'customers'. Their **main source of income** is money raised from taxpayers by central or local government. They are accountable to these taxpayers for the efficient use of funds when carrying out their services.

The main objective of most private sector companies is to **maximize the wealth** of their **owners** (ie shareholders). The international security company's financial objectives are typical for a private company, focusing on **growth in earnings per share** and obtaining a **target return on capital employed**. The company will be successful if it can earn a return on capital employed at least as good as similar risk investments. Growth in earnings per share is widely used as a **performance measure**, but can be manipulated and is best used as part of a package of measures.

Stakeholders

In the case of the police force, the **primary customers** are the **whole of the local community**, for whom they aim to reduce crime, promote safety and deliver justice. These people are more or less the same set as the tax payers who provide the funds, though the funds raised will come from central as well as local government.

Private sector companies will maximize profits by **concentrating on satisfying their customers**, considering the needs of other stakeholders (eg employees, suppliers, lenders) and managing their resources wisely.

441

Limiting factors

The police force provides its main services free. Because customers do not pay for specific services, **demand for services** is always likely to **outstrip supply**. The plans of the police force are therefore necessarily subject to cash limits. Recent developments in resource accounting attempt to remove the problems of being unable to move budget funds from one area or time period to another, but cash is still the major limiting factor to the services that can be carried out.

With private companies the **main limiting factor** is **not usually availability of cash** but **demand** for the **company's products or services**, which are not provided free but must be paid for at market rates. Therefore companies are always searching for new customers or new products to sell to them.

The international security company

Convergence of objectives

The objectives of public and private sector organisations have come closer in recent years. The public sector has **recognised the need** to be **more accountable** for taxpayers' money and has attempted to identify areas of its services that are **suitable for charging fees** to the public. Performance measures such as return on capital employed have been introduced. Areas of service suitable for privatization have been identified. The policing of football matches is a typical example.

For its part, the private sector has moved from purely shareholder-related objectives to recognising that other stakeholders can influence its success to a large extent. Commercial success depends on satisfying customers and managing the needs of customers, employees and the local community satisfactorily.

(b) **Police force commercial operations**

Effect of commercial operations on mainstream objectives

The main problem with running commercial operations within public sector organizations is that top management, who are concerned with maximizing available funds, might **spend too much of their time** on organizing these income-generating opportunities and be tempted to divert too many resources from mainstream operations. Thus police officers may be diverted from mainstream crime prevention activities during a big football game, for example, and this may leave weaknesses in normal crime patrols.

On the positive side, the visibility of friendly police at popular sporting events does a lot to **increase the confidence of the public** in the police force, thus contributing to their third objective. Also, if income from sports events is **reinvested** in mainstream services, in terms of manpower or improved systems, there can be real improvements in these services, thus reducing crime and promoting community safety.

Effect of possible privatization

If the policing of high profile public events were to be privatized, there would be a **number of losses and inconveniences** for the police force that would need to be considered when deciding the minimum tender price that would make privatization worthwhile.

(i) A **source of funds for investment** in mainstream policing services would be removed. **Additional funds** would need to be **advanced** by government to make up for this, or there would be a reduction in the quality of service.

(ii) The police would **lose the public relations advantage** of being seen to be present at major public events.

(iii) Even if a private security company patrolled the football matches, the **police** would still **have to be involved** if there were any incidents which led to the need for prosecution. These might be relatively small incidents, for example theft, as well as large scale disturbances by crowds.

(iv) There could also be a **confusion of the boundary** between **public and private responsibilities for policing**. The private company would operate according to the terms of a contract that it would refuse to step outside, thus possibly leaving many minor inconvenient problems to be covered by the police force.

Effect on stakeholder groups

Many of the stakeholders have voiced opposition to the privatization proposals. The effect on the various stakeholder groups can be summarized as follows:

(i)   **Senior officers and managers** will **request increases in government funding** to cover the loss of cash income from football policing and the other related disadvantages identified above.

(ii)   **Police officers and other employees** will **not be** in **favour** of the **privatisation** as they will lose overtime and other benefits (including free tickets to the football). This may cause hardship and unrest.

(iii) **The fee paying customers (football clubs and others)** will fear either that the **fees they are charged will rise**, or that the quality of service will decline because of the less comprehensive service offered by a private sector organization. They may fear may a drop in gate receipts from families. The boundary between security company and police force involvement will need to be carefully designed and explained.

(iv)   **Local suppliers** may fear that they will **lose out** because the international security company will source its supplies centrally.

(v)   **The local community (tax payers)** may fear that their **safety is less assured** than when the police force were directly involved.

(vi)   **The government** will **gain cash inflows** from privatizing the football and public events policing rights. In deciding the minimum price at which these rights can be sold, they must realistically take into account all identified problems, funding needs, and stakeholder fears and objections, including those identified above.

CIMA – Strategic Level

Paper P9

Management Accounting – Financial Strategy

Mock Examination 2

Instructions to candidates:

You are allowed three hours to answer this question paper.
In the real exam, you are allowed 20 minutes reading time before the examination begins during which you should read the question paper, and if you wish, make annotations on the question paper. However, you will **not** be allowed, **under any circumstances**, to open the answer book and start writing or use your calculator during this reading time.
You are strongly advised to carefully read the question requirement before attempting the question concerned.
Answer the ONE compulsory question in Section A.
Answer TWO of the FOUR questions in Section B.

DO NOT OPEN THIS PAPER UNTIL YOU ARE READY TO START UNDER EXAMINATION CONDITIONS

SECTION A – 50 marks

Answer this question

Question 1

Background

Ibsen is a privately-owned toy manufacturing company which has been trading for 12 years. It has 15 shareholders who each own an equal number of shares. Two of the shareholders are full-time managers in the company. The shareholders have discussed the possibility of a public flotation of shares on a number of occasions over the past five years, but have each time decided against the idea because it would conflict with many of their personal objectives for the company. However, some of the shareholders would now like to liquidate a proportion of their investment and believe the time might be right for a quotation on the London Stock Exchange.

Recent financial information

It is currently May 20X5. The company's accounting year ends on 31 December. Summary financial information for the five years 20X0–20X4 and forecast for 20X5 is shown below (all figures in millions of pounds Sterling).

INCOME STATEMENT (EXTRACTS)

	20X5 forecast	20X4	20X3	20X2	20X1	20X0
Revenue	220.0	215.0	170.0	150.0	125.0	115.0
Profit before tax and interest	36.0	25.0	27.0	26.0	23.0	21.0
Interest	4.0					
Taxation	10.6	8.2	8.9	8.6	7.6	7.0
Profit after interest and tax	21.4	16.8	18.1	17.4	15.4	14.0
Dividend payable	17.5	17.5	17.5	9.0	9.0	9.0

BALANCE SHEET (EXTRACTS)

Assets						
Non-current	124.0	85.0	66.0	60.0	55.0	50.0
Current (net of liabilities)	48.0	35.0	30.0	34.0	30.0	28.0
	172.0	120.0	96.0	94.0	85.0	78.0
Financing						
Authorised and issued ordinary share capital	30.0	30.0	30.0	30.0	30.0	30.0
Par value 50p						
Accumulated profits	97.0	90.0	66.0	64.0	55.0	48.0
10-year bank loan	45.0	–	–	–	–	–
Non-current	172.0	120.0	96.0	94.0	85.0	78.0

Notes

- The non-current assets were valued in 20X4.

- The average P/E ratio for companies in Ibsen's industry is currently 11.

- The company's marginal and average tax rate is 33%.

- The bank loan was taken out on 1 January 20X5. It is secured on the firm's premises and carries a variable rate of interest. The interest rate on similar loans made to companies with the same risk characteristics as Ibsen averaged 10% throughout 20X4.

- The shareholder's cost of equity is currently 14%.

Developments 20X5 to 20X9

Note. The information in this section of the scenario relates *only* to requirement (b) of the question.

The company is floated on the Stock Exchange during 20X5 at 300 pence per share. Assume it is now the year 20X9 and the company wishes to raise £250 million for the development and marketing of new products. The following information is relevant:

- There has been no change in issued ordinary share capital during the five years and no new debt has been raised. Earnings after interest and taxes in the year to 31 December 20X8 were £45 million.

- The original shareholders now own 20% of the issued shares; a further 20% is owned by three large institutional investors and the remaining 60% by a large number of small, private investors.

- P/E ratios have been as follows over the past 9 months.

	Ibsen	Industry
Present	18	16
3 months ago	15	16
6 months ago	14	15
9 months ago	16	15

The company is considering raising the £250 million by means of either a rights issue at 15% discount to the prevailing share price, or issuing convertible debt which would be convertible into ordinary shares in five years' time.

Required

(a) Assume you are a financial adviser to Ibsen *prior to flotation* in 20X5. Write a report to the Board which:

   (i) Explains the advantages and disadvantages of a public flotation. **(8 marks)**

   (ii) Recommends an issue price for the company if it decides to seek a stock market quotation

   Assume no change in issued share capital before flotation and that the existing shareholders are each prepared to sell 49% of their holding. **(15 marks)**

   (iii) Discusses the difficulties of setting a new issue price and recommends what other information should be considered by the company before deciding whether to proceed with the flotation

   (7 marks)

(b) Assume it is now 20X9 and you are advising the company on its need for new capital. Write a report to the Board which:

   (i) Advises a suitable rights issue price and calculates the theoretical ex-rights price **(6 marks)**

   (ii) Advises on the conversion terms for the issue of convertible debt. The return on unsecured debt is 10% in 20X9 **(8 marks)**

   (iii) Explains, briefly, the main advantages and disadvantages to a company such as Ibsen of raising finance via either a rights issue or convertible debt. Using your assumptions and calculations in (i) and (ii) above, recommend which of the two methods of financing is to be preferred by Ibsen in the circumstances **(6 marks)**

(Total = 50 marks)

SECTION B – 50 marks

Answer TWO questions ONLY

Question 2

Harry is Financial Manager of RP. He is nearing retirement. You have been appointed as his deputy with a view to taking over from him in 12 months' time.

The company is considering an investment in a new product which will cost €1,200,000 in new machinery and will result in profit before depreciation and tax of €375,000 per annum in real terms for five years. At the end of the five years, the machinery can be sold for its written-down tax value. The investment will require working capital of €100,000 in real terms from the start of year 1.

The following notes are relevant.

1 At the end of year 5, the total working capital can be released in cash back to the company.

2 Inflation is expected to be 4% per annum on all operating cash flows and working capital for the period under review. Working capital will not increase for any other reason.

3 The company pays tax at the rate of 30%. Tax is payable half in the year profits are earned, half a year later.

4 Tax relief is available on capital expenditure at 25% on a reducing balance. The company also depreciates its plant and equipment on this basis. The first claim is made in Year 1. The machine is sold at its tax written down value at the end of year 5..

5 Assume all cash flows occur at the end of the year *except* the purchase of the new machinery. This occurs at the beginning of the year.

6 The company's long-term capital structure is shown below.

	€'000
Ordinary shares €1 each	1,000
Reserves	8,794
	9,794
10% debenture (€100 par value)	1,000
	10,794

7 The current ex dividend market value of shares is 250c and the current ex interest market value of debentures is €95 per cent.

8 The debenture is redeemable in 3 years' time at par.

9 A dividend of 20c per share has just been paid on the shares. Dividends have grown consistently at 10% over the past few years, and this pattern is expected to continue.

Required

(a) Calculate the company's weighted average cost of capital.   **(7 marks)**

(b) Evaluate the investment using the company's WACC, as suggested by Harry. *Note.* If you are unable to complete part (a) of the question, you may assume a nominal cost of capital of 16%.   **(11 marks)**

(c) Whatever your own answer to part (b), assume the results of your financial evaluation suggest the investment is worthwhile (ie the NPV is positive). You think that some of Harry's assumptions are unrealistic. In particular, you are concerned about the uncertainty surrounding each year's cash flows and the use of the WACC as the discount rate.

Write a memo to Harry which explains how the evaluation might be refined, or developed, to overcome your concerns.   **(7 marks)**

Note. You are not required to revise your calculations for part (b) of the question to answer part (c) of the question.

(Total = 25 marks)

Question 3

This question concerns two organisations, one in the private sector and one in the public sector.

Organisation 1

This is a listed company in the electronics industry. Its stated financial objectives are twofold

- 'To increase earnings per share year-on-year by 10% per annum'
- 'To achieve a 25% per annum return on capital employed'

This company has an equity market capitalisation of £600 million. It also has a variety of debt instruments trading at a total value of £150 million.

Organisation 2

This organisation is a newly-established purchaser and provider of healthcare services in the public sector. The organisation' s legal status is a Trust.

Its total income of the current year will be almost £100 million. It is considering funding the building of a new healthcare centre via loan finance from the private sector. The total debt will be £15 million. Capital and interest will be repaid over 15 years at a variable rate of interest, currently 9% each year. The Trust's sole financial objective states simply 'to achieve financial balance during the year' . Its other objectives are concerned with qualitative factors such as 'providing high quality healthcare'.

Required

(a)   Discuss

    (i)   The reasons for the differences in the financial objectives of the two types of organisation given above; and

    (ii)   The main differences in the *business* risks involved in the achievement of their financial objectives and how these risks might be managed

    Use the scenario details given above to assist your answer wherever possible.   **(18 marks)**

(b)   Explain how the *financial* risks introduced into the public sector organisation by the use of private sector finance might affect the achievement of its objectives and comment on how these risks might be managed.
(7 marks)

(Total = 25 marks)

Question 4

PMS is an unlisted company with intentions of obtaining a stock market listing in the near future. The company is wholly equity financed at present but the directors are considering a new capital structure prior to it becoming a listed company.

PMS operates in an industry where the average asset beta is 1.2. The company's business risk is estimated to be similar to that of the industry as a whole. The current level of earnings before interest and taxes is €400,000. This earnings level is expected to be maintained for the foreseeable future.

The rate of return on riskless assets is at present 10% and the return on the market portfolio is 15%. These rates are post-tax and are expected to remain constant for the foreseeable future.

The finance director has recommended considering introducing debt into its capital structure by one of the following methods.

Scenario 1:   €500,000 10% Debentures at par, secured on land and buildings of the company
Scenario 2:   €1 million 12% Unsecured loan stock at par

The rate of tax is expected to remain at 33% and interest on debt is tax deductible.

Required

(a) Calculate, for *each* of the *two* options:

    (i)   Total market values and values of equity
    (ii)   Debt/equity ratios
    (iii) Cost of equity   **(15 marks)**

One of the other directors has suggested that PMS might consider raising €500,000 by means of an issue of convertible loan stock at par, with a coupon rate of 6%. He has stated that this would be preferable to the other debt options, or a rights issue which the Chief Executive favours. The loan stock would be redeemable in seven years' time. Prior to redemption, the loan stock may be converted at a rate of 35 ordinary shares per €100 nominal loan stock.

Current share price is €2.40.

Required

(b) (i)   Explain the term *conversion premium* and calculate the conversion premium at the date of issue implicit in the data given.   **(4 marks)**

    (ii)   Identify the advantages to PMS of issuing convertible loan stock instead of a rights issue to raise the necessary finance.   **(3 marks)**

    (iii) Explain why the market value of convertible loan stock is likely to be affected by the dividend policy of the issuing company.   **(3 marks)**

(Total = 25 marks)

Question 5

GSD Ltd is a private UK company owned by the two families that started the business in 20X0. The company produces organic food products for distribution in the domestic UK market using food products from UK farms. The company is experiencing a period of rapid growth, with revenue expected to rise by 15% in each of the following five years.

The company is hoping to retain a profit margin (profit before interest and taxes divided by revenue) of 30% throughout the next five years. The ratio of working capital to revenue is expected to remain constant, where working capital is inventories plus trade receivables less trade payables.

Interest is paid on the overdraft and bank loan at 6% per annum. Interest on the bank loan and overdraft is calculated on the balance outstanding at the beginning of the year. Corporation tax is paid one year in arrears at a rate of 30%, with a 100% tax allowance for capital expenditure in the year in which it is incurred. In arriving at operating profit, depreciation is charged at 25% on a reducing balance basis based on year-end balances.

Extracts from the management accounts of GSD Ltd on 31 December 20X4 are as follows:

Balance sheet as at 31 December 20X4

	£m
Property, plant and equipment	15
Working capital	9
	24
Share capital (50p ordinary)	10
Retained earnings	4
Long-term borrowings (bank loan)	8
Short-term borrowings (overdraft)	1
Current tax payable	1
	24

Income statement for the year ended 31 December 20X4

Revenue	45.0
Profit before interest and taxes	13.5
Dividend paid in 20X4	50p a share

Capital expenditure plans are for expenditure on property, plant and equipment of £10 million in 20X5, £10 million in 20X6 and £7 million in each of years 20X7 to 20X9. No disposals of property, plant and equipment are expected in this period.

Shareholders expect a year-on-year increase in dividends of 5%. Any funds deficit in the year will be funded by overdraft and any surplus funds used to reduce the overdraft. However, with the increased demands on the funds of the business to finance growth, the directors are concerned that they may exceed the overdraft limit of £1.5 million. They may, therefore, need to negotiate an increase in the bank loan, although the bank has indicated that it would not accept gearing higher than 70% based on book values where gearing is defined as long and short term borrowings (including overdraft) divided by equity. The shareholders have indicated that they do not wish to inject any additional capital into the business.

Required

(a)   Construct the balance sheet, income statement and a cash flow analysis of the company for each of the years 20X5 and 20X6 and advise the company on the extent of any additional funding requirement in that period. In your answer, round figures to the nearest £100,000. **(16 marks)**

(b)   Discuss the interrelationships between financing, investment and dividend strategies with reference to the liquidity requirements of GSD Ltd. Include in your discussion how each could be adapted to meet the company's liquidity requirements in the years 20X5 and 20X6 and provide a recommendation. **(9 marks)**

(Total = 25 marks)

Answers

**DO NOT TURN THIS PAGE UNTIL YOU HAVE
COMPLETED THE MOCK EXAM**

A PLAN OF ATTACK

We've already established that you've been told to do it 101 times, so it is of course superfluous to tell you for the 102nd time to **Take a good look at the paper before diving in to answer questions**. Then work out **which questions to do**, the **order** in which to attempt and spend the remainder of the 20 minutes' reading time going through **Question 1**.

The next step

You may be thinking that this paper is a lot more straightforward than the first mock exam; however, having sailed through the first mock, you may think this paper is actually rather difficult.

Option 1 (Don't like this paper)

If you are challenged by this paper, it may be best to get the optional questions done before tackling the case study **Question 1**. Don't forget though that you will need half the time to answer the case study.

- **Question 2** is heavily calculation based and is time-pressured. Part (b) calculations are easier than part (a) so you might want to just use a reasonable discount rate in (b) if you can't finish the WACC calculation for (a) in time. There are 7 marks available in part (c) for a straightforward discussion so make sure you leave enough time.

- You need to bring in your knowledge from P3 and P6 in **Question 3**.

- **Question 4** is again heavily calculation-based, and time-pressured. However you won't need to finish the calculations to be able to answer part (b).

- **Question 5** part (a) is a straightforward forecasting question which needs a methodical, logical approach.

- Start with part (a) of **Question 1,** it should be a straightforward discussion. Look for clues in the scenario to help you with the calculations in (ii). The calculations in (b) are quite straightforward.

Option 2 (This paper's alright)

Are you sure it is? If you are then that's encouraging. You'll feel even happier when you've got the compulsory question out the way, so you should consider doing **Question 1** first.

- Don't run over time on the calculations in **Question 1**, there are far more marks available for good quality discussion. You must make sure throughout that your discussion is relevant to Ibsen.

- The main danger in **Question 2** is running over time. Be disciplined and move on if you struggle with any of the calculations.

- **Question 3** is a pure discussion question and it is very important to carefully plan your answer. Make sure that your discussion is always applied to the specific organisations in the question.

- **Question 4** has some challenging calculations and the main danger again is running over time. Make sure you leave sufficient time for the discussion in part (b).

- Again be strict with timing in **Question 5**. Make sure you tailor your answers to GSD in part (b).

Once more

You must **allocate your time** according to the marks for the question in total, and for the parts of the questions. And you must also **follow the requirements exactly**.

Finished with fifteen minutes to spare?

Looks like you slipped up on the time allocation. However if you have, make sure you don't waste the last few minutes; go back to **any parts of questions that you didn't finish** because you ran out of time.

Forget about it!

Forget about what? Excellent, you already have.

Question 1

(a) To: Board of Directors of Ibsen
     From: Financial Adviser
     Date: 20 January 20X5
     Subject: Proposed stock exchange flotation

(i) **Advantages and disadvantages of public flotation**

It is helpful to separate the **position** of the company from that of its **existing shareholders** when considering the merits of flotation.

Effects on the existing shareholders

(1) They are able to sell all or part of their holdings. In the case of Ibsen, each shareholder owns 4m shares. This is a **sizeable holding** which it would be difficult to **sell privately**. Since some of the shareholders wish to realise their investment, a public flotation would be in their interests.

(2) A **wider market** will be created for the **remaining shares**. Even if some of the shareholders in Ibsen do not wish to sell at the moment, a flotation will make it easier for them to do so in the future if their personal position changes.

(3) A **quotation** provides a **ready share price**, which lessens the uncertainties of inheritance tax by avoiding the problems of valuing unquoted shares.

(4) They will experience a **dilution of control**, which could mean that the company develops in ways that they would not have wished. Although it is currently proposed that only 49% of the shares should be released, dilution will still occur. The shareholders should consider releasing a higher percentage of their holdings since this would improve the price that could be expected on flotation.

Effects on the company

(1) Flotation may lead to the shares being perceived as a **less risky investment**. This will mean that a better credit standing is obtained, which should make it easier to borrow money. The extra prominence and status given to listed companies might also help Ibsen to generate new business by attracting new customers.

(2) **Additional shares** can be **issued more easily** at a later date. It is difficult for companies to expand beyond a certain size without getting a quotation because of the difficulty of raising enough funds.

(3) Flotation will be an **expensive process** and will mean that the company has to comply with the stringent Stock Exchange regulations. It will put extra administrative burdens on the management.

(4) The **profits and performance** of the company will be much more in **the public eye** and the company cannot afford to show poor results without attracting considerable criticism. This can lead to the development of short-term pressures leading to decisions that are not in the best long-term interests of the business.

(5) The company will be able to **offer share option schemes** to its employees which should assist in the recruitment and retention of good staff.

(ii) **The issue price**

Possible approaches that can be used to arrive at an issue price include the following.

Dividend valuation model

This can be expressed as: $MV = \dfrac{d_0(1+g)}{(k_e - g)}$

where   MV (ex div) is the current market price
d_0 is the current net dividend = £17.5m/60m = 29.2 pence per share
k_e is the shareholders' cost of capital = 14%
g is the expected annual growth of dividend payments

Although the company has had a policy up to now of **stable dividends**, it is unlikely that this will be appropriate following flotation since investors will expect to see some level of growth in their income from the investment. A number of approaches could be taken to estimate a suitable dividend growth rate, but one method is to base it on the rate of growth in distributable profits for the period 20X0 to 20X4. The 20X5 figures will be excluded since these are only an estimate, and forecast an unusually sharp increase in profits for the year, which may or may not be realistic.

Year	Profit	Profit increase	% increase
20X0	14.0		
20X1	15.4	1.4	10.0
20X2	17.4	2.0	13.0
20X3	18.1	0.7	4.0
20X4	16.8	−1.3	−7.2

Alternative solution

$$g = \sqrt[4]{\dfrac{20X4\ dividend}{20X0\ dividend}} - 1$$

$$= \sqrt[4]{\dfrac{16.8}{14.0}} - 1 = 4.66\%$$

Average rate of increase = **5.0%**

This can now be used in the dividend valuation model:

$$MV = \dfrac{29.2(1+0.05)}{(0.14-0.05)} = £3.41 \text{ per share}$$

Net asset value

At the end of 20X4 the net assets amounted to £120m, and the number of shares in issue was 60m. This gives a theoretical share price of **£2.00**.

P/E basis

The average P/E ratio for companies in Ibsen's industry is currently 11. However, Ibsen is unlikely to achieve this P/E ratio on the initial flotation since the company is not well established and known on the market.

For the purposes of arriving at an offer price therefore, a discount will be applied to the P/E ratio of 10%, giving a ratio of 10. Earnings per share at the end of 20X4 amounted to £16.8m/60m = 28 pence per share. The theoretical share price on this basis is therefore £2.80 (£0.28 × 10).

Differences in methods of calculations

The methods of calculation show a **significant variation** in the theoretical share price. This is because they view the company from different perspectives.

(1)   The **net asset value** basis provides what is effectively a break-up valuation, which is not appropriate for valuing the shares on flotation.

(2)   While the **P/E method** is based on comparison with other firms in the industry, it is still **backward looking**, is over-influenced by the 20X4 dip in profits, and takes no account of future growth projections.

(3)   The **dividend valuation** model is therefore the preferred method since it is based on **projections of the earnings** that are likely to accrue to shareholders in the future. However, the shares may need to be offered at a discount to the calculated price to make them attractive to potential investors.

(iii)   **Further pricing issues**

(1)   Although calculations based on the fundamental value of the company are useful in establishing an appropriate level for pricing the issue, the **actual price** to be used must also take into account other factors. Possibly the most important of these is the **current mood** of the market – whether there is an optimistic view of equity performance – and the level of demand for equity investment.

(2)   **Current and projected economic conditions** will also play a part in determining the likely success of the issue. For example, if it is widely expected that the manufacturing sector is heading for recession, this will make the shares less attractive, regardless of the company's track record. If the company has a significant level of exports, or is reliant on imported raw materials, then global economic conditions will also assume more importance.

(3)   In view of the positive projections for 20X5, it might be worth waiting until these results are confirmed before **floating** the company. If these projections are realised, this would have a significant impact on the level of price that the shares might be expected to achieve.

(b) To: Board of Directors of Ibsen
From: Financial Adviser
Date: 20 May 20X9
Subject: Proposed new capital issue

(i) Rights issue pricing

The first step in establishing the rights issue price is to calculate the current share price. There are still 60m shares in issue, and the most recent earnings figure is £45m, giving an earnings per share of 75 pence. At the current P/E ratio of 18, this implies a share price of £13.50 (18 × 75p).

It is proposed to price the rights issue at a discount of 15% to the current share price, thus giving an issue price of **£11.48.** Since the company needs to raise £250m, this means that the number of shares to be issued must be **21,777,000.**

Existing shares 60m × £13.50 = £810m

New shares 21.777m × £11.48 = £250m

Total market capitalisation £1,060m

Total number of shares in issue = 60m + 21.777m = 81.777m

Theoretical ex-rights price = £1,060m ÷ 81.777m = **£12.96**

(ii) Conversion terms

(1) The primary factor influencing the pricing of convertibles is the **forecast level of the share price at the date of conversion**. These forecasts must focus on the expected level of earnings growth during the period up to the exercise date, and any anticipated changes to the cost of capital. The average rate of earnings growth since flotation has been around 28% ($\sqrt[3]{\dfrac{45}{21.4}} - 1$) and if this level of growth continues, earnings in five years' time would be around £198m. The P/E ratio over the last year has averaged 15.75, which is slightly above the industry average.

(2) If it is assumed that there is **no significant change in P/E ratios** over the five-year period, a P/E ratio of say 16 would give an expected share price of (198/60) × 16 = approximately £52.80. Conversion terms would therefore be 1.9 shares per £100 of loan stock. However, it must be realised that this is the **minimum number of shares** that could be **promised** in order to make conversion attractive. In practice, a larger number should be offered to compensate for the risk of returns being lower than anticipated, and to make the issue attractive to investors. It is therefore suggested that between four and five shares per £100 loan stock should be offered.

(3) The exact terms of the conversion will also be related to the **coupon rate of the debt** – although the coupon rate on convertibles is generally below the market rate, there is a **trade-off** between the **size of the discount** and the **generosity of the conversion terms**. To summarise, the **total package** of interest and conversion rights must be **sufficiently attractive** to ensure the success of the issue, and also appropriate to the company in terms of the timing and level of servicing costs, and the effect on the dividend requirements after conversion.

(iii) The relative merits of a rights issue as compared with convertible debt

(1) The immediate question is effectively a choice between issuing **equity or debt.** The current market capitalisation of the company is £810m (£45m × 18), and it has long term debt of only £45m. The gearing level is therefore currently extremely low at only 5.5%. The effect of the convertible issue would be to increase gearing in the short term to 36.4% ((£250m + £45m) ÷ £810m). Although this is a significant increase, 36.4% would still be a perfectly reasonable level of gearing for the majority of companies.

(2)   The key factor in determining whether or not this would be reasonable for Ibsen is the ease with which it would be able to **service the debt.** If it is assumed that the coupon rate is 9% (a small discount to the market rate) the annual interest charge would be £22.5m, giving an interest cover on the current earnings level of 2 times (in fact the real level of cover would be higher, but it is not known what the tax charge for the year is). Provided that Ibsen can continue to achieve the assumed rate of earnings growth, and that the volatility of earnings is not too great, the debt option is attractive because it allows the company to take advantage of the tax relief on debt interest.

(3)   However, the company must also consider the implications of **failing to achieve the forecast level of performance**. If the new project fails to deliver as anticipated and earnings performance is poor, the cost of servicing the debt could become a problem, and in this situation it is also unlikely that the share price would reach the anticipated level. The effect of this would be that holders of the debt might choose to opt for redemption rather than conversion, and this in turn will place a further financial burden on the company.

(4)   Thus the safest option would be to make a **rights issue**, but although this would reduce downside risk, it would also limit the level of profits that are available to shareholders by earnings dilution and by foregoing the tax relief on the debt interest. The directors must therefore determine exactly what their position is in relation to **financial risk**, and they must also make careful, detailed and realistic **forecasts** of business performance over the next few years before making their decision.

Question 2

Text references. The calculation of weighted average cost of capital is explained in Chapter 9 and the calculation of NPV in Chapter 18.

Top tips. Hopefully in (a) you remembered to take the **post-tax cost** of debt, and also remembered that the debt is redeemable and hence its cost should be calculated using the IRR formula.

In (b) the tax cash flow is calculated by taking 50% of the current year's profit, 50% of the previous year's profit. Your answer should have indicated this, but writing out the tax calculations in full is probably not a good use of time. As the tax allowance calculations are more complex, you should show those in detail. Showing the working capital calculations in detail should hopefully minimise the chances of your making mistakes in this area. (Remember it is the **change** or **increment** in working capital levels you include each year in the DCF calculation, not the value at the year-end.)

In (c) your discussion should focus on the strengths and weaknesses of the technique; you should assume that the information used is the best that can be estimated at the time of the evaluation. However the fact that the company is using 'best guesses' doesn't mean that uncertainty analysis cannot be employed. Note also that several factors (assumed constant) could well vary significantly over the time of the project (risk, technology).

It is unlikely that a question will be set using quarterly accounting for tax, but this question gives you practice just in case you encounter it in this paper or in TOPCIMA.

Easy marks. The working capital calculation in (b) is easier so it's worth doing that first. The discussion in (c) offers a lot of potential scope for mark-scoring, so make sure you leave yourself enough time for it by:

•   Using a reasonable rate in (b) if you don't have time to finish the WACC calculation in (a).
•   Not getting bogged down in the tax calculations in (b).

(a) **Cost of equity**

$$k_{eg} = \frac{d_0(1+g)}{P_0} + g$$

$$= \frac{20(1+0.1)}{250} + 0.1$$

$$= 18.8\%$$

Cost of debt can be estimated by comparing the current market value of the debt with the discounted payments due to be made by the company up to the redemption date.

Year	Cash flow	8% discount factor	PV	10% discount factor	PV
	€		€		€
0	(95)	1.000	(95)	1.000	(95)
1-3	10 (1 − 0.3)	2.577	18.04	2.487	17.41
3	100	0.794	79.40	0.751	75.10
			2.44		(2.49)

Interpolating

Post tax cost of debt, $k_{dnet} = 8\% + \dfrac{2.44}{2.44 + 2.49} \times (10 - 8)$

$$= 9.0\%$$

$$\text{WACC} = k_{eg}\left[\frac{V_E}{V_E + V_D}\right] + k_{dnet}\left[\frac{V_D}{V_E + V_D}\right]$$

$$= 18.8\left(\frac{250}{250 + 95}\right) + 9\left(\frac{95}{250 + 95}\right)$$

$$= 16.1\%, \text{ say } 16\%$$

(b)

	0	1	2	3	4	5	6
	€'000	€'000	€'000	€'000	€'000	€'000	€'000
Profit (nominal values)		390.0	405.6	421.8	438.7	456.2	
Tax (30%)		(58.5)	(119.3)	(124.1)	(129.1)	(134.2)	(68.4)
Capital outlay	(1,200.0)						
Machinery sale (W1)						284.8	
Tax allowances (W1)		45.0	78.8	59.1	44.3	33.3	14.2
Working capital	(100.0)	(4.0)	(4.2)	(4.3)	(4.5)	117.0	
Net cash flow	(1,300.0)	372.5	360.9	352.5	349.4	757.1	(54.2)
16% factor	1.000	0.862	0.743	0.641	0.552	0.476	0.410
Present value	(1,300.0)	321.1	268.1	226.0	192.9	360.4	(22.2)
PV cumulative	(1,300.0)	(978.9)	(710.8)	(484.8)	(291.9)	68.5	46.3

NPV is therefore **positive** €46,300.

Workings

1   *Tax allowances and resale value*

		€'000	Time
1st allowance	1,200 × 25% × 30%	90.0	1/2
2nd allowance	75% of previous	67.5	2/3
3rd allowance	75% of previous	50.6	3/4
4th allowance	75% of previous	38.0	4/5
5th allowance	75% of previous	28.5	5/6

There is no balancing allowance since the machinery is sold at its written down value.

Written down value = €1,200,000 × 0.75^5 = £284,766

2   *Working capital requirements*

Time	0	1	2	3	4	5
	€'000	€'000	€'000	€'000	€'000	€'000
Amounts	100.0	104.0	108.2	112.5	117.0	
Increment	(100.0)	(4.0)	(4.2)	(4.3)	(4.5)	117.0

(c)   To: Financial Manager
       From: Deputy Financial Manager
       Date: 12 May 20X8
       Subject: Evaluation of proposed new product investment

Evaluation of project

The financial evaluation of the proposed investment on the original basis suggests that the project will just about be viable since the NPV at the end of six years is positive. However, the size of the **profit** is relatively small in relation to the size of the project, and it is worth considering the **assumptions** underlying the evaluation to ensure that these are appropriate. Otherwise, we run the risk of **making a loss**. Areas that merit further work include the following.

Use of the WACC as the discount rate

The **WACC approximates** to the **overall cost of capital** to the business. However, this investment amounts to €1.3 million (including working capital), and is therefore a relatively large investment. We should therefore consider whether undertaking the project would in itself affect the cost of capital to the business. If it does, then the WACC should be adjusted to take account of this. Further, it is assumed that the project carries the same level of risk as the existing operations. If the risk profile is different, then the cost of capital should be adjusted to reflect this.

The timescale of the project

The project is evaluated over a six-year time frame, taking into account the tax effects, which is a long time in forecasting terms. In practice it is unlikely that the **same discount rate** will be **appropriate** to the **whole of this period**, and it would be helpful to adjust the current WACC for the expected movements in the general economic situation, and in particular the level of interest rates during that period.

The nature of the cash flows

Single values have been used for each element of the cash flow projections. In practice, each of the different elements is likely to be subject to **different levels of risk**. For example, the projected level of sales could be affected by the speed of technological change within the industry as well as by more general economic influences. We should therefore attempt to estimate the **levels of uncertainty** in the forecast cash flows. The most likely cash flows can then be reduced in line with our perceived risk aversion before being discounted at a rate appropriate to each year.

The sensitivities inherent in the project

It is likely that certain elements within the cash flow projections are **more important** than **others** in determining the eventual outcome of the project. It would therefore be useful to undertake some form of **sensitivity analysis** to identify both the key variables and the likely impact of their deviating from forecasts on the financial outcome of the project.

I would be happy to discuss any of these areas further with you, and look forward to receiving your comments.

Question 3

Text references. Chapter 2 covers objectives of organisations and financial risk of debt finance is covered in Chapter 10.

Top tips. In (a) (i), the financial profit-seeking objectives of a private sector company are fundamental to its success, whereas for a non-profit making public sector trust, finance acts mainly as a constraint. The answer also needed to bring out the responsibility of a private company being to its shareholders, and the responsibility of the health trust being to a wider stakeholder base. In (a) (ii), the private company's main business risk is falling demand, whereas that of the public sector healthcare trust is excess demand. Risk management knowledge from P3, in particular monitoring and risk reduction, is useful. In (b) higher than expected interest payments can force a reduction in the services offered; however the risk of this happening might not be great.

Easy marks. The question is easier if you can bring in knowledge from P3 and P6.

Examiner's comments. In (a) some candidates confused the public sector with public limited companies, and confused business and financial risk.

(a) (i) **Differences in financial objectives of the two types of organisation**

The differences in financial objectives arise from the differences in **ownership, stakeholders** and **overall objectives** of the two types of organisation.

(1) **Electronics company**

The financial objectives for the electronics company are concerned with **profitability** and the **generation of cash surpluses** and **returns for investors**. As with all listed private sector companies, these are key organisational objectives and performance measures, provided that they are linked to the risks being taken by the business. Shareholders, who provide the major source of finance for the business, have freedom of choice as to where they can invest their funds and will wish to direct them to those organisations that provide the best opportunities for return at any given risk level.

- Growth in **earnings per share** is regarded as an important yardstick for shareholders.

- Shareholders are also seeking an adequate return for their investment, measured most directly by **return on capital employed.** The return on the investments that the company makes should be comparable with similar risk investments.

(2) **Healthcare service trust**

The public sector trust has **no profit motive**. It receives funds from its main provider, the government, in return for achieving a **range of objectives**, most of which are concerned with **value for money** (effectiveness and quality of output), some of which are **political** and only a few of which are **financial**. Sometimes the government will levy a **financial charge** on money it has advanced for **capital investment**, but this is usually low compared with market borrowing rates. In financial terms, the trust's outputs (ie provision of health care) can often only be measured in cost terms because the services are provided free to customers, in line with government policy.

Profit and financial balance

(1) **Electronics company**

Although criticisms can be raised about both of the stated financial objectives (eg they are **not linked** to **risk measures**, they can **result in unfair comparisons** between companies, they may encourage short term thinking, see (ii) below) these objectives are indicative that for private sector companies the pursuit of profit is an overriding objective which is generally absent from the public sector's control framework. In competitive markets, **sales prices** and **demand** reflect the value that customers put on the company's products and the profit-seeking motive will encourage organisations to search for **improved effectiveness in production and quality of services** given.

(2) **Healthcare service trust**

Government budgeting is very much concerned with **allocating cash** to organisations and requiring them to achieve **defined outputs within the cash limits**. As a result the trust's key financial objective is to 'achieve **financial balance** during the year', that is to ensure that there is **no overspending** and that the available cash is spent appropriately. The fact that services are provided cheaply or free means that there is usually a **large excess of demand over supply** and in this situation, the financial objective usually becomes a constraint limiting the volume of work which the trust can handle.

Stakeholders

(1) **Electronics company**

From the company's point of view, a powerful argument can also be made that the **pursuit of profit** will **encourage the satisfaction** of **other stakeholders' goals.** For example profit cannot be made in the long run unless customers are satisfied with the product, the company adopts an ethical stance and does not alienate public opinion, employees' remuneration packages are motivating, and suppliers are paid on time. Whereas arguments can be made against all of these assertions, it cannot be denied that profit-based financial objectives are key to the success of a private sector organisation.

(2) **Healthcare service trust**

Because of the excess of **demand over supply**, there will be **difficulties** in **balancing the needs of stakeholders**, as discussed in (ii) below.

(ii) **Differences in business risks and how these risks might be managed**

The private sector company's main business risks are concerned with **falling demand** because products are less attractive to customers than those of its competitors. In contrast, the public sector trust's main risk is from disputes over methods of operation in a situation of **excess demand** from customers.

Risks

(1) **Electronics company**

The private sector company's stated financial objectives may, if followed blindly, lead to actions that harm the business. For example:

- Short term cost cutting can **improve profit**, earnings per share and return on capital employed; this may involve **sacrificing development** of new improved products with resulting failure in the longer term.

- Failure to invest in new fixed assets can **improve return on capital employed**, but will again harm longer term business success.

465

(2) **Healthcare service trust**

As indicated above, the financial objective of the public sector health service trust acts as a constraint resulting in **excess demand** for its **services** which cannot be alleviated by customer price increases. The consequent business risks include:

- **Rationing** between customers (potential patients) is unfairly carried out.

- The **general level of services deteriorates** as attempts are made to reduce service costs or increase through-put on existing staff levels.

- **Political interference** or **changes in policy reduce the effectiveness** of trust plans.

- **Capital investment** is **wasted** because no funds are allocated for ongoing running costs (eg new hospitals remain unused).

Risk management

(1) **Electronics company**

Business risk management will involve many techniques including:

- **Continuing reviews** of products and markets; investment on innovation

- **Quality management** approaches

- **Continuing dialogue with stakeholders**: shareholders, customers, employees, suppliers, local community, etc.

- **Insurance, security and other risk reduction activities**

(2) **Healthcare service trust**

Risk management techniques include:

- **Clear policies** and effective management of customer priorities

- A continuing drive for **value for money** (VFM) from internal and external service suppliers; this involves continuous monitoring techniques and special internal audit exercises

- Exercising **market choice** to buy the **most effective health services**

- Constant monitoring of the relevant **political environment** and, if necessary, lobbying

- **Matching capital investment plans** with **increased running costs** for sustainability

(b) **Current position**

The healthcare service trust wishes to fund a new healthcare centre using a £15 million variable interest rate loan from the private sector. Interest and repayment will need to be made out of the trust's income from the government. At current interest rates, these service payments will be relatively small in comparison with total income of £100 million per year. Equal annual repayments would be £15m/8.061 = £1.86 million, or less than 2% of income. The interest rate is relatively low because the loan is effectively underwritten by the government.

Additional financial risk

Nevertheless, there will be an **additional financial risk**. The government may not pay for the loan interest specifically but expect it to be found out of **overall trust income**. If **interest rates rise substantially**, there may have to be corresponding cuts in services. At the margin, key new 'flagship projects' may need to be postponed or abandoned.

Elimination of risk

To eliminate this risk the trust could try to **negotiate a fixed interest loan** with the lender, or to arrange for a **cap to the interest rate** by using an option. Such arrangements would result in higher initial annual payments but would eliminate or reduce the risk of payments rising above an acceptable limit.

Extension of repayment

If the variable rate loan is accepted and interest rates rise, it may be possible to agree with the lender that **repayment** could be **extended** over a longer period – 20 to 30 years is a reasonable possibility with the government acting as guarantor.

Other measures

The additional cash requirements may **need to be found out of improved efficiencies**, lowered purchase prices, or reductions in services offered.

Question 4

Text references. The cost of capital is covered in Chapter 9 and the capital asset pricing model calculation is explained in Chapter 12. Convertible loan stock is covered in Chapter 6.

Top tips. In part (a) make clear the theoretical basis for your calculations. The traditional view and the Modigliani/Miller (MM) approach have different implications for company values at different levels of gearing. It is also helpful to state any assumptions made about the dividend policy. It is useful to calculate the income statement under the different scenarios as a preliminary to finding the market values and cost of equity.

In (b) (ii) you are only asked about the advantages of issuing convertible loan stock; the principal feature is short-term benefits from being able to raise funds at limited cost, with possibly adverse consequences (dilution of earnings, change in control) only happening long-term.

Easy marks. (b) is rather easier than (a), particularly the discussion parts (b) (i) and (ii).

(a) **CAPM**

The purpose of raising the money is not stated. In the absence of details of a project, we assume that it is for restructuring. The first step is to calculate the present cost of equity using the **capital asset pricing model** (CAPM):

$k_e = R_f + [R_m - R_f] \beta$

where k_e = cost of equity (expected return)
   R_f = risk free rate of return (10%)
   β = beta value (1.2)
   R_m = market rate of return (15%)

In this case: k_e = $10 + (15 - 10) \times 1.2$
          = 16%

Dividend valuation model

This cost of equity can now be applied in the **dividend valuation model** to find the **total market value** of the firm. It is assumed that all earnings are distributed as dividend; earnings and therefore dividends do not grow.

$P_0 = d_0/k_e$

where P_0 = market value
   d_0 = current level of dividends (post tax)
   k_e = cost of equity
   P_0 = $400,000 \times 0.67/0.16$
     = €1.675m

(i) **Scenarios**

The situation under the different scenarios can be summarised as follows.

	Current €'000	Scen 1 €'000	Scen 2 €'000
Profit before interest and tax	400.0	400.0	400.0
Less interest	0.0	50.0	120.0
	400.0	350.0	280.0
Less tax at 33%	132.0	115.5	92.4
Distributable profits	268.0	234.5	187.6

Modigliani and Miller

According to the basic theory of capital structure developed by **Modigliani and Miller**, the market value of a firm is independent of capital structure. When tax is introduced into the calculations, the market value of the firm will increase as debt is added to the capital mix because of the present value of the **tax shield** on interest payments. This can be expressed as:

$V_g = V_u + TB_c$

where V_g = market value of the geared company

V_u = market value of the ungeared company

TB_c = value of tax shield

In this case:

	Current €'000	Scen 1 €'000	Scen 2 €'000
V_u	1,675	1,675	1,675
D	0	500	1,000
T	33%	33%	33%
TB_c	0	165	330
Total market value	1,675	1,840	2,005

The value of the equity can now be found:

$E = V_g - D$

Scenario 1: €1.84m – €0.5m = €1.34m

Scenario 2: €2.005m – €1.0m = €1.005m

(ii) The ratio of **debt to equity** is given by D/E:

Scenario 1: 500/1,340 = 37.3%

Scenario 2: 1,000/1,005 = 99.5%

(iii) We calculate a geared beta for both scenarios:

$$\beta_u = \beta_g \frac{V_E}{V_E + V_D(1-t)} + \beta_d \frac{V_D(1-t)}{V_E + V_D(1-t)}$$

SCENARIO 1:

β_d is zero as return = 10%, risk free rate

$$\beta_u = \beta_g \frac{V_E}{V_E + V_D(1-t)}$$

$$1.2 = \beta_g \frac{1.34}{1.34 + 0.5(1-0.33)}$$

$$\beta_g = 1.2 \left(\frac{1.34 + 0.5(1-0.33)}{1.34} \right)$$

$$= 1.5$$

Substituting into CAPM:

$k_e = 10 + (15 - 10)\ 1.5$
$= 17.5\%$

SCENARIO 2:

β_d is not zero, as return (12%) is higher than the risk free rate

Use CAPM to find β_d

$12\% = 10\% + (15 - 10)\ \beta_d$

$\beta_d = 0.4$

$1.2 = \beta_g\ \dfrac{1.005}{1.005 + 1(1 - 0.33)} + 0.4\ \dfrac{1(1 - 0.33)}{1.005 + 1(1 - 0.33)}$

$\beta_g = 1.67\ (1.2 - 0.16)$
$= 1.74$

Substituting into CAPM

$k_e = 10 + (15 - 10)\ 1.74$
$= 18.7\%$

Alternative working

Assuming that all distributable profits are paid as dividends, the **cost of equity** can be found using:

$k_e = d_0/P_0$

where: k_e = cost of equity
         d_0 = dividend (distributable profit above)
         P_0 = market value of equity

Scenario 1: 234.5/1,340 = 17.5%
Scenario 2: 187.6/1,005 = 18.7%

(b)   (i)   **Conversion premium**

The **conversion premium** is the **difference** between the **issue value** of the **stock** and the **conversion value** as at the date of issue. In other words it is the measure of the additional expense involved in buying shares via the convertible stock as compared with buying the shares on the open market immediately.

In this case, €100 loan stock can be converted into 35 ordinary shares. The **effective price** of these shares is therefore €2.86 (€100/35) per share.

The **current market price** of the shares is €2.40. The **conversion premium** is therefore €2.86 – €2.40 = **46 cents**. This can also be expressed in percentage terms as **19%** (0.46/2.40).

       (ii)   **Advantages of issuing convertible loan stock**

       (1)   **Convertibles** should be **cheaper than equity** because they offer greater security to the investor. This may make them particularly attractive in fast growing but high-risk companies.

       (2)   **Issue costs** are **lower** for loan stock than for equity.

       (3)   **Interest** on the **loan stock** is **tax deductible**, unlike dividends on ordinary shares.

       (4)   There is **no immediate change** in the **existing structure** of control, although this will change over time as conversion rights are exercised.

       (5)   There is no **immediate dilution** in **earnings** and **dividends per share**.

(iii) **Dividend policy**

Dividend policy is one of the major factors which determines the share price. Under the **dividend valuation model**, the share price is held to be directly related both to the current dividend and to the expected future growth in dividends:

$$p_0 = \frac{d_0(1+g)}{(k_e - g)}$$

Impact of dividend growth

Thus it can be seen that dividend growth is important in determining the likely market value of the shares. As has already been discussed above, the market value of the shares is very important in determining the price of convertibles, and therefore the dividend policy of the company will have an important effect on the value of convertible stock.

Question 5

Text references. Forecasts are revised in Chapter 3 and the inter-relationships between financing, investment and dividend decisions are discussed in Chapter 1.

Top tips. The format of the cash flow statement in (a) is fairly flexible. The best approach is to set out the proformas and try to fill in as many figures as possible, then do the more complicated workings (for which 5 marks were available between the two).

In (b) the relatively short-term nature of the funding requirement needs to be brought out. Although the question scenario says that the shareholders don't appear willing to subscribe new capital, it's legitimate to point out briefly that they may not have a choice.

Easy marks. The various possibilities in (b) offer the chance to score well, **provided** your answers were tailored to GSD.

Examiner's comments. Generally candidates were able to produce the financial statements and attempt the more complicated calculations, although depreciation was often ignored. Some overlooked the requirement to give advice on the extent of any extra funding required. Answers to (b) were too general, not focused on the situation described. In particular comments on dividend signalling and sale of shares to outsiders were irrelevant as GSD is unquoted.

(a) **Balance sheets, income statements and cash flow analysis for 20X5 and 20X6**

Income statement y/e 31 December	20X5	20X6	
	£m	£m	
Revenue	51.8	59.6	Up 15%
Profit before interest and tax	15.5	17.9	30% of revenue
Interest on bank loan	(0.5)	(0.5)	6% × £8m
Interest on overdraft	(0.1)	(0.2)	6% × opening balance
Profit before tax	14.9	17.2	
Taxation (W2)	(3.4)	(4.3)	
Profit after tax	11.5	12.9	
Dividend	(10.5)	(11.0)	Up 5%
Profit for the year retained	1.0	1.9	
Retained earnings brought forward	4.0	5.0	
Retained earnings carried forward	5.0	6.9	

Balance Sheet at 31 December	20X5	20X6	
	£m	£m	
Property, plant and equipment (W1)	18.7	21.5	
Working capital	10.4	11.9	20% × revenue
	29.1	33.4	
Share capital (50p ordinary)	10.0	10.0	
Retained earnings	5.0	6.9	
Long term borrowings (bank loan)	8.0	8.0	
Short term borrowings (overdraft)	2.7	4.2	
Current tax payable	3.4	4.3	
	29.1	33.4	

Cash flow for y/e 31 December	20X5	20X6	
Profit before interest and tax	15.5	17.9	
Add back: depreciation	6.3	7.2	
Funds generated by operations	21.8	25.1	
Less: Increase in working capital	(1.4)	(1.5)	
Cash generated by operations	20.4	23.6	
Payments: Tax	(1.0)	(3.4)	previous year's tax is paid
Interest	(0.6)	(0.7)	
Dividend	(10.5)	(11.0)	
Purchase of non-current assets	(10.0)	(10.0)	
Net cash flow	(1.7)	(1.5)	
Overdraft brought forward	(1.0)	(2.7)	
Overdraft carried forward	(2.7)	(4.2)	

Working 1	20X5	20X6
Property plant and equipment	£m	£m
Balance brought forward	15.0	18.7
Acquisitions	10.0	10.0
	25.0	28.7
Depreciation 25%	(6.3)	(7.2)
Balance carried forward	18.7	21.5

Working 2	20X5	20X6
Taxation	£m	£m
Profit before tax	14.9	17.2
Add back depreciation	6.3	7.2
Purchase of non-current assets	(10.0)	(10.0)
	11.2	14.4
Tax @ 30%	(3.4)	(4.3)

Overdraft limit

The **overdraft limit** is £1.5 million. This is exceeded by the end of 20X5 and increases during 20X6. The maximum shortfall (end of 20X6) is £4.2m – £1.5m = £2.7m.

Gearing

The **book value of gearing** (long and short term borrowings divided by equity) is 71% in 20X5 (10.7/15) and 72% in 20X6 (12.2/16.9). Both these figures exceed the figure that the bank considers the maximum possible.

(b)   **Financing, investment and dividend strategies**

The results of the financial plans show that the company has reached the limit of its borrowing capacity. It therefore has a choice between **cutting its investment plans** or **finding alternative sources of finance,** one of which is restricting shareholders' dividends. Thus the investment, financing and dividend decisions are all inter-related.

Need for investment

GSD is predicted to **show increasing profits** and its return on total assets (profit before tax divided by total assets) is forecast at a healthy 51% in both years. Its priority is therefore to continue with its investment plans. Any decision to delay the investment could allow competitors to gain an advantage and may reduce opportunities for future funding.

Bank loan

To continue with investment plans, funds must be raised. Although the gearing is in excess of what the bank considered desirable, GSD would approach the bank on the grounds that most of the loan will be repaid in 20X7 and the company expects positive cash flows as shown below.

	20X7	
	£m	
Profit before interest and tax	20.5	17.9×1.15
Add back: Depreciation	7.1	$(21.5 + 7) \times 25\%$
Less: Increase in working capital	(1.8)	$(59.6 \times 1.15 \times 20\%) - 11.9$
Cash generated by operations	25.8	
Payments: Tax	(4.3)	20X6 tax charge
Interest	(0.7)	$(8.0 + 4.2) \times 6\%$
Dividend	(11.6)	11.0×1.05
Purchase of non-current assets	(7.0)	
Net cash flow	2.2	

Need for equity funds

If further borrowing is impossible without impairing relationships with the bank, the company must seek equity funds. The type of equity funds sought will depend partly on whether the funds shortfall is seen as temporary or permanent.

Dividend restrictions

If the company's investment plans are limited to **£7 million** for each of 20X7 to 20X9, then the **funding requirement** is likely to **fall rapidly** assuming profitability is maintained. In this case, it would be best to cover the shortfall in 20X5 and 20X6 by reducing the dividends from the budgeted 5% annual growth. This could easily provide sufficient funds to cover the shortfall for the two years. Such a restriction would, however, need to be **agreed by directors** with the family shareholders. Some family shareholders will be dependent on their dividend income, but might be persuaded that it is in their best interest to sell some of their shares to other members and reinvest elsewhere.

Share issue

If the company predicts that additional expansion plans and investment will arise in 20X7 and beyond then, although continued reduction in dividends might be able to provide the necessary finance, it might be better to attempt to seek new cash from shareholders by way of a **rights issue.** This would enable those who wish to invest to **subscribe for new shares**, whereas other family members may wish to sell their rights and effectively reduce their shareholdings.

CIMA – Strategic Level

Paper P9

Management Accounting – Financial Strategy

Mock Examination 3

Instructions to candidates:

You are allowed three hours to answer this question paper.
In the real exam, you are allowed 20 minutes reading time before the examination begins during which you should read the question paper, and if you wish, make annotations on the question paper. However, you will **not** be allowed, **under any circumstances**, to open the answer book and start writing or use your calculator during this reading time.
You are strongly advised to carefully read the question requirement before attempting the question concerned.
Answer the ONE compulsory question in Section A.
Answer TWO of the FOUR questions in Section B.

DO NOT OPEN THIS PAPER UNTIL YOU ARE READY TO START UNDER EXAMINATION CONDITIONS

SECTION A – 50 MARKS

Answer this question
Read the scenario and answer the question

Question 1

Scenario

SHINE

Business background

SHINE is a publicly owned multinational group based in Germany with its main business centred on the production and distribution of gas and electricity to industrial and domestic consumers. It has recently begun investing in research and development in relation to renewable energy, exploiting solar, wave or wind energy to generate electricity.

Corporate objectives

Developing renewable energy sources is an important non-financial objective for the SHINE Group in order to protect and enhance the group's reputation. Renewable energy projects have been given a high profile in recent investor communications and television advertising campaigns.

Wind farm investment project

The latest renewable energy project under consideration is the development of a wind farm in the USA. This would involve the construction of 65 wind powered electricity generators which would be owned and operated by a new, local subsidiary entity and electricity that is generated by the farm would be sold to the local electricity grid. A suitable site, subject to planning permission, has been located.

Forecast operating cash flows for the project are as follows:

	Year(s)	US$ million
Initial investment (including working capital)	0	200
Residual value	4	50
Pre-tax operating net cash inflows	1 to 4	70

Other relevant data and assumptions:

- The initial investment is expected to be made on 30 November 20X6 and cash flows will arise at any point in the year.

- However, in any net present value (NPV) exercise, all cash flows should be assumed to arise on 31 December of each year.

- The local tax rate in the USA for this industry is set at a preferential rate of 10% to encourage environmentally-friendly projects rather than the normal rate of 25%.

- Tax is payable in the year in which it arises.

- No tax depreciation allowances are available.

- No additional tax is payable in Germany under the terms of the double tax treaties with the USA.

- Net cash flows are to be paid to the German parent entity as dividends at the end of each year.

Uncertainties affecting the outcome of the project

There is some uncertainty over the US tax rate over the period of the project, with extensive discussion at local government level about raising the tax rate to 25% with immediate effect. A vote will be taken in the next six months to decide whether to retain the preferential 10% tax rate, or to increase it to 25%. Once the vote has been taken and a decision made, the tax rate will not be open for debate again for at least four years.

Economic forecasters expect the value of the euro to either stay constant against the value of the US dollar for the next four years or to strengthen by 7% per annum. Assume that there is an equal probability of each of these two different exchange rate forecasts.

There is also significant risk to the project from strong objections to the wind farm scheme from local farmers in the USA who are concerned about the impact of acid water run-off from boring holes for the 65 windmills. In addition, there are a number of executive holiday homes nearby whose owners are objecting to the visual impact of the windmills.

Investment criteria

The SHINE Group evaluates foreign projects of this nature based on a euro cost of capital of 12% which reflects the risk profile of the proposed investment.

Extracts from the forecast financial statements for the SHINE Group at 31 December 20X6, the end of the current financial year:

	€ million	€ million
Assets		
Total assets		28,000
Equity and liabilities		
Equity		
Share capital (3,000 million €1 ords)	3,000	
Retained earnings	8,300	
		11,300
Non-current liabilities		
Floating rate borrowings		4,000
Current liabilities		12,700
		28,000

Alternative financing methods

The SHINE Group aims to maintain the group gearing ratio (debt as a proportion of debt plus equity) below 40% based on book values.

The following alternative methods are being considered by the SHINE parent entity for financing the new investment:

- Long-term borrowings denominated in euro.
- Long-term borrowings denominated in US dollars.

Required

(a) Calculate the NPV of the cash flows for the proposed investment for **each** of the following four possible scenarios:

- Constant exchange rate and a tax rate of 10%.

- Constant exchange rate and a tax rate of 25%.

- The euro to strengthen against the US dollar by 7% a year and a tax rate of 10%.

- The euro to strengthen against the US dollar by 7% a year and a tax rate of 25%.

In each case, assume that the exchange rate at year 0 is US$1·10 = €1·00. **(12 marks)**

(b)   Prepare the forecast balance sheet of the SHINE Group on 31 December 20X6, incorporating the project under each of the two alternative financing structures and each of the following two exchange rate scenarios A and B:

Date	Exchange rates under scenario A	Exchange rates under scenario B
30 November 20X6 (date of the initial investment and arrangement of financing)	US$1·10 = €1·00	US$1·10 = €1·00
31 December 20X6 (financial reporting/balance sheet date)	US$1·10 = €1·00 (no change)	US$1·40 = €1·00

Assume that no other project cash flows occur until 20X7.   **(8 marks)**

(c)   Write a report addressed to the Directors of the SHINE Group in which you, as Finance Director, address the following issues relating to the evaluation and implementation of the proposed wind farm project:

   (i)   Discuss the internal and external constraints affecting the investment decision and advise the SHINE Group how to proceed. In your answer, include reference to your calculations in part (a) above.
   (9 marks)

   (ii)   Discuss the comparative advantages of each of the two proposed alternative financing structures and advise the SHINE group which one to adopt. In your answer include reference to your results in part (b) above, and further analysis and discussion of the impact of each proposed financial structure on the group's balance sheet.   **(9 marks)**

   (iii) Discuss the differing roles and responsibilities of the treasury department and finance department in evaluating and implementing the US project and the interaction of the two departments throughout the process.   **(8 marks)**

Marks available for structure and presentation in Question 1.   **(4 marks)**

(Total = 50 marks)

SECTION B – 50 marks

Answer only TWO of the FOUR questions

Question 2

AB is a telecommunications consultancy based in Europe that trades globally. It was established 15 years ago. The four founding shareholders own 25% of the issued share capital each and are also executive directors of the entity. The shareholders are considering a flotation of AB on a European stock exchange and have started discussing the process and a value for the entity with financial advisers. The four founding shareholders, and many of the entity's employees, are technical experts in their field, but have little idea how entities such as theirs are valued.

Assume you are one of AB's financial advisors. You have been asked to estimate a value for the entity and explain your calculations and approach to the directors. You have obtained the following information.

Summary financial data for the past three years and forecast revenue and costs for the next two years is as follows:

Income Statement for the years ended 31 March

	Actual			Forecast	
	20X4	20X5	20X6	20X7	20X8
	€ million	€ million	€ million	€ million	€ million
Revenue	125.0	137.5	149.9	172.0	198.0
Less:					
Cash operating costs	37.5	41.3	45.0	52.0	59.0
Depreciation	20.0	22.0	48.0	48.0	48.0
Pre-tax earnings	67.5	74.2	56.9	72	91
Taxation	20.3	22.3	17.1	22	27

Balance Sheet at 31 March

	20X4	20X5	20X6
	€ million	€ million	€ million
Assets			
Non-current assets			
Property, plant and equipment	150	175	201
Current assets	48	54	62
	198	229	263
Equity and liabilities			
Equity			
Share capital (Shares of €1)	30	30	30
Retained earnings	148	179	203
	178	209	233
Current liabilities	20	20	30
	198	229	263

Note: The book valuations of non-current assets are considered to reflect current realisable values.

Other information/assumptions

- Growth in after tax cash flows for 20X9 and beyond (assume indefinitely) is expected to be 3% per annum. Cash operating costs can be assumed to remain at the same percentage of revenue as in previous years. Depreciation will fluctuate but, for purposes of evaluation, assume the 20X8 charge will continue indefinitely. Tax has been payable at 30% per annum for the last three years. This rate is expected to continue for the foreseeable future and tax will be payable in the year in which the liability arises.

- The average P/E ratio for telecommunication entities' shares quoted on European stock exchanges has been 12·5 over the past 12 months. However, there is a wide variation around this average and AB might be able to command a rating up to 30% higher than this.

- An estimated cost of equity capital for the industry is 10% after tax.

- The average pre-tax return on total assets for the industry over the past 3 years has been 15%.

Required

(a)   Calculate a range of values for AB, in total and per share, using methods of valuation that you consider appropriate. Where relevant, include an estimate of value for intellectual capital.   **(12 marks)**

(b)   Discuss the methods of valuation you have used, explaining the relevance of each method to an entity such as AB. Conclude with a recommendation of an approximate flotation value for AB, in total and per share.

(13 marks)

(Total = 25 marks)

A report format is **not** required for this question.

Question 3

VCI is a venture capital investor that specialises in providing finance to small but established businesses. At present, its expected average pre-tax return on equity investment is a nominal 30% per annum over a five-year investment period.

YZ is a typical client of VCI. It is a 100% family owned transport and distribution business whose shares are unlisted. The company sustained a series of losses a few years ago, but the recruitment of some professional managers and an aggressive marketing policy returned the company to profitability. Its most recent accounts show revenue of $105 million and profit before interest and tax of $28·83 million. Other relevant information is as follows:

- For the last three years dividends have been paid at 40% of earnings and the directors have no plans to change this payout ratio.

- Taxation has averaged 28% per annum over the past few years and this rate is likely to continue.

- The directors are forecasting growth in earnings and dividends for the foreseeable future of 6% per annum.

- YZ's accountants estimated the entity's cost of equity capital at 10% some years ago. The data they worked with was incomplete and now out of date. The current cost could be as high as 15%.

Extracts from its most recent balance sheet **at 31 March 20X6** are shown below.

	$ million
Assets	
Non-current assets	
Property, plant and equipment	35·50
Current assets	4.50
	40·00
Equity and liabilities	
Equity	
Share capital (Nominal value of 10 cents)	2.25
Retained earnings	18.00
	20.25
Non-current liabilities	
7% Secured bond repayable in ten years' time	15.00
Current liabilities	4.75
	19.75
	40.00

Note: The entity's vehicles are mainly financed by operating leases.

YZ has now reached a stage in its development that requires additional capital of $25 million. The directors, and major shareholders, are considering a number of alternative forms of finance. One of the alternatives they are considering is venture capital funding and they have approached VCI. In preliminary discussions, VCI has suggested it might be able to finance the necessary $25 million by purchasing a percentage of YZ's equity. This will, of course, involve YZ issuing new equity.

Required

(a) Assume you work for VCI and have been asked to evaluate the potential investment.

   (i) Using YZ's forecast of growth and its estimates of cost of capital, calculate the number of new shares that YZ will have to issue to VCI in return for its investment and the percentage of the entity VCI will then own. Comment briefly on your result. **(9 marks)**

   (ii) Evaluate exit strategies that might be available to VCI in five years' time and their likely acceptability to YZ. **(6 marks)**

Note: Use sensible roundings in your calculations.

(b)   Discuss the advantages and disadvantages to an established business such as YZ of using a venture capital entity to provide finance for expansion as compared with long term debt. Advise YZ about which type of finance it should choose, based on the information available so far.   **(10 marks)**

(Total = 25 marks)

A report format is **not** required for this question.

Question 4

CD is a furniture manufacturer based in the UK. It manufactures a limited range of furniture products to a very high quality and sells to a small number of retail outlets worldwide.

At a recent meeting with one of its major customers it became clear that the market is changing and the final consumer of CD's products is now more interested in variety and choice rather than exclusivity and exceptional quality.

CD is therefore reviewing two mutually exclusive alternatives to apply to a selection of its products:

Alternative 1

To continue to manufacture, but expand its product range and reduce its quality. The net present value (NPV), internal rate of return (IRR) and modified internal rate of return (MIRR) for this alternative have already been calculated as follows:

NPV   =   £1·45 million using a nominal discount rate of 9%

IRR   =   10·5%

MIRR   =   Approximately 13·2%   → investing e less than WACC ?

Alternative 2

To import furniture carcasses in 'flat packs' from the USA. The imports would be in a variety of types of wood and unvarnished. CD would buy in bulk from its US suppliers, assemble and varnish the furniture and re-sell, mainly to existing customers. An initial investigation into potential sources of supply and costs of transportation has already been carried out by a consultancy entity at a cost of £75,000.

CD's Finance Director has provided estimates of net sterling and US$ cash flows for this alternative. These net cash flows, in **real** terms, are shown below.

Year	0	1	2	3
US$m	(25.00)	2.60	3.80	4.10
£m	0	3.70	4.20	4.60

The following information is relevant:

- CD evaluates all its investments using nominal sterling cash flows and a nominal discount rate. All non-UK customers are invoiced in US$. US$ nominal cash flows are converted to sterling at the forward rate and discounted at the UK nominal rate.

- For the purposes of evaluation, assume the entity has a three year time horizon for investment appraisals.

- Based on recent economic forecasts, inflation rates in the US are expected to be constant at 4% per annum. UK inflation rates are expected to be 3% per annum. The current exchange rate is £1 = US$1·6.

Note: Ignore taxation.

Required

Assume that you are the Financial Manager of CD.

(a)   Calculate the net present value (NPV), internal rate of return (IRR) and (approximate) modified internal rate of return (MIRR) of alternative 2. **(12 marks)**

(b)   Briefly discuss the appropriateness and possible advantages of providing MIRRs for the evaluation of the two alternatives. **(4 marks)**

(c)   Evaluate the two alternatives and recommend which alternative the entity should choose. Include in your answer some discussion about what other criteria could or should be considered before a final decision is taken. **(9 marks)**

(Total = 25 marks)

A report format is **not** required for this question.

Question 5

(a) CCC is a local government entity. It is financed almost equally by a combination of central government funding and local taxation. The funding from central government is determined largely on a *per capita* (per head of population) basis, adjusted to reflect the scale of deprivation (or special needs) deemed to exist in CCC's region. A small percentage of its finance comes from the private sector, for example from renting out City Hall for private functions.

CCC's main objectives are:

- To make the region economically prosperous and an attractive place to live and work;
- To provide service excellence in health and education for the local community.

DDD is a large, listed entity with widespread commercial and geographical interests. For historic reasons, its headquarters are in CCC's region. This is something of an anomaly as most entities of DDD's size would have their HQ in a capital city, or at least a city much larger than where it is.

DDD has one financial objective: To increase shareholder wealth by an average 10% per annum. It also has a series of non-financial objectives that deal with how the entity treats other stakeholders, including the local communities where it operates.

DDD has total net assets of $1·5 billion and a gearing ratio of 45% (debt to debt plus equity), which is typical for its industry. It is currently considering raising a substantial amount of capital to finance an acquisition.

Required

Discuss the criteria that the two very different entities described above have to consider when setting objectives, recognising the needs of each of their main stakeholder groups. Make some reference in your answer to the consequences of each of them failing to meet its declared objectives. **(13 marks)**

(b) MS is a private entity in a computer-related industry. It has been trading for six years and is managed by its main shareholders, the original founders of the entity. Most of the employees are also shareholders, having been given shares as bonuses. None of the shareholders has attempted to sell shares in the entity so the problem of placing a value on them has not arisen. Dividends have been paid every year at the rate of 60 cents per share, irrespective of profits. So far, profits have always been sufficient to cover the dividend at least once but never more than twice.

MS is all-equity financed at present although $15 million new finance is likely to be required in the near future to finance expansion. Total net assets as at the last balance sheet date were $45 million.

Required

Discuss and compare the relationship between dividend policy, investment policy and financing policy in the context of the small entity described above, MS, and DDD, the large listed entity described in part (a)

(12 marks)

(Total = 25 marks)

Answers

DO NOT TURN THIS PAGE UNTIL YOU HAVE
COMPLETED THE MOCK EXAM

A PLAN OF ATTACK

We've already established that you've been told to do it 102 times, so it is of course superfluous to tell you for the 103rd time to **Take a good look at the paper before diving in to answer questions**. Then work out **which questions to do**, the **order** in which to attempt and spend the remainder of the 20 minutes' reading time going through **Question 1**.

The next step

You may be thinking that this paper is a lot more straightforward than the first two mock exams; however, having sailed through the first two mocks, you may think this paper is actually rather difficult.

Option 1 (Don't like it)

If you think this paper is quite tough, it may be best to do the optional questions before tackling the case study **Question 1**. Don't forget though that you **must** leave one and a half hours to answer the case study.

- **Question 2** is a business valuation question which you can expect in this paper. The calculations have some tricky parts but over half of the marks are available for a straightforward discussion.

- The calculations in **Question 3** may look daunting as you might not know where to start. There are however plenty of marks available if you have a good knowledge of venture capital.

- **Question 4** is a good choice if you have done enough practice on investment appraisal involving inflation and exchange rates. There are also quite a few marks available for using your knowledge of business strategy.

- **Question 5** doesn't involve any calculations so may tempt you for that reason alone. However, the requirements make it clear that your answers must be very clearly put in the context of the specific organisations mentioned in the question.

- Part (a) of **Question 1** has some relatively easy calculations which you should be able to tackle. There are 4 easy marks available for structure and presentation in this question so set out a proper report format in part (c) and write as many well structured points as you can, making sure you specifically answer the questions.

Option 2 (It's a pleasant surprise)

Are you sure it is? If you are then that's encouraging. You'll feel even happier when you've got the compulsory question out the way, so you should consider doing **Question 1** first.

- Don't run over time on the calculations in **Question 1** as you could take more time than necessary doing unnecessary laborious calculations for each scenario. The report will take you quite a long time to write and is worth 30 marks.

- **Question 2** may look like a standard valuation question but there are some difficult aspects such as intellectual capital and depreciation which you will need to be careful with.

- The majority of marks in **Question 3** are for discussion on venture capital so only do this question if you have sufficient knowledge of this form of finance.

- Make sure you know how to do MIRR calculations before choosing **Question 4.**

- The main danger in **Question 5** is not to tie your answer into the scenarios firmly enough. A general waffle will not please the examiner!

Once, once more

You must **allocate your time** according to the marks for the question in total, and for the parts of the questions. And you must also **follow the requirements exactly**.

Finished with fifteen minutes to spare?

Looks like you slipped up on the time allocation. However if you have, make sure you don't waste the last few minutes; go back to **any parts of questions that you didn't finish** because you ran out of time.

Forget about it!

Just wipe it from your mind.

Question 1

Text references. Investment appraisal methods are covered in Chapter 18 and the role of the Treasury department in Chapter 14.

Top tips. Parts (a) and (b) are straightforward calculations that need a logical, methodical approach. Save time by only doing the calculations necessary. For example, do not write out a complete NPV calculation for the second scenario. Part (c)(iii) is **not** asking you to write everything you know about treasury and finance departments. Make sure you answer the actual question.

Easy marks. Part (a) consists of very straightforward NPV calculations for twelve marks. Part (b) has some unusual calculations but is straightforward as long as you can remember what to do with an exchange rate gain.

Four marks are available for structure and presentation so use clear tables for the calculations and a proper format in part (b).

(a) **NPV of the cash flows for the investment**

Scenario 1: Constant exchange rate; tax rate 10%

	Year	$m	Ex. rate $/€	€m	12% discount factors	PV €m
Initial investment	0	(200)	1.10	(181.8)	1.000	(181.8)
Residual value	4	50	1.10	45.4	0.636	28.9
Pre-tax operating net cash inflows	1 to 4	70	1.10	63.6	3.037	193.2
Tax on operating cash flows	1 to 4	(7)	1.10	(6.4)	3.037	(19.4)
NPV						20.9

The NPV is positive: **€20.9 million**.

Scenario 2: Constant exchange rate; tax rate 25%

The figures will be the same except that the tax on operating cash flows is 15% higher. Thus the NPV will be 20.9 – [19.4 × 15/10] = 20.9 – 29.1 = **€(8.2 million)**.

Scenario 3: Euro strengthens against dollar by 7% a year; tax rate 10%

The exchange rate is found by multiplying by 1.07 each year.

	Year	$m	Ex. rate	€m	12%	PV
Initial investment	0	(200)	1.10	(181.8)	1.000	(81.8)
After tax cash flows (90%)	1	63	1.18	53.4	0.893	47.7
"	2	63	1.26	50.0	0.797	39.9
"	3	63	1.35	46.7	0.712	33.2
"	4	63	1.44	43.8	0.636	27.8
Residual value	4	50	1.44	34.7	0.636	22.1
NPV						(11.1)

The NPV is negative: **€(11.1 million)**.

Scenario 4: Euro strengthens against dollar by 7% a year; tax rate 25%

	Year	$m	Ex. rate	€m	12%	PV
Initial investment	0	(200)	1.10	(181.8)	1.000	(181.8)
After tax cash flows (75%)	1	52.5	1.18	44.5	0.893	39.7
"	2	52.5	1.26	41.7	0.797	33.2
"	3	52.5	1.35	38.9	0.712	27.7
"	4	52.5	1.44	36.5	0.636	23.2
Residual value	4	50	1.44	34.7	0.636	22.1
						(35.9)

The NPV is negative: **€(35.9 million)**.

(b) **Forecast balance sheet of the SHINE group at 31 December 20X6**

1 **Financing with long term borrowings denominated in euros**

Investment assets will be translated at the exchange rate which applies when they were acquired. The cost of the investment is $200 million. At 30 November 20X6 this is 200 / 1.1 = €182 million.

The loan to buy these assets is denominated in euros: €182 million. The balance sheet will be the same under both exchange rate scenarios.

	€ million
Total assets	28,182
Equity	
Share capital	3,000
Retained earnings	8,300
	11,300
Non-current liabilities	
Floating rate borrowings: Euros	4,182
Current liabilities	12,700
Total equity and liabilities	28,182
Gearing: Debt / (Debt + Equity) (4,182/11,300 + 4,182)	27%

2 **Financing with long term borrowings denominated in US dollars**

Under both exchange rate scenarios, the investment assets will be translated at 1.1, giving €182 million, as above.

The US $200 million loan is translated at the rate applying on the balance sheet date, 31 December 20X6. Under scenario A this translates to €182 million, but under scenario B it is 200 / 1.40 = €143 million, giving an exchange rate gain of €39 million, which is added to reserves. The two scenarios are shown below.

Scenario	A	B
	€ million	€ million
Total assets	28,182	28,182
Equity		
Share capital	3,000	3,000
Retained earnings	8,300	8,300
Exchange rate gain		39
	11,300	11,339
Non-current liabilities		
Floating rate borrowings: Euros	4,000	4,000
US dollars	182	143
	4,182	4,143
Current liabilities	12,700	12,700
Total equity and liabilities	28,182	28,182
Gearing: Debt / (Debt + Equity)	27%	27%

(c)   To: Board of Directors, SHINE Group

        From: Finance Director

Evaluation and implementation of the proposed wind farm project

Introduction

The proposed wind farm project enables SHINE to further the key objective of developing renewable energy sources. The purpose behind this objective is not just to make high financial returns but also to protect and enhance our reputation as a socially and environmentally caring global energy organisation. As such, the project is assured extensive media coverage following recent television and investor campaigns.

This report offers advice and opinions on three areas:

- Constraints affecting the investment decision
- The alternative proposed financing structures
- The inter-related roles of the treasury and finance departments when making decisions of this type

(i)   **Internal and external constraints affecting the investment decision**

        Within the SHINE organisation, the investment decision is constrained by internal constraints:

        (1)   **The need to achieve the purpose behind the renewable resources objective**

                The ultimate objective is good publicity for the Group. We must be prepared to invest in achieving this and in managing any factors that may potentially damage this publicity. The potential objections from the local community are key risks that must be managed (see below).

        (2)   **The need to achieve a reasonable financial return from the project**

                Although the financial returns are not required to be high, we cannot, as a public company, afford to make high losses on projects of this type. This would damage shareholder confidence.

        (3)   **Incomplete knowledge and skills**

                We are dealing with technological areas that are relatively new to us and we also suffer from a lack of knowledge of the local laws and culture. Steps will need to be taken to fill this information gap.

        (4)   **Management time and resources**

                Development of these cutting-edge projects uses up considerable amounts of management time at all levels. It is difficult to quantify this effect, but the danger is that existing profitable business suffers. Effective project management is essential.

        A number of external constraints on the project are emerging:

        (1)   **Local protest – farmers**

                A group of farmers is concerned with the possibility of acid water from boreholes, and we need to explore ways in which this can be **prevented**, and the associated **costs** of doing so.

        (2)   **Local protest – executive homeowners**

                The damage done to the previously unspoiled views from these homes cannot be avoided. We need to **defuse** this protest before it gains momentum in the local community, and this may require compensation or purchase of some of the properties.

        (3)   **Risk of future tax increases**

                The tax on this type of project is at the moment at a preferential rate of 10%, but the local government is seriously considering abolishing this concession, which would raise the tax rate to 25%. Our calculations (see part (a)) show that this would be likely to cost between €25 – €30 million and would **remove any chance of a positive financial return**. We need to

491

consult with local experts and make a strategic decision whether to live with this risk or to take positive steps to **mitigate** it, for example by setting up or assisting a local lobby group, or by negotiating a project-specific tax concession.

(4)   **Exchange rate risk**

As with all foreign projects we run the risk that the currency in which we expect to earn profits (US dollars) will decline against our home currency (Euro). Our calculations show that a steady strengthening of the euro against the dollar of 7% per year for four years would cost between €28 – €30 million. This risk can be **mitigated** by financing the project with a US dollar loan, as explained in (ii) below.

(5)   **Volatility of energy prices**

Risks for this project are estimated to be normal for our business.

(ii)   **Proposed alternative financing structures**

Two financing structures have been proposed by treasury department: long term borrowing in either euros or US dollars. Both of these methods pass the test that **gearing** (debt divided by the total of equity plus debt) should not become greater then 40%.

The differences between these methods are:

*   They may have different **interest costs** in real terms; and
*   They certainly have different effects on overall **exchange rate risk**.

Interest costs

As regards **interest costs**, a careful comparison must be made before making a decision. If borrowing in one currency appears cheaper than in another, this effect can and will often be removed by movements in the exchange rate between the currencies. Nevertheless there can be differences between the real interest costs of the loans, for example because the company may have a **comparative advantage** when borrowing in its own main currency, the euro.

Exchange rate risk

As regards **exchange rate risk**, a US dollar loan will be subject to substantial exchange gains or losses in response to **currency movements**, and these show up as **translation** gains or losses in the balance sheet (see calculation (b2) above), and real gains or losses in **cash flows** (economic exposure).

However when the US dollar loan is used to finance a project that generates income in the same currency (US dollars), exchange losses on the earnings are substantially offset by exchange gains on the loan. Similarly exchange gains on the earnings are substantially offset by exchange losses on the loan. This compensating effect is known as a '**currency hedge**' and has the effect of making overall cash flows more predictable and less risky if the company borrows in the same currency as the project earnings.

By contrast, the euro loan has no risk in itself (see calculation (b1) above), but fails to provide any hedge against exchange risk on the US dollar earnings of the project, so that the overall combination of project and finance is more **risky** if the company borrows in euros than if it borrows in dollars.

Recommendation

The **objective** of this project is to **avoid making losses** rather than to make high profits. The hedging effect of the US dollar loan will help achieve this and we therefore recommend that the project should be financed by borrowing in US dollars.

(iii) **Roles of treasury and finance departments in appraisal and implementation of the project**

The roles of these two departments are interrelated during the appraisal of the project, and during project planning and implementation.

Project appraisal

During the project appraisal stage, the role of the finance department is to use information from the project forecasts to make projections of annual cash flows and profits, over the whole of the project life. These are then analysed in statements of profitability, cash flow and project appraisal, including net present value computations. Project and activity forecasts are assessed against alternatives in order to decide the **best course of action** at each stage.

During the appraisal stage, the treasury department considers the financial implications of alternative sources of project finance. The treasury department attempts to balance the cost of finance against its risk, including the appropriate mix between long term and short term finance, equity and debt (gearing) and financial risk, interest rate risk and currency risk.

The decision information produced by these two departments is inter-related. For example, foreign projects are often best financed by loans in the same currency (see (ii) above), and the borrowing capacity of a project can make it worthwhile even if its base case NPV is not good.

Project planning

Once a project has received permission to proceed, the finance department will assist with **preparation of detailed budgets** and devising an accounting and monitoring system that will produce the required **performance information** for all stakeholders.

The treasury department will make arrangements for **raising** the necessary finance, as decided during the appraisal stage, and for setting up procedures for monitoring and handling cash, managing working capital and currency and interest rate risk.

Project implementation

During project implementation, the finance department monitors financial records of actual operations against budgets and feeds back information to project managers, in order to seek explanations of variances and to encourage improvements or changes to plan where necessary.

The treasury department similarly monitors cash, working capital, currency risk and interest rate risk. It reviews financing options throughout the project. For example there may be opportunities to terminate loans and refinance, or to enter into swaps

Question 2

Text references. Business valuation is covered in Chapter 15.

Top tips. This looks like a relatively standard business valuation question but there are some tricky elements. The technical expertise mentioned means there is intellectual capital which needs to be valued. An alternative valuation to the one presented here would be to deduct current liabilities from the total assets. Depreciation needs to be dealt with in a calculation of the present value of free cash flow.

Easy marks. Part (b) requires a straightforward explanation of business valuation methods but you **must** make sure you explain the **relevance** to AB.

(a) **Asset valuations**

The net realisable value of AB's net assets at 20X6 is equal to the book value of its equity: **€233 million**.

However, this value excludes one of AB's main assets, its intellectual capital value. One way of estimating this is to use the industry information on return on total assets.

For the industry as a whole, the average pre-tax return on total assets for the past 3 years has been 15%. AB's average pre-tax earnings for 20X4-6 was (67.5 + 74.2 + 56.9)/3 = €66.2 million. Applying a 15% capitalisation rate, gives a total asset value of 66.2/15% = €441 million, an excess of €178 million over AB's total asset value at 20X6 of €263 million.

Thus the net asset value, including intellectual capital value, is 233 + 178 = **€411 million**.

P/E basis valuation

The telecommunications average P/E has been 12.5, but it is thought that AB's P/E may be up to 30% higher, i.e. 16.25. These two P/E's are applied to AB's after tax earnings in the table below: the actual results for 20X6 and the forecast results for 20X7.

		20X6 €m	20X7 €m
Pre-tax earnings		56.9	72.0
Tax		17.1	22.0
After tax earnings		39.8	50.0
Apply P/E	12.5	497.5	625.0
Apply P/E	16.25	646.8	812.5

Using this method, the value of the company is between **€498 million** and **€813 million**.

Present value of free cash flow

There are several definitions of free cash flow, and the calculation shown here is one illustrative approach.

The cash flows for 20X7, 20X8, 20X9 and beyond are shown below.

	20X7 €m	20X8 €m	20X9 and beyond €m
Pre-tax earnings	72	91	
Tax 30%	(22)	(27)	
After tax earnings	50	64	
Add back depreciation	48	48	
After tax cash flows	98	112	115.36 growing at 3% p.a. indefinitely

In 20X9 onwards the after tax cash flows are assumed to grow at 3% per annum (given). As the company has no borrowings, the present value of these cash flows is found by discounting at the cost of equity capital, 10% p.a.

The perpetuity from 20X9 onwards has a present value at the end of 20X8 of $\dfrac{\text{Earnings}(1+g)}{r-g} =$

115.36/(0.10 – 0.03) = €1,648 million. The present value at end of 20X6 of the cash flows from 20X7 onwards is:

		€m	10% factors	€m
Year 1:	20X7	98.0	0.909	89.1
Year 2:	20X8	112.0	0.826	92.5
	Perpetuity	1648.0	0.826	1361.2
				1542.8

After tax cash flows are available for reinvestment and distribution. As depreciation is assumed to be constant to perpetuity, it may be assumed that capital investment each year is equal to depreciation. Thus the present value of capital investment cash flows is 48/0.1 = €480 million.

Although it is not really material, investment in working capital should also be computed. In 20X7 this is likely to be 3% of (current assets – current liabilities) = 3% × €32 million = €0.96 million, growing at 3% p.a., which has a present value to perpetuity of 0.96(1 + 0.03)/(0.10 – 0.03) = €14 million.

The present value of free cash flow available to equity is 1543 – 480 – 14 = **€1,049 million**

Range of values for AB

Using different valuation bases, the range of values for AB is summarised as follows:

	Total	Per share
Value of tangible net assets	€233 million	€7.77
Value of net assets including intellectual capital	€411 million	€13.70
Price/earnings ratio based valuation	€497.5 to €812.5 million	€16.58 to €27.08
Present value of free cash flows	€1,049 million	€34.97

(b) **Valuation methods**

All assets, including businesses, can be valued on several bases, the chief of which are **realisable value**, **replacement cost** and **economic value**.

The economic value of an business is the net present value of cash flows expected to be generated by the business. For a going concern this will usually be considerably **higher** than the net realisable value or the replacement cost of the business assets, and this is the justification for staying in business.

This is borne out by the figures for AB, where asset based valuations are low compared with the economic values, represented by the P/E and free cash flow valuations.

Tangible net assets

The **value of tangible net assets** gives a **minimum value** for the business and represents the cash that could be raised if the business was wound up, tangible assets sold and cash collected and paid out to creditors. As such it is only relevant to AB's potential flotation value to the extent that it shows investors this minimum value in the event of a severe downturn in business.

Assets including intellectual capital

The **asset value including intellectual capital** is an attempt to recognise that for consultancy companies much of the value is tied up in the **knowledge and skills of its employees**, rather than in plant and machinery. Hence the value is significantly higher than that of the tangible net assets alone. The relevance of intellectual capital value to the business value depends on the extent to which it belongs to the business as opposed to individual employees. If AB wishes to obtain a flotation, it is wise to tie in key employees with contracts and to ensure that all key processes are patented or copyrighted where possible.

Price-earnings ratio

The most **popular** method for making a going concern valuation is to multiply estimated equity earnings by an agreed Price/Earnings ratio. For AB this gives a wide range of possible values, depending on the estimates of earnings and on the P/E ratio used. The method is **simplistic** and makes only crude adjustments for key valuation factors such as expected growth rate, business risk and financial risk.

Free cash flow

The **free cash flow method** attempts to compute the **present value of cash available** to equity after making specific adjustments for investment in fixed assts and working capital. In practice, the method would be carried out more rigorously, with capital expenditure budgets specifically examined. As AB is an all equity company and its risk profile is assumed to be unchanged in the future, the discount rate used is the cost of equity capital, which is the minimum required rate of return on equity. This valuation method therefore produces an estimate of the **maximum** price that new investors would pay for the company.

Conclusion

An average of the range of values would be approximately €600m or €20 per share and this is arguably as valid a valuation as any that have been presented.

In practice all business values are subject to **negotiation**, and the figures calculated are only **guides** for investors and the company managers. If the directors of AB decide that they would like to float the company, the ultimate price would depend on supply and demand, which in turn depends on market-wide conditions as well as the availability of specific alternative routes, such as potential sale of the business to other companies.

Question 3

> **Text references.** Venture capital is covered in Chapter 16 and business valuation in Chapter 15.
>
> **Top tips.** Your difficulty with this question may be knowing where to start! The easiest way is to set out the results for YZ and then use the value of dividends in the dividend valuation model to work out the value of the company.
>
> **Easy marks.** The discussions in parts (a) (ii) and (b) are straightforward, provided you know enough about venture capital.

(a)   (i)   **Issue of shares to VCI**

A summary of YZ's results for the year ended 31 March 20X6 shows the following:

	$m
Revenue	105.00
Profit before interest and tax	28.83
Interest: 7% × $15m	1.05
Profit before tax	27.78
Tax: 28%	7.78
Profit after tax	20.00
Dividends: 40%	8.00
Retained earnings	12.00

Valuing the company on the basis of the dividend valuation model, and a constant growth rate of 6% per annum gives the following:

Cost of equity	Company value = $\dfrac{d_0(1+g)}{ke-g}$	No of shares	Value per share
10%	$8m × 1.06/(0.1 − 0.06) = $212 million	22.5	$9.42
15%	$8m × 1.06/(0.15 − 0.06) = $94 million	22.5	$4.18

To raise an additional $25 million, the number of shares issued to VCI will be as follows:

If cost of equity is 10%: $25m/$9.42 = 2.65 million shares, say **2.7 million** (= 11% of equity).
If cost of equity is 15%: $25m/$4.18 = 5.98 million shares, say **6.0 million** (= 21% of equity).

The above calculation for the value of the company, and hence the number of new shares that would be issued to VCI, is subject to **considerable uncertainty**, both for the **growth rate** (6% to perpetuity is high) and for the **cost of equity** capital (which needs to be investigated in more detail).

Ultimately the number of shares issued has to be **negotiated** with VCI, which seeks a 30% pre-tax rate of return on equity. Based on last year's pre-tax profits of $27.78 million, this would imply a rough company valuation of 27.78/0.3 = $93 million, ie the lower of the two figures above. However, the existence of alternative financing strategies for YZ will have a major influence on the negotiation process.

(ii)   **Possible exit strategies available to VCI**

Like all venture capital companies, VCI will look for an 'exit route' for its investment within the medium term, in this case 5 years. This may take a number of forms:

(1)   **Flotation of the equity shares**

This would be on a stock exchange or other equity market (eg over the counter market). This will involve placing VCI's shares, and probably some of the shares of existing shareholders, with institutional shareholders who take longer term equity interests than venture capital companies. This is likely to be feasible if YZ **maintains its growth rate** and will enable the existing shareholders to maintain control if they wish, or to sell out if they wish.

(2) **Sale of the company to another company**

A reasonable bid from, say, a competitor will enable VCI to realise its investment. This will cause the existing shareholders to lose control, which may or may not be in line with their personal objectives, depending on the price offered and the possibility of continuing involvement with the company.

(3) **A management buy-in**

A new management team may wish to purchase VCI's shares on condition that they have significant **influence** over company management.

(4) **Sale of VCI's stake to the company's existing shareholders and managers**

A management buy-out may be feasible for YZ if results have not been as good as expected and VCI has decided to **liquidate** its investment.

(b) **Venture equity capital**

Venture capital companies are in business to take **medium term interests** (say 5 years) in **growing** companies. At least part of the finance offered is usually an **equity stake**, combined with a seat on the board of directors.

The **advantage** of equity finance is that the **financial risk** of the company in relation to fluctuations in profits is kept to a minimum. In good years, shareholders receive high dividends, but in poorer years, there is **no liability** to keep paying high dividends. This enables the board of directors to take reasonable **business risks** without worrying about the short term costs of finance. Use of equity also makes future borrowing easier, if it is required at some stage.

However, venture capital companies normally look for companies with **high growth potential**. This is unlikely to be the case for YZ in its present state. To satisfy the venture capital company, which will have a **significant influence over board policy**, YZ would probably need to embark on a strategy of **acquisition for growth** combined with **cost savings** from economies of scale. This may not be in line with the current thinking of the board, who might prefer the steadier growth strategy that they have at the moment.

Debt finance

As an alternative, the company has considered raising more **long term debt finance**. The advantages of debt are that (i) **management control** does not change; and (ii) it has a **cheaper** direct cost than equity, especially because interest is a tax deductible expense. Against this is the problem that too much debt **increases financial risk**, forcing the directors to be become more **risk averse** in their business strategies. Also lenders may require a **charge** on the company's assets, especially if overall borrowing is high.

AB's existing long term borrowing is $15 million and its total assets less current liabilities are about $35 million. The motor vehicles, which are the life-blood of the company's business, are not owned, but on short **term operating leases**. Consequently, raising $25 million entirely by borrowing would probably be unwise.

Although the existing gearing ratio (Debt/Debt + Equity) is less than 10% in market values, it is 43% in book values which may deter lenders.

Recommendation

The recommendation is that for the proposed $25 million expansion the company should consider **increasing its equity capital**. Unless existing shareholders are able to finance a rights issue, this is likely to mean seeking venture capital finance from a venture capital company or from private investors.

Additional borrowing could then be used to purchase sufficient motor vehicles to generate the company's core income, leaving the remainder on operating leases. This would generate cost savings with little increase in risk. An alternative to borrowing would be to switch to **finance leases** for the core vehicles.

Question 4

> **Text references.** Investment appraisal methods are covered in Chapter 18.
>
> **Top tips.** You need to look carefully for the important information in this question. You are given inflation rates in both countries so your first step should be to calculate expected exchange rates using the purchasing power parity formula. The net cash flows are in **real** terms so need to be converted into **nominal** cash flows.
>
> Use your knowledge of business strategy from P6 in the discussion in part (c).
>
> **Easy marks.** The twelve marks for the calculations in part (a) are relatively easy to achieve if you have done enough practice on questions involving inflation and exchange rates and are confident with MIRR.

(a) **Appraisal of alternative 2**

Exchange rates

The future dollar/pound exchange rates for years 1 to 3 can be predicted using the purchasing power parity formula.

Future exchange rate \$/£ = current exchange rate \$/£ $\times$ [(1 + US inflation rate)/(1 + UK inflation rate)] ^{n} where n is the number of years in the future.

Thus, future exchange rate \$/£ = 1.600 $\times$ [1.04/1.03] ^{n}

Year	0	1	2	3
Exchange rate forecast US\$ / £	1.600	1.616	1.631	1.647

Net present value computation

Year	0	1	2	3
US\$m real cash flows	(25.00)	2.60	3.80	4.10
US\$m nominal cash flows (inflation 4% p.a.)	(25.00)	2.70	4.11	4.61
Exchange rate	1.600	1.616	1.631	1.647
US nominal cash flows in £m	(15.63)	1.67	2.52	2.80
£m real cash flows		3.70	4.20	4.60
£m nominal cash flows (inflation 3% p.a.)		3.81	4.46	5.03
Total nominal cash flows in £m	(15.63)	5.48	6.98	7.83
9% discount factors	1	0.917	0.842	0.772
Present value £m	(15.63)	5.03	5.88	6.04
Net present value	1.32			

The NPV of the project is **£1.32 million** positive.

Internal rate of return

The IRR can be found by trial discount rates and interpolation. If the discount rate is 15%, the NPV is £(0.43) million.

Year	0	1	2	3
Total nominal cash flows in £m	(15.63)	5.48	6.98	7.83
15% factors	1	0.870	0.756	0.658
PV	(15.63)	4.77	5.28	5.15
NPV	(0.43)			

By interpolation the IRR is 9% + (15% − 9%) $\times$ 1.32/(1.32 + 0.43) = **13.5% p.a.**

Modified internal rate of return

This is found by compounding the cash inflows forward to the end of the project at the cost of capital, 9%.

		£m		Year 3 value £m
Outlay:	Year 0	(15.63)		
Inflows:	Year 1	5.48	$\times 1.09^2$	6.51
	Year 2	6.98	$\times 1.09$	7.61
	Year 3	7.83		7.83
				21.95

The 3 year rate that links the 15.63 outlay and the 21.95 inflow is found from the discount tables.

15.63 / 21.95 = 0.712, which represents a discount rate of 12% for 3 years.

Thus the MIRR is **12%**.

(b) **Advantages of MIRR**

MIRR has the advantage over IRR that it assumes the **reinvestment rate** is the **company's cost of capital**. IRR assumes that the reinvestment rate is the IRR itself, which is usually untrue.

In many cases where there is conflict between the NPV and IRR methods, the MIRR will give the same indication as NPV, which is the **correct theoretical method**. This helps when explaining the appraisal of a project to managers, who often find the concept of rate of return easier to understand than that of net present value.

Disadvantages of MIRR

However, MIRR, like all rate of return methods, suffers from the problem that it may lead an investor to reject a project which has a **lower rate of return** but, because of its size, generates a **larger increase in wealth**.

In the same way, a **high-return** project with a **short life** may be preferred over a **lower-return** project with a longer life.

(c) **Evaluation of the two alternatives**

Summary of the appraisal results

Alternative	1	2
NPV at 9%	£1.45 m	£1.32 m
IRR	10.5%	13.5%
MIRR	13.2%	12.0%

All other things being equal, the project to be accepted should be the one with the higher NPV, that is Alternative 1. NPV shows the absolute amount by which the project is forecast to **increase shareholders' wealth**, and is theoretically more sound than the IRR and MIRR methods.

In this case the MIRR method backs up the NPV, but the IRR gives the opposite indication. This 'conflict' arises because IRR makes the wrong **assumption** about reinvestment rates (see (ii) above).

Before making a decision, however, there are a number of other important factors that must be taken into consideration.

Alternative 1

- Alternative 1 has a high risk of lowering the firm's reputation for quality and causing confusion among the customer base. The overall effect may be to **lose existing customers** but not to gain many new ones.

- It also removes the **focus** from the business. Marketing a wider range of products may be more difficult than is anticipated and may stretch resources.

BPP
LEARNING MEDIA

Alternative 2

- Alternative 2 represents a fundamental change in the nature of the business from a niche manufacturer to a **value added** distributor.

- The firm may be able to add successfully its **brand reputation for quality** to mass market products, but this will only be possible if the US 'flat packs' are of guaranteed quality and consistency, and the varnishing and assembly work are carried out to a high standard.

- The change in the nature of the firm's work may require **substantial new equipment**.

- This alternative may also result in a **loss of skilled workers**, with the risk of lower quality.

Given the similarity in the NPVs between the two projects, the decision will almost certainly depend on non-financial factors

Question 5

Top tips. To avoid irrelevant waffle, it is essential to plan a discussion question such as this and continually check you are applying your comments to the specific entities in the scenarios.

Easy marks. There are plenty of marks available for sensible use of your financial and general knowledge.

(a) **Objective setting criteria**

CCC local government

CCC local government exists to **provide services** for its community. Its outputs cannot usually be expressed in financial terms, but nevertheless need to be quantified so far as possible, and continually **monitored** against the costs of provision.

Stakeholders

The council has a complex mix of **stakeholders**. It is directed by a group of local politicians, controlled by the political party that won the last local election, which may be the same or different from the party in power in central government. The politicians are assisted by management executives who are required to keep their political views **separate** from their jobs.

Customers

The customers are members of the local community: individuals, groups, businesses and other organisations. The council's job is to set a budget that **prioritises** competing claims for services between these customers, and then to deliver **efficiently** the services for which it has budgeted. It focuses on services that are not provided by central government or the private sector, including sanitation, local roads and large parts of the health and education services.

The consequences for the council of failing to deliver adequate services is that the customers will start to **express dissatisfaction**, often by starting lobby groups and contacting the media (local newspapers, radio and television), and will get their chance to vote the councillors out of office at the next local election. Hence the importance of the key objective to **provide service excellence** – especially in health and education, to which the public are politically very sensitive.

Financiers

The financiers of the local government are ultimately local and national taxpayers (individual and corporate), the national taxpayers providing finance through central government. Although they vary in political outlook, taxpayers all wish to obtain **value for money in services**. Some form pressure groups who monitor the service provision of local government and attend its public meetings. The local government's objective of creating a prosperous community depends on satisfying taxpayers as well as customers.

In local government the consequences of failing to meet taxpayers' demands can be less or more important than failing to meet customers' objectives; as voting power in an election does not depend on how much tax an individual pays. However, the central government, acting on behalf of national taxpayers, has **substantial power** over the activities of local government, sets boundaries on its activities, monitors its activities and caps national funding if local expenditure is considered too high.

Employees

The employees of local government require **adequate compensation** for their work, usually lower than in equivalent private sector jobs. Their salary scales are usually outside of the control of the individual local authority and they may not be rewarded by **financial bonuses**, but are more likely to be **motivated** by teamwork, good working conditions and a sense of doing a good job. The consequences of failing to meet the objective of good working conditions is that good employees will leave, resulting in poorer service delivery and ultimate dissatisfaction from customers and taxpayers.

DDD

Unlike governments, private sector businesses produce goods and services with a monetary (sales) value which can be directly compared with the cost of production and delivery. Hence businesses have '**profit making**' as their primary objective, and this is ultimately measured by valuing the **wealth of their owners**, the shareholders. DDD's primary objective is to increase shareholder wealth by an average of 10% per annum.

Shareholders

The vast majority of shareholders of a large listed company have no executive power, having appointed **directors** to run the business on their behalf. Because these directors have enormous decision making powers, it is usually beneficial to **reward** them in ways that are related to furtherance of shareholders' objectives, such as share options or other forms of bonus schemes. The consequences of failing to reward directors in appropriate ways is that they can **pursue their own objectives** which may be more concerned with prestige than equity value. Ultimately, however, if the directors fail to achieve satisfactory returns for shareholders, the share price will drop and the directors may be removed from office, or the company will find itself subject to a **takeover bid** which will force a change in management.

Customers

Clearly the directors cannot create shareholder wealth by focusing solely on shareholders. They must match the company's products to customers. Hence **market intelligence** and **customer care** become major non-financial objectives for most companies. The consequences of failing to look after customers are that sales, profits and share price will fall rapidly.

Suppliers and lenders

The company must also work with its **suppliers** of goods and services to ensure that these are procured when and where required and at the right price. CCC is less likely to state an objective relating to suppliers than to customers but the failure to treat suppliers fairly (e.g. by delaying payments) may have **adverse consequences** for delivery schedules and input prices. As regards lenders, it is usual for companies to state objectives concerned with managing the cost of finance but no statement is necessary concerning the fair treatment of lenders as there are usually obvious financial consequences if, for example, service payments are delayed.

Employees

The company is certain to state **non-financial objectives** concerning its employees, usually concerned with fair remuneration rates, good working conditions, opportunities, and consultation over matters that affect employees. A company with the size and geographical spread of DDD, that may outsource substantial parts of its production to suppliers, must also be particularly sensitive to **working conditions** at those suppliers. Even if they are legally not responsible for those conditions, bad publicity can result from being associated with them if, for example, child labour is being used.

Local community

Finally, the company will probably state objectives relating to working with the local community to improve prosperity. In this respect the objectives of CCC and DDD overlap. On the negative side, DDD must be careful to minimise pollution of the local environment (e.g. waste, smoke, noise) or will risk lawsuits and significant adverse publicity. On the positive side, the company may decide to support local community activities and charitable events, including providing donations to educational and health facilities.

(b) **Dividend, investment and financing policies for MS and DDD**

Dividend policy

The shareholders of MS obtain cash returns from their investment entirely through dividends, which have been **constant and predictable** over the company's six year life. For the founding shareholders the dividends now probably form a substantial part of their annual rewards from the company, while other employees are likely to regard their dividends as annual bonuses.

The value of the company's shares has undoubtedly increased over the last few years, but no shareholders have yet attempted to realise these gains by selling their shares, even though this might in theory represent a more **tax efficient way** of receiving returns. The practical difficulties of selling effectively lower the sales price and act as a deterrent. Thus the ideal dividend policy for MS is to continue paying dividends at the same level as now, and hopefully building in some dividend growth in the future, but this policy must be weighed against **financing needs** (see below).

Because shares in listed companies can easily be sold, the shareholders of DDD will be less concerned than those of MS if dividends are restricted in order to finance investments. They can easily make up the cash shortfall by selling their shares to make **capital gains**. Nevertheless, dividend policy is regarded as important in listed companies because it is part of the way that the directors give **information** to investors and manage market expectations. They will usually aim for a **smooth** stream of dividends reflecting underlying **long term growth trends**.

Investment policy

For a specialised private company like MS, investment usually means **expansion** of the existing business by direct capital investment in assets and working capital. Opportunities for acquiring other businesses will occur, but the size of these acquisitions will be limited by the need to **finance** in cash.

DDD will have a wider range of investment opportunities because its activities are diversified and because its shares are listed. In particular, **growth by acquisition** of other businesses is much easier because the company can offer its shares as purchase consideration.

DDD experts will continually be appraising potential projects in the context of the company's strategic objectives. They will use a range of investment appraisal techniques using market based parameters (e.g. cost of capital and beta factors).

These appraisal techniques are less relevant to MS. A private company's cost of capital is not easy to estimate directly and investment appraisal, if it is formally carried out, will often focus as much on **profit forecasts** as on discounted cash flow.

Financing policy

For both companies, finance can be raised in three main ways:

    (i)   Equity funds: restricting the dividend payout
    (ii)   Equity funds: share issues
    (iii) Borrowing

MS wishes to finance a $15 million expansion of its business, equivalent to one third of its existing assets. Restricting the dividend payout would not raise enough for this project and, as argued above, would reduce the only cash return that the shareholders receive on their investment. To reduce the dividend substantially would require agreement between the company directors/shareholders and careful explanation to employees that a sacrifice now would pay off in the longer run.

A rights issue of new shares to existing shareholders in existing proportions would be difficult to get agreement on, but the shareholders may give permission for new shares to be purchased by just those who wish to subscribe. This may raise sufficient cash but, equally, it may also change the **relative ownership** of the company.

As the company is all-equity financed, borrowing $15 million would be feasible, bringing the gearing to approximately 25%, which is below the level where the directors need be concerned about excess **financial risk**. The relatively cheap interest and issue costs of debt, combined with the tax relief on interest paid, make **borrowing** a good source of finance for MS's expansion. Although the company really needs a long term loan at a fixed interest rate, for private companies the most feasible borrowing sources are banks, which usually offer medium term loans at floating rate, and this is the route the company will probably take.

DDD needs a **substantial** amount of capital to finance an acquisition. Again, restriction of the company's dividend will not by itself provide sufficient cash, and may send the wrong signal to the market about

BPP
LEARNING MEDIA

performance prospects. In this case an issue of **new shares** in DDD to the target company's shareholders is very suitable. No cash need be involved and there is no increased risk from borrowing. A decision would need to be made about whether the target company would have any representation of the board of DDD.

DDD could also consider **borrowing** in order to acquire the target company for cash, but this may increase gearing to beyond the desired level. A further alternative would be to offer a **mix of equity and cash**, borrowing to raise the cash portion of the purchase consideration.

Mathematical tables, exam formulae and international terminology

PRESENT VALUE TABLE

Present value of 1.00 unit of currency, that is $(1+r)^{-n}$ where r = interest rate, n = number of periods until payment or receipt.

Periods (n)					Interest rates (r)					
	1%	2%	3%	4%	5%	6%	7%	8%	9%	10%
1	0.990	0.980	0.971	0.962	0.952	0.943	0.935	0.926	0.917	0.909
2	0.980	0.961	0.943	0.925	0.907	0.890	0.873	0.857	0.842	0.826
3	0.971	0.942	0.915	0.889	0.864	0.840	0.816	0.794	0.772	0.751
4	0.961	0.924	0.888	0.855	0.823	0.792	0.763	0.735	0.708	0.683
5	0.951	0.906	0.863	0.822	0.784	0.747	0.713	0.681	0.650	0.621
6	0.942	0.888	0.837	0.790	0.746	0.705	0.666	0.630	0.596	0.564
7	0.933	0.871	0.813	0.760	0.711	0.665	0.623	0.583	0.547	0.513
8	0.923	0.853	0.789	0.731	0.677	0.627	0.582	0.540	0.502	0.467
9	0.914	0.837	0.766	0.703	0.645	0.592	0.544	0.500	0.460	0.424
10	0.905	0.820	0.744	0.676	0.614	0.558	0.508	0.463	0.422	0.386
11	0.896	0.804	0.722	0.650	0.585	0.527	0.475	0.429	0.388	0.350
12	0.887	0.788	0.701	0.625	0.557	0.497	0.444	0.397	0.356	0.319
13	0.879	0.773	0.681	0.601	0.530	0.469	0.415	0.368	0.326	0.290
14	0.870	0.758	0.661	0.577	0.505	0.442	0.388	0.340	0.299	0.263
15	0.861	0.743	0.642	0.555	0.481	0.417	0.362	0.315	0.275	0.239
16	0.853	0.728	0.623	0.534	0.458	0.394	0.339	0.292	0.252	0.218
17	0.844	0.714	0.605	0.513	0.436	0.371	0.317	0.270	0.231	0.198
18	0.836	0.700	0.587	0.494	0.416	0.350	0.296	0.250	0.212	0.180
19	0.828	0.686	0.570	0.475	0.396	0.331	0.277	0.232	0.194	0.164
20	0.820	0.673	0.554	0.456	0.377	0.312	0.258	0.215	0.178	0.149

Periods (n)					Interest rates (r)					
	11%	12%	13%	14%	15%	16%	17%	18%	19%	20%
1	0.901	0.893	0.885	0.877	0.870	0.862	0.855	0.847	0.840	0.833
2	0.812	0.797	0.783	0.769	0.756	0.743	0.731	0.718	0.706	0.694
3	0.731	0.712	0.693	0.675	0.658	0.641	0.624	0.609	0.593	0.579
4	0.659	0.636	0.613	0.592	0.572	0.552	0.534	0.516	0.499	0.482
5	0.593	0.567	0.543	0.519	0.497	0.476	0.456	0.437	0.419	0.402
6	0.535	0.507	0.480	0.456	0.432	0.410	0.390	0.370	0.352	0.335
7	0.482	0.452	0.425	0.400	0.376	0.354	0.333	0.314	0.296	0.279
8	0.434	0.404	0.376	0.351	0.327	0.305	0.285	0.266	0.249	0.233
9	0.391	0.361	0.333	0.308	0.284	0.263	0.243	0.225	0.209	0.194
10	0.352	0.322	0.295	0.270	0.247	0.227	0.208	0.191	0.176	0.162
11	0.317	0.287	0.261	0.237	0.215	0.195	0.178	0.162	0.148	0.135
12	0.286	0.257	0.231	0.208	0.187	0.168	0.152	0.137	0.124	0.112
13	0.258	0.229	0.204	0.182	0.163	0.145	0.130	0.116	0.104	0.093
14	0.232	0.205	0.181	0.160	0.141	0.125	0.111	0.099	0.088	0.078
15	0.209	0.183	0.160	0.140	0.123	0.108	0.095	0.084	0.074	0.065
16	0.188	0.163	0.141	0.123	0.107	0.093	0.081	0.071	0.062	0.054
17	0.170	0.146	0.125	0.108	0.093	0.080	0.069	0.060	0.052	0.045
18	0.153	0.130	0.111	0.095	0.081	0.069	0.059	0.051	0.044	0.038
19	0.138	0.116	0.098	0.083	0.070	0.060	0.051	0.043	0.037	0.031
20	0.124	0.104	0.087	0.073	0.061	0.051	0.043	0.037	0.031	0.026

CUMULATIVE PRESENT VALUE TABLE

This table shows the present value of 1.00 unit of currency per annum, receivable or payable at the end of each year for n years $\dfrac{1-(1+r)^{-n}}{r}$.

Periods (n)	Interest rates (r)									
	1%	2%	3%	4%	5%	6%	7%	8%	9%	10%
1	0.990	0.980	0.971	0.962	0.952	0.943	0.935	0.926	0.917	0.909
2	1.970	1.942	1.913	1.886	1.859	1.833	1.808	1.783	1.759	1.736
3	2.941	2.884	2.829	2.775	2.723	2.673	2.624	2.577	2.531	2.487
4	3.902	3.808	3.717	3.630	3.546	3.465	3.387	3.312	3.240	3.170
5	4.853	4.713	4.580	4.452	4.329	4.212	4.100	3.993	3.890	3.791
6	5.795	5.601	5.417	5.242	5.076	4.917	4.767	4.623	4.486	4.355
7	6.728	6.472	6.230	6.002	5.786	5.582	5.389	5.206	5.033	4.868
8	7.652	7.325	7.020	6.733	6.463	6.210	5.971	5.747	5.535	5.335
9	8.566	8.162	7.786	7.435	7.108	6.802	6.515	6.247	5.995	5.759
10	9.471	8.983	8.530	8.111	7.722	7.360	7.024	6.710	6.418	6.145
11	10.368	9.787	9.253	8.760	8.306	7.887	7.499	7.139	6.805	6.495
12	11.255	10.575	9.954	9.385	8.863	8.384	7.943	7.536	7.161	6.814
13	12.134	11.348	10.635	9.986	9.394	8.853	8.358	7.904	7.487	7.103
14	13.004	12.106	11.296	10.563	9.899	9.295	8.745	8.244	7.786	7.367
15	13.865	12.849	11.938	11.118	10.380	9.712	9.108	8.559	8.061	7.606
16	14.718	13.578	12.561	11.652	10.838	10.106	9.447	8.851	8.313	7.824
17	15.562	14.292	13.166	12.166	11.274	10.477	9.763	9.122	8.544	8.022
18	16.398	14.992	13.754	12.659	11.690	10.828	10.059	9.372	8.756	8.201
19	17.226	15.679	14.324	13.134	12.085	11.158	10.336	9.604	8.950	8.365
20	18.046	16.351	14.878	13.590	12.462	11.470	10.594	9.818	9.129	8.514

Periods (n)	Interest rates (r)									
	11%	12%	13%	14%	15%	16%	17%	18%	19%	20%
1	0.901	0.893	0.885	0.877	0.870	0.862	0.855	0.847	0.840	0.833
2	1.713	1.690	1.668	1.647	1.626	1.605	1.585	1.566	1.547	1.528
3	2.444	2.402	2.361	2.322	2.283	2.246	2.210	2.174	2.140	2.106
4	3.102	3.037	2.974	2.914	2.855	2.798	2.743	2.690	2.639	2.589
5	3.696	3.605	3.517	3.433	3.352	3.274	3.199	3.127	3.058	2.991
6	4.231	4.111	3.998	3.889	3.784	3.685	3.589	3.498	3.410	3.326
7	4.712	4.564	4.423	4.288	4.160	4.039	3.922	3.812	3.706	3.605
8	5.146	4.968	4.799	4.639	4.487	4.344	4.207	4.078	3.954	3.837
9	5.537	5.328	5.132	4.946	4.772	4.607	4.451	4.303	4.163	4.031
10	5.889	5.650	5.426	5.216	5.019	4.833	4.659	4.494	4.339	4.192
11	6.207	5.938	5.687	5.453	5.234	5.029	4.836	4.656	4.486	4.327
12	6.492	6.194	5.918	5.660	5.421	5.197	4.988	4.793	4.611	4.439
13	6.750	6.424	6.122	5.842	5.583	5.342	5.118	4.910	4.715	4.533
14	6.982	6.628	6.302	6.002	5.724	5.468	5.229	5.008	4.802	4.611
15	7.191	6.811	6.462	6.142	5.847	5.575	5.324	5.092	4.876	4.675
16	7.379	6.974	6.604	6.265	5.954	5.668	5.405	5.162	4.938	4.730
17	7.549	7.120	6.729	6.373	6.047	5.749	5.475	5.222	4.990	4.775
18	7.702	7.250	6.840	6.467	6.128	5.818	5.534	5.273	5.033	4.812
19	7.839	7.366	6.938	6.550	6.198	5.877	5.584	5.316	5.070	4.843
20	7.963	7.469	7.025	6.623	6.259	5.929	5.628	5.353	5.101	4.870

EXAM FORMULAE

Valuation models

(i)   Irredeemable preference share, paying a constant annual dividend, d, in perpetuity, where P_0 is the ex-div value:

$$P_0 = \frac{d}{k_{pref}}$$

(ii)   Ordinary (equity) share, paying a constant annual dividend, d, in perpetuity, where P_0 is the ex-div value:

$$P_0 = \frac{d}{k_e}$$

(iii)   Ordinary (equity) share, paying an annual dividend, d, growing in perpetuity at a constant rate, g, where P_0 is the ex-div value:

$$P_0 = \frac{d_1}{k_e - g} \text{ or } P_0 = \frac{d_0[1+g]}{k_e - g}$$

(iv)   Irredeemable (undated) debt, paying annual after tax interest, i(1 − t), in perpetuity, where P_0 is the ex-interest value:

$$P_0 = \frac{i[1-t]}{k_{d\,net}}$$

or, without tax:

$$P_0 = \frac{i}{k_d}$$

(v)   Total value of the geared firm, V_g (based on MM):

$$V_g = V_u + TB_c$$

(vi)   Future value S, of a sum X, invested for n periods, compounded at r% interest:

$$S = X[1 + r]^n$$

(vii)   Present value of 1.00 payable or receivable in n years, discounted at r% per annum:

$$PV = \frac{1}{[1+r]^n}$$

(viii)   Present value of an annuity of 1.00 per annum, receivable or payable for n years, commencing in one year, discounted at r% per annum:

$$PV = \frac{1}{r}\left[1 - \frac{1}{[1+r]^n}\right]$$

(ix)   Present value of 1.00 per annum, payable or receivable in perpetuity, commencing in one year, discounted at r% per annum:

$$PV = \frac{1}{r}$$

(x)   Present value of 1.00 per annum, receivable or payable, commencing in one year, growing in perpetuity at a constant rate of g% per annum, discounted at r% per annum:

$$PV = \frac{1}{r - g}$$

Cost of capital

(i) Cost of irredeemable preference capital, paying an annual dividend d in perpetuity, and having a current ex-div price P_0:

$$k_{pref} = \frac{d}{P_0}$$

(ii) Cost of irredeemable debt capital, paying annual net interest $i(1-t)$, and having a current ex-interest price P_0:

$$k_{d\,net} = \frac{i[1-t]}{P_0}$$

(iii) Cost of ordinary (equity) share capital, paying an annual dividend d in perpetuity, and having a current ex div price P_0:

$$k_e = \frac{d}{P_0}$$

(iv) Cost of ordinary (equity) share capital, having a current ex div price, P_0, having just paid a dividend, d_0, with the dividend growing in perpetuity by a constant g% per annum:

$$k_e = \frac{d_1}{P_0} + g \ \text{ or } k_e = \frac{d_0[1+g]}{P_0} + g$$

(v) Cost of ordinary (equity) share capital, using the CAPM:

$$k_e = R_f + [R_m - R_f]\beta$$

(vi) Cost of ordinary (equity) share capital in a geared firm, (no tax):

$$k_{eg} = k_0 + [k_0 - k_d]\frac{V_D}{V_E}$$

(vii) Cost of ordinary (equity) share capital in a geared firm, (with tax):

$$k_{eg} = k_{eu} + [k_{eu} - k_d]\frac{V_D[1-t]}{V_E}$$

(viii) Weighted average cost of capital, k_0:

$$k_0 = k_{eg}\left[\frac{V_E}{V_E + V_D}\right] + k_d\left[\frac{V_D}{V_E + V_D}\right]$$

(ix) Adjusted cost of capital (MM formula)

$$k_{adj} = k_{eu}[1 - tL] \text{ or } r^* = r[1 - T^*L]$$

In the following formula, β_u is used for an ungeared β, and β_g is used for a geared β:

(x) β_u from β_g, taking β_d as zero, (no tax):

$$\beta_u = \beta_g\left[\frac{V_E}{V_E + V_D}\right]$$

(xi) If β_d is not zero:

$$\beta_u = \beta_g\left[\frac{V_E}{V_E + V_D}\right] + \beta_d\left[\frac{V_D}{V_E + V_D}\right]$$

(xii) β_u from β_g, taking β_d as zero, (with tax):

$$\beta_u = \beta_g \left[\frac{V_E}{V_E + V_D[1-t]} \right]$$

(xiii) Adjusted discount rate to use in international capital budgeting using interest rate parity

$$\frac{1+\text{annual discount rate C\$}}{1+\text{annual discount rate Euro}} = \frac{\text{Exchange rate in 12 months' time C\$/Euro}}{\text{Spot rate C\$/Euro}}$$

Other formulae

(i)   Purchasing power parity (Law of one price)

$$\text{Forward rate US\$/£} = \text{Spot US\$/£} \times \frac{1+\text{US inflation rate}}{1+\text{UK inflation rate}}$$

(ii)   Interest rate parity (International Fisher effect)

$$\text{Forward rate US\$/£} = \text{Spot US\$/£} \times \frac{1+\text{nominal US interest rate}}{1+\text{nominal UK interest rate}}$$

(iii)   Link between nominal (money) and real interest rates

[1 + nominal (money) rate] = [1 + real interest rate][1 + inflation rate]

(iv)   Equivalent annual cost

$$\text{Equivalent annual cost} = \frac{\text{PV of costs over n years}}{\text{n year annuity factor}}$$

(v)   Theoretical ex-rights price

$$\text{TERP} = \frac{1}{N+1} \left[(N \times \text{Cumrights price}) + \text{Issue price} \right]$$

(vi)   Value of a right

$$\text{Value of a right} = \frac{\text{Rights on price} - \text{Issue price}}{N+1}$$

or

$$\frac{\text{Theoretical ex rights price} - \text{Issue price}}{N}$$

where N = number of rights required to buy one share.

International Accounting Terminology and Formats

Terminology

Below is a short list of the most important terms you are likely to use or come across, together with their international equivalents.

UK term	International term
Profit and loss account	Income statement
Profit and loss reserve (in balance sheet)	Accumulated profits
Turnover	Revenue
Debtor account	Account receivable
Debtors (eg 'debtors have increased')	Receivables
Debtor	Customer
Creditor account	Account payable
Creditors (eg 'creditors have increased')	Payables
Creditor	Supplier
Debtors control account	Receivables control account
Creditors control account	Payables control account
Stock	Inventory
Fixed asset	Non-current asset (generally). Tangible fixed assets are also referred to as 'property, plant and equipment'.
Long-term liability	Non-current liability
Provision (eg for depreciation)	Allowance (You will sometimes see 'provision' used too.)
General ledger	Nominal ledger
VAT	Sales tax
Debentures	Loan notes
Preference shares/dividends	Preferred shares/dividends

Formats

Note that the financial statements are generally expressed in dollars rather than pounds.

In general the format for the income statement (international) is the same as the profit and loss account (UK) except for a couple of differences in terminology. Here is a simple example, with the differences highlighted.

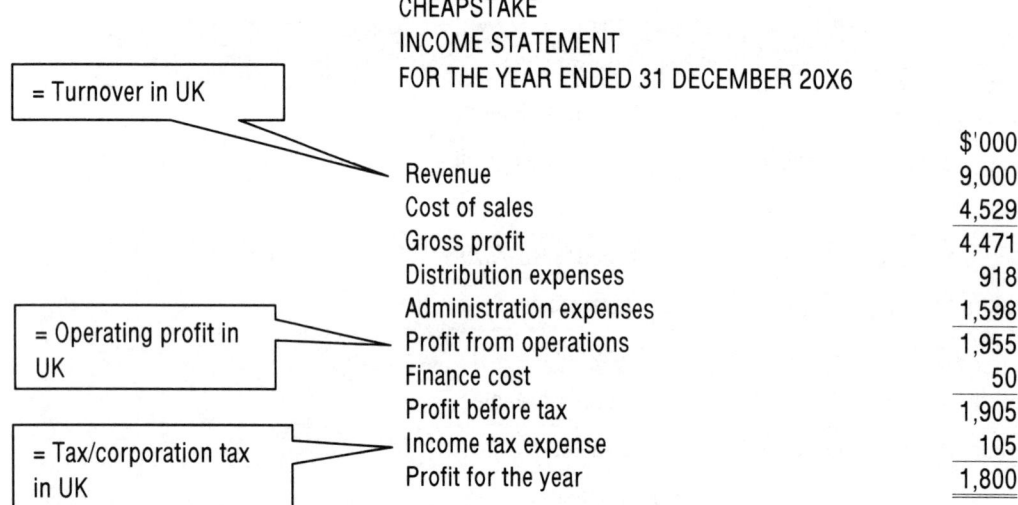

CHEAPSTAKE
INCOME STATEMENT
FOR THE YEAR ENDED 31 DECEMBER 20X6

= Turnover in UK

= Operating profit in UK

= Tax/corporation tax in UK

	$'000
Revenue	9,000
Cost of sales	4,529
Gross profit	4,471
Distribution expenses	918
Administration expenses	1,598
Profit from operations	1,955
Finance cost	50
Profit before tax	1,905
Income tax expense	105
Profit for the year	1,800

The format of the balance sheet is different from the UK. **Instead of having net assets (assets less liabilities) equal to capital and reserves, it has total assets in the top half equal to equity and liabilities in the bottom half.**

CHEAPSTAKE
BALANCE SHEET AS AT 31 DECEMBER 20X6

ASSETS	$'000	$'000
Non-current assets		
Intangible asset: goodwill		270
Tangible assets: property and plant		2,720
		2,990
Current assets		
Inventory	1,950	
Receivables	1,544	
Bank	200	
		3,694
		6,684
EQUITY AND LIABILITIES		
Capital and reserves		
$1 Ordinary shares		400
10% preferred shares		600
Revaluation reserve		350
Accumulated profits		2,274
		3,624
Non-current liabilities		
5% Loan notes	1,000	
Deferred tax	120	1,120
Current liabilities		1,940
		6,684

(As you can see, assets = capital plus liabilities, rather than assets less liabilities = capital.)

Review Form & Free Prize Draw - Paper P9 Management Accounting - Financial Strategy (1/07)

All original review forms from the entire BPP range, completed with genuine comments, will be entered into one of two draws on 31 July 2007 and 31 January 2008. The names on the first four forms picked out on each occasion will be sent a cheque for £50.

Name: _____   **Address**: _____

_____

_____

How have you used this Kit?
(Tick one box only)

☐ Home study (book only)

☐ On a course: college _____

☐ With 'correspondence' package

☐ Other _____

Why did you decide to purchase this Kit?
(Tick one box only)

☐ Have used the complementary Study text

☐ Have used other BPP products in the past

☐ Recommendation by friend/colleague

☐ Recommendation by a lecturer at college

☐ Saw advertising

☐ Other _____

During the past six months do you recall seeing/receiving any of the following?
(Tick as many boxes as are relevant)

☐ Our advertisement in *Financial Management*

☐ Our advertisement in *Pass*

☐ Our advertisement in *PQ*

☐ Our brochure with a letter through the post

☐ Our website www.bpp.com

Which (if any) aspects of our advertising do you find useful?
(Tick as many boxes as are relevant)

☐ Prices and publication dates of new editions

☐ Information on product content

☐ Facility to order books off-the-page

☐ None of the above

Which BPP products have you used?

Text	☐	Success CD	☐	Learn Online	☐
Kit	☑	i-Learn	☐	Home Study Package	☐
Passcard	☐	i-Pass	☐	Home Study PLUS	☐

Your ratings, comments and suggestions would be appreciated on the following areas.

	Very useful	Useful	Not useful
Passing CIMA exams	☐	☐	☐
Passing P9	☐	☐	☐
Planning your question practice	☐	☐	☐
Questions	☐	☐	☐
Top Tips etc in answers	☐	☐	☐
Content and structure of answers	☐	☐	☐
'Plan of attack' in mock exams	☐	☐	☐
Mock exam answers	☐	☐	☐

Overall opinion of this Kit   Excellent ☐   Good ☐   Adequate ☐   Poor ☐

Do you intend to continue using BPP products?   Yes ☐   No ☐

The BPP author of this edition can be e-mailed at: julietgood@bpp.com

Please return this form to: Nick Weller, CIMA Publishing Manager, BPP Learning Media Ltd, FREEPOST, London, W12 8BR

Review Form & Free Prize Draw (continued)

TELL US WHAT YOU THINK

Please note any further comments and suggestions/errors below.

Free Prize Draw Rules

1   Closing date for 31 July 2007 draw is 30 June 2007. Closing date for 31 January 2008 draw is 31 December 2007.

2   Restricted to entries with UK and Eire addresses only. BPP employees, their families and business associates are excluded.

3   No purchase necessary. Entry forms are available upon request from BPP Professional Education. No more than one entry per title, per person. Draw restricted to persons aged 16 and over.

4   Winners will be notified by post and receive their cheques not later than 6 weeks after the relevant draw date.

5   The decision of the promoter in all matters is final and binding. No correspondence will be entered into.